A READING APPRENTICESHIP
APPRENTICESHIP
Literature

A READING
APPRENTICESHIP
Literature

Norman A. Brittin

Hollifield Professor of English Literature
Auburn University

HOLT, RINEHART AND WINSTON, INC.
New York   Chicago   San Francisco
Atlanta   Dallas   Montreal   Toronto

Preface

Like *A Writing Apprenticeship* (New York: Holt, Rinehart and Winston, Inc., 1968), its companion textbook for freshman composition, *A Reading Apprenticeship* is a practical text intended to lead students to learn by doing. Its objective is to teach the skills with which students can read imaginative literature with understanding and enjoyment.

For thousands of years people have had literature to enjoy, whatever else they may or may not have had. Literature has been one of the most important means of helping man extend his understanding of how living beings respond to the world. The beings represented in literature have almost always been human beings faced by the problems or pressures of life. Various forms of literature, such as epics, tragedies, stories, and novels, are, essentially, artistic devices for revealing human character under pressure. The spectacle of human character faced by decisions and forced into responses under pressure is a fascinating one; for generation after generation listeners and readers find that this spectacle captures their imagination and teases them into thought. And these results are all gained with words; for literature is an art, the art of design in words. The fascination of human responses to every conceivable situation of life cannot be completely and effectively communicated unless the words are artistically selected and arranged.

Each type of literature is designed in certain ways. The reader who can understand literature best, respond to it most enthusiastically, and appreciate it most deeply is one who has read a fair amount of several kinds of literature, paying attention to the basic principles governing the works read; thus, he will develop his judgment and taste regarding literature.

This reader will be developing knowledge and judgment in much the same way as a person who watches excellent performers in baseball, football, tennis, or golf. Such a spectator comes to know a good deal about the art of playing these games, and every time he sees a new game he can make accurate judgments about what went on and whether the performance of the players was excellent or not.

Reading literature takes skill, and skill depends on experience. In this light we may think of the student as an apprentice in the field of reading. Like any other apprentice he must first learn the names of the elements of his trade and then learn how to handle the tools and materials used, so that eventually he can perform the more complicated jobs of a master workman. A carpenter's apprentice learns how to measure and saw boards accurately and how to hammer in nails straight and true. With enough experience he can become a carpenter and build a house. A football player learns a bit by watching as a boy, more as a member of a high-school squad, and more still by playing college football. But, even if he never plays, a boy may learn about football by attending games, watching them closely, analyzing them, and discussing them with other people. The apprentice reader of literature will develop his reading abilities and his judgment in a similar way.

We have estimated that the reading apprenticeship for which this book has been prepared will be a course of a few months. The material presented here has been carefully selected to represent the most significant types of imaginative literature for twentieth-century readers. Thus this book contains twenty short stories, one full-length play and two one-act plays, and nearly one hundred poems. The works have been selected for their variety of interest, their high level of excellence in terms of artistic achievement, and their usefulness in the classroom. Although among the poems a good many classic English pieces appear, the bulk of the selections comes from the twentieth century.

In addition to the literature a considerable amount of study apparatus has been included in this book. Before each of the three main divisions there is a brief introduction: on short stories, on drama, and on poetry. Also, a few of the works have been analyzed. The analyses provide examples of the questions that experienced readers ask about things they read and of ways in which these questions are answered. Material is included after the other selections to help the student study and understand them. This material consists mainly of questions, but the type of question varies according to the difficulty and position of the selection. At times a good deal of help—explanations and factual information—has been furnished in addition to the questions. Many of the questions are on matters of detail and require close reading, but others, at appropriate points, are broader and more general. Another helpful feature is the arrangement of the stories and poems in such a way that there are many opportunities for fruitful comparison among them.

Reading the selections carefully and formulating answers to the questions will give students the experience necessary to become more skillful and more knowledgeable readers. The more skill and knowledge they have, the more their reading will excite them and please them. By the time they have completed this reading apprenticeship, students should be able to meet future reading challenges, whether self-chosen or imposed by the world.

N. A. B.

Auburn, Alabama
September 1970

Contents

PREFACE   V

section one

SHORT STORIES	Reading Short Stories 3
JOHN COLLIER	*The Chaser* 4
JACK LONDON	*Lost Face* 13
AMBROSE BIERCE	*The Story of a Conscience* 24
HERNANDO TÉLLEZ	*Just Lather, That's All* 30
LERONE BENNETT, JR.	*The Convert* 35
BERNARD MALAMUD	*The Cost of Living* 48
ALFREDO MARQUERÍE	*Self-Service Elevator* 56
CARSON MC CULLERS	*The Jockey* 64
ELIZABETH BOWEN	*Careless Talk* 72
ANTON CHEKHOV	*After the Theater* 77
FRANK O'CONNOR	*The Ugly Duckling* 81
CONRAD AIKEN	*Farewell! Farewell! Farewell!* 95
RAY BRADBURY	*The Wonderful Ice Cream Suit* 111
HEINRICH BÖLL	*The Thrower-Away* 130
ROALD DAHL	*My Lady Love, My Dove* 139
JOHN UPDIKE	*Should Wizard Hit Mommy?* 152
PAUL BRODEUR	*The Spoiler* 158
FLANNERY O'CONNOR	*Everything That Rises Must Converge* 170
ERVIN D. KRAUSE	*The Snake* 183
JOYCE CAROL OATES	*First Views of the Enemy* 191

section two

PLAYS	Reading Plays 203
JOHN MILLINGTON SYNGE	*Riders to the Sea* 211
ARTHUR MILLER	*A View from the Bridge* 222
SEAN O'CASEY	*Bedtime Story* 275

section three

POEMS   Reading Poems   297

ELEMENTS OF NATURE

RICHARD HUGHES   *Winter*   305
EDMUND BLUNDEN   *Water Moment*   309
CONRAD AIKEN   *Keep in the Heart the Journal Nature*
                 Keeps   310

SOUND EFFECTS

FREDERICK ROBERT HIGGINS   *Song for the Clatter Bones*   313
JAMES JOYCE   *On the Beach at Fontana*   316
OGDEN NASH   *The Turtle*   317
ALFRED, LORD TENNYSON   *In Memoriam VII*   318
JOHN UPDIKE   *Player Piano*   319
GERARD MANLEY HOPKINS   *Inversnaid*   320
PHILIP BOOTH   *Crossing*   321
STEPHEN SPENDER   *The Express*   323

BALLADS AND NEAR BALLADS

ANONYMOUS   *Lord Randal*   325
ANONYMOUS   *Hind Horn*   327
ANONYMOUS   *Helen of Kirconnell*   329
LOUIS SIMPSON   *Carentan O Carentan*   331
CHARLES CAUSLEY   *Ballad of the Bread Man*   333
ROBERT GRAVES   *A Frosty Night*   335
KARL SHAPIRO   *Nostalgia*   337

SONNETS AND NEAR SONNETS

WILLIAM SHAKESPEARE   *Sonnet 73*   339
JOHN KEATS   *When I Have Fears That I May Cease*
              To Be   341
ROBINSON JEFFERS   *Promise of Peace*   343
E. E. CUMMINGS   *you shall above all things be glad and*
                  young   344
DANTE GABRIEL ROSSETTI   *Lilith*   345
ARCHIBALD MACLEISH   *Contemporary Portrait*   346

INCIDENTS

KARL SHAPIRO   *Auto Wreck*   348
ROBERT HAYDEN   *The Whipping*   350
JOYCE CAROL OATES   *A Girl at the Center of Her Life*   351
ANNE SEXTON   *Two Sons*   353
PHILIP LARKIN   *Reasons for Attendance*   355
ROBERT FROST   *Mending Wall*   356
RICHARD WILBUR   *Juggler*   358

CHARACTER AND CHARACTER ANALYSIS

EDWIN ARLINGTON ROBINSON | *Miniver Cheevy*   360
EVE MERRIAM | *Ruth*   362
GWENDOLYN BROOKS | *A Song in the Front Yard*   364
GEORGE BARKER | *To My Mother*   365
ROBERT BROWNING | *My Last Duchess*   366
EMILY BRONTË | *I Am the Only Being*   369
HENRY DAVID THOREAU | *Sic Vita*   370
DAVID HOLBROOK | *Me and the Animals*   371
DELMORE SCHWARTZ | *The Heavy Bear Who Goes with Me*   372

IMAGES

WILLIAM CARLOS WILLIAMS | *The Storm*   374
TU FU | *Overlooking the Desert*   376
SYLVIA PLATH | *Balloons*   377
LANGSTON HUGHES | *Troubled Woman*   379
MALCOLM LOWRY | *Happiness*   380
PHILIP LARKIN | *Coming*   381
GEORGE LOVE | *The Noonday April Sun*   382
ELEANOR MUNRO | *Spring*   383
W. S. MERWIN | *As by Water*   384

EXPERIENCES OF BEAUTY

EDMUND WALLER | *Go, Lovely Rose*   385
EZRA POUND | *Envoi (1919)*   386
EDGAR ALLAN POE | *To Helen*   387
JOHN KEATS | *On First Looking into Chapman's Homer*   389
EDNA ST. VINCENT MILLAY | *On Hearing a Symphony of Beethoven*   391
JOHN KEATS | *Ode on a Grecian Urn*   392

LOVE

WILLIAM SHAKESPEARE | *Sonnet 116*   395
EMILY DICKINSON | *The Soul Selects Her Own Society*   396
WILLIAM SHAKESPEARE | *Sonnet 55*   398
JOHN DONNE | *A Valediction: Forbidding Mourning*   400
ARCHIBALD MACLEISH | *"Not Marble nor the Gilded Monuments"*   402
ROBERT BURNS | *My Love is Like a Red Red Rose*   404
ROBERT FROST | *The Silken Tent*   405

DEATH IN WAR

JAMES SHIRLEY | *The Glories of Our Blood and State*   407
RALPH WALDO EMERSON | *Concord Hymn*   409
E. E. CUMMINGS | *next to of course god america i*   412

A. E. HOUSMAN   *Here Dead Lie We*   413
A. J. M. SMITH   *What Is That Music High in the Air?*   414

DEATH

EMILY DICKINSON   *One Dignity Delays for All*   415
WILLIAM WORDSWORTH   *She Dwelt among the Untrodden Ways*   417
EDNA ST. VINCENT MILLAY   *Elegy*   418
ALFRED, LORD TENNYSON   *In Memoriam XI*   419
WILLIAM JAY SMITH   *Funeral*   421
DYLAN THOMAS   *Do Not Go Gentle into That Good Night*   422

THE MODERN WORLD: SOCIAL CRITICISM

JOHN MASEFIELD   *Cargoes*   424
AE (GEORGE WILLIAM RUSSELL)   *New York*   425
JOHN PRESS   *Cities*   426
PHILIP BOOTH   *Siasconset Song*   427
RANDALL JARRELL   *A Lullaby*   428
LOUIS SIMPSON   *A Story about Chicken Soup*   429
DANIEL HOFFMAN   *The Arrival*   431
ANTHONY HECHT   *"More Light! More Light!"*   433
WILLIAM JAY SMITH   *Bay-Breasted Barge Bird*   434
W. H. AUDEN   *The Managers*   436
PETER PORTER   *Your Attention Please*   439

THE HUMAN SITUATION: VALUES

A. E. HOUSMAN   *Terence, This Is Stupid Stuff*   442
DANIEL HOFFMAN   *In Humbleness*   445
THEODORE ROETHKE   *"Long Live the Weeds"*   446
RICHARD EBERHART   *Recollection of Childhood*   447
BORIS PASTERNAK   *The Nobel Prize*   448
THOM GUNN   *On the Move*   449
RICHARD WILBUR   *A Fire-Truck*   451
TED HUGHES   *Thrushes*   453
HENRY WADSWORTH LONGFELLOW   *The Tide Rises, the Tide Falls*   454
GENE BARO   *The Horsemen*   455
JOHN WAIN   *The New Sun*   456
RICHARD EBERHART   *The Horse Chestnut Tree*   457
WILLIAM BUTLER YEATS   *A Prayer for My Daughter*   459
ROBERT LOWELL   *Waking Early Sunday Morning*   462

INDEX   467

SECTION ONE

SHORT STORIES

Reading Short Stories

I

The tale or story has a long history, but the form of fiction known as the short story only developed during the last 150 years. A great number of authors, including many of the most famous, have written short stories, and through their efforts the genre has not only attained high artistic excellence but become quite diversified. Every phase of life is treated in the short story, and in many modes, ranging from the photographically realistic to the fantastic and from the literal to the highly symbolic. Short stories vary not only in subject matter but also in technique, purpose, mood, and effect. When Edgar Allan Poe reviewed Nathaniel Hawthorne's *Twice-Told Tales* in 1842, he emphasized how important it was that a writer should conceive "with deliberate care, a certain unique or single *effect* to be wrought out," and then should invent incidents and combine events to bring about "this preconceived effect."

After Poe writers were more aware of the significance of working for that single effect, and consequently they paid much attention to the elements of plot. The majority of short story writers have composed well-plotted stories. But the best writers of the short story have in mind an ideal of functional efficiency and simplicity similar to that of modern architecture. "Less is more," a leading modern architect has said. Working in this spirit, many twentieth-century writers have abandoned the concept of feeling it their duty to *tell* the reader a great deal and have adopted the technique of describing significant details that *imply* more to the reader. Some writers have gone even farther in this direction by eliminating plot complications and focusing intently on a single character in a single situation dominated by a single mood. Thus they have experimented in achieving effects more subtle and poetic, more lyrical, than had been achieved earlier.

Although in any particular story one element may have more importance than other elements, we normally expect to find in short stories the basic elements of fiction: *Characters* are placed in a relationship, and they live through a series of events constituting a *plot*. The incidents of the plot take place in a *setting*. Each author relates a story in a certain *style*, and by means of the total story projects a *theme*.

In order to understand these and other terms useful in discussing short stories, and in order to understand how to read short stories effectively, it will be instructive to analyze a very brief and compact modern story, "The Chaser," by John Collier.

II

The Chaser

JOHN COLLIER

Alan Austen, as nervous as a kitten, went up certain dark and creaky stairs in the neighborhood of Pell Street, and peered about for a long time on the dim landing before he found the name he wanted written obscurely on one of the doors.

He pushed open this door, as he had been told to do, and found him- 5
self in a tiny room, which contained no furniture but a plain kitchen table, a rocking-chair, and an ordinary chair. On one side of the dirty buff-colored walls were a couple of shelves, containing in all perhaps a dozen bottles and jars.

An old man sat in the rocking-chair, reading a newspaper. Alan, 10
without a word, handed him the card he had been given. "Sit down, Mr. Austen," said the old man very politely. "I am glad to make your acquaintance."

"Is it true," asked Alan, "that you have a certain mixture that has—er—quite extraordinary effects?" 15

"My dear sir," replied the old man, "my stock in trade is not very large—I don't deal in laxatives and teething mixtures—but such as it is, it is varied. I think nothing I sell has effects which could be precisely described as ordinary."

"Well, the fact is——" began Alan. 20

"Here, for example," interrupted the old man, reaching for a bottle from the shelf. "Here is a liquid as colorless as water, almost tasteless, quite imperceptible in coffee, milk, wine, or any other beverage. It is also quite imperceptible to any known method of autopsy."

"Do you mean it is a poison?" cried Alan, very much horrified. 25

"Call it a glove-cleaner if you like," said the old man indifferently. "Maybe it will clean gloves. I have never tried. One might call it a life-cleaner. Lives need cleaning sometimes."

"I want nothing of that sort," said Alan.

"Probably it is just as well," said the old man. "Do you know the 30 price of this? For one teaspoonful, which is sufficient, I ask five thousand dollars. Never less. Not a penny less."

"I hope all your mixtures are not as expensive," said Alan apprehensively.

"Oh dear, no," said the old man. "It would be no good charging that 35 sort of price for a love potion, for example. Young people who need a love potion very seldom have five thousand dollars. Otherwise they would not need a love potion."

"I am glad to hear that," said Alan.

"I look at it like this," said the old man. "Please a customer with one 40 article, and he will come back when he needs another. Even if it *is* more costly. He will save up for it, if necessary."

"So," said Alan, "you really do sell love potions?"

"If I did not sell love potions," said the old man, reaching for another bottle, "I should not have mentioned the other matter to you. It is only 45 when one is in a position to oblige that one can afford to be so confidential."

"And these potions," said Alan. "They are not just—just—er——"

"Oh, no," said the old man. "Their effects are permanent, and extend far beyond casual impulse. But they include it. Bountifully, insistently. 50 Everlastingly."

"Dear me!" said Alan, attempting a look of scientific detachment. "How very interesting!"

"But consider the spiritual side," said the old man.

"For indifference," said the old man, "they substitute devotion. For 55 scorn, adoration. Give one tiny measure of this to the young lady—its flavor is imperceptible in orange juice, soup, or cocktails—and however gay and giddy she is, she will change altogether. She will want nothing but solitude, and you."

"I can hardly believe it," said Alan. "She is so fond of parties." 60

"She will not like them any more," said the old man. "She will be afraid of the pretty girls you may meet."

"She will actually be jealous?" cried Alan in a rapture. "Of me?"

"Yes, she will want to be everything to you."

"She is, already. Only she doesn't care about it."   65

"She will, when she has taken this. She will care intensely. You will be her sole interest in life."

"Wonderful!" cried Alan.

"She will want to know all you do," said the old man. "All that has happened to you during the day. Every word of it. She will want to know   70 what you are thinking about, why you smile suddenly, why you are looking sad."

"That is love!" cried Alan.

"Yes," said the old man. "How carefully she will look after you! She will never allow you to be tired, to sit in a draught, to neglect your   75 food. If you are an hour late, she will be terrified. She will think you are killed, or that some siren has caught you."

"I can hardly imagine Diana like that!" cried Alan, overwhelmed with joy.

"You will not have to use your imagination," said the old man.   80 "And, by the way, since there are always sirens, if by any chance you *should*, later on, slip a little, you need not worry. She will forgive you, in the end. She will be terribly hurt, of course, but she will forgive you— in the end."

"That will not happen," said Alan fervently.   85

"Of course not," said the old man. "But, if it did, you need not worry. She would never divorce you. Oh, no! And, of course, she herself will never give you the least, the very least, grounds for—uneasiness."

"And how much," said Alan, "is this wonderful mixture?"

"It is not as dear," said the old man, "as the glove-cleaner, or life-   90 cleaner, as I sometimes call it. No. That is five thousand dollars, never a penny less. One has to be older than you are, to indulge in that sort of thing. One has to save up for it."

"But the love potion?" said Alan.

"Oh, that," said the old man, opening the drawer in the kitchen   95 table, and taking out a tiny, rather dirty-looking phial. "That is just a dollar."

"I can't tell you how grateful I am," said Alan, watching him fill it.

"I like to oblige," said the old man. "Then customers come back, later in life, when they are rather better off, and want more expensive   100 things. Here you are. You will find it very effective."

"Thank you again," said Alan. "Good-by."

"*Au revoir*," said the old man.

ANALYSIS

An experienced reader will immediately notice words in the first sentence that give signals about the setting of the story and about the main character. Many readers will recognize the neighborhood of Pell

Street as a part of New York's Chinatown; this is the general setting. The terms describing the specific setting—"dark and creaky stairs," "dim landing," "written obscurely"—have a suggestion of something mysterious, something not quite respectable, perhaps sinister. They reinforce the associations of Chinatown as a place with such qualities. Thus the author has created a mood, or *atmosphere*, in his opening sentence. It is quite a different atmosphere from that of a sunny day in a park or of a new, shiny office building.

In the second paragraph the author describes with a few details the room that Alan Austen enters; these details let us visualize it. It certainly does not impress us as a setting for "big business" or even a successful enterprise, especially at the time represented, which is evidently the present day.

With his first hundred words the author has established his setting and given it a particular atmosphere. He has also begun to show us his main character, or *protagonist*. This person is a man, "as nervous as a kitten." We know that he has been given some directions, but obviously he has never before visited the place where he finds himself, and so his curiosity about it is as natural as ours. But what are his directions about, and why is he so nervous? Since we do not know, the author has created *suspense* in our minds. But the protagonist is in suspense too. Thus as the protagonist discovers more about the situation, we will also discover more; as his suspense is relieved, ours will be also.

As soon as possible, every author has to let his readers know who his characters are, what the relationships are between them, and what situation they are concerned with. This early part of a story is called the *exposition*. So in this story the author proceeds with his exposition. Collier's protagonist at once encounters an old man, the other speaking character of the story. Through their conversation we find out what the peculiar situation is—that the old man sells potions and that Alan Austen, a young man with little money, is interested in buying a love potion in order to help him win the love of a girl named Diana.

In fact, through the dialogue of the two characters, almost as in a play, the rest of the story is revealed. The reader is able to "watch"—in imagination—the characters as if they were actors upon a stage. Through signals in the text (much like stage directions) the author indicates how the characters respond, what actions they perform, and how they feel. However, we are told more about Alan Austen's feelings than about the old man's. Every author must decide from what *point of view* he is going to tell his story. If this story were told by Alan Austen, it would not be quite the same as it is. If it were told by the old man, the story would be still different. For example, it would be harder to include the atmospheric material "dark and creaky stairs," and "written obscurely." It would not be easy for the old man to notice, and provide the information, that his visitor was "as nervous as a kitten." The author has told us this very economically. If the story were told from the old man's point of view, some of the economy would be lost. As it is, the author tells the story in the third person, but he makes minimum use of his privilege of *omniscience*, of knowing everything about all the characters.

Collier does tell us that his protagonist is nervous. We can infer from Alan's questions that he is curious and skeptical about the effectiveness of potions. He is "very much horrified" at what the old man says about the "life-cleaner." A bit later he attempts "a look of scientific detachment"; and he becomes more and more excited and delighted as he hears how the potion will affect his beloved. Collier lets us know that he is "in a rapture" and finally "overwhelmed with joy." But these are the only places where the author has informed us about Alan's feelings.

Thus in a short time—perhaps fifteen minutes?—Alan has changed from a nervous and skeptical young man to a fervent believer in the potion; his only question—and the final bit of suspense—is whether he can afford it. The change has been rapid but not abrupt. In many stories we can pick out a precise *turning point* after which the plot is bound to turn out as it does. Here it is not easy to do so. Perhaps when Alan cries "Wonderful!" after being told that he will be Diana's "sole interest in life," he has taken the turn to positive commitment.

This means that his suspicions and disbelief have been overcome by his desire to possess the potion, the means of letting him possess the previously unattainable Diana. The *conflict* within him between desire and skepticism has been settled; it has been won by desire. Conflict is an element in most fiction. Often it occurs between one person and another or between a human being and an animal. In many stories there is conflict between a human being and the forces of nature or the forces of society. Much fiction also deals with internal conflicts (very often in addition to the other conflicts mentioned), such as between a desire for success and a sense of honor, between fear and a love of admiration, or between sensitivity over social disapproval and one's own integrity. The two characters of "The Chaser" are not engaged in a conflict, though they do have contrasting attitudes. Nor are we shown a conflict between Alan and Diana, though his struggle to win her is fundamental to the narrative. The conflict is within Alan, and this internal conflict is resolved as we have pointed out.

When a storyteller creates a plot, he shows a character or characters living through significant incidents that are connected by cause and effect. In a longer story than this there would be more incidents and more *complications* of plot. But in a story this short, the plot is uncomplicated. Because Alan desires to win Diana, he visits a seller of potions. Because the old man wishes to sell Alan a more profitable potion later, he convinces the lover that his potions are effective. The effect of his convincing explanation is that Alan buys the love potion.

The part of a plot before the turning point is often called the *rising action.* In longer stories plot complications would appear in this part. The turning point is thought of as the peak of a pyramid, and the part after it is called the *falling action.* At the end comes the *resolution* (also called *dénouement*, a French word meaning "untying of the knots"). The falling action of this story is very brief; the only important point is to reassure Alan that the price is cheap. The *dénouement* is that Alan buys some liquid in a phial. Everything the old man has said implies that Alan will use it and thus win Diana. Now our suspense is over; we know what Alan did and why he decided to do it. We perceive, too, something important concerning love.

The old man's comments also imply that a future conflict will arise in Alan, but the young lover remains unaware of the significance of these comments. The main point of the short story is provided by the old man's comments about the "life-cleaner" at five thousand dollars a teaspoonful that his satisfied customers return "later in life" to buy and their connection with his predictions of Diana's intensely devoted interest, love, and care. These sinister implications regarding the future give meaning to the title of the story and to its ending. A chaser is a drink, such as water, that takes away the taste of another drink, such as whisky. Diana's chaser will be a second potion, the "life-cleaner," which horrifies the protagonist at first but which at the end he is uninterested in. He says good-bye, but the old man replies *Au revoir,* "until we see each other again." It is ironical that the fervent young lover should return, and for such a purpose, but the old man knows that he will be back.

Thus the theme is projected. In the discussion of literature theme means an idea about life, or some conviction about the makeup of man, society, or the universe. The projection of the theme requires the whole story to make it effective. Alan's infatuation blinds him to the fact that Diana's excessively possessive and jealous devotion, which he is so happy to secure by the love potion, will eventually become so cloying and hateful that he will destroy her. The desperate lover will have turned into a desperate man—a husband desperate to free himself, to make his life "clean." The theme of "The Chaser" is that an intensely desired thing can, because of the very qualities that make it seem so overwhelmingly desirable, turn into something hated with an equal emotional intensity.

This theme is bitterly ironical. We feel the *irony* because there is so great an incongruity between the blind desire of the pursuing lover, who identifies love with being "her sole interest in life," and the later loathing, which we as well as the old man can see as the inevitable outcome of Diana's smothering, exclusive possessiveness. Because this is the theme, the reader cannot, of course, react skeptically and scoff at love potions or say he does not believe in magic. The reader must accept as true every word that the old man says.

So far we have discussed "The Chaser" in terms of characters, setting, plot, and theme. There remains the important element of style.

It is largely through style that the author has achieved the effect he aimed at, which is the perception of the bitter irony regarding love—irony mingled no doubt with a kind of wry regret. Most of the words of this story are put in the old man's mouth. He speaks unemotionally, in a dry and businesslike tone; his voice is, as it were, the voice of wisdom and age, too wise in the ways of the world to be impressed. There are ironic implications in his statements, as, for example, when he says: "Young people who need a love potion very seldom have five thousand dollars. Otherwise they would not need a love potion." He is implying that affections are secured by money, an idea opposite to young people's ideals of romantic love. The old man piles up a formidable list of things that Diana will do; like items in a column of figures, they are presented in parallel grammatical structures. In contrast, Alan is made to speak emotionally; his words, though few, are punctuated with exclamation points. Toward the end the author also underlines the old man's dry, indifferent attitude by giving him a manner of offhand understatement. Concerning the "life-cleaner," he says: "One has to be older than you are, to indulge in that sort of thing"; but they come back "when they are rather better off, and want more expensive things." To Alan the love potion has become "this wonderful mixture"; but the old man says, " 'Oh, that,' . . . taking out a tiny, rather dirty-looking phial. 'That is just a dollar.' "

According to the ideal, an author's style in each work should be in keeping with his purpose. Whatever his effect may be, it is accomplished by arrangements of words. Ideally the words should be perfectly adjusted to achieve the desired effect. Among the several qualities for which "The Chaser" may be praised, John Collier's style is not the least.

"The Chaser" is a good example of the modern short story that provides the reader a revelation of some phase of life by letting him observe a brief picture of a significant happening. All the elements of such a story have been so economically and efficiently combined—they interact so well together—that the story itself is a triumphant little work of art.

III

The short stories that follow have been arranged so that there is a movement from a relatively simple kind of story, in which plot, danger, and physical conflict are dominant, toward stories that are more subtle, less plot-oriented, and more concerned with emotion, internal conflict, psychological reactions, and ideas. But these are matters of varied emphases, and the arrangement is by no means rigid or dogmatic. The stories also illustrate differing techniques and differing points of view.

To read stories effectively, one needs always to pay close attention to the early, expository part; but inevitably a reader will follow different lines of interest with different stories—now plot, now character, now theme or atmosphere or emotion. Titles sometimes are clearly informative; such titles as "The Jockey," "The Thrower-Away," and "My Lady Love, My Dove" would seem to point to a strong character interest, whereas "The Story of a Conscience," "Careless Talk," and "The Cost of Living" suggest a predominating idea. But many titles are meant more to arouse interest and wonder than to inform.

The experienced reader knows that the setting chosen for an action is often extremely significant; many stories, in fact, could not plausibly take place except in the given setting. It is very important that the setting of Aiken's "Farewell! Farewell! Farewell!" is a passenger ship; both "The Jockey" and "Careless Talk" have eating places for their setting, and for each story the setting provides a special atmosphere. The different settings of "Just Lather, That's All" and "Self-Service Elevator" are intimately related with other elements of the stories; and the unusual plot of "Lost Face" could only be worked out in such an exotic setting as the one London uses.

To follow the causally interlinked, suspenseful events of a story is a basic activity of every reader; but an effective reader of modern stories must be aware also of the significance of the few events in stories where not much happens—where the quality of the revelation is more important than the excitements of plot. Revelation of character in stories fascinates us; to discover what a character really is (whatever he may say and how he may say it) provides a main satisfaction in many modern stories. Thus the picture of husbands and wives in "My Lady Love, My Dove" that the reader can construct after Arthur Beauchamp tells about one evening in his home is humorously ironic and yet almost horrifying. In some stories the reader will find that characters are not merely individuals; they stand as representatives of human types, of human attitudes, or perhaps of all mankind. The Negro undertaker in "The Convert" represents many men who find themselves impelled finally to take a stand for civil rights; Chekhov's Nadia in "After the Theater" is practically a personification of adolescence as Martinez is of all romantic young men in "The Wonderful Ice Cream Suit"; and the protagonist of "The Snake" is given a means to discover, along with the reader, that he is Everyman.

An author must bring us his story through words and words alone. Therefore, his choice of a point of view and of the tone in which the story is told is very important. The earnest manner of the protagonist telling his story in "The Thrower-Away" is essential to its satirical effect just as the guarded understatement of Arthur Beauchamp is essential for the irony of "My Lady Love, My Dove." The gay, informal style of "The Wonderful Ice Cream Suit" is completely different from the grave, almost biblical tone of "The Snake." The appreciative reader is aware of these varying stylistic qualities and can perceive why the spare, restrained style of "The Jockey" goes with Carson McCullers' choice of the objective point of view as well as why Joyce Carol Oates, although also writing in a vivid, concrete way, must enter the mind of her protagonist in "First Views of the Enemy."

Finally, every reader must hope that although he finds it useful and even necessary to analyze stories, he can put the parts back together and perceive how they operate like members of one body to form a functioning artistic whole. This means that it will simultaneously please and enlighten us about life.

Lost Face

JACK LONDON

It was the end. Subienkow had travelled a long trail of bitterness and horror, homing like a dove for the capitals of Europe, and here, farther away than ever, in Russian America, the trail ceased. He sat in the snow, arms tied behind him, waiting the torture. He stared curiously before him at a huge Cossack, prone in the snow, moaning in his pain. The men had 5 finished handling the giant and turned him over to the women. That they exceeded the fiendishness of the men, the man's cries attested.

Subienkow looked on, and shuddered. He was not afraid to die. He had carried his life too long in his hands, on that weary trail from Warsaw to Nulato, to shudder at mere dying. But he objected to the torture. It 10 offended his soul. And this offence, in turn, was not due to the mere pain he must endure, but to the sorry spectacle the pain would make of him. He knew that he would pray, and beg, and entreat, even as Big Ivan and the others that had gone before. This would not be nice. To pass out bravely and cleanly, with a smile and a jest—ah! that would have been the 15 way. But to lose control, to have his soul upset by the pangs of the flesh, to screech and gibber like an ape, to become the veriest beast—ah, that was what was so terrible.

There had been no chance to escape. From the beginning, when he dreamed the fiery dream of Poland's independence, he had become a 20 puppet in the hands of Fate. From the beginning, at Warsaw, at St. Petersburg, in the Siberian mines, in Kamtchatka, on the crazy boats of the fur-thieves, Fate had been driving him to this end. Without doubt, in the foundations of the world was graved this end for him—for him, who was so fine and sensitive, whose nerves scarcely sheltered under his skin, who 25 was a dreamer, and a poet, and an artist. Before he was dreamed of, it had been determined that the quivering bundle of sensitiveness that constituted him should be doomed to live in raw and howling savagery, and to die in this far land of night, in this dark place beyond the last boundaries of the world. 30

He sighed. So that thing before him was Big Ivan—Big Ivan the giant, the man without nerves, the man of iron, the Cossack turned freebooter of the seas, who was as phlegmatic as an ox, with a nervous system so low that what was pain to ordinary men was scarcely a tickle to him. Well, well, trust these Nulato Indians to find Big Ivan's nerves and trace them to 35 the roots of his quivering soul. They were certainly doing it. It was inconceivable that a man could suffer so much and yet live. Big Ivan was

paying for his low order of nerves. Already he had lasted twice as long
as any of the others.

Subienkow felt that he could not stand the Cossack's sufferings much 40
longer. Why didn't Ivan die? He would go mad if that screaming did not
cease. But when it did cease, his turn would come. And there was Yakaga
awaiting him, too, grinning at him even now in anticipation—Yakaga,
whom only last week he had kicked out of the fort, and upon whose face
he had laid the lash of his dog-whip. Yakaga would attend to him. 45
Doubtlessly Yakaga was saving for him more refined tortures, more ex-
quisite nerve-racking. Ah! that must have been a good one, from the way
Ivan screamed. The squaws bending over him stepped back with laughter and clapping of hands. Subienkow saw the monstrous thing that had
been perpetrated, and began to laugh hysterically. The Indians looked at 50
him in wonderment that he should laugh. But Subienkow could not stop.

This would never do. He controlled himself, the spasmodic twitch-
ings slowly dying away. He strove to think of other things, and began reading back in his own life. He remembered his mother and his father,
and the little spotted pony, and the French tutor who had taught him 55
dancing and sneaked him an old worn copy of Voltaire. Once more he saw
Paris, and dreary London, and gay Vienna, and Rome. And once more he
saw that wild group of youths who had dreamed, even as he, the dream
of an independent Poland with a king of Poland on the throne at Warsaw.
Ah, there it was that the long trail began. Well, he had lasted longest. One 60
by one, beginning with the two executed at St. Petersburg, he took up the
count of the passing of those brave spirits. Here one had been beaten to
death by a jailer, and there, on that blood-stained highway of the exiles,
where they had marched for endless months, beaten and maltreated by
their Cossack guards, another had dropped by the way. Always it had been 65
savagery—brutal, bestial savagery. They had died—of fever, in the mines,
under the knout. The last two had died after the escape, in the battle
with the Cossacks, and he alone had won to Kamtchatka with the stolen
papers and the money of a traveller he had left lying in the snow.

It had been nothing but savagery. All the years, with his heart in 70
studios, and theatres, and courts, he had been hemmed in by savagery. He
had purchased his life with blood. Everybody had killed. He had killed
that traveller for his passports. He had proved that he was a man of
parts by duelling with two Russian officers on a single day. He had had to
prove himself in order to win to a place among the fur-thieves. He had had 75
to win to that place. Behind him lay the thousand-years-long road
across all Siberia and Russia. He could not escape that way. The only way
was ahead, across the dark and icy sea of Behring to Alaska. The way had
led from savagery to deeper savagery. On the scurvy-rotten ships of the
fur-thieves, out of food and out of water, buffeted by the interminable 80
storms of that stormy sea, men had become animals. Thrice he had sailed

east from Kamtchatka. And thrice, after all manner of hardship and suffering, the survivors had come back to Kamtchatka. There had been no outlet for escape, and he could not go back the way he had come, for the mines and the knout awaited him.　85

Again, the fourth and last time, he had sailed east. He had been with those who first found the fabled Seal Islands; but he had not returned with them to share the wealth of furs in the mad orgies of Kamtchatka. He had sworn never to go back. He knew that to win to those dear capitals of Europe he must go on. So he had changed ships and remained in the 90 dark new land. His comrades were Slavonian hunters and Russian adventurers, Mongols and Tartars and Siberian aborigines; and through the savages of the new world they had cut a path of blood. They had massacred whole villages that refused to furnish the fur-tribute; and they, in turn, had been massacred by ships' companies. He, with one Finn, had been the 95 sole survivors of such a company. They had spent a winter of solitude and starvation on a lonely Aleutian isle, and their rescue in the spring by another fur-ship had been one chance in a thousand.

But always the terrible savagery had hemmed him in. Passing from ship to ship, and ever refusing to return, he had come to the ship that ex- 100 plored south. All down the Alaska coast they had encountered nothing but hosts of savages. Every anchorage among the beetling islands or under the frowning cliffs of the mainland had meant a battle or a storm. Either the gales blew, threatening destruction, or the war canoes came off, manned by howling natives with the war-paint on their faces, who came 105 to learn the bloody virtues of the sea-rovers' gunpowder. South, south they had coasted, clear to the myth-land of California. Here, it was said, were Spanish adventurers who had fought their way up from Mexico. He had had hopes of those Spanish adventurers. Escaping to them, the rest would have been easy—a year or two, what did it matter more or less—and he 110 would win to Mexico, then a ship, and Europe would be his. But they had met no Spaniards. Only had they encountered the same impregnable wall of savagery. The denizens of the confines of the world, painted for war, had driven them back from the shores. At last, when one boat was cut off and every man killed, the commander had abandoned the quest and 115 sailed back to the north.

The years had passed. He had served under Tebenkoff when Michael-ovski Redoubt was built. He had spent two years in the Kuskokwim country. Two summers, in the month of June, he had managed to be at the head of Kotzebue Sound. Here, at this time, the tribes assembled for 120 barter; here were to be found spotted deerskins from Siberia, ivory from the Diomedes, walrus skins from the shores of the Arctic, strange stone lamps, passing in trade from tribe to tribe, no one knew whence, and, once, a hunting-knife of English make; and here, Subienkow knew, was the school in which to learn geography. For he met Eskimos from Norton 125

Sound, from King Island and St. Lawrence Island, from Cape Prince of Wales, and Point Barrow. Such places had other names, and their distances were measured in days.

It was a vast region these trading savages came from, and a vaster region from which, by repeated trade, their stone lamps and that steel knife had come. Subienkow bullied, and cajoled, and bribed. Every far-journeyer or strange tribesman was brought before him. Perils unaccountable and unthinkable were mentioned, as well as wild beasts, hostile tribes, impenetrable forests, and mighty mountain ranges; but always from beyond came the rumor and the tale of white-skinned men, blue of eye and fair of hair, who fought like devils and who sought always for furs. They were to the east—far, far to the east. No one had seen them. It was the word that had been passed along.

It was a hard school. One could not learn geography very well through the medium of strange dialects, from dark minds that mingled fact and fable and that measured distances by "sleeps" that varied according to the difficulty of the going. But at last came the whisper that gave Subienkow courage. In the east lay a great river where were these blue-eyed men. The river was called the Yukon. South of Michaelovski Redoubt emptied another great river which the Russians knew as the Kwikpak. These two rivers were one, ran the whisper.

Subienkow returned to Michaelovski. For a year he urged an expedition up the Kwikpak. Then arose Malakoff, the Russian half-breed, to lead the wildest and most ferocious of the hell's broth of mongrel adventurers who had crossed from Kamtchatka. Subienkow was his lieutenant. They threaded the mazes of the great delta of the Kwikpak, picked up the first low hills on the northern bank, and for half a thousand miles, in skin canoes loaded to the gunwales with trade-goods and ammunition, fought their way against the five-knot current of a river that ran from two to ten miles wide in a channel many fathoms deep. Malakoff decided to build the fort at Nulato. Subienkow urged to go farther. But he quickly reconciled himself to Nulato. The long winter was coming on. It would be better to wait. Early the following summer, when the ice was gone, he would disappear up the Kwikpak and work his way to the Hudson Bay Company's posts. Malakoff had never heard the whisper that the Kwikpak was the Yukon, and Subienkow did not tell him.

Came the building of the fort. It was enforced labor. The tiered walls of logs arose to the sighs and groans of the Nulato Indians. The lash was laid upon their backs, and it was the iron hand of the freebooters of the sea that laid on the lash. There were Indians that ran away, and when they were caught they were brought back and spread-eagled before the fort, where they and their tribe learned the efficacy of the knout. Two died under it; others were injured for life; and the rest took the lesson to heart and ran away no more. The snow was flying ere the fort was finished, and then it was the time for furs. A heavy tribute was laid upon the tribe.

Blows and lashings continued, and that the tribute should be paid, the women and children were held as hostages and treated with the barbarity that only the fur-thieves knew.

Well, it had been a sowing of blood, and now was come the harvest. The fort was gone. In the light of its burning, half the fur-thieves had 175 been cut down. The other half had passed under the torture. Only Subienkow remained, or Subienkow and Big Ivan, if that whimpering, moaning thing in the snow could be called Big Ivan. Subienkow caught Yakaga grinning at him. There was no gainsaying Yakaga. The mark of the lash was still on his face. After all, Subienkow could not blame him, but he dis- 180 liked the thought of what Yakaga would do to him. He thought of appealing to Makamuk, the head-chief; but his judgment told him that such appeal was useless. Then, too, he thought of bursting his bonds and dying fighting. Such an end would be quick. But he could not break his bonds. Caribou thongs were stronger than he. Still devising, another 185 thought came to him. He signed for Makamuk, and that an interpreter who knew the coast dialect should be brought.

"Oh, Makamuk," he said, "I am not minded to die. I am a great man, and it were foolishness for me to die. In truth, I shall not die. I am not like these other carrion." 190

He looked at the moaning thing that had once been Big Ivan, and stirred it contemptuously with his toe.

"I am too wise to die. Behold, I have a great medicine. I alone know this medicine. Since I am not going to die, I shall exchange this medicine with you." 195

"What is this medicine?" Makamuk demanded.

"It is a strange medicine."

Subienkow debated with himself for a moment, as if loath to part with the secret.

"I will tell you. A little bit of this medicine rubbed on the skin makes 200 the skin hard like a rock, hard like iron, so that no cutting weapon can cut it. The strongest blow of a cutting weapon is a vain thing against it. A bone knife becomes like a piece of mud; and it will turn the edge of the iron knives we have brought among you. What will you give me for the secret of the medicine?" 205

"I will give you your life," Makamuk made answer through the interpreter.

Subienkow laughed scornfully.

"And you shall be a slave in my house until you die."

The Pole laughed more scornfully. 210

"Untie my hands and feet and let us talk," he said.

The chief made the sign; and when he was loosed Subienkow rolled a cigarette and lighted it.

"This is foolish talk," said Makamuk. "There is no such medicine. It cannot be. A cutting edge is stronger than any medicine." 215

The chief was incredulous, and yet he wavered. He had seen too many deviltries of fur-thieves that worked. He could not wholly doubt.

"I will give you your life; but you shall not be a slave," he announced.

"More than that."

Subienkow played his game as coolly as if he were bartering for a 220 foxskin.

"It is a very great medicine. It has saved my life many times. I want a sled and dogs, and six of your hunters to travel with me down the river and give me safety to one day's sleep from Michaelovski Redoubt."

"You must live here, and teach us all of your deviltries," was the reply. 225

Subienkow shrugged his shoulders and remained silent. He blew cigarette smoke out on the icy air, and curiously regarded what remained of the big Cossack.

"That scar!" Makamuk said suddenly, pointing to the Pole's neck, where a livid mark advertised the slash of a knife in a Kamtchatkan brawl. 230 "The medicine is not good. The cutting edge was stronger than the medicine."

"It was a strong man that drove the stroke." (Subienkow considered.) "Stronger than you, stronger than your strongest hunter, stronger than he." 235

Again, with the toe of his moccasin, he touched the Cossack—a grisly spectacle, no longer conscious—yet in whose dismembered body the pain-racked life clung and was loath to go.

"Also, the medicine was weak. For at that place there were no berries of a certain kind, of which I see you have plenty in this country. The 240 medicine here will be strong."

"I will let you go down river," said Makamuk; "and the sled and the dogs and the six hunters to give you safety shall be yours."

"You are slow," was the cool rejoinder. "You have committed an offence against my medicine in that you did not at once accept my terms. 245 Behold, I now demand more. I want one hundred beaver skins." (Makamuk sneered.) "I want one hundred pounds of dried fish." (Makamuk nodded, for fish were plentiful and cheap.) "I want two sleds—one for me and one for my furs and fish. And my rifle must be returned to me. If you do not like the price, in a little while the price will grow." 250

Yakaga whispered to the chief.

"But how can I know your medicine is true medicine?" Makamuk asked.

"It is very easy. First, I shall go into the woods——"

Again Yakaga whispered to Makamuk, who made a suspicious dis- 255 sent.

"You can send twenty hunters with me," Subienkow went on. "You see, I must get the berries and the roots with which to make the medicine. Then, when you have brought the two sleds and loaded on them the fish and the beaver skins and the rifle, and when you have told off the six 260 hunters who will go with me—then, when all is ready, I will rub the medicine on my neck, so, and lay my neck there on that log. Then can your strongest hunter take the axe and strike three times on my neck. You yourself can strike the three times."

Makamuk stood with gaping mouth, drinking in this latest and most 265 wonderful magic of the fur-thieves.

"But first," the Pole added hastily, "between each blow I must put on fresh medicine. The axe is heavy and sharp, and I want no mistakes."

"All that you have asked shall be yours," Makamuk cried in a rush of acceptance. "Proceed to make your medicine."   270

Subienkow concealed his elation. He was playing a desperate game, and there must be no slips. He spoke arrogantly.

"You have been slow. My medicine is offended. To make the offence clean you must give me your daughter."

He pointed to the girl, an unwholesome creature, with a cast in one 275 eye and a bristling wolf-tooth. Makamuk was angry, but the Pole remained imperturbable, rolling and lighting another cigarette.

"Make haste," he threatened. "If you are not quick, I shall demand yet more."

In the silence that followed, the dreary northland scene faded from 280 before him, and he saw once more his native land, and France, and, once, as he glanced at the wolf-toothed girl, he remembered another girl, a singer and a dancer, whom he had known when first as a youth he came to Paris.

"What do you want with the girl?" Makamuk asked.

"To go down the river with me." Subienkow glanced her over criti- 285 cally. "She will make a good wife, and it is an honor worthy of my medicine to be married to your blood."

Again he remembered the singer and dancer and hummed aloud a song she had taught him. He lived the old life over, but in a detached, impersonal sort of way, looking at the memory-pictures of his own life as if 290 they were pictures in a book of anybody's life. The chief's voice, abruptly breaking the silence, startled him.

"It shall be done," said Makamuk. "The girl shall go down the river with you. But be it understood that I myself strike the three blows with the axe on your neck."   295

"But each time I shall put on the medicine," Subienkow answered, with a show of ill-concealed anxiety.

"You shall put the medicine on between each blow. Here are the hunters who shall see you do not escape. Go into the forest and gather your medicine."   300

Makamuk had been convinced of the worth of the medicine by the Pole's rapacity. Surely nothing less than the greatest of medicines could enable a man in the shadow of death to stand up and drive an old-woman's bargain.

"Besides," whispered Yakaga, when the Pole, with his guard, had 305

disappeared among the spruce trees, "when you have learned the medicine you can easily destroy him."

"But how can I destroy him?" Makamuk argued. "His medicine will
not let me destroy him."

"There will be some part where he has not rubbed the medicine," 310
was Yakaga's reply. "We will destroy him through that part. It may be his
ears. Very well; we will thrust a spear in one ear and out the other. Or it
may be his eyes. Surely the medicine will be much too strong to rub on his
eyes."

The chief nodded. "You are wise, Yakaga. If he possesses no other 315
devil-things, we will then destroy him."

Subienkow did not waste time in gathering the ingredients for his
medicine. He selected whatsoever came to hand such as spruce needles,
the inner bark of the willow, a strip of birch bark, and a quantity of
moss-berries, which he made the hunters dig up for him from beneath the 320
snow. A few frozen roots completed his supply, and he led the way back
to camp.

Makamuk and Yakaga crouched beside him, noting the quantities
and kinds of the ingredients he dropped into the pot of boiling water.

"You must be careful that the moss-berries go in first," he explained. 325

"And—oh, yes, one other thing—the finger of a man. Here, Yakaga,
let me cut off your finger."

But Yakaga put his hands behind him and scowled.

"Just a small finger," Subienkow pleaded.

"Yakaga, give him your finger," Makamuk commanded.   330

"There be plenty of fingers lying around," Yakaga grunted, indicating
the human wreckage in the snow of the score of persons who had been
tortured to death.

"It must be the finger of a live man," the Pole objected.

"Then shall you have the finger of a live man." Yakaga strode over 335
to the Cossack and sliced off a finger.

"He is not yet dead," he announced, flinging the bloody trophy in
the snow at the Pole's feet. "Also, it is a good finger, because it is large."

Subienkow dropped it into the fire under the pot and began to sing.
It was a French lovesong that with great solemnity he sang into the brew. 340

"Without these words I utter into it, the medicine is worthless," he
explained. "The words are the chiefest strength of it. Behold, it is ready."

"Name the words slowly, that I may know them," Makamuk commanded.

"Not until after the test. When the axe flies back three times from my 345
neck, then will I give you the secret of the words."

"But if the medicine is not good medicine?" Makamuk queried
anxiously.

Subienkow turned upon him wrathfully.

"My medicine is always good. However, if it is not good, then do by 350 me as you have done to the others. Cut me up a bit at a time, even as you have cut him up." He pointed to the Cossack. "The medicine is now cool. Thus, I rub it on my neck, saying this further medicine."

With great gravity he slowly intoned a line of the "Marseillaise," at the same time rubbing the villainous brew thoroughly into his neck.   355

An outcry interrupted his play-acting. The giant Cossack, with a last resurgence of his tremendous vitality, had arisen to his knees. Laughter and cries of surprise and applause arose from the Nulatos, as Big Ivan began flinging himself about in the snow with mighty spasms.

Subienkow was made sick by the sight, but he mastered his qualms 360 and made believe to be angry.

"This will not do," he said. "Finish him, and then we will make the test. Here, you, Yakaga, see that his noise ceases."

While this was being done, Subienkow turned to Makamuk.

"And remember, you are to strike hard. This is not baby-work. Here, 365 take the axe and strike the log, so that I can see you strike like a man."

Makamuk obeyed, striking twice, precisely and with vigor, cutting out a large chip.

"It is well." Subienkow looked about him at the circle of savage faces that somehow seemed to symbolize the wall of savagery that had hemmed 370 him about ever since the Czar's police had first arrested him in Warsaw. "Take your axe, Makamuk, and stand so. I shall lie down. When I raise my hand, strike, and strike with all your might. And be careful that no one stands behind you. The medicine is good, and the axe may bounce from off my neck and right out of your hands."   375

He looked at the two sleds, with the dogs in harness, loaded with furs and fish. His rifle lay on top of the beaver skins. The six hunters who were to act as his guard stood by the sleds.

"Where is the girl?" the Pole demanded. "Bring her up to the sleds before the test goes on."   380

When this had been carried out, Subienkow lay down in the snow, resting his head on the log like a tired child about to sleep. He had lived so many dreary years that he was indeed tired.

"I laugh at you and your strength, O Makamuk," he said. "Strike, and strike hard."   385

He lifted his hand. Makamuk swung the axe, a broadaxe for the squaring of logs. The bright steel flashed through the frosty air, poised for a perceptible instant above Makamuk's head, then descended upon Subienkow's bare neck. Clear through flesh and bone it cut its way, biting deeply into the log beneath. The amazed savages saw the head bounce a yard 390 away from the blood-spouting trunk.

There was a great bewilderment and silence, while slowly it began to dawn in their minds that there had been no medicine. The fur-thief had outwitted them. Alone, of all their prisoners, he had escaped the torture. That had been the stake for which he played. A great roar of laughter went 395 up. Makamuk bowed his head in shame. The fur-thief had fooled him. He had lost face before all his people. Still they continued to roar out their laughter. Makamuk turned, and with bowed head stalked away. He knew that thenceforth he would be no longer known as Makamuk. He would be Lost Face; the record of his shame would be with him until he   400 died; and whenever the tribes gathered in the spring for the salmon, or in the summer for the trading, the story would pass back and forth across the camp-fires of how the fur-thief died peaceably, at a single stroke, by the hand of Lost Face.

"Who was Lost Face?" he could hear, in anticipation, some insolent   405 young buck demand. "Oh, Lost Face," would be the answer, "he who once was Makamuk in the days before he cut off the fur-thief's head."

QUESTIONS

1. What has the author told us in the ninety words of the first paragraph regarding a character, the setting (place and time), and the situation?
2. What important elements in the character of Subienkow are brought out in the second and third paragraphs? Is Subienkow the protagonist? What cause is suggested for his situation?
3. What are the elements of suspense in the opening paragraphs of the story?
4. What information in lines 31–39 throws more light on the situation?
5. By what method has the author introduced the material of lines 52–187? What does this material contribute to the story? Why does Subienkow leave home to travel "a long trail of bitterness and horror"? What makes the trail bitter and horrible?
6. Which words emphasize the quality of the experiences he has lived through? Why is it difficult for him to learn the geography necessary for him to get back to Europe? Who are the "white-skinned men" mentioned in line 135?
7. According to lines 162–187, why is Subienkow now in a hopeless situation?
8. Where does the exposition end and the action proper of the story begin?
9. Which characters are in conflict? Describe the nature of the conflict.
10. In line 220 Subienkow is said to be playing "his game." Check the stages of the bartering game as it proceeds, from line 197 to line 295.
11. What do lines 229–232 represent in terms of suspense?
12. What important psychological point is made in lines 301–304? What further information is provided by lines 305–316? What is the function of lines 323–324?
13. What produces the irony and grotesque humor of lines 326–342?
14. Why should London bother to mention Big Ivan again? Note that in

lines 356–363 the part about Big Ivan is not told very specifically. Why should London use such general terms?

15. What is demonstrated by the specific details in lines 376–378?
16. What is Subienkow's purpose in speaking the words of lines 384–385?
17. How is the conflict resolved? What is the *dénouement* of the plot? What elements of character, setting, and situation make the *dénouement* believable?
18. Summarize the plot of the story.
19. Why could London not tell the story from Subienkow's point of view? Why does he have to include thoughts and feelings of the Indians?
20. What theme is projected by this story?
21. Try to analyze London's style. Which does he use the more: general and abstract words or specific and concrete ones? Does he chiefly use short or long sentences? What qualities do his choices give to his style?

The Story of a Conscience

AMBROSE BIERCE

I

Captain Parrol Hartroy stood at the advanced post of his picket-guard, talking in low tones with the sentinel. This post was on a turnpike which bisected the captain's camp, a half-mile in rear, though the camp was not in sight from that point. The officer was apparently giving the soldier certain instructions—was perhaps merely inquiring if all were quiet in 5 front. As the two stood talking a man approached them from the direction of the camp, carelessly whistling, and was promptly halted by the soldier. He was evidently a civilian—a tall person, coarsely clad in the home-made stuff of yellow gray, called "butternut," which was men's only wear in the latter days of the Confederacy. On his head was a slouch felt hat, once white, 10 from beneath which hung masses of uneven hair, seemingly unacquainted with either scissors or comb. The man's face was rather striking; a broad forehead, high nose, and thin cheeks, the mouth invisible in the full dark beard, which seemed as neglected as the hair. The eyes were large and had that steadiness and fixity of attention which so frequently mark a consid- 15 ering intelligence and a will not easily turned from its purpose—so say those physiognomists who have that kind of eyes. On the whole, this was a man whom one would be likely to observe and be observed by. He carried a walking-stick freshly cut from the forest and his ailing cowskin boots were white with dust. 20

"Show your pass," said the Federal soldier, a trifle more imperiously perhaps than he would have thought necessary if he had not been under the eye of his commander, who with folded arms looked on from the roadside.

"'Lowed you'd rec'lect me, Gineral," said the wayfarer tranquilly, 25 while producing the paper from the pocket of his coat. There was something in his tone—perhaps a faint suggestion of irony—which made his elevation of his obstructor to exalted rank less agreeable to that worthy warrior than promotion is commonly found to be. "You-all have to be purty pertickler, I reckon," he added, in a more conciliatory tone, as if in 30 half-apology for being halted.

Having read the pass, with his rifle resting on the ground, the soldier handed the document back without a word, shouldered his weapon, and returned to his commander. The civilian passed on in the middle of the road, and when he had penetrated the circumjacent Confederacy a few 35

yards resumed his whistling and was soon out of sight beyond an angle in
the road, which at that point entered a thin forest. Suddenly the officer
undid his arms from his breast, drew a revolver from his belt and sprang
forward at a run in the same direction, leaving his sentinel in gaping astonishment at his post. After making to the various visible forms of nature 40
a solemn promise to be damned, that gentleman resumed the air of
stolidity which is supposed to be appropriate to a state of alert military
attention.

II

Captain Hartroy held an independent command. His force consisted
of a company of infantry, a squadron of cavalry, and a section of artillery, 45
detached from the army to which they belonged, to defend an important
defile in the Cumberland Mountains in Tennessee. It was a field officer's
command held by a line officer promoted from the ranks, where he had
quietly served until "discovered." His post was one of exceptional peril;
its defense entailed a heavy responsibility and he had wisely been given 50
corresponding discretionary powers, all the more necessary because of
his distance from the main army, the precarious nature of his com-
munications and the lawless character of the enemy's irregular troops in-
festing that region. He had strongly fortified his little camp, which em-
braced a village of a half-dozen dwellings and a country store, and had 55
collected a considerable quantity of supplies. To a few resident civilians of
known loyalty, with whom it was desirable to trade, and of whose services
in various ways he sometimes availed himself, he had given written passes
admitting them within his lines. It is easy to understand that an abuse of
this privilege in the interest of the enemy might entail serious conse- 60
quences. Captain Hartroy had made an order to the effect that any one so
abusing it would be summarily shot.

While the sentinel had been examining the civilian's pass the captain had eyed the latter narrowly. He thought his appearance familiar and
had at first no doubt of having given him the pass which had satisfied the 65
sentinel. It was not until the man had got out of sight and hearing that his
identity was disclosed by a revealing light from memory. With soldierly
promptness of decision the officer had acted on the revelation.

III

To any but a singularly self-possessed man the apparition of an officer
of the military forces, formidably clad, bearing in one hand a sheathed 70
sword and in the other a cocked revolver, and rushing in furious pursuit,
is no doubt disquieting to a high degree; upon the man to whom the pursuit was in this instance directed it appeared to have no other effect than
somewhat to intensify his tranquillity. He might easily enough have es-

caped into the forest to the right or the left, but chose another course of 75
action—turned and quietly faced the captain, saying as he came up: "I
reckon ye must have something to say to me, which ye disremembered.
What mout it be, neighbor?"

But the "neighbor" did not answer, being engaged in the unneigh-
borly act of covering him with a cocked pistol.   80

"Surrender," said the captain as calmly as a slight breathlessness from
exertion would permit, "or you die."

There was no menace in the manner of this demand; that was all in the
matter and in the means of enforcing it. There was, too, something not altogether reassuring in the cold gray eyes that glanced along the barrel of 85
the weapon. For a moment the two men stood looking at each other in
silence; then the civilian, with no appearance of fear—with as great apparent unconcern as when complying with the less austere demand of the
sentinel—slowly pulled from his pocket the paper which had satisfied
that humble functionary and held it out, saying: 90

"I reckon this 'ere parss from Mister Hartroy is——"

"The pass is a forgery," the officer said, interrupting. "I am Captain
Hartroy—and you are Dramer Brune."

It would have required a sharp eye to observe the slight pallor of
the civilian's face at these words, and the only other manifestation attesting 95
their significance was a voluntary relaxation of the thumb and fingers holding the dishonored paper, which, falling to the road, unheeded, was rolled
by a gentle wind and then lay still, with a coating of dust, as in humiliation
for the lie that it bore. A moment later the civilian, still looking unmoved
into the barrel of the pistol, said: 100

"Yes, I am Dramer Brune, a Confederate spy, and your prisoner. I
have on my person, as you will soon discover, a plan of your fort and its
armament, a statement of the distribution of your men and their number,
a map of the approaches, showing the positions of all your outposts. My
life is fairly yours, but if you wish it taken in a more formal way than by 105
your own hand, and if you are willing to spare me the indignity of march-
ing into camp at the muzzle of your pistol, I promise you that I will
neither resist, escape, nor remonstrate, but will submit to whatever penalty may be imposed."

The officer lowered his pistol, uncocked it, and thrust it into its place 110
in his belt. Brune advanced a step, extending his right hand.

"It is the hand of a traitor and a spy," said the officer coldly, and did
not take it. The other bowed.

"Come," said the captain, "let us go to camp; you shall not die until
to-morrow morning."   115

He turned his back upon his prisoner, and these two enigmatical
men retraced their steps and soon passed the sentinel, who expressed his
general sense of things by a needless and exaggerated salute to his commander.

IV

Early on the morning after these events the two men, captor and cap- 120
tive, sat in the tent of the former. A table was between them on which
lay, among a number of letters, official and private, which the captain had
written during the night, the incriminating papers found upon the spy.
That gentleman had slept through the night in an adjoining tent, unguarded. Both, having breakfasted, were now smoking. 125

"Mr. Brune," said Captain Hartroy, "you probably do not understand
why I recognized you in your disguise, nor how I was aware of your name."

"I have not sought to learn, Captain," the prisoner said with quiet
dignity.

"Nevertheless I should like you to know—if the story will not offend. 130
You will perceive that my knowledge of you goes back to the autumn of
1861. At that time you were a private in an Ohio regiment—a brave and
trusted soldier. To the surprise and grief of your officers and comrades you
deserted and went over to the enemy. Soon afterward you were captured
in a skirmish, recognized, tried by court-martial and sentenced to be shot. 135
Awaiting the execution of the sentence you were confined, unfettered,
in a freight car standing on a side track of a railway."

"At Grafton, Virginia," said Brune, pushing the ashes from his cigar
with the little finger of the hand holding it, and without looking up.

"At Grafton, Virginia," the captain repeated. "One dark and stormy 140
night a soldier who had just returned from a long, fatiguing march was put
on guard over you. He sat on a cracker box inside the car, near the door,
his rifle loaded and the bayonet fixed. You sat in a corner and his orders
were to kill you if you attempted to rise."

"But if I *asked* to rise he might call the corporal of the guard." 145

"Yes. As the long silent hours wore away the soldier yielded to the demands of nature: he himself incurred the death penalty by sleeping at his
post of duty."

"You did."

"What! you recognize me? you have known me all along?" 150

The captain had risen and was walking the floor of his tent, visibly
excited. His face was flushed, the gray eyes had lost the cold, pitiless look
which they had shown when Brune had seen them over the pistol barrel;
they had softened wonderfully.

"I knew you," said the spy, with his customary tranquillity, "the mo- 155
ment you faced me, demanding my surrender. In the circumstances it
would have been hardly becoming in me to recall these matters. I am perhaps a traitor, certainly a spy; but I should not wish to seem a suppliant."

The captain had paused in his walk and was facing his prisoner. There
was a singular huskiness in his voice as he spoke again. 160

"Mr. Brune, whatever your conscience may permit you to be, you
saved my life at what you must have believed the cost of your own. Until

I saw you yesterday when halted by my sentinel I believed you dead—thought that you had suffered the fate which through my own crime you might easily have escaped. You had only to step from the car and leave 165
me to take your place before the firing-squad. You had a divine compassion. You pitied my fatigue. You let me sleep, watched over me, and as the time drew near for the relief-guard to come and detect me in my crime, you gently waked me. Ah, Brune, Brune, that was well done—that was great—that——" 170

The captain's voice failed him; the tears were running down his face and sparkled upon his beard and his breast. Resuming his seat at the table, he buried his face in his arms and sobbed. All else was silence.

Suddenly the clear warble of a bugle was heard sounding the "assembly." The captain started and raised his wet face from his arms; it had 175
turned ghastly pale. Outside, in the sunlight, were heard the stir of the men falling into line; the voices of the sergeants calling the roll; the tapping of the drummers as they braced their drums. The captain spoke again:

"I ought to have confessed my fault in order to relate the story of 180
your magnanimity; it might have procured you a pardon. A hundred times I resolved to do so, but shame prevented. Besides, your sentence was just and righteous. Well, Heaven forgive me! I said nothing, and my regiment was soon afterward ordered to Tennessee and I never heard about you." 185

"It was all right, sir," said Brune, without visible emotion; "I escaped and returned to my colors—the Confederate colors. I should like to add that before deserting from the Federal service I had earnestly asked a discharge, on the ground of altered convictions. I was answered by punishment." 190

"Ah, but if I had suffered the penalty of my crime—if you had not generously given me the life that I accepted without gratitude you would not be again in the shadow and imminence of death."

The prisoner started slightly and a look of anxiety came into his face. One would have said, too, that he was surprised. At that moment a 195
lieutenant, the adjutant, appeared at the opening of the tent and saluted. "Captain," he said, "the battalion is formed."

Captain Hartroy had recovered his composure. He turned to the officer and said: "Lieutenant, go to Captain Graham and say that I direct him to assume command of the battalion and parade it outside the parapet. 200
This gentleman is a deserter and a spy; he is to be shot to death in the presence of the troops. He will accompany you, unbound and unguarded."

While the adjutant waited at the door the two men inside the tent rose and exchanged ceremonious bows, Brune immediately retiring.

Half an hour later an old negro cook, the only person left in camp 205
except the commander, was so startled by the sound of a volley of musketry that he dropped the kettle that he was lifting from a fire. But for his

consternation and the hissing which the contents of the kettle made among the embers, he might also have heard, nearer at hand, the single pistol shot with which Captain Hartroy renounced the life which in con- 210 science he could no longer keep.

In compliance with the terms of a note that he left for the officer who succeeded him in command, he was buried, like the deserter and spy, without military honors; and in the solemn shadow of the mountain which knows no more of war the two sleep well in long-forgotten graves.   215

QUESTIONS

1. Which character receives most attention in section I of the story? What is significant about him? What action in section I creates surprise and suspense?
2. What important points are made in the two paragraphs of section II?
3. What accounts for the quiet behavior of Brune when the captain is pursuing him? Why is the captain willing to turn his back upon Brune at the end of section III?
4. What does their conversation reveal about the relation of the captain to Brune? Why does the captain weep? What causes his face to turn "ghastly pale" (176)?[1] What does the captain blame himself for?
5. To what extent are we prepared for the captain's final decisions? Is he a cruel and ungrateful man?
6. What forces conflict in this story? How do you interpret the meaning of the title?
7. Which of Bierce's sentences best illustrate that he uses a formal and dignified style? Do you note a few places where the writing is a bit ironic?—for example, his reference to physiognomists in the first paragraph and the soldier's solemn promise in the fourth paragraph.

[1] Numbers in parentheses throughout Section One of the book denote lines in the story being discussed.

Just Lather, That's All

HERNANDO TÉLLEZ

He said nothing when he entered. I was passing the best of my razors back and forth on a strop. When I recognized him I started to tremble. But he didn't notice. Hoping to conceal my emotion, I continued sharpening the razor. I tested it on the meat of my thumb, and then held it up to the light. At that moment he took off the bullet-studded belt that his gun 5 holster dangled from. He hung it up on a wall hook and placed his military cap over it. Then he turned to me, loosening the knot of his tie, and said, "It's hot as hell. Give me a shave." He sat in the chair.

I estimated he had a four-day beard. The four days taken up by the latest expedition in search of our troops. His face seemed reddened, burned 10 by the sun. Carefully, I began to prepare the soap. I cut off a few slices, dropped them into the cup, mixed in a bit of warm water, and began to stir with the brush. Immediately the foam began to rise. "The other boys in the group should have this much beard, too." I continued stirring the lather. 15

"But we did all right, you know. We got the main ones. We brought back some dead, and we've got some others still alive. But pretty soon they'll all be dead."

"How many did you catch?" I asked.

"Fourteen. We had to go pretty deep into the woods to find them. 20 But we'll get even. Not one of them comes out of this alive, not one."

He leaned back on the chair when he saw me with the lather-covered brush in my hand. I still had to put the sheet on him. No doubt about it, I was upset. I took a sheet out of a drawer and knotted it around my customer's neck. He wouldn't stop talking. He probably thought I was in sym- 25 pathy with his party.

"The town must have learned a lesson from what we did the other day," he said.

"Yes," I replied, securing the knot at the base of his dark, sweaty neck. 30

"That was a fine show, eh?"

"Very good," I answered, turning back for the brush. The man closed his eyes with a gesture of fatigue and sat waiting for the cool caress of the soap. I had never had him so close to me. The day he ordered the

"Just Lather, That's All," by Hernando Téllez, translated by Donald A. Yates from *Great Spanish Short Stories*, selected and introduced by Angel Flores, copyright 1962. Dell Publishing Co., Inc. Reprinted by permission of Angel Flores.

whole town to file into the patio of the school to see the four rebels hang- 35
ing there, I came face to face with him for an instant. But the sight of the
mutilated bodies kept me from noticing the face of the man who had directed it all, the face I was now about to take into my hands. It was not an
unpleasant face, certainly. And the beard, which made him seem a bit
older than he was, didn't suit him badly at all. His name was Torres. Cap- 40
tain Torres. A man of imagination, because who else would have thought
of hanging the naked rebels and then holding target practice on certain
parts of their bodies? I began to apply the first layer of soap. With his
eyes closed, he continued. "Without any effort I could go straight to sleep,"
he said, "but there's plenty to do this afternoon." I stopped the lathering 45
and asked with a feigned lack of interest: "A firing squad?" "Something
like that, but a little slower." I got on with the job of lathering his beard.
My hands started trembling again. The man could not possibly realize it,
and this was in my favor. But I would have preferred that he hadn't come.
It was likely that many of our faction had seen him enter. And an enemy 50
under one's roof imposes certain conditions. I would be obliged to shave
that beard like any other one, carefully, gently, like that of any customer, taking pains to see that no single pore emitted a drop of blood.
Being careful to see that the little tufts of hair did not lead the blade
astray. Seeing that his skin ended up clean, soft, and healthy, so that 55
passing the back of my hand over it I couldn't feel a hair. Yes, I was
secretly a rebel, but I was also a conscientious barber, and proud of the
preciseness of my profession. And this four-days' growth of beard was
a fitting challenge.

I took the razor, opened up the two protective arms, exposed the 60
blade and began the job, from one of the sideburns downward. The
razor responded beautifully. His beard was inflexible and hard, not too
long, but thick. Bit by bit the skin emerged. The razor rasped along,
making its customary sound as fluffs of lather mixed with bits of hair gathered along the blade. I paused a moment to clean it, then took up the 65
strop again to sharpen the razor, because I'm a barber who does things
properly. The man, who had kept his eyes closed, opened them now, removed one of his hands from under the sheet, felt the spot on his face
where the soap had been cleared off, and said, "Come to the school today
at six o'clock." "The same thing as the other day?" I asked horrified. "It 70
could be better," he replied. "What do you plan to do?" "I don't know yet.
But we'll amuse ourselves." Once more he leaned back and closed his
eyes. I approached him with the razor poised. "Do you plan to punish
them all?" I ventured timidly. "All." The soap was drying on his face. I had
to hurry. In the mirror I looked toward the street. It was the same as ever: 75
the grocery store with two or three customers in it. Then I glanced at the
clock: two-twenty in the afternoon. The razor continued on its downward stroke. Now from the other sideburn down. A thick, blue beard.
He should have let it grow like some poets or priests do. It would suit him

well. A lot of people wouldn't recognize him. Much to his benefit, I 80
thought, as I attempted to cover the neck area smoothly. There, for sure,
the razor had to be handled masterfully, since the hair, although softer,
grew into little swirls. A curly beard. One of the tiny pores could be
opened up and issue forth its pearl of blood. A good barber such as I
prides himself on never allowing this to happen to a client. And this was 85
a first-class client. How many of us had he ordered shot? How many of us
had he ordered mutilated? It was better not to think about it. Torres did
not know that I was his enemy. He did not know it nor did the rest. It
was a secret shared by very few, precisely so that I could inform the
revolutionaries of what Torres was doing in the town and of what he was 90
planning each time he undertook a rebel-hunting excursion. So it was going
to be very difficult to explain that I had him right in my hands and let him
go peacefully—alive and shaved.

The beard was now almost completely gone. He seemed younger, less
burdened by years than when he had arrived. I suppose this always hap- 95
pens with men who visit barber shops. Under the stroke of my razor Torres
was being rejuvenated—rejuvenated because I am a good barber, the best
in the town, if I may say so. A little more lather here, under his chin, on
his Adam's apple, on this big vein. How hot it is getting! Torres must be
sweating as much as I. But he is not afraid. He is a calm man, who is not 100
even thinking about what he is going to do with the prisoners this afternoon. On the other hand I, with this razor in my hands, stroking and re-
stroking his skin, trying to keep blood from oozing from these pores, can't
even think clearly. Damn him for coming, because I'm a revolutionary and
not a murderer. And how easy it would be to kill him. And he deserves it. 105
Does he? No! What the devil! No one deserves to have someone else make
the sacrifice of becoming a murderer. What do you gain by it? Nothing.
Others come along and still others, and the first ones kill the second ones
and they the next ones and it goes on like this until everything is a sea of
blood. I could cut this throat just so, zip! zip! I wouldn't give him time to 110
complain and since he has his eyes closed he wouldn't see the glistening
knife blade or my glistening eyes. But I'm trembling like a real murderer.
Out of his neck a gush of blood would spout onto the sheet, on the chair,
on my hands, on the floor. I would have to close the door. And the blood
would keep inching along the floor, warm, ineradicable, uncontainable, 115
until it reached the street, like a little scarlet stream. I'm sure that one
solid stroke, one deep incision, would prevent any pain. He wouldn't
suffer. But what would I do with the body? Where would I hide it? I
would have to flee, leaving all I have behind, and take refuge far away, far,
far away. But they would follow until they found me. "Captain Torres' 120
murderer. He slit his throat while he was shaving him—a coward." And
then on the other side. "The avenger of us all. A name to remember. (And
here they would mention my name.) He was the town barber. No one
knew he was defending our cause."

And what of all this? Murderer or hero? My destiny depends on the 125 edge of this blade. I can turn my hand a bit more, press a little harder on the razor, and sink it in. The skin would give way like silk, like rubber, like the strop. There is nothing more tender than human skin and the blood is always there, ready to pour forth. A blade like this doesn't fail. It is my best. But I don't want to be a murderer, no sir. You came to me for a 130 shave. And I perform my work honorably. . . . I don't want blood on my hands. Just lather, that's all. You are an executioner and I am only a barber. Each person has his own place in the scheme of things. That's right. His own place.

Now his chin had been stroked clean and smooth. The man sat up 135 and looked into the mirror. He rubbed his hands over his skin and felt it fresh, like new.

"Thanks," he said. He went to the hanger for his belt, pistol and cap. I must have been very pale; my shirt felt soaked. Torres finished adjusting the buckle, straightened his pistol in the holster and after auto- 140 matically smoothing down his hair, he put on the cap. From his pants pocket he took out several coins to pay me for my services. And he began to head toward the door. In the doorway he paused for a moment, and turning to me he said:

"They told me that you'd kill me. I came to find out. But killing isn't 145 easy. You can take my word for it." And he headed on down the street.

QUESTIONS

1. What is the meaning of "our troops" (10), "his party" (26), "four rebels" (35), "our faction" (50)? What is the setting of the story? At what point has the reader been provided with enough information to understand the general background of the story?
2. What reasons does the barber have to tremble and be upset?
3. What idea of Captain Torres' character is developed as the barber continues shaving? What reasons does the barber have for hating Torres?
4. What kind of challenge does Torres represent to the barber? The barber says, "He wouldn't stop talking." Why does Torres talk as he does?
5. How is the idea of taking pride in one's work significant?
6. What does the barber mean by "No one deserves to have someone else make the sacrifice of becoming a murderer"?
7. Identify the conflicts in the story, external and internal.
8. As the barber sweats through his dilemma, what causes him to decide as he does? Has he rationalized to reach his decision? Does he prove himself a coward? a hero? a virtuous man?
9. The barber makes numerous statements about Captain Torres. Which ones are definitely incorrect?

10. After Torres' final speech, how would you contrast the two characters?
11. What is the meaning of the title? State the theme of the story.
12. Discuss the artistry with which the author handled his materials so as to create a strong and lasting effect in only about two thousand words.

The Convert

LERONE BENNETT, JR.

A man don't know what he'll do, a man don't know what he is till he gets his back pressed up against a wall. Now you take Aaron Lott: there ain't no other way to explain the crazy thing he did. He was going along fine, preaching the gospel, saving souls, and getting along with the white folks; and then, all of a sudden, he felt wood pressing against his 5 back. The funny thing was that nobody knew he was hurting till he preached that Red Sea sermon where he got mixed up and seemed to think Mississippi was Egypt. As chairman of the deacons board, I felt it was my duty to reason with him. I appreciated his position and told him so, but I didn't think it was right for him to push us all in a hole. The 10 old fool—he just laughed.

"Brother Booker," he said, "the Lord—He'll take care of me."

I knew then that that man was heading for trouble. And the very next thing he did confirmed it. The white folks called the old fool downtown to bear witness that the colored folks were happy. And you know 15 what he did: he got down there amongst all them big white folks and he said: "Things ain't gonna change here overnight, but they gonna change. It's inevitable. The Lord wants it."

Well sir, you could have bought them white folks for a penny. Aaron Lott, pastor of the Rock of Zion Baptist Church, a man white folks had 20 said was wise and sound and sensible, had come close—too close—to saying that the Supreme Court was coming to Melina, Mississippi. The surprising thing was that the white folks didn't do nothing. There was a lot of mumbling and whispering but nothing bad happened till the terrible morning when Aaron came a-knocking at the door of my funeral home. 25 Now things had been tightening up—you could feel it in the air—and I didn't want no part of no crazy scheme and I told him so right off. He walked on past me and sat down on the couch. He had on his preaching clothes, a shiny blue suit, a fresh starched white shirt, a black tie, and his Sunday black shoes. I remember thinking at the time that Aaron was too 30 black to be wearing all them dark clothes. The thought tickled me and I started to smile but then I noticed something about him that didn't seem quite right. I ran my eyes over him closely. He was kinda middle-sized and he had a big clean-shaven head, a big nose, and thin lips. I stood there looking at him for a long time but I couldn't figure out what it was 35 till I looked at his eyes; they were burning bright, like bulbs do just before they go out. And yet he looked contented, like his mind was resting some-wheres else.

"I wanna talk with you, Booker," he said, glancing sideways at my wife. "If you don't mind, Sister Brown——"   40

Sarah got up and went into the living quarters. Aaron didn't say noth-ing for a long time; he just sat there looking out the window. Then he spoke so soft I had to strain my ears to hear.

"I'm leaving for the Baptist convention," he said. He pulled out his gold watch and looked at it. "Train leaves in 'bout two hours."   45

"I know *that*, Aaron."

"Yeah, but what I wanted to tell you was that I ain't going Jim Crow. I'm going first class, Booker, right through the white waiting room. That's the law."

A cold shiver ran through me.   50

"Aaron," I said, "don't you go talking crazy now."

The old fool laughed, a great big body-shaking laugh. He started talking 'bout God and Jesus and all that stuff. Now, I'm a God-fearing man myself, but I holds that God helps those who help themselves. I told him so.   55

"You can't mix God up with these white folks," I said. "When you start to messing around with segregation, they'll burn you up and the Bible, too."

He looked at me like I was Satan.

"I sweated over this thing," he said. "I prayed. I got down on my   60 knees and I asked God not to give me this cup. But He said I was the one. I heard Him, Booker, right here—he tapped his chest—in my heart."

The old fool's been having visions, I thought. I sat down and tried to figure out a way to hold him, but he got up, without saying a word, and started for the door.   65

"Wait!" I shouted. "I'll get my coat."

"I don't need you," he said. "I just came by to tell you so you could tell the board in case something happened."

"You wait," I shouted, and ran out of the room to get my coat.

We got in his beat-up old Ford and went by the parsonage to get   70 his suitcase. Rachel—that was his wife—and Jonah were sitting in the liv-ing room, wringing their hands. Aaron got his bag, shook Jonah's hand, and said, "Take care of your Mamma, boy." Jonah nodded. Aaron hugged Rachel and pecked at her cheek. Rachel broke down. She throwed her arms around his neck and carried on something awful. Aaron shoved her away.   75

"Don't go making no fuss over it, woman. I ain't gonna be gone for-ever. Can't a man go to a church meeting 'thout women screaming and crying."

He tried to make light of it, but you could see he was touched by the way his lips trembled. He held his hand out to me, but I wouldn't take it.   80

I told him off good, told him it was a sin and a shame for a man of God to be carrying on like he was, worrying his wife and everything.

"I'm coming with you," I said. "Somebody's gotta see that you don't make a fool of yourself."

He shrugged, picked up his suitcase, and started for the door. Then 85 he stopped and turned around and looked at his wife and his boy and from the way he looked I knew that there was still a chance. He looked at the one and then at the other. For a moment there, I thought he was going to cry, but he turned, quick-like, and walked out of the door.

I ran after him and tried to talk some sense in his head. But he shook 90 me off, turned the corner, and went on up Adams Street. I caught up with him and we walked in silence, crossing the street in front of the First Baptist Church for whites, going on around the Confederate monument where, once, they hung a boy for fooling around with white women.

"Put it off, Aaron," I begged. "Sleep on it." 95

He didn't say nothing.

"What you need is a vacation. I'll get the board to approve, full pay and everything."

He smiled and shifted the suitcase over to his left hand. Big drops of sweat were running down his face and spotting up his shirt. His eyes 100 were awful, all lit up and burning.

"Aaron, Aaron, can't you hear me?"

We passed the feed store, Bill Williams' grocery store, and the movie house.

"A man's gotta think about his family, Aaron. A man ain't free. Didn't 105 you say that once, didn't you?"

He shaded his eyes with his hand and looked into the sun. He put the suitcase on the ground and checked his watch.

"Why don't you think about Jonah?" I asked. "Answer that. Why don't you think about your own son?" 110

"I am," he said. "That's exactly what I'm doing, thinking about Jonah. Matter of fact, he started *me* to thinking. I ain't never mentioned it before, but the boy's been worrying me. One day we was downtown here and he asked me something that hurt. 'Daddy,' he said, 'how come you ain't a man?' I got mad, I did, and told him: 'I am a man.' He said 115 that wasn't what he meant. 'I mean,' he said, 'how come you ain't a man where white folks concerned.' I couldn't answer him, Booker. I'll never forget it till the day I die. I couldn't answer my own son, and I been preaching forty years."

"He don't know nothing 'bout it," I said. "He's hot-headed, like my 120 boy. He'll find out when he grows up."

"I hopes not," Aaron said, shaking his head. "I hopes not."

Some white folks passed and we shut up till they were out of hearing. Aaron, who was acting real strange, looked up in the sky and moved his lips. He came back to himself, after a little bit, and he said: "This thing 125 of being a man, Booker, is a big thing. The Supreme Court can't make you a man. The NAACP can't do it. God Almighty can do a lot, but even He can't do it. Ain't nobody can do it but you."

He said that like he was preaching and when he got through he was all filled up with emotion and he seemed kind of ashamed—he was a man 130 who didn't like emotion outside the church. He looked at his watch, picked up his bag, and said, "Well, let's git it over with."

We turned into Elm and the first thing I saw at the end of the Street was the train station. It was an old red building, flat like a slab. A group of white men were fooling around in front of the door. I couldn't make them 135 out from that distance, but I could tell they weren't the kind of white folks to be fooling around with.

We walked on, passing the dry goods store, the barber shop, and the new building that was going up. Across the street from that was the sheriff's office. I looked in the window and saw Bull Sampson sitting at his 140 desk, his feet propped up on a chair, a fat brown cigar sticking out of his mouth. A ball about the size of a sweet potato started burning in my stomach.

"Please Aaron," I said. "Please. You can't get away with it. I know how you feel. Sometimes I feel the same way myself, but I wouldn't risk my neck 145 to do nothing for these niggers. They won't appreciate it; they'll laugh at you."

We were almost to the station and I could make out the faces of the men sitting on the benches. One of them must have been telling a joke. He finished and the group broke out laughing.   150

I whispered to Aaron: "I'm through with it. I wash my hands of the whole mess."

I don't know whether he heard me or not. He turned to the right without saying a word and went on in the front door. The string-beany man who told the joke was so shocked that his cigarette fell out of his 155 mouth.

"Y'all see that," he said. "Why, I'll——"

"Shut up," another man said. "Go git Bull."

I kept walking, fast, turned at the corner, and ran around to the colored waiting room. When I got in there, I looked through the ticket window and 160 saw Aaron standing in front of the clerk. Aaron stood there for a minute or more, but the clerk didn't see him. And that took some not seeing. In that room, Aaron Lott stood out like a pig in a chicken coop.

There were, I'd say, about ten or fifteen people in there, but didn't none of them move. They just sat there, with their eyes glued on Aaron's 165 back. Aaron cleared his throat. The clerk didn't look up; he got real busy with some papers. Aaron cleared his throat again and opened his mouth to speak. The screen door of the waiting room opened and clattered shut.

It got real quiet in that room, hospital quiet. It got so quiet I could hear my own heart beating. Now Aaron knew who opened that door, but 170 he didn't bat an eyelid. He turned around real slow and faced High Sheriff Sampson, the baddest man in South Mississippi.

Mr. Sampson stood there with his legs wide open, like the men you see on television. His beefy face was blood-red and his gray eyes were rattlesnake hard. He was mad; no doubt about it. I had never seen him so 175 mad.

"Preacher," he said, "you done gone crazy?" He was talking low-like and mean.

"Nosir," Aaron said. "Nosir, Mr. Sampson."

"What you think you doing?" 180

"Going to St. Louis, Mr. Sampson."

"You must done lost yo' mind, boy."

Mr. Sampson started walking towards Aaron with his hand on his gun. Twenty or thirty men pushed through the front door and fanned out over the room. Mr. Sampson stopped about two paces from Aaron and looked 185 him up and down. That look had paralyzed hundreds of niggers; but it didn't faze Aaron none—he stood his ground.

"I'm gonna give you a chance, preacher. Git on over to the nigger side and git quick."

"I ain't bothering nobody, Mr. Sampson." 190

Somebody in the crowd yelled: "Don't reason wit' the nigger, Bull. Hit 'em."

Mr. Sampson walked up to Aaron and grabbed him in the collar and throwed him up against the ticket counter. He pulled out his gun.

"Did you hear me, deacon. I said, 'Git.'" 195

"I'm going to St. Louis, Mr. Sampson. That's cross state lines. The court done said——"

Aaron didn't have a chance. The blow came from nowhere. Laying there on the floor with blood spurting from his mouth, Aaron looked up at Mr. Sampson and he did another crazy thing: he grinned. Bull Sampson 200 jumped up in the air and came down on Aaron with all his two hundred pounds. It made a crunchy sound. He jumped again and the mob, maddened by the blood and heat, moved in to help him. They fell on Aaron like mad dogs. They beat him with chairs; they beat him with sticks; they beat him with guns. 205

Till this day, I don't know what come over me. The first thing I know I was running and then I was standing in the middle of the white waiting room. Mr. Sampson was the first to see me. He backed off, cocked his pistol, and said: "Booker, boy, you come one mo' step and I'll kill you. What's a matter with you niggers today? All y'all gone crazy?" 210

"Please don't kill him," I begged. "You ain't got no call to treat him like that."

"So you saw it all, did you? Well, then, Booker you musta saw the nigger preacher reach for my gun?"

"He didn't do that, Mr. Sampson," I said. "He didn't——" 215

Mr. Sampson put a big hairy hand on my tie and pulled me to him.

"Booker," he said sweetly. "You saw the nigger preacher reach for my gun, didn't you?"

I didn't open my mouth—I couldn't I was so scared—but I guess my eyes answered for me. Whatever Mr. Sampson saw there musta con- 220 vinced him 'cause he threw me on the floor besides Aaron.

"Git this nigger out of here," he said, "and be quick about it."

Dropping to my knees, I put my hand on Aaron's chest; I didn't feel nothing. I felt his wrist; I didn't feel nothing. I got up and looked at them white folks with tears in my eyes. I looked at the women, sitting crying on 225 the benches. I looked at the men. I looked at Mr. Sampson. I said, "He was a good man."

Mr. Sampson said, "Move the nigger."

A big sigh came out of me and I wrung my hands.

Mr. Sampson said, "Move the nigger." 230

He grabbed my tie and twisted it, but I didn't feel nothing. My eyes were glued to his hands; there was blood under the fingernails, and the fingers—they looked like fat little red sausages. I screamed and Mr. Sampson flung me down on the floor.

He said, *"Move the nigger."* 235

I picked Aaron up and fixed his body over my shoulder and carried him outside. I sent for one of my boys and we dressed him up and put him away real nice-like and Rachel and the boy came and they cried and carried on and yet, somehow, they seemed prouder of Aaron than ever before. And the colored folks—they seemed proud, too. Crazy niggers. 240 Didn't they know? Couldn't they see? It hadn't done no good. In fact, things got worse. The Northern newspapers started kicking up a stink and Mr. Rivers, the solicitor, announced they were going to hold a hearing. All of a sudden, Booker Taliaferro Brown became the biggest man in that town. My phone rang day and night; I got threats, I got promises, and I 245 was offered bribes. Everywhere I turned somebody was waiting to ask me: "Whatcha gonna do? Whatcha gonna say?" To tell the truth, I didn't know myself. One day I would decide one thing and the next day I would decide another.

It was Mr. Rivers and Mr. Sampson who called my attention to that. 250 They came to my office one day and called me a shifty, no-good nigger. They said they expected me to stand by "my statement" in the train station that I saw Aaron reach for the gun. I hadn't said no such thing, but Mr. Sampson said I said it and he said he had witnesses who heard me say it. "And if you say anything else," he said, "I can't be responsible for your 255 health. Now you know"—he put that bloody hand on my shoulder and he smiled his sweet death smile—"you *know* I wouldn't threaten you, but the boys"—he shook his head—"the boys are real worked up over this one."

It was long about then that I began to hate Aaron Lott. I'm ashamed to admit it now, but it's true: I hated him. He had lived his life; he had made 260 his choice. Why should he live my life, too, and make me choose? It wasn't fair; it wasn't right; it wasn't Christian. What made me so mad was the fact that nothing I said would help Aaron. He was dead and it wouldn't help one whit for me to say that he didn't reach for that gun. I tried to explain that to Rachel when she came to my office, moaning and crying, 265 the night before the hearing.

"Listen to me, woman," I said. "Listen. Aaron was a good man. He lived a good life. He did a lot of good things, but he's *dead, dead, dead!* Nothing I say will bring him back. Bull Sampson's got ten niggers who are going to swear on a stack of Bibles that they saw Aaron reach for 270 that gun. It won't do me or you or Aaron no good for me to swear otherwise."

What did I say that for? That woman liked to had a fit. She got down on her knees and she begged me to go with Aaron.

"Go wit' him," she cried. "Booker. *Booker!* If you's a man, if you's a 275 father, if you's a friend, go wit' Aaron."

That woman tore my heart up. I ain't never heard nobody beg like that.

"Tell the truth, Booker," she said. "That's all I'm asking. Tell the truth." 280

"Truth!" I said. "Hah! That's all you niggers talk about: truth. What do you know about truth? Truth is eating good and sleeping good. Truth is living, Rachel. Be loyal to the living."

Rachel backed off from me. You would have thought that I had cursed her or something. She didn't say nothing; she just stood there 285 pressed against the door. She stood there saying nothing for so long that my nerves snapped.

"Say something," I shouted. "Say something—anything!"

She shook her head, slowly at first, and then her head started moving like it wasn't attached to her body. It went back and forth, back and 290 forth, back and forth. I started towards her, but she jerked open the door and ran out into the night, screaming.

That did it. I ran across the room to the filing cabinet, the bottom drawer, and took out a dusty bottle of Scotch. I started drinking, but the more I drank the soberer I got. I guess I fell asleep 'cause I dreamed I buried 295 Rachel and that everything went along fine until she jumped out of the casket and started screaming. I came awake with a start and knocked over the bottle. I reached for a rag and my hand stopped in midair.

"Of course," I said out loud and slammed my fist down on the Scotch-soaked papers. 300

I didn't see nothing.

Why didn't I think of it before?

I didn't see nothing.

Jumping up, I walked to and fro in the office. Would it work? I rehearsed it in my mind. All I could see was Aaron's back. I don't know 305 whether he reached for the gun or not. All I know is that *for some reason* the men beat him to death.

Rehearsing the thing in my mind, I felt a great weight slip off my shoulders. I did a little jig in the middle of the floor and went upstairs to my bed, whistling. Sarah turned over and looked me up and down.   310

"What you happy about?"

"Can't a man be happy?" I asked.

She sniffed the air, said, "Oh," turned over, and mumbled something in her pillow. It came to me then for the first time that she was 'bout the only person in town who hadn't asked me what I was going to do. I   315 thought about it for a little while, shrugged, and fell into bed with all my clothes on.

When I woke up the next morning, I had a terrible headache and my tongue was a piece of sandpaper. For a long while, I couldn't figure out what I was doing laying there with all my clothes on. Then it came to me: 320 this was the big day. I put on my black silk suit, the one I wore for big funerals, and went downstairs to breakfast. I walked into the dining room without looking and bumped into Russell, the last person in the world I wanted to see. He was my only child, but he didn't act like it. He was al- ways finding fault. He didn't like the way I talked to Negroes; he didn't like   325 the way I talked to white folks. He didn't like this; he didn't like that. And to top it off, the young whippersnapper wanted to be an artist. Undertaking wasn't good enough for him. He wanted to paint pictures.

I sat down and grunted.

"Good morning, Papa." He said it like he meant it. He wants some-   330 thing, I thought, looking him over closely, noticing that his right eye was swollen.

"You been fighting again, boy?"

"Yes, Papa."

"You younguns. Education—that's what it is. Education! It's ruining   335 you."

He didn't say nothing. He just sat there, looking down when I looked up and looking up when I looked down. This went on through the grits and the eggs and the second cup of coffee.

"Whatcha looking at?" I asked.   340

"Nothing, Papa."

"Whatcha thinking?"

"Nothing, Papa."

"You lying, boy. It's written all over your face."

He didn't say nothing.   345

I dismissed him with a wave of my hand, picked up the paper, and turned to the sports page.

"What are you going to do, Papa?"

The question caught me unawares. I know now that I was expecting

it, that I wanted him to ask it; but he put it so bluntly that I was flabber- 350
gasted. I pretended I didn't understand.

"Do 'bout what, boy? Speak up!"

"About the trial, Papa."

I didn't say nothing for a long time. There wasn't much, in fact, I
could say; so I got mad.   355

"Questions, questions, questions," I shouted. "That's all I get in
this house—questions. You never have a civil word for your pa. I go out
of here and work my tail off and you keep yourself shut up in that room
of yours looking at them fool books and now soon as your old man gets his
back against the wall you join the pack. I expected better than that of 360
you, boy. A son ought to back his pa."

That hurt him. He picked up the coffee pot and poured himself
another cup of coffee and his hand trembled. He took a sip and watched
me over the rim.

"They say you are going to chicken out, Papa."   365

"Chicken out? What that mean?"

"They're betting you'll 'Tom.'"

I leaned back in the chair and took a sip of coffee.

"So they're betting, huh?" The idea appealed to me. "Crazy niggers—
they'd bet on a funeral."   370

I saw pain on his face. He sighed and said: "I bet, too, Papa."

The cup fell out of my hand and broke, spilling black water over the
tablecloth.

"You did what?"

"I bet you wouldn't 'Tom.'"   375

"You little fool." I fell out laughing and then I stopped suddenly and
looked at him closely. "How much you bet?"

"One hundred dollars."

I stood up.

"You're lying," I said. "Where'd you get that kind of money?"   380

"From Mamma."

"Sarah!" I shouted. "Sarah! You get in here. What kind of house you
running, sneaking behind my back, giving this boy money to gamble
with?"

Sarah leaned against the door jamb. She was in her hot iron mood. 385
There was no expression on her face. And her eyes were hard.

"I gave it to him, Booker," she said. "They called you an Uncle Tom.
He got in a fight about it. He wanted to bet on you, Booker. *He* believes
in you."

Suddenly I felt old and used up. I pulled a chair to me and sat down. 390

"Please," I said, waving my hand. "Please. Go away. Leave me alone.
Please."

I sat there for maybe ten or fifteen minutes, thinking, praying. The

phone rang. It was Mr. Withers, the president of the bank. I had put in
for a loan and it had been turned down, but Mr. Withers said there'd 395
been a mistake. "New fellow, you know," he said, clucking his tongue.
He said he knew that it was my lifelong dream to build a modern funeral
home and to buy a Cadillac hearse. He said he sympathized with that
dream, supported it, thought the town needed it, and thought I deserved
it. "The loan will go through," he said. "Drop by and see me this morning 400
after the hearing."

When I put that phone down, it was wet with sweat. I couldn't turn
that new funeral home down and Mr. Withers knew it. My father had
raised me on that dream and before he died he made me swear on a
Bible that I would make it good. And here it was on a platter, just for a 405
word, a word that wouldn't hurt nobody.

I put on my hat and hurried to the courthouse. When they called
my name, I walked in with my head held high. The courtroom was packed.
The white folks had all the seats and the colored folks were standing in
the rear. Whoever arranged the seating had set aside the first two rows 410
for white men. They were sitting almost on top of each other, looking
mean and uncomfortable in their best white shirts.

I walked up to the bench and swore on the Bible and took a seat.
Mr. Rivers gave me a little smile and waited for me to get myself set.

"State your name," he said. 415

"Booker Taliaferro Brown." I took a quick look at the first two rows
and recognized at least ten of the men who killed Aaron.

"And your age?"

"Fifty-seven."

"You're an undertaker?" 420

"Yessir."

"You been living in this town all your life?"

"Yessir."

"You like it here, don't you, Booker?"

Was this a threat? I looked Mr. Rivers in the face for the first time. 425
He smiled.

I told the truth. I said, "Yessir."

"Now, calling your attention to the day of May 17th, did anything
unusual happen on that day?"

The question threw me. I shook my head. Then it dawned on me. 430
He was talking about——

"Yessir," I said. "That's the day Aaron got——" Something in Mr.
Rivers' face warned me and I pulled up—"that's the day of the trouble at
the train station."

Mr. Rivers smiled. He looked like a trainer who'd just put a monkey 435
through a new trick. You could feel the confidence and the contempt
oozing out of him. I looked at his prissy little mustache and his smiling
lips and I got mad. Lifting my head a little bit, I looked him full in the

eyes; I held the eyes for a moment and I tried to tell the man behind the
eyes that I was a man like him and that he didn't have no right to be   440
using me and laughing about it. But he didn't get the message. The bas-
tard—he chuckled softly, turned his back to me, and faced the audience.

"I believe you were with the preacher that day."

The water was getting deep. I scroonched down in my seat, closed
the lids of my eyes, and looked dense.   445

"Yessir, Mr. Rivers," I drawled. "Ah was, Ah was."

"Now, Booker—" he turned around—"I believe you tried to keep
the nigger preacher from getting out of line."

I hesitated. It wasn't a fair question. Finally, I said: "Yessir."

"You begged him not to go in the white side?"   450

"Yessir."

"And when that failed, you went over to *your* side—the *colored*
side—and looked through the window?"

"Yessir."

He put his hand in his coat pocket and studied my face.   455

"You saw *everything*, didn't you?"

"Just about." A muscle on the inside of my thigh started tingling.

Mr. Rivers shuffled some papers he had in his hand. He seemed to be
thinking real hard. I pushed myself against the back of the chair. Mr.
Rivers moved close, quick, and stabbed his finger into my chest.   460

"Booker, did you see the nigger preacher reach for Mr. Sampson's
gun?"

He backed away, smiling. I looked away from him and I felt my heart
trying to tear out of my skin. I looked out over the courtroom. It was still;
wasn't even a fly moving. I looked at the white folks in front and the col-   465
ored folks in back and I turned the question over in my mind. While I was
doing that, waiting, taking my time, I noticed, out of the corner of my eye,
that the smile on Mr. Rivers' face was dying away. Suddenly, I had a terrible
itch to know what that smile would turn into.

I said, "Nosir."   470

Mr. Rivers stumbled backwards like he had been shot. Old Judge
Sloan took off his glasses and pushed his head out over the bench. The
whole courtroom seemed to be leaning in to me and I saw Aaron's widow
leaning back with her eyes closed and it seemed to me at that distance
that her lips were moving in prayer.   475

Mr. Rivers was the first to recover. He put his smile back on and he
acted like my answer was in the script.

"You mean," he said, "that you didn't see it. It happened so quickly
that you missed it?"

I looked at the bait and I ain't gonna lie: I was tempted. He knew as   480
well as I did what I meant, but he was gambling on my weakness. I had
thrown away my funeral home, my hearse, everything I owned, and he
was standing there like a magician, pulling them out of a hat, one at a

time, dangling them, saying: "Looka here, looka here, don't they look pretty?" I was on top of a house and he was betting that if he gave me a 485 ladder I would come down. He was wrong, but you can't fault him for trying. He hadn't never met no nigger who would go all the way. I looked him in the eye and went the last mile.

"Aaron didn't reach for that gun," I said. "Them people, they just fell on——" 490

"Hold it," he shouted. "I want to remind you that there are laws in this state against perjury. You can go to jail for five years for what you just said. Now I know you've been conferring with those NAACP fellows, but I want to remind you of the statements you made to Sheriff Sampson and me. Judge—" he dismissed me with a wave of his hand—"Judge, this *man*—" 495 he caught himself and it was my turn to smile—"this *boy* is lying. Ten niggers have testified that they saw the preacher reach for the gun. Twenty white people saw it. You've heard their testimony. I want to withdraw this witness and I want to reserve the right to file perjury charges against him." 500

Judge Sloan nodded. He pushed his bottom lip over his top one.

"You can step down," he said. "I want to warn you that perjury is a very grave offense. You——"

"Judge, I didn't——"

"Nigger!" He banged his gavel. "Don't you interrupt me. Now git 505 out of here."

Two guards pushed me outside and waved away the reporters. Billy Giles, Mr. Sampson's assistant, came out and told me Mr. Sampson wanted me out of town before sundown. "And he says you'd better get out before the Northern reporters leave. He won't be responsible for your safety after 510 that."

I nodded and went on down the stairs and started out the door.

"Booker!"

Rachel and a whole line of Negroes were running down the stairs. I stepped outside and waited for them. Rachel ran up and throwed her 515 arms around me. "It don't take but one, Booker," she said. "It don't take but one." Somebody else said: "They whitewashed it, they whitewashed it, but you spoiled it for 'em."

Russell came out then and stood over to the side while the others crowded around to shake my hands. Then the others sensed that he was 520 waiting and they made a little aisle. He walked up to me kind of slow-like and he said, "Thank you, sir." That was the first time in his whole seventeen years that that boy had said "sir" to me. I cleared my throat and when I opened my eyes Sarah was standing beside me. She didn't say nothing; she just put her hand in mine and stood there. It was long about 525 then, I guess, when I realized that I wasn't seeing so good. They say I cried, but I don't believe a word of it. It was such a hot day and the sun was shining so bright that the sweat rolling down my face blinded me. I

wiped the sweat out of my eyes and some more people came up and said
a lot of foolish things about me showing the white folks and following in 530
Aaron's footsteps. I wasn't doing no such fool thing. Ol' Man Rivers just
put the thing to me in a way it hadn't been put before—man to man. It
was simple, really. Any man would have done it.

QUESTIONS

1. At what points does the author establish the setting and the issue on which Booker and Aaron conflict?
2. Explain Booker's and Aaron's conflicting attitudes on this issue. How do they differ about their sons?
3. What impressions does the author create of the people at the station and of Sheriff Sampson?
4. In terms of the main conflict in the story, what is the purpose of the scene in the white waiting room?
5. What does the narrator mean by "All of a sudden, Booker Taliaferro Brown became the biggest man in that town"?
6. Describe the stages of the conflict within Booker.
7. How was Mr. Rivers instrumental in deciding that conflict for Booker?
8. The story begins and ends on the idea of being a man. What is its theme, in terms of this idea?
9. At the resolution of the story what has Booker lost and won?
10. In what spirit does he speak at the end? Why do you think the author chose to have Booker tell the story?

The Cost of Living

BERNARD MALAMUD

Winter had fled the city streets but Sam Tomashevsky's face, when
he stumbled into the back room of his grocery store, was a blizzard. Sura,
who was sitting at the round table eating bread and salted tomato, looked
up in fright and the tomato turned a deeper red. She gulped the bite she
had bitten and with pudgy fist socked her chest to make it go down. 5
The gesture already was one of mourning for she knew from the wordless
sight of him there was trouble.

"My God," Sam croaked.

She screamed, making him shudder, and he fell wearily into a chair.
Sura was standing, enraged and frightened. 10

"Speak, for God's sake."

"Next door," Sam muttered.

"What happened next door?"—upping her voice.

"Comes a store!"

"What kind of a store?" The cry was piercing. 15

He waved his arms in rage. "A grocery comes next door."

"Oi." She bit her knuckle and sank down moaning. It could not have
been worse.

They had, all winter, been haunted by the empty store. An Italian
shoemaker had owned it for years and then a streamlined shoe-repair 20
shop had opened up next block where they had three men in red smocks
hammering away in the window and everyone stopped to look. Pellegrino's business had slackened off as if someone were shutting a faucet,
and one day he had looked at his workbench and when everything
stopped jumping, it loomed up ugly and empty. All morning he had sat 25
motionless, but in the afternoon he put down the hammer he had been
clutching and got his jacket and an old darkened Panama hat a customer
had never called for when he used to do hat cleaning and blocking; then
he went into the neighborhood, asking among his former customers for
work they might want done. He collected two pairs of shoes, a man's 30
brown and white ones for summer-time and a fragile pair of ladies' dancing
slippers. At the same time, Sam found his own soles and heels had been
worn paper thin for being so many hours on his feet—he could feel the

cold floorboards under him as he walked—and that made three pairs all
together, which was what Mr. Pellegrino had that week—and another 35
pair the week after. When the time came for him to pay next month's
rent he sold everything to a junkman and bought candy to peddle with
in the streets; but after a while no one saw the shoemaker any more, a
stocky man with round eyeglasses and a bristling moustache, wearing a
summer hat in wintertime.   40

When they tore up the counters and other fixtures and moved them
out, when the store was empty except for the sink glowing in the rear,
Sam would occasionally stand there at night, everyone on the block but
him closed, peering into the window exuding darkness. Often, while
gazing through the dusty plate glass, which gave him back the image 45
of a grocer gazing out, he felt as he had when he was a boy in Ka-
menets-Podolskiy and going, three of them, to the river; they would, as
they passed, swoop a frightened glance into a tall wooden house, eerily
narrow, topped by a strange double-steepled roof, where there had once
been a ghastly murder and now the place was haunted. Returning late, at 50
times in early moonlight, they walked a distance away, speechless, listening to the ravenous silence of the house, room after room fallen into
deeper stillness, and in the midmost a pit of churning quiet from which, if
you thought about it, all evil erupted. And so it seemed in the dark re-
cesses of the empty store, where so many shoes had been leathered 55
and hammered into life, and so many people had left something of themselves in the coming and going, that even in emptiness the store contained
some memory of their vanished presences, unspoken echoes in declining
tiers, and that in a sense was what was so frightening. Afterwards when
Sam went by the store, even in daylight he was afraid to look, and 60
quickly walked past, as they had the haunted house when he was a boy.

But whenever he shut his eyes the empty store was stuck in his mind,
a long black hole eternally revolving so that while he slept he was not
asleep but within revolving: what if it should happen to me? What if
after twenty-seven years of eroding toil (he should years ago have got 65
out), what if after all of that, your own store, a place of business . . . after
all the years, the years, the multitude of cans he had wiped off and
packed away, the milk cases dragged in like rocks from the street before
dawn in freeze or heat; insults, petty thievery, doling of credit to the
impoverished by the poor; the peeling ceiling, fly-specked shelves, puffed 70
cans, dirt, swollen veins; the back-breaking sixteen-hour day like a heavy
hand slapping, upon awakening, the skull, pushing the head to bend the
body's bones; the hours; the work, the years, my God, and where is my
life now? Who will save me now, and where will I go, where? Often he
had thought these thoughts, subdued after months; and the garish FOR 75
RENT sign had yellowed and fallen in the window so how could any one
know the place was to let? But they did. Today when he had all but

laid the ghost of fear, a streamer in red cracked him across the eyes:
National Grocery Will Open Another Of Its Bargain Price Stores On
These Premises, and the woe went into him and his heart bled.   80

At last Sam raised his head and told her, "I will go to the landlord
next door."

Sura looked at him through puffy eyelids. "So what will you say?"

"I will talk to him."

Ordinarily she would have said, "Sam, don't be a fool," but she let   85
him go.

Averting his head from the glare of the new red sign in the window,
he entered the hall next door. As he laboured up the steps the bleak
light from the skylight fell on him and grew heavier as he ascended. He
went unwillingly, not knowing what he would say to the landlord.   90
Reaching the top floor he paused before the door at the jabbering in
Italian of a woman bewailing her fate. Sam already had one foot on the top
stair, ready to descend, when he heard the coffee advertisement and
realized it had been a radio play. Now the radio was off, the hallway
oppressively silent. He listened and at first heard no voices inside so he   95
knocked without allowing himself to think any more. He was a little frightened and lived in suspense until the slow heavy steps of the landlord, who
was also the barber across the street, reached the door, and it was—after
some impatient fumbling with the lock—opened.

When the barber saw Sam in the hall he was disturbed, and Sam at   100
once knew why he had not been in the store even once in the past two
weeks. However, the barber became cordial and invited Sam to step into
the kitchen where his wife and a stranger were seated at the table eating
from piled-high plates of spaghetti.

"Thanks," said Sam shyly. "I just ate."   105

The barber came out into the hall, shutting the door behind them.
He glanced vaguely down the stairway and then turned to Sam. His
movements were unresolved. Since the death of his son in the war he
had become absent-minded; and sometimes when he walked one had the
impression he was dragging something.   110

"Is it true?" Sam asked in embarrassment, "What it says downstairs
on the sign?"

"Sam," the barber began heavily. He stopped to wipe his mouth with
the napkin he held in his hand and said, "Sam, you know this store I had
no rent for it for seven months?"   115

"I know."

"I can't afford. I was waiting for maybe a liquor store or a hardware
but I don't have no offers from them. Last month this chain-store make
me an offer and then I wait five weeks for something else. I had to take
it, I couldn't help myself."   120

Shadows thickened in the growing darkness. In a sense Pellegrino
was present, standing with them at the top of the stairs.

"When will they move in?" Sam sighed.

"Not till May."

The grocer was too faint to say anything. They stared at each other, not knowing what to suggest. But the barber forced a laugh and said the chain-store wouldn't hurt Sam's business.

"Why not?"

"Because you carry different brands of goods and when the customers want those brands they go to you."

"Why should they go to me if my prices are higher?"

"A chain-store brings more customers and they might like things that you got."

Sam felt ashamed. He didn't doubt the barber's sincerity but his stock was meagre and he could not imagine chain-store customers interested in what he had to sell.

Holding Sam by the arm, the barber told him in confidential tones of a friend who had a meat store next to an A & P Supermarket and was making out very well.

Sam tried hard to believe he would make out well but couldn't.

"So did you sign with them the lease yet?" he asked.

"Friday," said the barber.

"Friday?" Sam had a wild hope. "Maybe," he said, trying to hold it down, "maybe I could find you, before Friday, a new tenant?"

"What kind of a tenant?"

"A tenant," Sam said.

"What kind of store is he interested?"

Sam tried to think. "A shoe store," he said.

"Shoemaker?"

"No, a shoe store where they sell shoes."

The barber pondered it. At last he said if Sam could get a tenant he wouldn't sign the lease with the chain-store.

As Sam descended the stairs the light from the top-floor bulb diminished on his shoulders but not the heaviness, for he had no one in mind to take the store.

However, before Friday he thought of two people. One was the red-haired salesman for a wholesale grocery jobber, who had lately been recounting his investments in new stores; but when Sam spoke to him on the phone he said he was only interested in high-income grocery stores, which was no solution to the problem. The other man he hesitated to call, because he didn't like him. That was I. Kaufman, a former dry-goods merchant, with a wart under his left eyebrow. Kaufman had made some fortunate real estate deals and had become quite wealthy. Years ago he and Sam had stores next to one another on Marcy Avenue in Williamsburg. Sam took him for a lout and was not above saying so, for which Sura often ridiculed him, seeing how Kaufman had progressed and where Sam was. Yet they stayed on comparatively good terms, perhaps because the grocer

never asked for favours. When Kaufman happened to be around in the
Buick, he usually dropped in, which Sam increasingly disliked, for Kaufman
gave advice without stint and Sura sandpapered it in when he had left. 170

Despite qualms he telephoned him. Kaufman was pontifically surprised and said yes he would see what he could do. On Friday morning
the barber took the red sign out of the window so as not to prejudice a
possible deal. When Kaufman marched in with his cane that forenoon,
Sam, who for once, at Sura's request, had dispensed with his apron, ex- 175
plained to him they had thought of the empty store next door as perfect
for a shoe store because the neighbourhood had none and the rent was
reasonable. And since Kaufman was always investing in one project or another they thought he might be interested in this. The barber came over
from across the street and unlocked the door. Kaufman clomped into the 180
empty store, appraised the structure of the place, tested the floor, peered
through the barred window into the back yard, and squinting, totalled
with moving lips how much shelving was necessary and at what cost. Then
he asked the barber how much rent and the barber named a modest figure.

Kaufman nodded sagely and said nothing to either of them there, but 185
back in the grocery store he vehemently berated Sam for wasting his time.

"I didn't want to make you ashamed in front of the goy," he said in
anger, even his wart red, "but who do you think, if he is in his right mind,
will open a shoe store in this stinky neighbourhood?"

Before departing, he gave good advice the way a tube bloops tooth- 190
paste and ended by saying to Sam, "If a chain-store grocery comes in
you're finished. Get out of here before the birds pick the meat out of your
bones."

Then he drove off in his Buick. Sura was about to begin a commen-
tary but Sam pounded his fist on the table and that ended it. That evening 195
the barber pasted the red sign back on the window, for he had signed the
lease.

Lying awake nights, Sam knew what was going on inside the store,
though he never went near it. He could see carpenters sawing the sweet-
smelling pine that willingly yielded to the sharp shining blade and be- 200
came in tiers the shelves rising to the ceiling. The painters arrived, a long
man and a short one he was positive he knew, their faces covered with paint
drops. They thickly calcimined the ceiling and painted everything in
bright colours, impractical for a grocery but pleasing to the eye. Electri-
cians appeared with fluorescent lamps which obliterated the yellow dark- 205
ness of globed bulbs; and then the fixture men hauled down from their
vans the long marble-top counters and a gleaming enamelled refrigerator
containing three windows, for cooking, medium, and best butter; and a
case of frozen foods, creamy white, the latest thing. As he was admiring it
all, he thought he turned to see if anyone was watching him, and when he 210
had reassured himself and turned again to look through the window it
had been whitened so he could see nothing more. He had to get up then

to smoke a cigarette and was tempted to put on his pants and go in slippers quietly down the stairs to see if the window was really soaped. That it might be kept him back so he returned to bed, and being still un- able to sleep, he worked until he had polished, with a bit of rag, a small hole in the centre of the white window, and enlarged that till he could see everything clearly. The store was assembled now, spic and span, roomy, ready to receive the goods; it was a pleasure to come in. He whispered to himself this would be good if it was for me, but then the alarm banged in his ear and he had to get up and drag in the milk cases. At eight A.M. three enormous trucks rolled down the block and six young men in white duck jackets jumped off and packed the store in seven hours. All day Sam's heart beat so hard he sometimes fondled it with his hand as though trying to calm a wild bird that wanted to fly away.

When the chain-store opened in the middle of May, with a horse-shoe wreath of roses in the window, Sura counted up that night and pro-claimed they were ten dollars short; which wasn't so bad, Sam said, till she reminded him ten times six was sixty. She openly wept, sobbing they must do *something*, driving Sam to a thorough wiping of the shelves with wet clothes she handed him, oiling the floor, and washing, inside and out, the front window, which she redecorated with white tissue paper from the five-and-ten. Then she told him to call the wholesaler, who read off this week's specials; and when they were delivered, Sam packed three cases of cans in a towering pyramid in the window. Only no one seemed to buy. They were fifty dollars short the next week and Sam thought if it stays like this we can exist, and he cut the price of beer, lettering with black crayon on wrapping paper a sign for the window that beer was re-duced in price, selling fully five cases more that day, though Sura nagged what was the good of it if they made no profit—lost on paper bags—and the customers who came in for beer went next door for bread and canned goods? Yet Sam still hoped, but the next week they were seventy-two behind, and in two weeks a clean hundred. The chain-store, with a manager and two clerks, was busy all day but with Sam there was never, any more, anything resembling a rush. Then he discovered that they car-ried, next door, every brand he had and many he hadn't, and he felt for the barber a furious anger.

That summer, usually better for his business, was bad, and the fall was worse. The store was so silent it got to be a piercing pleasure when someone opened the door. They sat long hours under the unshaded bulb in the rear, reading and rereading the newspaper and looking up hopefully when anyone passed by in the street, though trying not to look when they could tell he was going next door. Sam now kept open an hour longer, till midnight, although that wearied him greatly, but he was able, during the extra hour, to pick up a dollar or two among the housewives who had run out of milk or needed a last-minute loaf of bread for school sandwiches. To cut expenses he put out one of the two lights in the window and a lamp in the store. He had the phone removed, bought his paper bags from pedlars, shaved every second day and, although he would not admit it, ate less. Then in an unexpected burst of optimism he ordered eighteen 260 cases of goods from the jobber and filled the empty sections of his shelves with low-priced items clearly marked, but as Sura said, who saw them if nobody came in? People he had seen every day for ten, fifteen, even twenty years, disappeared as if they had moved or died. Sometimes when he was delivering a small order somewhere, he saw a former customer 265 who either quickly crossed the street, or ducked the other way and walked around the block. The barber, too, avoided him and he avoided the barber. Sam schemed to give short weight on loose items but couldn't bring himself to. He considered canvassing the neighbourhood from house to house for orders he would personally deliver but then remembered Mr. 270 Pellegrino and gave up the idea. Sura, who had all their married life nagged him, now sat silent in the back. When Sam counted the receipts for the first week in December he knew he could no longer hope. The wind blew outside and the store was cold. He offered it for sale but no one would take it.   275

One morning Sura got up and slowly ripped her cheeks with her fingernails. Sam went across the street for a haircut. He had formerly had his hair cut once a month but now it had grown ten weeks and was thickly pelted at the back of the neck. The barber cut it with his eyes shut. Then Sam called an auctioneer who moved in with two lively assistants and a 280 red auction flag that flapped and furled in the icy breeze as though it were a holiday. The money they got was not a quarter of the sum needed to pay the creditors. Sam and Sura closed the store and moved away. So long as he lived he would not return to the old neighbourhood, afraid his store was standing empty, and he dreaded to look through the window.   285

QUESTIONS

1. Horace, the Roman poet, advised writers to begin by plunging into the midst of things. "Don't begin with the egg," he said. Like many other stories and plays, this story plunges into the midst of things. What impression is created by Sam's entrance and the conversation that follows?

2. Note the statement that Sam and Sura "had, all winter, been haunted by the empty store." (19) What does this mean? How does the story of Pellegrino's experience explain the fears of the Tomashev-skys?

3. Sam's feeling about the vacant store is related to his feelings about a house he knew as a boy. What is the relationship?

4. Where did Sam live as a boy? What kind of background did he probably have?

5. What is the setting of this story?

6. Lines 62–80 are important. Most of the material in them represents Sam's thoughts, a kind of whirlpool of worries and memories, given as a modified stream of consciousness. What has Sam's life been like? Which details most affect the reader's feelings, and how?

7. If we skip lines 19–80, we continue the action of the story with no break. But what do these lines contribute that is essential to Malamud's purpose? What part of "Lost Face" do they resemble?

8. What are the barber's feelings toward Sam about renting the store?

9. How does Sam's interview with the barber create suspense?

10. How does Kaufman's report on opening a shoe store affect the plot?

11. Why does Malamud show what goes on at the new store as a kind of nightmare for Sam? (198–225) Why does Sam never go near it?

12. What do Sura's attempts at improvement reveal about the situation?

13. What are the steps from Sam's first decline in income to his closing of the store?

14. At what time of year does Sam close the store? For the purposes of the story, is it a suitable time? Explain.

15. Analyze the last paragraph. What is the significance of its parts in the lives of Sam and Sura?

16. Very briefly summarize the plot from the initial incident through the rising action, turning point, falling action, and *dénouement*.

17. Malamud presents this story almost entirely from the protagonist's point of view. Where does he tell a little about the feelings and thoughts of other characters?

18. What do you think the title "The Cost of Living" signifies?

19. How do the characters determine the style of the conversations? Demonstrate with examples from speeches. Which of the following groups of lines is written in the most vivid style: 19–40, 41–61, 62–80, 87–99, 171–184, 198–225, 248–275?

20. Against what is Sam in conflict? He works hard and makes efforts to survive—why is he defeated? Because of his character? Compare the element of conflict in this story with that of a preceding story.

Self-Service Elevator

ALFREDO MARQUERÍE

He had opened the elevator door to let the young lady enter first, but he could not get a clear view of her face. Once inside that vertical vehicle's community cloister he asked the question which has become almost a ritual:

"What floor?" 5

He pressed the button, and the elevator started up. In situations like this Luis was always conscious of a strange sensation. A chance encounter with a woman in this kind of captive balloon gave him a sort of anxiety state. "Here"—he would say to himself—"is a case of unavoidable and enforced intimacy. Two people who perhaps have never seen or spoken to 10 each other, and who may separate afterwards and never meet again for all eternity, live together face to face for a few moments in a cramped cubicle, prying into each other's lives even in spite of themselves, because in the brief time the trip lasts they have nothing else to do but to stare and to theorize about one another." 15

But on that occasion Luis had, from the very beginning, the distinct feeling that the girl with whom he was sharing the little lift was clearly not a stranger. With a single glance his mind had registered admiration of her taste in clothes: two solid colors—the maroon of her tailored suit and the green of her gloves, hat, purse and shoes—made his 20 quick evaluation easier and faster. In a moment, then, it was possible for him to devote his glances to her face, which was as smooth as porcelain and had lips like fresh red fruit. Her thin eyebrows arched over a pair of dark eyes that contrasted with her long, natural-blonde hair, light as honey and fine as spun gold. 25

"Where have I seen this dark-eyed blonde before?" he began to wonder.

The girl was not paying the slightest attention to Luis. She seemed preoccupied or lost in thought, and she had a far-away, diamond-like sheen in her unseeing eyes. 30

Luis' whole thought-process had been more than fast: it had been fleeting, not more than a few seconds in duration. Before he reached the first floor he was sure he knew his chance travelling companion.

Suddenly the elevator jerked to a halt. They hadn't reached the second floor, and through the glass in the door they could see the wall and the elevator cables.

"What happened?" asked the dark-eyed blonde.

The tone and inflection of her voice as she asked the question enabled him to identify the young lady and to place her precisely in a definite period of his youthful past. Luis was delighted with his discovery, and rejoiced inwardly at this identification, as one usually does when relieved of the almost physical torture of knowing someone without being quite able to place him. This inner satisfaction kept him from answering her question immediately, kept him from returning to reality so he could pay attention to what was happening and to what she was saying. Finally, after realizing that the elevator had suddenly stopped, he answered stupidly:

"Well, you can see: this old crate has stopped."

"What can the trouble be?"

Luis, glad of the mishap that had given him a pretext for conversation, shrugged his shoulders and replied, "I don't know. A power failure, maybe. Or else somebody has opened a door. I'm going to try something."

He went to press one of the buttons, but the girl made a timid, frightened gesture and stopped him with her gloved hand: "No! Please!"

"Are you afraid?"

"Suppose we drop down all of a sudden?"

"Oh, no! I'm going to press the up-button."

He tried several, but the elevator didn't budge. He smiled soothingly: "Nothing happened, you see?"

"Yes, but we're not moving."

"Now let's see. I'm going to press the emergency button."

The electric alarm in the box on the staircase clanged loud and long. From below came the thick voice of the porter, like a great glob from a gushing spout: "What's the matter?"

Putting his mouth near the crack in the door, Luis replied, "We're stuck between floors!"

The voice from the ground floor counselled caution: "Don't open the door. I'm going to try the down-button."

The preliminary click sounded clearly, but the elevator did not start down.

The girl commented: "This is not funny at all."

Luis seemed quite amused by the incident, and the comment was no doubt intended to reproach him for the satisfaction betrayed by his ill-concealed smile.

They heard the wheezing porter pant up the steps one by one, and heard him try the buttons on each floor without success. Finally, from the very top of the staircase came this almost sensational announcement:

"The cables have come loose and are twisted. There is no danger, understand, but you'll have to wait a while. I'm going to put in an emergency call."   80

The girl's ashen face no longer showed annoyance or distress, but sheer panic. With contorted features and wide-opened eyes, and her mouth twisted into a frightened grimace, she uttered just three syllables:

"Oh, my God!" And then she crossed herself devoutly.

Luis felt himself obliged to calm her, and to try to restore her peace 85
of mind. He began to bring into play all kinds of arguments, and to employ his most persuasive tone of voice:

"Come on, now; just calm down! Please don't worry. This happens lots of times."

"But won't we crash down?"   90

"Heavens, no! You heard what he said; it's just that the cables are tangled."

"Now what will be done?"

"Well, they'll come and untangle them."

"Will they be long?"   95

Luis consulted his wrist watch gravely, like a doctor taking someone's pulse: "Fifteen minutes to get here, another fifteen to get us out . . . It's two o'clock now . . . We should be free by half past two."

"You sound as though we were in jail!"

"Well, we certainly are imprisoned here."   100

"I should say so! I'm furious!"

"Furious? Why?"

"Surely this can't seem pleasant to you?"

"This mishap has given me the great pleasure of your company."

"This isn't exactly the occasion for compliments."   105

"Quite to the contrary, I believe that a case like this, or one similar to it—a fire or a shipwreck, for example—is precisely where one can reveal his good upbringing. In that connection, let me tell you a story about. . . ."

"This is no time for stories! Appealing to your good upbringing, I beg you to. . . ."   110

Luis made a gesture like a good man wronged, and then said jokingly:

"Señorita, please! Aren't you forgetting that you are in my power, and that even though you may scream at the top of your lungs nobody can come to help you? Believe me, if this hadn't happened by accident, I'd have arranged it with the greatest of pleasure. This is a trick for catching 115
dark-eyed little blondes that I intend to begin putting into practice with the help of my porter friends."

"It certainly is quite a scheme!"

"Come, now! Are you still worried and nervous?"

"Do you think I should start dancing for joy?"   120

"But could you tell me the reason for your displeasure, aside from the delay involved?"

"That's very simple. First of all, the danger. . . ."

"There isn't any. The service men will come and raise the elevator
easily."   125
"Then, I'm going to be late at the office."
"Let them know."
"How?"
"By calling to the porter. Use your wireless telephone, the good old
voice system that I used before."   130
At that instant Luis suddenly remembered her name: Alba Vélez.
And to surprise her, he shouted loudly: "Hey, porter! Señorita Alba Vélez
wants you to. . . ."
She stifled a startled cry: "Oh! You know me?"
". . . tell her office that she's been kidnapped and is being held pris-   135
oner in this elevator!"
Then, turning to the girl and making an exaggerated, mock-heroic
bow, he explained: "Of course I know you. I've known you for many
years."
"From the islands, perhaps?"[1]   140
"Exactly right."
"Do you come from there?"
"No, but I lived there for a while, quite near your house."
"In the capital?"
"Naturally."   145
"But I don't remember you."
It occurred to Luis that for a joke, just to make the half-hour's wait
in the elevator amusing, he should give a false name. He said:
"My name is Dámaso Jelez."
"I still don't remember you."   150
"I've often met you and your sisters."
"The poor girls are dead now."
"I'm truly sorry."
There were a few painful moments of silence. Alba finally renewed
the conversation: 155
"I'm alone now, and working. But tell me: with whom did you used
to associate there in the islands?"
The joke could be kept going on its merry way with surprising com-
plications and digressions: Alba didn't recognize him. Luis could have
some unexpected fun by playing with his own real name, so he said: 160
"I used to go around with Luis Martín."
"Oh, that fellow! I remember him, all right!" she exclaimed.
"What ever became of him?" asked the real Luis with the most in-
nocent expression in the world.
"Bah! He's a hopeless case, a crackpot, a scoundrel."   165
When he heard this revelation he felt an irrepressible urge to inter-

---

[1] These could be the Balearics, where the author was born, or the Canary Islands.

rupt such insults, and was on the point of shouting, "Be careful, there! I'm Luis Martín!" But he succeeded in restraining himself. The expression of alarm and surprise on his face made her suspect something, however.   170

Alba said, "Are you still a friend of his?"

Luis reacted quickly, and dissembled:

"Who, me? I don't know a thing about the fellow. But where do you get your information?"

"Oh, from friends of his, and from his sister."   175

"From my . . . from his friends?"

Alba became talkative. She decided to sit down on the still-motionless elevator's red velvet-covered bench. Luis did the same. The girl continued talking, more and more confidentially:

"You see, Luis Martín's sister is a very good family friend, and she al-   180
ways keeps us posted on his activities. Luis is a young man with absolutely no stability or steadfastness of purpose. Women laugh at him, and have fooled him frightfully. He just throws his money away. First he's riding high, then he's absolutely broke. He has tried I don't know how many lines of business: automobiles, radio . . . he prefers modern things. But   185
he always makes a mess of it. His friends say he's a lunatic, that he tires of everything right away, and that he is incapable of being serious about anything. Occasionally luck is with him, and he makes some money. But as soon as he has to pay steady attention to what he's doing, he's hopelessly lost."   190

The points that Alba was making, while essentially true, contained such distortions of the facts and were such an unkind caricature of his life that Luis felt obliged to protest:

"That's not what I hear."

"Oh, no?"   195

"The information that reaches me through friends is that Luis has indeed tried several lines of business, some with good results and others which were less fortunate. But I don't believe he is an unstable person; he is a man who gets involved in very complicated business activities and therefore he sometimes succeeds and sometimes fails. Now, as to   200
women. . . ."

Alba interrupted: "About that point everyone is in agreement. Surely you're not going to defend him? Not only does his sister say so, but also Alicia, a girl from our part of the country . . . you may know her. . . ."

"Yes, slightly."   205

"Well, she was engaged to Martín and can tell you what a laugh she had at his expense. She had another boy friend at the same time, and Luis never even caught on at all: he believed every excuse she gave him as if it were Gospel truth. And I don't know how many things he bought for her: wrist watches, pocketbooks, dresses . . . Then one day she pretended to   210 be angry because he came late, and they broke off the engagement. 'This simpleton Luis,' she said, 'has been buying me my whole trousseau.' What a laugh we had!"

Luis thought about Alicia, and not even by recalling very carefully the details of his foolish engagement could he recollect that cruel trick. 215 But the facts were true, without a doubt. Through the medium of his joke he was coming to some startling and unsuspected conclusions about the world and himself. He pressed on, morbidly:

"And you say that his sister. . . ."

"Oh, his sister is the one who has the worst opinion of him. Of 220 course, he helps her financially, but here is how she puts it: 'What's the difference if he's generous with me? He spends so much on other people . . . Basically, it isn't pity that I feel for him: it's scorn.' "

Inwardly Luis made a firm resolve to hold his sister to a strict accounting for such slanderous remarks. But together with this desire for 225 vengeance came a special uneasiness. He would never have thought that people—his own family and outsiders—had such an opinion of him. He could never have imagined the existence of such ideas about himself, nor that these ideas were in such general circulation. He fell silent, and began to think: "Yes, indeed; we certainly don't know ourselves. Can we really 230 be as others see us? In fact, if I hadn't tried this experiment of hiding my identity, and if I hadn't asked the questions I did, I should have gone on to my dying day without knowing what other people were thinking of me. And wouldn't I have been happier not knowing? I wonder how many others have had this same experience? We are deceived by those 235 around us. We don't believe what our enemies say about us because their opinions are lowered or biased by envy or hate; nor can we give any weight to what friends state in our presence, because personal considerations and flattery usually twist the truth. But what my friends and my sister are saying must be true. I have never seen myself in such a clear, 240 hard mirror; it had never occurred to me to listen behind closed doors. I must be—I am—'that fellow' Alba described, but in another incarnation, different and distinct from the one I had supposed."

"You've fallen very quiet and thoughtful. What's the matter?" said Alba. 245

Martín tried to cover up: "Could you believe it? I've caught your fear of a possible sudden fall of this cage we're stuck in."

"Oh, you said 'possible' fall."

"Now don't get nervous again. There is no such possibility."

"Then why did that word slip out?" 250

"How do I know? I probably meant something else; I must have been absorbed in my thoughts."

"I, too, was thinking of our conversation about Martín. The subject isn't really worth it, though. At least it's been a good excuse for a chat."

Swallowing his deep chagrin with great difficulty, Martín felt obliged 255
to say: "It wasn't necessary to fall back on any pretext in order to spend a
delightful moment talking with you."

"Very gallant."

"But listen! Here come our rescuers!"

On the staircase could be heard the steps of the service men going 260
up to straighten out the cables and repair the elevator. Alba clapped her
hands joyfully:

"This has all the thrill of an episode in a book or an adventure film.
I remember a novel in which a girl was being saved from a fire, and the
chapter that described the moment when the firemen appeared at the 265
window sill among the smoke and flames."

"You have quite an imagination."

"Perhaps less than other girls may age. But with today's incident I
now have something to tell about."

The cable pulleys creaked overhead, and after a few unsuccessful 270
starts the elevator rose with two sudden jerks until it reached the floor
level. Alba hardly realized it.

Martín said simply: "We're there!"

Alba sighed: "Good! That wasn't so bad, thank Heaven."

He opened the door, and went out into the hall after the young lady. 275
Holding out his hand, he said: "Friends?"

"I should say so! And thanks for the chat; without you I'd have
died of fright."

Smiling happily, Alba went up the staircase with bird-like little 280
hops, and was soon lost to view beyond the first landing.

Martín stayed where he was for a while, standing next to the door of
the elevator from which he had emerged—as if reborn—into a strange
new world, to an unusual understanding of his own personality, to a re-
discovery of himself.

"Am I the same man as before?" he wondered. No more than a few 285
minutes separated him from 'before,' but Luis understood why it is said
that there are minutes that count as centuries, that have the function,
value and meaning of eternity. A man can have two lives, one unknown,
the other recently discovered. . . .

He summed up his ideas with the thought: "How young I am! I 290
have just been born!"

QUESTIONS

1. We read in this story about what happened to a man during a single
   half-hour of his life. In what setting, and with whom, has the author
   chosen to place the man?
2. In early paragraphs we find the following terms: "community clois-

ter," "captive balloon," "enforced intimacy," "cramped cubicle." Why is the situation emphasized in this way?

3. In what relation to his companion does Luis discover himself? Explain how this relationship leads him to think of the joke that will make the half hour amusing.

4. Luis is thinking of having fun: "The joke would be kept going . . . with surprising complications. . . ." He does not know how surprising a complication will immediately appear. This is an example of dramatic irony, when something a character says turns out to have a meaning different from what he expected. Explain how the "joke" takes an ironic turn.

5. What pressure is Luis under to give the joke away?

6. How much truth is there in what Alba tells about him? What are his reactions to the things she says?

7. In lines 217–218 we are told that "he was coming to some startling and unsuspected conclusions about the world and himself." What are his conclusions about the world? about himself? In which paragraph are they brought out specifically? Why does he feel "morbid" in continuing the conversation?

8. Luis remembers Alba from his "youthful past" (40), and he believes that then he was different, "in another incarnation" (242). Toward the end he feels "as if reborn" (282). Reborn to what? What discovery has he made? What is the difference between his new incarnation and the person he was before he talked to Alba?

9. Explain the *dénouement* of the story. What unexpected thing has happened to the protagonist in half an hour? How would you state the theme of the story?

10. We might call this a story of awakening, rebirth, or initiation. If we call it an "initiation story," in what sense has the protagonist been initiated?

The Jockey

CARSON MCCULLERS

The jockey came to the doorway of the dining-room, then after a moment stepped to one side and stood motionless, with his back to the wall. The room was crowded, as this was the third day of the season and all the hotels in the town were full. In the dining-room bouquets of August roses scattered their petals on the white table linen and from the adjoining 5 bar came a warm, drunken wash of voices. The jockey waited with his back to the wall and scrutinized the room with pinched, crêpy eyes. He examined the room until at last his eyes reached a table in a corner diagonally across from him, at which three men were sitting. As he watched, the jockey raised his chin and tilted his head back to one side, his dwarfed 10 body grew rigid, and his hands stiffened so that the fingers curled inward like grey claws. Tense against the wall of the dining-room, he watched and waited in this way.

He was wearing a suit of green Chinese silk that evening, tailored precisely and the size of a costume outfit for a child. The shirt was yellow, the 15 tie striped with pastel colours. He had no hat with him and wore his hair brushed down in a stiff, wet bang on his forehead. His face was drawn, ageless, and grey. There were shadowed hollows at his temples and his mouth was set in a wiry smile. After a time he was aware that he had been seen by one of the three men he had been watching. But the jockey did 20 not nod; he only raised his chin still higher and hooked the thumb of his tense hand in the pocket of his coat.

The three men at the corner table were a trainer, a bookie, and a rich man. The trainer was Sylvester—a large, loosely built fellow with a flushed nose and slow blue eyes. The bookie was Simmons. The rich man was the 25 owner of a horse named Seltzer, which the jockey had ridden that afternoon. The three of them drank whisky with soda, and a white-coated waiter had just brought on the main course of the dinner.

It was Sylvester who first saw the jockey. He looked away quickly, put down his whisky glass, and nervously mashed the tip of his red nose with 30 his thumb. "It's Bitsy Barlow," he said. "Standing over there across the room. Just watching us."

"Oh, the jockey," said the rich man. He was facing the wall and he half turned his head to look behind him. "Ask him over."

"God no," Sylvester said.   35

"He's crazy," Simmons said. The bookie's voice was flat and without inflection. He had the face of a born gambler, carefully adjusted, the expression a permanent deadlock between fear and greed.

"Well, I wouldn't call him that exactly," said Sylvester. "I've known him a long time. He was O.K. until about six months ago. But if he goes on   40 like this, I can't see him lasting another year. I just can't."

"It was what happened in Miami," said Simmons.

"What?" asked the rich man.

Sylvester glanced across the room at the jockey and wet the corner of his mouth with his red, fleshy tongue. "An accident. A kid got hurt on   45 the track. Broke a leg and a hip. He was a particular pal of Bitsy's. An Irish kid. Not a bad rider, either."

"That's a pity," said the rich man.

"Yeah. They were particular friends," Sylvester said. "You would always find him up in Bitsy's hotel room. They would be playing rummy   50 or else lying on the floor reading the sports page together."

"Well, those things happen," said the rich man.

Simmons cut into his beefsteak. He held his fork prongs downward on the plate and carefully piled on mushrooms with the blade of his knife. "He's crazy," he repeated. "He gives me the creeps."   55

All the tables in the dining-room were occupied. There was a party at the banquet table in the centre, and green-white August moths had found their way in from the night and fluttered about the clear candle flames. Two girls wearing flannel slacks and blazers walked arm in arm across the room into the bar. From the main street outside came the echoes of   60 holiday hysteria.

"They claim that in August Saratoga is the wealthiest town per capita in the world." Sylvester turned to the rich man. "What do you think?"

"I wouldn't know," said the rich man. "It may very well be so."

Daintily, Simmons wiped his greasy mouth with the tip of his fore-   65 finger. "How about Hollywood? And Wall Street——"

"Wait," said Sylvester. "He's decided to come over here."

The jockey had left the wall and was approaching the table in the corner. He walked with a prim strut, swinging out his legs in a half-circle with each step, his heels biting smartly into the red velvet carpet on   70 the floor. On the way over he brushed against the elbow of a fat woman in white satin at the banquet table; he stepped back and bowed with dandified courtesy, his eyes quite closed. When he had crossed the room he drew up a chair and sat at a corner of the table, between Sylvester and the rich man, without a nod of greeting or a change in his set, grey   75 face.

"Had dinner?" Sylvester asked.

"Some people might call it that." The jockey's voice was high, bitter, clear.

Sylvester put his knife and fork down carefully on his plate. The rich 80
man shifted his position, turning sidewise in his chair and crossing his
legs. He was dressed in twill riding pants, unpolished boots, and a shabby
brown jacket—this was his outfit day and night in the racing season, although he was never seen on a horse. Simmons went on with his dinner.

"Like a spot of seltzer water?" asked Sylvester. "Or something like 85
that?"

The jockey didn't answer. He drew a gold cigarette case from his
pocket and snapped it open. Inside were a few cigarettes and a tiny
gold penknife. He used the knife to cut a cigarette in half. When he had
lighted his smoke he held up his hand to a waiter passing by the table. 90
"Kentucky bourbon, please."

"Now listen, Kid," said Sylvester.

"Don't Kid me."

"Be reasonable. You know you got to behave reasonable."

The jockey drew up the left corner of his mouth in a stiff jeer. His 95
eyes lowered to the food spread out on the table, but instantly he looked
up again. Before the rich man was a fish casserole, baked in a cream sauce
and garnished with parsley. Sylvester had ordered eggs Benedict. There
was asparagus, fresh buttered corn, and a side dish of wet black olives. A
plate of French-fried potatoes was in the corner of the table before the 100
jockey. He didn't look at the food again, but kept his pinched eyes on
the centre-piece of full-blown lavender roses. "I don't suppose you remember a certain person by the name of McGuire," he said.

"Now, listen," said Sylvester.

The waiter brought the whisky, and the jockey sat fondling the glass 105
with his small, strong, callused hands. On his wrist was a gold link bracelet that clinked against the table edge. After turning the glass between his
palms, the jockey suddenly drank the whisky neat in two hard swallows.
He set down the glass sharply. "No, I don't suppose your memory is that
long and extensive," he said.   110

"Sure enough, Bitsy," said Sylvester. "What makes you act like this?
You hear from the kid today?"

"I received a letter," the jockey said. "The certain person we were
speaking about was taken out from the cast on Wednesday. One leg is two
inches shorter than the other one. That's all."   115

Sylvester clucked his tongue and shook his head. "I realize how you
feel."

"Do you?" The jockey was looking at the dishes on the table. His gaze
passed from the fish casserole to the corn, and finally fixed on the plate
of fried potatoes. His face tightened and quickly he looked up again. A 120
rose shattered and he picked up one of the petals, bruised it between his
thumb and forefinger, and put it in his mouth.

"Well, those things happen," said the rich man.

The trainer and the bookie had finished eating, but there was food

left on the serving dishes before their plates. The rich man dipped his 125
buttery fingers in his water glass and wiped them with his napkin.

"Well," said the jockey. "Doesn't somebody want me to pass them
something? Or maybe perhaps you desire to re-order. Another hunk of
beefsteak, gentlemen, or——"

"Please," said Sylvester. "Be reasonable. Why don't you go on up- 130
stairs?"

"Yes, why don't I?" the jockey said.

His prim voice had risen higher and there was about it the sharp
whine of hysteria.

"Why don't I go up to my god-damn room and walk around and write 135
some letters and go to bed like a good boy? Why don't I just——" He
pushed his chair back and got up. "Oh, foo," he said. "Foo to you. I want a
drink."

"All I can say is it's your funeral," said Sylvester. "You know what
it does to you. You know well enough." 140

The jockey crossed the dining-room and went into the bar. He ordered a Manhattan, and Sylvester watched him stand with his heels pressed
tight together, his body hard as a lead soldier's, holding his little finger
out from the cocktail glass and sipping the drink slowly.

"He's crazy," said Simmons. "Like I said." 145

Sylvester turned to the rich man. "If he eats a lamb chop, you can
see the shape of it in his stomach a hour afterward. He can't sweat things
out of him any more. He's a hundred and twelve and a half. He's gained
three pounds since we left Miami."

"A jockey shouldn't drink," said the rich man. 150

"The food don't satisfy him like it used to and he can't sweat it out.
If he eats a lamb chop, you can watch it tooching out in his stomach and
it don't go down."

The jockey finished his Manhattan. He swallowed, crushed the cherry
in the bottom of the glass with his thumb, then pushed the glass away 155
from him. The two girls in blazers were standing at his left, their faces
turned toward each other, and at the other end of the bar two touts had
started an argument about which was the highest mountain in the world.
Everyone was with somebody else; there was no other person drinking
alone that night. The jockey paid with a brand-new fifty-dollar bill and 160
didn't count the change.

He walked back to the dining-room and to the table at which the three
men were sitting, but he did not sit down. "No, I wouldn't presume to
think your memory is that extensive," he said. He was so small that the
edge of the table top reached almost to his belt, and when he gripped 165
the corner with his wiry hands he didn't have to stoop. "No, you're too
busy gobbling up dinners in dining-rooms. You're too——"

"Honestly," begged Sylvester. "You got to behave reasonable."

"Reasonable! Reasonable!" The jockey's grey face quivered, then set

in a mean, frozen grin. He shook the table so that the plates rattled, and 170
for a moment it seemed that he would push it over. But suddenly he
stopped. His hand reached out toward the plate nearest to him and deliberately he put a few of the French-fried potatoes in his mouth. He
chewed slowly, his upper lip raised, then he turned and spat out the
pulpy mouthful on the smooth red carpet which covered the floor. "Lib- 175
ertines," he said, and his voice was thin and broken. He rolled the word in
his mouth, as though it had a flavour and a substance that gratified him.
"You libertines," he said again, and turned and walked with his rigid
swagger out of the dining-room.

Sylvester shrugged one of his loose, heavy shoulders. The rich man 180
sopped up some water that had been spilled on the tablecloth, and they
didn't speak until the waiter came to clear away.

ANALYSIS

Setting   The setting of the story is a hotel dining room one evening
in August during the racing season at Saratoga Springs. The atmosphere of
free spending, looseness, and self-indulgence is first put before us in the
third sentence: "Bouquets of August roses scattered their petals on the
white table linen and from the adjoining bar came a warm, drunken wash
of voices." Later the roses are called "full-blown lavender roses"; they are
rich but have reached a flaccid, stale condition and are on the point of corruption. The lush wealth of the hotel is further suggested by the remark:
"They claim that in August Saratoga is the wealthiest town per capita in
the world."

Characters   The secondary characters, three men at a corner table,
blend perfectly with the atmosphere. They are indulging themselves with
whiskey and soda and a rich dinner. Description of these men, kept to a
minimum, has the function of characterizing them in thematic opposition
to the protagonist, Bitsy Barlow, the jockey. Sylvester, the trainer with the
"loose, heavy shoulders," shows most plainly the effects of indulgence.
He has a "red nose," and his inclination to sensuality is suggested by his
"red, fleshy tongue." In a sense he is the most important of the three secondary characters, for the author elects to have him tell the most about
McGuire's accident and to show some interest in Barlow's condition and
future. In fact, he is the only one who talks to the jockey. He knows how
close Barlow and McGuire were, foresees Barlow's having to quit racing
within a year, understands that he has a weight problem, and advises him
not to drink.

As a contrasting extreme, Simmons, the bookie, merely calls Barlow
crazy and takes no interest in the jockey's problems. His voice—"flat and
without inflection"—parallels his indifference. The rich man, on hearing
about McGuire's accident, says: "That's a pity" and "Those things happen."
These are trite phrases that do not really disguise the speaker's shell of

unconcern. The rich man has a casual interest in hearing why Barlow behaves abnormally for a jockey, but he is critical and dogmatic rather than sympathetic. "A jockey shouldn't drink," he says. In his scale of values professional and prudential considerations come before friendship or sentiment.

The three secondary characters expect a jockey to live according to a set pattern: a jockey must live a life of abstention in order to keep his weight down and succeed on the track. The contrast between the jockey's life and their easy and indulgent lives is brought out by the description of their dinners. Sylvester has eggs Benedict with corn and French fried potatoes; Simmons eats beefsteak and mushrooms; the rich man, who owns the horse that the jockey has ridden and who dresses like a rider but is "never seen on a horse," has a fish casserole with a cream sauce. All these are rich, caloric meals. We are not told what the jockey ate for dinner, but he ate abstemiously; when asked if he has had dinner, he replies bitterly: "Some people might call it that." Ordinarily his sensual pleasures are minimized: he cuts a cigarette in two.

The special discipline of his life isolates him from most people much as army life cuts a soldier off from civilians—who have no compunction about accepting the sacrifice of his life for their protection. The difference between the secondary characters and the protagonist is brought out by bodily details: Sylvester's "red, fleshy tongue," Simmons' "greasy mouth," and the rich man's "buttery fingers." These are rather offensive items and suggest a gross opposite of abstemiousness and fastidiousness. Several details describing the jockey show the contrast: his drawn face, his "wiry smile," his "small, strong, callused hands" (later "wiry hands"), his "prim voice," his suit "tailored precisely," and, most effective of all—"his body hard as a lead soldier's."

Situation and Plot The three secondary characters represent the racing "system"; all of them are dependent for their economic existence on jockeys who win; trainer, bookie, and owner have a living because of what men like Barlow and McGuire can do. A fake horseman can own horseflesh; it is only a small step to owning another chattel—a jockey. But while the representatives of the system feel entitled to live soft, jockeys have to accept conditions of hard discipline for their benefit. In fact, the jockey's sacrifices are ignored or taken for granted. In terms of sense gratification the secondary characters are "haves," the jockeys are expected to be "have-nots." Sylvester assumes that Barlow will drink "seltzer water. . . . Or something like that"; the jockey's challenge to the system is manifested by his ordering "Kentucky bourbon." Plot incidents are very few. The ordering of the whiskey is the turning point of the slight plot.

Nevertheless, we are aware of much tension during the short time that elapses in the story. In terms of money Barlow is evidently successful: he has a gold cigarette case and a gold link bracelet, and after paying for his drinks with a fifty-dollar bill he does not count the change.

But he is the only person in the bar who drinks alone. Without his one friend McGuire (and McGuire, we might say, is like a soldier injured in the service of the system), Barlow has a terrible problem of loneliness, which coupled with his worry and grief over McGuire's disability is driving him to relieve his tensions by drinking. All four men know that his increasing weight and his drinking imperil his existence as a jockey. But his growing disgust with the callousness of the system of racing drives him to defiance expressed through sarcasm, drinking, and his actions in the dining room.

Perhaps the simile of the lead soldier has more than merely descriptive significance. The jockey-soldier is a plaything of the system. But the soldier has sensibilities. Now that friendship and orderly discipline, once proudly or at least stoically accepted, have been replaced by disorder and sorrow, Barlow can no longer restrain himself from revolt. His mutinous disgust is dramatized by the sarcasms he addresses to Sylvester and company and by his attack on them for their unconcern about men while they are "busy gobbling up dinners." He feels that he is being patronized: he resents being called "Kid." He resents their self-gratification with the food that at once enthralls and repels him. His feelings are expressed through the stiff mock-elegance and heavy irony with which he offers them extra portions though they are replete and are leaving food uneaten: "Another hunk of beefsteak, gentlemen. . . ." The coarseness of "hunk" contrasts with his pseudo-politeness.

Barlow also resents Sylvester's advice to be reasonable and "go on upstairs." He feels that he is being treated like a child. He approaches hysteria as he visualizes his room. The room that once would have been warm with the companionship of McGuire is now a "god-damn room." Being a "good boy" means writing letters there or going to bed. The intolerable loneliness and loss which incite his rebellion are suggested most of all by Barlow's remark about the room.

Point of View and Style   Miss McCullers writes this story from an objective, or dramatic, point of view. At least three reasons recommend the author's choice of a strictly dramatic point of view: (1) to use any other point of view would lengthen the story; (2) Barlow is presented as somewhat inarticulate; (3) and the cold, restrained style of presentation suits exactly the jockey's experience meeting the hard wall of indifference. Miss McCullers writes with an economy that reenforces the bleakness of the jockey's situation. This is a report; we are told how the characters look, what they do, and what they say, but not a word about their thoughts and feelings. Feelings and attitudes must be inferred from the report. Thus we understand that Simmons is completely without feeling, as is the rich man. Sylvester has at least an inkling of what Barlow is experiencing, but his feelings are unengrossed. On hearing that McGuire is permanently crippled, Sylvester says, "I realize how you feel," but the jockey's "Do you?" while he peers at the fried potatoes immediately shows that Sylvester remains far from anything that could properly be called a *realization*. Barlow, on the other hand, is grief-stricken and bitterly resentful of the system that leads him to rebellion. So Simmons calls him crazy, the rich man callously shrugs off the jockey's troubles, and Sylvester fumblingly tries to persuade Barlow to act in his own interest. This means reconciling himself to the system, and Barlow meets the test of character by remaining intransigent.

Theme   The jockey's increasing estrangement from the system is symbolized by his not sitting down with the men when he returns from the bar. His gathering indignation as he approaches the limit of his moral endurance is shown by his quivering gray face and his shaking of the table. The author focuses her story of character on the dramatic moment when Barlow's contempt for the self-indulgent, tough-hearted representatives of the system receives climactic expression in his spitting of the greasy potatoes on the rug (he has had to restrain himself from swallowing them) and his denunciatory "you libertines."

In this *dénouement* the three men remain silent, evidently feeling some onus of Barlow's criticism. Perhaps Barlow will be down and out within a year. But we are to understand that they deserve their punishment from Barlow, a better man. The theme is that a better man is he who, although like Barlow suffering bitterly from isolation and loneliness, is yet capable of love and of instinctual resentment against indifference, injustice, and inhumanity.

"The Jockey" is another variation on the main theme of Carson McCullers' writing, the theme of "human loneliness" or "spiritual isolation." It is a masterly story of character, the thematic implications of which are unerringly derived from placing in contrast two opposite ways of life.

Careless Talk

ELIZABETH BOWEN

"How good, how kind, *how* thoughtful!" said Mary Dash. "I can't
tell you what a difference they will make! And you brought them like this
all the way from Shepton Mallet in the train?" She looked helpless. "Where
do you think I had better put them? This table's going to be terribly small
for four, and *think*, if one of Eric Farnham's sweeping gesticulations . . ." 5
She signalled a waiter. "I want these put somewhere for me till the end
of lunch. *Carefully*," she added. "They are three eggs." The waiter bowed
and took the parcel away. "I do hope they will be all right," said Mrs.
Dash, looking suspiciously after him. "But at least they'll be quieter with
the hats, or something. I expect you see how crowded everywhere is?" 10
Joanna looked round the restaurant and saw. The waiters had to melt
to get past the backs of the chairs; between the net-curtained windows,
drowsy with August rain, mirrors reflected heads in smoke and electric
light and the glitter of buttons on uniforms. Every European tongue
struck its own note, with exclamatory English on top of all. As fast as people 15
went wading out people came wading in, and so many greeted each other
that Joanna might easily have felt out of it. She had not lunched in
London for four months and could not resist saying so to her friend.
"Honestly, you haven't deteriorated," said Mary. Herself, she was
looking much as ever, with orchids pinned on to her last year's black. 20
"Then how lucky I caught you just today! And I'm glad the others will
be late. The only men one likes now are always late. While it's still just you
and me, there's so much to say. I don't know what I've done without you,
Joanna." She fixed enraptured eyes on Joanna's face. "For instance, can
you tell me what's become of the Stones?" 25
"No, I'm afraid I can't. I. . . ."
"And Edward and I were wondering if you could tell us about the
Hickneys. I know they are somewhere in Dorset or Somerset. They're not
by any chance anywhere near you?. . . Well, never mind. Tell me about
yourself." 30
But at this point Eric Farnham joined them. "You don't know how
sorry I am," he said. "I was kept. But you found the table all right. Well,
Joanna, this couldn't be nicer, could it?"

From *Ivy Gripped the Steps*, by Elizabeth Bowen. Copyright 1941, 1946 by Elizabeth
Bowen. Reprinted by permission of Alfred A. Knopf, Inc.

"Isn't she looking radiant?" said Mary Dash. "We have been having the most tremendous talk."

Eric was now at the War Office, and Joanna, who had not seen him in uniform before, looked at him naïvely, twice. He reminded her of one of the pictures arrived at in that paper game when, by drawing on folded-over paper, you add to one kind of body an intriguingly wrong kind of head. He met her second look kindly through his shell-rimmed glasses. "How do you think the war is going?" she said.

"Oh, we mustn't ask him things," said Mary quickly. "He's doing most frightfully secret work." But this was lost on Eric, who was consulting his wrist watch. "As Ponsonby's later than I am," he said, "that probably means he'll be pretty late. Though God knows what they do at that Ministry. I propose not waiting for Ponsonby. First of all, what will you two drink?"

"Ponsonby?" Joanna said.

"No, I don't expect you'd know him. He's only been about lately," said Mary. "He's an expert; he's very interesting."

"He could be," said Eric. "He was at one time. But he's not supposed to be interesting just now." The drinks came; then they got together over the *cartes du jour*. Ponsonby did not arrive till just after the potted shrimps. "This is dreadful," he said. "I do hope you'll forgive me. But things keep on happening, you know." He nodded rapidly round to several tables, then dropped exhausted into his place. "Eat?" he said. "Oh, really, anything—shrimps. After that, whatever you're all doing."

"Well, Mary's for grouse," said Eric. Ponsonby, after an instant of concentration, said, "In that case, grouse will do me fine."

"Now you must talk to Joanna," said Mary Dash. "She's just brought me three eggs from the country and she's longing to know about everything."

Ponsonby gave Joanna a keen, considering look. "Is it true," he said, "that in the country there are no cigarettes at all?"

"I believe there are sometimes some. But I don't——"

"There are. Then that alters everything," said Ponsonby. "How lucky you are!"

"I got my hundred this morning," said Eric, "from my regular man. But those will have to last me to Saturday. I can't seem to cut down, somehow. Mary, have you cut down?"

"I've got my own, if that's what you mean," said she. "I just got twenty out of my hairdresser." She raised her shilling-size portion of butter from its large bed of ice and spread it tenderly over her piece of toast. "Now, what is your news?" she said. "Not that I'm asking anything, of course."

"I don't think anything's happened to me," said Eric, "or that anything else has happened that you wouldn't know about. When I say happened I mean *happened,* of course. I went out of London for one night; everywhere outside London seemed to me very full. I must say I was glad to be home again." He unlocked his chair from the chair behind him, 80 looked at the grouse on his plate, then took up his knife and fork.

"Eric," said Mary, after a minute, "the waiter's trying to tell you there's no more of that wine *en carafe.*"

"Bring it in a bottle then. I wonder how much longer——"

"Oh, my dear, so do *I,*" said Mary. "One daren't think about that. 85 Where we were dining last night they already had several numbers scratched off the wine list. Which reminds me. Edward sent you his love."

"Oh, how *is* Edward?" Joanna said. "What is he doing?"

"Well, I'm not strictly supposed to say. By the way, Eric, I asked Joanna, and she doesn't know where the Stones *or* the Hickneys are." 90

"In the case of the Hickneys, I don't know that it matters."

"Oh, don't be inhuman. You know you're not!"

"I must say," said Eric, raising his voice firmly, "I do like London now a lot of those people have gone. Not *you,* Joanna; we all miss you very much. Why don't you come back? You've no idea how nice it is." 95

Joanna, colouring slightly, said, "I've got no place left to come back to. Belmont Square——"

"Oh, my Lord, yes," he said. "I did hear about your house. I was so sorry. Completely? . . . Still, you don't want a house, you know. None of us live in houses. You could move in on someone. Sylvia has moved in 100 on Mona——"

"That's not a good example," said Mary quickly. "Mona moved out almost at once and moved in on Isobel, but the worst of that is that now Isobel wants her husband back, and meanwhile Sylvia's taken up with a young man, so Mona can't move back to her own flat. But what would 105 make it difficult for Joanna is having taken on all those hens. Haven't you?"

"Yes, and I have evacuees——"

"But we won't talk about those, will we?" said Mary quickly. "Any more than you would want to hear about bombs. I think one great rule is never to bore each other. Eric, *what's* that you are saying to Ponsonby?" 110

Eric and Ponsonby had seized the occasion to exchange a few rapid remarks. They stopped immediately. "It was quite boring," Ponsonby explained.

"I don't believe you," said Mary. "These days everything's frightfully interesting. Joanna, you must be feeling completely dazed. Will everyone 115 ask you things when you get home?"

"The worst of the country these days," said Joanna, "is everyone gets so wrapped up in their own affairs."

"Still, surely they must want to know about us? I suppose London is too much the opposite," said Mary. "One lives in a perfect whirl of ideas. 120 Ponsonby, who was that man I saw you with at the Meunière? I was certain I knew his face."

"That was a chap called Odgers. Perhaps he reminded you of somebody else? We were talking shop. I think that's a nice place, don't you? I
always think they do veal well. That reminds me, Eric. Was your friend 125
the other evening a Pole, or what?"

"The fact is I hardly know him," said Eric. "I'm never quite sure of
his name myself. He's a Pole all right, but Poles aren't really my thing. He
was quite interesting, as a matter of fact; he had quite a line of his own on
various things. Oh, well, it was nothing particular . . . No, I can't do you 130
Poles, Mary. Warrington's really the man for Poles."

"I know he is, but he keeps them all up his sleeve. You do know
about Edward and the Free French? I hope it didn't matter my having
told you that, but Edward took it for granted that you already knew."

Ponsonby recoiled from his wrist-watch. "Good heavens," he said, 135
"it *can't* be as late as this? If it is, there's someone waiting for me."

"Look," said Eric, "I'll hurry on coffee."

"You know," Mary added anxiously, "you really can't concentrate
without your coffee. Though I know we mustn't be difficult. It's like this
all the time," she said to Joanna. "Have *you* got to hurry, Eric?"   140

"I needn't exactly hurry. I just ought to keep an eye on the time."

"I'll do that for you," Mary said. "I'd love to. You see you've hardly
had a word with Joanna, and she's wanting so much to catch up with life.
I tell you one thing that *is* worrying me: that waiter I gave Joanna's lovely
eggs to hasn't been near this table again. Do you think I put temptation 145
right in his way? Because, do you know, all the time we've been talking
I've been thinking up a new omelette I want to make. One's mind gets like
that these days," she said to Joanna. "One seems able to think of twenty
things at one time. Eric, do you think you could flag the *maître d'hôtel*? I
don't know how I'd feel if I lost three eggs."   150

QUESTIONS

1. The author informed the public that this story and others were written
    in London "between the spring of 1941 and the late autumn of 1944."
    Various details indicate the setting: which ones indicate the place?
    the era?
2. Which words in the second paragraph make very vivid and specific the
    situation in which Joanna and Mary are meeting?
3. Certain details let the reader know the historical circumstances that
    are affecting the characters. In terms of hardships and dislocations,
    what is the significance of: the three eggs; Mary's "orchids pinned on
    to her last year's black"; Eric wearing his uniform; Ponsonby's question
    about cigarettes in the country; Joanna's having evacuees?
4. How does the author contrast Mary and Joanna? In characterizing
    them, consider their remarks and questions, such as (1) "I don't know

what I've done without you, Joanna"; (2) "We have been having the most tremendous talk"; (3) "How do you think the war is going?" (4) "I just got twenty out of my hairdresser"; (5) "Oh, how *is* Edward?" (6) "I think one great rule is never to bore each other"; (7) "The worst of the country these days . . . is everyone gets so wrapped up in their own affairs"; (8) "I suppose London is too much the opposite. . . . One lives in a perfect whirl of ideas."

5. In the light of the whole story, which of the items quoted in Question 4 are the most ironical?

6. What do the shrimps, grouse, butter, and wine contribute to our knowledge of, and judgment of, the characters?

7. What other story in this text has the same point of view? Why is that point of view an artistically successful device for this kind of story?

8. The story has given us a brief look at four people. Think of what has been revealed about them, and state the theme of the story. How is the title related to the theme?

After the Theater

ANTON CHEKHOV

When Nadia Zelenina came home with her mother from the theater, where they had been watching a performance of *Eugene Onegin*, she went to her own room, slipped quickly out of her dress, and wearing only a petticoat and a white bodice, sat down at the table in a great hurry and began to write a letter in the manner of Tatiana: "I love you," she wrote, 5 "but you have no love for me—none at all!"

A moment later she burst out laughing.

She was only sixteen, and in all her life she had never been in love. She knew that Gorny, an officer, and Gruzdev, a student, were both in love with her, but now, having seen the opera, she was inclined to doubt 10 that they loved her. To be unloved and unhappy—how interesting that was! How beautiful, poetic, and touching, when one was hopelessly in love with someone who was completely indifferent. What was interesting about Onegin was that he was incapable of loving, and what was enchanting about Tatiana was that she was hopelessly in love. If they had loved each 15 other with an identical passion and were completely happy together, how boring!

"You must never again confess your love for me," Nadia went on writing, thinking of Gorny, the officer. "I cannot believe your words. You are clever, well educated, serious, you have a great talent, and maybe a 20 brilliant future awaits you. As for me, I am only an insignificant and uninteresting young woman, and you yourself know perfectly well that I would only be a hindrance in your life; and though you were attracted to me, and thought you had found your ideal in me, still it was all a mistake, and even now you are saying to yourself in despair: 'Why did I ever 25 meet that girl?' Only your goodness of heart prevents you from admitting it!"

At this point Nadia began to feel sorry for herself. She burst into tears, but continued writing: "If it were not so hard for me to leave my mother and my brother, I would take the veil and wander away wherever my 30 feet led me. Then you would be free to love someone else. Oh, if only I were dead!"

Through her tears she could no longer see what she had written. Tiny rainbows trembled on the floor, on the table, on the ceiling, and it

seemed to Nadia that she was looking through a prism. Impossible to go on 35
writing. She threw herself back in her armchair and began thinking of
Gorny.

Goodness, how attractive, how fascinating men were! Nadia remembered Gorny's beautiful expression during a discussion on music: so com-
pelling, so tender, so deferential, and he had difficulty subduing the pas- 40
sion in his voice. In society, where an icy pride and an air of indifference
are the marks of a good education and fine breeding, he tried to conceal
his feelings, but without success, and everyone knew how devoted he
was—how passionately devoted—to music. Those never-ending discus-
sions on music, and the loud criticisms of ignoramuses, kept him in a con- 45
stant state of tension, so that he appeared to be awed, timid, and silent.
He played the piano with the flair of a professional pianist, and if he
had not been an officer, he would certainly have become a famous musician.

The tears dried on Nadia's cheeks. She remembered now that Gorny 50
had declared his love for her during a symphony concert, and then
again downstairs near the cloakroom, where they were chilled by the
strong draft which came at them from all sides.

"I am so glad you have at last made the acquaintance of the student
Gruzdev," she wrote. "He is a very clever man, and I am sure you will be 55
friends. Yesterday he came to see us, and stayed until two. We were all so
happy—I am sorry you could not join us. He said some very remarkable things."

Nadia laid her arms on the table, and rested her head on them. Her
hair fell over the letter. It occurred to her that the Student Gruzdev was 60
also in love with her, and deserved a letter as much as Gorny. But then—
she wondered—perhaps after all she should be writing to Gruzdev. An un-
reasoning joy stirred in her heart: at first it was a very small joy, and
rolled about in her heart like a little rubber ball, but it became more
powerful and vaster, and at last poured out of her like a fountain. She had 65
forgotten Gorny and Gruzdev. She was confused; but her joy grew and
spread from her heart into her hands and feet, and it seemed that a gentle
and refreshing wind was fanning her face and lifting her hair. Her shoulders
shook with silent laughter, the table shook, the lamp chimney trembled.
Her tears were sprinkled on the letter she was writing. She could not 70
control her laughter and so, to prove that she was not laughing for no reason at all, she quickly thought of something funny.

"Oh, what an amusing poodle!" she exclaimed, feeling faint with laughter. "What an amusing poodle!"

She remembered how on the previous day Gruzdev had romped 75
with Maxim, the family poodle, after they had taken tea together, and
later he told her the story of a clever poodle who chased a raven round
the garden. Suddenly the raven stopped, looked round, and said: "Stinker!"
The poodle was completely unaware that the raven was trained, and be-

came terribly confused, running away with a look of utter bewilderment. 80
After a while he began to bark.

"No, it would be much better to fall in love with Gruzdev," Nadia
decided, and she tore up the letter.

Her thoughts turned to the student, of his love for her and her love
for him, and soon her thoughts went wandering, and she found herself 85
thinking of many things: of her mother, of the street, of the pencil, of the
piano. . . . She thought of all these things with joy, and it seemed to her
that everything was good and splendid and beautiful, and her joy spoke to
her, saying there was much more to come, and in a little while it would be
still better. Soon spring would come, and then it would be summer, and she 90
would go with her mother to Gorbiky, and then Gorny would come for
the holidays, take her for walks in the garden, and flirt with her. And then
Gruzdev would come. They would play croquet and bowls, and he would
tell her funny stories and others that would leave her dumb with astonishment. Passionately she longed for the garden, the darkness, the clear 95
sky, the stars. Once more her shoulders shook with laughter: the room
seemed to fill with aromatic scents, and a twig was tapping against the
windowpane.

She went to her bed and sat down, and then not knowing what to
do with the joy that was flooding into her heart, she gazed at the icon 100
which hung at the head of her bed, and murmured: "Dear God, dear God,
dear God!"

QUESTIONS

1. Tatiana, the heroine of Pushkin's novel in verse *Eugene Onegin,* is a
   famous figure in Russian literature. How has the 16-year-old Nadia
   been influenced by her? What makes Nadia "burst out laughing"?
2. What does she think of Gorny? Is she in love with him? What im-
   presses her most about him?
3. How does Nadia's mood change after she begins to think of Gruzdev?
4. Why does she think that "in a little while it would be still better"?
   What appears to be the reason for her feeling of joy and bewilderment
   as the story ends?
5. Is there any reason why this story should not be told by the protagonist in the first person? or objectively, like the stories of McCullers
   and Bowen? What point of view does Chekhov use?
6. What amount of time elapses in this story? What happens? What
   makes the story interesting? How does Chekhov's insight into human
   nature relate to the story?
7. This is an example of a story in which, we may say, a door is swung
   open so that we see the protagonist at a revealing moment. Why did
   Chekhov choose this particular moment to show us something about
   Nadia? Is she under special pressures? What is revealed to us?

8. Do you think Nadia is a sentimental girl? Is the story a sentimental story?

9. Would you call the story poetic? If so, give evidence. Or would you call it realistic? If so, give evidence.

The Ugly Duckling

FRANK O'CONNOR

I

Mick Courtney had known Nan Ryan from the time he was fourteen or fifteen. She was the sister of his best friend, and youngest of a family of four in which she was the only girl. He came to be almost as fond of her as her father and brothers were; she had practically lost her mother's re- 5 gard by inheriting her father's looks. Her ugliness indeed was quite endearing. She had a stocky, sturdy figure and masculine features all crammed into a feminine container till it bulged. None of her features was really bad, and her big, brown, twinkling eyes were delightful, but they made a group that was almost comic.

Her brothers liked her spirit; they let her play with them while any of 10 them was of an age for play, and, though she suffered from night-panics and Dinny broke the maternal rule by letting her into his bed, they never told. He, poor kid, would be wakened in the middle of the night by Nan's pulling and shaking. "Dinny, Dinny," she would hiss fiercely, "I have 'em again!" "What are they this time?" Dinny would ask drowsily. "Li-i- 15 ons!" she would reply in a blood-curdling tone, and then lie for half an hour in his arms, contracting her toes and kicking spasmodically while he patted and soothed her.

She grew up a tomboy, fierce, tough, and tearless, fighting in Dinny's gang, which contested the old quarry on the road with the hill-tribes 20 from the slum area above it; and this was how Mick was to remember her best; an ugly, stocky little Amazon, leaping from rock to rock, hurling stones in an awkward but effective way and screaming deadly insults at the enemy and encouragement to her own side.

He could not have said when she gave up fighting, but between twelve 25 and fourteen she became the pious one in a family not remarkable for piety; always out at Mass or diving into church on her way from school to light candles and make novenas. Afterwards it struck Mick that it might have been an alternative to getting in Dinny's bed, for she still suffered from night-fears, only now when they came on she grabbed her rosary 30 beads instead.

It amused him to discover that she had developed something of a crush on himself. Mick had lost his faith, which in Cork is rather similar

to a girl's loss of her virtue and starts the same sort of flutterings among
the quiet ones of the opposite sex. Nan would be waiting for him at the   35
door in the evening, and when she saw him would begin to jump down
the steps one by one with her feet together, her hands stiff at her sides,
and her pigtail tossing.

"How are the novenas coming on, Nan?" he would ask with amusement.   40

"Fine!" she would reply in a shrill, expressionless voice. "You're on
your way."

"I'll come quietly."

"You think you won't, but I know better. I'm a fierce pray-er."

Another stiff jump took her past him.   45

"Why don't you do it for the blacks, Nan?"

"I'm doing it for them too, sure."

But though her brothers could ease the pangs of childhood for her,
adolescence threw her on the mercy of life. Her mother, roly-poly of a
woman who went round a great deal with folded arms, thus increasing   50
the impression of curves and rolls, was still a beauty, and did her best to
disguise Nan's ugliness, a process that mystified her husband who could
see nothing lacking in the child except her shaky mathematics.

"I'm no blooming beauty," Nan would cry with an imitation of a
schoolboy's toughness whenever her mother tried to get her out of the   55
rough tweeds and dirty pullovers she fancied into something more feminine.

"The dear knows you're not," her mother would say, folding her
arms with an expression of resignation. "I don't suppose you want to advertise it though."   60

"Why wouldn't I advertise it?" Nan would cry, squaring up to her.
"I don't want any of your dirty old men."

"You needn't worry, child. They'll let you well alone."

"Let them!" Nan would say, scowling. "I don't care. I want to be a
nun."   65

All the same it made her self-conscious about friendships with girls
of her own age, even pious ones like herself. They too would have boys
around, and the boys wanted nothing to do with Nan. Though she carefully
avoided all occasion for a slight, even the hint of one was enough to make
her brooding and resentful, and then she seemed to become hideous and   70
shapeless and furtive. She slunk round the house with her shoulders up
about her ears, her red-brown hair hanging loose and a cigarette glued
loosely to her lower lip. Suddenly and inexplicably she would drop some
quite nice girl she had been friendly with for years and never even speak
of her again. It gave her the reputation of being cold and insincere, but as   75
Dinny in his shrewd, old-mannish way observed to Mick, she made her
real friends among older women and even sick people—"all seventy or

paralysed" as he put it. Yet, even with these she tended to be jealous and exacting.

Dinny didn't like this, and his mother thought it was awful, but Nan 80 paid no attention to their views. She had become exceedingly obstinate in a way that did not suit either her age or her sex, and it made her seem curiously angular, almost masculine, as though it were the psychological aspect of her ugliness. She had no apparent shyness and stalked in and out of a room, swinging her arms like a boy. Her conversation changed too, 85 and took on the tone of an older woman's. It was not dull—she was far too brainy to be dull—but it was too much on one key—"crabbed" to use a local word—and it did not make the sharp distinctions young people's conversation makes between passion and boredom. Dinny and Mick could be very bored indeed in one another's company, but suddenly some 90 topic would set flame to their minds, and they would walk the streets by the hour with their coats buttoned up, arguing.

Her father was disappointed when she refused to go to college. When she did go to work it was in a dress shop, a curious occupation for a girl whose only notions of dress were a trousers and jersey. 95

II

Then one night something happened that electrified Mick. It was more like a transformation scene in a pantomime than anything in his experience. Later, of course, he realized that it had not happened like that at all. It was just that, as usual with those one has known too well, he had ceased to observe Nan, had taken her too much for granted, and the 100 change in her had come about gradually and imperceptibly till it forced itself on his attention in the form of a shock.

Dinny was upstairs and Mick and she were arguing. Though without formal education, Mick was a well-read man, and he had no patience with Nan's literary tastes which were those of her aged and invalid acquaintances 105 —popular novels and biographies. As usual he made fun of her and as usual she grew angry. "You're so damn superior, Mick Courtney," she said with a scowl and went to search for the book they had discussed in the big mahogany bookcase, which was one of the handsome pieces of furniture her mother took pride in. Laughing, Mick got up and stood beside her, 110 putting his arm round her shoulder as he would have done at any other time. She misunderstood the gesture for she leaned back on his shoulder and offered herself to be kissed. At that moment only did he realize that she had turned into a girl of startling beauty. He did not kiss her. Instead, he dropped his arm and looked at her incredulously. She gave him 115 a malicious grin and went on with her search.

For the rest of the evening he could not take his eyes from her. Now he could easily analyse the change for himself. He remembered that she had been ill with some type of fever and had come out of it white and thin. Then she had seemed to shoot up, and now he saw that during her illness 120 her face had lengthened and one by one each of those awkward lumps of feature had dropped into place and proportion till they formed a perfect structure that neither age nor illness could any longer quite destroy. It was not in the least like her mother's type of beauty which was round and soft and eminently pattable. It was like a translation of her father's 125 masculinity, tight and strained and almost harsh, and she had deliberately emphasized it by the way she pulled her hair back in a tight knot, exposing the rather big ears. Already it had begun to affect her gait because she no longer charged about a room, swinging her arms like a sergeant-major. At the same time she had not yet learned to move gracefully, and 130 she seemed to drift rather than walk, and came in and went out in profile as though afraid to face a visitor or turn her back on him. And he wondered again at the power of habit that causes us to live with people historically, with faults or virtues that have long disappeared to every eye but our own. 135

For twelve months Mick had been going steadily with a nice girl from Sunday's Well and in due course he would have married her. Mick was that sort; a creature of habit who controlled circumstances by simplifying them down to a routine—the same restaurant, the same table, the same waitress, and the same dish. It enabled him to go on with his own thoughts. 140 But whenever anything did happen to disturb this routine it was like a convulsion of Nature for him; even his favourite restaurant became a burden and he did not know what to do with his evenings and week-ends. The transformation of Nan into a beauty had a similar effect on him. Gradually he dropped the nice girl from Sunday's Well without a word 145 of explanation or apology and went more and more to the Ryans, where he had a feeling of not being particularly welcome to anyone but Dinny and—sometimes at least—to Nan herself.

She had plenty of admirers without him. Mr. Ryan, a tall, bald, noisy man with an ape-like countenance of striking good nature, enjoyed 150 it as proof that sensible men were not put off by a girl's mathematics— he, poor man, had noticed no change whatever in his daughter. Mrs. Ryan had no such pleasure. Naturally, she had always cared more for her sons, but they had not brought home with them attractive young men who were compelled to flirt with her, and now Nan took an almost perverse 155 delight in keeping the young men and her mother apart. Beauty had brought out what ugliness had failed to do—a deep resentment of her mother that at times went too far for Mick's taste. Occasionally he saw it in a reversion to a heavy, stolid, almost stupid air that harked back to her childhood, sometimes in a sparkle of wit that had malice in it. She made 160 up for this by what Mick thought of as an undue consideration for her father. Whenever he came into the room, bellowing and cheerful, her face lit up.

She had ceased to wear the rough masculine tweeds she had always preferred and to Mick's eye it was not a change for the better. She had developed a passion for good clothes without an understanding of them, and she used powder and lipstick in the lavish tasteless manner of a girl of twelve.

But if he disapproved of her taste in dress, he hated her taste in men. What left Dinny bored made Mick mad. He and Nan argued about this in the same way they argued about books. "Smoothies," he called her admirers to her face. There was Joe Lyons, the solicitor, a suave, dark-haired young man with mysterious slit-like eyes who combined a knowledge of wines with an intellectual Catholicism, and Matt Healy, a little leprechaun of a butter merchant who had a boat and rattled on cheerfully about whisky and "dames." The pair of them could argue for a full half-hour about a particular make of car or a Dublin hotel without, so far as Mick could see, ever uttering one word of sense, and obviously Lyons despised Healy as a chatter-box and Healy despised Lyons as a fake, while both of them despised Mick. They thought he was a character, and whenever he tried to discuss religion or politics with them they listened with an amusement that made him furious.

"I stick to Mick against the day the Revolution comes," said Healy with his leprechaun's laugh.

"No," Lyons said, putting his arm patronizingly about Mick, "Mick will have nothing to do with revolutions."

"Don't be too sure," said Healy, his face lit up with merriment. "Mick is a *sans-culotte*. Isn't that the word, Mick?"

"I repeat no," said Lyons with his grave smile. "I know Mick. Mick is a wise man. Mind," he added solemnly, raising his finger, "I didn't say an intelligent man. I said a wise one. There's a difference."

Mick could not help being angry. When they talked that way to Dinny he only blinked politely and drifted upstairs to his book or his gramophone, but Mick stayed and grew mad. He was hard-working but unambitious; too intelligent to value the things commonplace people valued, but too thin-skinned to ignore their scorn at his failure to do so.

Nan herself had no objection to being courted by Mick. She was still under the influence of her childish infatuation, and it satisfied her vanity to be able to indulge it. She was an excellent companion, active and intelligent, and would go off for long walks with him over the hills through the fields to the river. They would end up in a public house in Glanmire or Little Island, though she soon stopped him trying to be extravagant in the manner of Lyons and Healy. "I'm a whisky drinker, Mick," she would say with a laugh. "You're not a whisky buyer." She could talk for an hour over a glass of beer, but when Mick tried to give their conversation a sentimental turn she countered with a bluff practicality that shocked him.

"Marry you?" she exclaimed with a laugh. "Who died and left you the fortune?"

"Why, do I have to have a fortune?" he asked quietly, though he was 210 stung by her good-natured contempt.

"Well, it would be a help if you're thinking of getting married," she replied with a laugh. "As long as I remember my family, we never seem to have been worried by anything else."

"Of course, if you married Joe Lyons, you wouldn't have to worry," 215 he said with a hint of a sneer.

"From my point of view, that would be a very good reason," she said.

"A classy car and St. Thomas Aquinas," Mick went on, feeling like a small boy but unable to stop himself. "What more could a girl ask?"

"You resent people having cars, don't you?" she asked, leaning her el- 220 bows on the table and giving him a nasty look. "Don't you think it might help if you went and got one for yourself?"

The worldly, middle-aged tone, particularly when linked with the Ryan go-getting, could be exceedingly destructive. There was something else that troubled him, too, though he was not sure why. He had always liked 225 to pose a little as a man of the world, but Nan could sometimes shock him badly. There seemed to be depths of sensuality in her that were out of character. He could not believe that she really intended it, but she could sometimes inflame him with some sudden violence or coarseness as no ordinary girl could do.   230

Then one evening when they were out together, walking in the Lee Fields, he noticed a change in her. She and another girl had been spending a few days in Glengarriffe with Lyons and Healy. She did not want to talk of it, and he had the feeling that something about it had disappointed her. She was different; brooding, affectionate, and intense. She pulled off 235 her shoes and stockings and sat with her feet in the river, her hands joined between her knees while she gazed at the woods on the other side of the river.

"You think too much of Matt and Joe," she said, splashing her feet. "Why can't you feel sorry for them?"   240

"Feel sorry for them?" he repeated, so astonished that he burst into a laugh. She turned her head and her brown eyes rested on him with a strange innocence.

"If you weren't such an old agnostic, I'd say pray for them."

"For what?" he asked, still laughing. "Bigger dividends?"   245

"The dividends aren't much use to them," she said. "They're both bored. That's why they like me—I don't bore them. They don't know what to make of me. . . . Mind," she added, laughing in her enthusiastic way, "I love money, Mick Courtney. I love expensive clothes and flashy dinners and wines I can't pronounce the names of, but they don't take 250 me in. A girl who was brought up as I was needs more than that to take her in."

"What is it you need?" asked Mick.

"Why don't you go and do something?" she asked with sudden gravity.   255

"What?" he replied with a shrug.

"What?" she asked, waving her hands. "What do I care? I don't even know what you care about. I don't mind if you make a mess of it. It's not failure I'm afraid of. It's just getting stuck in the mud, not caring for anything. Look at Daddy! You may not think so, but I know he's a brilliant 260 man, and he's stuck. Now he hopes the boys will find out whatever secret there is and do all the things he couldn't do. That doesn't appeal to me."

"Yes," Mick agreed thoughtfully, lighting a cigarette and answering himself rather than her. "I know what you mean. I dare say I'm not ambitious. I've never felt the need for being ambitious. But I fancy I 265 could be ambitious for someone else. I'd have to get out of Cork though. Probably to Dublin. There's nothing here in my line."

"Dublin would do me fine," she said with satisfaction. "Mother and I would get on much better at that distance."

He said nothing for a few moments, and Nan went on splashing 270 gaily with her feet.

"Is that a bargain then?" he asked.

"Oh, yes," she said, turning her big soft eyes on him. "That's a bargain. Don't you know I was always mad about you?"

Their engagement made a big change in Mick. He was, as I have said, 275 a creature of habit, a man who lived by associations. He really knew the city in a way that few of us knew it, its interesting corners and queer characters, and the idea of having to exchange it for a place of no associations at all was more of a shock to him than it would have been to any of us; but though at certain times it left him with a lost feeling, at others it restored 280 to him a boyish excitement and gaiety as though the trip he was preparing for was some dangerous voyage from which he might not return, and when he lit up like that he became more attractive, reckless, and innocent. Nan had always been attracted by him; now she really admired and loved him.   285

All the same she did not discontinue her outings with her other beaux. In particular, she remained friendly with Lyons, who was really fond of her and believed that she wasn't serious about marrying Mick. He was, as she said, a genuinely kind man, and was shocked at the thought that so beautiful a girl should even consider cooking and washing clothes on a 290 clerk's income. He went to her father about it, and explained patiently to him that it would mean social extinction for Nan, and would even have gone to Mick himself but that Nan forbade it. "But he can't do it, Nan," he protested earnestly. "Mick is a decent man. He can't do that to you." "He can't like hell," said Nan, chuckling and putting her head on Lyons's 295 chest. "He'd send me out on the streets to keep himself in fags."

These minor infidelities did not in the least worry Mick, who was almost devoid of jealousy. He was merely amused by her occasional lies and evasions and even more by the fits of conscience that followed them.

"Mick," she asked between anger and laughter, "why do I tell you all 300 these lies? I'm not naturally untruthful, am I? I didn't go to confession on Saturday night. I went out with Joe Lyons instead. He still believes I'm going to marry him, and I would, too, if only he had a brain in his head. Mick, why can't you be attractive like that?"

But if Mick didn't resent it, Mrs. Ryan resented it on his behalf, 305 though she resented his complaisance even more. She was sufficiently feminine to know she might have done the same herself, and to feel that if she had, she would need correction. No man is ever as anti-feminist as a really feminine woman.

No, it was Nan's father who exasperated Mick, and he was sensible 310 enough to realize that he was being exasperated without proper cause. When Joe Lyons lamented Nan's decision to Tom Ryan as though it were no better than suicide, the old man was thunderstruck. He had never mixed in society himself which might be the reason that he had never got any-where in life.   315

"You really think it would come to that, Joe?" he asked, scowling.

"But consider it for yourself, Mr. Ryan," pleaded Joe, raising that warning finger of his. "Who is going to receive them? They can always come to my house, but I'm not everybody. Do you think they'll be invited to the Healys? I say, the moment they marry, Matt will drop them, and I 320 won't blame him. It's a game, admitted, but you have to play it. Even I have to play it, and my only interest is in philosophy."

By the end of the evening Tom Ryan had managed to persuade him-self that Mick was almost a ne'er-do-well and certainly an adventurer. The prospect of the Dublin job did not satisfy him in the least. He wanted to 325 know what Mick proposed to do then. Rest on his oars? There were ex-aminations he could take which would ensure his chances of promotion. Tom would arrange it all and coach him himself.

At first Mick was amused and patient; then he became sarcastic, a great weakness of his whenever he was forced on the defensive. Tom 330 Ryan, who was as incapable as a child of understanding sarcasm, rubbed his bald head angrily and left the room in a flurry. If Mick had only hit him over the head, as his wife did whenever he got on her nerves, Tom would have understood that he was only relieving his feelings, and liked him the better for it. But sarcasm was to him a sort of silence, a denial of atten- 335 tion that hurt him bitterly.

"I wish you wouldn't speak to Daddy like that," Nan said one night when her father had been buzzing about Mick with syllabuses he had re-fused even to look at.

"I wish Daddy would stop arranging my life for me," Mick said 340 wearily.

"He only means it in kindness."

"I didn't think he meant it any other way," Mick said stiffly. "But I wish he'd get it into his head that I'm marrying you, not him."

"I wouldn't be too sure of that either, Mick," she said angrily.   345

"Really, Nan!" he said reproachfully. "Do you want me to be pushed round by your old man?"

"It's not only that," she said, rising and crossing the room to the fireplace. He noticed that when she lost her temper, she suddenly seemed to lose command of her beauty. She scowled, bowed her head, and walked   350 with a heavy guardsman's tread. "It's just as well we've had this out, because I'd have had to tell you anyway. I've thought about it enough, God knows. I can't possibly marry you."

Her tone was all that was necessary to bring Mick back to his own tolerant, reasonable self.   355

"Why not?" he asked gently.

"Because I'm scared, if you want to know." And just then, looking down at him, she seemed scared.

"Of marriage?"

"Of marriage as well." He noticed the reservation.   360

"Of me, also?"

"Oh, of marriage and you and myself," she said explosively. "Myself most of all."

"Afraid you may kick over the traces?" he asked with affectionate mockery.   365

"You think I wouldn't?" she hissed, with clenched fists, her eyes narrowing and her face looking old and grim. "You don't understand me at all, Mick Courtney," she added, with a sort of boyish braggadocio that made her seem again like the little tomboy he had known. "You don't even know the sort of things I'm capable of. You're wrong for me. I al-   370 ways knew you were."

Mick treated the scene lightly as though it were merely another of their disagreements, but when he left the house he was both hurt and troubled. Clearly there was a side of her character that he did not understand, and he was a man who liked to understand things, if only so that   375 he could forget about them and go on with his own thoughts. Even on the familiar hill-street with the gas-lamp poised against the night sky, he seemed to be walking a road without associations. He knew Nan was unhappy and felt it had nothing to do with the subject of their quarrel. It was unhappiness that had driven her into his arms in the first place, and   380 now it was as though she were being driven out again by the same wind. He had assumed rather too complacently that she had turned to him in the first place because she had seen through Lyons and Healy, but now he felt that her unhappiness had nothing to do with them either. She was desperate about herself rather than them. It struck him that she might   385 easily have been tempted too far by Lyons's good looks and kindness. She was the sort of passionate girl who could very easily be lured into an indiscretion and who would then react from it in loathing and self-disgust. The very thought that this might be the cause moved him to a passion of protective tenderness, and before he went to bed he wrote and posted 390 an affectionate letter, apologizing for his rudeness to her father and promising to consider her feelings more in the future.

In reply, he got a brief note, delivered at his house while he was at work. She did not refer at all to his letter, and told him that she was marrying Lyons. It was a dry note, and, for him, full of suppressed malice. 395 He left his own house and met Dinny on the way up to call for him. From Dinny's gloomy air Mick saw that he knew all about it. They went for one of their usual country walks, and only when they were sitting in a country pub over their beer did Mick speak of the breach.

Dinny was worried and his worry made him rude, and through the 400 rudeness Mick seemed to hear the voices of the Ryans discussing him. They hadn't really thought much of him as a husband for Nan but had been prepared to put up with him on her account. At the same time there was no question in their minds but that she didn't really care for Lyons and was marrying him only in some mood of desperation induced 405 by Mick. Obviously, it was all Mick's fault.

"I can't really imagine what I did," Mick said reasonably. "Your father started bossing me and I was rude to him. I know that, and I told Nan I was sorry."

"Oh, the old man bosses us all, and we're all rude," said Dinny. "It's 410 not that."

"Then it's nothing to do with me," Mick said doggedly.

"Maybe not," replied Dinny without conviction. "But whatever it is, the harm is done. You know how obstinate Nan is when she takes an idea into her head." 415

"And you don't think I should see her and ask her?"

"I wouldn't," said Dinny, looking at Mick directly for the first time. "I don't think Nan will marry you, old man, and I'm not at all sure but that it might be the best thing for you. You know I'm fond of her but she's a curious girl. I think you'll only hurt yourself worse than you're hurt al- 420 ready."

Mick realized that Dinny, for whatever reasons, was advising him to quit, and for once he was in a position to do so. With the usual irony of events, the job in Dublin he had been seeking only on her account had been offered to him, and he would have to leave at the end of the month. 425

This, which had seemed an enormous break with his past, now turned out to be the very best solace for his troubled mind. Though he missed old friends and familiar places more than most people, he had the sensitiveness of his type to any sort of novelty, and soon ended by wondering how he could ever have stuck Cork for so long. Within twelve months he 430 had met a nice girl called Eilish and married her. And though Cork people might be parochial, Eilish believed that anything that didn't happen between Glasnevin and Terenure had not happened at all. When he talked to her of Cork her eyes simply glazed over.

So entirely did Cork scenes and characters fade from his memory that it came as a shock to him to meet Dinny one fine day in Grafton Street. Dinny was on his way to his first job in England, and Mick at once invited him home. But before they left town they celebrated their reunion in Mick's favourite pub off Grafton Street. Then he could ask the question that had sprung to his mind when he caught sight of Dinny's face.

"How's Nan?"

"Oh, didn't you hear about her?" Dinny asked with his usual air of mild surprise. "Nan's gone into a convent, you know."

"Nan?" repeated Mick. "Into a convent?"

"Yes," said Dinny. "Of course, she used to talk of it when she was a kid, but we never paid much attention. It came as a surprise to us. I fancy it surprised the convent even more," he added dryly.

"For God's sake!" exclaimed Mick. "And the fellow she was engaged to—Lyons?"

"Oh, she dropped him inside a couple of months," said Dinny with distaste. "I never thought she was serious about him anyway. The fellow is a damned idiot."

Mick went on with his drink, suddenly feeling embarrassed and strained. A few minutes later he asked with the pretence of a smile:

"You don't think if I'd hung on she might have changed her mind?"

"I dare say she might," Dinny replied sagaciously. "I'm not so sure it would have been the best thing for you though," he added kindly. "The truth is, I don't think Nan is the marrying kind."

"I dare say not," said Mick, but he did not believe it for an instant. He was quite sure that Nan was the marrying kind, and that nothing except the deep unhappiness that had first united and then divided them had kept her from marrying. But what that unhappiness was about he still had no idea, and he saw that Dinny knew even less than he did.

Their meeting had brought it all back, and at intervals during the next few years it returned again to his mind, disturbing him. It was not that he was unhappy in his own married life—a man would have to have something gravely wrong with him to be unhappy with a girl like Eilish—but sometimes in the morning when he kissed her at the gate and went swinging down the ugly modern avenue towards the sea, he would think of the river or the hills of Cork and of the girl who had seemed to have none of his pleasure in simple things, whose decisions seemed all to have been dictated by some inner torment.

III

Then, long after, he found himself alone in Cork, tidying up things after the death of his father, his last relative there, and was suddenly

plunged back into the world of his childhood and youth, wandering like 475
a ghost from street to street, from pub to pub, from old friend to old
friend, resurrecting other ghosts in a mood that was half anguish, half
delight. He walked out to Blackpool and up Goulding's Glen only to find that
the big mill-pond had all dried up, and sat on the edge remembering winter days when he was a child and the pond was full of skaters, and sum- 480
mer nights when it was full of stars. His absorption in the familiar made
him peculiarly susceptible to the poetry of change. He visited the Ryans
and found Mrs. Ryan almost as good-looking and pattable as ever, though
she moaned sentimentally about the departure of the boys, her disappointment with Nan and her husband's growing crankiness.   485

When she saw him to the door she folded her arms and leaned
against the jamb.

"Wisha, Mick, wouldn't you go and see her?" she asked reproachfully.

"Nan?" said Mick. "You don't think she'd mind?"   490

"Why would she mind, boy?" Mrs. Ryan said with a shrug. "Sure the
girl must be dead for someone to talk to! Mick, boy, I was never one for
criticizing religion, but God forgive me, that's not a natural life at all. I
wouldn't stand it for a week. All those old hags!"

Mick, imagining the effect of Mrs. Ryan on any well-organized con- 495
vent, decided that God would probably not hold it too much against her,
but he made up his mind to visit Nan. The convent was on one of the
steep hills outside the city with a wide view of the valley from its front
lawn. He was expecting a change but her appearance in the ugly convent
parlour startled him. The frame of white linen and black veil gave her 500
strongly marked features the unnatural relief of a fifteenth-century German portrait. And the twinkle of the big brown eyes convinced him of
an idea that had been forming slowly in his mind through the years.

"Isn't it terrible I can't kiss you, Mick?" she said with a chuckle. "I
suppose I could really, but our old chaplain is a terror. He thinks I'm the 505
New Nun. He's been hearing about her all his life, but I'm the first he's
run across. Come into the garden where we can talk," she added with an
awed glance at the holy pictures on the walls. "This place would give you
the creeps. I'm at them the whole time to get rid of that Sacred Heart.
It's Bavarian, of course. They love it."   510

Chattering on, she rustled ahead of him on to the lawn with her
head bowed. He knew from the little flutter in her voice and manner that
she was as pleased to see him as he was to see her. She led him to a
garden seat behind a hedge that hid them from the convent and then
grabbed in her enthusiastic way at his hand.   515

"Now, tell me all about you," she said. "I heard you were married
to a very nice girl. One of the sisters went to school with her. She says
she's a saint. Has she converted you yet?"

"Do I look as if she had?" he asked with a pale smile.

"No," she replied with a chuckle. "I'd know that agnostic look of yours anywhere. But you needn't think you'll escape me all the same."

"You're a fierce pray-er," he quoted, and she burst into a delighted laugh.

"It's true," she said. "I am. I'm a terror for holding on."

"Really?" he asked mockingly. "A girl that let two men slip in—what was it? a month?"

"Ah, that was different," she said with sudden gravity. "Then there were other things at stake. I suppose God came first." Then she looked at him slyly out of the corner of her eye. "Or do you think I'm only talking nonsense?"

"Don't you? What else is it?" he asked.

"I'm not really," she said. "Though I sometimes wonder myself how it all happened," she added with a rueful shrug. "And it's not that I'm not happy here. You know that?"

"Yes," he said quietly. "I've suspected that for quite a while."

"My," she said with a laugh, "you *have* changed!"

He had not needed her to say that she was happy, nor did he need her to tell him why. He knew that the idea that had been forming in his mind for the last year or two was the true one, and that what had happened to her was not something unique and inexplicable. It was something that happened to others in different ways. Because of some inadequacy in themselves—poverty or physical weakness in men, poverty or ugliness in women—those with the gift of creation built for themselves a rich interior world; and when the inadequacy disappeared and the real world was spread before them with all its wealth and beauty, they could not give their whole heart to it. Uncertain of their choice, they wavered between goals; were lonely in crowds, dissatisfied amid noise and laughter, unhappy even with those they loved best. The interior world called them back, and for some it was a case of having to return there or die.

He tried to explain this to her, feeling his own lack of persuasiveness and at the same time aware that she was watching him keenly and with amusement, almost as though she did not take him seriously. Perhaps she didn't, for which of us can feel, let alone describe, another's interior world? They sat there for close on an hour, listening to the convent bells calling one sister or another, and Mick refused to stay for tea. He knew convent tea parties, and had no wish to spoil the impression that their meeting had left on him.

"Pray for me," he said with a smile as they shook hands.

"Do you think I ever stopped?" she replied with a mocking laugh, and he strode quickly down the shady steps to the lodgegate in a strange mood of rejoicing, realizing that however the city might change, that old love-affair went on unbroken in a world where disgust or despair would never touch it, and would continue to do so till both of them were dead.

QUESTIONS

1. What sort of story does the title lead you to expect? After you have read the story, explain what new variation O'Connor has given to an old tale.

2. O'Connor divides his story into three parts. Note that sections I and III are very short, and section II is much longer. Explain what goes on in each part, and show the subparts of section II. Explain the proportioning of the parts.

3. In what way was Nan Ryan unattractive? In what ways did she seem attractive?

4. Describe the pressures put on Mick Courtney during his association with the Ryan family. Why were there conflicts between Mick and Nan, Mick and Lyons, Mick and Tom Ryan?

5. Toward the end of section II Mick has the opportunity to go to Dublin to work. O'Connor says this happened "with the usual irony of events." Explain the irony.

6. Where is the turning point that affects the whole lives of the characters? How long a time elapses in this story? Why can it not be compressed into a shorter period?

7. Just before the story ends Mick tries to explain his idea about a contrast of an "interior world" and the "real world." How does this contrast account for what happened to Nan?

8. In what sense can the old love affair go on unbroken?

Farewell! Farewell! Farewell!

CONRAD AIKEN

I

Margaret O'Brien dreamed that she woke up late—the alarm clock on the table by her bed said eight o'clock—she couldn't account for it, and jumped out of bed in a panic. The Converses expected breakfast at eight-thirty. She flew down to the kitchen, without stopping to put up her hair or wash her face, and rushed to the stove. It was out. The grate was 5 full of half-burned coal and ashes, cold, and she dumped out the whole thing; a cloud of dust filled the air, and she began to cough. Then she found that the kindling box was empty, and that she would have to go down to the cellar and get some. She stuffed newspapers into the grate, flung her hair over her left shoulder, and went to the door which led 10 down to the cellar. It was locked or stuck. She pulled at the knob, wrestled with it, shook it violently; and just at that moment she heard Mrs. Converse's voice in the distance, calling her: *"Margaret!—Margaret!—Margaret!"* The bell began ringing furiously and prolongedly in the indicator over the sink, and she turned around and saw all the little arrows 15 jumping at once. Someone—perhaps Mr. Converse—was running down the front stairs, running and singing. The voice trailed off forlornly, with the sinister effect of a train whistle. A door slammed—Mr. Converse had gone off without waiting for his breakfast—and she woke up.

Sweet hour, what a dream! She rubbed her hand across her forehead, 20 looked up, and saw something unfamiliar over her head; it was the upper bunk of the stateroom, with long leaded slats of wood to support the mattress. Then there was a rack with a life-belt in it. Of course; she was on a steamship, going to Ireland. How funny! She relaxed, smiled, turned her head on the hard little pillow, and looked across to the other bunk; and 25 there was Katy looking back at her and grinning. The ship gave a long, slow lurch, and the hooked door rattled twice on its brass hook. She put her hand quickly to her mouth.

"Gosh, what a dream I had!" she said. "I'm going to get out of this, or I'll be sick." 30

"Me, too," said Katy. "You could cut the air with a knife."

"What time is it, I wonder?"

Katy slid a bare leg out from under the bedclothes.

"I don't know," she said. "I heard a gong, but I don't know if it was the first or the second."   35

II

It was a lovely day, and the ocean was beautiful. It was much smoother than they had expected it to be, too—a lazy blue swell with fish-scale sparkles on it. A sailing ship went by on the south, with very white sails, and tiny rowboats hung up on the decks, and one hanging over the stern. They could see a little man running along the deck and then hauling up a 40 bunch of flags, some kind of signal. It was the kind of day when it is warm, almost hot, in the sun, but cold in the shade. They walked round and round the decks, after eating some oranges, and wished there was something to do. At eleven o'clock the band began playing in the lounge, and they went in for a cup of beef-tea. The room was crowded, and chil- 45 dren were falling over people's legs. Some women were playing cards at a table. The deck-steward went round with a tray of beef-tea cups and crackers.

While they were drinking their beef-tea they saw him again—the gentleman who had the room next to theirs; he just looked into the lounge 50 for a minute, with a book under his arm, and then went out again. He was the nicest man on the ship: so refined-looking, so much of a gentleman, with a queer, graceful, easy way of walking and such nice blue eyes. He reminded Margaret a little of Mr. Converse, but he was younger; he couldn't have been more than thirty. She thought it would be nice to talk to him, 55 but she supposed he wouldn't come near her. He had been keeping aloof from everyone, all the way over, reading most of the time, or walking alone on the deck with that book under his arm, and never wearing a hat.

"I'd like to talk to that man," she said, putting down the cup under her chair.   60

"Well, why don't you?" said Katy. "I guess he wouldn't bite you."

"He looks like Mr. Converse; I guess he's shy."

"I don't see what's the matter with Pat, if you want to talk to somebody."

"Oh, Pat's all right. . . ."   65

Pat, however, was in the steerage, and when Margaret wanted to talk to him they had to go down the companionway to the forward deck. It was all right, but it did seem a pity, when you were in the second cabin, to be spending so much time down in the steerage. And Katy had taken up with old man Diehl, the inventor, who was in the second cabin. He 70 was after her all the time to play cards or walk on the deck or sit and talk in the smoking room. It was all right for Katy, but not much fun for Margaret. She couldn't always be tagging along with them, and she didn't like

to feel that Mr. Diehl was paying for her glass of Guinness every time they
had a drink.   75

A crowd of people rushed out to the decks, and others went to the
windows, pointing; so they went out too, to see what the excitement was
about. It was only another steamer coming from the opposite direction,
with black smoke pouring out of its smokestacks. They walked along to the
place where they played shovelboard, but some kids had it; so then they   80
didn't know what to do. They looked down at the steerage deck, and
there were Pat and the girls having a dance. Pat was playing his concertina. His black curly hair was blowing in the wind, and he looked up
and saw them. He jerked his head backward as a signal to them to come
down, so they did. They danced for a while, and one of the girls passed   85
round a box of candy.

"I guess you think you're too good for us," said Pat, grinning.

"No, we don't," Margaret said. "But they don't like to have us going
up and down these stairs. It's against the rules of the ship."

"Ah, tell it to the marines," said Pat.   90

He shut up his eyes and began playing "The Wearing of the Green,"
beating time with his foot on the deck.

"I hear Katy has a swell sweetheart," one of the girls said.

They talked about old man Diehl, and how he always carried around
the blueprints of his inventions with him, and showed them all the time to 95
everybody in the smoking room. Katy said she liked his voice; such a
deep rumble, it carried all over the dining room—you could hear it above
everything else, even the music. And it wasn't that he was talking loudly,
either. He seemed to have lots of money. His daughter was with him,
very pretty, but with a bad heart. She was kind of stuck-up, and wouldn't   100
have anything to do with Katy, and was always dragging the old man out
of the smoking room on one excuse or another. But she looked very pretty
at the dance in that orchid dress.

"I guess he made a lot of money out of those inventions," said Katy.

"What did he invent?" one of the girls asked.   105

"One of those amusement things they have at Coney Island," said
Katy.

Just then the whistle blew for noon, deafening everybody, and the
steerage passengers had their dinner at noon, so they began going away.
Pat strapped up his concertina and ran his hand through his hair.   110

"So long," he said. "Give us a look again, when you haven't got any
swell company."

He dived down the dark little companionway, and they were left
alone.

As they went up the stairs Margaret said that Pat gave her a head-   115
ache. He made her tired. He made her sick.

III

At lunch there was something of a treat. A special table had been put on the little platform where the band usually played—the piano had been pushed back—and a swell party was being given there. It was, in fact, the wedding breakfast, after a mock wedding which had taken place 120
in the dining saloon just before lunch. They had come in just as it was over and old Mr. Diehl was in the act of kissing the bride, who was Mr. Carter dressed up in a girl's dress. The bridegroom was Miss Diehl dressed in a man's tuxedo. They all sat, eight people, at the round table on the platform, and they had several bottles of wine. Miss Diehl was 125
wearing a white yachting cap to keep up her hair, which was pulled up to look like a man's.

"Your friend is there," said Katy, giving Margaret a nudge with her elbow.

And, sure enough, he was. He was sitting at the opposite side, next to 130
Mr. Carter, and he looked as if he weren't enjoying himself at all. He kept sipping his wine and smiling in an uneasy sort of way, as if he were very much embarrassed. Most of the time he was looking down at the dishes before him. The rest of the party were making a lot of noise, talking and laughing and making jokes and slapping each other on the back. Then 135
Mr. Diehl made a speech, toward the end, and the bridegroom got up and proposed a toast. Several toasts were drunk and speeches made, and they tried to get the nice man to get up and speak, but he blushed and resisted and sat still, though Mr. Carter tried to push him out of his chair.

"He's awful good-looking," said Margaret.   140

"Suit yourself," said Katy. "To my idea, he's too quiet-seeming."

"I wish he'd look at me once."

"Well, if you keep on staring at him like you are, he will, and then he'll be scared to death."

All the same, she felt as if she couldn't keep her eyes off him, she 145
didn't know why; there was something very appealing about his face. His blue eyes were very kind and wise-looking, and he had a way of smiling to himself all the time as if he were having all sorts of humorous thoughts. She felt that he was very superior to all those other people, but he was too nice to show it. In fact, he was superior to everyone else on the ship. There 150
was something important about him.

And then, all of a sudden—she didn't know just how it happened— he was looking at her. There were two tables in between, and lots of other people he might have looked at, and a branch of a palm tree that almost got in the way, but in spite of all these obstacles there could be no doubt 155
about it: he was looking straight at her. A sort of shock went through her, and she felt herself blushing. But she kept her nerve, and looked back at him without in the least changing her expression, which she knew had been one of frank admiration. In fact, she felt her eyes widening a little,

and a special kind of brightness going into them. And the strangest thing 160
of all was the way he met this: he looked quickly away, but only for a moment; and then he looked right back again, while with one hand he fid-
dled with his glass of water. He looked at her almost as if he had suddenly recognized her, though of course they had never met before. His
eyes brightened, in fact, in exactly the same way that hers had done; they 165
brightened and widened, and he seemed to be unable to look away again.
So they looked at each other for about two or three minutes like this, as
if they were the only two people in the whole room. It was almost as if
they were signaling to each other. Then Mr. Carter apparently said
something to him, and he turned his head away. 170

"Well, he looked at me," she said to Katy, "and something happened."

"What do you mean, something happened?"

"I don't know, but it gave me a funny feeling. I think he likes me
the same way I like him."

"Don't be too sure," said Katy. "Anyway, he isn't looking at you now." 175

"No, I know he isn't; but he was, just the same. It was a long look, and
I felt all over as if I was melting."

"I guess what you need is some air," said Katy, "or else both of you'll
have to be locked up."

IV

They roamed the decks again after lunch, and sat for a while in the sun 180
parlor at the back, in wicker chairs, watching the stern of the ship swoop
up and down in quarter-circles against the sea, which seemed to be coming right up over the ship but never did; and for a while the old deckhand,
a sailor with a nice white beard, stood with his pail in his hand and talked
to them about the "old country." He also told them about a hawk that had 185
been blown on to the ship. It was exhausted, he said. It had probably
been chasing some other bird and followed it out to sea, and then didn't
know how to get back. It stayed on one of the masts for a while, and
they put out food for it, and then the next day they found it on the bow,
huddled up against an iron thwart. It fought when they came near it, 190
and it wouldn't eat, so they decided they'd better kill it. Finally, one of
the sailors threw his hat over it and jumped on it, and killed it.

"Oh, what a shame!" said Margaret. "I think that's a shame."

The old sailor grinned, half embarrassed.

"We get hardened to it," he said. "There's always birds like that 195
coming aboard, you know, and they never live. Those little yellowbirds,
for instance. You can feed them, but they die just the same, and you might
as well heave 'em overboard and be done with it. They get so tame, or
scared maybe, that they'll come hoppin' right in here amongst these
chairs." 200

After a while he went away, carrying his sponge in one hand and his pail in the other, walking very slowly, as if there was lots of time. Katy opened her magazine and began reading. Every now and then she turned a page, but she hadn't turned many when Margaret noticed that she was fast asleep. The twins went by, with their short skirts blowing way up 205 round their skinny little legs, and then came Mr. Carter and Miss Diehl, in their proper clothes again. They brought the peg and began playing quoits. They were having a good time—just as they were going to throw the quoit the ship would give a slant and the quoit would go wild. They would laugh and stagger about. The noise finally waked up Katy. She 210 yawned and stretched, and wanted as usual to know what time it was. The sky was clouding up and the wind seemed colder, so they decided to go and sit in the lounge. Margaret wanted to be doing something, but she didn't know what there was they could do.

"What are you so restless for?" said Katy. 215

"I'm not restless; only I get so sick of just sitting round and watching the water go by."

"Well, it *is* kind of monotonous, at that," said Katy.

They took a look down at the steerage deck, but there was nobody there, probably because it was getting chilly. In the steerage you got all 220 the wind.

What she really wanted was to see the nice man, but she couldn't exactly go looking for him. She hoped he would be in the lounge, and when she saw that he wasn't she thought of suggesting to Katy that they go to the smoking room, but she didn't quite have the nerve to do it. In- 225 stead they settled down in a corner and listened to the music and had their tea and watched the people and yawned. Margaret felt unhappy. It wasn't only because she wanted to see him; it was just as much because she was bored with being on a ship. Every day was like Sunday. After a while you got tired of walking around the decks and sitting here and sitting 230 there and drinking tea or beef-tea and going to the dining saloon for another meal that was just like the last. The stewards were all the time trying to flirt with them, too.

All the same, she didn't see how it could just end there, after a look like that—it didn't seem natural at all. But would he do anything about it? 235 Most probably he was too shy. He might even be so shy that he would try to keep out of her way. Or he might think that she was trying to kidnap him or something. She thought of that look again, and felt herself blushing just the way she did at the time. If any look had a meaning, that look did. There was no getting away from that. 240

"I'll be back in a minute," she said, suddenly jumping up.

She walked quickly out of the lounge without knowing at all where she was going—she just felt that she had to be doing something, going somewhere, anything but just sitting still. She felt excited, too, as she pushed open the door that led out to the deck—it had been shut for the 245 night—and launched herself out into the wind. It was just getting dark. The water was black, with patches of moving white, and seemed to be slid- ing past the ship much faster than it did in the daytime. She walked briskly round the deck, keeping an eye out for other pedestrians, but 250 there was nobody about. She tried the other two decks, but they too were deserted. Then she stood hesitating. After all, she didn't have the least idea of what to say to him if she met him—or whether she would find any excuse for it, or way of doing it. In fact, she wasn't sure that that was what she wanted. She just wanted to see him. Perhaps he was in the smok- 255 ing room. She turned and went down a companionway to the lower deck again, and then round the sun parlor to the smoking room. She went in and stood near the door, as if she just wanted to look round for someone, and surveyed the whole room. Old man Diehl was standing by the bar with Mr. Carter and two other men; he seemed to be a little drunk. They 260 were telling smutty stories. The bar-steward saw her and warned them, and they lowered their voices. Two other men were sitting in armchairs, facing the artificial fire; neither of them was the man she was looking for. And there was no one else in the room. She returned to the sun parlor, which looked very forlorn with its deserted wicker chairs under electric lights, 265 facing the darkness and emptiness of the sea, and sat down. Suddenly she felt defeated and miserable. She didn't want to see Katy or anybody— she didn't want to go down to dinner. She would excuse herself with a headache and go to bed. . . . 270

V

At lunch the next day she said she was going to speak to him if she died for it. She would ask him to join them in a game of whist. They could get old man Diehl to make the fourth, in case he accepted. Katy was skeptical but resigned.

"Anybody'd think you were in love with him," she said.

Margaret laughed and blushed. 275

"Oh, no," she said. "But I'd like to talk to him just the same. After lunch I'm going to find him if I have to comb the whole ship. He must be somewhere."

They had seen him only once in the morning—as usual he was walking the deck for his half-hour's constitutional. He passed them sev- 280 eral times, and looked at them with interest but without speaking. Mar- garet said she thought he wanted to speak but was too bashful. He had that everlasting blue book under his arm, and his fair hair was all on end with the wind. Then he had disappeared again.

After lunch, accordingly, they went straight to the lounge and got a 285 table, and Katy spoke to Mr. Diehl. Mr. Diehl said he would be in the smoking room and they could find him there any time in case they wanted a game. Katy got the cards and sat down at the table, and Margaret started off to make her search; and just at that very minute he came in and sat 290 down at the other side of the room and opened his book. She didn't know whether he had seen them or not.

She walked right up to him, smiling, and stood in front of him and looked down at him.

"Would you care to join us in a game of whist?" she said.   295

He closed his book and looked up.

"Oh, it's you, is it?" he said, smiling.

She gave a laugh.

"Yes, it's me, large as life and twice as natural!"

He stood up, tucking the book under his arm.   300

"As a matter of fact," he said, "I never played whist in my life. Is it anything like bridge?"

"I don't know, but I guess if you can play bridge you can play whist."

They stood very close to each other, swaying with the ship, and again they found themselves looking into each other's eyes as they had done the 305 day before at lunch. Margaret almost regretted that they had planned the whist game for it was now obvious that otherwise she could have him all to herself.

"All right," he said, again smiling, "if you can stand it I can."

She led him over to the table and introduced him to Katy. He said 310 his name was Camp. Katy got up and went in pursuit of Mr. Diehl, and they sat down.

"You'd better be my partner," she said, "and then I can show you as we go along."

She took the chair opposite his and began shuffling the cards, at the 315 same time looking at him. A feeling of extraordinary happiness came over her—she had never in her life felt so happy, or so much as if her whole happiness was in her eyes. And the queer thing was that she somehow knew that he was in the same state of mind.

"What do you do with yourself all the time?" she asked. "You hardly 320 ever seem to be anywhere round."

"Most of the time I've been in the smoking room playing chess," he said. "But I've also been working a good deal in my stateroom. I've got some work that has to be finished before we get to Liverpool. And there's only two more days."   325

Margaret felt a sharp pain in her breast.

"I get off at Queenstown," she said. "Tomorrow night."

"*Do* you?"

He accented the first word, and looked at her with a curious helplessness. They both dropped their eyes and became silent.   330

At that moment Katy brought Mr. Diehl and introduced him, and the game began. Margaret and Katy explained how it went to Mr. Camp, with a good deal of laughter. Mr. Diehl gave Mr. Camp a cigar.

"What's your line of business, Mr. Camp?" he said.

Mr. Camp said that he was an architect. He was going over to super- 335
intend the construction of a new office building that an American firm was
putting up in London. Margaret felt a thrill. She slid her right foot forward under the table, so that the toe of her slipper touched something.
Then Mr. Camp, after a moment, caught her foot between his two feet
and squeezed it firmly, and they looked at each other and smiled.   340

VI

At four o'clock the deck-steward brought them tea, and Mr. Diehl
began telling them in his deep voice, with a slight German accent, how he
had come to America at the age of sixteen and worked in railroad repair
shops. He said he was sixty-eight years old and strong as an ox, and he
looked it. He told Mr. Camp about his Whirligig Car, at Coney Island, and 345
how he got the idea for it in his work on trucks in the railroad yards. Now
it had made him a fortune, and he was going over to Blackpool and South-
port to put them in there.

Margaret couldn't listen. She was impatient. She wanted to go off
alone with Mr. Camp. She pressed his foot hard, under the table, and 350
smiled at him. But he didn't take the hint, or couldn't think what to do.
It was Katy who saved the day. She got up and suggested that they all
take a stroll—it was a lovely warm day and a shame to be indoors. Besides,
the lounge was getting stuffy.

"Come on, then, Katy!" said Mr. Diehl.   355

He jumped up and gave her his arm with mock gallantry—the sort of
thing he was always doing—and they started off.

"Shall we walk too—or shall we stay here?" said Mr. Camp.

"Whatever you like," said Margaret.

"I feel terribly separated from you, without your foot," he said, laugh- 360
ing. "But I suppose we ought to get a breath of air."

They climbed up to the top deck and began walking to and fro. He
didn't offer to take her arm, but walked rather distantly beside her. At
first they couldn't think of much to say—they talked about the whist game
and Mr. Diehl, but not as if they were really interested in these things. 365
Margaret felt as if she wouldn't be able to think straight till she took his
arm, so after a few turns on the deck she did so.

"That's better," she said simply.

"Much!"

"Tell me," she said, "if I hadn't spoken to you, would you ever have 370
spoken to me?"

"That's what I came into the lounge for," he answered. "Ever since
lunch yesterday I've been wondering what on earth to do about it. I'm
kind of shy, and these things don't come natural to me. But I thought, if I

went into the lounge, some kind of opportunity might occur. That's what I   375
was there for. But I was terribly relieved when *you* started it off."

"You must think I'm very bold."

"Good Lord, no! You had a little more courage than I did, that's all."

They talked then about Ireland, and she told him that she was going
back to visit her mother for the summer. She was a cook, she said, and   380
her employer, Mr. Converse, who was very nice, had given her three months
off and paid her passage to Queenstown. She had been in Brooklyn for
ten years. She was twenty-five. He asked her if she was married, and she
said no.

"I am," he said.   385

She felt again that pain in her breast.

"I thought you were," she said, looking intently at him.

He wanted to know why she thought so, and they stood and leaned
against the railing, with their shoulders touching and their faces very
close. His eyes, she noticed, were even bluer than the sea. She couldn't   390
tell him why she thought so, exactly—it was just something about him.

"A woman can almost always tell when a man's married," she said. "But
I'm glad you told me, all the same."

"I believe in being honest, especially at a time like this."

"How do you mean, at a time like this?"   395

He gave her a queer look—the corners of his mouth were twisting a
little, as if he were under a strain, but there was a twinkle in his eyes.

"You know what I mean," he said.

"No, honest, I don't!"

"Well, you certainly ought to," he said. He turned around and put his   400
arms on the railing and stared down at the water. "I mean the way we feel
about each other."

She held her breath. He had said it so nicely and so quietly, and
without even trying to hold her hand.

"How do you know we do!" she said, smiling.   405

He smiled back at her.

"All right—let's see you look me in the eye and tell me that we
don't!"

She looked away from him, sobering.

"We oughtn't to be talking like this," she answered. "What about your   410
wife? You know it isn't right."

"Of course it isn't . . . Or is it? . . . I don't know."

"What does your religion tell you?" she said.

"I haven't got any."

"Well, I have. I'm a Catholic."   415

"Do you go to confession?"

"Sure, I do."

They were silent. She was half-sorry she had rebuked him, and half-glad. But he had to know how she felt, even if it hurt her to tell him. She didn't want him to get any false ideas. After a minute, as he didn't say anything, but just went on staring at the water, she turned and looked at him. He was resting his chin on his hands.

"Would you like to walk some more?" she asked, almost timidly.

They walked round and round the deck, while slowly the sunset behind them faded and the sky darkened. He said that he always thought the sea sounded louder at night, and she stopped to listen to it, to see if it was true. She said she couldn't see any difference, or any reason why there should be any. They talked about Katy and Mr. Diehl. Miss Diehl, she said, was likely to die most any time—she had a very bad heart. But she insisted on doing everything just as if there wasn't anything the matter with her. Everybody at the dance had been scared that she would just drop down on the floor all of a sudden. Her face had got very white.

"Let's go down and find Katy," she suggested.

They went down the ladder to the lower deck and found them sitting in the sun parlor, holding hands.

"Is *that* what you're doing!" said Margaret.

Mr. Diehl gave his deep rumble of a laugh. "I've got a pretty nice little girl," he said, patting Katy's shoulder.

Margaret and Mr. Camp sat down at the other side of the veranda. He pulled his chair up close to hers and she dropped her hand on her knee, where he couldn't help seeing it. He put his own on top of it after a moment, and they just sat still without saying anything for a long while. He stroked her thumb with one of his fingers, to and fro, and the smooth hollow between the thumb and forefinger, and she felt as if she were being hypnotized. Once in a while he would slip his finger up her sleeve and touch the inner side of her wrist. And once in a while, as if accidentally, he would stroke her knee. She knew he wouldn't try to kiss her.

"My stateroom is next door to yours," he said, after a time. "If you should want me for anything in the night, don't hesitate to come in."

There was a pause.

"I don't think there's anything I'd want," she answered. "Unless one of us was to be sick, or something like that."

"Well, if there's anything at all," he said.

She tried to withdraw her hand, but he held on to it. She gave up struggling and allowed it to remain in his. She felt unhappy again.

"I always try to think the best of people," she said. "I'm sure you didn't mean anything wrong by that."

He didn't reply, but instead, after a pause, put his other hand on her forearm and gave it a squeeze.

"You're awfully nice, Margaret," he said. "If I were free, I'd like to marry you."

She shut her eyes, and didn't know whether to believe him or not.

VII

After dinner she had a good cry in her bunk, while Katy sat and
talked to her, and from time to time wet the washcloth to put on her eyes.
The ship was making a terrible noise, blowing off steam, which was a good   465
thing, as it prevented the neighbors from hearing her. Two of the bedroom
stewards were hanging round in the corridor outside. Now and then she
could hear them laughing. Katy sat on the camp-chair and argued with
her.

"You just put him out of your mind," she said.   470
"But I can't. You think it's easy, Katy, but it isn't."
"I told you how it would be from the beginning, Peg, and you
wouldn't listen to me. He doesn't care anything for you—don't kid yourself. He isn't our kind at all. You know how it is with that kind of man.
He may soft-soap you, but really he looks down on us, and if he met us   475
anywhere at home he wouldn't even speak to us."

Margaret moved her head from side to side on the pillow—back and
forth, back and forth.

"No," she said, "he isn't like that. He's in love with me. He doesn't
despise me because I'm a cook."   480
"Don't kid yourself. He might think so right now, when there's nobody else for him to fool with, but that's all there is to it. What's the use
getting all upset about it anyway, with him a married man!"

Margaret blew her nose and sat up.

"It's awful hot in here," she said.   485
"I tell you what, you need a little excitement to take your mind off
this business. Let's get a glass of stout and then go down and have a bit of
a dance with Pat and the girls."

Margaret was helpless, apathetic. She didn't care one way or the
other, and she was too tired to resist. She bathed her eyes in the wash-   490
basin, rubbed her cheeks with the towel, and tidied up her hair. Maybe
Katy was right—maybe he really didn't care for her at all. He shouldn't
have said that about her coming to his stateroom; though, of course, men's
views were so different about those things.

She felt better after the glass of stout, and they went down the dark   495
companionway to the steerage deck—the whole crowd was out there in
the moonlight, Pat with his concertina, another boy with his mouth organ.
Two of the men were whirling a skipping rope, and the girls were taking
turns in seeing how fast they could skip and how long they could keep
it up. A lot of people were sitting along the canvas-covered hatch.   500
Katy had a try at it, and the very first thing the rope caught her skirt
and lifted it way up so that her knickers showed, and everybody laughed.
Katy didn't mind at all. She laughed as much as anybody did. She was a
good sport. There was an English girl, about eighteen, who was the best
at it—she would take a running start into the rope and put her hands on   505

her hips and jump as if she was possessed. They couldn't down her at all, and everybody clapped her when finally one of the men dropped his end of the rope.

Pat tuned up on his concertina and they began to dance. A tall young fellow named Jim, who was a carpenter, asked Margaret to dance 510 with him, and before she had time to make up her mind about it he had grabbed her and she was dancing with him and having a good time. They had a fox-trot first, and after that there was a jig, and in the middle of this, just when she had bumped into Katy and they were both laughing, she happened to look up at the second-cabin deck, and there was Mr. Camp, 515 looking down. She waved her hand at him.

"Come on down!" she shouted to him.

He shook his head and smiled; Mr. Carter was standing with him. Jim yanked her hand and whirled her round, and when she looked up again he was gone. 520

VIII

They spent the morning in packing, and getting their landing cards, and writing letters. He wasn't at breakfast when they were, and she took Katy's advice and kept out of his way. At lunch she avoided looking in his direction—she knew he was there, and Katy said he kept looking toward her, but she wouldn't look back. She guessed Katy was right. If he had really 525 cared, he would have come down and danced with them. He was probably a snob, just as Katy said he was. After lunch she went back to the stateroom, and didn't go out till she heard they were sailing along close to the coast of Ireland; so she went up on deck. There was a crowd all along the railing, and she and Katy wedged themselves in and stared at the 530 cliffs and green slopes and watched the little steam trawlers wallowing up and down in what looked like a smooth sea. A tremendous lot of seagulls were flying over the ship, swooping down to the water for the swill that was flung overboard, and all of them mewing like cats. The idea of landing at Queenstown was beginning to be exciting. Her mother and 535 uncle would probably come in from Tralee to meet her, and she supposed they would all spend the night in some hotel in Queenstown.

When they went in for their last tea she rather hoped that Mr. Camp would turn up, but he didn't. By this time, most likely, he saw that she was avoiding him, and was keeping himself out of her track. Maybe his 540 feelings were hurt. She was restless, unhappy, excited, and, try as she would, she couldn't stop thinking about him. She gulped down her two cups of tea as if she were in a hurry; but then she couldn't find anything to be in a hurry for. Her trunk was packed, her bag was all strapped and labeled, there was nothing to do. The orchestra came in and began play- 545 ing. The sound of the music made her feel like crying. Katy said she was going to see if there was a night train out of Queenstown for the north. She got down a timetable from the shelves and looked at it, but couldn't make head or tail of it. Then two of the ladies at their table came with menus on which they were getting all their acquaintances to sign their 550 names. She and Katy signed their names and said goodbye, in case they shouldn't meet again, for it wasn't certain whether they would have supper on board or not. The rumor was that they would get into Queenstown harbor about six o'clock, in which case the Queenstown passengers would have to wait and have their supper in Queenstown. 555

It was after dark when finally the ship swung into the harbor. They felt the engine stopping, and ran out on deck. They could see the lights all round them, and a long row of especially bright ones; there was the hotel, and another ship waiting a little way off—waiting, as they were, for the tenders to come out. Everything seemed very still, now that the en- 560 gines were stopped; it was almost as if something was wrong with the ship, —unnatural. Everybody seemed to talk in lower voices. The harbor water was quieter than the ocean; it just lapped a little against the side of the ship, and there was a long narrow rowboat which had come out and was lying against the bow with two men in it, one of them giving an 565 occasional flourish with a long oar. A light was played on them from the ship, so that they stood out very clear against the blackness of the water. Then at last they saw the tenders coming out, and they decided they had better go down and see about their things.

It was just after they had tipped the steward, and he had gone off with 570 the trunks, and just when they heard the tender coming alongside, that Mr. Camp suddenly came to their stateroom door.

"I've just dropped in to say goodbye," he said, putting his hand against one side of the doorway.

Katy saw how it was, and said she had to go out for a minute, leaving 575 them alone. Mr. Camp stepped in then, and shut the door behind him. He put out his hand and she took it, and they shook hands for a minute, feeling embarrassed.

"Goodbye, Margaret," he said.

"Goodbye, Mr. Camp." 580

"I've been hunting for you all day," he said. "Why did you hide yourself from me?"

"I thought it was better," she said.

She felt the tears coming into her eyes and was ashamed. He suddenly put his arms around her and kissed her. She tried to turn her face away from 585 him, and he just kissed her cheek two or three times, lightly. His arms were holding her very hard. Then he kissed her once on the mouth.

"You musn't," she said. "You're a married man."

They looked at each other for what seemed like a long while, and then they heard someone coming to the door and he let her go. Katy and 590 the steward were there. It was time to go. Mr. Diehl came running up too, and she hurriedly put on her hat and coat. Mr. Diehl took Katy's bag from the steward, and Mr. Camp picked up hers from the camp-chair.

They followed the other passengers and stewards with bags along the corridor, went through the first-cabin dining saloon, and then came out 595 on to a deck where an iron door had been swung open and the gangway made fast. There was a great crowd there, and two officers standing at the top of the gangway taking the landing cards. Mr. Diehl gave Katy her handbag and tried to kiss her, right there before everybody, and she gave a screech and tried to run, but he caught her and kissed her. Then 600 she started down the steep gangway under the bright lights. Mr. Camp handed Margaret her bag and shook hands with her again.

"Here's my address," he said. "Write me a letter some time, if you feel like it."

He gave her a slip of paper, and she tucked it under her glove.   605
"Goodbye," she said.
"Goodbye."

She turned and went gingerly down the gangway, taking short steps. When she got to the deck of the tender she didn't look for Katy, but walked right to the stern of the boat, where there was a semicircular 610 bench, and put down her bag, and then stood and looked up at the ship. It seemed enormous, and at first she couldn't make out where the second-cabin decks were at all. The band was playing somewhere above her, in the night, and the decks were lined with people waving handkerchiefs. They were shouting, too. She ran her eyes to and fro over the crowds, 615 looking for Mr. Camp, but she couldn't find him, anywhere. Maybe he wouldn't come. Then the gangway was hauled down, the bells rang, and the tender began chugging.

Just at that minute she finally saw him. He had got a little open space of railing all to himself, and was leaning way out, waving his arm. She 620 felt as if her heart was going to break, and threw him three long kisses, and he threw three long kisses back. The steamship whistle began blowing, the tender drew away very fast, but she could still see him waving his arm. Then she couldn't see any more, because the tears came into her eyes, and she sat down and waited for Katy to come, and turned her head 625 away from the ship and wished she were dead.

QUESTIONS

1. Aiken begins "in the midst of things" with Margaret's dream. What does this reveal about Margaret? What else that is significant comes out in section I? What does the author accomplish through this dream-device?

2. In section II we learn things about other characters: Katy, Mr. Diehl, the refined-looking man in the next cabin, and Pat. Why has the

author created each of these characters? Why does Margaret feel displeased with Pat?

3. What point of view does the author adopt? Why?
4. How does section III advance the plot? Why should it be followed by a kind of retarding effect in section IV?
5. What elements of "delayed exposition" come out in sections V and VI? How do Margaret and Mr. Camp feel the pressure of time in section V?
6. What great significance does section VI have?
7. How do Margaret's and Katy's views differ concerning Mr. Camp? What part do differences of social class play in the story? What part does chance play?
8. After section VI why is the rest of the action inevitable? What effect is created by the final paragraph?
9. Where does the chief emphasis of this story fall, on plot or on emotion? What kind of enlightenment about human nature does the story give us?
10. Compare this story with "The Ugly Duckling" or with "After the Theater."

The Wonderful Ice Cream Suit

RAY BRADBURY

It was summer twilight in the city, and out front of the quiet-clicking
pool hall three young Mexican-American men breathed the warm air and
looked around at the world. Sometimes they talked and sometimes they
said nothing at all but watched the cars glide by like black panthers on the
hot asphalt or saw trolleys loom up like thunderstorms, scatter lightning, 5
and rumble away into silence.

"Hey," sighed Martínez at last. He was the youngest, the most sweetly
sad of the three. "It's a swell night, huh? Swell."

As he observed the world it moved very close and then drifted away
and then came close again. People, brushing by, were suddenly across the 10
street. Buildings five miles away suddenly leaned over him. But most of
the time everything—people, cars, and buildings—stayed way out on the
edge of the world and could not be touched. On this quiet warm summer
evening Martínez's face was cold.

"Nights like this you wish . . . lots of things."   15

"Wishing," said the second man, Villanazul, a man who shouted books
out loud in his room but spoke only in whispers on the street. "Wishing is
the useless pastime of the unemployed."

"Unemployed?" cried Vamenos, the unshaven. "Listen to him! We
got no jobs, no money!"   20

"So," said Martínez, "we got no friends."

"True." Villanazul gazed off toward the green plaza where the palm
trees swayed in the soft night wind. "Do you know what I wish? I wish
to go into that plaza and speak among the businessmen who gather there
nights to talk big talk. But dressed as I am, poor as I am, who would listen? 25
So, Martínez, we have each other. The friendship of the poor is real friendship. We——"

But now a handsome young Mexican with a fine thin mustache strolled
by. And on each of his careless arms hung a laughing woman.

"*Madre mía!*" Martínez slapped his own brow. "How does that one rate 30
two friends?"

"It's his nice new white summer suit." Vamenos chewed a black
thumbnail. "He looks sharp."

Martínez leaned out to watch the three people moving away, and

then at the tenement across the street, in one fourth-floor window of which, 35
far above, a beautiful girl leaned out, her dark hair faintly stirred by the
the wind. She had been there forever, which was to say for six weeks. He
had nodded, he had raised a hand, he had smiled, he had blinked rapidly,
he had even bowed to her, on the street, in the hall when visiting friends,
in the park, downtown. Even now, he put his hand up from his waist and 40
moved his fingers. But all the lovely girl did was let the summer wind stir
her dark hair. He did not exist. He was nothing.

"*Madre mía!*" He looked away and down the street where the man
walked his two friends around a corner. "Oh, if just I had one suit, one! I
wouldn't need money if I *looked* okay." 45

"I hesitate to suggest," said Villanazul, "that you see Gómez. But he's
been talking some crazy talk for a month now about clothes. I keep on saying I'll be in on it to make him go away. That Gómez."

"Friend," said a quiet voice.

"Gómez!" Everyone turned to stare. 50

Smiling strangely, Gómez pulled forth an endless thin yellow ribbon
which fluttered and swirled on the summer air.

"Gómez," said Martínez, "what are you doing with that tape measure?"

Gómez beamed. "Measuring people's skeletons."

"Skeletons!" 55

"Hold on." Gómez squinted at Martínez. "*Caramba!* Where you *been*
all my life! Let's try *you!*"

Martínez saw his arm seized and taped, his leg measured, his chest
encircled.

"Hold still!" cried Gómez. "Arm—perfect. Leg—chest—*perfecto!* 60
Now quick, the height! There! Yes! Five foot five! You're in! Shake!" Pump-
ing Martínez's hand, he stopped suddenly. "Wait. You got . . . ten bucks?"

"I have!" Vamenos waved some grimy bills. "Gómez, measure me!"

"All I got left in the world is nine dollars and ninety-two cents." Martínez searched his pockets. "That's enough for a new suit? Why?" 65

"Why? Because you got the right skeleton, that's why!"

"Señor Gómez, I don't hardly know you——"

"Know me? You're going to live with me! Come on!"

Gómez vanished into the poolroom. Martínez, escorted by the polite
Villanazul, pushed by an eager Vamenos, found himself inside. 70

"Domínguez!" said Gómez.

Domínguez, at a wall telephone, winked at them. A woman's voice
squeaked on the receiver.

"Manulo!" said Gómez.

Manulo, a wine bottle tilted bubbling to his mouth, turned. 75

Gómez pointed at Martínez.

"At last we found our fifth volunteer!"

Domínguez said, "I got a date, don't bother me——" and stopped.
The receiver slipped from his fingers. His little black telephone book full

of fine names and numbers went quickly back into his pocket. "Gómez, 80 you——?"

"Yes, yes! Your money, now! *Ándale!*"

The woman's voice sizzled on the dangling phone.

Domínguez glanced at it uneasily.

Manulo considered the empty wine bottle in his hand and the liquor- 85 store sign across the street.

Then very reluctantly both men laid ten dollars each on the green velvet pool table.

Villanazul, amazed, did likewise, as did Gómez, nudging Martínez. Martínez counted out his wrinkled bills and change. Gómez flourished the 90 money like a royal flush.

"Fifty bucks! The suit costs sixty! All we need is ten bucks!"

"Wait," said Martínez. "Gómez, are we talking about *one* suit? *Uno?*"

"*Uno!*" Gómez raised a finger. "One wonderful white ice cream summer suit! White, white as the August moon!" 95

"But who will own this one suit?"

"Me!" said Manulo.

"Me!" said Domínguez.

"Me!" said Villanazul.

"Me!" cried Gómez. "*And* you, Martínez. Men, let's show him. Line 100 up!"

Villanazul, Manulo, Domínguez, and Gómez rushed to plant their backs against the poolroom wall.

"Martínez, you too, the other end, line up! Now, Vamenos, lay that billiard cue across our heads!" 105

"Sure, Gómez, sure!"

Martínez, in line, felt the cue tap his head and leaned out to see what was happening. "Ah!" he gasped.

The cue lay flat on all their heads, with no rise or fall, as Vamenos slid it along, grinning. 110

"We're all the same height!" said Martínez.

"The same!" Everyone laughed.

Gómez ran down the line, rustling the yellow tape measure here and there on the men so they laughed even more wildly.

"Sure!" he said. "It took a month, four weeks, mind you, to find four 115 guys the same size and shape as me, a month of running around measuring. Sometimes I found guys with five-foot-five skeletons, sure, but all the meat on their bones was too much or not enough. Sometimes their bones were too long in the legs or too short in the arms. Boy, all the bones! I tell you! But now, five of us, same shoulders, chests, waists, arms, and as for weight? 120 Men!"

Manulo, Domíguez, Villanazul, Gómez, and at last Martínez stepped onto the scales which flipped ink-stamped cards at them as Vamenos, still smiling wildly, fed pennies. Heart pounding, Martínez read the cards.

"One hundred thirty-five pounds . . . one thirty-six . . . one thirty-three   125
. . . one thirty-four . . . one thirty-seven . . . a miracle!"

"No," said Villanazul simply, "Gómez."

They all smiled upon that genius who now circled them with his arms.

"Are we not fine?" he wondered. "All the same size, all the same dream   130
—the suit. So each of us will look beautiful at least one night each week, eh?"

"I haven't looked beautiful in years," said Martínez. "The girls run away."

"They will run no more, they will freeze," said Gómez, "when they see   135
you in the cool white summer ice cream suit."

"Gómez," said Villanazul, "just let me ask one thing."

"Of course, *compadre*."

"When we get this nice new white ice cream summer suit, some night you're not going to put it on and walk down to the Greyhound bus in it   140
and go live in El Paso for a year in it, are you?"

"Villanazul, Villanazul, how can you say that?"

"My eye sees and my tongue moves," said Villanazul. "How about the *Everybody Wins!* Punchboard Lotteries you ran and you kept running when nobody won? How about the United Chili Con Carne and Frijole   145
Company you were going to organize and all that ever happened was the rent ran out on a two-by-four office?"

"The errors of a child now grown," said Gómez. "Enough! In this hot weather someone may buy the special suit that is made just for us that stands waiting in the window of SHUMWAY'S SUNSHINE SUITS! We have fifty   150
dollars. Now we need just one more skeleton!"

Martínez saw the men peer around the pool hall. He looked where they looked. He felt his eyes hurry past Vamenos, then come reluctantly back to examine his dirty shirt, his huge nicotined fingers.

"Me!" Vamenos burst out at last. "My skeleton, measure it, it's great!   155
Sure, my hands are big, and my arms, from digging ditches! But——"

Just then Martínez heard passing on the sidewalk outside that same terrible man with his two girls, all laughing together.

He saw anguish move like the shadow of a summer cloud on the faces of the other men in this poolroom.   160

Slowly Vamenos stepped onto the scales and dropped his penny. Eyes closed, he breathed a prayer.

"*Madre mía*, please . . ."

The machinery whirred; the card fell out. Vamenos opened his eyes.

"Look! One thirty-five pounds! Another miracle!"   165

The men stared at his right hand and the card, at his left hand and a soiled ten-dollar bill.

Gómez swayed. Sweating, he licked his lips. Then his hand shot out, seized the money.

"The clothing store! The suit! *Vamos!*"   170

Yelling, everyone ran from the poolroom.

The woman's voice was still squeaking on the abandoned telephone. Martínez, left behind, reached out and hung the voice up. In the silence he shook his head. "*Santos,* what a dream! Six men," he said, "one suit. What will come of this? Madness? Debauchery? Murder? But I go with 175 God. Gómez, wait for me!"

Martínez was young. He ran fast.

Mr. Shumway, of SHUMWAY'S SUNSHINE SUITS, paused while adjusting a tie rack, aware of some subtle atmospheric change outside his establishment.   180

"Leo," he whispered to his assistant. "Look . . ."

Outside, one man, Gómez, strolled by, looking in. Two men, Manulo and Domínguez, hurried by, staring in. Three men, Villanazul, Martínez, and Vamenos, jostling shoulders, did the same.

"Leo." Mr. Shumway swallowed. "Call the police!"   185

Suddenly six men filled the doorway.

Martínez, crushed among them, his stomach slightly upset, his face feeling feverish, smiled so wildly at Leo that Leo let go the telephone.

"Hey," breathed Martínez, eyes wide. "There's a great suit over there!"

"No." Manulo touched a lapel. "*This* one!"   190

"There is only one suit in all the world!" said Gómez coldly. "Mr. Shumway, the ice cream white, size thirty-four, was in your window just an hour ago! It's gone! You didn't——"

"Sell it?" Mr. Shumway exhaled. "No, no. In the dressing room. It's still on the dummy."   195

Martínez did not know if he moved and moved the crowd or if the crowd moved and moved him. Suddenly they were all in motion. Mr. Shumway, running, tried to keep ahead of them.

"This way, gents. Now which of you . . . ?"

"All for one, one for all!" Martínez heard himself say, and laughed. 200 "We'll all try it on!"

"All?" Mr. Shumway clutched at the booth curtain as if his shop were a steamship that had suddenly tilted in a great swell. He stared.

That's it, thought Martínez, look at our smiles. Now, look at the skeletons behind our smiles! Measure here, there, up, down, yes, do you 205 *see?*

Mr. Shumway saw. He nodded. He shrugged.

"All!" He jerked the curtain. "There! Buy it, and I'll throw in the dummy free!"

Martínez peered quietly into the booth, his motion drawing the others 210 to peer too.

The suit was there.

And it was white.

Martínez could not breathe. He did not want to. He did not need to. He was afraid his breath would melt the suit. It was enough, just looking. 215

But at last he took a great trembling breath and exhaled, whispering, "*Ay. Ay, caramba!*"

"It puts out my eyes," murmured Gómez.

"Mr. Shumway," Martínez heard Leo hissing. "Ain't it dangerous precedent, to sell it? I mean, what if everybody bought *one* suit for *six* people?" 220

"Leo," said Mr Shumway, "you ever hear one single fifty-nine-dollar suit make so many people happy at the same time before?"

"Angels' wings," murmured Martínez. "The wings of white angels."

Martínez felt Mr. Shumway peering over his shoulder into the booth. The pale glow filled his eyes. 225

"You know something, Leo?" he said in awe. "That's a *suit!*"

Gómez, shouting, whistling, ran up to the third-floor landing and turned to wave to the others, who staggered, laughed, stopped, and had to sit down on the steps below.

"Tonight!" cried Gómez. "Tonight you move in with me, eh? Save 230 rent as well as clothes, eh? Sure! Martínez you got the suit?"

"Have I?" Martínez lifted the white gift-wrapped box high. "From us to us! *Ay-hah!*"

"Vamenos, you got the dummy?"

"Here!" 235

Vamenos, chewing an old cigar, scattering sparks, slipped. The dummy, falling, toppled, turned over twice and banged down the stairs.

"Vamenos! Dumb! Clumsy!"

They seized the dummy from him. Stricken, Vamenos looked about as if he'd lost something. 240

Manulo snapped his fingers. "Hey, Vamenos, we got to celebrate! Go borrow some wine!"

Vamenos plunged downstairs in a whirl of sparks.

The others moved into the room with the suit, leaving Martínez in the hall to study Gómez's face. 245

"Gómez, you look sick."

"I am," said Gómez. "For what have I done?" He nodded to the shadows in the room working about the dummy. "I pick Domínguez, a devil with the women. All right. I pick Manulo, who drinks, yes, but who sings as sweet as a girl, eh? Okay. Villanazul reads books. You, you go wash 250 behind your ears. But then what do I do? Can I wait? No! I got to buy that suit! So the last guy I pick is a clumsy slob who has the right to wear *my* suit——" He stopped, confused. "Who gets to wear *our* suit one night a week, fall down in it, or not come in out of the rain in it! Why, why, why did I do it!" 255

"Gómez," whispered Villanazul from the room. "The suit is ready. Come see if it looks as good using *your* light bulb."

Gómez and Martínez entered.

And there on the dummy in the center of the room was the phosphorescent, the miraculously white-fired ghost with the incredible lapels, the precise stitching, the neat buttonholes. Standing with the white illumination of the suit upon his cheeks, Martínez suddenly felt he was in church. White! White! It was white as the whitest vanilla ice cream, as the bottled milk in tenement halls at dawn. White as a winter cloud all alone in the moonlit sky late at night. Seeing it here in the warm summer-night room made their breath almost show on the air. Shutting his eyes, he could see it printed on his lids. He knew what color his dreams would be this night.

"White . . ." murmured Villanazul. "White as the snow on that mountain near our town in Mexico, which is called the Sleeping Woman."

"Say that again," said Gómez.

Villanazul, proud yet humble, was glad to repeat his tribute.

". . . white as the snow on the mountain called——"

"I'm back!"

Shocked, the men whirled to see Vamenos in the door, wine bottles in each hand.

"A party! Here! Now tell us, who wears the suit first tonight? Me?"

"It's too late!" said Gómez.

"Late! It's only nine-fifteen!"

"Late?" said everyone, bristling. "Late?"

Gómez edged away from these men who glared from him to the suit to the open window.

Outside and below it was, after all, thought Martínez, a fine Saturday night in a summer month and through the calm warm darkness the women drifted like flowers on a quiet stream. The men made a mournful sound.

"Gómez, a suggestion." Villanazul licked his pencil and drew a chart on a pad. "You wear the suit from nine-thirty to ten, Manulo till ten-thirty, Domínguez till eleven, myself till eleven-thirty, Martínez till midnight, and——"

"Why me *last*?" demanded Vamenos, scowling.

Martínez thought quickly and smiled. "After midnight is the *best* time, friend."

"Hey," said Vamenos, "that's right. I never thought of that. Okay."

Gómez sighed. "All right. A half hour each. But from now on, remember, we each wear the suit just one night a week. Sundays we draw straws for who wears the suit the extra night."

"Me!" laughed Vamenos. "I'm lucky!"

Gómez held onto Martínez, tight.

"Gómez," urged Martínez, "you first. Dress."

Gómez could not tear his eyes from that disreputable Vamenos. At last, impulsively, he yanked his shirt off over his head. "Ay-yeah!" he howled. "*Ay-yeee!*"

Whisper rustle . . . the clean shirt.

"Ah . . . !"

How clean the new clothes feel, thought Martínez, holding the coat ready. How clean they sound, how clean they smell!   305

Whisper . . . the pants . . . the tie, rustle . . . the suspenders. Whisper . . . now Martínez let loose the coat, which fell in place on flexing shoulders.

"*Ole!*"

Gómez turned like a matador in his wondrous suit-of-lights.

"*Ole,* Gómez, *ole!*"   310

Gómez bowed and went out the door.

Martínez fixed his eyes to his watch. At ten sharp he heard someone wandering about in the hall as if they had forgotten where to go. Martínez pulled the door open and looked out.

Gómez was there, heading for nowhere.   315

He looks sick, thought Martínez. No, stunned, shook up, surprised, many things.

"Gómez! This is the place!"

Gómez turned around and found his way through the door.

"Oh, friends, friends," he said. "Friends, what an experience! This   320
suit! This suit!"

"Tell us, Gómez!" said Martínez.

"I can't, how can I say it!" He gazed at the heavens, arms spread, palms up.

"*Tell* us, Gómez!"   325

"I have no words, no words. You must see, yourself! Yes, you must see——" And here he lapsed into silence, shaking his head until at last he remembered they all stood watching him. "Who's next? Manulo?"

Manulo, stripped to his shorts, leapt forward.

"Ready!"   330

All laughed, shouted, whistled.

Manulo, ready, went out the door. He was gone twenty-nine minutes and thirty seconds. He came back holding to doorknobs, touching the wall, feeling his own elbows, putting the flat of his hand to his face.

"Oh, let me tell you," he said. "*Compadres*, I went to the bar, eh, to 335
have a drink? But no, I did not go in the bar, do you hear? I did not drink. For as I walked I began to laugh and sing. Why, why? I listened to myself and asked this. Because. The suit made me feel better than wine ever did. The suit made me drunk, drunk! So I went to the *Guadalajara Refritería* instead and played the guitar and sang four songs, very high! The suit, ah, 340
the suit!"

Domínguez, next to be dressed, moved out through the world, came back through the world.

The black telephone book! thought Martínez. He had it in his hands when he left! Now, he returns, hands empty! What? What?   345

"On the street," said Domínguez, seeing it all again, eyes wide, "on the street I walked, a woman cried, 'Domínguez, is that *you*?' Another said, 'Domínguez? No, Quetzalcoatl, the Great White God come from the East,' do you hear? And suddenly I didn't want to go with six women or eight, no. One, I thought. One! And to this one, who knows *what* I would say? 'Be 350 mine!' Or 'Marry me!' *Caramba!* This suit is dangerous! But I did not care! I live, I live! Gómez, did it happen this way with you?"

Gómez, still dazed by the events of the evening, shook his head. "No, no talk. It's too much. Later. Villanazul . . . ?"

Villanazul moved shyly forward.   355

Villanazul went shyly out.

Villanazul came shyly home.

"Picture it," he said, not looking at them, looking at the floor, talking to the floor. "The Green Plaza, a group of elderly businessmen gathered under the stars and they are talking, nodding, talking. Now one of them 360 whispers. All turn to stare. They move aside, they make a channel through which a white-hot light burns its way as through ice. At the center of the great light is this person. I take a deep breath. My stomach is jelly. My voice is very small, but it grows louder. And what do I say? I say, 'Friends. Do you know Carlyle's *Sartor Resartus*? In that book we find *his* Philoso- 365 phy of Suits. . . .' "

And at last it was time for Martínez to let the suit float him out to haunt the darkness.

Four times he walked around the block. Four times he paused beneath the tenement porches, looking up at the window where the light was 370 lit; a shadow moved, the beautiful girl was there, not there, away and gone, and on the fifth time there she was on the porch above, driven out by the summer heat, taking the cooler air. She glanced down. She made a gesture.

At first he thought she was waving to him. He felt like a white explosion that had riveted her attention. But she was not waving. Her hand 375 gestured and the next moment a pair of dark-framed glasses sat upon her nose. She gazed at him.

Ah, ah, he thought, so that's it. So! Even the blind may see this suit! He smiled up at her. He did not have to wave. And at last she smiled back. She did not have to wave either. Then, because he did not know what else 380 to do and he could not get rid of this smile that had fastened itself to his cheeks, he hurried, almost ran, around the corner, feeling her stare after him. When he looked back she had taken off her glasses and gazed now with the look of the nearsighted at what, at most, must be a moving blob of light in the great darkness here. Then for good measure he went around 385 the block again, through a city so suddenly beautiful he wanted to yell, then laugh, then yell again.

Returning, he drifted, oblivious, eyes half closed, and seeing him in the door, the others saw not Martínez but themselves come home. In that moment, they sensed that something had happened to them all.   390

"You're late!" cried Vamenos, but stopped. The spell could not be broken.

"Somebody tell me," said Martínez. "Who am I?"

He moved in a slow circle through the room.

Yes, he thought, yes, it's the suit, yes, it had to do with the suit and them all together in that store on this fine Saturday night and then here, laughing and feeling more drunk without drinking as Manulo said himself, as the night ran and each slipped on the pants and held, toppling, to the others and, balanced, let the feeling get bigger and warmer and finer as each man departed and the next took his place in the suit until now here stood Martínez all splendid and white as one who gives orders and the world grows quiet and moves aside.

"Martínez, we borrowed three mirrors while you were gone. Look!"

The mirrors, set up as in the store, angled to reflect three Martínezes and the echoes and memories of those who had occupied this suit with him and known the bright world inside this thread and cloth. Now, in the shimmering mirror, Martínez saw the enormity of this thing they were living together and his eyes grew wet. The others blinked. Martínez touched the mirrors. They shifted. He saw a thousand, a million white-armored Martínezes march off into eternity, reflected, re-reflected, forever, indomitable, and unending.

He held the white coat out on the air. In a trance, the others did not at first recognize the dirty hand that reached to take the coat. Then:

"Vamenos!"

"Pig!"

"You didn't wash!" cried Gómez. "Or even shave, while you waited! *Compadres*, the bath!"

"The bath!" said everyone.

"No!" Vamenos flailed. "The night air! I'm dead!"

They hustled him yelling out and down the hall.

Now here stood Vamenos, unbelievable in white suit, beard shaved, hair combed, nails scrubbed.

His friends scowled darkly at him.

For was it not true, thought Martínez, that when Vamenos passed by, avalanches itched on mountaintops? If he walked under windows, people spat, dumped garbage, or worse. Tonight now, this night, he would stroll beneath ten thousand wide-opened windows, near balconies, past alleys. Suddenly the world absolutely sizzled with flies. And here was Vamenos, a fresh-frosted cake.

"You sure look keen in that suit, Vamenos," said Manulo sadly.

"Thanks." Vamenos twitched, trying to make his skeleton comfortable where all their skeletons had so recently been. In a small voice Vamenos said, "Can I go now?"

"Villanazul!" said Gómez. "Copy down these rules."

Villanazul licked his pencil.   435

"First," said Gómez, "don't fall down in that suit, Vamenos!"

"I won't."

"Don't lean against buildings in that suit."

"No buildings."

"Don't walk under trees with birds in them in that suit. Don't smoke.   440
Don't drink——"

"Please," said Vamenos, "can I *sit down* in this suit?"

"When in doubt, take the pants off, fold them over a chair."

"Wish me luck," said Vamenos.

"Go with God, Vamenos."   445

He went out. He shut the door.

There was a ripping sound.

"Vamenos!" cried Martínez.

He whipped the door open.

Vamenos stood with two halves of a handkerchief torn in his hands,   450
laughing.

"Rrrip! Look at your faces! Rrrip!" He tore the cloth again. "Oh, oh,
your faces, your faces! Ha!"

Roaring, Vamenos slammed the door, leaving them stunned and alone.

Gómez put both hands on top of his head and turned away. "Stone   455
me. Kill me. I have sold our souls to a demon!"

Villanazul dug in his pockets, took out a silver coin, and studied it
for a long while.

"Here is my last fifty cents. Who else will help me buy back Vamenos'
share of the suit?"   460

"It's no use." Manulo showed them ten cents. "We got only enough
to buy the lapels and the buttonholes."

Gómez, at the open window, suddenly leaned out and yelled.
"Vamenos! No!"

Below on the street, Vamenos, shocked, blew out a match and threw   465
away an old cigar butt he had found somewhere. He made a strange gesture to all the men in the window above, then waved airily and saun-
tered on.

Somehow, the five men could not move away from the window. They
were crushed together there.   470

"I bet he eats a hamburger in that suit," mused Villanazul. "I'm thinking of the mustard."

"Don't!" cried Gómez. "No, no!"

Manulo was suddenly at the door.

"I need a drink, bad."   475

"Manulo, there's wine here, that bottle on the floor——"

Manulo went out and shut the door.

A moment later Villanazul stretched with great exaggeration and
strolled about the room.

"I think I'll walk down to the plaza, friends." 48

He was not gone a minute when Domínguez, waving his black book at the others, winked and turned the doorknob.

"Domínguez," said Gómez.

"Yes?"

"If you see Vamenos, by accident," said Gómez, "warn him away from 48 Mickey Murrillo's Red Rooster Café. They got fights not only *on* TV but *out front* of the TV too."

"He wouldn't go into Murrillo's," said Domínguez. "That suit means too much to Vamenos. He wouldn't do anything to hurt it."

"He'd shoot his mother first," said Martínez. 49

"Sure he would."

Martínez and Gómez, alone, listened to Domínguez's footsteps hurry away down the stairs. They circled the undressed window dummy.

For a long while, biting his lips, Gómez stood at the window, looking out. He touched his shirt pocket twice, pulled his hand away, and then at 49 last pulled something from the pocket. Without looking at it, he handed it to Martínez.

"Martínez, take this."

"What is it?"

Martínez looked at the piece of folded pink paper with print on it, 50 with names and numbers. His eyes widened.

"A ticket on the bus to El Paso three weeks from now!"

Gómez nodded. He couldn't look at Martínez. He stared out into the summer night.

"Turn it in. Get the money," he said. "Buy us a nice white panama hat 50 and a pale blue tie to go with the white ice cream suit, Martínez. Do that."

"Gómez——"

"Shut up. Boy, is it hot in here! I need air."

"Gómez. I am touched. Gómez——"

But the door stood open. Gómez was gone. 51

Mickey Murrillo's Red Rooster Café and Cocktail Lounge was squashed between two big brick buildings and, being narrow, had to be deep. Outside, serpents of red and sulphur-green neon fizzed and snapped. Inside, dim shapes loomed and swam away to lose themselves in a swarming night sea. 51

Martínez, on tiptoe, peeked through a flaked place on the red-painted front window.

He felt a presence on his left, heard breathing on his right. He glanced in both directions.

"Manulo! Villanazul!" 52

"I decided I wasn't thirsty," said Manulo. "So I took a walk."

"I was just on my way to the plaza," said Villanazul, "and decided to go the long way around."

As if by agreement, the three men shut up now and turned together to peer on tiptoe through various flaked spots on the window. 525

A moment later, all three felt a new very warm presence behind them and heard still faster breathing.

"Is our white suit in there?" asked Gómez's voice.

"Gómez!" said everybody, surprised. "Hi!"

"Yes!" cried Domínguez, having just arrived to find his own peephole. 530 "There's the suit! And, praise God, Vamenos is still *in* it!"

"I can't see!" Gómez squinted, shielding his eyes. "What's he *doing?*"

Martínez peered. Yes! There, way back in the shadows, was a big chunk of snow and the idiot smile of Vamenos winking above it, wreathed in smoke. 535

"He's smoking!" said Martínez.

"He's drinking!" said Domínguez.

"He's eating a taco!" reported Villanazul.

"A *juicy* taco," added Manulo.

"No," said Gómez. "No, no, no. . . ." 540

"Ruby Escuadrillo's with him!"

"Let me see that!" Gómez pushed Martínez aside.

Yes, there was Ruby! Two hundred pounds of glittering sequins and tight black satin on the hoof, her scarlet fingernails clutching Vamenos' shoulder. Her cowlike face, floured with powder, greasy with lipstick, hung 545 over him!

"That hippo!" said Domínguez. "She's crushing the shoulder pads. Look, she's going to sit on his lap!"

"No, no, not with all that powder and lipstick!" said Gómez. "Manulo, inside! Grab that drink! Villanazul, the cigar, the taco! Domínguez, date 550 Ruby Escuadrillo, get her away. *Ándale*, men!"

The three vanished. leaving Gómez and Martínez to stare, gasping, through the peephole.

"Manulo, he's got the drink, he's *drinking* it!"

"*Ay!* There's Villanazul, he's got the cigar, he's eating the taco!" 555

"Hey, Domínguez, he's got Ruby! What a *brave* one!"

A shadow bulked through Murrillo's front door, traveling fast.

"Gómez!" Martínez clutched Gómez's arm. "That was Ruby Escuadrillo's boy friend, Toro Ruíz. If he finds her with Vamenos, the ice cream suit will be covered with blood, *covered* with blood——" 560

"Don't make me nervous," said Gómez. "Quickly!"

Both ran. Inside they reached Vamenos just as Toro Ruíz grabbed about two feet of the lapels of that wonderful ice cream suit.

"Let go of Vamenos!" said Martínez.

"Let go that *suit!*" corrected Gómez. 565

Toro Ruíz, tap-dancing Vamenos, leered at these intruders.

Villanazul stepped up shyly.

Vilanazul smiled. "Don't hit him. Hit me."

Toro Ruíz hit Villanazul smack on the nose.

Villanazul, holding his nose, tears stinging his eyes, wandered off.   570

Gómez grabbed one of Toro Ruíz's arms, Martínez the other.

"Drop him, let go, *cabrón, coyote, vaca!*"

Toro Ruíz twisted the ice cream suit material until all six men screamed in mortal agony. Grunting, sweating, Toro Ruíz dislodged as many as climbed on. He was winding up to hit Vamenos when Villanazul   575 wandered back, eyes streaming.

"Don't hit him. Hit me!"

As Toro Ruíz hit Villanazul on the nose, a chair crashed on Toro's head.

"*Ai!*" said Gómez.   580

Toro Ruíz swayed, blinking, debating whether to fall. He began to drag Vamenos with him.

"Let go!" cried Gómez. "Let go!"

One by one, with great care, Toro Ruíz's banana-like fingers let loose of the suit. A moment later he was ruins at their feet.   585

"*Compadres*, this way!"

They ran Vamenos outside and set him down where he freed himself of their hands with injured dignity.

"Okay, okay. My time ain't up. I still got two minutes and, let's see— ten seconds."   590

"What!" said everybody.

"Vamenos," said Gómez, "you let a Guadalajara cow climb on you, you pick fights, you smoke, you drink, you eat tacos, and *now* you have the nerve to say your time ain't up?"

"I got two minutes and one second left!"   595

"Hey, Vamenos, you sure look sharp!" Distantly, a woman's voice called from across the street.

Vamenos smiled and buttoned the coat.

"It's Ramona Álvarez! Ramona, wait!" Vamenos stepped off the curb.

"Vamenos," pleaded Gómez. "What can you do in one minute and"—   600 he checked his watch—"forty seconds!"

"Watch! Hey, Ramona!"

Vamenos loped.

"Vamenos, look out!"

Vamenos, surprised, whirled, saw a car, heard the shriek of brakes.   605

"No," said all five men on the sidewalk.

Martínez heard the impact and flinched. His head moved up. It looks like white laundry, he thought, flying through the air. His head came down.

Now he heard himself and each of the men make a different sound. Some swallowed too much air. Some let it out. Some choked. Some groaned.   610 Some cried aloud for justice. Some covered their faces. Martínez felt his own fist pounding his heart in agony. He could not move his feet.

"I don't want to live," said Gómez quietly. "Kill me, someone."

Then, shuffling, Martínez looked down and told his feet to walk, stag- 615
ger, follow one after the other. He collided with other men. Now they were
trying to run. They ran at last and somehow crossed a street like a deep
river through which they could only wade, to look down at Vamenos.

"Vamenos!" said Martínez. "You're alive!"

Strewn on his back, mouth open, eyes squeezed tight, tight, Vamenos
motioned his head back and forth, back and forth, moaning.   620

"Tell me, tell me, oh, tell me, tell me."

"Tell you what, Vamenos?"

Vamenos clenched his fists, ground his teeth.

"The suit, what have I done to the suit, the suit, the suit!"

The men crouched lower.   625

"Vamenos, it's . . . why, it's *okay!*"

"You lie!" said Vamenos. "It's torn, it must be, it must be, it's torn, all
around, *underneath?*"

"No." Martínez knelt and touched here and there. "Vamenos, all
around, underneath even, it's okay!"   630

Vamenos opened his eyes to let the tears run free at last. "A miracle,"
he sobbed. "Praise the saints!" He quieted at last. "The car?"

"Hit and run." Gómez suddenly remembered and glared at the empty
street. "It's good he didn't stop. We'd have——"

Everyone listened.   635

Distantly a siren wailed.

"Someone phoned for an ambulance."

"Quick!" said Vamenos, eyes rolling. "Set me up! Take off our coat!"

"Vamenos——"

"Shut up, idiots!" cried Vamenos. "The coat, that's it! Now, the pants, 640
the pants, quick, quick, *peónes!* Those doctors! You seen movies? They
rip the pants with razors to get them off! They don't *care!* They're
maniacs! Ah, God, quick, quick!"

The siren screamed.

The men, panicking, all handled Vamenos at once.   645

"Right leg, *easy*, hurry, cows! Good! Left leg, now, left, you hear,
there, easy, *easy!* Ow, God! Quick! Martínez, your pants, take them off!"

"What?" Martínez froze.

The siren shrieked.

"Fool!" wailed Vamenos. "All is lost! Your pants! Give me!"   650

Martínez jerked at his belt buckle.

"Close in, make a circle!"

Dark pants, light pants flourished on the air.

"Quick, here come the maniacs with the razors! Right leg on, left leg,
there!"   655

"The zipper, cows, zip my zipper!" babbled Vamenos.

The siren died.

"*Madre mía,* yes, just in time! They arrive." Vamenos lay back down and shut his eyes. "*Gracias.*"

Martínez turned, nonchalantly buckling on the white pants as the 660 interns brushed past.

"Broken leg," said one intern as they moved Vamenos onto a stretcher.

"*Compadres,*" said Vamenos, "don't be mad with me."

Gómez snorted. "Who's mad?"

In the ambulance, head tilted back, looking out at them upside down, 665 Vamenos faltered.

"*Compadres,* when . . . when I come from the hospital . . . am I still in the bunch? You won't kick me out? Look, I'll give up smoking, keep away from Murrillo's, swear off women———"

"Vamenos," said Martínez gently, "don't promise nothing."   670

Vamenos, upside down, eyes brimming wet, saw Martínez there, all white now against the stars.

"Oh, Martínez, you sure look great in that suit. *Compadres,* don't he look *beautiful?*"

Villanazul climbed in beside Vamenos. The door slammed. The four 675 remaining men watched the ambulance drive away.

Then, surrounded by his friends, inside the white suit, Martínez was carefully escorted back to the curb.

In the tenement, Martínez got out the cleaning fluid and the others stood around, telling him how to clean the suit and, later, how not to have 680 the iron too hot and how to work the lapels and the crease and all. When the suit was cleaned and pressed so it looked like a fresh gardenia just opened, they fitted it to the dummy.

"Two o'clock," murmured Villanazul. "I hope Vamenos sleeps well. When I left him at the hospital, he looked good."   685

Manulo cleared his throat. "Nobody else is going out with that suit tonight, huh?"

The others glared at him.

Manulo flushed. "I mean . . . it's late. We're tired. Maybe no one will use the suit for forty-eight hours, huh? Give it a rest. Sure. Well. Where 690 do we sleep?"

The night being still hot and the room unbearable, they carried the suit on its dummy out and down the hall. They brought with them also some pillows and blankets. They climbed the stairs toward the roof of the tenement. There, thought Martínez, is the cooler wind, and sleep.   695

On the way, they passed a dozen doors that stood open, people still perspiring and awake, playing cards, drinking pop, fanning themselves with movie magazines.

I wonder, thought Martínez. I wonder if——— Yes!

On the fourth floor, a certain door stood open.   700

The beautiful girl looked up as the men passed. She wore glasses and when she saw Martínez she snatched them off and hid them under her book.

The others went on, not knowing they had lost Martínez, who seemed stuck fast in the open door.

For a long moment he could say nothing. Then he said: 705

"José Martínez."

And she said:

"Celia Obregón."

And then both said nothing.

He heard the men moving up on the tenement roof. He moved to 710 follow.

She said quickly, "I saw you tonight!"

He came back.

"The suit," he said.

"The suit," she said, and paused. "But not the suit."   715

"Eh?" he said.

She lifted the book to show the glasses lying in her lap. She touched the glasses.

"I do not see well. You would think I would wear my glasses, but no. I walk around for years now, hiding them, seeing nothing. But tonight, 720 even without the glasses, I see. A great whiteness passes below in the dark. So white! And I put on my glasses quickly!"

"The suit, as I said," said Martínez.

"The suit for a little moment, yes, but there is another whiteness above the suit."   725

"Another?"

"Your teeth! Oh, such white teeth, and so many!"

Martínez put his hand over his mouth.

"So happy, Mr. Martínez," she said. "I've not often seen such a happy face and such a smile."   730

"Ah," he said, not able to look at her, his face flushing now.

"So, you see," she said quietly, "the suit caught my eye, yes, the whiteness filled the night below. But the teeth were much whiter. Now, I have forgotten the suit."

Martínez flushed again. She, too, was overcome with what she had 735 said. She put her glasses on her nose, and then took them off, nervously, and hid them again. She looked at her hands and at the door above his head.

"May I——" he said, at last.

"May you——"

"May I call for you," he asked, "when next the suit is mine to wear?" 740

"Why must you wait for the suit?" she said.

"I thought——"

"You do not need the suit," she said.

"But——"

"If it were just the suit," she said, "anyone would be fine in it. But 745
no, I watched. I saw many men in that suit, all different, this night. So again
I say, you do not need to wait for the suit."

"*Madre mía, madre mía!*" he cried happily. And then, quieter, "I will
need the suit for a little while. A month, six months, a year. I am uncertain.
I am fearful of many things. I am young."   750

"That is as it should be," she said.

"Good night, Miss——"

"Celia Obregón."

"Celia Obregón," he said, and was gone from the door.

The others were waiting on the roof of the tenement. Coming up 755
through the trapdoor, Martínez saw they had placed the dummy and the
suit in the center of the roof and put their blankets and pillows in a circle
around it. Now they were lying down. Now a cooler night wind was blowing here, up in the sky.

Martínez stood alone by the white suit, smoothing the lapels, talking 760
half to himself.

"Ay, *caramba*, what a night! Seems ten years since seven o'clock, when
it all started and I had no friends. Two in the morning. I got all *kinds* of
friends. . . ." He paused and thought, Celia Obregón, Celia Obregón.
". . . all kinds of friends," he went on. "I got a room, I got clothes. You tell 765
me. You know what?" He looked around at the men lying on the rooftop,
surrounding the dummy and himself. "It's funny. When I wear this suit, I
know I will win at pool, like Gómez. A woman will look at me like Domínguez. I will be able to sing like Manulo, sweetly. I will talk fine politics like
Villanazul. I'm strong as Vamenos. So? So, tonight, I am more than Mar- 770
tínez. I am Gómez, Manulo, Domínguez, Villanazul, Vamenos. I am everyone. Ay . . . ay . . ." He stood a moment longer by this suit which could
save all the ways they sat or stood or walked. This suit which could move
fast and nervous like Gómez or slow and thoughtfully like Villanazul or
drift like Domínguez, who never touched ground, who always found a wind 775
to take him somewhere. This suit which belonged to them but which also
owned them all. This suit that was—what? A parade.

"Martínez," said Gómez. "You going to sleep?"

"Sure. I'm just thinking."

"What?"   780

"If we ever get rich," said Martínez softly, "it'll be kind of sad. Then
we'll all have suits. And there won't be no more nights like tonight. It'll
break up the old gang. It'll never be the same after that."

The men lay thinking of what had just been said.

Gómez nodded gently.   785

"Yeah . . . it'll never be the same . . . after that."

Martinez lay down on his blanket. In darkness, with the others, he
faced the middle of the roof and the dummy, which was the center of
their lives.

And their eyes were bright, shining, and good to see in the dark as 790 the neon lights from nearby buildings flicked on, flicked off, flicked on, flicked off, revealing and then vanishing, revealing and then vanishing, their wonderful white vanilla ice cream summer suit.

QUESTIONS

1. What is the setting of the story?
2. The story is about a group of young men. What makes them feel frustrated? Why does Martínez say "we got no friends"? What plan does Gómez have to help them? Why is it necessary to include Vamenos in the plan?
3. Among the six men, which ones stand out? What is the reason why each one does?
4. What effect does wearing the new suit have on each man?
5. The story is presented in several scenes. What significant thing happens in each scene?
6. Which parts of the story are especially comical?
7. What is the climax of his companions' concern about Vamenos?
8. What wonderful things does Martínez discover? At the end how have things changed for him?
9. How would you describe the mood of the story?
10. What sort of style does Bradbury use here? Is it loose and slangy? realistic? poetic? sentimental? formal?
11. Why did Bradbury choose the setting that he used?

The Thrower-Away

HEINRICH BÖLL

For the last few weeks I have been trying to avoid people who might
ask me what I do for a living. If I really had to put a name to my occupation, I would be forced to utter a word which would alarm people. So I
prefer the abstract method of putting down my confession on paper.

Until recently I would have been prepared at any time to make an oral 5
confession. I almost insisted. I called myself an inventor, a scholar, even a
student, and, in the melodramatic mood of incipient intoxication, an unrecognized genius. I basked in the cheerful fame which a frayed collar
can radiate; arrogantly, as if it were mine by right, I exacted reluctant
credit from suspicious shopkeepers who watched margarine, ersatz coffee 10
and cheap tobacco disappear into my pockets; I reveled in my unkempt
appearance, and at breakfast, lunch and dinner I drank the nectar of Bo-
hemian life: the bliss of knowing one is not conforming.

But for the past few weeks I have been boarding the streetcar every
morning just before 7:30 at the corner of the Roonstrasse; like everyone 15
else I meekly hold out my season ticket to the conductor. I have on a gray
double-breasted suit, a striped shirt, a dark-green tie, I carry my sandwiches in a flat aluminum box and hold the morning paper, lightly rolled,
in my hand. I look like a citizen who has managed to avoid introspection.
After the third stop I get up to offer my seat to one of the elderly 20
working women who have got on at the housing settlement. Having sacrificed my seat on the altar of social compassion, I continue to read the
newspaper standing up, now and again letting myself be heard in the
capacity of arbitrator when morning irritation is inclined to make people
unjust. I correct the worst political and historical errors (by explaining, 25
for instance, that there is a certain difference between SA and USA); as
soon as anyone puts a cigarette to his lips I discreetly hold my lighter in
front of his nose and, with the aid of the tiny but dependable flame, light
his morning cigarette for him. Thus I complete the picture of a well-
groomed fellow-citizen who is still young enough for people to say he "has 30
nice manners."

I seem to have been successful in donning the mask which makes it
impossible to ask me about my occupation. I am evidently taken for an

educated businessman dealing in attractively packaged and agreeably smelling articles such as coffee, tea or spices, or in valuable small ob- 35 jects which are pleasing to the eye such as jewelry or watches; a man who practices his profession in a nice old-fashioned office with dark oil paint- ings of merchant forebears hanging on the walls, who phones his wife about ten, who knows how to imbue his apparently impassive voice with that hint of tenderness which betrays affection and concern. Since I also 40 participate in the usual jokes and do not refrain from laughing when every morning at the Lohengrinstrasse the clerk from City Hall shouts out "When does the next swan leave?," since I do not withhold my comments concerning either the events of the day or the results of the football pools, I am obviously regarded as someone who, although pros- 45 perous (as can be seen from his suit material), has an attitude toward life which is deeply rooted in the principles of democracy. An air of integrity encases me the way the glass coffin encased Snow White.

When a passing truck provides the streetcar window with a back- ground for a moment, I check up on the expression on my face: isn't it per- 50 haps rather too pensive, almost verging on the sorrowful? I assiduously erase the remnants of brooding and do my best to give my face the ex- pression I want it to wear: neither reserved nor familiar, neither superficial nor profound.

My camouflage seems to be successful, for when I get out at the 55 Marienplatz and dive into the maze of streets in the Old Town, where there is no lack of nice old-fashioned offices, where notaries and lawyers abound, no one suspects that I pass through a rear entrance into the UBIA building—a firm that can boast of supporting 350 people and of insuring the lives of 400,000. The commissionaire greets me with a smile 60 at the delivery entrance, I walk past him, go down to the basement, and start in on my work, which has to be completed by the time the employees come pouring into the offices at 8:30. The activity that I pursue every morning between 8 and 8:30 in the basement of this respected establish- ment is devoted entirely to destruction. I throw away. 65

It took me years to invent my profession, to endow it with mathe- matical plausibility. I wrote treatises; graphs and charts covered—and still cover—the walls of my apartment. For years I climbed along abscissas and up ordinates, wallowed in theories, and savored the glacial ecstasy of solving formulas. Yet since practicing my profession and seeing my the- 70 ories come to life, I am filled with a sense of sadness such as may come over a general who finds himself obliged to descend from the heights of strategy to the plains of tactics.

I enter my workroom, exchange my jacket for a gray smock, and immediately set to work. I open the mailbags which the commissionaire 75 has already picked up earlier from the main post office, and I empty them into the two wooden bins which, constructed according to my design,

hang to the right and left on the wall over my worktable. This way I only
need to stretch out my hands, somewhat like a swimmer, and begin
swiftly to sort the mail.   80

First I separate the circulars from the letters, a purely routine job,
since a glance at the postage suffices. At this stage a knowledge of the postal
tariff renders hesitation unnecessary. After years of practice I am able to
complete this phase within half an hour, and by this time it is half past
eight and I can hear the footsteps of the employees pouring into the offices 85
overhead. I ring for the commissionaire, who takes the sorted letters to the
various departments. It never fails to sadden me, the sight of the commissionaire carrying off in a metal tray the size of a briefcase the remains
of what had once filled three mailbags. I might feel triumphant, for this,
the vindication of my theory of throwing away, has for years been the   90
objective of my private research; but, strangely enough, I do not feel
triumphant. To have been right is by no means always a reason for rejoicing.

After the departure of the commissionaire there remains the task of
examining the huge pile of printed matter to make sure it contains no
letter masquerading behind the wrong postage, no bill mailed as a cir-   95
cular. This work is almost always superfluous, for the probity of the mail-
ing public is nothing short of astounding. I must admit that here my calculations were incorrect: I had overestimated the number of postal de-
frauders.

Rarely has a post card, a letter or a bill sent as printed matter escaped 100
my notice; about half past nine I ring for the commissionaire, who takes
the remaining objects of my careful scrutiny to the departments.

The time has now come when I require some refreshment. The commissionaire's wife brings me my coffee, I take my sandwich out of the
flat aluminum box, sit down for my break, and chat with the commis-   105
sionaire's wife about her children. Is Alfred doing somewhat better in
arithmetic? Has Gertrude been able to catch up in spelling? Alfred is not
doing any better in arithmetic, whereas Gertrude has been able to catch
up in spelling. Have the tomatoes ripened properly, are the rabbits plump,
and was the experiment with the melons successful? The tomatoes have   110
not ripened properly, but the rabbits are plump, while the experiment
with the melons is still undecided. Serious problems, such as whether
one should stock up on potatoes or not, matters of education, such as
whether one should enlighten one's children or be enlightened by them,
are the subjects of our intense consideration.   115

Just before eleven the commissionaire's wife leaves, and usually she
asks me to let her have some travel folders. She is collecting them, and I
smile at her enthusiasm, for I have retained tender memories of travel folders. As a child I also collected travel folders, I used to fish them out of my
father's waste-paper basket. Even as a boy it bothered me that my father   120
would take mail from the mailman and throw it into the waste-paper
basket without looking at it. This action wounded my innate propensity

for economy: there was something that had been designed, set up, printed, put in an envelope, and stamped, that had passed through the mysterious channels by which the postal service actually causes our mail to arrive at our addresses; it was weighted with the sweat of the draftsman, the writer, the printer, the office boy who had stuck on the stamps; on various levels and in various tariffs it had cost money: all this only to end—without being deemed worthy of so much as a glance—in a waste-paper basket?

At the age of eleven I had already adopted the habit of taking out of the waste-paper basket, as soon as my father had left for the office, whatever had been thrown away. I would study it, sort it, and put it away in a chest which I used to keep toys in. Thus by the time I was twelve I already possessed an imposing collection of wine-merchants' catalogues, as well as prospectuses on naturopathy and natural history. My collection of travel folders assumed the dimensions of a geographical encyclopedia; Dalmatia was as familiar to me as the Norwegian fjords, Scotland as close as Zakopane, the forests of Bohemia soothed me while the waves of the Atlantic disquieted me; hinges were offered me, houses and buttons, political parties asked for my vote, charities for my money; lotteries promised me riches, religious sects poverty. I leave it to the reader's imagination to picture what my collection was like when at the age of seventeen, suddenly bored with it all, I offered my collection to a junk dealer who paid me 7 marks and 60 pfennigs for it.

Having finished school, I embarked in my father's footsteps and set my foot on the first rung of the civil service ladder. With the 7 marks and 60 pfennigs I bought a package of squared paper and three colored crayons, and my attempt to gain a foothold in the civil service turned into a laborious detour, for a happy thrower-away was slumbering in me while I filled the role of an unhappy junior clerk. All my free time was devoted to intricate calculations.

Stop-watch, pencil, slide-rule, squared paper, these were the props of my obsession; I calculated how long it took to open a circular of small, medium or large size, with or without pictures, give it a quick glance, satisfy oneself of its uselessness, and then throw it in the waste-paper basket, a process requiring a minimum of five seconds and a maximum of twenty-five; if the circular is at all attractive, either the text or the pictures, several minutes, often a quarter of an hour, must be allowed for this. By conducting bogus negotiations with printing firms, I also worked out the minimum production costs for circulars. Indefatigably I checked the results of my studies and adjusted them (it did not occur to me until two years later that the time of the cleaning-women who have to empty the waste-paper baskets had to be included in my calculations); I applied the results of my research to firms with ten, twenty, a hundred or more employees; and I arrived at results which an expert on economics would not have hesitated to describe as alarming.

Obeying my sense of loyalty, I began by offering my results to my superiors; although I had reckoned with the possibility of ingratitude, I was nevertheless shocked at the extent of that ingratitude. I was accused of neglecting my duties, suspected of nihilism, pronounced "a mental 170 case," and discharged. To the great sorrow of my kind parents, I abandoned my promising career, began new ones, broke these off too, forsook the warmth of the parental hearth, and, as I have already said, eked out my existence as an unrecognized genius. I took pleasure in the humiliation of vainly peddling my invention, and spent years in a blissful state of 175 being anti-social, so consistently that my punch-card in the central files which had long ago been punched with the symbol for "mental case" was now stamped with the confidential symbol for "antisocial."

In view of these circumstances, it can readily be imagined what a shock it was when the obviousness of my results at last became obvious 180 to someone else—the manager of UBIA, how deeply humiliated I was to have to wear a dark-green tie, yet I must continue to go around in disguise as I am terrified of being found out. I try anxiously to give my face the proper expression when I laugh at the Lohengrin joke, since there is no greater vanity than that of the wags who populate the streetcar every 185 morning. Sometimes, too, I am afraid the streetcar may be full of people who the previous day have done work which I am about to destroy that very morning: printers, typesetters, draftsmen, writers who compose the wording of advertisements, commercial artists, envelope stuffers, packers, apprentices of all kinds. From 8 to 8:30 every morning I ruthlessly destroy 190 the products of respected paper mills, worthy printing establishments, brilliant commercial artists, the texts of talented writers; coated paper, glossy paper, copperplate, I take it all, just as it comes from the mailbag, and without the faintest sentimentality tie it up into handy bundles for the waste-paper dealer. In the space of one hour I destroy the output of 195 200 work-hours and save UBIA a further 100 hours, so that altogether (here I must lapse into my own jargon) I achieve a concentrate of 1:300.

When the commissionaire's wife leaves with the empty coffeepot and the travel folders, I knock off. I wash my hands, exchange my smock for my jacket, pick up the morning paper, and leave the UBIA building by the 200 rear entrance. I stroll through the town and wonder how I can escape from tactics and get back into strategy. That which intoxicated me as a formula, I find disappointing, since it can be performed so easily. Strategy translated into action can be carried out by hacks. I shall probably establish schools for throwers-away. I may possibly also attempt to have throw- 205 ers-away placed in post offices, perhaps even in printing establishments; an enormous amount of energy, valuable commodities, and intelligence could be utilized as well as postage saved; it might even be feasible to conceive, compose, and set brochures up in type but not print them. These are all problems still requiring a lot of study.   210

However, the mere throwing away of mail as such has almost ceased to interest me; any improvements on that level can be worked out by means of the basic formula. For a long time now I have been devoting my attention to calculations concerning wrapping paper and the process of wrapping: this is virgin territory where nothing has been done, here one can strive to spare humanity those unprofitable efforts under the burden of which it is groaning. Every day billions of throwing-away movements are made, energies are dissipated which, could they but be utilized, would suffice to change the face of the earth. It would be a great advantage if one were permitted to undertake experiments in department stores; should one dispense with the wrapping process altogether, or should one post an expert thrower-away right next to the wrapping table who unwraps what has just been wrapped and immediately ties the wrapping paper into bundles for the waste-paper dealer? These are problems meriting some thought. In any case it has struck me that in many shops the customers implore the clerk not to wrap the purchased article, but that they have to submit to having it wrapped. Clinics for nervous diseases are rapidly filling with patients who complain of an attack of nerves whenever they unwrap a bottle of perfume or a box of chocolates, or open a packet of cigarettes, and at the moment I am making an intensive study of a young man from my neighborhood who earned his living as a book reviewer but at times was unable to practice his profession because he found it impossible to undo the twisted wire tied around the parcel, and even when he did find himself equal to this physical exertion, he was incapable of penetrating the massive layer of gummed paper with which the corrugated paper is stuck together. The man appears deeply disturbed and has now gone over to reviewing the books unread and placing the parcels on his bookshelves without unwrapping them. I leave it to the reader's imagination to depict for himself the effect of such a case on our intellectual life.

While walking through the town between eleven and one I observe all sorts of details: I spend some time unobtrusively in the department stores, hovering around the wrapping tables; I stand in front of tobacco shops and pharmacies and note down minor statistics; now and again I even purchase something, so as to allow the senseless procedure to be performed on myself and to discover how much effort is required actually to take possession of the article one wishes to own.

So between eleven and one in my impeccable suit I complete the picture of a man who is sufficiently prosperous to afford a bit of leisure—who at about one o'clock enters a sophisticated little restaurant, casually chooses the most expensive meal, and scribbles some hieroglyphics on his beer coaster which could equally well be stock quotations or flights of poetry; who knows how to praise or decry the quality of the meat with arguments which betray the connoisseur to even the most blasé waiter; who, when it comes to choosing dessert, hesitates with a knowing air between cake, ice cream and cheese; and who finishes off his scribblings with a flourish which proves that they were stock quotations after all.

Shocked at the results of my calculations I leave the little restaurant. My expression becomes more and more thoughtful while I search for a small café where I can pass the time till three o'clock and read the evening 260 paper. At three I re-enter the UBIA building by the rear door to take care of the afternoon mail, which consists almost exclusively of circulars. It is a matter of scarcely fifteen minutes to pick out the ten or twelve letters; I don't even have to wash my hands after it, I just brush them off, take the letters to the commissionaire, leave the building, and at the 265 Marienplatz board the streetcar, glad that on the way home I do not need to laugh at the Lohengrin joke. When the dark tarpaulin of a passing truck makes a background for the streetcar window, I can see my face: it is relaxed; that is to say pensive, almost brooding, and I relish the fact that I do not have to put on any other face, for at this hour none of my morn- 270 ing fellow-travelers has finished work. I get out at the Roonstrasse, buy some fresh rolls, a piece of cheese or sausage, some ground coffee, and walk up to my little apartment, the walls of which are hung with graphs and charts, with hectic curves: between the abscissas and ordinates I capture the lines of a fever going up and up; not a single one of my curves 275 goes down, not a single one of my formulas has the power to soothe me. I groan under the burden of my vision of economics, and while the water is boiling for the coffee I place my slide-rule, my notes, pencil and paper in readiness.

My apartment is sparsely furnished, it looks more like a laboratory. I 280 drink my coffee standing up and hastily swallow a sandwich, the epicure I was at noon is now a thing of the past. Wash hands, light a cigarette, then I set my stop-watch and unwrap the nerve tonic I bought that morn- ing on my stroll through the town: outer wrapping paper, cellophane covering, carton, inside wrapping paper, directions for use secured by a 285 rubber band: thirty-seven seconds. The nervous energy consumed in un- wrapping exceeds the nervous energy which the tonic promises to impart to me, but there may be subjective reasons for this which I shall disre- gard in my calculations. One thing is certain: the wrapping is worth more than the contents, and the cost of the twenty-five yellow tablets is 290 out of all proportion to their value. But these are considerations verging on the moral aspect, and I would prefer to keep away from morality altogether. My field of speculation is one of pure economics.

Numerous articles are waiting to be unwrapped by me, many slips of paper are waiting to be evaluated; green, red, blue ink, everything is 295 ready. It is usually late by the time I get to bed, and as I fall asleep I am haunted by my formulas, whole worlds of useless paper roll over me; some formulas explode like dynamite, the noise of the explosion sounds like a burst of laughter: it is my own, my laughter at the Lohengrin joke origi- nating in my fear of the clerk from City Hall. Perhaps he has access to 300 the punch-card file, has picked out my card, discovered that it con- tains not only the symbol for "mental case" but the second, more dangerous one for "antisocial." There is nothing more difficult to fill than a tiny hole like that in a punch-card; perhaps my laughter at the Lohengrin joke is the price I have to pay for my anonymity. I would not like 305 to admit face to face what I find easier to do in writing: that I am a thrower-away.

QUESTIONS

1. What questions do the first two paragraphs bring to the reader's mind? How does the situation of the speaker as presented in the third paragraph contrast with that in the second paragraph?
2. *Lohengrinstrasse* means Lohengrin Street. In Wagner's opera *Lohengrin*, the knight Lohengrin is conveyed in a boat drawn by a swan. What is the point of the clerk's joke? What is the point of the speaker's "I . . . do not refrain from laughing" at it?
3. What do lines 55–102 contribute to the development of the story?
4. What does the protagonist's "propensity for economy" lead him to do? What was the object of the "intricate calculations" that took up all his free time?
5. Why was he discharged from his civil service job? Why did the discharge shock him? What further shock did he receive some years later? Why is he afraid to tell people what he works at?
6. Why does he wish to "escape from tactics and get back into strategy"? What is the basis of the suggestions he makes in lines 204–209? Is the reader expected to find these suggestions reasonable, practicable, insane, ridiculous, laudable, antisocial, or what?
7. In lines 176–178 the protagonist says that his "punch-card in the central files" described him as a mental case and an antisocial person. Why did he receive this designation? Do you think it is correct? Do you think he may also be a fanatic, a martyr, or an "unrecognized genius"?
8. What questions regarding twentieth-century society are raised by lines 211–240? What do you judge the purpose of the author to be in this story?
9. In what sense does the protagonist lead an easy life? a hard life?
10. If his ideas were put into practice, how would the world be changed?
11. What kind of character has the author created here? Consider these passages from the last three paragraphs: "not a single one of my formulas has the power to soothe me"; "my apartment . . . looks more like a laboratory"; "there may be subjective reasons for this"; "I would prefer to keep away from morality altogether"; "there is nothing more difficult to fill than a tiny hole like that in a punch-card." Why is such a character necessary to the author's purpose in the story?
12. What elements of conflict, of irony, and of satire do you find in the story?

13. Describe Böll's style in the story. Why is it a perfect style for his purpose here?

14. Elizabeth Bowen's "Careless Talk" is also a satirical story, but it is told from the objective point of view. Explain how Bowen's and Böll's different satirical purposes require different points of view and different tones in the two stories.

My Lady Love, My Dove

ROALD DAHL

It has been my habit for many years to take a nap after lunch. I settle myself in a chair in the living room with a cushion behind my head and my feet up on a small square leather stool, and I read until I drop off.

On this Friday afternoon, I was in my chair and feeling as comfortable as ever with a book in my hands—an old favorite, Doubleday and Westwood's "The Genera of Diurnal Lepidoptera"—when my wife, who has never been a silent lady, began to talk to me from the sofa opposite. "These two people," she said, "what time are they coming?"

I made no answer, so she repeated the question, louder this time.

I told her politely that I didn't know.

"I don't think I like them very much," she said. "Especially him."

"No dear, all right."

"Arthur. I said I don't think I like them very much."

I lowered my book and looked across at her lying with her feet up on the sofa, flipping over the pages of some fashion magazine. "We've only met them once," I said.

"A dreadful man, really. Never stopped telling jokes or stories, or something."

"I'm sure you'll manage them very well, dear."

"And she's pretty frightful, too. When do you think they'll arrive?"

Somewhere around six o'clock, I guessed.

"But don't *you* think they're awful?" she asked, pointing at me with her finger.

"Well . . ."

"They're *too* awful, they really are."

"We can hardly put them off now, Pamela."

"They're absolutely the end," she said.

"Then why did you ask them?" The question slipped out before I could stop myself and I regretted it at once, for it is a rule with me never to provoke my wife if I can help it. There was a pause, and I watched her face, waiting for the answer—the big white face that to me was something so strange and fascinating there were occasions when I could hardly bring myself to look away from it. In the evenings sometimes—working on her embroidery, or painting those small intricate flower pictures—the

face would tighten and glimmer with a subtle inward strength that was 35
beautiful beyond words, and I would sit and stare at it minute after minute
while pretending to read. Even now, at this moment, with that compressed
acid look, the frowning forehead, the petulant curl of the nose. I had to
admit that there was a majestic quality about this woman, something splendid, almost stately; and so tall she was, far taller than I—although today, in 40
her fifty-first year, I think one would have to call her big rather than tall.

"You know very well why I asked them," she answered sharply. "For
bridge, that's all. They play an absolutely first-class game, and for a decent
stake." She glanced up and saw me watching her. "Well," she said, "that's
about the way you feel too, isn't it?"   45

"Well, of course, I . . ."

"Don't be a fool, Arthur."

"The only time I met them I must say they did seem quite nice."

"So is the butcher."

"Now Pamela, dear—please. We don't want any of that."   50

"Listen," she said, slapping down the magazine on her lap, "you saw
the sort of people they were as well as I did. A pair of stupid climbers
who think they can go anywhere just because they play good bridge."

"I'm sure you're right dear, but what I don't honestly understand is
why——"   55

"I keep telling you—so that for once we can get a decent game. I'm
sick and tired of playing with rabbits. But I really can't see why I should
have these awful people in the house."

"Of course not, my dear, but isn't it a little late now——"

"Arthur?"   60

"Yes?"

"Why for God's sake do you always argue with me. You *know* you disliked them as much as I did."

"I really don't think you need worry, Pamela. After all, they seemed
quite a nice well-mannered young couple."   65

"Arthur, don't be pompous." She was looking at me hard with those
wide gray eyes of hers, and to avoid them—they sometimes made me
quite uncomfortable—I got up and walked over to the French windows
that led into the garden.

The big sloping lawn out in front of the house was newly mown, 70
striped with pale and dark ribbons of green. On the far side, the two
laburnums were in full flower at last, the long golden chains making a
blaze of colour against the darker trees beyond. The roses were out too,
and the scarlet begonias, and in the long herbaceous border all my lovely
hybrid lupins, columbine, delphinium, sweet William, and the huge, 75
pale, scented iris. One of the gardeners was coming up the drive from his
lunch. I could see the roof of his cottage through the trees, and beyond
it to one side, the place where the drive went out through the iron gates
on the Canterbury road.

My wife's house. Her garden. How beautiful it all was! How peaceful! Now, if only Pamela would try to be a little less solicitous of my welfare, less prone to coax me into doing things for my own good rather than for my own pleasure, then everything would be heaven. Mind you, I don't want to give the impression that I do not love her—I worship the very air she breathes—or that I can't manage her, or that I am not the captain of my ship. All I am trying to say is that she can be a trifle irritating at times, the way she carries on. For example, those little mannerisms of hers—I do wish she would drop them all, especially the way she has of pointing a finger at me to emphasize a phrase. You must remember that I am a man who is built rather small, and a gesture like this, when used to excess by a person like my wife, is apt to intimidate. I sometimes find it difficult to convince myself that she is not an overbearing woman.

"Arthur!" she called. "Come here."

"What?"

"I've just had a most marvellous idea. Come here."

I turned and went over to where she was lying on the sofa.

"Look," she said, "do you want to have some fun?"

"What sort of fun?"

"With the Snapes."

"Who are the Snapes?"

"Come on," she said. "Wake up. Henry and Sally Snape. Our weekend guests."

"Well?"

"Now listen. I was lying here thinking how awful they really are . . . the way they behave . . . him with his jokes and her like a sort of love-crazed sparrow . . ." She hesitated, smiling slyly, and for some reason, I got the impression she was about to say a shocking thing. "Well—if that's the way they behave when they're in front of us, then what on earth must they be like when they're alone together?"

"Now wait a minute, Pamela——"

"Don't be an ass, Arthur. Let's have some fun—some real fun for once—tonight." She had half raised herself up off the sofa, her face bright with a kind of sudden recklessness, the mouth slightly open, and she was looking at me with two round gray eyes, a spark dancing slowly in each.

"Why shouldn't we?"

"What do you want to do?"

"Why, it's obvious. Can't you see?"

"No, I can't."

"All we've got to do is put a microphone in their room."

I admit I was expecting something pretty bad, but when she said this I was so shocked I didn't know how to answer.

"That's exactly what we'll do," she said.

"Here!" I cried. "No. Wait a minute. You can't do that."

"Why not?"

"That's about the nastiest trick I ever heard of. It's like—why, it's like 125
listening at keyholes, or reading letters, only far far worse. You don't
mean this seriously, do you?"

"Of course I do."

I knew how much she disliked being contradicted, but there were
times when I felt it necessary to assert myself, even at considerable risk. 130
"Pamela," I said, snapping the words out sharply, "I forbid you to do it!"

She took her feet down from the sofa and sat up straight. "What in
God's name are you trying to pretend to be, Arthur? I simply don't understand you."

"That shouldn't be too difficult." 135

"Tommyrot! I've known you to do lots of worse things than this before
now."

"Never!"

"Oh yes I have. What makes you suddenly think you're a so much
nicer person than I am?" 140

"I've never done things like that."

"All right my boy," she said, pointing her finger at me like a pistol.
"What about that time at the Milfords' last Christmas? Remember? You
nearly laughed your head off and I had to put my hand over your mouth
to stop them hearing us. What about that for one?" 145

"That was different," I said. "It wasn't our house. And they weren't our
guests."

"It doesn't make any difference at all." She was sitting very upright,
staring at me with those round gray eyes, and the chin was beginning to
come up high in a peculiarly contemptuous manner. "Don't be such a 150
pompous hyprocrite," she said. "What on earth's come over you?"

"I really think it's a pretty nasty thing, you know, Pamela. I honestly do."

"But listen, Arthur. I'm a *nasty* person. And so are you—in a secret
sort of way. That's why we get along together." 155

"I never heard such nonsense."

"Mind you, if you've suddenly decided to change your character
completely, that's another story."

"You've got to stop talking this way, Pamela."

"You see," she said, "if you really *have* decided to reform, then what 160
on earth am I going to do?"

"You don't know what you're saying."

"Arthur, how could a nice person like you want to associate with a
stinker?"

I sat myself down slowly in the chair opposite her, and she was watch- 165
ing me all the time. You understand, she was a big woman, with a big
white face, and when she looked at me hard, as she was doing now, I became—how shall I say it—surrounded, almost enveloped by her, as
though she were a great tub of cream and I had fallen in.

"You don't honestly want to do this microphone thing, do you?" 170
"But of course I do. It's time we had a bit of fun around here. Come on, Arthur. Don't be so stuffy."

"It's not right, Pamela."

"It's just as right"—up came the finger again—"just as right as when you found those letters of Mary Proberts' in her purse and you read them 175 through from beginning to end."

"We should never have done that."

"*We!*"

"You read them afterwards, Pamela."

"It didn't harm anyone at all. You said so yourself at the time. And 180 this one's no worse."

"How would *you* like it if someone did it to *you?*"

"How could I *mind* if I didn't know it was being done. Come on, Arthur. Don't be so flabby."

"I'll have to think about it." 185

"Maybe the great radio engineer doesn't know how to connect the mike to the speaker?"

"That's the easiest part."

"Well, go on then. Go on and do it."

"I'll think about it and let you know later." 190

"There's no time for that. They might arrive any moment."

"Then I won't do it. I'm not going to be caught red-handed."

"If they come before you're through, I'll simply keep them down here. No danger. What's the time anyway?"

It was nearly three o'clock. 195

"They're driving down from London," she said, "and they certainly won't leave till after lunch. That gives you plenty of time."

"Which room are you putting them in?"

"The big yellow room at the end of the corridor. That's not too far away, is it?" 200

"I suppose it could be done."

"And by the bye," she said, "where are you going to have the speaker?"

"I haven't said I'm going to do it yet."

"My God!" she cried, "I'd like to see someone try and stop you now. You ought to see your face. It's all pink and excited at the very prospect. 205 Put the speaker in our bedroom, why not? But go on—and hurry."

I hesitated. It was something I made a point of doing whenever she tried to order me about, instead of asking nicely. "I don't like it, Pamela."

She didn't say any more after that; she just sat there, absolutely still, watching me, a resigned, waiting expression on her face, as though she were 210 in a long queue. This, I knew from experience, was a danger signal. She was like one of those bomb things with the pin pulled out, and it was only a matter of time before—bang! and she would explode. In the silence that followed, I could almost hear her ticking.

So I got up quietly and went out to the workshop and collected a 215
mike and a hundred and fifty feet of wire. Now that I was away from her, I
am ashamed to admit that I began to feel a bit of excitement myself, a tiny
warm prickling sensation under the skin, near the tips of my fingers. It
was nothing much, mind you—really nothing at all. Good heavens, I experience the same thing every morning of my life when I open the paper 220
to check the closing prices on two or three of my wife's larger stockhold-
ings. So I wasn't going to get carried away by a silly joke like this. At
the same time, I couldn't help being amused.

I took the stairs two at a time and entered the yellow room at the end
of the passage. It had the clean, unlived-in appearance of all guest rooms, 225
with its twin beds, yellow satin bedspreads, pale-yellow walls, and golden-
colored curtains. I began to look around for a good place to hide the mike.
This was the most important part of all, for whatever happened, it must
not be discovered. I thought first of the basket of logs by the fireplace. Put
it under the logs. No—not safe enough. Behind the radiator? On top 230
of the wardrobe? Under the desk? None of these seemed very professional to me. All might be subject to chance inspection because of a
dropped collar stud or something like that. Finally, with considerable
cunning, I decided to put it inside of the springing of the sofa. The sofa
was against the wall, near the edge of the carpet, and my lead wire could 235
go straight under the carpet over to the door.

I tipped up the sofa and slit the material underneath. Then I tied the
microphone securely up among the springs, making sure that it faced the
room. After that, I led the wire under the carpet to the door. I was calm
and cautious in everything I did. Where the wire had to emerge from 240
under the carpet and pass out of the door, I made a little groove in the
wood so that it was almost invisible.

All this, of course, took time, and when I suddenly heard the crunch
of wheels on the gravel of the drive outside, and then the slamming of
car doors and the voices of our guests, I was still only halfway down the 245
corridor, tacking the wire along the skirting. I stopped and straightened up,
hammer in hand, and I must confess that I felt afraid. You have no idea
how unnerving that noise was to me. I experienced the same sudden
stomachy feeling of fright as when a bomb once dropped the other side
of the village during the war, one afternoon, while I was working quietly 250
in the library with my butterflies.

Don't worry, I told myself. Pamela will take care of these people.
She won't let them come up here.

Rather frantically, I set about finishing the job, and soon I had the
wire tacked all along the corridor and through into our bedroom. Here, 255
concealment was not so important, although I still did not permit myself to
get careless because of the servants. So I laid the wire under the carpet and
brought it up unobtrusively into the back of the radio. Making the final
connections was an elementary technical matter and took me no time at all.

Well—I had done it. I stepped back and glanced at the little radio. 260
Somehow, now, it looked different—no longer a silly box for making noises
but an evil little creature that crouched on the tabletop with a part of its
own body reaching out secretly into a forbidden place far away. I switched
it on. It hummed faintly but made no other sound. I took my bedside
clock, which had a loud tick, and carried it along to the yellow room and 265
placed it on the floor by the sofa. When I returned, sure enough the radio
creature was ticking away as loudly as if the clock were in the room—even
louder.

I fetched back the clock. Then I tidied myself up in the bathroom,
returned my tools to the workshop, and prepared to meet the guests. But 270
first, to compose myself, and so that I would not have to appear in front
of them with the blood, as it were, still wet on my hands, I spent five
minutes in the library with my collection. I concentrated on a tray of the
lovely *Vanessa cardui*—the "painted lady"—and made a few notes for a
paper I was preparing entitled "The Relation between Color Pattern and 275
Framework of Wings," which I intended to read at the next meeting of our
society in Canterbury. In this way I soon regained my normal grave, at-
tentive manner.

When I entered the living room, our two guests, whose names I could
never remember, were seated on the sofa. My wife was mixing drinks.   280
"Oh, *there* you are, Arthur," she said. "Where *have* you been?"
I thought this was an unnecessary remark. "I'm so sorry," I said to the
guests as we shook hands. "I was busy and forgot the time."
"We all know what *you've* been doing," the girl said, smiling wisely.
"But we'll forgive him, won't we, dearest?"   285
"I think we should," the husband answered.
I had a frightful, fantastic vision of my wife telling them, amidst
roars of laughter, precisely what I had been doing upstairs. She *couldn't*—
she *couldn't* have done that! I looked round at her and she too was smiling
as she measured out the gin.   290
"I'm sorry we disturbed you," the girl said.
I decided that if this was going to be a joke then I'd better join in
quickly, so I forced myself to smile with her.
"You must let us see it," the girl continued.
"See what?"   295
"Your collection. Your wife says that they are absolutely beautiful."
I lowered myself slowly into a chair and relaxed. It was ridiculous to be
so nervous and jumpy. "Are you interested in butterflies?" I asked her.
"I'd love to see yours, Mr. Beauchamp."
The Martinis were distributed and we settled down to a couple of 300
hours of talk and drink before dinner. It was from then on that I began to
form the impression that our guests were a charming couple. My wife,
coming from a titled family, is apt to be conscious of her class and breeding,
and is often hasty in her judgment of strangers who are friendly toward

her—particularly tall men. She is frequently right, but in this case I felt 305
that she might be making a mistake. As a rule, I myself do not like tall men
either; they are apt to be supercilious and omniscient. But Henry Snape—
my wife had whispered his name—struck me as being an amiable simple
young man with good manners whose main preoccupation, very properly,
was Mrs. Snape. He was handsome in a long-faced, horsy sort of way, with 310
dark-brown eyes that seemed to be gentle and sympathetic. I envied him
his fine mop of black hair, and caught myself wondering what lotion he
used to keep it looking so healthy. He did tell us one or two jokes, but
they were on a high level and no one could have objected.

"At school," he said, "they used to call me Scervix. Do you know 315
why?"

"I haven't the least idea," my wife answered.

"Because cervix is Latin for nape."

This was rather deep and it took me a while to work out.

"What school was that, Mr. Snape?" my wife asked. 320

"Eton," he said, and my wife gave a quick little nod of approval. Now
she will talk to him, I thought, so I turned my attention to the other one,
Sally Snape. She was an attractive girl with a bosom. Had I met her fifteen
years earlier I might well have gotten myself into some sort of trouble. As
it was, I had a pleasant enough time telling her all about my beautiful but- 325
terflies. I was observing her closely as I talked, and after a while I began to
get the impression that she was not, in fact, quite so merry and smiling a girl
as I had been led to believe at first. She seemed to be coiled in herself,
as though with a secret she was jealously guarding. The deep-blue eyes
moved too quickly about the room, never settling or resting on one thing 330
for more than a moment; and over all her face, though so faint that they
might not even have been there, those small downward lines of sorrow.

"I'm so looking forward to our game of bridge," I said finally changing the subject.

"Us too," she answered. "You know we play almost every night, we 335
love it so."

"You are extremely expert, both of you. How did you get to be so
good?"

"It's practice," she said. "That's all. Practice, practice, practice."

"Have you played in any championships?" 340

"Not yet, but Henry wants very much for us to do that. It's hard work,
you know, to reach that standard. Terribly hard work." Was there not
here, I wondered, a hint of resignation in her voice? Yes, that was probably
it, he was pushing her too hard, making her take it too seriously, and the
poor girl was tired of it all. 345

At eight o'clock, without changing, we moved in to dinner. The
meal went well, with Henry Snape telling us some very droll stories.
He also praised my Richebourg '34 in a most knowledgeable fashion,

which pleased me greatly. By the time coffee came, I realized that I had grown to like these two youngsters immensely, and as a result I began to feel uncomfortable about this microphone business. It would have been all right if they had been horrid people, but to play this trick on two such charming young persons as these filled me with a strong sense of guilt. Don't misunderstand me. I was not getting cold feet. It didn't seem necessary to stop the operation. But I refused to relish the prospect openly as my wife seemed now to be doing, with covert smiles and winks and secret little noddings of the head.

Around nine-thirty, feeling comfortable and well fed we returned to the large living room to start our bridge. We were playing for a fair stake— ten shillings a hundred—so we decided not to split families, and I partnered my wife the whole time. We all four of us took the game seriously, which is the only way to take it, and we played silently, intently, hardly speaking at all except to bid. It was not the money we played for. Heaven knows, my wife had enough of that, and so apparently did the Snapes. But among experts it is almost traditional that they play for a reasonable stake.

That night the cards were evenly divided, but for once my wife played badly, so we got the worst of it. I could see that she wasn't concentrating fully, and as we came along toward midnight she began not even to care. She kept glancing up at me with those large gray eyes of hers, the eyebrows raised, the nostrils curiously open, a little gloating smile around the corners of her mouth.

Our opponents played a fine game. Their bidding was masterly, and all through the evening they made only one mistake. That was when the girl badly overestimated her partner's hand and bid six spades. I doubled and they went three down, vulnerable, which cost them eight hundred points. It was just a momentary lapse, but I remember that Sally Snape was very put out by it, even though her husband forgave her at once, kissing her hand across the table and telling her not to worry.

Around twelve-thirty my wife announced that she wanted to go to bed.

"Just one more rubber?" Henry Snape said.

"No, Mr. Snape. I'm tired tonight. Arthur's tired, too. I can see it. Let's all go to bed."

She herded us out of the room and we went upstairs, the four of us together. On the way up, there was the usual talk about breakfast and what they wanted and how they were to call the maid. "I think you'll like your room," my wife said. "It has a view right across the valley, and the sun comes to you in the morning around ten o'clock."

We were in the passage now, standing outside our own bedroom door, and I could see the wire I had put down that afternoon and how it ran along the top of the skirting down to their room. Although it was nearly the same color as the paint, it looked very conspicuous to me.

"Sleep well," my wife said. "Sleep well, Mrs. Snape. Good night, Mr. Snape." I followed her into our room and shut the door.   395

"Quick!" she cried. "Turn it on!" My wife was always like that, frightened that she was going to miss something. She had a reputation, when she went hunting—I never go myself—of always being right up with the hounds whatever the cost to herself or her horse for fear that she might miss a kill. I could see she had no intention of missing this one.   400

The little radio warmed up just in time to catch the noise of their door opening and closing again.

"There!" my wife said. "They've gone in." She was standing in the center of the room in her blue dress, her hands clasped before her, her head craned forward, intently listening, and the whole of the big white   405
face seemed somehow to have gathered itself together, tight like a wineskin.

Almost at once the voice of Henry Snape came out of the radio, strong and clear. "You're just a goddam little fool," he was saying, and this voice was so different from the one I remembered, so harsh and unpleasant, it made me jump. "The whole bloody evening wasted! Eight hundred points   410
—that's four pounds!"

"I got mixed up," the girl answered. "I won't do it again, I promise."

"What's *this?*" my wife said. "What's going on?" Her mouth was wide open now, the eyebrows stretched up high, and she came quickly over to the radio and leaned forward, ear to the speaker. I must say I felt rather   415
excited myself.

"I promise, I promise I won't do it again," the girl was saying.

"We're not taking any chances," the man answered grimly. "We're going to have another practice right now."

"Oh no, please! I couldn't stand it!"   420

"Look," the man said, "all the way out here to take money off this rich bitch and you have to go and mess it up."

My wife's turn to jump.

"The second time this week," he went on.

"I promise I won't do it again."   425

"Sit down. I'll sing them out and you answer."

"No, Henry, *please!* Not all five hundred of them. It'll take three hours."

"All right, then. We'll leave out the finger positions. I think you're sure of those. We'll just do the basic bids, showing honor tricks."   430

"Oh, Henry, must we? I'm so tired."

"It's absolutely essential you get them perfect," he said. "We have a game every day next week, you know that. And we've got to eat."

"What is this?" my wife whispered. "What on earth is it?"

"Shhh!" I said. "Listen!"   435

"All right," the man's voice was saying. "Now we'll start from the beginning. Ready?"

"Oh Henry, *please.*" She sounded very near to tears.

"Come on, Sally. Pull yourself together."

Then, in a quite different voice, the one we had been used to hearing in the living room, Henry Snape said, "*One* club." I noticed that there was a curious lilting emphasis on the word "one," the first part of the word drawn out long.

"Ace queen of clubs," the girl replied wearily. "King jack of spades. No hearts, and ace jack of diamonds."

"And how many cards to each suit? Watch my finger positions carefully."

"You said we could miss those."

"Well—if you're quite sure you know them?"

"Yes, I know them."

A pause, then "A *club.*"

"King jack of clubs," the girl recited. "Ace of spades. Queen jack of hearts, and ace queen of diamonds."

Another pause, then "I'll say *one* club."

"Ace king of clubs . . ."

"My heavens alive!" I cried. "It's a bidding code! They show every card in the hand!"

"Arthur, it couldn't be!"

"It's like those men who go into the audience and borrow something from you and there's a girl blindfolded on the stage, and from the way he phrases the question she can tell him exactly what it is—even a railway ticket, and what station it's from."

"It's impossible!"

"Not at all. But it's tremendous hard work to learn. Listen to them."

"I'll go *one heart*," the man's voice was saying.

"King queen ten of hearts. Ace jack of spades. No diamonds. Queen jack of clubs . . ."

"And you see," I said, "he tells her the *number* of cards he has in each suit by the position of his fingers."

"How?"

"I don't know. You heard him saying about it."

"My *God*, Arthur! Are you sure that's what they're doing?"

"I'm afraid so." I watched her as she walked quickly over to the side of the bed to fetch a cigarette. She lit it with her back to me and then swung round, blowing the smoke up at the ceiling in a thin stream. I knew we were going to have to do something about this, but I wasn't quite sure what because we couldn't possibly accuse them without revealing the source of our information. I waited for my wife's decision.

"Why Arthur," she said slowly, blowing out clouds of smoke. "Why, this is a *mar-vellous* idea. D'you think *we* could learn to do it?"

"What!"

"Of course. Why not?"

"Here! No! Wait a minute, Pamela . . ." But she came swiftly across

the room, right up close to me where I was standing, and she dropped
her head and looked down at me—the old look of a smile that wasn't a   485
smile, at the corners of the mouth, and the curl of the nose, and the big
full gray eyes staring at me with their bright black centers, and then they
were gray, and all the rest was white flecked with hundreds of tiny red
veins—and when she looked at me like this, hard and close, I swear to
you it made me feel as though I were drowning.   490

"Yes," she said. "Why not?"

"But Pamela . . . Good heavens . . . No . . . After all . . ."

"Arthur, I do wish you wouldn't *argue* with me all the time. That's
exactly what we'll do. Now, go fetch a deck of cards; we'll start right
away."   495

QUESTIONS

1. List details that give indications of Pamela's character. A few among
   many: "apt to be conscious of her class and breeding"; "those little
   mannerisms of hers"; " 'I'm a *nasty* person' "; "right up with the
   hounds . . . for fear that she might miss a kill."

2. List details that reveal Arthur's character. A few among many: "I
   am a man who is built rather small"; "during the war . . . while I was
   working quietly in the library with my butterflies"; "it is a rule with
   me never to provoke my wife if I can help it"; "couldn't help being
   amused."

3. During the argument between Arthur and Pamela she tells him:
   "Don't be such a pompous hypocrite," and a bit later she suggests
   that he would have to reform to be a nice person. How nice a person
   is he? Do you think he is a pompous hypocrite? What are the differences of character between husband and wife?

4. We are given much information about Pamela, Arthur, and their relationship—all from Arthur's point of view. Suppose Arthur and his
   situation were described by Pamela—or by a neighbor; how would
   that account differ from Arthur's? Why is it necessary for Dahl's
   purpose that the story be told from Arthur's point of view?

5. What are the significant things in the story up to the moment when
   the guests arrive? What are the essential points of the action there-
   after?

6. What question, asked by Pamela, provides the motivation for the
   essential decision on which the plot turns?

7. What is the chief device to create suspense in the story?

8. What is gained by slowing down the narrative and telling all the
   details of installing the microphone?

9. Bridge playing is important in the story. What was the real reason
   for the "hint of resignation" in Sally Snape's voice over the bridge

playing? During the game why did Pamela play badly and not care? But the guests' "bidding was masterly." Why was it so good?

10. What accounts for the difference in Henry Snape's voice during the bedroom scene? How much evidence is required for the realization that comes to Arthur as he listens to the loudspeaker? When the answer to Pamela's question (question 6) is revealed, what ironical surprise does Pamela, and the reader, receive? How have we been prepared for this revelation?

11. Arthur feels that he and Pamela are in an awkward situation; he "knew we were going to have to do something about this." Why is Pamela's response a surprising one? Has it been prepared for?

12. Compare the two couples in regard to honesty and deceitfulness. After reading the resolution of the story, what moral judgment would you give on each couple?

13. There is much irony in the story. Point out three significant examples.

14. How much does understatement account for the irony? Give examples of understatement. Is it the most significant element of Dahl's style in this story? What other qualities does the style have?

15. What impression does the title make on you after having read the story?

Should Wizard Hit Mommy?

JOHN UPDIKE

In the evenings and for Saturday naps like today's, Jack told his daughter Jo a story out of his head. This custom, begun when she was two, was itself now nearly two years old, and his head felt empty. Each new story was a slight variation of a basic tale: a small creature, usually named Roger (Roger Fish, Roger Squirrel, Roger Chipmunk), had some problem and 5 went with it to the wise old owl. The owl told him to go to the wizard, and the wizard performed a magic spell that solved the problem, demanding in payment a number of pennies greater than the number Roger Creature had but in the same breath directing the animal to a place where the extra pennies could be found. Then Roger was so happy 10 he played many games with other creatures, and went home to his mother just in time to hear the train whistle that brought his daddy home from Boston. Jack described their supper, and the story was over. Working his way through this scheme was especially fatiguing on Saturday, because Jo never fell asleep in naps any more, and knowing this made the 15 rite seem futile.

The little girl (not so little any more; the bumps her feet made under the covers were halfway down the bed, their big double bed that they let her be in for naps and when she was sick) had at last arranged herself, and from the way her fat face deep in the pillow shone in the sunlight 20 sifting through the drawn shades, it did not seem fantastic that something magic would occur, and she would take her nap like an infant of two. Her brother, Bobby, was two, and already asleep with his bottle. Jack asked, "Who shall the story be about today?"

"Roger . . ." Jo squeezed her eyes shut and smiled to be thinking she 25 was thinking. Her eyes opened, her mother's blue. "Skunk," she said firmly.

A new animal; they must talk about skunks at nursery school. Having a fresh hero momentarily stirred Jack to creative enthusiasm. "All right," he said. "Once upon a time, in the deep dark woods, there was a tiny little 30 creature name of Roger Skunk. And he smelled very bad——"

"Yes," Jo said.

"He smelled so bad none of the other little woodland creatures would play with him." Jo looked at him solemnly; she hadn't foreseen

this. "Whenever he would go out to play," Jack continued with zest, re- 35
membering certain humiliations of his own childhood, "all of the other
tiny animals would cry, 'Uh-oh, here comes Roger Stinky Skunk," and they
would run away, and Roger Skunk would stand there all alone, and two
little round tears would fall from his eyes." The corners of Jo's mouth
drooped down and her lower lip bent forward as he traced with a fore- 40
finger along the side of her nose the course of one of Roger Skunk's tears.

"Won't he see the owl?" she asked in a high and faintly roughened
voice.

Sitting on the bed beside her, Jack felt the covers tug as her legs
switched tensely. He was pleased with this moment—he was telling her 45
something true, something she must know—and had no wish to hurry on.
But downstairs a chair scraped, and he realized he must get down to help
Clare paint the living-room woodwork.

"Well, he walked along very sadly and came to a very big tree, and in
the tiptop of the tree was an enormous wise old owl."   50

"Good."

"'Mr. Owl,' Roger Skunk said, 'all the other little animals run away
from me because I smell so bad.' 'So you do,' the owl said. 'Very, very
bad.' 'What can I do?' Roger Skunk said, and he cried very hard."

"The wizard, the wizard," Jo shouted, and sat right up, and a Little 55
Golden Book spilled from the bed.

"Now, Jo. Daddy's telling the story. Do you want to tell Daddy the
story?"

"No. You me."

"Then lie down and be sleepy."   60

Her head relapsed onto the pillow and she said, "Out of your head."

"Well. The owl thought and thought. At last he said, 'Why don't you
go see the wizard?' "

"Daddy?"

"What?"   65

"Are magic spells *real?*" This was a new phase, just this last month, a
reality phase. When he told her spiders eat bugs, she turned to her
mother and asked, "Do they *really?*" and when Clare told her God was in
the sky and all around them, she turned to her father and insisted, with a
sly yet eager smile, "Is He *really?*"   70

"They're real in stories," Jack answered curtly. She had made him
miss a beat in the narrative. "The owl said, 'Go through the dark woods,
under the apple trees, into the swamp, over the crick——' "

"What's a crick?"

"A little river. 'Over the crick, and there will be the wizard's house.' 75
And that's the way Roger Skunk went, and pretty soon he came to a
little white house, and he rapped on the door." Jack rapped on the window
sill, and under the covers Jo's tall figure clenched in an infantile thrill.
"And then a tiny little old man came out, with a long white beard and a

pointed blue hat, and said, 'Eh? Whatzis? Whatcher want? You smell 80
awful.'" The wizard's voice was one of Jack's own favorite effects; he did
it by scrunching up his face and somehow whining through his eyes,
which felt for the interval rheumy. He felt being an old man suited him.

"'I know it,' Roger Skunk said, 'and all the little animals run away
from me. The enormous wise owl said you could help me.'   85

"'Eh? Well, maybe. Come on in. Don't git too close.' Now, inside,
Jo, there were all these magic things, all jumbled together in a big dusty
heap, because the wizard did not have any cleaning lady."

"Why?"

"Why? Because he was a wizard, and a very old man."   90

"Will he die?"

"No. Wizards don't die. Well, he rummaged around and found an old
stick called a magic wand and asked Roger Skunk what he wanted to smell
like. Roger thought and thought and said, 'Roses.'"

"Yes. Good," Jo said smugly.   95

Jack fixed her with a trancelike gaze and chanted in the wizard's
elderly irritable voice:

"Abracadabry, hocus-poo,
Roger Skunk, how do you do,
Roses, boses, pull an ear,   100
Roger Skunk, you never fear:
    Bingo!"

He paused as a rapt expression widened out from his daughter's
nostrils, forcing her eyebrows up and her lower lip down in a wide noise-
less grin, an expression in which Jack was startled to recognize his wife 105
feigning pleasure at cocktail parties. "And all of a sudden," he whispered,
"the whole inside of the wizard's house was full of the smell of—*roses!*
'Roses!' Roger Fish cried. And the wizard said, very cranky, 'That'll be
seven pennies.'"

"Daddy."   110

"What?"

"Roger *Skunk*. You said Roger Fish."

"Yes. Skunk."

"You said Roger *Fish*. Wasn't that silly?"

"Very silly of your stupid old daddy. Where was I? Well, you know 115
about the pennies."

"Say it."

"O.K. Roger Skunk said, 'But all I have is four pennies,' and he began
to cry." Jo made the crying face again, but this time without a trace of
sincerity. This annoyed Jack. Downstairs some more furniture rumbled. 120
Clare shouldn't move heavy things; she was six months pregnant. It would
be their third.

"So the wizard said, 'Oh, very well. Go to the end of the lane and turn around three times and look down the magic well and there you will find three pennies. Hurry up.' So Roger Skunk went to the end of the lane and turned around three times and there in the magic well were *three pennies*! So he took them back to the wizard and was very happy and ran out into the woods and all the other little animals gathered around him because he smelled so good. And they played tag, baseball, football, basketball, lacrosse, hockey, soccer, and pick-up-sticks."

"What's pick-up-sticks?"

"It's a game you play with sticks."

"Like the wizard's magic wand?"

"Kind of. And they played games and laughed all afternoon and then it began to get dark and they all ran home to their mommies."

Jo was starting to fuss with her hands and look out of the window, at the crack of day that showed under the shade. She thought the story was all over. Jack didn't like women when they took anything for granted; he liked them apprehensive, hanging on his words. "Now, Jo, are you listening?"

"Yes."

"Because this is very interesting. Roger Skunk's mommy said, 'What's that awful smell?' "

"Wha-at?"

"And Roger Skunk said, 'It's me, Mommy. I smell like roses.' And she said, 'Who made you smell like that?' And he said, 'The wizard,' and she said, 'Well, of all the nerve. You come with me and we're going right back to that very awful wizard.' "

Jo sat up, her hands dabbling in the air with genuine fright. "But Daddy, then he said about the other little animals run *away!*" Her hands skittered off, into the underbrush.

"All right. He said, 'But Mommy, all the other little animals run away,' and she said, 'I don't care. You smelled the way a little skunk should have and I'm going to take you right back to that wizard,' and she took an umbrella and went back with Roger Skunk and hit that wizard right over the head."

"No," Jo said, and put her hand out to touch his lips, yet even in her agitation did not quite dare to stop the source of truth. Inspiration came to her. "Then the wizard hit *her* on the head and did not change that little skunk back."

"No," he said. "The wizard said 'O.K.' and Roger Skunk did not smell of roses any more. He smelled very bad again."

"But the other little amum—*oh!*—amum———"

"Joanne. It's Daddy's story. Shall Daddy not tell you any more stories?" Her broad face looked at him through sifted light, astounded. "This is what happened, then. Roger Skunk and his mommy went home and they heard *Woo-oo, woooo-oo* and it was the choo-choo train bringing Daddy Skunk home from Boston. And they had lima beans, pork chops, celery, liver, mashed potatoes, and Pie-Oh-My for dessert. And when Roger Skunk was in bed Mommy Skunk came up and hugged him 170 and said he smelled like her little baby skunk again and she loved him very much. And that's the end of the story."

"But Daddy."

"What?"

"Then did the other little ani-mals run away?"   175

"No, because eventually they got used to the way he was and did not mind it at all."

"What's evenshiladee?"

"In a little while."

"That was a stupid mommy."   180

"It was *not*," he said with rare emphasis, and believed, from her expression, that she realized he was defending his own mother to her, or something as odd. "Now I want you to put your big heavy head in the pillow and have a good long nap." He adjusted the shade so not even a crack of day showed, and tiptoed to the door, in the pretense that she was 185 already asleep. But when he turned, she was crouching on top of the covers and staring at him. "Hey. Get under the covers and fall faaast asleep. Bobby's asleep."

She stood up and bounced gingerly on the springs. "Daddy."

"What?"   190

"Tomorrow, I want you to tell me the story that that wizard took that magic wand and hit that mommy"—her plump arms chopped fiercely —"right over the head."

"No. That's not the story. The point is that the little skunk loved his mommy more than he loved aaalll the other little animals and she knew 195 what was right."

"No. Tomorrow you say he hit that mommy. Do it." She kicked her legs up and sat down on the bed with a great heave and complaint of springs, as she had done hundreds of times before, except that this time she did not laugh. "Say it, Daddy."   200

"Well, we'll see. Now at least have a rest. Stay on the bed. You're a good girl."

He closed the door and went downstairs. Clare had spread the newspapers and opened the paint can and, wearing an old shirt of his on top of her maternity smock, was stroking the chair rail with a dipped brush. 205 Above him footsteps vibrated and he called, "*Joanne*. Shall I come up there and spank you?" The footsteps hesitated.

"That was a long story," Clare said.

"The poor kid," he answered, and with utter weariness watched his wife labor. The woodwork, a cage of moldings and rails and baseboards all 210 around them, was half old tan and half new ivory and he felt caught in an ugly middle position, and though he as well felt his wife's presence in the cage with him, he did not want to speak with her, work with her, touch her, anything.

QUESTIONS

1. What does the first paragraph bring out that is essential to the story?
2. What pressures does Jack feel on the Saturday of the story?
3. Why is it important for the author's purpose that Jo is almost four years old (not older or younger)? Where is the significance of her age hinted at?
4. How is the story Jack tells related to his own childhood? What values in life do you think Jack's mother tried to teach him?
5. By telling his story in (what seems to Jo) an unusual way, is Jack trying to help her understand life better (telling her "something she must know"), or is he trying to hurt or punish her? What would be his motives in either case?
6. How does Jack feel toward women? What things in Jo's behavior startle and annoy him? Is he also annoyed with Clare for the same things?
7. What does the story about Roger Skunk have to do with the relation of the individual and society? with the relation of mothers and children? Why do Jack and Jo disagree about the outcome of that story? Why does Jo insist that the wizard should "hit that mommy"?
8. Has Jack been "defending his own mother to her"? If so, on what grounds? Why should the author couple this idea with "something as odd"? Since becoming a father, has he changed his attitude toward his mother? In what contrasting ways does he see the past and the present?
9. From the clues given, what do you think are the psychological pressures on Jack from his mother, wife, and daughter?
10. What conflicts, open and concealed, can be perceived in this story?
11. What symbolism do you see in the final paragraph? What is the nature of Jack's ambiguous situation? What effect does the end of the story produce?

The Spoiler

PAUL BRODEUR

Stephen Drew saw the shaggy-haired skiers when he was riding up the chair lift for his first run of the day. They came hurtling toward him over the lip of a steep face—three of them, strung out across the trail that plunged down the mountain beside the liftline. Hatless, wearing tattered Levis and baggy sweaters, and not deigning to make the slightest speed 5 checks, they came straight on, skiing powerfully and gracelessly, bounding high into the air from the tops of moguls and landing heavily and often wavering off balance until, exploding off other moguls, they seemed miraculously to regain their equilibrium in flight. Stephen turned his attention to one skier who was racing perilously close to the steel towers 10 that supported the chair-lift cable, and saw the wind-burned face of a young man in his early twenties—a blunt, openmouthed face that was surrounded by a thick mane of red hair, which, covering his ears and most of his forehead, was kept out of his eyes only because it was streaming backward in the wake of his tremendous speed. The red-headed skier was past 15 him in an instant, yet Stephen had the sensation that he had not passed beneath him but over him, like an avalanche or a jet plane. Turning in the chair, he watched the youth and his companions disappear over the lip of another face, emerge again as specks far down the mountain, and finally pass from view behind a screen of fir trees. 20

Stephen saw the shaggy-haired skiers again half an hour later, when he was halfway down the mountain. He had stopped to rest and was looking back to watch an instructor—a model of skiing grace—lead his class of students over a tortuous series of moguls when he heard a joyous shout from far above him and, glancing up the mountain, saw the red-headed 25 skier silhouetted, arms outflung and skis apart, against the blue January sky as he came over the lip of another face. This time, however, the youth caught an edge when he landed and, teetering out of control, plunged into the midst of the skiing class, narrowly missing a girl in yellow stretch pants before he finally righted himself and came to a ragged stop a few 30 yards below Stephen. Now, ignoring his two companions, who, whooping at his plight, swept past and disappeared, the red-headed skier leaned forward, thrust his weight against his poles, which bent in protest, and, shaking his head as if to clear it, spat into the snow between the tips of

his skis. An instant later, Stephen's view of him was interrupted as the 35
ski instructor passed between them with a straight downhill plunge and
two quick finishing waggles. Placing himself directly in front of the red-
headed youth, the instructor also leaned forward on his poles and, in a
shrill German accent, began to scream slowly spaced words that seemed
to ricochet off the hardpacked snow. 40

"If . . . I . . . effer . . . shall . . . see . . . such . . . foolishness . . .
again . . . you . . . shall . . . be . . . taken . . . from . . . this . . . moun-
t-a-a-ahn!" he shouted in a rising crescendo of outrage. "Haff . . . you . . .
a-ahnderstood . . . me?"

For a moment, the two figures remained motionless, bent toward 45
one another like a pair of stags locked in combat; then the shaggy-haired
skier lifted his head and looked the ski instructor in the face. For a long
time, he simply stared at the instructor without the slightest expression,
but just before he pushed off down the mountain he gave a faint grin that
Stephen interpreted as a smirk of contempt. 50

With a surge of energy that seemed to be the residue of anger, the
ski instructor began sidestepping briskly up the mountain to rejoin his
class. When he drew abreast of Stephen, however, he paused for breath
and, in a voice still full of rage, shouted, "They care not for any thing,
this kind of people! They haff no idea what means responsibility! If he 55
has fallen, that one, he can only haff badly hurt this girl in my class!"

Stephen nodded in agreement, but made no reply. There was something in the instructor's shrilly enunciated Teutonic anger that seemed
improbable and out of place on this tree-covered mountain in Vermont.
Besides, Stephen had been watching the shaggy-haired skier, who was 60
plummeting down the mountainside with the same reckless abandon as before, and, remembering that he himself had skied with a certain abandon
at the age of twenty, had been thinking with regret that the sensation of
such speed was something he would never come close to experiencing
again. He had, in fact, been in the process of acknowledging to himself 65
that there were certain things he was past doing, because of fear. Not that
he really wanted to ski beyond the brink of control, but to admit that he
was past it and afraid to try was something else again, for, at thirty-five,
Stephen considered himself a young man whose courage was still intact.
Now, resuming his train of thought as the instructor resumed his climb, 70
he realized that he envied the shaggy-haired youth who, envying no one
and emulating nothing—not even the grace of ski instructors—skied only
against himself, and in so doing conquered fear. Was it just a question
of age? Stephen wondered. But once again the voice of the instructor in-
truded upon his reverie. It was a calm voice now, completely under control, 75
and fading away as he called soothingly back to the students, who trailed
him down the mountain.

"So remember, always in our linked turns we lock the knees together,
and we dip up . . . and then down . . . and so-o-o-o . . ."

Stephen did not see the shaggy-haired skiers on the slopes again. At 80 three o'clock, he took a final run down the mountain and found his wife, Marilyn, waiting for him outside the base lodge. She was sitting in the afternoon sun, looking very pretty in the new blue-and-white ski outfit he had bought her for the trip, and Stephen paused to admire her. Then, as he bent over to release his safety bindings, he realized that she had not 85 brought the baby with her. "How's little Petey?" he asked.

"I left him with the sitter," Marilyn said proudly, as if she were announcing an achievement. "He's fine."

Stephen kicked his boots free of the bindings. Afterward, he strapped his skis together, placed them on his shoulder, and followed Marilyn 90 through a parking lot to the place where she had left their car.

"Can we ski together tomorrow?" she asked, smiling.

"Of course!" he replied with a laugh. "Isn't that why we came up here—to ski?"

Marilyn nodded, but the smile had left her face. "The girl seems very 95 good," she said sombrely. "Her name is Janice Pike. She's got funny bleached hair, but she's intelligent and competent, and Petey took to her right away. I spent the whole morning and most of the afternoon with them, and I've given her careful instructions about everything. I really don't think we have to worry."   100

"Then we won't worry," Stephen replied lightly. "Does the girl know we'll want her for the next few days?"

"Yes, and she's delighted about that. Evidently she needs the money."

They had reached the car, and after fastening his skis to the roof rack Stephen got inside, opened the door on Marilyn's side, and started up the 105 engine. As they drove through the valley that led south, toward Worthington, Marilyn continued to tell him about the sitter.

"I've given Janice the telephone number at the base lodge so we could be paged if we were needed," she went on. "She, of course, knows all the doctors in the vicinity. Oh, and she's familiar with the house 110 we're staying in, which makes me especially happy because of the stove and everything. It turns out the caretaker often hires her to clean up the place after weekends."

"I'd say we were lucky," Stephen said, glancing carefully at his wife. She has become more and more like me, he thought. She tries to think of 115 all the awful possibilities.

"One thing worries me, though," Marilyn was saying.

"What's that?"

"Where the house is," she replied. "I mean it's so isolated. Not that I think anything would happen, but what if it did?"   120

Stephen reached across the seat and touched her arm. "Don't give in to that, baby," he said gently. But as they drove on through the valley, he realized that his words of admonition were a form of self-address. They had lost their first child—a boy of two—in an absurd accident, a year before. Little Peter had been born five months later, at the end of June, 125 and except on rare occasions, when he had been safely tucked into his crib for the night and their neighbor, Mrs. Murphy, could come over to sit for them, they had never left him with anyone. Now, having been lent the use of a small chalet by friends in Boston, they had come skiing with the idea of spelling one another at the task of caring for the baby. (He 130 would ski in the mornings and she in the afternoons—not an ideal solution, perhaps, but all they hoped for.) When they arrived in Worthington, the night before, they telephoned the caretaker, who came to open up the house. The caretaker was friendly and garrulous—a country handyman whose dealings with the winter sporting crowd had coated his native 135 astuteness with a certain veneer of assurance.

"Your wife ski, too?" he asked, glancing at the baby.

"Yes," Stephen answered.

"Then you're goin' to need a sitter, ain't you?"

"Yes," Stephen replied, though he and Marilyn had scarcely both- 140 ered to discuss the possibility. "It would be nice if we could ski together," he added, glancing at her.

"I know just the girl," the caretaker said. "She's nineteen and real experienced. Lives in town. Why'nt I have her call you in the morning?"

"Fine," said Stephen. "I'd appreciate that." 145

After the caretaker left, he turned to Marilyn. "There's no harm in trying her out, is there?" he said.

Now, turning off the highway at a point midway between the mountain and the town, Stephen drove over a dirt road that wound up the side of the valley through thick stands of spruce and pine trees. The road was a 150 washboard affair, bordered by high snowbanks that had been thrown up by plows, and the heavy growth had plunged it into premature shadow. There were half a dozen forks and turnoffs on the way to the house, and, realizing for the first time that none of them was marked, Stephen suddenly found himself wondering how the girl could possibly give direc- 155 tions to summon help. He imagined her trying to remember all the twists and turns as precious minutes slipped away. "Don't give in to that," he had told Marilyn, sitting beside him. But he had merely been talking to himself.

The chalet, a prefabricated structure with two sides consisting of 160 panel picture windows, was hidden from the road by a wooded knoll, and was reached by a narrow, rutted driveway that first passed before a similar dwelling, fifty yards away, which was unoccupied. The driveway ended in a cul-de-sac at the second house, where Stephen turned the car around and parked it. When he and Marilyn came through the door, they found the 165 sitter watching television and Petey playing happily on the tile floor at her feet.

Ten minutes later, Stephen set out to drive Janice Pike home. As they descended over the washboard road toward the valley, the girl lit a cigarette, stubbed it out, and immediately lit another. To make conver- 170 sation, Stephen asked her if she had always lived in Worthington.

Janice Pike shook her head, which tossed the bleached, teased mop of hair that crowned it, and blew out a cloud of smoke. "For a year after high school, I worked over to Brattleboro," she replied. "Waitressing."

"How did you like Brattleboro?"   175

"I liked it a lot. I have a boy friend there."

"What made you come back?"

"My family," she replied. "They want me to settle down, you know?"

"What about your boy friend?"

"Oh, he drives over to see me weekends. He's a plumber's apprentice 180 and he got himself a car this year."

They had reached the valley highway and were driving past a series of ski lodges, restaurants, and roadhouses. "I suppose there's a lot doing here on weekends," Stephen said.

"Yeah, but we just seem to drive around," replied the girl morosely, 185 and looked out the window. "Saturday night, we were driving around and I never saw so many cars parked out in front of these places," she went on. "I guess people must really be having a swell time in them. I mean little bitsy joints with just a guitar player or something and about twenty cars out front!"   190

Stephen glanced sidewise at Janice Pike, and decided that her hair was teased into its absurd pile as an antidote to boredom. Now he imagined her having worked over it for hours, only to drive around and look wistfully through the windshield of the apprentice plumber's car at lights in the windows of ski lodges. "You should get your boy friend to take you dancing 195 in some of these places," he said.

"Yeah, but they're supposed to be kind of wild," she replied, with more yearning, however, than disapproval. "I mean a lot of the fellows who come skiing here are real maniacs, you know?"

"No kidding," Stephen said.   200

"Look, I wasn't going to say anything because your wife seems awful worried about leaving the baby and everything, but a whole carload of guys drove up to the house this afternoon. They sat out front awhile, honking and waving at me. Then they went over to the other house and left some skis and stuff inside and drove away. I'm pretty sure the care- 205 taker doesn't know they're there, and I was a little worried 'cause they looked kind of wild, you know, but maybe they were just out for fun."

"Sure," Stephen said. "Probably a lark of some kind."

"Yeah, well, I kept the door locked anyway."

"That's a good idea," Stephen replied.   210

They had arrived in Worthington, a village built at the conjunction of two roads that crossed through the mountains, and packed with shabby frame houses. Following the girl's directions, Stephen drove to the lower end of town, where, next to a small stream and the gutted remnants of a factory that had once been used to manufacture wooden boxes, there stood 215 a particularly ramshackle dwelling with a sagging roof, peeling shingles, and a veranda that was evolving into debris. For a moment, Stephen studied the house in silence; then, embarrassed, he took out his wallet and turned to the girl. "How much do we owe you, Janice?" he asked.

"Your wife picked me up at ten o'clock, so that would make about six 220 hours I worked," she replied.

"And what do you charge by the hour?" Stephen asked.

"Fifty cents?"

Stephen looked again at the decrepit house, and winced. "Tell you what, Janice, let's call it eight hours," he said, handing her four one-dol- 225 lar bills. "I'll come by for you tomorrow morning at nine."

"Oh, lovely!" she cried. "Thank you!" Now, jumping out of the car, she climbed the porch steps and, skirting a large hole where several rotten planks had fallen through, waved at Stephen and went into the house.

"Thank *you!*" Stephen called after her. A child of Appalachia, he 230 thought as he turned the car around and headed back through town. He drove more quickly on the return trip, anxious to take a bath, have a drink, and play with Petey before his bedtime. He was happy with anticipation. For the first time in a year, he sensed that he and Marilyn were on the brink of resuming life. He told himself that it was a good thing they had 235 decided to come skiing, and that they had been able to bring themselves to leave little Petey with the girl. They must not give in to the temptation to overprotect him. Yes, above all, they must not allow his life and theirs to be forever colored by tragedy. Entangled in these thoughts, Stephen was surprised when, fifteen minutes later, he came upon a black Volks- 240 wagen sitting in the driveway that led up to the house. The Volkswagen was badly battered at the fenders and wore a bent Florida license plate, and it had been parked carelessly, in such a way that it half blocked the drive. Putting his car into second gear, Stephen drove slowly around it; then, glancing toward the porch of the other house, he saw that there were 245 three young men sitting on it in deck chairs. The young men were drinking beer from cans, and, looking closer, Stephen saw that one of them was, unmistakably, the shaggy, red-headed youth he had seen on the mountain. None of the young men bothered to look at the passing car, but as Stephen drove by the redhead gave a flip of his wrist that sent his beer 250 can over the porch railing and into a snowbank.

When he drew up before the house of his friends, Stephen parked the car, got out, and stood beside it for several minutes as he tried to decide what the three shaggy-haired skiers were doing in the other chalet. Perhaps the caretaker is allowing them to stay there in return for some 255 chores, he thought. Or perhaps the caretaker is making money on the side with an illicit rental. But what if, as Janice Pike seemed to imply, the young men had simply broken into the place? Stephen thought of them catching sight of Janice's bleached hair through the picture window, and for a moment he toyed with the idea of telephoning the caretaker. Then he decided against it. Their honking at Janice was like their skiing, the parking of their car in the middle of the driveway, and the red-headed youth's disposal of his beer can. It was thoughtless, nothing more—just thoughtlessness. You're getting old, Stephen told himself. What's the point of spoiling other people's fun? But when he went into the house, he did not mention the presence of the shaggy-haired skiers to Marilyn.

In the morning, the sun was shining brilliantly in a cloudless sky. When Stephen left the house to pick up Janice Pike, the black Volkswagen was still parked before the other chalet. It was there when he returned with the girl, half an hour later, so he asked her if it was the same car that had honked at her the day before.

She took a deep drag on her cigarette, and nodded. "Yeah, that's the one," she replied. "I know from the dented fenders. They must be wild drivers, huh?"

Stephen looked quickly at Janice Pike. Had he detected a slight note of admiration in her voice, or was it his imagination? Everything was "wild" to this country girl, or was it simply that, out of sheer boredom, she hoped her life might become so? "Look, Janice," he said. "I don't want to mention anything about this to my wife, but on the other hand I don't want to spend my day worrying, either. So I'll speak frankly to you— O.K.?"

"Sure, but you don't have to worry, Mr. Drew. I'll keep the door locked—you can count on that."

"Fine," Stephen said, and glanced at her hair. "But maybe you'd better stay away from the window as much as possible. I mean, just don't be sitting too conspicuously next to it."

"Oh, sure," the girl replied. "O.K."

"And I'll phone you every couple of hours from the base lodge," Stephen said. "Just to make certain things are all right."

When they went into the house, Marilyn went over a list of things she had made out for Janice to do. "Petey's lunch is on the stove," she said. "You'll just have to heat it up. If he balks at eating the beef mush, dip each spoonful into his banana-dessert mush. It sometimes works. He woke up at seven this morning, which means he'll be ready for his nap any time now. After lunch, of course, he'll take another nap. If it's still sunny when he wakes up from that one, bundle him into his snowsuit and take him outside for some air."

"No," Stephen said quickly. "Don't have him go out today."

"But if it's nice and sunny—"

Stephen shook his head, picked up an armload of jackets, poles, and 300
ski boots, and started out the door. "A day or two won't matter," he said
over his shoulder. "And I'll feel better if he stays inside."

When Stephen reached the car, he put the jackets, poles, and boots
into the back and climbed in behind the wheel. He was about to start the
engine when he heard the sharp crack of a rifle. The report sounded close 305
by, but in the cold, dazzling brilliance of the morning light he could not
be sure how close. Leaving the car door open, he listened intently, heard
several more shots, and recognized the explicitly neat sound of a .22-
calibre rifle. The shots seemed to be coming from the far side of the next
house, but he could detect no movement there. When Marilyn climbed 310
into the car, he started up the engine and drove slowly down the driveway.

"Really, Stephen, you shouldn't interfere that way," Marilyn said.
"Why on earth shouldn't the girl take Petey out for some air?"

"There's a reason," Stephen said absently, but they were drawing
abreast of the other house, and he was not paying Marilyn any real atten- 315
tion, for at that moment the three young men, led by the shaggy red-
headed youth, came around a corner from the back. The redhead was
carrying a rifle, which, when he saw the car, he seemed to thrust out of
sight between his body and the wall of the house. They must be there illegally, Stephen thought. He wondered if Marilyn had seen the weapon, 320
but a moment later he realized that she had not.

"Goodness!" she exclaimed. "Who are *they*—beatniks?"

Stephen nodded his head, and turned to study the young men as he
drove past. Unshaven and bleary-eyed, they seemed to have recently
risen after a night of heavy drinking, and now they gave the car bold 325
looks of appraisal that, because of their brazenness, also seemed to be defensive. Looking back, Stephen saw them duck quickly into the house. He
was more certain than ever now that they had broken into it, but as he
continued down the drive it was the rifle that stayed in his mind. He
knew that it was against the law in almost every state to shoot a rifle so 330
close to inhabited places. He wondered if he should not call the police.

"What's the matter?" Marilyn asked.

"Nothing," he told her.

His mind, however, was in ferment. The harsh vibrations of the washboard road that descended into the valley triggered his brain into con- 335
juring up visions of catastrophe. Helplessly, he imagined the young men
firing at a beer can, the bullet ricocheting off a rock, piercing the picture
window behind which little Petey sat playing, or, perhaps, striking the
girl and causing one of her interminable cigarettes to fall, smoldering,
upon a scatter rug. . . . "They haff no idea what means responsibility," the 340
outraged ski instructor had said. The sentence repeated itself within
him endlessly.

"You're awfully silent," Marilyn remarked when they reached the highway.

"It's nothing," he told her again, and, stepping hard on the accelera- 345
tor, drove quickly toward the mountain, already planning to telephone Janice Pike the moment they arrived. The miles seemed to pass slowly, however, and soon they found themselves behind a line of cars bearing other skiers to the slopes. When finally they reached the parking lot at the base lodge, he jumped from the car, unstrapped Marilyn's skis, 350 and handed them to her. Then, as he reached inside the car for her boots and poles, he deliberately pushed his own boots out of sight beneath the seat.

"Damn!" he said, straightening up. "I've left my boots behind."

Marilyn made a grimace of sympathy and pain.   355

"Why don't you take a few runs on the beginner's slope," he told her. "It'll get you in the swing of things. I won't be more than half an hour—forty minutes at the most."

He scarcely waited to hear her assent, but, jumping into the car, started the engine, threw it into first gear, and tore away. There was no 360 traffic on the road leading from the mountain, but the sun, rising higher in the sky, shed a brilliant light that, rebounding from the snow and glinting off the hood of the car, found its way into his eyes. The light—a sharp, metallic intrusion—cut into him, exposing his fear as a surgeon's scalpel lays open tissue to disclose a nerve, and now, as the valley broadened, so 365 did the range of awful possibilities that haunted his mind.

When he swerved into the driveway, twenty minutes later, he jammed the car into second gear, topped the knoll with a roar, and swept past the first chalet and the Volkswagen, which was still parked, half blocking the road, before it. He was squinting through the windshield, hoping to get a 370 glimpse of Janice Pike's massive blond coiffure in the picture window, when, dead ahead, walking toward him down the middle of the drive, he saw the shaggy redheaded youth. Stephen slammed on the brakes and brought the car to an abrupt halt; then, taking a deep breath, he was amazed to find himself filling with a curious kind of relief—the kind of 375 relief that comes when the worst is apparent and no longer in the realm of fantasy—for the shaggy-haired youth, who was standing just ahead of the front bumper and looking at him without expression, was holding a rifle over his shoulder with one hand and the hind legs of a blood-spattered snowshoe hare with the other. Stephen's gaze travelled along the barrel 380 of the rifle that, draped carelessly over the young man's shoulder, was pointing in the direction of the picture window, where he could see Janice Pike, holding little Peter. He got out of the car, walked toward the redheaded youth, and stopped directly in front of him.

"Is the rifle loaded?" he asked. He was looking into the young man's 385 eyes, which were deep blue, and the sound of his voice came back to him as an alien presence—a cold breath that was still as the icicles hanging perilously from the roof of the house.

The shaggy-haired youth made no reply, but gave the snowshoe hare a shake so that—as if gore were in itself sufficient answer—its bloody 390 carcass was swung ever so slightly in Stephen's direction.

"Look where the rifle's pointing," Stephen said. Every instinct in him wanted to make a lunge for it, but fear of causing the weapon to discharge deterred him, and this terrible fear, plus the studied unconcern of the young man's face, unnerved him. He felt his control unravelling 395 like a ball of twine. "Damn you," he said in a hoarse whisper. "*Look where it's pointing!*"

The shaggy-haired youth gave a quick sidewise glance toward the picture window; then he looked at Stephen again and shrugged. "Relax," he said. "The safety's on."   400

Cursing him, Stephen told him to take the rifle off his shoulder.

For a moment, the shaggy-haired youth looked at Stephen with the same detachment with which he had stared into the face of the angry ski instructor; then, with taunting slowness, he swung the rifle from his shoulder in a lazy arc and rested the tip of the barrel against the top of his 405 shoe. "Man, you've gone and lost your cool," he told Stephen, and calmly pulled the trigger. Afterward, he gave an insolent grin and, to further affirm the fact that the safety was on, allowed the weight of the rifle to be suspended from his forefinger, which was still curled around the trigger.

Stephen looked at the unafraid, contemptuous face before him and, a 410 second later, struck it. The blow—a roundhouse swing—landed just in front of the ear on the sideburn and knocked the shaggy-haired youth into a sitting position in the middle of the driveway. The rifle fell to the ground, and, stooping quickly, Stephen picked it up and pushed the safety button off.   415

The shaggy-haired youth had not uttered a sound, but when he saw Stephen pick up the rifle and push the safety button off his mouth fell open, and the look of fear that Stephen hoped to see—desperately *wanted* to see—came over his face and filled his eyes. Sitting there, rubbing the side of his head with one hand and still clutching the bloody hare with the 420 other, he suddenly looked like a small boy about to cry.

"Listen, man," he said in a voice that croaked. "Like we're low on funds, you know, and the rabbit's just for eating."

"Shut up!" Stephen replied. He wanted silence simply because he was trying to figure out what he should do next.   425

"So maybe it's out of season," the young man went on. "What d'you care? You're not a game warden."

"Shut up!" Stephen said again, but as he looked down at the youth he felt some of the anger and hatred draining out of him.

"Look, the house wasn't even locked! It was just sitting there, like 430 waiting for us, and the rifle was standing in the corner behind the door."

"The rabbit and the house have nothing to do with it," Stephen told him. "It's my *child*, you fool! You were pointing the rifle at my *child!*"

"But nothing *happened!*" said the shaggy-haired youth, shaking his head in puzzlement and protest. "I mean, like, if nothing's happened—" 435

"Something's going to happen now," Stephen told him quietly. "Here's what's going to happen. You and your friends are going to pack up and be out of here in five minutes. You are only going to have five minutes—d'you understand?—and if you are not, the lot of you, out of here for good in five minutes, I am going to make damn sure you'll be here 440 when the state police arrive. Now get on your feet and get moving."

The shaggy-haired youth did as he was told and, still clutching the snowshoe hare, stumbled off down the driveway to the other house. A moment later, Stephen saw a curtain being parted in the kitchen window and a pair of disembodied faces looking out at him. Suddenly he felt im- 445 mensely weary. Glancing at his watch, he leaned against the fender of his car and waited.

Five minutes later, the young men had finished packing the Volkswagen. Stephen watched them in silence as, casting nervous glances in his direction like hired men anxious to please, they threw the last of their 450 belongings into the back of the car. He was struck by the idea that they, who had skied without fear, were now dancing to the macabre tune of his own fear, but he derived no satisfaction from it. Presently the red-headed youth came out of the house, closed the door behind him, and, picking up the hare from the porch, walked around the front of the car to 455 the driver's side. At this point, he hesitated, as if debating with himself; then he tossed the hare into some bushes and looked toward Stephen.

For several moments, he stood there, gazing at Stephen with profound reproach, as if what had happened between them was caused by a gulf of misunderstanding that was far too deep to ever be bridged. Then, with a 460 sad shake of his head, he got in behind the wheel, started the engine, and drove away.

Leaning against his car, Stephen listened as the Volkswagen growled toward the valley in second gear. He continued listening until the sound of its engine faded into silence; then he turned and walked toward the 465 house where Janice Pike, still holding the baby at the picture window, was looking out at him with horror and awe. He was thinking that he would not return the rifle to the other house until he and Marilyn and little Peter left for good. He was trembling slightly as he reached the door, but he did not know whether it was with the aftermath of rage or 470 with a mixture of relief and regret. He told himself, however, that even now the shaggy-haired skiers were probably heading for some other mountain, where, bounding high into the air with arms outflung and whoops of joy, they would continue to escape from care.

QUESTIONS

1. How does the first encounter with the red-haired young man and his skiing companions affect Stephen Drew? What view does Stephen take of himself (68–69)? Why does he envy the young man?

2. Why are Stephen and his wife so concerned about their child? What forewarning of complications does Janice Pike give Stephen?

3. What are Stephen's reactions when he sees the three young skiers at the house next to his? When he sees them next morning, what makes him think that perhaps he should call the police?

4. By what means is Stephen (as well as the reader) put in suspense? What does he do to relieve his suspense?

5. Where has the author arranged the climactic encounter between Stephen and the red-haired youth? Why is it necessary to have it there?

6. What is the issue that brings them into violent conflict? Explain how each man feels during the encounter. What makes Stephen knock the younger man down?

7. What is reasonable about each man's position? How is each one unreasonable?

8. Why does Stephen not feel more satisfaction in his victory over his opponent? What does the last sentence suggest regarding Stephen's attitude?

9. After finding that the young men are next door, Stephen decides not to report them; he thinks, "What's the use of spoiling other people's fun?" How do you relate this and the resolution of the story to the title? To whom should the title be applied?

10. What causes Stephen to feel fear and the young man to be practically fearless? Does the story reveal an unchanging truth about an inevitable "generation gap," or is this a special case?

11. In which element does the author create the greatest interest: plot, character, or theme? State the theme that the story projects.

Everything That Rises Must Converge

FLANNERY O'CONNOR

Her doctor had told Julian's mother that she must lose twenty pounds on account of her blood pressure, so on Wednesday nights Julian had to take her downtown on the bus for a reducing class at the Y. The reducing class was designed for working girls over fifty, who weighed from 165 to 200 pounds. His mother was one of the slimmer ones, but she said ladies 5 did not tell their age or weight. She would not ride the buses by herself at night since they had been integrated, and because the reducing class was one of her few pleasures, necessary for her health, and *free*, she said Julian could at least put himself out to take her, considering all she did for him. Julian did not like to consider all she did for him, but every Wednes- 10 day night he braced himself and took her.

She was almost ready to go, standing before the hall mirror, putting on her hat, while he, his hands behind him, appeared pinned to the door frame, waiting like Saint Sebastian for the arrows to begin piercing him. The hat was new and had cost her seven dollars and a half. She kept 15 saying, "Maybe I shouldn't have paid that for it. No, I shouldn't have. I'll take it off and return it tomorrow. I shouldn't have bought it."

Julian raised his eyes to heaven. "Yes, you should have bought it," he said. "Put it on and let's go." It was a hideous hat. A purple velvet flap came down on one side of it and stood up on the other; the rest of it 20 was green and looked like a cushion with the stuffing out. He decided it was less comical than jaunty and pathetic. Everything that gave her pleasure was small and depressed him.

She lifted the hat one more time and set it down slowly on top of her head. Two wings of gray hair protruded on either side of her florid face, 25 but her eyes, sky-blue, were as innocent and untouched by experience as they must have been when she was ten. Were it not that she was a widow who had struggled fiercely to feed and clothe and put him through school and who was supporting him still, "until he got on his feet," she might have been a little girl that he had to take to town. 30

"It's all right, it's all right," he said. "Let's go." He opened the door himself and started down the walk to get her going. The sky was a dying violet and the houses stood out darkly against it, bulbous liver-colored monstrosities of a uniform ugliness though no two were alike. Since this had been a fashionable neighborhood forty years ago, his mother persisted in thinking they did well to have an apartment in it. Each house had a narrow collar of dirt around it in which sat, usually, a grubby child. Julian walked with his hands in his pockets, his head down and thrust forward and his eyes glazed with the determination to make himself completely numb during the time he would be sacrificed to her pleasure.

The door closed and he turned to find the dumpy figure, surmounted by the atrocious hat, coming toward him. "Well," she said, "you only live once and paying a little more for it, I at least won't meet myself coming and going."

"Some day I'll start making money," Julian said gloomily—he knew he never would—"and you can have one of those jokes whenever you take the fit." But first they would move. He visualized a place where the nearest neighbors would be three miles away on either side.

"I think you're doing fine," she said, drawing on her gloves. "You've only been out of school a year. Rome wasn't built in a day."

She was one of the few members of the Y reducing class who arrived in hat and gloves and who had a son who had been to college. "It takes time," she said, "and the world is in such a mess. This hat looked better on me than any of the others, though when she brought it out I said, 'Take that thing back. I wouldn't have it on my head,' and she said, 'Now wait till you see it on,' and when she put it on me, I said, "We-ull,' and she said, 'If you ask me, that hat does something for you and you do something for the hat, and besides,' she said, 'with that hat, you won't meet yourself coming and going.'"

Julian thought he could have stood his lot better if she had been selfish, if she had been an old hag who drank and screamed at him. He walked along, saturated in depression, as if in the midst of his martyrdom he had lost his faith. Catching sight of his long, hopeless, irritated face, she stopped suddenly with a grief-stricken look, and pulled back on his arm. "Wait on me," she said. "I'm going back to the house and take this thing off and tomorrow I'm going to return it. I was out of my head. I can pay the gas bill with that seven-fifty."

He caught her arm in a vicious grip. "You are not going to take it back," he said. "I like it."

"Well," she said, "I don't think I ought . . ."

"Shut up and enjoy it," he muttered, more depressed than ever.

"With the world in the mess it's in," she said, "it's a wonder we can enjoy anything. I tell you, the bottom rail is on the top."

Julian sighed.

"Of course," she said, "if you know who you are, you can go anywhere." She said this every time he took her to the reducing class. "Most of them in it are not our kind of people," she said, "but I can be gracious to anybody. I know who I am."

"They don't give a damn for your graciousness," Julian said savagely. "Knowing who you are is good for one generation only. You haven't the 80 foggiest idea where you stand now or who you are."

She stopped and allowed her eyes to flash at him. "I most certainly do know who I am," she said, "and if you don't know who you are, I'm ashamed of you."

"Oh hell," Julian said.   85

"Your great-grandfather was a former governor of this state," she said. "Your grandfather was a prosperous landowner. Your grandmother was a Godhigh."

"Will you look around you," he said tensely, "and see where you are now?" and he swept his arm jerkily out to indicate the neighborhood, 90 which the growing darkness at least made less dingy.

"You remain what you are," she said. "Your great-grandfather had a plantation and two hundred slaves."

"There are no more slaves," he said irritably.

"They were better off when they were," she said. He groaned to see 95 that she was off on that topic. She rolled onto it every few days like a train on an open track. He knew every stop, every junction, every swamp along the way, and knew the exact point at which her conclusion would roll majestically into the station: "It's ridiculous. It's simply not realistic. They should rise, yes, but on their own side of the fence."   100

"Let's skip it," Julian said.

"The ones I feel sorry for," she said, "are the ones that are half white. They're tragic."

"Will you skip it?"

"Suppose we were half white. We would certainly have mixed feel- 105 ings."

"I have mixed feelings now," he groaned.

"Well let's talk about something pleasant," she said. "I remember going to Grandpa's when I was a little girl. Then the house had double stairways that went up to what was really the second floor—all the cooking was 110 done on the first. I used to like to stay down in the kitchen on account of the way the walls smelled. I would sit with my nose pressed against the plaster and take deep breaths. Actually the place belonged to the Godhighs but your grandfather Chestny paid the mortgage and saved it for them. They were in reduced circumstances," she said, "but reduced or 115 not, they never forgot who they were."

"Doubtless that decayed mansion reminded them," Julian muttered. He never spoke of it without contempt or thought of it without longing. He had seen it once when he was a child before it had been sold. The double stairways had rotted and been torn down. Negroes were living in it. 120 But it remained in his mind as his mother had known it. It appeared in his dreams regularly. He would stand on the wide porch, listening to the rustle of oak leaves, then wander through the high-ceilinged hall into the parlor that opened onto it and gaze at the worn rugs and faded draperies.

It occurred to him that it was he, not she, who could have appreciated it. 125
He preferred its threadbare elegance to anything he could name and it was
because of it that all the neighborhoods they had lived in had been a torment to him—whereas she had hardly known the difference. She called
her insensitivity "being adjustable."

"And I remember the old darky who was my nurse, Caroline. There 130
was no better person in the world. I've always had a great respect for my
colored friends," she said. "I'd do anything in the world for them and
they'd . . ."

"Will you for God's sake get off that subject?" Julian said. When he
got on a bus by himself, he made it a point to sit down beside a Negro, 135
in reparation as it were for his mother's sins.

"You're mighty touchy tonight," she said. "Do you feel all right?"

"Yes I feel all right," he said. "Now lay off."

She pursed her lips. "Well, you certainly are in a vile humor," she observed. "I just won't speak to you at all." 140

They had reached the bus stop. There was no bus in sight and Julian,
his hands still jammed in his pockets and his head thrust forward,
scowled down the empty street. The frustration of having to wait on the
bus as well as ride on it began to creep up his neck like a hot hand. The
presence of his mother was borne in upon him as she gave a pained sigh. 145
He looked at her bleakly. She was holding herself very erect under the
preposterous hat, wearing it like a banner of her imaginary dignity.
There was in him an evil urge to break her spirit. He suddenly unloosened
his tie and pulled it off and put it in his pocket.

She stiffened. "Why must you look like *that* when you take me to 150
town?" she said. "Why must you deliberately embarrass me?"

"If you'll never learn where you are," he said, "you can at least learn
where I am."

"You look like a—thug," she said.

"Then I must be one," he murmured. 155

"I'll just go home," she said. "I will not bother you. If you can't do a
little thing like that for me . . ."

Rolling his eyes upward, he put his tie back on. "Restored to my
class," he muttered. He thrust his face toward her and hissed, "True culture
is in the mind, the *mind*," he said, and tapped his head, "the mind." 160

"It's in the heart," she said, "and in how you do things and how you
do things is because of who you *are*."

"Nobody in the damn bus cares who you are."

"I care who I am," she said icily.

The lighted bus appeared on top of the next hill and as it approached, 165
they moved out into the street to meet it. He put his hand under her
elbow and hoisted her up on the creaking step. She entered with a little
smile, as if she were going into a drawing room where everyone had been
waiting for her. While he put in the tokens, she sat down on one of the
broad front seats for three which faced the aisle. A thin woman with pro- 170

truding teeth and long yellow hair was sitting on the end of it. His mother moved up beside her and left room for Julian beside herself. He sat down and looked at the floor across the aisle where a pair of thin feet in red and white canvas sandals were planted.

His mother immediately began a general conversation meant to attract 175 anyone who felt like talking. "Can it get any hotter?" she said and removed from her purse a folding fan, black with a Japanese scene on it, which she began to flutter before her.

"I reckon it might could," the woman with the protruding teeth said, "but I know for a fact my apartment couldn't get no hotter."   180

"It must get the afternoon sun," his mother said. She sat forward and looked up and down the bus. It was half filled. Everybody was white. "I see we have the bus to ourselves," she said. Julian cringed.

"For a change," said the woman across the aisle, the owner of the red and white canvas sandals. "I come on one the other day and they were 185 thick as fleas—up front and all through."

"The world is in a mess everywhere," his mother said. "I don't know how we've let it get in this fix."

"What gets my goat is all those boys from good families stealing automobile tires," the woman with the protruding teeth said. "I told my boy, 190 I said you may not be rich but you been raised right and if I ever catch you in any such mess, they can send you on to the reformatory. Be exactly where you belong."

"Training tells," his mother said. "Is your boy in high school?"

"Ninth grade," the woman said.   195

"My son just finished college last year. He wants to write but he's selling typewriters until he gets started," his mother said.

The woman leaned forward and peered at Julian. He threw her such a malevolent look that she subsided against the seat. On the floor across the aisle there was an abandoned newspaper. He got up and got it and 200 opened it out in front of him. His mother discreetly continued the conversation in a lower tone but the woman across the aisle said in a loud voice, "Well that's nice. Selling typewriters is close to writing. He can go right from one to the other."

"I tell him," his mother said, "that Rome wasn't built in a day."   205

Behind the newspaper Julian was withdrawing into the inner compartment of his mind where he spent most of his time. This was a kind of mental bubble in which he established himself when he could not bear to be a part of what was going on around him. From it he could see out and judge but in it he was safe from any kind of penetration from without. 210 It was the only place where he felt free of the general idiocy of his fellows. His mother had never entered it but from it he could see her with absolute clarity.

The old lady was clever enough and he thought that if she had started from any of the right premises, more might have been expected of her. 215

She lived according to the laws of her own fantasy world, outside of which he had never seen her set foot. The law of it was to sacrifice herself for him after she had first created the necessity to do so by making a mess of things. If he had permitted her sacrifices, it was only because her lack of foresight had made them necessary. All of her life had been a struggle to 220 act like a Chestny without the Chestny goods, and to give him everything she thought a Chestny ought to have; but since, said she, it was fun to struggle, why complain? And when you had won, as she had won, what fun to look back on the hard times! He could not forgive her that she had enjoyed the struggle and that she thought *she* had won. 225

What she meant when she said she had won was that she had brought him up successfully and had sent him to college and that he had turned out so well—good looking (her teeth had gone unfilled so that his could be straightened), intelligent (he realized he was too intelligent to be a success), and with a future ahead of him (there was of course no 230 future ahead of him). She excused his gloominess on the grounds that he was still growing up and his radical ideas on his lack of practical experience. She said he didn't yet know a thing about "life," that he hadn't even entered the real world—when already he was as disenchanted with it as a man of fifty. 235

The further irony of all this was that in spite of her, he had turned out so well. In spite of going to only a third-rate college, he had, on his own initiative, come out with a first-rate education; in spite of growing up dominated by a small mind, he had ended up with a large one; in spite of all her foolish views, he was free of prejudice and unafraid to face facts. 240 Most miraculous of all, instead of being blinded by love for her as she was for him, he had cut himself emotionally free of her and could see her with complete objectivity. He was not dominated by his mother.

The bus stopped with a sudden jerk and shook him from his meditation. A woman from the back lurched forward with little steps and barely 245 escaped falling in his newspaper as she righted herself. She got off and a large Negro got on. Julian kept his paper lowered to watch. It gave him a certain satisfaction to see injustice in daily operation. It confirmed his view that with a few exceptions there was no one worth knowing within a radius of three hundred miles. The Negro was well dressed and carried a brief- 250 case. He looked around and then sat down on the other end of the seat where the woman with the red and white canvas sandals was sitting. He immediately unfolded a newspaper and obscured himself behind it. Julian's mother's elbow at once prodded insistently into his ribs. "Now you see why I won't ride on these buses by myself," she whispered. 255

The woman with the red and white canvas sandals had risen at the same time the Negro sat down and had gone further back in the bus and taken the seat of the woman who had got off. His mother leaned forward and cast her an approving look.

Julian rose, crossed the aisle, and sat down in the place of the woman 260 with the canvas sandals. From this position, he looked serenely across at his mother. Her face had turned an angry red. He stared at her, making his eyes the eyes of a stranger. He felt his tension suddenly lift as if he had openly declared war on her.

He would have liked to get in conversation with the Negro and to talk 265 with him about art or politics or any subject that would be above the comprehension of those around them, but the man remained entrenched behind his paper. He was either ignoring the change of seating or had never noticed it. There was no way for Julian to convey his sympathy.

His mother kept her eyes fixed reproachfully on his face. The woman 270 with the protruding teeth was looking at him avidly as if he were a type of monster new to her.

"Do you have a light?" he asked the Negro.

Without looking away from his paper, the man reached in his pocket and handed him a packet of matches. 275

"Thanks," Julian said. For a moment he held the matches foolishly. A NO SMOKING sign looked down upon him from over the door. This alone would not have deterred him; he had no cigarettes. He had quit smoking some months before because he could not afford it. "Sorry," he muttered and handed back the matches. The Negro lowered the paper and gave 280 him an annoyed look. He took the matches and raised the paper again.

His mother continued to gaze at him but she did not take advantage of his momentary discomfort. Her eyes retained their battered look. Her face seemed to be unnaturally red, as if her blood pressure had risen. Julian allowed no glimmer of sympathy to show on his face. Having got the 285 advantage, he wanted desperately to keep it and carry it through. He would have liked to teach her a lesson that would last her a while, but there seemed no way to continue the point. The Negro refused to come out from behind his paper.

Julian folded his arms and looked stolidly before him, facing her but 290 as if he did not see her, as if he had ceased to recognize her existence. He visualized a scene in which, the bus having reached their stop, he would remain in his seat and when she said, "Aren't you going to get off?" he would look at her as at a stranger who had rashly addressed him. The corner they got off on was usually deserted, but it was well lighted and it 295 would not hurt her to walk by herself the four blocks to the Y. He decided to wait until the time came and then decide whether or not he would let her get off by herself. He would have to be at the Y at ten to bring her back, but he could leave her wondering if he was going to show up. There was no reason for her to think she could always depend on him. 300

He retired again into the high-ceilinged room sparsely settled with large pieces of antique furniture. His soul expanded momentarily but then he became aware of his mother across from him and the vision shriveled. He studied her coldly. Her feet in little pumps dangled like a child's and did not quite reach the floor. She was training on him an exaggerated 305 look of reproach. He felt completely detached from her. At that moment he could with pleasure have slapped her as he would have slapped a particularly obnoxious child in his charge.

He began to imagine various unlikely ways by which he could teach her a lesson. He might make friends with some distinguished Negro pro- 310 fessor or lawyer and bring him home to spend the evening. He would be entirely justified but her blood pressure would rise to 300. He could not push her to the extent of making her have a stroke, and moreover, he had never been successful at making any Negro friends. He had tried to strike up an acquaintance on the bus with some of the better types, with 315 ones that looked like professors or ministers or lawyers. One morning he had sat down next to a distinguished-looking dark brown man who had answered his questions with a sonorous solemnity but who had turned out to be an undertaker. Another day he had sat down beside a cigar-smoking Negro with a diamond ring on his finger, but after a few stilted 320 pleasantries, the Negro had rung the buzzer and risen, slipping two lottery tickets into Julian's hand as he climbed over him to leave.

He imagined his mother lying desperately ill and his being able to secure only a Negro doctor for her. He toyed with that idea for a few minutes and then dropped it for a momentary vision of himself participating 325 as a sympathizer in a sit-in demonstration. This was possible but he did not linger with it. Instead, he approached the ultimate horror. He brought home a beautiful suspiciously Negroid woman. Prepare yourself, he said. There is nothing you can do about it. This is the woman I've chosen. She's intelligent, dignified, even good, and she's suffered and she hasn't 330 thought it *fun.* Now persecute us, go ahead and persecute us. Drive her out of here, but remember, you're driving me too. His eyes were narrowed and through the indignation he had generated, he saw his mother across the aisle, purple-faced, shrunken to the dwarf-like proportions of her moral nature, sitting like a mummy beneath the ridiculous banner of 335 her hat.

He was tilted out of his fantasy again as the bus stopped. The door opened with a sucking hiss and out of the dark a large, gaily dressed, sullen-looking colored woman got on with a little boy. The child, who might have been four, had on a short plaid suit and a Tyrolean hat with 340 a blue feather in it. Julian hoped that he would sit down beside him and that the woman would push in beside his mother. He could think of no better arrangement.

As she waited for her tokens, the woman was surveying the seating possibilities—he hoped with the idea of sitting where she was least wanted. 345 There was something familiar-looking about her but Julian could not place what it was. She was a giant of a woman. Her face was set not only to meet opposition but to seek it out. The downward tilt of her large lower lip was like a warning sign: DON'T TAMPER WITH ME. Her bulging figure was encased in a green crepe dress and her feet overflowed in red shoes. She had 350

on a hideous hat. A purple velvet flap came down on one side of it and
stood up on the other; the rest of it was green and looked like a cushion
with the stuffing out. She carried a mammoth red pocketbook that bulged
throughout as if it were stuffed with rocks.   355

To Julian's disappointment, the little boy climbed up on the empty
seat beside his mother. His mother lumped all children, black and white,
into the common category, "cute," and she thought little Negroes were on
the whole cuter than little white children. She smiled at the little boy as
he climbed on the seat.   360

Meanwhile the woman was bearing down upon the empty seat beside Julian. To his annoyance, she squeezed herself into it. He saw his
mother's face change as the woman settled herself next to him and he
realized with satisfaction that this was more objectionable to her than it
was to him. Her face seemed almost gray and there was a look of dull recog- 365
nition in her eyes, as if suddenly she had sickened at some awful con-
frontation. Julian saw that it was because she and the woman had, in a
sense, swapped sons. Though his mother would not realize the symbolic
significance of this, she would feel it. His amusement showed plainly on
his face.   370

The woman next to him muttered something unintelligible to herself. He was conscious of a kind of bristling next to him, a muted growling
like that of an angry cat. He could not see anything but the red pocketbook
upright on the bulging green thighs. He visualized the woman as she had
stood waiting for her tokens—the ponderous figure, rising from the red   375
shoes upward over the solid hips, the mammoth bosom, the haughty
face, to the green and purple hat.

His eyes widened.

The vision of the two hats, identical, broke upon him with the radi-
ance of a brilliant sunrise. His face was suddenly lit with joy. He could   380
not believe that Fate had thrust upon his mother such a lesson. He gave
a loud chuckle so that she would look at him and see that he saw. She
turned her eyes on him slowly. The blue in them seemed to have turned
a bruised purple. For a moment he had an uncomfortable sense of her
innocence, but it lasted only a second before principle rescued him.   385
Justice entitled him to laugh. His grin hardened until it said to her as
plainly as if he were saying aloud: Your punishment exactly fits your
pettiness. This should teach you a permanent lesson.

Her eyes shifted to the woman. She seemed unable to bear looking at
him and to find the woman preferable. He became conscious again of the   390
bristling presence at his side. The woman was rumbling like a volcano
about to become active. His mother's mouth began to twitch slightly at
one corner. With a sinking heart, he saw incipient signs of recovery on
her face and realized that this was going to strike her suddenly as funny
and was going to be no lesson at all. She kept her eyes on the woman and
an amused smile came over her face as if the woman were a monkey that   395

had stolen her hat. The little Negro was looking up at her with large fascinated eyes. He had been trying to attract her attention for some time.

"Carver!" the woman said suddenly. "Come heah!"

When he saw that the spotlight was on him at last, Carver drew his feet up and turned himself toward Julian's mother and giggled.   400

"Carver!" the woman said. "You heah me? Come heah!"

Carver slid down from the seat but remained squatting with his back against the base of it, his head turned slyly around toward Julian's mother, who was smiling at him. The woman reached a hand across the aisle and snatched him to her. He righted himself and hung backwards on her 405 knees, grinning at Julian's mother. "Isn't he cute?" Julian's mother said to the woman with the protruding teeth.

"I reckon he is," the woman said without conviction.

The Negress yanked him upright but he eased out of her grip and shot across the aisle and scrambled, giggling wildly, onto the seat beside his 410 love.

"I think he likes me," Julian's mother said, and smiled at the woman. It was the smile she used when she was being particularly gracious to an inferior. Julian saw everything lost. The lesson had rolled off her like rain on a roof.   415

The woman stood up and yanked the little boy off the seat as if she were snatching him from contagion. Julian could feel the rage in her at having no weapon like his mother's smile. She gave the child a sharp slap across his leg. He howled once and then thrust his head into her stomach and kicked his feet against her shins. "Be-have," she said vehemently.   420

The bus stopped and the Negro who had been reading the newspaper got off. The woman moved over and set the little boy down with a thump between herself and Julian. She held him firmly by the knee. In a moment he put his hands in front of his face and peeped at Julian's mother through his fingers.   425

"I see yoooooooo!" she said and put her hand in front of her face and peeped at him.

The woman slapped his hand down. "Quit yo' foolishness," she said, "before I knock the living Jesus out of you!"

Julian was thankful that the next stop was theirs. He reached up and 430 pulled the cord. The woman reached up and pulled it at the same time. Oh my God, he thought. He had the terrible intuition that when they got off the bus together, his mother would open her purse and give the little boy a nickel. The gesture would be as natural to her as breathing. The bus stopped and the woman got up and lunged to the front, dragging the child, 435 who wished to stay on, after her. Julian and his mother got up and followed. As they neared the door, Julian tried to relieve her of her pocketbook.

"No," she murmured, "I want to give the little boy a nickel."

"No!" Julian hissed. "No!"   440

She smiled down at the child and opened her bag. The bus door opened and the woman picked him up by the arm and descended with him, hanging at her hip. Once in the street she set him down and shook him.

Julian's mother had to close her purse while she got down the bus step but as soon as her feet were on the ground, she opened it again and began to rummage inside. "I can't find but a penny," she whispered, "but it looks like a new one."

"Don't do it!" Julian said fiercely between his teeth. There was a streetlight on the corner and she hurried to get under it so that she could better see into her pocketbook. The woman was heading off rapidly down the street with the child still hanging backward on her hand.

"Oh little boy!" Julian's mother called and took a few quick steps and caught up with them just beyond the lamppost. "Here's a bright new penny for you," and she held out the coin, which shone bronze in the dim light.

The huge woman turned and for a moment stood, her shoulders lifted and her face frozen with frustrated rage, and stared at Julian's mother. Then all at once she seemed to explode like a piece of machinery that had been given one ounce of pressure too much. Julian saw the black fist swing out with the red pocketbook. He shut his eyes and cringed as he heard the woman shout, "He don't take nobody's pennies!" When he opened his eyes, the woman was disappearing down the street with the little boy staring wide-eyed over her shoulder. Julian's mother was sitting on the sidewalk.

"I told you not to do that," Julian said angrily. "I told you not to do that!"

He stood over her for a minute, gritting his teeth. Her legs were stretched out in front of her and her hat was on her lap. He squatted down and looked her in the face. It was totally expressionless. "You got exactly what you deserved," he said. "Now get up."

He picked up her pocketbook and put what had fallen out back in it. He picked the hat up off her lap. The penny caught his eye on the sidewalk and he picked that up and let it drop before her eyes into the purse. Then he stood up and leaned over and held his hands out to pull her up. She remained immobile. He sighed. Rising above them on either side were black apartment buildings, marked with irregular rectangles of light. At the end of the block a man came out of a door and walked off in the opposite direction. "All right," he said, "suppose somebody happens by and wants to know why you're sitting on the sidewalk?"

She took the hand and, breathing hard, pulled heavily up on it and then stood for a moment, swaying slightly as if the spots of light in the darkness were circling around her. Her eyes, shadowed and confused, finally settled on his face. He did not try to conceal his irritation. "I hope this teaches you a lesson," he said. She leaned forward and her eyes raked his face. She seemed trying to determine his identity. Then, as if she

found nothing familiar about him, she started off with a headlong movement in the wrong direction.

"Aren't you going on to the Y?" he asked.

"Home," she muttered.

"Well, are we walking?"   490

For answer she kept going. Julian followed along, his hands behind
him. He saw no reason to let the lesson she had had go without backing it up with an explanation of its meaning. She might as well be made
to understand what had happened to her. "Don't think that was just an
uppity Negro woman," he said. "That was the whole colored race which 495
will no longer take your condescending pennies. That was your black double. She can wear the same hat as you, and to be sure," he added gratui-
tously (because he thought it was funny), "it looked better on her than
it did on you. What all this means," he said, "is that the old world is
gone. The old manners are obsolete and your graciousness is not worth a 500
damn." He thought bitterly of the house that had been lost for him. "You
aren't who you think you are," he said.

She continued to plow ahead, paying no attention to him. Her hair
had come undone on one side. She dropped her pocketbook and took no
notice. He stooped and picked it up and handed it to her but she did not 505
take it.

"You needn't act as if the world had come to an end," he said, "because it hasn't. From now on you've got to live in a new world and face a
few realities for a change. Buck up," he said, "it won't kill you."

She was breathing fast.   510

"Let's wait on the bus," he said.

"Home," she said thickly.

"I hate to see you behave like this," he said. "Just like a child. I
should be able to expect more of you." He decided to stop where he was
and make her stop and wait for a bus. "I'm not going any farther," he said, 515
stopping. "We're going on the bus."

She continued to go on as if she had not heard him. He took a few
steps and caught her arm and stopped her. He looked into her face and
caught his breath. He was looking into a face he had never seen before. "Tell
Grandpa to come get me," she said.   520

He stared, stricken.

"Tell Caroline to come get me," she said.

Stunned, he let her go and she lurched forward again, walking as if
one leg were shorter than the other. A tide of darkness seemed to be
sweeping her from him. "Mother!" he cried. "Darling, sweetheart, wait!" 525
Crumpling, she fell to the pavement. He dashed forward and fell at her
side, crying, "Mamma, Mamma!" He turned her over. Her face was fiercely
distorted. One eye, large and staring, moved slightly to the left as if it had
become unmoored. The other remained fixed on him, raked his face again,
found nothing and closed.   530

"Wait here, wait here!" he cried and jumped up and began to run for help toward a cluster of lights he saw in the distance ahead of him. "Help, help!" he shouted, but his voice was thin, scarcely a thread of sound. The lights drifted farther away the faster he ran and his feet moved numbly as if they carried him nowhere. The tide of darkness seemed to   535 sweep him back to her, postponing from moment to moment his entry into the world of guilt and sorrow.

QUESTIONS

1. What information do we get from the first paragraph about Julian and his mother? How does their talk about her hat extend our knowledge of both characters?

2. Why is Julian so impatient with his mother on the questions of "knowing who you are" and of integration of races?

3. What do we learn about her from her vocabulary: "the old darky," for instance, and "my colored friends"?

4. What does Julian's action with his necktie represent?

5. What is the significance of their different views of culture—"in the mind"; "in the heart"?

6. Where does the exposition end and the action proper of the story begin?

7. What do you take to be the main difference between Julian's world "of complete objectivity" and his mother's "fantasy world"? What opinion of Julian are we likely to form as we are told about his fantasies?

8. Why does Julian move to the opposite side of the bus? The author says, "He would have liked to teach her a lesson. . . ." What lesson? Why is it hard for him to teach her such a lesson?

9. What symbolic parallelism is brought out by the two identical hats and the relation of the two mothers and their sons? What may we infer is going on in the minds of the two women as they ride?

10. Why are both Julian and the child's mother so exasperated by Julian's mother's behavior?

11. Does the middle part of the story plausibly bring about the resolution?

12. When she is sitting on the sidewalk, what revelation has come to Julian's mother? After he pulls her up, why does she pay no attention to him? Has she learned her lesson at last? What lesson has Julian learned? Why should he have to enter a world of guilt and sorrow?

13. From what point of view is the story told? Why can it not be told from Julian's mother's point of view?

14. Discuss the story as an effective dramatization of the "generation gap" and the pain that such a gap can cause.

15. What is the meaning of the title?

The Snake

ERVIN D. KRAUSE

I was thinking of the heat and of water that morning when I was plowing the stubble field far across the hill from the farm buildings. It had
grown hot early that day, and I hoped that the boy, my brother's son,
would soon come across the broad black area of plowed ground, carrying
the jar of cool water. The boy usually was sent out at about that time with 5
the water, and he always dragged an old snow-fence lath or a stick along,
to play with. He pretended that the lath was a tractor and he would drag
it through the dirt and make buzzing, tractor sounds with his lips.

I almost ran over the snake before I could stop the tractor in time.
I had turned at the corner of the field and I had to look back to raise the 10
plow and then to drop it again into the earth, and I was thinking of the
boy and the water anyway, and when I looked again down the furrow, the
snake was there. It lay half in the furrow and half out, and the front
wheels had rolled nearly up to it when I put in the clutch. The tractor
was heavily loaded with the weight of the plow turning the earth, and 15
the tractor stopped instantly.

The snake slid slowly and with great care from the new ridge the
plow had made, into the furrow and did not go any further. I had never
liked snakes much, I still had that kind of quick panic that I'd had as a
child whenever I saw one, but this snake was clean and bright and very 20
beautiful. He was multi-colored and graceful and he lay in the furrow and
moved his arched and tapered head only so slightly. Go out of the furrow,
snake, I said, but he did not move at all. I pulled the throttle of the tractor
in and out, hoping to frighten him with the noise, but the snake only
flicked its black, forked tongue and faced the huge tractor wheel, without 25
fright or concern.

I let the engine idle then, and I got down and went around the wheel
and stood beside it. My movement did frighten the snake and it raised its
head and trailed delicately a couple of feet and stopped again, and its
tongue was working very rapidly. I followed it, looking at the brilliant 30
colors on its tubular back, the colors clear and sharp and perfect, in orange
and green and brown diamonds the size of a baby's fist down its back, and
the diamonds were set one within the other and interlaced with glistening
jet-black. The colors were astonishing, clear and bright, and it was as if the
body held a fire of its own, and the colors came through that transparent 35

flesh and skin, vivid and alive and warm. The eyes were clear and black and
the slender body was arched slightly. His flat and gracefully tapered head
lifted as I looked at him and the black tongue slipped in and out of that
solemn mouth.

You beauty, I said, I couldn't kill you. You are much too beautiful. I   40
had killed snakes before, when I was younger, but there had been no
animal like this one, and I knew it was unthinkable that an animal such as
that should die. I picked him up, and the length of him arched very carefully and gracefully and only a little wildly, and I could feel the coolness of
that radiant, fire-colored body, like splendid ice, and I knew that he had   45
eaten only recently because there were two whole and solid little lumps
in the forepart of him, like fieldmice swallowed whole might make.

The body caressed through my hands like cool satin, and my hands,
usually tanned and dark, were pale beside it, and I asked it where the
fire colors could come from the coolness of that body. I lowered him so   50
he would not fall and his body slid out onto the cool, newly-plowed
earth, from between my pale hands. The snake worked away very slowly
and delicately and with a gorgeous kind of dignity and beauty, and he
carried his head a little above the rolled clods. The sharp, burning colors
of his body stood brilliant and plain against the black soil, like a target.   55

I felt good and satisfied, looking at the snake. It shone in its bright
diamond color against the sun-burned stubble and the crumbled black
clods of soil and against the paleness of myself. The color and beauty of
it were strange and wonderful and somehow alien, too, in that dry and
dusty and uncolored field.   60

I got on the tractor again and I had to watch the plow closely because the field was drawn across the long hillside and even in that good
soil there was a danger of rocks. I had my back to the corner of the trian-
gular field that pointed towards the house. The earth was a little heavy and
I had to stop once and clean the plowshares because they were not scour-   65
ing properly, and I did not look back towards the place until I had turned
the corner and was plowing across the upper line of the large field, a long
way from where I had stopped because of the snake.

I saw it all at a glance. The boy was there at the lower corner of the
field, and he was in the plowed earth, stamping with ferocity and a kind   70
of frenzied impatience. Even at that distance, with no sound but the
sound of the tractor, I could tell the fierce mark of brutality on the boy.
I could see the hunched-up shoulders, the savage determination, the dance
of his feet as he ground the snake with his heels, and the pirouette of his
arms as he whipped at it with the stick.   75

Stop it, I shouted, but the lumbering and mighty tractor roared on,
above anything I could say. I stopped the tractor and I shouted down to the
boy, and I knew he could hear me, for the morning was clear and still, but
he did not even hesitate in that brutal, murdering dance. It was no use.
I felt myself tremble, thinking of the diamond light of that beauty I had   80

held a few moments before, and I wanted to run down there and halt, if I could, that frenetic pirouette, catch the boy in the moment of his savagery, and save a glimmer, a remnant, of that which I remembered, but I knew it was already too late. I drove the tractor on, not looking down there; I was afraid to look for fear the evil might still be going on. My head began to ache, and the fumes of the tractor began to bother my eyes, and I hated the job suddenly, and I thought, there are only moments when one sees beautiful things, and these are soon crushed, or they vanish. I felt the anger mount within me.

The boy waited at the corner, with the jar of water held up to me in his hands, and the water had grown bubbly in the heat of the morning. I knew the boy well. He was eleven and we had done many things together. He was a beautiful boy, really, with finely-spun blonde hair and a smooth and still effeminate face, and his eyelashes were long and dark and brushlike, and his eyes were blue. He waited there and he smiled as the tractor came up, as he would smile on any other day. He was my nephew, my brother's son, handsome and warm and newly-scrubbed, with happiness upon his face and his face resembled my brother's and mine as well.

I saw then, too, the stake driven straight and hard into the plowed soil, through something there where I had been not long before.

I stopped the tractor and climbed down and the boy came eagerly up to me. "Can I ride around with you?" he asked, as he often did, and I had as often let him be on the tractor beside me. I looked closely at his eyes, and he was already innocent; the killing was already forgotten in that clear mind of his.

"No, you cannot," I said, pushing aside the water jar he offered to me. I pointed to the splintered, upright stake. "Did you do that?" I asked.

"Yes," he said, eagerly, beginning a kind of dance of excitement. "I killed a snake; it was a big one." He tried to take my hand to show me.

"Why did you kill it?"

"Snakes are ugly and bad."

"This snake was very beautiful. Didn't you see how beautiful it was?"

"Snakes are ugly," he said again.

"You saw the colors of it, didn't you? Have you ever seen anything like it around here?"

"Snakes are ugly and bad, and it might have bitten somebody, and they would have died."

"You know there are no poisonous snakes in this area. This snake could not harm anything."

"They eat chickens sometimes," the boy said. "They are ugly and they eat chickens and I hate snakes."

"You are talking foolishly," I said. "You killed it because you wanted to kill it, for no other reason."

"They're ugly and I hate them," the boy insisted. "Nobody likes snakes."

"It was beautiful," I said, half to myself.

The boy skipped along beside me, and he was contented with what he had done.

The fire of the colors was gone; there was a contorted ugliness now; the colors of its back were dull and gray-looking, torn and smashed in, and dirty from the boy's shoes. The beautifully-tapered head, so delicate and so cool, had been flattened as if in a vise, and the forked tongue splayed out of the twisted, torn mouth. The snake was hideous, and I remembered, even then, the cool, bright fire of it only a little while before, and I thought perhaps the boy had always seen it dead and hideous like that, and had not even stopped to see the beauty of it in its life.

I wrenched the stake out, that the boy had driven through it in the thickest part of its body, between the colored diamond crystals. I touched it and the coolness, the ice-feeling, was gone, and even then it moved a little, perhaps a tiny spasm of the dead muscles, and I hoped that it was truly dead, so that I would not have to kill it. And then it moved a little more, and I knew the snake was dying, and I would have to kill it there. The boy stood off a few feet and he had the stake again and he was racing innocently in circles, making the buzzing tractor sound with his lips.

I'm sorry, I thought to the snake, for you were beautiful. I took the broken length of it around the tractor and I took one of the wrenches from the tool-kit and I struck its head, not looking at it, to kill it at last, for it could never live.

The boy came around behind me, dragging the stake. "It's a big snake, isn't it?" he said. "I'm going to tell everybody how big a snake I killed."

"Don't you see what you have done?" I said. "Don't you see the difference now?"

"It's an ugly, terrible snake," he said. He came up and was going to push at it with his heavy shoes. I could see the happiness in the boy's eyes, the gleeful brutality.

"Don't," I said. I could have slapped the boy. He looked up at me, puzzled, and he swayed his head from side to side. I thought, you little brute, you nasty, selfish, little beast, with brutality already developed within that brain and in those eyes. I wanted to slap his face, to wipe forever the insolence and brutal glee from his mouth, and I decided then, very suddenly, what I would do.

I drew the snake up and I saw the blue eyes of the boy open wide and change and fright, and I stepped towards him as he cringed back, and I shouted, "It's alive, it's alive!" and I looped the tube of the snake's body around the boy's neck.

The boy shrieked and turned in his terror and ran, and I followed a few steps, shouting after him, "It's alive, it's alive, alive!"

The boy gasped and cried out in his terror and he fled towards the distant house, stumbling and falling and rising to run again, and the dead snake hung on him, looped around his neck, and the boy tore at it, but it would not fall off.

The little brute, I thought, the little cruel brute, to hurt and seek to kill something so beautiful and clean, and I couldn't help smiling and feeling satisfied because the boy, too, had suffered a little for his sav- 175 ageness, and I felt my mouth trying to smile about it. And I stopped suddenly and I said, oh God, with the fierce smile of brutality frightening my face, and I thought, oh God, oh God. I climbed quickly onto the tractor and I started it and pulled the throttle open to drown the echoes of the boy shrieking down there in the long valley. I was trembling and I could 180 not steer the tractor well, and I saw that my hands were suffused and flushed, red with a hot blood color.

ANALYSIS

The critical reader of "The Snake" quickly notices the workmanlike way in which the author has constructed his story. The first paragraph makes the necessary point that the boy is due to come to the field carrying not only the water but a stick. In the second paragraph the snake appears, and the third to seventh paragraphs dwell on the animal, presenting a very favorable impression of it and emphasizing its beauty, dignity, and grace. It is accepted as one of God's creatures with no sinister implications attached to it. The eighth paragraph has an expository purpose: the storyteller explains what he was doing that kept him from knowing what was happening across the field. Thus the first eight paragraphs have introduced the man, the boy, and the snake in believable circumstances.

The middle section of the story extends from the ninth paragraph up to the final paragraph; it presents the boy's killing of the snake, the anger of the man, the argument, the description of the dead snake contrasting with the description in earlier paragraphs of the live one, the man's regret, his rising hatred, his decision to punish, and the punishment.

In the final paragraph the *dénouement* occurs: the protagonist's realization of his own sin.

Each of the first two parts logically results in the next part. The protagonist admits that when younger he had killed snakes, and we know that the boy is due to come; so his killing of the snake is not unexpected. The admiration of the protagonist for the snake's beauty leads to his treatment of the boy. His action then results in his realization of his own brutality.

The substantial middle part creates the most suspense and develops the most interest. First, the response of the protagonist to the killing of the snake is brought out in lines 69–75. His judgment of this act is set forth with unmistakable clearness; the significant words are "ferocity," "frenzied," "fierce," "brutality," "savage." In line 85 he says, "I was afraid to look for fear the evil might still be going on." For him the killing of the snake is "the evil"—he regards it as a really monstrous act. What will he do now? This is the question that sustains the reader's suspense.

After the description of the boy's actions the reader may feel surprised to learn that the boy is beautiful, his face effeminate, his eyes blue. He seems, like the snake, a beautiful little animal; and the last clause describing him brings out his resemblance to others in the family. The uncle acknowledges the family likeness; the fact that uncle and nephew look alike makes probable the likeness of their actions.

But the boy, we are told, "was already innocent." The killing of the snake means nothing to him in terms of responsibility or guilt, and the conversation that follows demonstrates how firmly prejudiced the boy is in his opinion of snakes, having picked up his ideas from his elders and never given attention to facts or to the actual appearance of a snake. He cannot realize at all how he has shattered a creation of beauty and how sadly different the battered snake looks from the creature his uncle admired. In his own eyes, he has done a brave thing, an action that should be approved and even admired by his elders. The author makes several deliberate contrasts to bring out the man's regretful perceptions: "the colors of its back were dull and gray-looking" (instead of having *fire*); "the beautifully-tapered head . . . had been *flattened*"; the "tongue *splayed* out of the twisted, torn mouth." The boy can only say, "It's an ugly, terrible snake," and we know, as the uncle conjectures, that he has never seen it any other way.

The uncle accused him: "You killed it because you wanted to kill it, for no other reason," and now he finds "gleeful brutality" in the boy's eyes. The boy's shocking (should we call it inhuman?) response triggers the climax. The man wishes to punish the boy and teach him a lesson by making him feel great fear—not only to punish him but to take revenge on him for having spoiled the pleasure that the uncle took in the life and beauty of the snake. His looping the snake around the boy's neck is the climax. It makes the uncle have a feeling of satisfaction—but this is momentary, for immediately there rush upon him the revulsion and realization that constitute the resolution.

The resolution of the story comes about as a result of a combination of character and circumstances. The boy scarcely has a character; he behaves wantonly in accordance with the prejudices he has picked up. The man is more developed. He has the usual feeling of affection for his handsome nephew; but he also has an esthetic sense: he can admire the snake. He has a conscience; and he is pleased with himself as a good man. So the bringing together of snake and boy and the death of the snake constitute the circumstances putting pressure on the protagonist and giving him a character test. Without it he could not have the realization that concludes the story.

In that moment of discovery (James Joyce would call it an *epiphany*, or "showing forth") the protagonist finds that he also has in himself the evil desire to be brutal and to hurt ("the fierce smile of brutality") instead of to understand and to forgive. His flushed, red hands symbolize his guilt; it is almost as if he has taken the blood of his nephew. That evil which, according to the Bible, was introduced into Eden by the snake still remains in the human heart. It is ironic that what we tritely think of as "brute" conduct should be essentially human. The repeated "oh God" probably signifies that man needs the grace of God to remove that everlasting taint of sin passed all the way down from the Garden of Eden.

The author has done well to tell the story in the first person from the protagonist's point of view. Telling it in this way is an assurance of veracity; the protagonist admits that he "had never liked snakes much," and so his admiration of the particular snake in the story—"clean and bright and very beautiful"—is sincere and convincing. His explaining how he felt upon punishing the boy, his moment of self-discovery, and his description of his responses to it constitute a confession that is all the more believable as it is revealed by the guilty party without interpretation.

"The Snake" is written very economically, for characters and plot are held to a minimum, and the action is compressed to a few minutes of conflict. Yet neither man nor boy will be the same after this incident. Part of the author's skill consists in his focusing upon this *telling* point in their lives.

In most stories the characters have names; we might wonder why the characters of "The Snake" remain unnamed. In view of the author's intentions they do not need names—or, rather, it is better to leave them unnamed, therefore less individualized, and therefore more representative. More than the characters in most stories, they are universal figures representing mankind. The widespread prejudice against snakes, the fact that the characters are unnamed, the feeling of the boy that he has acted rightly, and the anger of the man all give the story universality.

Should "The Snake" then be called an allegory? No! It does not have the exact correspondences found in allegory. In strict allegory, for example, as in Bunyan's *Pilgrim's Progress*, Christian, a pilgrim on his way to the Celestial City, who encounters Giant Despair and is imprisoned in Doubting Castle is meant to represent any Christian man who lives his life hoping to attain salvation but who at times feels doubts and is afflicted by despair. "The Snake" does, however, have a kind of mythic or fable quality, part of which is due to the presence in the story of the snake itself. If Krause had written about a small alligator, he would not have achieved the same effect. The snake appears in the story of the Garden of Eden; it has a very old mythic lineage, and because of its long history of sinister associations it takes on a symbolic importance here that is in keeping with the universality and the theme of the story.

Both human characters are guilty of hatred and violence. Precisely as the uncle is feeling the satisfaction of the just punisher, he realizes his guilt. The theme of the story is that the propensity of mankind to sin has not been eradicated.

The author's style is fitting for that theme. It is a simple style resembling that of a folktale or of the Bible. The second paragraph furnishes a good example of Krause's additive manner; here and throughout the story many of his clauses are connected by *and*. Such writing suggests the traditional manner of a storyteller. This style also renders clearly and specifically the details of the experience and has the dignity of simple honesty.

"The Snake" contains no more than 2600 words, but every word counts. It is written economically, yet with enough length to produce an intense and lasting effect—an effect of grim pathos that reinforces the theme, which is projected not didactically or moralistically, but dramatically.

First Views of the Enemy

JOYCE CAROL OATES

Just around the turn, the road was alive. First to assault the eye was a profusion of heads, black-haired, bobbing, and a number of straw hats that looked oddly professional—like straw hats in a documentary film; and shirts and overalls and dresses, red, yellow, beflowered, dotted, striped, some bleached by the sun, some stiff and brilliant, just bought and worn 5 proudly out of the store. The bus in which they were traveling—a dead dark blue, colored, yet without any color—was parked half on the clay road and half in the prickly high grass by the ditch. Its old-fashioned hood was open, yanked cruelly up and doubled on itself, and staring into its greasy, dust-flecked tangle of parts was the driver, the only fair, brown- 10 haired one of the bunch. Annette remembered later that as her station wagon moved in astonishment toward them, the driver looked up and straight at her: a big indifferent face, curious without interest, smeared with grease, as if deliberately to disguise himself. No kin of yours, lady, no kin! he warned contemptuously. 15

Breaking from a group of children, running with arms out for a mock embrace, a boy of about seven darted right toward Annette's car. The boy's thick black hair, curled with sweat, plastered onto his forehead, framed a delicate, cruelly tanned face, a face obviously dead white beneath its tan: great dark eyes, expanded out of proportion, neat little brows 20 like angels' brows—that unbelievable and indecent beauty of children exploited for art—a pouting mouth, still purple at the corners from the raspberries picked and hidden for the long bus ride, these lips now turning as Annette stared into a hilarious grin and crying out at her and the stricken child who cringed beside her, legs already drawn up flatly 25 at the knees——

In agony the brakes cried, held: the scene, dizzy with color, rocked with the car, down a little, back up, giddily, helplessly, while dust exploded up on all sides. "Mommy!" Timmy screamed, fascinated by the violence, yet his wail was oddly still and drawn out, and his eyes never 30 once turned to his mother. The little Mexican boy had disappeared in front of the car. Still the red dust arose, the faces at the bus jerked around together, white eyes, white teeth, faces were propelled toward the windows of the bus, empty a second before. "God, God," Annette mur-

mured; she had not yet released the steering wheel, and on it her fingers 35
began to tighten as if they might tear the wheel off, hold it up to defend
her and her child, perhaps even to attack.

A woman in a colorless dress pushed out of the crowd, barefooted
in the red clay, pointed her finger at Annette and shouted something—
gleefully. She shook her fist, grinning, others grinned behind her; the bus 40
driver turned back to his bus. Annette saw now the little boy on the
other side of the road, popping up safe in the ditch and jumping frantically—though the sharp weeds must have hurt his feet—and laughing,
yelling, shouting as if he were insane. The air rang with shouts, with
laughter. A good joke. What was the joke? Annette's brain reeled with 45
shock, sucked for air as if drowning. Beside her Timmy wailed softly, but
his eyes were fastened on the boy in the ditch. "He's safe, he's safe,"
Annette whispered. But others ran toward her now—big boys, tall but
skinny, without shirts. How their ribs seemed to run with them, sliding
up and down inside the dark tanned flesh with the effort of their legs! 50
Even a few girls approached, hard dark faces, already aged, black hair
matted and torn about their thin shoulders. They waved and cried, "Missus! Missus!" Someone even shouted, "Cadillac!" though her station wagon,
already a year old, was far from being a Cadillac. As if to regain attention,
the little boy in the ditch picked up something, a handful of pebbles, 55
and threw it at the car, right beneath Timmy's pale gaping face. A bab-
ble of Spanish followed, more laughter, the barefoot woman who must have
been the boy's mother strode mightily across the road, grabbed the boy,
shook him in an extravagant mockery of punishment: sucked her lips at
him, made spitting motions, rubbed his head hard with the palm of her 60
hand—this hurt, Annette saw with satisfaction, for the child winced in
spite of his bravado. At the bus the American man's back swelled
damply and without concern beneath his shirt; he did not even glance
around.

Annette leaned to the window, managed a smile. "Please let me 65
through," she called. Her voice surprised her, it sounded like a voice
without body or identity, channeled in over a radio.

The boys made odd gestures with their hands, not clenching them
into fists, but instead striking with the edges of their hands, knifelike, into
the air. Their teeth grinned and now, with them so close (the bravest 70
were at her fender), Annette could see how discolored their teeth were,
though they had seemed white before. They must have been eating dirt!
she thought vaguely. "Please let me through," she said. Beside her, Timmy
sat in terror. She wanted to reach over and put her hand over his eyes,
hide this sight from him—this mob of dirty people, so hungry their 75
tongues seemed to writhe in their mouths, their exhaustion turned to
frenzy. "Missus! Missus! *Si, si,* Cadillac!" the boys yelled, pounding on
the front of the car. The women, men, even very old people—with frail
white hair—watched, surprised and pleased at being entertained.

"Please. Please." Suddenly Annette pressed on the horn: what con- 80
fidence that sound inspired! The boys hesitated, moved back. She toyed
with the accelerator, wanting to slam down on it, to escape. But suppose
one of them were in the way. . . . The horror of that falling thud, the
vision of blood sucked into red clay, stilled her nervousness, made her
inch the big car forward slowly, slowly. And in the back, those unmis- 85
takable bags of groceries, what would be showing at the tops? Maybe tomatoes, pears, strawberries—perhaps picked by these people a few days
ago—maybe bread, maybe meat—Annette's face burned with something
more than shame. But when she spoke, her voice showed nothing. "Let
me through, please. Let me through." She sounded cool and still.   90

Then she was past. The station wagon picked up speed. Behind her
were yells, cries no longer gleeful, now insulted, vicious: in the mirror
fists, shouting faces, the little boy running madly into the cloud of dust
behind the car. He jerked something back behind his head, his skinny
elbow swung, and with his entire body he sent a mud rock after the car 95
that hit the back window square, hard, and exploded. With her fingers
still frozen to the steering wheel, Annette sped home.

Beside her the child, fascinated, watched the familiar road as if seeing
it for the first time. That tender smile was something strange; Annette
did not like it. Annette herself, twitching with fear, always a nervous 100
woman, electric as the harassed or the insanely ill are, saw with shock
that her face in the mirror was warm and possessed. That was she, then, and
not this wild, heart-thumping woman afraid of those poor children in the
road. . . . Her eyes leaped home, her mind anticipated its haven. Already,
straightening out of a turn, she could see it: the long, low orange brick 105
home, trees behind the house not yet big enough for shade, young trees,
a young house, a young family. Cleared out of the acres of wheat and
wood and grass fields on either side, a surprise to someone driving by,
looking for all the world as if it and its fine light green grass, so thin as
to look unreal, and its Hercules fence had been picked up somewhere far 110
away and dropped down here. Two miles away, on the highway that
paralleled this road, there were homes something like this, but on this
road there were only, a half-mile ahead, a few farmhouses, typical, some
shacks deserted and not deserted, and even a gas station and store; otherwise nothing. Annette felt for the first time the insane danger of this 115
location, and heard with magical accuracy her first question when her
husband had suggested it: "But so far out. . . . Why do you want it so far
out?" City children, both of them, the hot rich smell of sunlight and
these soundless distances had never been forbidding, isolating. Instead,
each random glance at the land strengthened in them a sense of their own 120
cleverness. Children of fortune, to withdraw from their comfortable
pasts, to raise a child in such safety!—It was fifteen miles to the nearest
town where Annette did her shopping and Timmy went to school, and
fifty miles to the city where her husband worked.

Annette turned in the driveway, drove slowly into the garage. Still in   125
a trance, angry at herself, she got out of the car but stood with her hand
still lingering on the steering wheel. A thin, fashionably thin young
woman, for years more woman than girl, in a white dress she stood with
a remote, vague smile, hand lightly on the wheel, mind enticed by something she could not name. Perplexed, incredulous: in spite of the enor-   130
mity of what threatened (the migrant workers were hardly a mile away),
she felt slowed and meaningless, her inertia touched even Timmy, who
usually jumped out of the car and slammed the door. If only he would do
this and she could cry, "Timmy! *Please!*" calm might be restored. But no,
he climbed down on his side like a little old man, he pushed the door back   135
indifferently so that it gave a feeble click and did not even close all the
way. For a while mother and son stood on opposite sides of the car; Annette could tell that Timmy did not move and was not even looking at
her. Then his footsteps began. He ran out of the garage.

Annette was angry. Only six, he understood her, he knew what was   140
to come next: he was to help her with the packages, with the doors, open
the cupboards in the kitchen, he would be in charge of putting things
into the refrigerator. As if stricken by a sudden bad memory, Annette
stood in the garage, waiting for her mind to clear. What was there in
Timmy's running out? For an instant she felt betrayed—as if he cherished   145
the memory of that strange little boy and ran out to keep it from her.
She remembered the early days of her motherhood, how contemptuous
she had been of herself, of what she had accomplished—a baby she refused to look at, a husband neurotic with worry, a waiting life of motherhood so oppressive that she felt nausea contemplating it: is this what I   150
have become? What is this baby to me? Where am I? Where am *I*? Impassioned, a month out of college and fearful, in spite of her attractiveness,
that she would never be married, Annette had taken the dangerous gamble of tearing aside her former life, rejecting the familiar possessions and
patterns that had defined her, and had plunged, with that intense con-   155
fident sharp-voiced young man, into a new life she was never quite sure
had not betrayed the old, stricken the old: her parents, her lovely mother,
now people to write to, send greeting cards to, hint vaguely at visiting
to. . . .

Sighing, she began to move. She took the packages out of the car,   160
went outside (the heat was not brilliant), put them down, and, with
deft angry motions in case Timmy was secretly watching, pulled down the
garage door and locked it. "There!" But when she turned, her confidence was distracted. She stared at the house. Shrubbery hiding the
concrete slab—basements were not necessary this far south—rosebushes   165
bobbing roses, vulnerable, insanely gaudy, the great picture window that
made her think, always, someone was slyly watching her, even the faint
professional sweep of grass out to the road—all these in their elaborate
planned splendor shouted mockery at her, mockery at themselves, as if

they were safe from destruction! Annette fought off the inertia again, it 170
passed close by her, a whiff of something like death; the same darkness
that had bothered her in the hospital, delivered of her child. She left the
packages against the garage (though the ice cream in its special package
might be melting) and, awkward in her high heels, hurried out the drive.
She shielded her eyes: nothing in sight down the road. It was a red clay 175
road, a country road that would never be paved, and she and her husband
had at first taken perverse pride in it. But it turned so, she had never noticed that before, and great bankings of foliage hid it, disguised its twist-
ings, so that she could see not more than a quarter mile away. Never before
had the land seemed so flat.   180

She hurried. At the gate the sun caught up with her, without ceremony. She struggled to swing the gate around (a few rusty, loosened
prongs had caught in the grass), she felt perspiration breaking out on
her body, itching and prickling her, under her arms, on her back. The
white dress must have hung damp and wrinkled about her legs. Panting 185
with the exertion, she managed to get the gate loose and drag it around;
it tilted down at a jocose angle, scraping the gravel; then she saw that
there was no lock, she would need a padlock, there was one in the garage
somewhere, and in the same instant, marveling at her stamina, she turned
back.   190

Hurrying up the drive, she thought again of the little Mexican boy.
She saw his luxurious face, that strange unhealthy grin inside his embracing arms—it sped toward her. Cheeks drawn in as if by age, eyes protruding with—it must have been hunger, dirty hands like claws reaching out,
grabbing, demanding what? What would they demand of her? If they 195
were to come and shout for her out in the road, if she were to offer them
—something—milk, maybe, the chocolate cookies Timmy loved so, maybe
even money? Would they go away then, would they thank her and run
back to their people? Would they continue their trip north, headed for
Oregon and Washington? What would happen? Violence worried the 200
look of the house, dizzied Annette! There were the yellow roses she
tended so fondly, rich and sprawling against the orange brick. In the
sunlight their petals, locked intricately inside one another, were vivid, glar-
ingly detailed, as if their secret life were swelling up in rage at her for
having so endangered their beauty.   205

There the packages lay against the garage, and seeing them, Annette
forgot about the padlock. She stooped and picked them up. When she
turned again she saw Timmy standing just inside the screen door. "Timmy,
open the——" she said, vexed, but he had already disappeared. Inside the
kitchen she slammed the bags down, fought back the impulse to cry, 210
stamped one heel on the linoleum so hard that her foot buzzed with
pain. "Timmy," she said, her eyes shut tight, "come out in this kitchen."

He appeared, carrying a comic book. That was for the look of it, of
course; he had not been reading. His face was wary. Fair, like his mother,

blond-toned, smart for his age, he had still about his quiet plump face 215
something that belonged to field animals, wood animals, shrewd, secret
creatures that had little to say for themselves. He read the newspaper
as his father did, cultivated the same thoughtful expression; encouraged,
he talked critically about his schoolteacher with a precocity that delighted
his father, frightened Annette (to her, even now, teachers were somehow 220
different from other people), he had known the days of the week, months
of the year, continents of the world, planets of the solar system, major
star groupings of the universe, at an astonishing age—as a child he approached professional perfection; but Annette, staring at him, was not
sure now that she could trust him. What if, when the shouting began 225
outside, when "Missus! Missus!" demanded her, Timmy ran out to them,
joined them, stared back at her in the midst of their white eyes and dirty
arms? They stared at each other as if this question had been voiced.

"You almost killed him," Timmy said.

His voice was soft. Its innocence showed that he knew how daring he 230
was; his eyes as well, neatly fringed by pale lashes, trembled slightly in
their gaze. "What?" said Annette. "What?"

The electric clock, built into the big white range, whirred in the
silence. Timmy swallowed, rustled his comic book, pretended to wipe his
nose—a throwback to a habit long outgrown—hoping to mislead her, 235
and looked importantly at the clock. "*He* hit the car. Two times," he said.

This was spoken differently. The ugly spell was over. "Yes, he certainly did," Annette said. She was suddenly busy. "He certainly did."
After a moment Timmy put down the comic book to help her. They
worked easily, in silence. Eyes avoided each other. But Annette felt fe- 240
verishly excited; something had been decided, strengthened. Timmy,
stooping to put vegetables in the bottom of the refrigerator, felt her
staring at him and peered up, his little eyebrows raised in a classic look of
wonder. "You going to call Daddy?" he said.

Annette had been thinking of this, but when Timmy suggested it, it 245
was exposed for what it was—a child's idea. "That won't be necessary," she
said. She folded bags noisily and righteously.

When they finished, mother and son wandered without enthusiasm
into the dining room, into the living room, as if they did not really want to
leave the kitchen. Annette's eyes flinched at what she saw: crystal, pol- 250
ished wood, white walls, aqua lampshades, white curtains, sand-toned rug,
detailed, newly cleaned, spreading regally across the room—surely no
one ever walked on that rug! That was what *they* would say if they saw it.
And the glassware off in the corner, spearlike, transparent green, a great
window behind it linking it with the green grass outside, denying a bar- 255
rier, inviting in sunlight, wind, anyone's eyes approaching—— Annette
went to the window and pulled the draw drapes shut; that was better;
she breathed gently, coaxed by the beauty of those drapes into a smile:
they were white, perfectly hung, sculpted superbly in generous swirl-

ing curves. And fireproof, if it came to that. . . . Annette turned. Timmy 260
stood before the big red swivel chair as if he were going to sit in it—he
did not—and looked at her with such a queer, pinched expression, in spite
of his round face, that Annette felt a sudden rush of shame. She was too
easily satisfied, too easily deluded. In all directions her possessions
stretched out about her, defining her, identifying her, and they were vul- 265
nerable and waiting, the dirt road led right to them; and she could be
lured into smiling! That must be why Timmy looked at her so strangely.
"I have something to do," she murmured, and went back to the dining
room. The window there was open; she pulled it down and locked it. She
went to the wall control and turned on the air conditioning. "Run, honey, 270
and close the windows," she said. "In your room."

She went into the bedroom, closed the windows there and locked
them. Outside there was nothing—smooth lawn, lawn furniture (fire-
engine red) grouped casually together, as if the chairs made of tubing and
spirals were having a conversation. Annette went into the bathroom, 275
locked that window, avoided her gaze in the mirror, went, at last, into
the "sewing room" that faced the road, and stood for a while staring out the
window. She had never liked the color of that clay, really—it stretched up
from Louisiana to Kentucky, sometimes an astonishing blood red, pulsat-
ing with heat. Now it ran watery in the sunlight at the bend. Nothing 280
there. Annette waited craftily. But still nothing. She felt that, as soon
as she turned away, the first black spots would appear—coarse black hair—
and the first splashes of color; but she could not wait. There was too much
yet to do.

She found Timmy in the living room again, still not sitting in the 285
chair. "I'll be right back, darling," she said. "Stay here. It's too hot outside for you. Put on the television—Mommy will be right back."

She got the clipping shears out of the closet and went outside, still
teetering in her high heels. There was no time to waste, no time. The yellow
rosebush was farthest away, but most important. She clipped roses off, a 290
generous amount of stem. Though hurried—every few seconds she had to
stare down the road—she took time to clip off some leaves as well. Then
she went to the red bushes, which now exclaimed at her ignorance: she
could see they were more beautiful, really, than the yellow roses. Red
more beautiful than yellow; yellow looked common, not stunning enough 295
against the house. It took her perhaps ten minutes, and even then she
had to tear her eyes away from the lesser flowers, over there in the circular
bed, she did not have time for them—unaccountably she was angry at
them, as if they had betrayed her already, grateful to the migrant workers who were coming to tear them to pieces! Their small stupid faces 300
nodded in the hot wind.

Timmy awaited her in the kitchen. He looked surprised at all the roses.
"The big vase," she commanded. In a flurry of activity, so pleased by
what she was doing that she did not notice the dozens of bleeding

scratches on her hands, she laid the roses on the cupboard, clipped at 305
leaves, arranged them, took down a slender copper vase and filled it with
water, forced some roses in, abandoned it when Timmy came in with the
milk-glass vase (wedding present from a remote aunt of hers). The smell
of roses filled the kitchen, sweetly drugged Annette's anxiety. Beauty,
beauty—it was necessary to have beauty, to possess it, to keep it around 310
oneself!—how well she understood that now.

Finished abruptly, she left the refuse on the cupboard and brought
the vases into the living room. She stood back from them, peered critically
. . . saw a stain on the wood of the table already, she must have spilled
some water. And the roses were not arranged well, too heavy, too many 315
flowers, an insane jumble of flowered faces, some facing one another nose
to nose, some staring down toward the water in the vase in an indecent
way, some at the ceiling, some at Annette herself. But there was no time
to worry over them, already new chores called to her, demanded her services. What should she do next?—The answer hit her like a blow; how 320
could she be so stupid? The doors were not even locked! Staggered by
this, she ran to the front door, with trembling fingers locked it. How
could she have overlooked this? Was something in her, some secret corner,
conspiring with the Mexicans down the road? She ran stumbling to the
back door—even that had been left open, it could have been seen from 325
the road! A few flies buzzed idly, she had no time for them. When she
appeared, panting, in the doorway, she saw Timmy by the big white vase
trying to straighten the flowers. . . . "Timmy," she said sharply, "you'll
cut yourself. Go away, go into the other room, watch television."

He turned at once but did not look at her. She watched him and felt, 330
then, that it was a mistake to speak that way to him—in fact, a deliberate
error, like forgetting about the doors; might not her child be separated
from her if they came, trapped in the other room? "No, no, Timmy," she
said, reaching out for him—he looked around, frightened—"no, come
here. Come here." He came slowly. His eyes showed trust; his mouth, 335
pursed and tightened, showed wariness, fear of that trust. Annette saw
all this—had she not felt the same way about him, wishing him dead as
soon as he was born?—and flicked it aside, bent to embrace him. "Darling,
I'll take care of you. Here. Sit here. I'll bring you something to eat."

He allowed her to help him sit at the dining room table. He was 340
strangely quiet, his head bowed. There was a surface mystery about that
quietness! Annette thought, in the kitchen, I'll get through that, I'll
prove myself to him. At first cunningly, then anxiously, she looked through
the refrigerator, touching things, rearranging things, even upsetting
things—a jar of pickles—and then came back carrying some strawberry 345
tarts, made just the day before, and the basket of new strawberries, and
some apples. "Here, darling," she said. But Timmy hesitated; while Annette's own mouth watered painfully, he could only blink in surprise.
Impatiently she said, "Here, eat it, eat them. You love them. *Here.*"

"No napkins," Timmy said fearfully. "Never mind napkins, or a tablecloth, 350
or plates," Annette said angrily—how slow her child seemed to her, like
one of those empty-faced children she often saw along the road, country
children, staring at her red car. "Here. Eat it. Eat it." When she turned
to go back to the kitchen, she saw him lifting one of the tarts slowly to
his mouth.   355

She came back almost immediately—bringing the package of ice
cream, two spoons, a basket of raspberries, a plate of sliced chicken wrapped
loosely in wax paper—— She was overcome by hunger. She pulled a
chair beside Timmy, who had not yet eaten—he stared gravely at her—
and began to eat one of the tarts. It convulsed her mouth, so delicious was 360
it, so sweet yet at the same time sour, tantalizing; she felt something like
love for it, jealousy for it, and was already reaching for another when
she caught sight of Timmy's stare. "Won't Daddy be home? Won't we
have dinner?" he pleaded.

But he paused. His lips parted moistly and he stared at his mother, 365
who smiled back at him, reassuring him, comforting him, pushing one of
the tarts toward him with her polished nails. Then something clicked in
his eyes. His lips damp with new saliva, he smiled at her, relieved,
pleased. As if a secret ripened to bursting between them, swollen with
passion, they smiled at each other. Timmy said, before biting into the 370
tart, "*He* can't hit the car again, it's all locked up." Annette said, gesturing
at him with sticky fingers, "Here, darling. Eat this. Eat. *Eat.*"

QUESTIONS

1. Note the vocabulary in the first three paragraphs, especially the
   verbs, through which many details of action, color, and sound are presented. Which words are the most vivid and concrete? What impressions do these words create?
2. What are Annette's feelings at the end of line 37? Where does the
   author provide information on Annette's personality?
3. Who are the people whom she meets on the road? What do they do
   for a living? In what terms does Annette see them? We are told in
   lines 88–89 that her "face burned with something more than shame."
   How do you interpret this?
4. Why do the people act as they do in lines 91–97? Do they look
   on Annette as an enemy?
5. What is the basis of her fears after she reaches home? When she
   looks at her attractive possessions in the living room, what does she
   think? Why does she hurriedly cut so many roses?
6. What items in the story reveal Annette's feeling that she is confronted by an "enemy"? Is Timmy also an enemy or a part of "the
   enemy"?

7. Afflicted by fears, what measures of protection does Annette take? What do her actions symbolize?

8. If the story exemplifies class conflict, in what terms should it be stated? What is the basis of the conflict between Timmy and his mother? What makes her "not sure . . . that she could trust him"? How is the conflict between Annette and Timmy related to the experience with the people on the road?

9. As mother and son put away the groceries, she feels that "something had been decided, strengthened." What causes her to feel that way? Later she is disturbed by his quietness, and she thinks, "I'll get through that, I'll prove myself to him." What does she think she has to prove?

10. What causes Annette to do the things she does in the final three paragraphs? How do mother and son feel at the end?

11. At what points would you divide the story into beginning (exposition), middle, and end?

12. What is the resolution of the story?

SECTION TWO

PLAYS

Reading Plays

I

A play is a story told in a particular way and intended for acting before an audience, frequently on a stage. When a play is presented, actors pretend to live through the events of the story, using appropriate body movements and gestures, and reciting words—that is, "speaking their lines" of dialogue. A performance of a play is the product of the combining of several arts: that of the scene designer, of the costumer, of the director, of the actors, and of the author who constructed the plot pattern of the play and wrote the dialogue and the stage directions.

No matter how well rehearsed a play is, every performance will be a little different from every other performance because of variations in the condition and spirit of the actors and because of variations in the response of audiences. The rapport established between actors and audience is a special thing. Audiences will respond differently to the "same" play in Boston, Seattle, New York, and Denver. Some audiences are ignorant and slow to respond, some are naïve and easily impressed, some are cold and hard to warm up. Other audiences are intelligent and perceptive, or, perhaps, oversophisticated and blasé, while others are enthusiastic and inspiring. Thus, because of the interaction between the cast and the audience, each performance of a play is a brief, unique experience; it lasts two or three hours and is gone.

Where, then, does the play exist? It exists for a time in the memories of the actors; in the script from which they learned their lines; and very often in the printed pages of a book. A reader's response to a play, however, will never be the same as that of a spectator. Readers will not feel what an audience feels in a darkened theater, and they will have to use their imagination to try to see something like the performance that the playwright intended. On the other hand, they can give freer play to their imagination, unhampered by bad acting or awkward staging, and they are also able to take in the play more slowly, to ponder over it if they like, and to go back if they choose and reread some passage before proceeding. So a reader may have a few advantages over a spectator.

Of course, reading a play is something like reading a story or a novel. But because of the conventions of the theater—the medium the playwright is using—a dramatist cannot write in the same way as a novelist. He cannot give descriptions, characterizations, and information about the history of his characters in the same free way that a novelist can. He cannot interpret and comment on their actions. Above all, he cannot enter the minds of the characters. Except for stage directions, every word he writes must be spoken by the actors. The characters' thoughts and feelings and any interpretations of character have to come out through speeches. Thus, a dramatist is forced by the operations of his medium to use the objective point of view, whereas a novelist or short story writer has other options.

II

In the early portion of his play a dramatist has to accomplish several important things. First, he has to choose where to begin. Horace, the Roman poet who gave advice on epic and dramatic construction, said: "Don't start with the egg." A playwright cannot spend much time on the early days of his characters. Plunge into the midst of things (*in medias res*), Horace advised. The dramatist may choose some exciting moment for his beginning in order to grip the attention of his audience. Shakespeare became very good at openings: he opens *Hamlet* with nervous sentinels watching for a ghost at midnight and *Romeo and Juliet* with a fray among members of the feuding Capulets and Montagues.

Having begun, a dramatist has to show his characters living in a particular setting and situation and make them act and talk convincingly according to their temperaments. He must also let the spectator or reader know something of what has gone on among them before the moment when they commence interacting on the stage and what their present relationships are. One couple may be in love; another may be planning divorce. One pair may have committed robbery; another, adultery; a third, murder. As his final duty, as soon as he reasonably can after presenting the characters, the dramatist must start the action of the play. And he must do all these things through dialogue.

This is a large order. Naturally, a skillful playwright fills it successfully. That is why he is called a playwright (from *play* + *wright*, "maker"), a craftsman who can *work* out the problems of dramatic construction. He must also accomplish his objectives in an interesting way. The style in which he writes must have distinction, whether of wit, poetry, atmosphere, or realism.

As a reader peruses the early part of a play—the first act, for instance —he must give his attention to these various matters, mentally organizing the information given him in the dialogue; the experienced reader may hardly be aware that he is doing so. Aristotle, in his *Poetics*, the cornerstone of European literary criticism, said that plot is the soul of drama. No doubt characterization is important; some characters—such as Shakespeare's Hamlet, Falstaff, and Richard III—stand out so memorably that we tend to minimize the plots in which they play their parts. But characters scarcely reveal themselves except through their decisions and actions, required by the pressures put on them in the plot. If plot is the soul of drama, the soul of plot is conflict. Outer conflicts, as between Hamlet and his uncle Claudius, and between the forces of Brutus and of Mark Antony in *Julius Caesar*, and inner conflicts as well, as those between conscience and the temptation to murder that rack Brutus and Macbeth so harshly, are the forces that the playwrights must create the semblance of, by means of his words, and then must manipulate in the course of his plot.

The plots of dramas, like the plots of novels and short stories, are often analyzed in similar terms. *Exposition* is the early part of the play, in which the dramatist introduces characters and gives the necessary information about their past and the relationships among them. The action proper consists of *complications*; it is called *rising action* because there are increasing tensions, risks, and suspense as the play proceeds. If we diagram the course of the plot with an outline of a pyramid, the action-line rises toward a high point. In many plays there is a *turning point* that we can see when we look back and consider the whole action, after which the fortunes of the characters went one way or another and things were bound to turn out as they did. In the *falling action* the characters are proceeding toward a solution to their problems in accordance with the pattern of earlier action. The *resolution* is the part at the end where the answers are revealed and all suspense is ended. Another term for resolution is *dénouement*, a French word meaning the untying of knots. In *Julius Caesar* the resolution shows the defeat and death of Brutus and Cassius brought about by the avenging forces of Mark Antony and Octavius Caesar. In the resolution of *As You Like It* three couples are married and the banished duke is restored to power. The pressures put upon the characters have been removed, and with the establishment of a new arrangement of things, life looks calmer even if less exciting.

But plot is not everything. If a dramatist expects his play to be remembered long and favorably, he must create characters that are interesting in one way or another. The reader of a play has to use his imagination in order to form a conception of each character, often without much help from the author. Some realistic playwrights of the nineteenth and twentieth centuries provide considerable information. Ibsen, for instance, tells us before a word is spoken in *John Gabriel Borkman*:

> Mrs. Gunhild Borkman sits on the sofa, knitting. She is an elderly lady, of cold, distinguished appearance, with stiff carriage and immobile features. Her hair is very grey, her delicate hands transparent. She is dressed in a gown of heavy dark silk, which had at one time been attractive, but is now somewhat worn and shabby. A woolen shawl is thrown over her shoulders.

But such aids to visualization are not common. Generally a reader knows only that some characters are older, some younger, and what their social or official positions are. Thus Molière, listing the dramatis personae of *The Miser*, lets us know only that Anselme is "the father of Valère and Marianne" and that Master Jacques is "cook and coachman to Harpagon." The reader must accumulate his impressions of their personalities from the dialogue that the playwright gives them to speak. Anyone reading *The Merchant of Venice* will quickly note the difference in tone between Antonio the merchant:

> I hold the world but as the world, Gratiano;
> A stage where every man must play a part,
> And mine a sad one;

and his friend Gratiano, who replies:

> Let me play the fool:
> With mirth and laughter let old wrinkles come.

A few words from the Prince of Morocco show what a boaster he is:

> I tell thee, lady, this aspect of mine
> Hath fear'd the valiant: by my love, I swear
> The best-regarded virgins of our clime
> Have loved it too.

How different in personality is Shylock:

> Well, Jessica, go in:
> Perhaps I will return immediately:
> Do as I bid you; shut doors after you:
> Fast bind, fast find. . . .

These are the words of a severe and careful man.

The creation of character by a dramatist is not essentially different from character creation by a novelist except that it must be more concentrated. Sinclair Lewis used more than four hundred pages to relate the story of Dr. Martin Arrowsmith's career, and Dickens devoted some eight hundred pages to the growing-up of David Copperfield. These characters become very real to every reader, and if they were transferred from novels to plays, they would be very real there too, but only dialogue could be used, and much would have to be omitted. At the opening of Chapter 19, David tells us:

> I am doubtful whether I was at heart glad or sorry, when my school-days drew to an end, and the time came for my leaving Doctor Strong's. I had been very happy there, I had a great attachment for the Doctor, and I was eminent and distinguished in that little world. For these reasons I was sorry to go; but for other reasons, unsubstantial enough, I was glad. . . . I try in vain to recall how I felt about it. . . .

If the novel were dramatized, a great deal of this sort of thing would have to be omitted. Dickens chose to have the protagonist tell his own story; but a dramatist could not use that point of view; he could adopt only the objective point of view, so that any of David's thoughts and feelings would have to be expressed in conversation with other characters, or possibly in soliloquy.

The main point for the reader of plays to remember is that drama is a highly specialized form of literature, that it has greater intensity than other types of fiction because it is more concentrated, and that it often calls for more exertion of imagination and thought than does the typical novel.

A full-length play is rather like a stripped-down novel comprising some one hundred pages; it is usually divided into two, three, four, or five acts. A one-act play, typically a product of the last three-quarters of a century in the serious theater, is likely to cover from fifteen to thirty pages. The one-act play is to the full-length play as the short story is to the novel, for it requires greater compression and greater attention to unity of effect. It must be composed with simplicity and directness, without any of the complexity of action found, for example, in some Shakespearean plays. It has few characters.

A one-act play must open at a point where the playwright can rouse interest about a significant matter. Within the first half-dozen speeches of *Riders to the Sea*, for example, we know that the women of a family fear that a son and brother has been drowned. The resolution must, of course, be very effective; it may be conveyed more by pantomime or tableau than by word, as is the ending of O'Casey's *Bedtime Story*. A one-acter must deal with a single situation; as in the short story, a brief interval of great significance is, so to speak, detached from the flow of life and exhibited so that we can see and understand how plot affects characters and how the characters, out of their very natures, make the plot. Thus its compression, its very limitations, make the effect of the one-act play intense and striking.

III

The two main types of drama are tragedy and comedy. Traditionally, epic and tragedy have been considered the greatest kinds of literature. Tragedy frequently portrays serious action with issues of life and death. Very often the tragic hero, and other characters as well, meet their deaths. Even if they do not, they undergo great pressures and suffering, and their lives are spoiled. It has been said that "tragedy is the artistic presentation of human suffering" (Dan S. Norton and Peters Rushton, *A Glossary of Literary Terms*). The dramatist is an artist; he does not depict suffering and bloodshed so that we will sadistically gloat over them; he presents suffering so that we can understand and sympathize with the kind of character who endures it. In the spectacle of his painful struggle we become aware of some of the mystery of human destiny.

Why, for example, should an excellent young man like Hamlet, "the expectancy and rose of the fair state," have to meet such an early death? Was there no honorable way for him to avoid the ruin of his life? How is it that men as fundamentally good and honorable as Brutus, Othello, and Oedipus became involved in situations from which there is no escape except death or horrible self-punishment? For ages Europeans have been fascinated by the questions that tragedies suggest. Is there a principle of evil in the universe that works against goodness and greatness? Is there something in the very nature of things that traps and defeats the heroic man when lesser men escape both inordinate pain and dramatic defeat? What kind of world is this in which Oedipus, who rose in the morning the idol of his people, is by nightfall a blind and hated outcast? Can this be a good world in which even good people are made to suffer so?

These are fundamental questions of metaphysics and religion. Tragedy presents situations that pose these questions; tragedy does not answer them, however. But the fact that tragedy projects these deep questions dramatically explains why tragedy is considered the greatest form of literature.

Tragedy brings spectacles of suffering and the unhappy waste of human resources before our pitying and horrified eyes. We can see that a tragic downfall grows from some combination of character and circumstances. The downfall is unfortunate; yet in the circumstances we would not have it otherwise. A man has to be a hero in order to have a tragic fate. If Romeo had said, "Well, I'm banished; it would be dangerous to try to see Juliet again, so I'll let her go—there must be plenty of attractive girls in Mantua," he would never have met a tragic fate—nor would he ever have gained our respect. So we pity the tragic hero, but we honor him for his distinction, for his heroic qualities. Although tense and inwardly racked by the tragic spectacle, we feel almost exalted that humanity has in it such inspiring possibilities of character. Not many writings can make us feel a sense of awe. Tragedy can.

Of all the animals, man is the only one that laughs. When his irreverent and life-affirming spirit of laughter expresses itself by dramatic means, the result is comedy. In the world of comedy the killjoy authoritarian who is stupidly sure of himself is the one to be laughed at, whether he is policeman or constable, doctor, lawyer, professor, stern father, or overbearing boss. The fussy wife and the critical mother-in-law are also resisted and criticized with laughter. In fact, the comic spirit makes fun of all kinds of excesses; whatever departs from the norms of society will receive its punishment through laughter. A tragic hero undergoes a fall, often from greatness, but the comic character cannot fall; he can only take a tumble.

Animals are different from human beings. They pursue lives of sensations, not of thoughts. They feel no sense of sin and no obligations to unseen worlds or remote ancestors. To them stealing or killing or sexual chastity are not problems. They never worry about being seen with the right people, buying a house on a better street, creating the right impressions, or being able to afford a new car or a frock in the latest fashion. There is no discrepancy between their aspirations and what they are: they are not hypocrites. If we were as unselfconscious as animals, we would not laugh either.

And if every detail of every phase of life were exactly as it should be, nothing would seem comic. When we perceive the gaps (Emerson called them the "yawning delinquencies of practice") between our concept of the ideal and what exists, our sense of humor breaks forth; we laugh.

So comedy performs a healthful function in society. It helps us assert a sense of reality and sincerity, and to punish or correct all kinds of pretensions. Louis Kronenberger, in *The Thread of Laughter*, wrote:

> Comedy is always jarring us with the evidence that we are no better than other people, and always comforting us with the knowledge that most other people are no better than we are. It makes us more critical but it leaves us more tolerant; and to that extent it performs a very notable social function.

To perform this function, comedy uses many figures with exaggerated traits of character, figures who depart from accepted norms. Those characters in comedy who come through with a minimum of ridicule, those who succeed in marrying the beautiful girl or the strong, handsome man are those who have a sense of humor, at least average common sense, and, best of all, a good heart.

There are several kinds of comedy: the boisterous physical fun of farce (getting a pie in the face or being found in the wrong bedroom); the witty exhibition of a social code in the comedy of manners; the satirical punishing of vice and folly in what is called corrective comedy; the exposure of ignorance and blunders in low comedy; and the charm of wit and intelligence in that high comedy which expresses what George Meredith called "the spirit of thoughtful laughter." This last kind of comedy best satisfies our maturest demands of this type of literature.

Some of these types may be mingled. In fact, comedy is seldom a pure form. Comic elements sometimes occur in tragedy. Comedy is a term that has been used of any play with a happy ending. In the English tradition of comedy it is often mixed with romance. In general, we think that tragedies end with deaths and comedies with weddings.

Besides tragedies and comedies, there are also many plays that lack the towering dignity and seriousness of tragedy and the gaiety of comedy but that represent problems of everyday living. The French term *drame* describes plays of this class, a class which has been gradually growing since the eighteenth century. Although, in the main, comedies and *drames* are constructed much like tragedies, the reader of nontragic plays is generally willing to accept more improbability in them than he will in tragedy. In tragedy the outcome is foreshadowed; we anticipate it; it must seem inevitable. Tragedy is no place for surprise endings, but a reader may enjoy them in comedy and *drame*.

Riders to the Sea

JOHN MILLINGTON SYNGE

Characters
MAURYA   *an old woman*
BARTLEY   *her son*
CATHLEEN   *her daughter*
NORA   *a younger daughter*
MEN AND WOMEN

SCENE   *An Island off the West of Ireland.*
Cottage kitchen, with nets, oil-skins, spinning-wheel, some new boards stand-
ing by the wall, etc. CATHLEEN, *a girl of about twenty, finishes kneading*
cake, and puts it down in the pot-oven by the fire; then wipes her hands,
and begins to spin at the wheel. NORA, *a young girl, puts her head in at*
the door.

NORA [*in a low voice*]   Where is she?
CATHLEEN   She's lying down, God help her, and may be sleeping, if she's
   able.
   [NORA *comes in softly, and takes a bundle from under her shawl.*]
CATHLEEN [*spinning the wheel rapidly*]   What is it you have?   5
NORA   The young priest is after bringing them. It's a shirt and a plain
   stocking were got off a drowned man in Donegal.
   [CATHLEEN *stops her wheel with a sudden movement, and leans out*
   to listen.]
NORA   We're to find out if it's Michael's they are, some time herself will   10
   be down looking by the sea.
CATHLEEN   How would they be Michael's, Nora? How would he go the
   length of that way to the far north?
NORA   The young priest says he's known the like of it. "If it's Michael's
   they are," says he, "you can tell herself he's got a clean burial by the   15
   grace of God, and if they're not his, let no one say a word about them,

for she'll be getting her death," says he, "with crying and lamenting."
[*The door which* NORA *half closed is blown open by a gust of wind.*]

CATHLEEN [*looking out anxiously*]   Did you ask him would he stop Bartley
going this day with the horses to the Galway fair?   20

NORA   "I won't stop him," says he, "but let you not be afraid. Herself does
be saying prayers half through the night, and the Almighty God won't
leave her destitute," says he, "with no son living."

CATHLEEN   Is the sea bad by the white rocks, Nora?

NORA   Middling bad, God help us. There's a great roaring in the west,   25
and it's worse it'll be getting when the tide's turned to the wind.
[*She goes over to the table with the bundle.*] Shall I open it now?

CATHLEEN   Maybe she'd wake up on us, and come in before we'd done.
[*coming to the table*] It's a long time we'll be, and the two of us crying.

NORA [*goes to the inner door and listens*]   She's moving about on the bed.   30
She'll be coming in a minute.

CATHLEEN   Give me the ladder, and I'll put them up in the turf-loft, the
way she won't know of them at all, and maybe when the tide turns
she'll be going down to see would he be floating from the east.
[*They put the ladder against the gable of the chimney;* CATHLEEN   35
goes up a few steps and hides the bundle in the turf-loft. MAURYA
comes from the inner room.]

MAURYA [*looking up at* CATHLEEN *and speaking querulously*]   Isn't it turf
enough you have for this day and evening?

CATHLEEN   There's a cake baking at the fire for a short space [*throwing   40
down the turf*] and Bartley will want it when the tide turns if he
goes to Connemara.
[NORA *picks up the turf and puts it round the pot-oven.*]

MAURYA [*sitting down on a stool at the fire*]   He won't go this day with
the wind rising from the south and west. He won't go this day, for the   45
young priest will stop him surely.

NORA   He'll not stop him, mother, and I heard Eamon Simon and Stephen
Pheety and Colum Shawn saying he would go.

MAURYA   Where is he itself?

NORA   He went down to see would there be another boat sailing in the   50
week, and I'm thinking it won't be long till he's here now, for the
tide's turning at the green head, and the hooker's tacking[1] from
the east.

CATHLEEN   I hear some one passing the big stones.

NORA [*looking out*]   He's coming now, and he in a hurry.   55

BARTLEY [*comes in and looks round the room; speaking sadly and quietly*]
Where is the bit of new rope, Cathleen, was bought in Connemara?

---

[1] A hooker is a one-masted fishing smack. To tack is to make a run obliquely against
the wind.

CATHLEEN [*coming down*]   Give it to him, Nora; it's on a nail by the white
boards. I hung it up this morning, for the pig with the black feet was
eating it.   60

NORA [*giving him a rope*]   Is that it, Bartley?

MAURYA   You'd do right to leave that rope, Bartley, hanging by the boards.
[BARTLEY *takes the rope.*] It will be wanting in this place, I'm telling you,
if Michael is washed up tomorrow morning, or the next morning, or
any morning in the week, for it's a deep grave we'll make him by   65
the grace of God.

BARTLEY [*beginning to work with the rope*]   I've no halter the way I can
ride down on the mare, and I must go now quickly. This is the one
boat going for two weeks or beyond it, and the fair will be a good
fair for horses I heard them saying below.   70

MAURYA   It's a hard thing they'll be saying below if the body is washed
up and there's no man in it to make the coffin, and I after giving a big
price for the finest white boards you'd find in Connemara. [*She looks
round at the boards.*]

BARTLEY   How would it be washed up, and we after looking each day for 75
nine days, and a strong wind blowing a while back from the west
and south?

MAURYA   If it wasn't found itself, that wind is raising the sea, and there
was a star up against the moon, and it rising in the night. If it was a
hundred horses, or a thousand horses you had itself, what is the price 80
of a thousand horses against a son where there is one son only?

BARTLEY [*working at the halter, to* CATHLEEN]   Let you go down each day,
and see the sheep aren't jumping in on the rye, and if the jobber comes
you can sell the pig with the black feet if there is a good price going.

MAURYA   How would the like of her get a good price for a pig?   85

BARTLEY [*to* CATHLEEN]   If the west wind holds with the last bit of the
moon let you and Nora get up weed enough for another cock for the
kelp. It's hard set we'll be from this day with no one in it but one
man to work.

MAURYA   It's hard set we'll be surely the day you're drownd'd with the 90
rest. What way will I live and the girls with me, and I an old woman
looking for the grave?
[BARTLEY *lays down the halter, takes off his old coat, and puts on a
newer one of the same flannel.*]

BARTLEY [*to* NORA]   Is she coming to the pier?   95

NORA [*looking out*]   She's passing the green head and letting fall her sails.

BARTLEY [*getting his purse and tobacco*]   I'll have half an hour to go down,
and you'll see me coming again in two days, or in three days, or
maybe in four days if the wind is bad.

MAURYA [*turning round to the fire, and putting her shawl over her head*] 100
Isn't it a hard and cruel man won't hear a word from an old woman,
and she holding him from the sea?

CATHLEEN   It's the life of a young man to be going on the sea, and who would listen to an old woman with one thing and she saying it over?

BARTLEY [*taking the halter*]   I must go now quickly. I'll ride down on the   105
red mare, and the gray pony'll run behind me. . . . The blessing of God on you. [*He goes out.*]

MAURYA [*crying out as he is in the door*]   He's gone now, God spare us, and we'll not see him again. He's gone now, and when the black night is falling I'll have no son left me in the world.   110

CATHLEEN   Why wouldn't you give him your blessing and he looking round in the door? Isn't it sorrow enough is on every one in this house without your sending him out with an unlucky word behind him, and a hard word in his ear?

[MAURYA *takes up the tongs and begins raking the fire aimlessly with-   115
out looking round.*]

NORA [*turning toward her*]   You're taking away the turf from the cake.

CATHLEEN [*crying out*]   The Son of God forgive us, Nora, we're after for-getting his bit of bread. [*She comes over to the fire.*]

NORA   And it's destroyed[2] he'll be going till dark night, and he after eating   120
nothing since the sun went up.

CATHLEEN [*turning the cake out of the oven*]   It's destroyed he'll be, surely. There's no sense left on any person in a house where an old woman will be talking forever.

[MAURYA *sways herself on her stool.*]   125

CATHLEEN [*cutting off some of the bread and rolling it in a cloth; to* MAURYA]
Let you go down now to the spring well and give him this and he passing. You'll see him then and the dark word will be broken, and you can say "God speed you," the way he'll be easy in his mind.

MAURYA [*taking the bread*]   Will I be in it as soon as himself?   130

CATHLEEN   If you go now quickly.

MAURYA [*standing up unsteadily*]   It's hard set I am to walk.

CATHLEEN [*looking at her anxiously*]   Give her the stick, Nora, or maybe she'll slip on the big stones.

NORA   What stick?   135

CATHLEEN   The stick Michael brought from Connemara.

MAURYA [*taking a stick* NORA *gives her*]   In the big world the old people do be leaving things after them for their sons and children, but in this place it is the young men do be leaving things behind for them that do be old. [*She goes out slowly.* NORA *goes over to the ladder.*]   140

CATHLEEN   Wait, Nora, maybe she'd turn back quickly. She's that sorry, God help her, you wouldn't know the thing she'd do.

NORA   Is she gone round by the bush?

CATHLEEN [*looking out*]   She's gone now. Throw it down quickly, for the Lord knows when she'll be out of it again.   145

[2] Half-dead.

NORA [*getting the bundle from the loft*]   The young priest said he'd be passing to-morrow, and we might go down and speak to him below if it's Michael's they are surely.

CATHLEEN [*taking the bundle*]   Did he say what way they were found?

NORA [*coming down*]   "There were two men," says he, "and they rowing 150 round with poteen before the cocks crowed, and the oar of one of them caught the body, and they passing the black cliffs of the north."

CATHLEEN [*trying to open the bundle*]   Give me a knife, Nora, the string's perished with the salt water, and there's a black knot on it you wouldn't loosen in a week.   155

NORA [*giving her a knife*]   I've heard tell it was a long way to Donegal.

CATHLEEN [*cutting the string*]   It is surely. There was a man in here a while ago—the man sold us that knife—and he said if you set off walking from the rocks beyond, it would be seven days you'd be in Donegal.   160

NORA   And what time would a man take, and he floating?

[CATHLEEN *opens the bundle and takes out a bit of a stocking. They look at them eagerly.*]

CATHLEEN [*in a low voice*]   The Lord spare us, Nora! isn't it a queer hard thing to say if it's his they are surely?   165

NORA   I'll get his shirt off the hook the way we can put the one flannel on the other. [*She looks through some clothes hanging in the corner.*] It's not with them, Cathleen, and where will it be?

CATHLEEN   I'm thinking Bartley put it on him in the morning, for his own shirt was heavy with the salt in it. [*pointing to the corner*] There's 170 a bit of a sleeve was of the same stuff. Give me that and it will do.

[*Nora brings it to her and they compare the flannel.*]

CATHLEEN   It's the same stuff, Nora; but if it is itself aren't there great rolls of it in the shops of Galway, and isn't it many another man may have a shirt of it as well as Michael himself?   175

NORA [*who has taken up the stocking and counted the stitches, crying out*] It's Michael, Cathleen, it's Michael; God spare his soul, and what will herself say when she hears this story, and Bartley on the sea?

CATHLEEN [*taking the stocking*]   It's a plain stocking.

NORA   It's the second one of the third pair I knitted, and I put up threescore 180 stitches, and I dropped four of them.

CATHLEEN [*counts the stitches*]   It's that number is in it. [*Crying out*] Ah, Nora, isn't it a bitter thing to think of him floating that way to the far north, and no one to keen him but the black hags that do be flying on the sea?   185

NORA [*swinging herself round, and throwing out her arms on the clothes*] And isn't it a pitiful thing when there is nothing left of a man who was a great rower and fisher, but a bit of an old shirt and a plain stocking?

CATHLEEN [*after an instant*]   Tell me is herself coming, Nora? I hear a little 19
sound on the path.

NORA [*looking out*]   She is, Cathleen. She's coming up to the door.

CATHLEEN   Put these things away before she'll come in. Maybe it's easier
she'll be after giving her blessing to Bartley, and we won't let on we've
heard anything the time he's on the sea.   19

NORA [*helping* CATHLEEN *to close the bundle*]   We'll put them here in the
corner.

[*They put them into a hole in the chimney corner.* CATHLEEN *goes
back to the spinning-wheel.*]

NORA   Will she see it was crying I was?   20

CATHLEEN   Keep your back to the door the way the light'll not be on you.

[NORA *sits down at the chimney corner, with her back to the door.*
MAURYA *comes in very slowly, without looking at the girls, and goes
over to her stool at the other side of the fire. The cloth with the bread
is still in her hand. The girls look at each other, and* NORA *points to the* 20
bundle of bread.]

CATHLEEN [*after spinning for a moment*]   You didn't give him his bit of
bread?

[MAURYA *begins to keen softly, without turning round.*]

CATHLEEN   Did you see him riding down?   21

[MAURYA *goes on keening.*]

CATHLEEN [*a little impatiently*]   God forgive you; isn't it a better thing
to raise your voice and tell what you seen, than to be making lamenta-
tion for a thing that's done? Did you see Bartley, I'm saying to you.

MAURYA [*with a weak voice*]   My heart's broken from this day.   21

CATHLEEN [*as before*]   Did you see Bartley?

MAURYA   I seen the fearfulest thing.

CATHLEEN [*leaves her wheel and looks out*]   God forgive you; he's riding
the mare now over the green head, and the gray pony behind him.

MAURYA [*starts, so that her shawl falls back from her head and shows her* 22
white tossed hair. With a frightened voice]   The gray pony behind
him.

CATHLEEN [*coming to the fire*]   What is it ails you, at all?

MAURYA [*speaking very slowly*]   I've seen the fearfulest thing any person
has seen, since the day Bride Dara seen the dead man with the child 22
in his arms.

CATHLEEN and NORA   Uah. [*They crouch down in front of the old woman
at the fire.*]

NORA   Tell us what it is you seen.

MAURYA   I went down to the spring well, and I stood there saying a 23
prayer to myself. Then Bartley came along, and he riding on the red
mare with the gray pony behind him. [*She puts up her hands, as if
to hide something from her eyes.*] The Son of God spare us, Nora!

CATHLEEN   What is it you seen?

MAURYA   I seen Michael himself.   235

CATHLEEN [*speaking softly*]   You did not, mother; it wasn't Michael you seen, for his body is after being found in the far north, and he's got a clean burial by the grace of God.

MAURYA [*a little defiantly*]   I'm after seeing him this day, and he riding and galloping. Bartley came first on the red mare; and I tried to say   240 "God speed you," but something choked the words in my throat. He went by quickly; and "the blessing of God on you," says he, and I could say nothing. I looked up then, and I crying, at the gray pony, and there was Michael upon it—with fine clothes on him, and new shoes on his feet.   245

CATHLEEN [*begins to keen*]   It's destroyed we are from this day. It's destroyed, surely.

NORA   Didn't the young priest say the Almighty God wouldn't leave her destitute with no son living?

MAURYA [*in a low voice, but clearly*]   It's little the like of him knows of   250 the sea. . . . Bartley will be lost now, and let you call in Eamon and make me a good coffin out of the white boards, for I won't live after them. I've had a husband, and a husband's father, and six sons in this house—six fine men, though it was a hard birth I had with every one of them and they coming to the world—and some of them were   255 found and some of them were not found, but they're gone now the lot of them. . . . There were Stephen, and Shawn, were lost in the great wind, and found after in the Bay of Gregory of the Golden Mouth, and carried up the two of them on the one plank, and in by that door. [*She pauses for a moment, the girls start as if they heard*   260 *something through the door that is half open behind them.*]

NORA [*in a whisper*]   Did you hear that, Cathleen? Did you hear a noise in the north-east?

CATHLEEN [*in a whisper*]   There's some one after crying out by the seashore.   265

MAURYA [*continues without hearing anything*]   There was Sheamus and his father, and his own father again, were lost in a dark night, and not a stick or sign was seen of them when the sun went up. There was Patch after was drowned out of a curragh that turned over. I was sitting here with Bartley, and he a baby, lying on my two knees, and   270 I seen two women, and three women, and four women coming in, and they crossing themselves, and not saying a word. I looked out then, and there were men coming after them, and they holding a thing in the half of a red sail, and water dripping out of it—it was a dry day, Nora—and leaving a track to the door. [*She pauses again with her*   275 *hand stretched out towards the door. It opens softly and old women begin to come in, crossing themselves on the threshold, and kneeling down in front of the stage with red petticoats over their heads.*]

MAURYA [*half in a dream, to* CATHLEEN]   Is it Patch, or Michael, or what is
it at all?   280

CATHLEEN   Michael is after being found in the far north, and when he is
found there how could he be here in this place?

MAURYA   There does be a power of young men floating round in the sea,
and what way would they know if it was Michael they had, or
another man like him, for when a man is nine days in the sea, and   285
the wind blowing, it's hard set his own mother would be to say what
man was it.

CATHLEEN   It's Michael, God spare him, for they're after sending us a
bit of his clothes from the far north. [*She reaches out and hands*
MAURYA *the clothes that belonged to Michael.* MAURYA *stands up*   290
slowly and takes them in her hand. NORA *looks out.*]

NORA   They're carrying a thing among them and there's water dripping
out of it and leaving a track by the big stones.

CATHLEEN [*in a whisper to the women who have come in*]   Is it Bartley
it is?   295

ONE OF THE WOMEN   It is surely, God rest his soul.
[*Two younger women come in and pull out the table. Then men carry
in the body of* BARTLEY, *laid on a plank, with a bit of sail over it, and
lay it on the table.*]

CATHLEEN [*to the women, as they are doing so*]   What way was he   300
drowned?

ONE OF THE WOMEN   The gray pony knocked him into the sea, and he
was washed out where there is a great surf on the white rocks.
[MAURYA *has gone over and knelt down at the head of the table. The
women are keening softly and swaying themselves with a slow move-*   305
ment. CATHLEEN *and* NORA *kneel at the other end of the table. The
men kneel near the door.*]

MAURYA [*raising her head and speaking as if she did not see the people
around her*]   They're all gone now, and there isn't anything more
the sea can do to me. . . . I'll have no call now to be up crying and   310
praying when the wind breaks from the south, and you can hear the
surf is in the east, and the surf is in the west, making a great stir
with the two noises, and they hitting one on the other. I'll have no
call now to be going down and getting Holy Water in the dark nights
after Samhain, and I won't care what way the sea is when the other   315
women will be keening. [*To* NORA] Give me the Holy Water, Nora,
there's a small sup still on the dresser.
[NORA *gives it to her.*]

MAURYA [*drops Michael's clothes across Bartley's feet, and sprinkles the
Holy Water over him*]   It isn't that I haven't prayed for you, Bartley,   320
to the Almighty God. It isn't that I haven't said prayers in the dark
night till you wouldn't know what I'd be saying; but it's a great rest I'll
have now, and it's time surely. It's a great rest I'll have now, and great

sleeping in the long nights after Samhain, if it's only a bit of wet flour we do have to eat, and maybe a fish that would be stinking. 325 [*She kneels down again, crossing herself, and saying prayers under her breath.*]

CATHLEEN [*to an old man*]   Maybe yourself and Eamon would make a coffin when the sun rises. We have fine white boards herself bought, God help her, thinking Michael would be found, and I have a new 330 cake you can eat while you'll be working.

THE OLD MAN [*looking at the boards*]   Are there nails with them?

CATHLEEN   There are not, Colum; we didn't think of the nails.

ANOTHER MAN   It's a great wonder she wouldn't think of the nails, and all the coffins she's seen made already.   335

CATHLEEN   It's getting old she is, and broken.

[MAURYA *stands up again very slowly and spreads out the pieces of* MICHAEL's *clothes beside the body, sprinkling them with the last of the Holy Water.*]

NORA [*in a whisper to* CATHLEEN]   She's quiet now and easy; but the day 340 Michael was drowned you could hear her crying out from this to the spring well. It's fonder she was of Michael, and would any one have thought that?

CATHLEEN [*slowly and clearly*]   An old woman will be soon tired with anything she will do, and isn't it nine days herself is after crying and 345 keening, and making great sorrow in the house?

MAURYA [*puts the empty cup downwards on the table, and lays her hands together on* BARTLEY's *feet*]   They're all together this time, and the end is come. May the Almighty God have mercy on Bartley's soul, and on Michael's soul, and on the souls of Sheamus and Patch, and 350 Stephen and Shawn—[*bending her head*]; and may He have mercy on my soul, Nora, and on the soul of every one is left living in the world. [*She pauses, and the keen rises a little more loudly from the women, then sinks away.*]

MAURYA [*continuing*]   Michael has a clean burial in the far north, by the 355 grace of the Almighty God. Bartley will have a fine coffin out of the white boards, and a deep grave surely. What more can we want than that? No man at all can be living forever, and we must be satisfied. [*She kneels down again and the curtain falls slowly.*]

QUESTIONS

1. How does the setting (an island) have influence in the story? In the description of the cottage kitchen, what detail does Synge draw attention to that might seem unusual?

2. What questions are brought up in the reader's mind by the talk about the bundle?

3. In the exposition what events have been mentioned or hinted at by

line 34? At what point have all the characters with names been introduced?

4. What effect is produced by the gust of wind blowing open the door? In what places is the weather mentioned? What is the state of the weather and why is it significant?

5. The setting is one of the Aran Islands, which do not have harbors. Consequently, horses and cows being taken to the mainland are made to swim through the treacherous currents of the sea out to ships in order to be loaded aboard. Why is the question of Bartley's going to Connemara so important? Explain the views of the following persons about his going: the young priest, Maurya, Cathleen, and Bartley himself.

6. Why does Bartley need the new rope?

7. What characters are in conflict? How does each character justify his or her position? Besides the conflict of characters what larger conflict envelops the action?

8. What evidences of superstition do you find in the play? How are superstitions significant for the action?

9. What is the effect of the speech of Maurya, lines 137–140? How does she say these lines—in exasperation, rebellion, resignation, bitterness, disgust?

10. What significant thing happens between the exit of Maurya at line 140 and her reentry at line 203? What produces suspense in this part of the play? What effect is produced by the girls' speeches, lines 182–189?

11. Why does Synge have Maurya begin and continue her *keening*, lines 209–214?

12. What is the significance of the responses made by Cathleen, line 246, and by Maurya, lines 250–253?

13. After Maurya's comment, lines 269–272, what idea is Synge projecting by having the women enter as they do at line 276? What event is foreshadowed by their entrance?

14. What element of fear is injected by Nora's words at lines 292–293?

15. What feelings are represented by the actions in lines 304–307?

16. Who is the loser in the conflict? Who feels the keenest agony? Why is Maurya "quiet now and easy" (line 340)? Which words of hers, from line 309 to line 325, express her feelings about these tragic experiences? In what spirit is the final speech spoken?

17. Who is the protagonist of the play?

18. Explain the meaning of the title of the tragedy.

19. How long a time elapses during the action of the play? Comment on the compression of the material.

20. Does the play have a turning point? What is the state of affairs at the resolution?

21. State the theme of the tragedy.

22. What particular elements of Synge's style impress you? What part is played by rhythm and repetition in creating his stylistic effects? Point to specific examples.
23. This play has been called a timeless tragedy or a tragedy representing unchanging human experience. Why does it deserve such comments on its universality?

A View from the Bridge

ARTHUR MILLER

Characters

LOUIS
MIKE
ALFIERI
EDDIE
CATHERINE
BEATRICE
MARCO
TONY
RODOLPHO
FIRST IMMIGRATION OFFICER
SECOND IMMIGRATION OFFICER
MR. LIPARI
MRS. LIPARI
TWO "SUBMARINES"
NEIGHBORS

ACT ONE

[*The street and house front of a tenement building. The front is skele-
tal entirely. The main acting area is the living room-dining room of
EDDIE'S apartment. It is a worker's flat, clean, sparse, homely. There is
a rocker down front; a round dining table at center, with chairs; and a
portable phonograph.*   5
*At back are a bedroom door and an opening to the kitchen; none of
these interiors are seen.*
At the right, forestage, a desk. This is MR. ALFIERI'S *law office.
There is also a telephone booth. This is not used until the last scenes,
so it may be covered or left in view.*   10

A *stairway leads up to the apartment, and then farther up to the next
story, which is not seen.*
*Ramps, representing the street, run upstage and off to right and left.
As the curtain rises,* LOUIS *and* MIKE, *longshoremen, are pitching coins
against the building at left.*   15
A distant foghorn blows.
Enter ALFIERI, *a lawyer in his fifties turning gray; he is portly, good-
humored, and thoughtful. The two pitchers nod to him as he passes.
He crosses the stage to his desk, removes his hat, runs his fingers
through his hair, and grinning, speaks to the audience.*]   20

ALFIERI   You wouldn't have known it, but something amusing has just
happened. You see how uneasily they nod to me? That's because I am
a lawyer. In this neighborhood to meet a lawyer or a priest on the
street is unlucky. We're only thought of in connection with disasters,
and they'd rather not get too close.   25

I often think that behind that suspicious little nod of theirs lie
three thousand years of distrust. A lawyer means the law, and in
Sicily, from where their fathers came, the law has not been a
friendly idea since the Greeks were beaten.

I am inclined to notice the ruins in things, perhaps because I was   30
born in Italy. . . . I only came here when I was twenty-five. In those
days, Al Capone, the greatest Carthaginian of all, was learning his
trade on these pavements, and Frankie Yale himself was cut precisely in half by a machine gun on the corner of Union Street, two
blocks away. Oh, there were many here who were justly shot by un-   35
just men. Justice is very important here.

But this is Red Hook, not Sicily. This is the slum that faces the
bay on the seaward side of Brooklyn Bridge. This is the gullet of New
York swallowing the tonnage of the world. And now we are quite
civilized, quite American. Now we settle for half, and I like it better.   40
I no longer keep a pistol in my filing cabinet.

And my practice is entirely unromantic.

My wife has warned me, so have my friends; they tell me the people in this neighborhood lack elegance, glamour. After all, who have
I dealt with in my life? Longshoremen and their wives, and fathers   45
and grandfathers, compensation cases, evictions, family squabbles—
the petty troubles of the poor—and yet . . . every few years there is
still a case, and as the parties tell me what the trouble is, the flat air
in my office suddenly washes in with the green scent of the sea, the
dust in this air is blown away and the thought comes that in some   50
Caesar's year, in Calabria perhaps or on the cliff at Syracuse, another
lawyer, quite differently dressed, heard the same complaint and sat
there as powerless as I, and watched it run its bloody course.

[EDDIE *has appeared and has been pitching coins with the men and*

is highlighted among them. He is forty—a husky, slightly overweight 55
longshoreman.]

This one's name was Eddie Carbone, a longshoreman working the docks from Brooklyn Bridge to the breakwater where the open sea begins.

[ALFIERI *walks into darkness.*] 60

EDDIE [*moving up steps into doorway*]   Well, I'll see ya, fellas.

[CATHERINE *enters from kitchen, crosses down to window, looks out.*]

LOUIS   You workin' tomorrow?

EDDIE   Yeah, there's another day yet on that ship. See ya, Louis.

[EDDIE *goes into the house, as light rises in the apartment.* CATHERINE 65
is waving to LOUIS *from the window and turns to him.*]

CATHERINE   Hi, Eddie!

[*Eddie is pleased and therefore shy about it; he hangs up his cap and jacket.*]

EDDIE   Where you goin' all dressed up? 70

CATHERINE [*running her hands over her skirt*]   I just got it. You like it?

EDDIE   Yeah, it's nice. And what happened to your hair?

CATHERINE   You like it? I fixed it different. [*Calling to kitchen*] He's here, B.!

EDDIE   Beautiful. Turn around, lemme see in the back. [*She turns for him*] 75
Oh, if your mother was alive to see you now! She wouldn't believe it.

CATHERINE   You like it, huh?

EDDIE   You look like one of them girls that went to college. Where you goin'?

CATHERINE [*taking his arm*]   Wait'll B. comes in, I'll tell you something. 80
Here, sit down. [*She is walking him to the armchair. Calling offstage*]
Hurry up, will you, B.?

EDDIE [*sitting*]   What's going on?

CATHERINE   I'll get you a beer, all right?

EDDIE   Well, tell me what happened. Come over here, talk to me. 85

CATHERINE   I want to wait till B. comes in. [*She sits on her heels beside him*] Guess how much we paid for the skirt.

EDDIE   I think it's too short, ain't it?

CATHERINE [*standing*]   No! not when I stand up.

EDDIE   Yeah, but you gotta sit down sometimes. 90

CATHERINE   Eddie, it's the style now. [*She walks to show him.*] I mean, if you see me walkin' down the street——

EDDIE   Listen, you been givin' me the willies the way you walk down the street, I mean it.

CATHERINE   Why? 95

EDDIE   Catherine, I don't want to be a pest, but I'm telling you you're walkin' wavy.

CATHERINE   I'm walkin' wavy?

EDDIE   Now don't aggravate me, Katie, you are walkin' wavy! I don't like the looks they're givin' you in the candy store. And with them new 100 high heels on the sidewalk—clack, clack, clack. The heads are turnin' like windmills.

CATHERINE   But those guys look at all the girls, you know that.

EDDIE   You ain't "all the girls."

CATHERINE   [*almost in tears because he disapproves*]   What do you want 105 me to do? You want me to——

EDDIE   Now don't get mad, kid.

CATHERINE   Well, I don't know what you want from me.

EDDIE   Katie, I promised your mother on her deathbed. I'm responsible for you. You're a baby, you don't understand these things. I mean like 110 when you stand here by the window, wavin' outside.

CATHERINE   I was wavin' to Louis!

EDDIE   Listen, I could tell you things about Louis which you wouldn't wave to him no more.

CATHERINE   [*trying to joke him out of his warning*]   Eddie, I wish there 115 was one guy you couldn't tell me things about!

EDDIE   Catherine, do me a favor, will you? You're gettin' to be a big girl now, you gotta keep yourself more, you can't be so friendly, kid. [*Calls*] Hey, B., what're you doin' in there? [*To Catherine*] Get her in here, will you? I got news for her.   120

CATHERINE   [*starting out*]   What?

EDDIE   Her cousins landed.

CATHERINE   [*clapping her hands together*]   No! [*She turns instantly and starts for the kitchen.*] B.! Your cousins!
[*Beatrice enters, wiping her hands with a towel.*]   125

BEATRICE   [*in the face of* CATHERINE's *shout*]   What?

CATHERINE   Your cousins got in!

BEATRICE   [*astounded, turns to* EDDIE]   What are you talkin' about? Where?

EDDIE   I was just knockin' off work before and Tony Bereli come over to me; he says the ship is in the North River.   130

BEATRICE   [*her hands are clasped at her breast; she seems half in fear, half in unutterable joy*]   They're all right?

EDDIE   He didn't see them yet, they're still on board. But as soon as they get off he'll meet them. He figures about ten o'clock they'll be here.

BEATRICE   [*sits, almost weak from tension*]   And they'll let them off the 135 ship all right? That's fixed, heh?

EDDIE   Sure, they give them regular seamen papers and they walk off with the crew. Don't worry about it, B., there's nothin' to it. Couple of hours they'll be here.

BEATRICE   What happened? They wasn't supposed to be till next Thursday. 140

EDDIE   I don't know; they put them on any ship they can get them out on. Maybe the other ship they was supposed to take there was some danger—What you cryin' about?

BEATRICE [*astounded and afraid*]   I'm—— I just—I can't believe it! I didn't
even buy a new tablecloth; I was gonna wash the walls——   145

EDDIE   Listen, they'll think it's a millionaire's house compared to the way
they live. Don't worry about the walls. They'll be thankful. [*To*
CATHERINE] Whyn't you run down buy a tablecloth. Go ahead, here.
[*He is reaching into his pocket.*]

CATHERINE   There's no stores open now.   150

EDDIE [*to* BEATRICE]   You was gonna put a new cover on the chair.

BEATRICE   I know—well, I thought it was gonna be next week! I was gonna
clean the walls, I was gonna wax the floors.
[*She stands disturbed.*]

CATHERINE [*pointing upward*]   Maybe Mrs. Dondero upstairs——   155

BEATRICE [*of the tablecloth*]   No, hers is worse than this one. [*Suddenly*]
My God, I don't even have nothin' to eat for them!
[*She starts for the kitchen.*]

EDDIE [*reaching out and grabbing her arm*]   Hey, hey! Take it easy.

BEATRICE   No, I'm just nervous, that's all. [*To* CATHERINE] I'll make the   160
fish.

EDDIE   You're savin' their lives, what're you worryin' about the tablecloth?
They probably didn't see a tablecloth in their whole life where they
come from.

BEATRICE [*looking into his eyes*]   I'm just worried about you, that's all I'm   165
worried.

EDDIE   Listen, as long as they know where they're gonna sleep.

BEATRICE   I told them in the letters. They're sleepin' on the floor.

EDDIE   Beatrice, all I'm worried about is you got such a heart that I'll
end up on the floor with you, and they'll be in our bed.   170

BEATRICE   All right, stop it.

EDDIE   Because as soon as you see a tired relative, I end up on the floor.

BEATRICE   When did you end up on the floor?

EDDIE   When your father's house burned down I didn't end up on the
floor?   175

BEATRICE   Well, their house burned down!

EDDIE   Yeah, but it didn't keep burnin' for two weeks!

BEATRICE   All right, look, I'll tell them to go someplace else.
[*She starts into the kitchen.*]

EDDIE   Now wait a minute. Beatrice! [*She halts. He goes to her.*] I just   180
don't want you bein' pushed around, that's all. You got too big a
heart. [*He touches her hand.*] What're you so touchy?

BEATRICE   I'm just afraid if it don't turn out good you'll be mad at me.

EDDIE   Listen, if everybody keeps his mouth shut, nothin' can happen.
They'll pay for their board.   185

BEATRICE   Oh, I told them.

EDDIE   Then what the hell. [*Pause. He moves.*] It's an honor, B. I mean
it. I was just thinkin' before, comin' home, suppose my father didn't

come to this country, and I was starvin' like them over there . . . and
I had people in America could keep me a couple of months? The man   190
would be honored to lend me a place to sleep.

BEATRICE [*There are tears in her eyes. She turns to* CATHERINE]   You see
what he is? [*She turns and grabs* EDDIE's *face in her hands.*] Mmm!
You're an angel! God'll bless you. [*He is gratefully smiling.*] You'll
see, you'll get a blessing for this!   195

EDDIE [*laughing*]   I'll settle for my own bed.

BEATRICE   Go, Baby, set the table.

CATHERINE   We didn't tell him about me yet.

BEATRICE   Let him eat first, then we'll tell him. Bring everything in.
[*She hurries* CATHERINE *out.*]   200

EDDIE [*sitting at the table*]   What's all that about? Where's she goin'?

BEATRICE   Noplace. It's very good news, Eddie. I want you to be happy.

EDDIE   What's goin' on?
[CATHERINE *enters with plates, forks.*]

BEATRICE   She's got a job.   205
[*Pause.* EDDIE *looks at* CATHERINE, *then back to* BEATRICE.]

EDDIE   What job? She's gonna finish school.

CATHERINE   Eddie, you won't believe it——

EDDIE   No——no, you gonna finish school. What kinda job, what do you
mean? All of a sudden you——   210

CATHERINE   Listen a minute, it's wonderful.

EDDIE   It's not wonderful. You'll never get nowheres unless you finish
school. You can't take no job. Why didn't you ask me before you take
a job?

BEATRICE   She's askin' you now, she didn't take nothin' yet.   215

CATHERINE   Listen a minute! I came to school this morning and the principal called me out of the class, see? To go to his office.

EDDIE   Yeah?

CATHERINE   So I went in and he says to me he's got my records, y'know?
And there's a company wants a girl right away. It ain't exactly a sec-   220
retary, it's a stenographer first, but pretty soon you get to be secretary. And he says to me that I'm the best student in the whole
class——

BEATRICE   You hear that?

EDDIE   Well why not? Sure she's the best.   225

CATHERINE   I'm the best student, he says, and if I want, I should take the
job and the end of the year he'll let me take the examination and he'll
give me the certificate. So I'll save practically a year!

EDDIE [*strangely nervous*]   Where's the job? What company?

CATHERINE   It's a big plumbing company over Nostrand Avenue.   230

EDDIE   Nostrand Avenue and where?

CATHERINE   It's someplace by the Navy Yard.

BEATRICE   Fifty dollars a week, Eddie.

EDDIE [*to* CATHERINE, *surprised*]   Fifty?

CATHERINE   I swear.   235

[*Pause.*]

EDDIE   What about all the stuff you wouldn't learn this year, though?

CATHERINE   There's nothin' more to learn, Eddie, I just gotta practice from now on. I know all the symbols and I know the keyboard. I'll just get faster, that's all. And when I'm workin' I'll keep gettin' better   240 and better, you see?

BEATRICE   Work is the best practice anyway.

EDDIE   That ain't what I wanted, though.

CATHERINE   Why! It's a great big company——

EDDIE   I don't like that neighborhood over there.   245

CATHERINE   It's a block and half from the subway, he says.

EDDIE   Near the Navy Yard plenty can happen in a block and a half. And a plumbin' company! That's one step over the water front. They're practically longshoremen.

BEATRICE   Yeah, but she'll be in the office, Eddie.   250

EDDIE   I know she'll be in the office, but that ain't what I had in mind.

BEATRICE   Listen, she's gotta go to work sometime.

EDDIE   Listen, B., she'll be with a lotta plumbers? And sailors up and down the street? So what did she go to school for?

CATHERINE   But it's fifty a week, Eddie.   255

EDDIE   Look, did I ask you for money? I supported you this long I support you a little more. Please, do me a favor, will ya? I want you to be with different kind of people. I want you to be in a nice office. Maybe a lawyer's office someplace in New York in one of them nice buildings. I mean if you're gonna get outa here then get out; don't   260 go practically in the same kind of neighborhood.

[*Pause.* CATHERINE *lowers her eyes.*]

BEATRICE   Go, Baby, bring in the supper. [CATHERINE *goes out.*] Think about it a little bit, Eddie. Please. She's crazy to start work. It's not a little shop, it's a big company. Some day she could be a secretary.   265 They picked her out of the whole class. [*He is silent, staring down at the tablecloth, fingering the pattern.*] What are you worried about? She could take care of herself. She'll get out of the subway and be in the office in two minutes.

EDDIE [*somehow sickened*]   I know that neighborhood, B., I don't like it.   270

BEATRICE   Listen, if nothin' happened to her in this neighborhood it ain't gonna happen noplace else. [*She turns his face to her.*] Look, you gotta get used to it, she's no baby no more. Tell her to take it. [*He turns his head away.*] You hear me? [*She is angering.*] I don't understand you; she's seventeen years old, you gonna keep her in the house   275 all her life?

EDDIE [*insulted*]   What kinda remark is that?

BEATRICE [*with sympathy but insistent force*]   Well, I don't understand when it ends. First it was gonna be when she graduated high school, so she graduated high school. Then it was gonna be when she learned 280 stenographer, so she learned stenographer. So what're we gonna wait for now? I mean it, Eddie, sometimes I don't understand you; they picked her out of the whole class, it's an honor for her.

[CATHERINE *enters with food, which she silently sets on the table. After a moment of watching her face,* EDDIE *breaks into a smile, but* 285 *it almost seems that tears will form in his eyes.*]

EDDIE   With your hair that way you look like a madonna, you know that? You're the madonna type. [*She doesn't look at him, but continues ladling out food onto the plates.*] You wanna go to work, heh, Madonna? 290

CATHERINE [*softly*]   Yeah.

EDDIE [*with a sense of her childhood, her babyhood, and the years*]   All right, go to work. [*She looks at him, then rushes and hugs him.*] Hey, hey! Take it easy! [*He holds her face away from him to look at her.*] What're you cryin' about? [*He is affected by her, but smiles his emo-* 295 *tion away.*]

CATHERINE [*sitting at her place*]   I just——[*Bursting out*] I'm gonna buy all new dishes with my first pay! [*They laugh warmly.*] I mean it. I'll fix up the whole house! I'll buy a rug!

EDDIE   And then you'll move away. 300

CATHERINE   No, Eddie!

EDDIE [*grinning*]   Why not? That's life. And you'll come visit on Sundays, then once a month, then Christmas and New Year's, finally.

CATHERINE [*grasping his arm to reassure him and to erase the accusation*] No, please! 305

EDDIE [*smiling but hurt*]   I only ask you one thing—don't trust nobody. You got a good aunt but she's got too big a heart, you learned bad from her. Believe me.

BEATRICE   Be the way you are, Katie, don't listen to him.

EDDIE [*to* BEATRICE—*strangely and quickly resentful*]   You lived in a house 310 all your life, what do you know about it? You never worked in your life.

BEATRICE   She likes people. What's wrong with that?

EDDIE   Because most people ain't people. She's goin' to work; plumbers; they'll chew her to pieces if she don't watch out. [*To* CATHERINE] 315 Believe me, Katie, the less you trust, the less you be sorry.

[EDDIE *crosses himself and the women do the same, and they eat.*]

CATHERINE   First thing I'll buy is a rug, heh, B.?

BEATRICE   I don't mind. [*To* EDDIE] I smelled coffee all day today. You unloadin' coffee today? 320

EDDIE   Yeah, a Brazil ship.

CATHERINE   I smelled it too. It smelled all over the neighborhood.

EDDIE   That's one time, boy, to be a longshoreman is a pleasure. I could work coffee ships twenty hours a day. You go down in the hold, y'know? It's like flowers, that smell. We'll bust a bag tomorrow, I'll bring you some. 325

BEATRICE   Just be sure there's no spiders in it, will ya? I mean it. [*She directs this to* CATHERINE, *rolling her eyes upward.*] I still remember that spider coming out of that bag he brung home. I nearly died.

EDDIE   You call that a spider? You oughta see what comes outa the bananas 330 sometimes.

BEATRICE   Don't talk about it!

EDDIE   I seen spiders could stop a Buick.

BEATRICE [*clapping her hands over her ears*]   All right, shut up!

EDDIE [*laughing and taking a watch out of his pocket*]   Well, who started 335 with spiders?

BEATRICE   All right, I'm sorry, I didn't mean it. Just don't bring none home again. What time is it?

EDDIE   Quarter nine. [*Puts watch back in his pocket.*]
[*They continue eating in silence.*] 340

CATHERINE   He's bringin' them ten o'clock, Tony?

EDDIE   Around, yeah. [*He eats.*]

CATHERINE   Eddie, suppose somebody asks if they're livin' here. [*He looks at her as though already she had divulged something publicly. Defensively*] I mean if they ask. 345

EDDIE   Now look, Baby, I can see we're gettin' mixed up again here.

CATHERINE   No, I just mean . . . people'll see them goin' in and out.

EDDIE   I don't care who sees them goin' in and out as long as you don't see them goin' in and out. And this goes for you too, B. You don't see nothin' and you don't know nothin'. 350

BEATRICE   What do you mean? I understand.

EDDIE   You don't understand; you still think you can talk about this to somebody just a little bit. Now lemme say it once and for all, because you're makin' me nervous again, both of you. I don't care if somebody comes in the house and sees them sleepin' on the floor, it never comes 355 out of your mouth who they are or what they're doin' here.

BEATRICE   Yeah, but my mother'll know——

EDDIE   Sure she'll know, but just don't you be the one who told her, that's all. This is the United States government you're playin' with now, this is the Immigration Bureau. If you said it you knew it, if you 360 didn't say it you didn't know it.

CATHERINE   Yeah, but Eddie, suppose somebody——

EDDIE   I don't care what question it is. You—don't—know—nothin'. They got stool pigeons all over this neighborhood they're payin' them every week for information, and you don't know who they are. It could be 365 your best friend. You hear? [*To* BEATRICE] Like Vinny Bolzano, remember Vinny?

BEATRICE Oh, yeah. God forbid.

EDDIE Tell her about Vinny. [*To* CATHERINE] You think I'm blowin' steam here? [*To* BEATRICE] Go ahead, tell her. [*To* CATHERINE] You was a 370 baby then. There was a family lived next door to her mother, he was about sixteen——

BEATRICE No, he was no more than fourteen, cause I was to his confirmation in Saint Agnes. But the family had an uncle that they were hidin' in the house, and he snitched to the Immigration. 375

CATHERINE The kid snitched?

EDDIE On his own uncle!

CATHERINE What, was he crazy?

EDDIE He was crazy after, I tell you that, boy.

BEATRICE Oh, it was terrible. He had five brothers and the old father. 380 And they grabbed him in the kitchen and pulled him down the stairs —three flights his head was bouncin' like a coconut. And they spit on him in the street, his own father and his brothers. The whole neighborhood was cryin'.

CATHERINE Ts! So what happened to him? 385

BEATRICE I think he went away. [*To* EDDIE] I never seen him again, did you?

EDDIE [*rises during this, taking out his watch*] Him? You'll never see him no more, a guy do a thing like that? How's he gonna show his face? [*To* CATHERINE, *as he gets up uneasily*] Just remember, kid, you can 390 quicker get back a million dollars that was stole than a word that you gave away. [*He is standing now, stretching his back.*]

CATHERINE Okay, I won't say a word to nobody, I swear.

EDDIE Gonna rain tomorrow. We'll be slidin' all over the decks. Maybe you oughta put something on for them, they be here soon. 395

BEATRICE I only got fish, I hate to spoil it if they ate already. I'll wait, it only takes a few minutes; I could broil it.

CATHERINE What happens, Eddie, when that ship pulls out and they ain't on it, though? Don't the captain say nothin'?

EDDIE [*slicing an apple with his pocket knife*] Captain's pieced off, what 400 do you mean?

CATHERINE Even the captain?

EDDIE What's the matter, the captain don't have to live? Captain gets a piece, maybe one of the mates, piece for the guy in Italy who fixed the papers for them, Tony here'll get a little bite. . . . 405

BEATRICE I just hope they get work here, that's all I hope.

EDDIE Oh, the syndicate'll fix jobs for them; till they pay 'em off they'll get them work every day. It's after the pay-off, then they'll have to scramble like the rest of us.

BEATRICE Well, it be better than they got there. 410

EDDIE Oh sure, well, listen. So you gonna start Monday, eh, Madonna?

CATHERINE [*embarrassed*]   I'm supposed to, yeah.

[EDDIE *is standing facing the two seated women. First* BEATRICE *smiles, then* CATHERINE, *for a powerful emotion is on him, a childish one and a knowing fear, and the tears show in his eyes—and they are shy before the avowal.*]   415

EDDIE [*sadly smiling, yet somehow proud of her*]   Well . . . I hope you have good luck. I wish you the best. You know that, kid.

CATHERINE [*rising, trying to laugh*]   You sound like I'm goin' a million miles!   420

EDDIE   I know. I guess I just never figured on one thing.

CATHERINE [*smiling*]   What?

EDDIE   That you would ever grow up. [*He utters a soundless laugh at himself, feeling his breast pocket of his shirt.*] I left a cigar in my other coat, I think. [*He starts for the bedroom.*]   425

CATHERINE   Stay here! I'll get it for you.

[*She hurries out. There is a slight pause, and* EDDIE *turns to* BEATRICE, *who has been avoiding his gaze.*]

EDDIE   What are you mad at me lately?

BEATRICE   Who's mad? [*She gets up, clearing the dishes.*]   I'm not mad.   430
[*She picks up the dishes and turns to him.*] You're the one is mad.
[*She turns and goes into the kitchen as* CATHERINE *enters from the bedroom with a cigar and a pack of matches.*]

CATHERINE   Here! I'll light it for you! [*She strikes a match and holds it to his cigar. He puffs. Quietly*] Don't worry about me, Eddie, heh?   435

EDDIE   Don't burn yourself. [*Just in time she blows out the match.*] You better go in help her with the dishes.

CATHERINE [*turns quickly to the table, and, seeing the table cleared, she says almost guiltily*]   Oh! [*She hurries into the kitchen, and as she exits there*]   I'll do the dishes, B.!   440

[*Alone,* EDDIE *stands looking toward the kitchen for a moment. Then he takes out his watch, glances at it, replaces it in his pocket, sits in the armchair, and stares at the smoke flowing out of his mouth.*

The lights go down, then come up on ALFIERI, *who has moved onto the forestage.*]   445

ALFIERI   He was as good a man as he had to be in a life that was hard and even. He worked on the piers when there was work, he brought home his pay, and he lived. And toward ten o'clock of that night, after they had eaten, the cousins came.

[*The lights fade on* ALFIERI *and rise on the street.*   450

Enter TONY, *escorting* MARCO *and* RODOLPHO, *each with a valise.* TONY *halts, indicates the house. They stand for a moment looking at it.*]

MARCO [*He is a square-built peasant of thirty-two, suspicious, tender, and quiet-voiced*]   Thank you.

TONY   You're on your own now. Just be careful, that's all. Ground floor.   455

MARCO   Thank you.

TONY [*indicating the house*]   I'll see you on the pier tomorrow. You'll go
to work.

[MARCO *nods.* TONY *continues on walking down the street.*]

RODOLPHO   This will be the first house I ever walked into in America! 460
Imagine! She said they were poor!

MARCO   Ssh! Come. [*They go to the door.*]

[MARCO *knocks. The lights rise in the room.* EDDIE *goes and opens
the door. Enter* MARCO *and* RODOLPHO, *removing their caps.* BEATRICE
and CATHERINE *enter from the kitchen. The lights fade in the street.*] 465

EDDIE   You Marco?

MARCO   Marco.

EDDIE   Come on in! [*He shakes* MARCO'S *hand.*]

BEATRICE   Here, take the bags!

MARCO [*nods, looks to the women and fixes on* BEATRICE. *Crosses to* BEA- 470
TRICE]   Are you my cousin?

[*She nods. He kisses her hand.*]

BEATRICE [*above the table, touching her chest with her hand*]   Beatrice.
This is my husband, Eddie. [*All nod.*] Catherine, my sister Nancy's
daughter. [*The brothers nod.*]   475

MARCO [*indicating* RODOLPHO]   My brother. Rodolpho. [RODOLPHO *nods.*
MARCO *comes with a certain formal stiffness to* EDDIE]   I want to tell
you now Eddie—when you say go, we will go.

EDDIE   Oh, no . . . [*Take's* MARCO'S *bag.*]

MARCO   I see it's a small house, but soon, maybe, we can have our own 480
house.

EDDIE   You're welcome, Marco, we got plenty of room here. Katie, give
them supper, heh? [*Exits into bedroom with their bags.*]

CATHERINE   Come here, sit down. I'll get you some soup.

MARCO [*as they go to the table*]   We ate on the ship. Thank you. [*To* EDDIE, 485
calling off to bedroom]   Thank you.

BEATRICE   Get some coffee. We'll all have coffee. Come sit down.

[RODOLPHO *and* MARCO *sit, at the table.*]

CATHERINE [*wondrously*]   How come he's so dark and you're so light,
Rodolpho?   490

RODOLPHO [*ready to laugh*]   I don't know. A thousand years ago, they say,
the Danes invaded Sicily.

[*Beatrice kisses* RODOLPHO. *They laugh as* EDDIE *enters.*]

CATHERINE [*to* BEATRICE]   He's practically blond!

EDDIE   How's the coffee doin'?   495

CATHERINE [*brought up*]   I'm gettin' it. [*She hurries out to kitchen.*]

EDDIE [*sits on his rocker*]   Yiz have a nice trip?

MARCO   The ocean is always rough. But we are good sailors.

EDDIE   No trouble gettin' here?

MARCO   No. The man brought us. Very nice man.   500

RODOLPHO [*to* EDDIE]   He says we start to work tomorrow. Is he honest?

EDDIE [*laughing*]   No. But as long as you owe them money, they will get you plenty of work. [*To* MARCO]   Yiz ever work on the piers in Italy?

MARCO   Piers? Ts—no.   505

RODOLPHO [*smiling at the smallness of his town*]   In our town there are no piers, only the beach, and little fishing boats.

BEATRICE   So what kinda work did yiz do?

MARCO [*shrugging shyly, even embarrassed*]   Whatever there is, anything.

RODOLPHO   Sometimes they build a house, or if they fix the bridge—Marco 510
is a mason and I bring him the cement. [*He laughs.*] In harvest time we work in the fields . . . if there is work. Anything.

EDDIE   Still bad there, heh?

MARCO   Bad, yes.

RODOLPHO [*laughing*]   It's terrible! We stand around all day in the piazza 515
listening to the fountain like birds. Everybody waits only for the train.

BEATRICE   What's on the train?

RODOLPHO   Nothing. But if there are many passengers and you're lucky you make a few lire to push the taxi up the hill.

[*Enter* CATHERINE; *she listens.*]   520

BEATRICE   You gotta push a taxi?

RODOLPHO [*laughing*]   Oh, sure! It's a feature in our town. The horses in our town are skinnier than goats. So if there are too many passengers we help to push the carriages up to the hotel. [*He laughs.*] In our town the horses are only for show.   525

CATHERINE   Why don't they have automobile taxis?

RODOLPHO   There is one. We push that too. [*They laugh.*] Everything in our town, you gotta push!

BEATRICE [*to* EDDIE]   How do you like that!

EDDIE [*to* MARCO]   So what're you wanna do, you gonna stay here in this 530
country or you wanna go back?

MARCO [*surprised*]   Go back?

EDDIE   Well, you're married, ain't you?

MARCO   Yes. I have three children.

BEATRICE   Three! I thought only one.   535

MARCO   Oh, no. I have three now. Four years, five years, six years.

BEATRICE   Ah . . . I bet they're cryin' for you already, heh?

MARCO   What can I do? The older one is sick in his chest. My wife—she feeds them from her own mouth. I tell you the truth, if I stay there they will never grow up. They eat the sunshine.   540

BEATRICE   My God. So how long you want to stay?

MARCO   With your permission, we will stay maybe a——

EDDIE   She don't mean in this house, she means in the country.

MARCO   Oh. Maybe four, five, six years, I think.

RODOLPHO [*smiling*]   He trusts his wife.   545

BEATRICE   Yeah, but maybe you'll get enough, you'll be able to go back quicker.

MARCO   I hope. I don't know. [*To* EDDIE] I understand it's not so good here either.

EDDIE   Oh, you guys'll be all right—till you pay them off, anyway. After 550 that, you'll have to scramble, that's all. But you'll make better here than you could there.

RODOLPHO   How much? We hear all kinds of figures. How much can a man make? We work hard, we'll work all day, all night——

[MARCO *raises a hand to hush him.*]   555

EDDIE   [*He is coming more and more to address* MARCO *only*]   On the average a whole year? Maybe—well, it's hard to say, see. Sometimes we lay off, there's no ships three four weeks.

MARCO   Three, four weeks!—Ts!

EDDIE   But I think you could probably—thirty, forty a week, over the 560 whole twelve months of the year.

MARCO   [*rises, crosses to* EDDIE]   Dollars.

EDDIE   Sure dollars.

[MARCO *puts an arm round* RODOLPHO *and they laugh.*]

MARCO   If we can stay here a few months, Beatrice——   565

BEATRICE   Listen, you're welcome, Marco——

MARCO   Because I could send them a little more if I stay here.

BEATRICE   As long as you want, we got plenty a room.

MARCO   [*his eyes are showing tears*]   My wife——[*To* EDDIE] My wife —I want to send right away maybe twenty dollars——   570

EDDIE   You could send them something next week already.

MARCO   [*He is near tears*]   Eduardo . . . [*He goes to* EDDIE, *offering his hand.*]

EDDIE   Don't thank me. Listen, what the hell, it's no skin off me. [*To* CATHE-RINE] What happened to the coffee?   575

CATHERINE   I got it on. [*To* RODOLPHO] You married too? No.

RODOLPHO   [*rises*]   Oh, no . . .

BEATRICE   [*to* CATHERINE]   I told you he——

CATHERINE   I know, I just thought maybe he got married recently.

RODOLPHO   I have no money to get married. I have a nice face, but no 580 money. [*He laughs.*]

CATHERINE   [*to* BEATRICE]   He's a real blond!

BEATRICE   [*to* RODOLPHO]   You want to stay here too, heh? For good?

RODOLPHO   Me? Yes, forever! Me, I want to be an American. And then I want to go back to Italy when I am rich, and I will buy a motorcycle. 585 [*He smiles.* MARCO *shakes him affectionately.*]

CATHERINE   A motorcycle!

RODOLPHO   With a motorcycle in Italy you will never starve any more.

BEATRICE   I'll get you coffee. [*She exits to the kitchen.*]

EDDIE   What you do with a motorcycle?   590
MARCO   He dreams, he dreams.
RODOLPHO [*to* MARCO]   Why? [*To* EDDIE]   Messages! The rich people in
   the hotel always need someone who will carry a message. But quickly,
   and with a great noise. With a blue motorcycle I would station myself in the courtyard of the hotel, and in a little while I would have   595
   messages.
MARCO   When you have no wife you have dreams.
EDDIE   Why can't you just walk, or take a trolley or sump'm?
   [*Enter* BEATRICE *with coffee.*]
RODOLPHO   Oh, no, the machine, the machine is necessary. A man comes   600
   into a great hotel and says, I am a messenger. Who is this man? He
   disappears walking, there is no noise, nothing. Maybe he will never
   come back, maybe he will never deliver the message. But a man who
   rides up on a great machine, this man is responsible, this man exists.
   He will be given messages. [*He helps* BEATRICE *set out the coffee*   605
   things.] I am also a singer, though.
EDDIE   You mean a regular——?
RODOLPHO   Oh, yes. One night last year Andreola got sick. Baritone. And
   I took his place in the garden of the hotel. Three arias I sang without
   a mistake! Thousand-lire notes they threw from the tables, money was   610
   falling like a storm in the treasury. It was magnificent. We lived six
   months on that night, eh, Marco?
   [MARCO *nods doubtfully.*]
MARCO   Two months.
   [EDDIE *laughs.*]   615
BEATRICE   Can't you get a job in that place?
RODOLPHO   Andreola got better. He's a baritone, very strong.
   [BEATRICE *laughs.*]
MARCO [*regretfully to* BEATRICE]   He sang too loud.
RODOLPHO   Why too loud?   620
MARCO   Too loud. The guests in that hotel are all Englishmen. They don't
   like too loud.
RODOLPHO [*to* CATHERINE]   Nobody ever said it was too loud!
MARCO   I say. It was too loud. [*To* BEATRICE] I knew it as soon as he started
   to sing. Too loud.   625
RODOLPHO   Then why did they throw so much money?
MARCO   They paid for your courage. The English like courage. But once
   is enough.
RODOLPHO [*to all but* MARCO]   I never heard anybody say it was too loud.
CATHERINE   Did you ever hear of jazz?   630
RODOLPHO   Oh, sure! I *sing* jazz.
CATHERINE [*rises*]   You could sing jazz?
RODOLPHO   Oh, I sing Napolidan, jazz, bel canto——I sing "Paper Doll,"
   you like "Paper Doll"?

CATHERINE   Oh, sure, I'm crazy for "Paper Doll." Go ahead, sing it. 635
[RODOLPHO *takes his stance after getting a nod of permission from*
MARCO, *and with a high tenor voice begins singing*]

I'll tell you boys it's tough to be alone,
And it's tough to love a doll that's not your own.
I'm through with all of them, 640
I'll never fall again,
Hey, boy, what you gonna do?
I'm gonna buy a paper doll that I can call my own,
A doll that other fellows cannot steal.

[EDDIE *rises and moves upstage.*] 645

And then those flirty, flirty guys
With their flirty, flirty eyes
Will have to flirt with dollies that are real——

EDDIE   Hey, kid—hey, wait a minute——
CATHERINE [*enthralled*]   Leave him finish, it's beautiful! [*To* BEATRICE] 650
He's terrific! It's terrific, Rodolpho.
EDDIE   Look, kid; you don't want to be picked up, do you?
MARCO   No—no! [*He rises.*]
EDDIE [*indicating the rest of the building*]   Because we never had no
singers here . . . and all of a sudden there's a singer in the house, 655
y'know what I mean?
MARCO   Yes, Yes. You'll be quiet, Rodolpho.
EDDIE [*He is flushed*]   They got guys all over the place, Marco. I mean.
MARCO   Yes. He'll be quiet. [*To* RUDOLPHO] You'll be quiet.
[RODOLPHO *nods.* EDDIE *has risen, with iron control, even a smile. He* 660
moves to CATHERINE.]
EDDIE   What's the high heels for, Garbo?
CATHERINE   I figured for tonight——
EDDIE   Do me a favor, will you? Go ahead.
[*Embarrassed now, angered,* CATHERINE *goes out into the bedroom.* 665
BEATRICE *watches her go and gets up; in passing, she gives* EDDIE *a*
cold look, restrained only by the strangers, and goes to the table to
pour coffee.]
EDDIE [*striving to laugh, and to* MARCO, *but directed as much to* BEATRICE]
All actresses they want to be around here. 670
RODOLPHO [*happy about it*]   In Italy too! All the girls.
[CATHERINE *emerges from the bedroom in low-heel shoes, comes to*
the table. RODOLPHO *is lifting a cup.*]
EDDIE [*He is sizing up* RODOLPHO, *and there is a concealed suspicion*]
Yeah, heh? 675

RODOLPHO   Yes! [*Laughs, indicating* CATHERINE]   Especially when they are so beautiful!

CATHERINE   You like sugar?

RODOLPHO   Sugar? Yes! I like sugar very much!

[EDDIE *is downstage, watching as she pours a spoonful of sugar into his cup, his face puffed with trouble, and the room dies.* 680

Lights rise on ALFIERI.]

ALFIERI   Who can ever know what will be discovered? Eddie Carbone had never expected to have a destiny. A man works, raises his family, goes bowling, eats, gets old, and then he dies. Now, as the weeks 685 passed, there was a future, there was a trouble that would not go away.

[*The lights fade on* ALFIERI, *then rise on* EDDIE *standing at the doorway of the house.* BEATRICE *enters on the street. She sees* EDDIE, *smiles at him. He looks away.* 690

She starts to enter the house when EDDIE *speaks.*]

EDDIE   It's after eight.

BEATRICE   Well, it's a long show at the Paramount.

EDDIE   They must've seen every picture in Brooklyn by now. He's supposed to stay in the house when he ain't working. He ain't supposed 695 to go advertising himself.

BEATRICE   Well, that's his trouble, what do you care? If they pick him up they pick him up, that's all. Come in the house.

EDDIE   What happened to the stenography? I don't see her practice no more. 700

BEATRICE   She'll get back to it. She's excited, Eddie.

EDDIE   She tell you anything?

BEATRICE [*comes to him, now the subject is opened*]   What's the matter with you? He's a nice kid, what do you want from him?

EDDIE   That's a nice kid? He gives me the heeby-jeebies. 705

BEATRICE [*smiling*]   Ah, go on, you're just jealous.

EDDIE   Of *him*? Boy, you don't think much of me.

BEATRICE   I don't understand you. What's so terrible about him?

EDDIE   You mean it's all right with you? That's gonna be her husband?

BEATRICE   Why? He's a nice fella, hard workin', he's a good-lookin' fella. 710

EDDIE   He sings on the ships, didja know that?

BEATRICE   What do you mean, he sings?

EDDIE   Just what I said, he sings. Right on the deck, all of a sudden, a whole song comes out of his mouth—with motions. You know what they're callin' him now? Paper Doll they're callin' him, Canary. He's 715 like a weird. He comes out on the pier, one-two-three, it's a regular free show.

BEATRICE   Well, he's a kid; he don't know how to behave himself yet.

EDDIE   And with that wacky hair; he's like a chorus girl or sump'm.

BEATRICE So he's blond, so—— 720

EDDIE I just hope that's his regular hair, that's all I hope.

BEATRICE You crazy or sump'm? [*She tries to turn him to her.*]

EDDIE [*He keeps his head turned away*] What's so crazy? I don't like his whole way.

BEATRICE Listen, you never seen a blond guy in your life? What about 725 Whitey Balso?

EDDIE [*turning to her victoriously*] Sure, but Whitey don't sing; he don't do like that on the ships.

BEATRICE Well, maybe that's the way they do in Italy.

EDDIE Then why don't his brother sing? Marco goes around like a man; 730 nobody kids Marco. [*He moves from her, halts. She realizes there is a campaign solidified in him.*] I tell you the truth I'm surprised I have to tell you all this. I mean I'm surprised, B.

BEATRICE [*She goes to him with purpose now*] Listen, you ain't gonna start nothin' here. 735

EDDIE I ain't startin' nothin', but I ain't gonna stand around lookin' at that. For that character I didn't bring her up. I swear, B., I'm surprised at you; I sit there waitin' for you to wake up but everything is great with you.

BEATRICE No, everything ain't great with me. 740

EDDIE No?

BEATRICE No. But I got other worries.

EDDIE Yeah. [*He is already weakening.*]

BEATRICE Yeah, you want me to tell you?

EDDIE [*in retreat*] Why? What worries you got? 745

BEATRICE When am I gonna be a wife again, Eddie?

EDDIE I ain't been feeling good. They bother me since they came.

BEATRICE It's almost three months you don't feel good; they're only here a couple of weeks. It's three months, Eddie.

EDDIE I don't know, B. I don't want to talk about it. 750

BEATRICE What's the matter, Eddie, you don't like me, heh?

EDDIE What do you mean, I don't like you? I said I don't feel good, that's all.

BEATRICE Well, tell me, am I doing something wrong? Talk to me.

EDDIE [*Pause. He can't speak, then*] I can't. I can't talk about it. 755

BEATRICE Well tell me what——

EDDIE I got nothin' to say about it!

[*She stands for a moment; he is looking off; she turns to go into the house.*]

EDDIE I'll be all right, B.; just lay off me, will ya? I'm worried about her. 760

BEATRICE The girl is gonna be eighteen years old, it's time already.

EDDIE B., he's taking her for a ride!

BEATRICE All right, that's her ride. What're you gonna stand over her

till she's forty? Eddie, I want you to cut it out now, you hear me?
I don't like it! Now come in the house.   765
EDDIE   I want to take a walk, I'll be in right away.
BEATRICE   They ain't goin' to come any quicker if you stand in the street.
It ain't nice, Eddie.
EDDIE   I'll be in right away. Go ahead. [*He walks off.*]
[*She goes into the house.* EDDIE *glances up the street, sees* LOUIS *and*   770
MIKE *coming, and sits on an iron railing.* LOUIS *and* MIKE *enter.*]
LOUIS   Wanna go bowlin' tonight?
EDDIE   I'm too tired. Goin' to sleep.
LOUIS   How's your two submarines?
EDDIE   They're okay.   775
LOUIS   I see they're gettin' work allatime.
EDDIE   Oh yeah, they're doin' all right.
MIKE   That's what we oughta do. We oughta leave the country and come
in under the water. Then we get work.
EDDIE   You ain't kiddin'.   780
LOUIS   Well, what the hell. Y'know?
EDDIE   Sure.
LOUIS   [*sits on railing beside* EDDIE]   Believe me, Eddie, you got a lotta
credit comin' to you.
EDDIE   Aah, they don't bother me, don't cost me nutt'n.   785
MIKE   That older one, boy, he's a regular bull. I seen him the other day
liftin' coffee bags over the Matson Line. They leave him alone he
woulda load the whole ship by himself.
EDDIE   Yeah, he's a strong guy, that guy. Their father was a regular
giant, supposed to be.   790
LOUIS   Yeah, you could see. He's a regular slave.
MIKE   [*grinning*]   That blond one, though——[EDDIE *looks at him.*] He's
got a sense of humor. [LOUIS *snickers.*]
EDDIE   [*searchingly*]   Yeah. He's funny——
MIKE   [*starting to laugh*]   Well he ain't exackly funny, but he's always like   795
makin' remarks like, y'know? He comes around, everybody's laughin'.
[LOUIS *laughs.*]
EDDIE   [*uncomfortably, grinning*]   Yeah, well . . . he's got a sense of humor.
MIKE   [*laughing*]   Yeah, I mean, he's always makin' like remarks, like,
y'know?   800
EDDIE   Yeah, I know. But he's a kid yet, y'know? He—he's just a kid, that's
all.
MIKE   [*geting hysterical with* LOUIS]   I know. You take one look at him—
everybody's happy. [LOUIS *laughs.*] I worked one day with him last
week over the Moore-MacCormack Line, I'm tellin' you they was all   805
hysterical. [LOUIS *and he explode in laughter.*]
EDDIE   Why? What'd he do?
MIKE   I don't know . . . he was just humorous. You never can remember

what he says, y'know? But it's the way he says it. I mean he gives
you a look sometimes and you start laughin'!   810
EDDIE   Yeah. [*Troubled*] He's got a sense of humor.
MIKE [*gasping*]   Yeah.
LOUIS [*rising*]   Well, we see ya, Eddie.
EDDIE   Take it easy.
LOUIS   Yeah. See ya.   815
MIKE   If you wanna come bowlin' later we're goin' Flatbush Avenue.
    [*Laughing, they move to exit, meeting* RODOLPHO *and* CATHERINE *en-
    tering on the street. Their laughter rises as they see* RODOLPHO, *who
    does not understand but joins in.* EDDIE *moves to enter the house as*
    LOUIS *and* MIKE *exit.* CATHERINE *stops him at the door.*]   820
CATHERINE   Hey, Eddie—what a picture we saw! Did we laugh!
EDDIE [*He can't help smiling at sight of her*]   Where'd you go?
CATHERINE   Paramount. It was with those two guys, y'know? That—
EDDIE   Brooklyn Paramount?
CATHERINE [*with an edge of anger, embarrassed before* RODOLPHO]   Sure, 825
    the Brooklyn Paramount. I told you we wasn't goin' to New York.
EDDIE [*retreating before the threat of her anger*]   All right, I only asked
    you. [*To* RODOLPHO]   I just don't want her hangin' around Times
    Square, see? It's full of tramps over there.
RODOLPHO   I would like to go to Broadway once, Eddie. I would like to 830
    walk with her once where the theaters are and the opera. Since I
    was a boy I see pictures of those lights.
EDDIE [*his little patience waning*]   I want to talk to her a minute, Rodolpho.
    Go inside, will you?
RODOLPHO   Eddie, we only walk together in the streets. She teaches me. 835
CATHERINE   You know what he can't get over? That there's no fountains
    in Brooklyn!
EDDIE [*smiling unwillingly*]   Fountains? [RODOLPHO *smiles at his own
    naïveté.*]
CATHERINE   In Italy he says, every town's got fountains, and they meet 840
    there. And you know what? They got oranges on the trees where he
    comes from, and lemons. Imagine—on the trees? I mean it's interest-
    ing. But he's crazy for New York.
RODOLPHO [*attempting familiarity*]   Eddie, why can't we go once to
    Broadway——?   845
EDDIE   Look, I gotta tell her something——
RODOLPHO   Maybe you can come too. I want to see all those lights. [*He
    sees no response in* EDDIE's *face. He glances at* CATHERINE.]   I'll walk
    by the river before I go to sleep. [*He walks off down the street.*]
CATHERINE   Why don't you talk to him, Eddie? He blesses you, and you 850
    don't talk to him hardly.
EDDIE [*enveloping her with his eyes*]   I bless you and you don't talk to
    me. [*He tries to smile.*]

CATHERINE   *I* don't talk to you? [*She hits his arm.*] What do you mean?

EDDIE   I don't see you no more. I come home you're runnin' around some-   855
place——

CATHERINE   Well, he wants to see everything, that's all, so we go . . .
You mad at me?

EDDIE   No. [*He moves from her, smiling sadly.*] It's just I used to come
home, you was always there. Now, I turn around, you're a big girl. I   860
don't know how to talk to you.

CATHERINE   Why?

EDDIE   I don't know, you're runnin', you're runnin', Katie. I don't think you
listening anymore to me.

CATHERINE [*going to him*]   Ah, Eddie, sure I am. What's the matter? You   865
don't like him?
[*Slight pause.*]

EDDIE [*turns to her*]   *You* like him, Katie?

CATHERINE [*with a blush but holding her ground*]   Yeah. I like him.

EDDIE [*his smile goes*]   You like him.   870

CATHERINE [*looking down*]   Yeah. [*Now she looks at him for the conse-
quences, smiling but tense. He looks at her like a lost boy.*] What're
you got against him? I don't understand. He only blesses you.

EDDIE [*turns away*]   He don't bless me, Katie.

CATHERINE   He does! You're like a father to him!   875

EDDIE [*turns to her*]   Katie.

CATHERINE   What, Eddie?

EDDIE   You gonna marry him?

CATHERINE   I don't know. We just been . . . goin' around, that's all. [*Turns
to him*] What're you got against him, Eddie? Please, tell me. What?   880

EDDIE   He don't respect you.

CATHERINE   Why?

EDDIE   Katie . . . if you wasn't an orphan, wouldn't he ask your father's
permission before he run around with you like this?

CATHERINE   Oh, well, he didn't think you'd mind.   885

EDDIE   He knows I mind, but it don't bother him if I mind, don't you
see that?

CATHERINE   No, Eddie, he's got all kinds of respect for me. And you too!
We walk across the street he takes my arm—he almost bows to me!
You got him all wrong, Eddie; I mean it, you——   890

EDDIE   Katie, he's only bowin' to his passport.

CATHERINE   His passport!

EDDIE   That's right. He marries you he's got the right to be an American
citizen. That's what's goin' on here. [*She is puzzled and surprised.*]
You understand what I'm tellin' you? The guy is lookin' for his break,   895
that's all he's lookin' for.

CATHERINE [*pained*]   Oh, no, Eddie, I don't think so.

EDDIE   You don't think so! Katie, you're gonna make me cry here. Is that a workin' man? What does he do with his first money? A snappy new jacket he buys, records, a pointy pair new shoes and his brother's kids are starvin' over there with tuberculosis? That's a hit-and-run guy, baby; he's got bright lights in his head, Broadway. Them guys don't think of nobody but theirself! You marry him and the next time you see him it'll be for a divorce! 900

CATHERINE   [*steps toward him*]   Eddie, he never said a word about his papers or—— 905

EDDIE   You mean he's supposed to tell you that?

CATHERINE   I don't think he's even thinking about it.

EDDIE   What's better for him to think about! He could be picked up any day here and he's back pushin' taxis up the hill! 910

CATHERINE   No, I don't believe it.

EDDIE   Katie, don't break my heart, listen to me.

CATHERINE   I don't want to hear it.

EDDIE   Katie, listen . . .

CATHERINE   He loves me! 915

EDDIE   [*with deep alarm*]   Don't say that, for God's sake! This is the oldest racket in the country——

CATHERINE   [*desperately, as though he had made his imprint*]   I don't believe it! [*She rushes to the house.*]

EDDIE   [*following her*]   They been pullin' this since the Immigration Law was put in! They grab a green kid that don't know nothin' and they—— 920

CATHERINE   [*sobbing*]   I don't believe it and I wish to hell you'd stop it!

EDDIE   Katie!

[*They enter the apartment. The lights in the living room have risen and* BEATRICE *is there. She looks past the sobbing* CATHERINE *at* EDDIE, *who, in the presence of his wife, makes an awkward gesture of eroded command, indicating* CATHERINE.] 925

EDDIE   Why don't you straighten her out?

BEATRICE   [*inwardly angered at his flowing emotion, which in itself alarms her*]   When are you going to leave her alone? 930

EDDIE   B., the guy is no good!

BEATRICE   [*suddenly, with open fright and fury*]   You going to leave her alone? Or you gonna drive me crazy? [*He turns, striving to retain his dignity, but nevertheless in guilt walks out of the house, into the street and away.* CATHERINE *starts into a bedroom.*]   Listen, Catherine. [CATHERINE *halts, turns to her sheepishly.*]   What are you going to do with yourself? 935

CATHERINE   I don't know.

BEATRICE   Don't tell me you don't know; you're not a baby any more, what are you going to do with yourself? 940

CATHERINE   He won't listen to me.

BEATRICE   I don't understand this. He's not your father, Catherine. I don't understand what's going on here.

CATHERINE [*as one who herself is trying to rationalize a buried impulse*]   945
What am I going to do, just kick him in the face with it?

BEATRICE   Look, honey, you wanna get married, or don't you wanna get married? What are you worried about, Katie?

CATHERINE [*quietly, trembling*]   I don't know B. It just seems wrong if
he's against it so much.   950

BEATRICE [*never losing her aroused alarm*]   Sit down, honey, I want to tell you something. Here, sit down. Was there ever any fella he liked for you? There wasn't, was there?

CATHERINE   But he says Rodolpho's just after his papers.

BEATRICE   Look, he'll say anything. What does he care what he says? If it   955
was a prince came here for you it would be no different. You know that, don't you?

CATHERINE   Yeah, I guess.

BEATRICE   So what does that mean?

CATHERINE [*slowly turns her head to* BEATRICE]   What?   960

BEATRICE   It means you gotta be your own self more. You still think you're a little girl, honey. But nobody else can make up your mind for you any more, you understand? You gotta give him to understand that he can't give you orders no more.

CATHERINE   Yeah, but how am I going to do that? He thinks I'm a baby.   965

BEATRICE   Because *you* think you're a baby. I told you fifty times already, you can't act the way you act. You still walk around in front of him in your slip——

CATHERINE   Well I forgot.

BEATRICE   Well you can't do it. Or like you sit on the edge of the bathtub   970
talkin' to him when he's shavin' in his underwear.

CATHERINE   When'd I do that?

BEATRICE   I seen you in there this morning.

CATHERINE   Oh . . . well, I wanted to tell him something and I——

BEATRICE   I know, honey. But if you act like a baby and he be treatin'   975
you like a baby. Like when he comes home sometimes you throw yourself at him like when you was twelve years old.

CATHERINE   Well I like to see him and I'm happy so I——

BEATRICE   Look, I'm not telling you what to do honey, but——

CATHERINE   No, you could tell me, B.! Gee, I'm all mixed up. See, I——   980
He looks so sad now and it hurts me.

BEATRICE   Well look Katie, if it's goin' to hurt you so much you're gonna end up an old maid here.

CATHERINE   No!

BEATRICE   I'm tellin' you, I'm not makin' a joke. I tried to tell you a cou-   985
ple of times in the last year or so. That's why I was so happy you

were going to go out and get work, you wouldn't be here so much, you'd be a little more independent. I mean it. It's wonderful for a whole family to love each other, but you're a grown woman and you're in the same house with a grown man. So you'll act different now, eh? 990

CATHERINE Yeah, I will. I'll remember.

BEATRICE Because it ain't only up to him, Katie, you understand? I told him the same thing already.

CATHERINE [*quickly*] What?

BEATRICE That he should let you go. But, you see, if only I tell him, he 995 thinks I'm just bawlin' him out, or maybe I'm jealous or somethin', you know?

CATHERINE [*astonished*] He said you was jealous?

BEATRICE No, I'm just sayin' maybe that's what he thinks. [*She reaches over to* CATHERINE's *hand; with a strained smile*] You think I'm jealous 1000 of you, honey?

CATHERINE No! It's the first I thought of it.

BEATRICE [*with a quiet sad laugh*] Well you should have thought of it before . . . but I'm not. We'll be all right. Just give him to understand; you don't have to fight, you're just——You're a woman, that's 1005 all, and you got a nice boy, and now the time came when you said good-by. All right?

CATHERINE [*strangely moved at the prospect*] All right. . . . If I can.

BEATRICE Honey . . . you gotta.

[CATHERINE, *sensing now an imperious demand, turns with some fear,* 1010 *with a discovery, to* BEATRICE. *She is at the edge of tears, as though a familiar world had shattered.*]

CATHERINE Okay.

[*Lights out on them and up on* ALFIERI, *seated behind his desk.*]

ALFIERI It was at this time that he first came to me. I had represented 1015 his father in an accident case some years before, and I was acquainted with the family in a casual way. I remember him now as he walked through my doorway——

[*Enter* EDDIE *down right ramp.*]

His eyes were like tunnels; my first thought was that he had com- 1020 mitted a crime,

[EDDIE *sits beside the desk, cap in hand, looking out.*]

but soon I saw it was only a passion that had moved into his body, like a stranger. [ALFIERI *pauses, looks down at his desk, then to* EDDIE *as though he were continuing a conversation with him.*] I don't quite 1025 understand what I can do for you. Is there a question of law somewhere?

EDDIE That's what I want to ask you.

ALFIERI Because there's nothing illegal about a girl falling in love with an immigrant. 1030

EDDIE Yeah, but what about it if the only reason for it is to get his papers?

ALFIERI   First of all you don't know that.

EDDIE   I see it in his eyes; he's laughin' at her and he's laughin' at me.

ALFIERI   Eddie, I'm a lawyer. I can only deal in what's provable. You understand that, don't you? Can you prove that?   103

EDDIE   *I know what's in his mind, Mr. Alfieri!*

ALFIERI   Eddie, even if you could prove that——

EDDIE   Listen . . . will you listen to me a minute? My father always said
you was a smart man. I want you to listen to me.

ALFIERI   I'm only a lawyer, Eddie.   104

EDDIE   Will you listen a minute? I'm talkin' about the law. Lemme just
bring out what I mean. A man, which he comes into the country
illegal, don't it stand to reason he's gonna take every penny and put
it, in the sock? Because they don't know from one day to another,
right?   104

ALFIERI   All right.

EDDIE   He's spendin'. Records he buys now. Shoes. Jackets. Y'understand
me? This guy ain't worried. This guy is *here.* So it must be that he's
got it all laid out in his mind already—he's stayin'. Right?

ALFIERI   Well? What about it?   105

EDDIE   All right. [*He glances at* ALFIERI, *then down to the floor.*] I'm talking
to you confidential, ain't I?

ALFIERI   Certainly.

EDDIE   I mean it don't go no place but here. Because I don't like to say
this about anybody. Even my wife I didn't exactly say this.   105

ALFIERI   What is it?

EDDIE   [*takes a breath and glances briefly over each shoulder*]   The guy ain't
right, Mr. Alfieri.

ALFIERI   What do you mean?

EDDIE   I mean he ain't right.   106

ALFIERI   I don't get you.

EDDIE   [*shifts to another position in the chair*]   Dja ever get a look at him?

ALFIERI   Not that I know of, no.

EDDIE   He's a blond guy. Like . . . platinum. You know what I mean?

ALFIERI   No.   106

EDDIE   I mean if you close the paper fast—you could blow him over.

ALFIERI   Well that doesn't mean——

EDDIE   Wait a minute, I'm tellin' you sump'm. He sings, see. Which is——
I mean it's all right, but sometimes he hits a note, see. I turn around.
I mean——high. You know what I mean?   107

ALFIERI   Well, that's a tenor.

EDDIE   I know a tenor, Mr. Alfieri. This ain't no tenor. I mean if you came
in the house and you didn't know who was singin', you wouldn't be
lookin' for him you be lookin' for her.

ALFIERI   Yes, but that's not——   107

EDDIE   I'm tellin' you sump'm, wait a minute. Please, Mr. Alfieri. I'm tryin' to bring out my thoughts here. Couple of nights ago my niece brings out a dress which it's too small for her, because she shot up like a light this last year. He takes the dress, lays it on the table, he cuts it up; one-two-three, he makes a new dress. I mean he looked so 1080 sweet there, like an angel—you could kiss him he was so sweet.

ALFIERI   Now look, Eddie——

EDDIE   Mr. Alfieri, they're laughin' at him on the piers. I'm ashamed. Paper Doll they call him. Blondie now. His brother thinks it's because he's got a sense of humor, see—which he's got—but that ain't what they're 1085 laughin'. Which they're not goin' to come out with it because they know he's my relative, which they have to see me if they make a crack, y'know? But I know what they're laughin' at, and when I think of that guy layin' his hands on her I could—I mean it's eatin' me out, Mr. Alfieri, because I struggled for that girl. And now he comes in my 1090 house and——

ALFIERI   Eddie, look—I have my own children. I understand you. But the law is very specific. The law does not . . .

EDDIE   [*with a fuller flow of indignation*]   You mean to tell me that there's no law a guy which he ain't right can go to work and marry a girl 1095 and——?

ALFIERI   You have no recourse in the law, Eddie.

EDDIE   Yeah, but if he ain't right, Mr. Alfieri, you mean to tell me——

ALFIERI   There is nothing you can do, Eddie, believe me.

EDDIE   Nothin'.   1100

ALFIERI   Nothing at all. There's only one legal question here.

EDDIE   What?

ALFIERI   The manner in which they entered the country. But I don't think you want to do anything about that, do you?

EDDIE   You mean——?   1105

ALFIERI   Well, they entered illegally.

EDDIE   Oh, Jesus, no, I wouldn't do nothin' about that, I mean——

ALFIERI   All right, then, let me talk now, eh?

EDDIE   Mr. Alfieri, I can't believe what you tell me. I mean there must be some kinda law which——   1110

ALFIERI   Eddie, I want you to listen to me. [*Pause.*] You know, sometimes God mixes up the people. We all love somebody, the wife, the kids—every man's got somebody that he loves, heh? But sometimes . . . there's too much. You know? There's too much, and it goes where it musn't. A man works hard, he brings up a child, sometimes it's a 1115 niece, sometimes even a daughter, and he never realizes it, but through the years—there is too much love for the daughter, there is too much love for the niece. Do you understand what I'm saying to you?

EDDIE   [*sardonically*]   What do you mean, I shouldn't look out for her 1120 good?

ALFIERI   Yes, but these things have to end, Eddie, that's all. The child has
to grow up and go away, and the man has to learn to forget. Because after all, Eddie—what other way can it end? [*Pause.*] Let her
go. That's my advice. You did your job, now it's her life; wish her   112
luck, and let her go. [*Pause.*] Will you do that? Because there's no
law, Eddie; make up your mind to it; the law is not interested in this.

EDDIE   You mean to tell me, even if he's a punk? If he's——

ALFIERI   There's nothing you can do.

   [EDDIE *stands.*]   113

EDDIE   Well, all right, thanks. Thanks very much.

ALFIERI   What are you going to do?

EDDIE   [*with a helpless but ironic gesture*]   What can I do? I'm a patsy,
what can a patsy do? I worked like a dog twenty years so a punk
could have her, so that's what I done. I mean, in the worst times, in   113
the worst, when there wasn't a ship comin' in the harbor, I didn't stand
around lookin' for relief—I hustled. When there was empty piers in
Brooklyn I went to Hoboken, Staten Island, the West Side, Jersey,
all over—because I made a promise. I took out of my own mouth to
give to her. I took out of my wife's mouth. I walked hungry plenty   114
days in this city! [*It begins to break through.*] And now I gotta sit
in my own house and look at a son-of-a-bitch punk like that—which
he came out of nowhere! I give him my house to sleep! I take the
blankets off my bed for him, and he takes and puts his dirty filthy
hands on her like a goddamn thief!   114

ALFIERI   [*rising*]   But, Eddie, she's a woman now.

EDDIE   He's stealing from me!

ALFIERI   She wants to get married, Eddie. She can't marry you, can she?

EDDIE   [*furiously*]   What're you talkin' about, marry me! I don't know what
the hell you're talkin' about!

   [*Pause.*]   115

ALFIERI   I gave you my advice, Eddie. That's it.

   [EDDIE *gathers himself. A pause.*]

EDDIE   Well, thanks. Thanks very much. It just—it's breakin' my heart,
y'know. I——   115

ALFIERI   I understand. Put it out of your mind. Can you do that?

EDDIE   I'm——[*He feels the threat of sobs, and with a helpless wave.*]
I'll see you around. [*He goes out up the right ramp.*]

ALFIERI   [*sits on desk*]   There are times when you want to spread an alarm,
but nothing has happened. I knew, I knew then and there—I could   1160
have finished the whole story that afternoon. It wasn't as though
there was a mystery to unravel. I could see every step coming, step
after step, like a dark figure walking down a hall toward a certain
door. I knew where he was heading for, I knew where he was going
to end. And I sat here many afternoons asking myself why, being an   1165
intelligent man, I was so powerless to stop it. I even went to a certain

old lady in the neighborhood, a very wise old woman, and I told
her, and she only nodded, and said, "Pray for him . . ." And so I—
waited here.

[*As lights go out on* ALFIERI, *they rise in the apartment where all are* 1170
finishing dinner. BEATRICE *and* CATHERINE *are clearing the table.*]

CATHERINE   You know where they went?

BEATRICE   Where?

CATHERINE   They went to Africa once. On a fishing boat. [EDDIE *glances*
at her.] It's true, Eddie.   1175

[BEATRICE *exits into the kitchen with dishes.*]

EDDIE   I didn't say nothin'. [*He goes to his rocker, picks up a newspaper.*]

CATHERINE   And I was never even in Staten Island.

EDDIE [*sitting with the paper*]   You didn't miss nothin'. [*Pause.* CATHERINE
takes dishes out.] How long that take you, Marco—to get to Africa? 1180

MARCO [*rising*]   Oh . . . two days. We go all over.

RODOLPHO [*rising*]   Once we went to Yugoslavia.

EDDIE [*to* MARCO]   They pay all right on them boats?

[BEATRICE *enters. She and* RODOLPHO *stack the remaining dishes.*]

MARCO   If they catch fish they pay all right. [*Sits on a stool.*]   1185

RODOLPHO   They're family boats, though. And nobody in our family
owned one. So we only worked when one of the families was sick.

BEATRICE   Y'know, Marco, what I don't understand—there's an ocean full
of fish and yiz are all starvin'.

EDDIE   They gotta have boats, nets, you need money.   1190

[CATHERINE *enters.*]

BEATRICE   Yeah, but couldn't they like fish from the beach? You see them
down Coney Island——

MARCO   Sardines.

EDDIE   Sure. [*Laughing*] How you gonna catch sardines on a hook?   1195

BEATRICE   Oh, I didn't know they're sardines. [*To* CATHERINE] They're sardines!

CATHERINE   Yeah, they follow them all over the ocean, Africa, Yugoslavia
. . . [*She sits and begins to look through a movie magazine.* RODOLPHO
joins her.]   1200

BEATRICE [*to* EDDIE]   It's funny, y'know. You never think of it, that sardines are swimming in the ocean! [*She exits to kitchen with dishes.*]

CATHERINE   I know. It's like oranges and lemons on a tree. [*To* EDDIE] I
mean you ever think of oranges and lemons on a tree?

EDDIE   Yeah, I know. It's funny. [*To* MARCO] I heard that they paint the 1205
oranges to make them look orange.

[BEATRICE *enters.*]

MARCO [*he has been reading a letter*]   Paint?

EDDIE   Yeah, I heard that they grow like green.

MARCO   No, in Italy the oranges are orange.   1210

RODOLPHO   Lemons are green.

EDDIE [*resenting his instruction*]   I know lemons are green, for Christ's sake, you see them in the store they're green sometimes. I said oranges they paint, I didn't say nothin' about lemons.

BEATRICE [*sitting; diverting their attention*]   Your wife is gettin' the money all right, Marco?   121

MARCO   Oh, yes. She bought medicine for my boy.

BEATRICE   That's wonderful. You feel better, heh?

MARCO   Oh, yes! But I'm lonesome.

BEATRICE   I just hope you ain't gonna do like some of them around here.   122 They're here twenty-five years, some men, and they didn't get enough together to go back twice.

MARCO   Oh, I know. We have many families in our town, the children never saw the father. But I will go home. Three, four years, I think.

BEATRICE   Maybe you should keep more here. Because maybe she thinks   122 it comes so easy you'll never get ahead of yourself.

MARCO   Oh, no, she saves. I send everything. My wife is very lonesome. [*He smiles shyly.*]

BEATRICE   She must be nice. She pretty? I bet, heh?

MARCO [*blushing*]   No, but she understand everything.   1230

RODOLPHO   Oh, he's got a clever wife!

EDDIE   I betcha there's plenty surprises sometimes when those guys get back there, heh?

MARCO   Surprises?

EDDIE [*laughing*]   I mean, you know—they count the kids and there's a   1235 couple extra than when they left?

MARCO   No—no . . . The women wait, Eddie. Most. Most. Very few surprises.

RODOLPHO   It's more strict in our town. [EDDIE *looks at him now.*] It's not so free.   1240

EDDIE [*rises, paces up and down*]   It ain't so free here either, Rodolpho, like you think. I seen greenhorns sometimes get in trouble that way —they think just because a girl don't go around with a shawl over her head that she ain't strict, y'know. Girl don't have to wear black dress to be strict. Know what I mean?   1245

RODOLPHO   Well, I always have respect——

EDDIE   I know, but in your town you wouldn't just drag off some girl without permission, I mean. [*He turns.*] You know what I mean, Marco? It ain't that much different here.

MARCO [*cautiously*]   Yes.   1250

BEATRICE   Well, he didn't exactly drag her off though, Eddie.

EDDIE   I know, but I seen some of them get the wrong idea sometimes. [*To* RODOLPHO] I mean it might be a little more free here but it's just as strict.

RODOLPHO   I have respect for her, Eddie. I do anything wrong?   1255

EDDIE   Look, kid, I ain't her father, I'm only her uncle——

BEATRICE   Well then, be an uncle then. [EDDIE *looks at her, aware of her criticizing force.*] I mean.

MARCO   No, Beatrice, if he does wrong you must tell him. [*To* EDDIE] What does he do wrong?   1260

EDDIE   Well, Marco, till he came here she was never out on the street twelve o'clock at night.

MARCO [*to* RODOLPHO]   You come home early now.

BEATRICE [*to* CATHERINE]   Well, you said the movie ended late, didn't you?

CATHERINE   Yeah.   1265

BEATRICE   Well, tell him, honey. [*To* EDDIE] The movie ended late.

EDDIE   Look, B., I'm just sayin'—he thinks she always stayed out like that.

MARCO   You come home early now, Rodolpho.

RODOLPHO [*embarrassed*]   All right, sure. But I can't stay in the house all the time, Eddie.   1270

EDDIE   Look, kid, I'm not only talkin' about her. The more you run around the more chance you're takin.' [*To* BEATRICE] I mean suppose he gets hit by a car or something. [*To* MARCO] Where's his papers, who is he? Know what I mean?

BEATRICE   Yeah, but who is he in the daytime, though? It's the same chance   1275
in the daytime.

EDDIE [*holding back a voice full of anger*]   Yeah, but he don't have to go lookin' for it, Beatrice. If he's here to work, then he should work; if he's here for a good time then he could fool around! [*To* MARCO] But I understood, Marco, that you was both comin' to make a livin' for   1280
your family. You understand me, don't you, Marco? [*He goes to his rocker.*]

MARCO   I beg your pardon, Eddie.

EDDIE   I mean, that's what I understood in the first place, see.

MARCO   Yes. That's why we came.   1285

EDDIE [*sits on his rocker*]   Well, that's all I'm askin'.
    [EDDIE *reads his paper. There is a pause, an awkwardness. Now* CATHERINE *gets up and puts a record on the phonograph—"Paper Doll."*]

CATHERINE [*flushed with revolt*]   You wanna dance, Rodolpho?   1290

RODOLPHO [*in deference to* EDDIE]   No, I—I'm tired.

BEATRICE   Go ahead, dance, Rodolpho.

CATHERINE   Ah, come on. They got a beautiful quartet, these guys. Come.
    [*She has taken his hand and he stiffly rises, feeling* EDDIE's *eyes on his back, and they dance.*]   1295

EDDIE [*to* CATHERINE]   What's that, a new record?

CATHERINE   It's the same one. We bought it the other day.

BEATRICE [*to* EDDIE]   They only bought three records. [*She watches them dance;* EDDIE *turns his head away.* MARCO *just sits there, waiting. Now* BEATRICE *turns to* EDDIE.] Must be nice to go all over in one of them   1300
fishin' boats. I would like that myself. See all them other countries?

EDDIE   Yeah.

BEATRICE [*to* MARCO]   But the women don't go along, I bet.

MARCO   No, not on the boats. Hard work.

BEATRICE   What're you got, a regular kitchen and everything?   130

MARCO   Yes, we eat very good on the boats—especially when Rodolpho comes along; everybody gets fat.

BEATRICE   Oh, he cooks?

MARCO   Sure, very good cook. Rice, pasta, fish, everything.

[EDDIE *lowers his paper.*]   131

EDDIE   He's a cook, too! [*Looking at* RODOLPHO] He sings, he cooks . . .
[RODOLPHO *smiles thankfully.*]

BEATRICE   Well it's good, he could always make a living.

EDDIE   It's wonderful. He sings, he cooks, he could make dresses . . .

CATHERINE   They get some high pay, them guys. The head chefs in all the   131.
big hotels are men. You read about them.

EDDIE   That's what I'm sayin'.

[CATHERINE *and* RODOLPHO *continue dancing.*]

CATHERINE   Yeah, well, I mean.

EDDIE [*to* BEATRICE]   He's lucky, believe me. [*Slight pause. He looks away,*   132�€
then back to BEATRICE.] That's why the water front is no place for
him. [*They stop dancing.* RODOLPHO *turns off phonograph.*] I mean
like me—I can't cook, I can't sing, I can't make dresses, so I'm on the
water front. But if I could cook, if I could sing, if I could make dresses,
I wouldn't be on the water front. [*He has been unconsciously twist-*   132.
ing the newspaper into a tight roll. They are all regarding him now;
he senses he is exposing the issue and he is driven on.] I would be
someplace else. I would be like in a dress store. [*He has bent the*
rolled paper and it suddenly tears in two. He suddenly gets up and
pulls his pants up over his belly and goes to MARCO.] What do you   133(
say, Marco, we go to the bouts next Saturday night. You never seen
a fight, did you?

MARCO [*uneasily*]   Only in the moving pictures.

EDDIE [*going to* RODOLPHO]   I'll treat yiz. What do you say, Danish? You
wanna come along? I'll buy the tickets.   133.

RODOLPHO   Sure. I like to go.

CATHERINE [*goes to* EDDIE; *nervously happy now*]   I'll make some coffee,
all right?

EDDIE   Go ahead, make some! Make it nice and strong. [*Mystified, she*
smiles and exits to kitchen. He is weirdly elated, rubbing his fists into   134(
his palms. He strides to MARCO.] You wait, Marco, you see some real
fights here. You ever do any boxing?

MARCO   No, I never.

EDDIE [*to* RODOLPHO]   Betcha you have done some, heh?

RODOLPHO   No.   134.

EDDIE   Well, come on, I'll teach you.

BEATRICE   What's he got to learn that for?

EDDIE   Ya can't tell, one a these days somebody's liable to step on his foot
or sump'm. Come on, Rodolpho, I show you a couple of passes. [*He
stands below table.*]   1350

BEATRICE   Go ahead, Rodolpho. He's a good boxer, he could teach you.

RODOLPHO [*embarrassed*]   Well, I don't know how to——[*He moves down
to* EDDIE.]

EDDIE   Just put your hands up. Like this, see? That's right. That's very
good, keep your left up, because you lead with the left, see, like this.   1355
[*He gently moves his left into* RODOLPHO'S *face.*] See? Now what you
gotta do is you gotta block me, so when I come in like that you—
[RODOLPHO *parries his left.*] Hey, that's very good! [RODOLPHO *laughs.*]
All right, now come into me. Come on.

RODOLPHO   I don't want to hit you, Eddie.   1360

EDDIE   Don't pity me, come on. Throw it, I'll show you how to block it.
[RODOLPHO *jabs at him, laughing. The others join.*] 'At's it. Come on
again. For the jaw right here. [RODOLPHO *jabs with more assurance.*]
Very good!

BEATRICE [*to* MARCO]   He's very good!   1365
[EDDIE *crosses directly upstage of* RODOLPHO.]

EDDIE   Sure, he's great! Come on, kid, put sump'm behind it, you can't
hurt me. [RODOLPHO, *more seriously, jabs at* EDDIE's *jaw and grazes it.*]
Attaboy.
[CATHERINE *comes from the kitchen, watches.*]   1370
Now I'm gonna hit you, so block me, see?

CATHERINE [*with beginning alarm*]   What are they doin'?
[*They are lightly boxing now.*]

BEATRICE [*she senses only the comradeship in it now*]   He's teachin' him;
he's very good!   1375

EDDIE   Sure, he's terrific! Look at him go! [RODOLPHO *lands a blow.*] 'At's it!
Now, watch out, here I come Danish! [*He feints with his left hand and
lands with his right. It mildly staggers* RODOLPHO. MARCO *rises.*]

CATHERINE [*rushing to* RODOLPHO]   Eddie!

EDDIE   Why? I didn't hurt him. Did I hurt you, kid? [*He rubs the back*   1380
of his hand across his mouth.]

RODOLPHO   No, no, he didn't hurt me. [*To* EDDIE *with a certain gleam and
a smile*] I was only surprised.

BEATRICE [*pulling* EDDIE *down into the rocker*]   That's enough, Eddie; he
did pretty good, though.   1385

EDDIE   Yeah. [*Rubbing his fists together*]   He could be very good, Marco.
I'll teach him again.
[MARCO *nods at him dubiously.*]

RODOLPHO   Dance, Catherine. Come. [*He takes her hand; they go to
phonograph and start it. It plays "Paper Doll."*]   1390
[RODOLPHO *takes her in his arms. They dance.* EDDIE *in thought sits*

in his chair, and MARCO *takes a chair, places it in front of* EDDIE, *and looks down at it.* BEATRICE *and* EDDIE *watch him.*]

MARCO   Can you lift this chair?

EDDIE   What do you mean?   1395

MARCO   From here. [*He gets on one knee with one hand behind his back, and grasps the bottom of one of the chair legs but does not raise it.*]

EDDIE   Sure, why not? [*He comes to the chair, kneels, grasps the leg, raises the chair one inch, but it leans over to the floor.*] Gee, that's hard, I never knew that. [*He tries again, and again fails.*] It's on an angle,   1400 that's why, heh?

MARCO   Here. [*He kneels, grasps, and with strain slowly raises the chair higher and higher, getting to his feet now.* RODOLPHO *and* CATHERINE *have stopped dancing as* MARCO *raises the chair over his head.*]

[MARCO *is face to face with* EDDIE, *a strained tension gripping his eyes*   1405 *and jaw, his neck stiff, the chair raised like a weapon over* EDDIE'S *head—and he transforms what might appear like a glare of warning into a smile of triumph, and* EDDIE's *grin vanishes as he absorbs his look.*]

[*Curtain*]   1410

ACT TWO

[*Light rises on* ALFIERI *at his desk.*]

ALFIERI   On the twenty-third of that December a case of Scotch whisky slipped from a net while being unloaded—as a case of Scotch whisky is inclined to do on the twenty-third of December on Pier Forty-one. There was no snow, but it was cold, his wife was out shopping. Marco   5 was still at work. The boy had not been hired that day; Catherine told me later that this was the first time they had been alone together in the house.

[*Light is rising on* CATHERINE *in the apartment.* RODOLPHO *is watching as she arranges a paper pattern on cloth spread on the table.*]   10

CATHERINE   You hungry?

RODOLPHO   Not for anything to eat. [*Pause.*] I have nearly three hundred dollars. Catherine?

CATHERINE   I heard you.

RODOLPHO   You don't like to talk about it any more?   15

CATHERINE   Sure, I don't mind talkin' about it.

RODOLPHO   What worries you, Catherine?

CATHERINE   I been wantin' to ask you about something. Could I?

RODOLPHO   All the answers are in my eyes, Catherine. But you don't look in my eyes lately. You're full of secrets. [*She looks at him. She seems*   20 *withdrawn.*] What is the question?

CATHERINE   Suppose I wanted to live in Italy.

RODOLPHO [*smiling at the incongruity*]   You going to marry somebody rich?

CATHERINE   No, I mean live there—you and me.   25

RODOLPHO [*his smile vanishing*]   When?

CATHERINE   Well . . . when we get married.

RODOLPHO [*astonished*]   You want to be an Italian?

CATHERINE   No, but I could live there without being Italian. Americans live there.   30

RODOLPHO   Forever?

CATHERINE   Yeah.

RODOLPHO [*crosses to rocker*]   You're fooling.

CATHERINE   No, I mean it.

RODOLPHO   Where do you get such an idea?   35

CATHERINE   Well, you're always saying it's so beautiful there, with the mountains and the ocean and all the——

RODOLPHO   You're fooling me.

CATHERINE   I mean it.

RODOLPHO [*goes to her slowly*]   Catherine, if I ever brought you home   40 with no money, no business, nothing, they would call the priest and the doctor and they would say Rodolpho is crazy.

CATHERINE   I know, but I think we would be happier there.

RODOLPHO   Happier! What would you eat? You can't cook the view!

CATHERINE   Maybe you could be a singer, like in Rome or——   45

RODOLPHO   Rome! Rome is full of singers.

CATHERINE   Well, I could work then.

RODOLPHO   Where?

CATHERINE   God, there must be jobs somewhere!

RODOLPHO   There's nothing! Nothing, nothing, nothing. Now tell me what   50 you're talking about. How can I bring you from a rich country to suffer in a poor country? What are you talking about? [*She searches for words.*] I would be a criminal stealing your face. In two years you would have an old, hungry face. When my brother's babies cry they give them water, water that boiled a bone. Don't you believe   55 that?

CATHERINE [*quietly*]   I'm afraid of Eddie here.

[*Slight pause.*]

RODOLPHO [*steps closer to her*]   We wouldn't live here. Once I am a citizen I could work anywhere and I would find better jobs and we would   60 have a house, Catherine. If I were not afraid to be arrested I would start to be something wonderful here!

CATHERINE [*steeling herself*]   Tell me something. I mean just tell me, Rodolpho—would you still want to do it if it turned out we had to go live in Italy? I mean just if it turned out that way.   65

RODOLPHO   This is your question or his question?

CATHERINE   I would like to know, Rodolpho. I mean it.

RODOLPHO   To go there with nothing.

CATHERINE   Yeah.

RODOLPHO   No. [*She looks at him wide-eyed.*] No.   70

CATHERINE   You wouldn't?

RODOLPHO   No; I will not marry you to live in Italy. I want you to be my
wife, and I want to be a citizen. Tell him that, or I will. Yes. [*He
moves about angrily.*] And tell him also, and tell yourself, please, that
I am not a beggar, and you are not a horse, a gift, a favor for a poor   75
immigrant.

CATHERINE   Well, don't get mad!

RODOLPHO   I am furious! [*Goes to her.*] Do you think I am so desperate?
My brother is desperate, not me. You think I would carry on my back
the rest of my life a woman I didn't love just to be an American? It's   80
so wonderful? You think we have no tall buildings in Italy? Electric
lights? No wide streets? No flags? No automobiles? Only work we don't
have. I want to be an American so I can work, that is the only wonder
here—work! How can you insult me, Catherine?

CATHERINE   I didn't mean that——   85

RODOLPHO   My heart dies to look at you. Why are you so afraid of him?

CATHERINE [*near tears*]   I don't know!

RODOLPHO   Do you trust me, Catherine? You?

CATHERINE   It's only that I——He was good to me, Rodolpho. You don't
know him; he was always the sweetest guy to me. Good. He razzes me   90
all the time but he don't mean it. I know. I would—just feel ashamed
if I made him sad. 'Cause I always dreamt that when I got married
he would be happy at the wedding, and laughin'—and now he's—
mad all the time and nasty—[*She is weeping.*] Tell him you'd live
in Italy—just tell him, and maybe he would start to trust you a little,   95
see? Because I want him to be happy; I mean—I like him, Rodolpho
—and I can't stand it!

RODOLPHO   Oh, Catherine—oh, little girl.

CATHERINE   I love you, Rodolpho, I love you.

RODOLPHO   Then why are you afraid? That he'll spank you?   100

CATHERINE   Don't, don't laugh at me! I've been here all my life. . . .
Every day I saw him when he left in the morning and when he came
home at night. You think it's so easy to turn around and say to a
man he's nothin' to you no more?

RODOLPHO   I know, but——   105

CATHERINE   You don't know; nobody knows! I'm not a baby, I know a lot
more than people think I know. Beatrice says to be a woman, but——

RODOLPHO   Yes.

CATHERINE   Then why don't she be a woman? If I was a wife I would
make a man happy instead of goin' at him all the time. I can tell a   110
block away when he's blue in his mind and just wants to talk to some-

body quiet and nice. . . . I can tell when he's hungry or wants a beer before he even says anything. I know when his feet hurt him, I mean I *know* him and now I'm supposed to turn around and make a stranger out of him? I don't know why I have to do that, I mean.   115

RODOLPHO   Catherine. If I take in my hands a little bird. And she grows and wishes to fly. But I will not let her out of my hands because I love her so much, is that right for me to do? I don't say you must hate him; but anyway you must go, mustn't you? Catherine?

CATHERINE [*softly*]   Hold me.   120

RODOLPHO [*clasping her to him*]   Oh, my little girl.

CATHERINE   Teach me. [*She is weeping.*] I don't know anything, teach me, Rodolpho, hold me.

RODOLPHO   There's nobody here now. Come inside. Come. [*He is leading her toward the bedrooms.*] And don't cry any more.   125
[*Light rises on the street. In a moment* EDDIE *appears. He is unsteady, drunk. He mounts the stairs. He enters the apartment, looks around, takes out a bottle from one pocket, puts it on the table. Then another bottle from another pocket, and a third from an inside pocket. He sees the pattern and cloth, goes over to it and touches it, and turns toward*   130 *upstage.*]

EDDIE   Beatrice? [*He goes to the open kitchen door and looks in.*] Beatrice? Beatrice?
[CATHERINE *enters from bedroom; under his gaze she adjusts her dress.*]   135

CATHERINE   You got home early.

EDDIE   Knocked off for Christmas early. [*Indicating the pattern*] Rodolpho makin' you a dress?

CATHERINE   No. I'm makin' a blouse.
[RODOLPRO *appears in the bedroom doorway.* EDDIE *sees him and his*   140 *arm jerks slightly in shock.* RODOLPHO *nods to him testingly.*]

RODOLPHO   Beatrice went to buy presents for her mother.
[*Pause.*]

EDDIE   Pack it up. Go ahead. Get your stuff and get outa here. [CATHERINE *instantly turns and walks toward the bedroom, and* EDDIE *grabs her*   145 *arm.*] Where you goin'?

CATHERINE [*trembling with fright*]   I think I have to get out of here, Eddie.

EDDIE   No, you ain't goin' nowheres, he's the one.

CATHERINE   I think I can't stay here no more. [*She frees her arm, steps back*   150 *toward the bedroom.*] I'm sorry, Eddie. [*She sees the tears in his eyes.*] Well, don't cry. I'll be around the neighborhood; I'll see you. I just can't stay here no more. You know I can't. [*Her sobs of pity and love for him break her composure.*] Don't you know I can't? You know that, don't you? [*She goes to him.*] Wish me luck. [*She clasps her hands*   155 *prayerfully.*] Oh, Eddie, don't be like that!

EDDIE   You ain't goin' nowheres.

CATHERINE   Eddie, I'm not going to be a baby any more! You——

[*He reaches out suddenly, draws her to him, and as she strives to free herself he kisses her on the mouth.*]   160

RODOLPHO   Don't! [*He pulls on* EDDIE's *arm.*] Stop that! Have respect for her!

EDDIE [*spun around by* RODOLPHO]   You want something?

RODOLPHO   Yes! She'll be my wife. That is what I want. My wife!

EDDIE   But what're you gonna be?   165

RODOLPHO   I show you what I be!

CATHERINE   Wait outside; don't argue with him!

EDDIE   Come on, show me! What're you gonna be? Show me!

RODOLPHO [*with tears of rage*]   Don't say that to me!

[RODOLPHO *flies at him in attack.* EDDIE *pins his arms, laughing, and*   170 *suddenly kisses him.*]

CATHERINE   Eddie! let go, ya hear me! I'll kill you! Leggo of him!

[*She tears at* EDDIE's *face and* EDDIE *releases* RODOLPHO. EDDIE *stands there with tears rolling down his face as he laughs mockingly at* RODOLPHO. *She is staring at him in horror.* RODOLPHO *is rigid. They are*   175 *like animals that have torn at one another and broken up without a decision, each waiting for the other's mood.*]

EDDIE [*to* CATHERINE]   You see? [*To* RODOLPHO] I give you till tomorrow, kid. Get outa here. Alone. You hear me? Alone.

CATHERINE   I'm going with him, Eddie. [*She starts toward* RODOLPHO.]   180

EDDIE [*indicating* RODOLPHO *with his head*]   Not with that. [*She halts, frightened. He sits, still panting for breath, and they watch him helplessly as he leans toward them over the table.*] Don't make me do nuttin', Catherine. Watch your step, submarine. By rights they oughta throw you back in the water. But I got pity for you. [*He moves un-*   185 *steadily toward the door, always facing* RODOLPHO.] Just get outa here and don't lay another hand on her unless you wanna go out feet first. [*He goes out of the apartment.*]

[*The lights go down, as they rise on* ALFIERI.]

ALFIERI   On December twenty-seventh I saw him next. I normally go   190 home well before six, but that day I sat around looking out my window at the bay, and when I saw him walking through my doorway, I knew why I had waited. And if I seem to tell this like a dream, it was that way. Several moments arrived in the course of the two talks we had when it occurred to me how—almost transfixed I had come to feel. I   195 had lost my strength somewhere. [EDDIE *enters, removing his cap, sits in the chair, looks thoughtfully out.*] I looked in his eyes more than I listened—in fact, I can hardly remember the conversation. But I will never forget how dark the room became when he looked at me; his eyes were like tunnels. I kept wanting to call the police, but nothing   200 had happened. Nothing at all had really happened. [*He breaks off and looks down at the desk. Then he turns to* EDDIE.] So in other words, he won't leave?

EDDIE   My wife is talkin' about renting a room upstairs for them. An old lady on the top floor is got an empty room.   205

ALFIERI   What does Marco say?

EDDIE   He just sits there. Marco don't say much.

ALFIERI   I guess they didn't tell him, heh? What happened?

EDDIE   I don't know; Marco don't say much.

ALFIERI   What does your wife say?   210

EDDIE   [*unwilling to pursue this*]   Nobody's talkin' much in the house. So what about that?

ALFIERI   But you didn't prove anything about him. It sounds like he just wasn't strong enough to break your grip.

EDDIE   I'm tellin' you I know—he ain't right. Somebody that don't want 215
it can break it. Even a mouse, if you catch a teeny mouse and you hold it in your hand, that mouse can give you the right kind of fight. He didn't give me the right kind of fight, I know it, Mr. Alfieri, the guy ain't right.

ALFIERI   What did you do that for, Eddie?   220

EDDIE   To show her what he is! So she would see, once and for all! Her mother'll turn over in the grave! [*He gathers himself almost peremptorily.*] So what do I gotta do now? Tell me what to do.

ALFIERI   She actually said she's marrying him?

EDDIE   She told me, yeah. So what do I do?   225
[*Slight pause.*]

ALFIERI   This is my last word, Eddie, take it or not, that's your business. Morally and legally you have no rights, you cannot stop it; she is a free agent.

EDDIE   [*angering*]   Didn't you hear what I told you?   230

ALFIERI   [*with a tougher tone*]   I heard what you told me, and I'm telling you what the answer is. I'm not only telling you now, I'm warning you—the law is nature. The law is only a word for what has a right to happen. When the law is wrong it's because it's unnatural, but in this case it is natural and a river will drown you if you buck it now. 235
Let her go. And bless her. [*A phone booth begins to glow on the opposite side of the stage; a faint, lonely blue.* EDDIE *stands up, jaws clenched.*] Somebody had to come for her, Eddie, sooner or later.
[EDDIE *starts turning to go and* ALFIERI *rises with new anxiety.*] You won't have a friend in the world, Eddie! Even those who understand 240
will turn against you, even the ones who feel the same will despise you! [EDDIE *moves off.*] Put it out of your mind! Eddie! [*He follows into the darkness, calling desperately.*]
[EDDIE *is gone. The phone is glowing in light now. Light is out on* ALFIERI. EDDIE *has at the same time appeared beside the phone.*] 245

EDDIE   Give me the number of the Immigration Bureau. Thanks. [*He dials.*] I want to report something. Illegal immigrants. Two of them. That's right. Four-forty-one Saxon Street, Brooklyn, yeah. Ground floor. Heh? [*With greater difficulty*] I'm just around the neighborhood, that's all. Heh?   250

[*Evidently he is being questioned further, and he slowly hangs up. He leaves the phone just as* LOUIS *and* MIKE *come down the street.*]

LOUIS   Go bowlin', Eddie?

EDDIE   No, I'm due home.

LOUIS   Well, take it easy.   255

EDDIE   I'll see yiz.

[*They leave him, exiting right, and he watches them go. He glances about, then goes up into the house. The lights go on in the apartment.* BEATRICE *is taking down Christmas decorations and packing them in a box.*]   260

EDDIE   Where is everybody? [BEATRICE *does not answer.*] I says where is everybody?

BEATRICE [*looking up at him, wearied with it, and concealing a fear of him*] I decided to move them upstairs with Mrs. Dondero.

EDDIE   Oh, they're all moved up there already?   265

BEATRICE   Yeah.

EDDIE   Where's Catherine? She up there?

BEATRICE   Only to bring pillow cases.

EDDIE   She ain't movin' in with them.

BEATRICE   Look, I'm sick and tired of it. I'm sick and tired of it!   270

EDDIE   All right, all right, take it easy.

BEATRICE   I don't wanna hear no more about it, you understand? Nothin'!

EDDIE   What're you blowin' off about? Who brought them in here?

BEATRICE   All right, I'm sorry; I wish I'd a drop dead before I told them to come. In the ground I wish I was.   275

EDDIE   Don't drop dead, just keep in mind who brought them in here, that's all. [*He moves about restlessly.*] I mean I got a couple of rights here. [*He moves, wanting to beat down her evident disapproval of him.*] This is my house here not their house.

BEATRICE   What do you want from me? They're moved out; what do you   280
want now?

EDDIE   I want my respect!

BEATRICE   So I moved them out, what more do you want? You got your house now, you got your respect.

EDDIE [*he moves about biting his lip*]   I don't like the way you talk to me,   285
Beatrice.

BEATRICE   I'm just tellin' you I done what you want!

EDDIE   I don't like it! The way you talk to me and the way you look at me. This is my house. And she is my niece and I'm responsible for her.

BEATRICE   So that's why you done that to him?   290

EDDIE   I done what to him?

BEATRICE   What you done to him in front of her; you know what I'm
talkin' about. She goes around shakin' all the time, she can't go to
sleep! That's what you call responsible for her?

EDDIE [*quietly*]   The guy ain't right, Beatrice. [*She is silent.*] Did you hear   295
what I said?

BEATRICE   Look, I'm finished with it. That's all. [*She resumes her work.*]

EDDIE [*helping her to pack the tinsel*]   I'm gonna have it out with you one
of these days, Beatrice.

BEATRICE   Nothin' to have out with me, it's all settled. Now we gonna be   300
like it never happened, that's all.

EDDIE   I want my respect, Beatrice, and you know what I'm talkin' about.

BEATRICE.   What?

[*Pause.*]

EDDIE [*finally his resolution hardens*]   What I feel like doin' in the bed   305
and what I don't feel like doin'. I don't want no——

BEATRICE   When'd I say anything about that?

EDDIE   You said, you said, I ain't deaf. I don't want no more conversations
about that, Beatrice. I do what I feel like doin' or what I don't feel
like doin'.   310

BEATRICE   Okay.

[*Pause.*]

EDDIE   You used to be different, Beatrice. You had a whole different way.

BEATRICE   *I'm* no different.

EDDIE   You didn't used to jump me all the time about everything. The last   315
year or two I come in the house I don't know what's gonna hit me.
It's a shootin' gallery in here and I'm the pigeon.

BEATRICE   Okay, okay.

EDDIE   Don't tell me okay, okay, I'm tellin' you the truth. A wife is supposed to believe the husband. If I tell you that guy ain't right don't   320
tell me he is right.

BEATRICE   But how do you know?

EDDIE   Because I know. I don't go around makin' accusations. He give
me the heeby-jeebies the first minute I seen him. And I don't like
you sayin' I don't want her marryin' anybody. I broke my back payin'   325
her stenography lessons so she could go out and meet a better class
of people. Would I do that if I didn't want her to get married? Sometimes you talk like I was a crazy man or sump'm.

BEATRICE   But she likes him.

EDDIE   Beatrice, she's a baby, how is she gonna know what she likes?   330

BEATRICE   Well, you kept her a baby, you wouldn't let her go out. I told you
a hundred times.

[*Pause.*]

EDDIE   All right. Let her go out, then.

BEATRICE   She don't wanna go out now. It's too late, Eddie.   335

[*Pause.*]

EDDIE   Suppose I told her to go out. Suppose I——

BEATRICE   They're going to get married next week, Eddie.

EDDIE [*his head jerks around to her*]   She said that?

BEATRICE   Eddie, if you want my advice, go to her and tell her good luck. 340
I think maybe now that you had it out you learned better.

EDDIE   What's the hurry next week?

BEATRICE   Well, she's been worried about him bein' picked up; this way
he could start to be a citizen. She loves him, Eddie. [*He gets up, moves
about uneasily, restlessly.*] Why don't you give her a good word? Be- 345
cause I still think she would like you to be a friend, y'know? [*He is
standing, looking at the floor.*] I mean like if you told her you'd go to
the wedding.

EDDIE   She asked you that?

BEATRICE   I know she would like it. I'd like to make a party here for her. 350
I mean there oughta be some kinda send-off. Heh? I mean she'll have
trouble enough in her life, let's start it off happy. What do you say?
Cause in her heart she still loves you, Eddie. I know it. [*He presses
his fingers against his eyes.*] What're you, cryin'? [*She goes to him,
holds his face.*] Go . . . whyn't you go tell her you're sorry? [CATHERINE 355
*is seen on the upper landing of the stairway, and they hear her de-
scending.*] There . . . she's comin' down. Come on, shake hands with
her.

EDDIE [*moving with suppressed suddenness*]   No, I can't, I can't talk to
her.   360

BEATRICE   Eddie, give her a break; a wedding should be happy!

EDDIE   I'm goin', I'm goin' for a walk.
[*He goes upstage for his jacket.* CATHERINE *enters and starts for the
bedroom door.*]

BEATRICE   Katie? . . . Eddie, don't go, wait a minute. [*She embraces* 365
EDDIE's *arm with warmth.*] Ask him, Katie. Come on, honey.

EDDIE   It's all right, I'm——[*He starts to go and she holds him.*]

BEATRICE   No, she wants to ask you. Come on, Katie, ask him. We'll have
a party! What're we gonna do, hate each other? Come on!

CATHERINE   I'm gonna get married, Eddie. So if you wanna come, the wed- 370
ding be on Saturday.
[*Pause.*]

EDDIE   Okay. I only wanted the best for you, Katie. I hope you know that.

CATHERINE   Okay. [*She starts out again.*]

EDDIE   Catherine? [*She turns to him.*] I was just tellin' Beatrice . . . if you 375
wanna go out, like . . . I mean I realize maybe I kept you home too
much. Because he's the first guy you ever knew, y'know? I mean now
that you got a job, you might meet some fellas, and you get a different idea, y'know? I mean you could always come back to him, you're
still only kids, the both of yiz. What's the hurry? Maybe you'll get 380
around a little bit, you grow up a little more, maybe you'll see dif-

ferent in a couple of months. I mean you be surprised, it don't have to
be him.

CATHERINE   No, we made it up already.

EDDIE [*with increasing anxiety*]   Katie, wait a minute.   385

CATHERINE   No, I made up my mind.

EDDIE   But you never knew no other fella, Katie! How could you make up
your mind?

CATHERINE   Cause I did. I don't want nobody else.

EDDIE   But, Katie, suppose he gets picked up.   390

CATHERINE   That's why we gonna do it right away. Soon as we finish the
wedding he's goin' right over and start to be a citizen. I made up my
mind, Eddie. I'm sorry. [*To* BEATRICE] Could I take two more pillow
cases for the other guys?

BEATRICE   Sure, go ahead. Only don't let her forget where they came from.   395
[CATHERINE *goes into a bedroom.*]

EDDIE   She's got other boarders up there?

BEATRICE   Yeah, there's two guys that just came over.

EDDIE   What do you mean, came over?

BEATRICE   From Italy. Lipari the butcher—his nephew. They come from   400
Bari, they just got here yesterday. I didn't even know till Marco and
Rodolpho moved up there before. [CATHERINE *enters, going toward
exit with two pillow cases.*] It'll be nice, they could all talk together.

EDDIE   Catherine! [*She halts near the exit door. He takes in* BEATRICE *too.*]
What're you, got no brains? You put them up there with two other   405
submarines?

CATHERINE   Why?

EDDIE [*in a driving fright and anger*]   Why! How do you know they're not
trackin' these guys? They'll come up for them and find Marco and
Rodolpho! Get them out of the house!   410

BEATRICE   But they been here so long already——

EDDIE   How do you know what enemies Lipari's got? Which they'd love
to stab him in the back?

CATHERINE   Well what'll I do with them?

EDDIE   The neighborhood is full of rooms. Can't you stand to live a couple   415
of blocks away from him? Get them out of the house!

CATHERINE   Well maybe tomorrow night I'll——

EDDIE   Not tomorrow, do it now. Catherine, you never mix yourself with
somebody else's family! These guys get picked up, Lipari's liable
to blame you or me and we got his whole family on our head. They got   420
a temper, that family.
[*Two men in overcoats appear outside, start into the house.*]

CATHERINE   How'm I gonna find a place tonight?

EDDIE   Will you stop arguin' with me and get them out! You think I'm always tryin' to fool you or sump'm? What's the matter with you, don't   425
you believe I could think of your good? Did I ever ask sump'm for

myself? You think I got no feelin's? I never told you nothin' in my
life that wasn't for your good. Nothin'! And look at the way you talk
to me! Like I was an enemy! Like I——[*A knock on the door. His
head swerves. They all stand motionless. Another knock.* EDDIE, *in a*   430
whisper, pointing upstage.] Go up the fire escape, get them out over
the back fence.

[CATHERINE *stands motionless, uncomprehending.*]

FIRST OFFICER [*in the hall*]   Immigration! Open up in there!

EDDIE   Go, go. Hurry up! [*She stands a moment staring at him in a realized*   435
horror.] Well, what're you lookin' at!

FIRST OFFICER   Open up!

EDDIE [*calling toward door*]   Who's that there?

FIRST OFFICER   Immigration, open up.

[EDDIE *turns, looks at* BEATRICE. *She sits. Then he looks at* CATHERINE.   440
With a sob of fury CATHERINE *streaks into a bedroom.*
Knock is repeated.]

EDDIE   All right, take it easy, take it easy. [*He goes and opens the door. The*
OFFICER *steps inside.*] What's all this?

FIRST OFFICER   Where are they?   445

[SECOND OFFICER *sweeps past and, glancing about, goes into the*
kitchen.]

EDDIE   Where's who?

FIRST OFFICER   Come on, come on, where are they? [*He hurries into the*
bedrooms.]   450

EDDIE   Who? We got nobody here. [*He looks at* BEATRICE, *who turns her*
head away. Pugnaciously, furious, he steps toward BEATRICE.] What's
the matter with you?

[FIRST OFFICER *enters from the bedroom, calls to the kitchen.*]

FIRST OFFICER   Dominick?   455

[*Enter* SECOND OFFICER *from kitchen.*]

SECOND OFFICER   Maybe it's a different apartment.

FIRST OFFICER   There's only two more floors up there. I'll take the front,
you go up the fire escape. I'll let you in. Watch your step up there.

SECOND OFFICER   Okay, right, Charley. [FIRST OFFICER *goes out apartment*   460
door and runs up the stairs.] This is Four-forty-one, isn't it?

EDDIE   That's right.

[SECOND OFFICER *goes out into the kitchen.*

EDDIE *turns to* BEATRICE. *She looks at him now and sees his terror.*]

BEATRICE [*weakened with fear*]   Oh, Jesus, Eddie.   465

EDDIE   What's the matter with *you?*

BEATRICE [*pressing her palms against her face*]   Oh, my God, my God.

EDDIE   What're you, accusin' me?

BEATRICE [*her final thrust is to turn toward him instead of running from*
him]   My God, what did you do?   470

[*Many steps on the outer stair draw his attention. We see the* FIRST

OFFICER *descending, with* MARCO, *behind him* RODOLPHO, *and* CATHE-
RINE *and the two strange immigrants, followed by* SECOND OFFICER.
BEATRICE *hurries to door.*]

CATHERINE [*backing down stairs, fighting with* FIRST OFFICER; *as they ap-*   475
pear on the stairs]   What do yiz want from them? They work, that's
all. They're boarders upstairs, they work on the piers.

BEATRICE [*to* FIRST OFFICER]   Ah, Mister, what do you want from them,
who do they hurt?

CATHERINE [*pointing to* RODOLPHO]   They ain't no submarines, he was born   480
in Philadelphia.

FIRST OFFICER   Step aside, lady.

CATHERINE   What do you mean? You can't just come in a house and——

FIRST OFFICER   All right, take it easy. [*To* RODOLPHO] What street were you
born in Philadelphia?   485

CATHERINE   What do you mean, what street? Could you tell me what
street you were born?

FIRST OFFICER   Sure. Four blocks away, One-eleven Union Street. Let's go,
fellas.

CATHERINE [*fending him off* RODOLPHO]   No, you can't! Now, get outa here!   490

FIRST OFFICER   Look, girlie, if they're all right they'll be out tomorrow. If
they're illegal they go back where they came from. If you want, get
yourself a lawyer, although I'm tellin' you now you're wasting your
money. Let's get them in the car, Dom. [*To the men*] Andiamo, Andiamo, let's go.   495

[*The men start, but* MARCO *hangs back.*]

BEATRICE [*from doorway*]   Who're they hurtin', for God's sake, what do you
want from them? They're starvin' over there, what do you want!
Marco!

[MARCO *suddenly breaks from the group and dashes into the room and*   500
faces EDDIE; BEATRICE *and* FIRST OFFICER *rush in as* MARCO *spits into*
EDDIE's *face.*

CATHERINE *runs into hallway and throws herself into* RODOLPHO's *arms.*
EDDIE, *with an enraged cry, lunges for* MARCO.]

EDDIE   Oh, you mother's——   505

[FIRST OFFICER *quickly intercedes and pushes* EDDIE *from* MARCO, *who*
stands there accusingly.]

FIRST OFFICER [*between them, pushing* EDDIE *from* MARCO]   Cut it out!

EDDIE [*over the* FIRST OFFICER's *shoulder, to* MARCO]   I'll kill you for that,
you son of a bitch!   510

FIRST OFFICER   Hey! [*Shakes him.*] Stay in here now, don't come out, don't
bother him. You hear me? Don't come out, fella.

[*For an instant there is silence. Then* FIRST OFFICER *turns and takes*
MARCO's *arm and then gives a last, informative look at* EDDIE. *As he*
and MARCO *are going out into the hall,* EDDIE *erupts.*]   515

EDDIE   I don't forget that, Marco! You hear what I'm sayin'?

[*Out in the hall,* FIRST OFFICER *and* MARCO *go down the stairs. Now, in the street,* LOUIS, MIKE, *and several neighbors including the butcher,* LIPARI—*a stout, intense, middle-aged man—are gathering around the stoop.*   520

LIPARI, *the butcher, walks over to the two strange men and kisses them. His wife, keening, goes and kisses their hands.* EDDIE *is emerging from the house shouting after* MARCO. BEATRICE *is trying to restrain him.*]

EDDIE   That's the thanks I get? Which I took the blankets off my bed for   525
yiz? You gonna apologize to me, Marco! *Marco!*

FIRST OFFICER [*in the doorway with* MARCO]   All right, lady, let them go.
Get in the car, fellas, it's over there.

[RODOLPHO *is almost carrying the sobbing* CATHERINE *off up the street, left.*]   530

CATHERINE   He was born in Philadelphia! What do you want from him?

FIRST OFFICER   Step aside, lady, come on now . . .

[*The* SECOND OFFICER *has moved off with the two strange men.* MARCO, *taking advantage of the* FIRST OFFICER'S *being occupied with* CATHERINE, *suddenly frees himself and points back at* EDDIE.]   535

MARCO   That one! I accuse that one!

[EDDIE *brushes* BEATRICE *aside and rushes out to the stoop.*]

FIRST OFFICER [*grabbing him and moving him quickly off up to the left street*]   Come on!

MARCO [*as he is taken off, pointing back at* EDDIE]   That one! He killed   540
my children! That one stole the food from my children!

[MARCO *is gone. The crowd has turned to* EDDIE.]

EDDIE [*to* LIPARI *and wife*]   He's crazy! I give them the blankets off my
bed. Six months I kept them like my own brothers!

[LIPARI, *the butcher, turns and starts up left with his arm around his*   545
wife.]

EDDIE   Lipari! [*He follows* LIPARI *up left.*] For Christ's sake, I kept them,
I give them the blankets off my bed!

[LIPARI *and wife exit.* EDDIE *turns and starts crossing down right to*
LOUIS *and* MIKE.]   550

EDDIE   Louis! *Louis!*

[LOUIS *barely turns, then walks off and exits down right with* MIKE.
Only BEATRICE *is left on the stoop.* CATHERINE *now returns, blank-eyed,
from offstage and the car.* EDDIE *calls after* LOUIS *and* MIKE.]

EDDIE   He's gonna take that back. He's gonna take that back or I'll kill   555
him! You hear me? I'll kill him! I'll kill him! [*He exits up street calling.*]

[*There is a pause of darkness before the lights rise, on the reception
room of a prison.* MARCO *is seated;* ALFIERI, CATHERINE, *and* RODOLPHO
standing.]   560

ALFIERI   I'm waiting, Marco, what do you say?

RODOLPHO   Marco never hurt anybody.

ALFIERI   I can bail you out until your hearing comes up. But I'm not going to do it, you understand me? Unless I have your promise. You're an honorable man, I will believe your promise. Now what do you say?   565

MARCO   In my country he would be dead now. He would not live this long.

ALFIERI   All right, Rodolpho—you come with me now.

RODOLPHO   No! Please, Mister. Marco—promise the man. Please, I want you to watch the wedding. How can I be married and you're in here?   570 Please, you're not going to do anything; you know you're not. [MARCO *is silent.*]

CATHERINE [*kneeling left of* MARCO]   Marco, don't you understand? He can't bail you out if you're gonna do something bad. To hell with Eddie. Nobody is gonna talk to him again if he lives to a hundred.   575 Everybody knows you spit in his face, that's enough, isn't it? Give me the satisfaction—I want you at the wedding. You got a wife and kids, Marco. You could be workin' till the hearing comes up, instead of layin' around here.

MARCO [*to* ALFIERI]   I have no chance?   580

ALFIERI [*crosses to behind* MARCO]   No, Marco. You're going back. The hearing is a formality, that's all.

MARCO   But him? There is a chance, eh?

ALFIERI   When she marries him he can start to become an American. They permit that, if the wife is born here.   585

MARCO [*looking at* RODOLPHO]   Well—we did something. [*He lays a palm on* RODOLPHO's *arm and* RODOLPHO *covers it.*]

RODOLPHO   Marco, tell the man.

MARCO [*pulling his hand away*]   What will I tell him? He knows such a promise is dishonorable.   590

ALFIERI   To promise not to kill is not dishonorable.

MARCO [*looking at* ALFIERI]   No?

ALFIERI   No.

MARCO [*gesturing with his head—this is a new idea*]   Then what is done with such a man?   595

ALFIERI   Nothing. If he obeys the law, he lives. That's all.

MARCO [*rises, turns to* ALFIERI]   The law? All the law is not in a book.

ALFIERI   Yes. In a book. There is no other law.

MARCO [*his anger rising*]   He degraded my brother. My blood. He robbed my children, he mocks my work. I work to come here, mister!   600

ALFIERI   I know, Marco——

MARCO   There is no law for that? Where is the law for that?

ALFIERI   There is none.

MARCO [*shaking his head, sitting*]   I don't understand this country.

ALFIERI   Well? What is your answer? You have five or six weeks you could   605 work. Or else you sit here. What do you say to me?

MARCO [*lowers his eyes. It almost seems he is ashamed.*]   All right.

ALFIERI   You won't touch him. This is your promise.

   [*Slight pause.*]

MARCO   Maybe he wants to apologize to me.   610

   [MARCO *is staring away.* ALFIERI *takes one of his hands.*]

ALFIERI   This is not God, Marco. You hear? Only God makes justice.

MARCO   All right.

ALFIERI [*nodding, not with assurance*]   Good! Catherine, Rodolpho, Marco, let us go.   615

   [CATHERINE *kisses* RODOLPHO *and* MARCO, *then kisses* ALFIERI's *hand.*]

CATHERINE   I'll get Beatrice and meet you at the church. [*She leaves quickly.*]

   [MARCO *rises.* RODOLPHO *suddenly embraces him.* MARCO *pats him on the back and* RODOLPHO *exits after* CATHERINE. MARCO *faces* ALFIERI.]   620

ALFIERI   Only God, Marco.

   [MARCO *turns and walks out.* ALFIERI *with a certain processional tread leaves the stage. The lights dim out.*

   The lights rise in the apartment. EDDIE *is alone in the rocker, rocking back and forth in little surges. Pause. Now* BEATRICE *emerges from a*   625 *bedroom. She is in her best clothes, wearing a hat.*]

BEATRICE [*with fear, going to* EDDIE]   I'll be back in about an hour, Eddie. All right?

EDDIE [*quietly, almost inaudibly, as though drained*]   What, have I been talkin' to myself?   630

BEATRICE   Eddie, for God's sake, it's her wedding.

EDDIE   Didn't you hear what I told you? You walk out that door to that wedding you ain't comin' back here, Beatrice.

BEATRICE   Why! What do you want?

EDDIE   I want my respect. Didn't you ever hear of that? From my wife?   635

   [CATHERINE *enters from bedroom.*]

CATHERINE   It's after three; we're supposed to be there already, Beatrice. The priest won't wait.

BEATRICE   Eddie. It's her wedding. There'll be nobody there from her family. For my sister let me go. I'm goin' for my sister.   640

EDDIE [*as though hurt*]   Look, I been arguin' with you all day already, Beatrice, and I said what I'm gonna say. He's gonna come here and apologize to me or nobody from this house is goin' into that church today. Now if that's more to you than I am, then go. But don't come back. You be on my side or on their side, that's all.   645

CATHERINE [*suddenly*]   Who the hell do you think you are?

BEATRICE   Sssh!

CATHERINE   You got no more right to tell nobody nothin'! Nobody! The rest of your life, nobody!

BEATRICE   Shut up, Katie! [*She turns* CATHERINE *around.*]   650

CATHERINE   You're gonna come with me!

BEATRICE   I can't Katie, I can't . . .

CATHERINE   How can you listen to him? This rat!

BEATRICE [*shaking* CATHERINE]   Don't you call him that!

CATHERINE [*clearing from* BEATRICE]   What're you scared of? He's a rat!   655
He belongs in the sewer!

BEATRICE   Stop it!

CATHERINE [*weeping*]   He bites people when they sleep! He comes when
nobody's lookin' and poisons decent people. In the garbage he belongs!   660

[EDDIE *seems about to pick up the table and fling it at her.*]

BEATRICE   No, Eddie! Eddie! [*To* CATHERINE] Then we all belong in the
garbage. You, and me too. Don't say that. Whatever happened we all
done it, and don't you ever forget it, Catherine. [*She goes to* CATHE-
RINE.] Now go, go to your wedding, Katie, I'll stay home. Go. God   665
bless you, God bless your children.

[*Enter* RODOLPHO.]

RODOLPHO   Eddie?

EDDIE   Who said you could come in here? Get outa here!

RODOLPHO   Marco is coming, Eddie. [*Pause.* BEATRICE *raises her hands in*   670
terror.] He's praying in the church. You understand? [*Pause.* RODOLPHO
advances into the room.] Catherine, I think it is better we go. Come
with me.

CATHERINE   Eddie, go away, please.

BEATRICE [*quietly*]   Eddie. Let's go someplace. Come. You and me. [*He has*   675
not moved.] I don't want you to be here when he comes. I'll get
your coat.

EDDIE   Where? Where am I goin'? This is my house.

BEATRICE [*crying out*]   What's the use of it! He's crazy now, you know the
way they get, what good is it! You got nothin' against Marco, you al-   680
ways liked Marco!

EDDIE   I got nothin' against Marco? Which he called me a rat in front of
the whole neighborhood? Which he said I killed his children! Where
you been?

RODOLPHO [*quite suddenly, stepping up to* EDDIE]   It is my fault, Eddie.   685
Everything. I wish to apologize. It was wrong that I do not ask your
permission. I kiss your hand. [*He reaches for* EDDIE's *hand, but* EDDIE
snaps it away from him.]

BEATRICE   Eddie, he's apologizing!

RODOLPHO   I have made all our troubles. But you have insult me too.   690
Maybe God understand why you did that to me. Maybe you did not
mean to insult me at all——

BEATRICE   Listen to him! Eddie, listen what he's tellin' you!

RODOLPHO   I think, maybe when Marco comes, if we can tell him we are
comrades now, and we have no more argument between us. Then   695
maybe Marco will not——

EDDIE   Now, listen——

CATHERINE   Eddie, give him a chance!

BEATRICE   What do you want! Eddie, what do you want!

EDDIE   I want my name! He didn't take my name; he's only a punk. 700
Marco's got my name—[*to* RODOLPHO] and you can run tell him, kid,
that he's gonna give it back to me in front of this neighborhood, or we
have it out. [*Hoisting up his pants*] Come on, where is he? Take me to
him.

BEATRICE   Eddie, listen——   705

EDDIE   I heard enough! Come on, let's go!

BEATRICE   Only blood is good? He kissed your hand!

EDDIE   What he does don't mean nothin' to nobody! [*To* RODOLPHO] Come
on! ⸳

BEATRICE   [*barring his way to the stairs*]   What's gonna mean somethin'? 710
Eddie, listen to me. Who could give you your name? Listen to me,
I love you, I'm talkin' to you, I love you; if Marco'll kiss your hand
outside, if he goes on his knees, what is he got to give you? That's not
what you want.

EDDIE   Don't bother me!   715

BEATRICE   You want somethin' else, Eddie, and you can never have her!

CATHERINE   [*in horror*]   B.!

EDDIE   [*shocked, horrified, his fists clenching*]   Beatrice!
[MARCO *appears outside, walking toward the door from a distant
point.*]   720

BEATRICE   [*crying out, weeping*]   The truth is not as bad as blood, Eddie!
I'm tellin' you the truth—tell her good-by forever!

EDDIE   [*crying out in agony*]   That's what you think of me—that I would
have such a thought? [*His fists clench his head as though it will
burst.*]   725

MARCO   [*calling near the door outside*]   Eddie Carbone!
[EDDIE *swerves about; all stand transfixed for an instant. People appear outside.*]

EDDIE   [*as though flinging his challenge*]   Yeah, Marco! Eddie Carbone.
Eddie Carbone. Eddie Carbone. [*He goes up the stairs and emerges* 730
from the apartment. RODOLPHO *streaks up and out past him and runs
to* MARCO.]

RODOLPHO   No, Marco, please! Eddie, please, he has children! You will
kill a family!

BEATRICE   Go in the house! Eddie, go in the house!   735

EDDIE   [*he gradually comes to address the people*]   Maybe he come to
apologize to me. Heh, Marco? For what you said about me in front
of the neighborhood? [*He is incensing himself and little bits of laughter even escape him as his eyes are murderous and he cracks his
knuckles in his hands with a strange sort of relaxation.*] He knows 740

that ain't right. To do like that? To a man? Which I put my roof over their head and my food in their mouth? Like in the Bible? Strangers I never seen in my whole life? To come out of the water and grab a girl for a passport? To go and take from your own family like from the stable—and never a word to me? And now accusations in the bar- 745 gain! [*Directly to* MARCO] Wipin' the neighborhood with my name like a dirty rag! I want my name, Marco. [*He is moving now, carefully, toward* MARCO.] Now gimme my name and we go together to the wedding.

BEATRICE *and* CATHERINE [*keening*]   Eddie! Eddie, don't! Eddie!   750

EDDIE   No, Marco knows what's right from wrong. Tell the people, Marco, tell them what a liar you are! [*He has his arms spread and* MARCO *is spreading his.*] Come on, liar, you know what you done! [*He lunges for* MARCO *as a great hushed shout goes up from the people.*]

[MARCO *strikes* EDDIE *beside the neck.*]   755

MARCO   Animal! You go on your knees to me!

[EDDIE *goes down with the blow and* MARCO *starts to raise a foot to stomp him when* EDDIE *springs a knife into his hand and* MARCO *steps back.* LOUIS *rushes in toward* EDDIE.]

LOUIS   Eddie, for Christ's sake!   760

[EDDIE *raises the knife and* LOUIS *halts and steps back.*]

EDDIE   You lied about me, Marco. Now say it. Come on now, say it!

MARCO   Anima-a-a-l!

[EDDIE *lunges with the knife.* MARCO *grabs his arm, turning the blade inward and pressing it home as the women and* LOUIS *and* MIKE *rush* 765 *in and separate them, and* EDDIE, *the knife still in his hand, falls to his knees before* MARCO. *The two women support him for a moment, calling his name again and again.*]

CATHERINE   Eddie, I never meant to do nothing bad to you.

EDDIE   Then why——Oh, B.!   770

BEATRICE   Yes, yes!

EDDIE   My B.!

[*He dies in her arms, and* BEATRICE *covers him with her body.* ALFIERI, *who is in the crowd, turns out to the audience. The lights have gone down, leaving him in a glow, while behind him the dull prayers of* 775 *the people and the keening of the women continue.*]

ALFIERI   Most of the time now we settle for half and and I like it better. But the truth is holy, and even as I know how wrong he was, and his death useless, I tremble, for I confess that something perversely pure calls to me from his memory—not purely good, but himself purely, 800 for he allowed himself to be wholly known and for that I think I will love him more than all my sensible clients. And yet, it is better to settle for half, it must be! And so I mourn him—I admit it—with a certain . . . alarm.

QUESTIONS FOR ACT I

1. Miller uses an ingenious setting. What advantages does the setting have in localizing the play and yet making it possible to assemble many characters in a believable way?

2. The action of the play is presented as a reliving of the memories of Alfieri. Whom does he introduce? What kind of comments does he make? What purposes are served by such a "chorus character"? Why has Miller made him a Sicilian instead of, say, a New Englander or a German? a lawyer instead of a longshoreman?

3. What information does his first speech (a kind of prologue) provide concerning the characters and their backgrounds?

4. What does his last sentence (after "and yet . . .") suggest about the action of the play and about the kind of play it is?

5. Try to define the relation of Eddie and Catherine as it is brought out in their conversation before Beatrice enters.

6. Catherine says, "I'll tell you something," but her piece of news is not announced for some time. By what means does Miller delay the announcement? Why is it better to delay it than to have it at once?

7. How is the arrival of Beatrice's cousins made to seem important to the Carbone family?

8. How do Eddie and Beatrice treat each other?

9. When the women finally announce the news about Catherine, what is Eddie's reaction? How has Miller prepared us for it? What conflict arises at this point? What reason does each character have for taking a certain position in the conflict? Why does Eddie give in to the women?

10. What further information is brought out about the situation of Beatrice's cousins? What particularly Sicilian attitudes are revealed in the conversation up to the arrival of Marco and Rodolpho? What does the story about Vinny Bolzano illustrate?

11. What contrasts has Miller created between the brothers, Marco and Rodolpho?

12. What is the reader to infer from Catherine's "You married too?," Beatrice's "I told you he———," and Catherine's emphasis on Rodolpho's being blond?

13. At what point in Act I does the exposition end and the action start?

14. Explain the basis of the growing conflict between Beatrice and Eddie.

15. What elements of Rodolpho's personality does Eddie disapprove of? When Eddie and Catherine talk about Rodolpho, what is the reason, according to Eddie, for Rodolpho's interest in her? How does this idea affect her? What part does Beatrice take in this matter?

16. When Eddie tells Alfieri that Rodolpho "ain't right," what assumptions has he made? What does he regard as "evidence"? What could be said on Rodolpho's side?

17. What has Alfieri decided about Eddie's motives regarding Rodolpho and Catherine? What has happened, subconsciously, to Eddie? What response does Eddie make to Alfieri's analysis: "there is too much love for the niece," and his advice: "Let her go"? What does Alfieri think will happen, and why does he feel powerless to stop it?

18. What does Eddie hope to demonstrate with the boxing lesson? What is demonstrated by it? What does the chair-lifting tableau at the close of Act I symbolize?

QUESTIONS FOR ACT II

1. We may say that tragedy results from a combination of circumstances and character. What have the circumstances of the Christmas season and the case of Scotch whisky to do with the events of the play on December 23? How do the character traits of Eddie, Catherine, and Rodolpho play a part in the conflict early in Act II?

2. What different views regarding the law do Eddie and Alfieri have? Interpret, for example, Alfieri's comments "the law is nature," or similar statements.

3. What does Eddie's call to the Immigration Bureau mean to him? How would other people regard it?

4. What concession does Eddie make, hoping to prevent or delay the marriage of Catherine and Rodolpho?

5. Why does Eddie become so concerned when he hears that Marco and Rodolpho will be living with the Liparis? What realization comes to Beatrice about Eddie?

6. What has the Sicilian code to do with the actions of Marco and Eddie just before the officers take Marco away? Do the neighbors believe Marco or Eddie?

7. Explain the difference of views expressed in Marco's "All the law is not in a book" and Alfieri's "Yes. In a book. There is no other law."

8. What are the implications of Alfieri's "Only God makes justice"? (Does the lawyer expect men to put up with injustices?) If Marco took this seriously, what would he do?

9. On what grounds does Eddie issue his ultimatum that Beatrice must not attend the wedding? Why does he feel pushed to act as he does?

10. What are Rodolpho and Beatrice trying to prevent? What attempt at prevention does each make?

11. By what means is the sense of impending and inevitable doom produced in this part of the play?

12. When Beatrice tells Eddie "the truth," is he really shocked and horrified? If so, how can he have been blind to what was obvious to others?

13. What drives Marco and Eddie on to their final conflict? Has Miller

prepared us in any way for the *dénouement*—that Marco can conquer an attacker who has a knife?

14. What ironies do you perceive in Eddie's downfall? Does Eddie act to save himself? If not to save himself, then to save what? Or does he act to destroy himself?

15. What different reasons can you find for Eddie's defeat? How complex are the forces that contribute to his downfall? Could nothing be done to prevent it? At what point did it become inevitable?

16. To what extent is Eddie, Catherine, Rodolpho each responsible for the tragedy?

17. Is Eddie an evil man or an essentially good man? If the latter, how could he be impelled to commit murder?

18. Who has the most insight into character? Who has the least?

19. According to Alfieri's closing comment, what makes Eddie memorable as a tragic hero? In contrast to Eddie, how would his "sensible clients" act? What is the significance of Alfieri's repeating "now we settle for half and I like it better"?

20. Consider that the play projects some idea regarding the nature of justice. Sir Francis Bacon called revenge "a kind of wild justice." Is the play presenting a contrast of the "wild justice" of the old system in which every man takes the law into his own hands and a higher code of officially approved justice (trial and punishment only as sanctioned by the courts)? What are the strengths and weaknesses of each kind of justice?

21. Consider that the play projects some idea regarding the nature of law. Where does law subsist: in God; in nature; in the statute books; in the hearts of men?

22. Consider that the play projects some idea regarding the nature of mankind. What is basic in that nature if men insist on making decisions that bring tragedy?

23 Is no one responsible for the tragedy? Are the characters the victims of circumstances or of something we can call Fate? victims of social forces? victims of the rigid codes they inherited from their ancestors? victims of a lack of self-knowledge?

24. Arthur Miller has written concerning the hero of modern tragedy: "It matters not at all whether the hero falls from a great height or a small one, whether he is highly conscious or only dimly aware of what is happening, whether his pride brings the fall or an unseen pattern written behind clouds; if the intensity, the human passion to surpass his given bounds, the fanatic insistence upon his self-conceived role— if these are not present there can only be an outline of tragedy but no living thing." (Introduction to *Arthur Miller's Collected Plays*. New York: The Viking Press, 1957, p. 33.) Think of Eddie Carbone in terms of intensity, passion and fanaticism, and discuss whether his tragedy is a "living thing."

Bedtime Story

An Anatole Burlesque in One Act

SEAN O'CASEY

JOHN JO MULLIGAN   *a clerk*
ANGELA NIGHTINGALE   *a gay lass*
DANIEL HALIBUT   *a clerk—friend to Mulligan*
MISS MOSSIE   *a very respectable lodging-house keeper*
A POLICEMAN
A DOCTOR
A NURSE

SCENE   *A bachelor-flat in Dublin.*
TIME   *The present.*

[*The sitting-room of the bachelor-flat rented by* JOHN JO MULLIGAN *from* MISS MOSSIE, *owner of one of the old houses of Dublin, decayed a little, but still sternly respectable, and kept presentable by her rigid attention to it. She has divided it into lodgings for respectable young gentlemen. A rather dull though lofty room. To the right is an ordi-* 5 *nary gas fire; over it a mantlepiece on which is a clock, flanked on either side by a coloured vase; over these, on the wall, a square, gilt-framed mirror. Further up, towards back, is a door leading to Mulligan's bedroom. By the back wall, near this door, is a small bookcase with a few books sprawled out on its shelves; and on top is a pale-* 10 *green vase holding a bunch of white pampas grass. To the left of this is a window, now heavily curtained with dull, brown hangings. In the window's centre is a stand holding a coloured flower-pot containing some kind of a palm plant. Further on is a picture of a whitewashed cottage, well thatched with straw, a brown pathway before the door,* 15 *with purple heather growing in tufts on its edges, and, in the distance, the dark-blue peaks of hills, all surmounted by a bright blue sky. In*

From *Collected Plays*, Vol. IV, by Sean O'Casey, by permission of Mrs. Casey, St. Martin's Press, Inc., Macmillan & Co. Ltd., London, and The Macmillan Company of Canada Limited.

the side wall on the left is the door leading to the rest of the house. On
this door several overcoats are hanging. To the left of it is an umbrella-
stand in which are a walking-stick and two umbrellas, one newer than 20
the other. Close to the fireplace is an armchair clad in dark-green
leather, and further away, at an angle, is a settee to hold two, clad in
the same colour. In the room's centre is a round table covered with
a red table-cloth. On the table are a photograph or two, a vase of
chrysanthemums, and a book, open, with its face turned down, so that 25
the place might not be lost when the reader left it aside. The room is
lighted from a bulb hanging from the centre of the ceiling; the light
is softened by being covered with a yellow parchment shade. A stand-
ard lamps stands of the floor a little way from the sitting-room door,
towards the window, its light mollified by a deeply-fringed red silk 30
shade. A key is sticking in the keyhole of the sitting-room door. A pair
of MULLIGAN's *tan shoes are beside the fireplace. It is three or four*
of a cold, sleety January morning.

The fire is unlit, the room in darkness, when, presently, the bedroom
door opens, and MULLIGAN *comes into the sitting-room, showing the* 35
way to himself by the light of an electric torch. He is but half dressed,
in blue shirt, bright-checked, baggy plus-fours, and coloured-top
stockings. He is a young man of twenty-four or -five; tall, but not thin.
His hair is almost blond, and he wears it brushed back from his fore-
head, which is too high for the rather stolid face, giving him, at times, 40
the look of a clown having a holiday. His upper lip has a close-cropped
moustache. He is a constitutionally frightened chap, never able to
take the gayer needs of life in his stride—though he would be glad to
do it, if he could; but he can never become convalescent from a futile
sense of sin. His clean-shaven face shows a very worried look. He 45
comes into the room cautiously, waving the light over the floor, the
table, the chairs, as if looking for something—as a matter of fact, he
is; then returns to the door to peep into the bedroom.]

MULLIGAN [*sticking his head into the room—in a cautious whisper*]   I can't
see the thing anywhere. Sure you left it out here? [*There is no reply* 50
to the question.] I say I can't find it anywhere out here. [*There is no*
reply. He mutters to himself as if half in prayer] I shouldn't have done
it; I shouldn't have done it! I musta been mad. Oh, forgive me! [*He*
clicks his tongue, and peeps into the room again.] Dtch! dtch! Gone
asleep again! [*Whispering*] Angela! Angela! [*In a louder whisper*] 55
Are you awake? Eh, Angela?

ANGELA [*within the room—sleepily*]   Wha'?

MULLIGAN [*echoing her*]   Wha', wha'! [*To himself*] Oh, it was a mad thing
to do. Miserere mei. [*Speaking into room with irritation*] Have you forgotten what you sent me out to get? [*Appealingly*] Please try to arouse 60
yourself, Angela!

ANGELA [*within*]   Wha'?

[*Silence again for a few moments while* MULLIGAN *flashes the light on to the clock.*]

MULLIGAN   It's going to four o'clock in the morning, Angela.   65

ANGELA [*within*]   Didja get the lipstick?

MULLIGAN [*testily*]   I've told you I can't see it anywhere.

ANGELA [*sleepily*]   Have another look—there's a dear. I know I left it out there somewhere.

MULLIGAN [*shivering a little*]   It's nothing like a tropical climate out here,   70 you know.

ANGELA [*sleepily*]   It's easy to li' the fire, isn't it?

[MULLIGAN *crosses to the fireplace, turns the gas tap, and sees that the meter wants another shilling. He irritatedly turns the tap off, and, crossing quickly back to the bedroom, knocks over the vase of flowers*   75 *on the table, sending the water spilling over the table and on to the floor.*]

MULLIGAN [*half to himself and half to* ANGELA—*with annoyance*]   There's the vase down! Wather into me shoes and all over the floor! [*Putting his head into the bedroom again*] I've knocked the vase down now!   80 The place is flooded! And I can't light the fire—the meter needs another shilling.

ANGELA [*sleepily*]   Look in me han'bag, somewhere about. Maybe there's a bob in it.

[*In desperation,* MULLIGAN *goes to the cupboard, opens it, takes out*   85 *a wallet from which he takes a shilling, goes back to fireplace, puts it in the slot, and lights the fire. Then he returns to the bedroom door.*]

MULLIGAN [*putting his head into the bedroom again*]   Angela, are you up yet? The whole place is flooded. [*He gets no answer.*] You're not going asleep again, are you? Angela!   90

ANGELA [*within—sleepily*]   What time is it?

MULLIGAN [*in a loud and impatient whisper*]   I told you long ago. It's going to four o'clock in the morning. That friend of mine I told you of, will be back any minute from his all-night dance, before you slip away, if you don't hurry.   95

ANGELA [*from within*]   And what if he is? If he knew what had been going on in here, he'd be sorry he ever went to the dance.

MULLIGAN   Looka, Angela, I don't feel a bit funny about it. We should never have done it. Please get up, and face the situation. Remember your solemn promise to slip off when things were still.   100

[ANGELA *appears at the door. She is a girl of twenty-five to twenty-seven, tall, trimly-formed, and not without dignity. He hair is auburn, inclining towards redness. She is something of a pagan.*

At present, she is dressed in her cami-knickers, covered by MULLI- GAN's *brown dressing-gown, and her bare feet are thrust into* MULLI-   105 GAN's *slippers. Far and away too good a companion of an hour, a year, or a life, for a fellow like* MULLIGAN.]

ANGELA [*from the doorway*]   D'ye like the dark because your deeds are evil, or what? Switch on the light for God's sake, man, and let's have a look at each other before you banish your poor Eve from her Mul-   110 ligan paradise.

MULLIGAN [*as he switches on the light*]   I was afraid someone outside might see it, stay to look, might hear our voices, and wonder.

ANGELA   Wonder at what?

MULLIGAN   At hearing a girl's voice in my room at this time of night or   115 morning.

ANGELA [*mockingly*]   And isn't it a sweet thing for a girl's voice to be heard in a man's room at this time o' the night or morning?

MULLIGAN [*almost tearfully*]   You know it's not; not as we're situated. You know you did wrong to practise on a body who didn't know enough.   120 Situated as we are, without divine warrant, it's not proper. We're in the midst of a violent sin, and you should be ashamed and sorry, instead of feeling sinfully gay about it. It's necessary to feel sorry for a sin of this kind.

ANGELA   You were quite gay when we were coming in, boy, weren't you?   125 You've had your few bright moments, and you've given a sparkle to your life, so don't spoil it all. It may well be more serious for me than it is for you. [*She shivers.*] Burrr! It's cold here! I'll come back when the room's warmer, and make myself ready to meet the respectable world.   130

[*She goes back into the bedroom, while he stands at the bedroom door for a few moments, not knowing what to do.*]

MULLIGAN [*eyes raised appealing to the ceiling*]   Oh, that one'll be well punished for her gaiety and carelessness in sin! Oh, when will I forget this night's doings? Shattering fall! The very next day after   135 me Novena too! [*He peeps into the bedroom.*] Don't get too cosy there, or you won't want to move. Move we must, and soon. [*He goes to the cupboard, relocks it, and puts the key in his pocket; then he goes to the armchair, sits down in it, and starts to put on his shoes. Putting on a shoe—in a half-prayer*] Sweet Saint Panteemalaria, get   140 me outa this without exposure. [*He clicks his tongue.*] Dtch dtch! Soaking wet! and I'll be a cautious goer from this out—I promise. [*He goes over to bedroom door again with but one shoe on, and peeps in.*] Angela, room's warm now; quite warm. The time's flying, mind you. [*There is no reply.*] Aw, God, have you gone to sleep again!   145 Please, Miss Nightingale, please have some regard for others!

ANGELA [*from within—sleepily*].   Did you find it?

MULLIGAN   Find what, find what?

ANGELA   Me lipstick you were looking for?

MULLIGAN   No, no, I didn't; must be in there somewhere.   150

ANGELA   I remember I had it when you had me perched on your lap. Remember?

MULLIGAN [*as if to someone in sitting-room*]   Oh, don't be reminding me of things! [*Into the bedroom*] No, I don't remember. Oh, for goodness sake, get up!   155

ANGELA   All right, all right. Put out a glass of wine, and I'll be out in a minute.

[MULLIGAN *goes to the cupboard, unlocks it, and takes out a bottle of wine and a glass. He locks the cupboard again, leaving the key in the keyhole. He goes to the table, fills out a glass of wine, and leaves* 160 *it, with the bottle, on the table, in readiness for* ANGELA.

He sits down in the armchair, puts on the other shoe, then winds a woollen muffler round his neck, puts on a pullover and coat that have been hanging over the back of a chair, and finally places a trilby hat on his head. As he does these things, he occasionally mutters to him- 165 *self.*]

MULLIGAN [*busy with the wine for* ANGELA]   Not a single thought has she for what might happen to me if discovery came. Utterly abandoned to her own intherests. [*As he sits in chair putting on the second shoe— in a full-blown prayer*] Oh, gentle Saint Camisolinus, guardianess of all   170 good young people, get between me and this petticoated demonsthrator of sinful delusion, and I'll be O.K. for evermore. I will, I promise! [ANGELA *comes into the room at last, and makes quick for the fire. She has put on her stockings—silk ones—and skirt, a short, well-tailored one of darkish green, with broad belt of dark red and black buckle.* 175 *She carries a brown jersey over her arm, and her shoes in her hand.*]

ANGELA [*throwing her shoes on to the armchair, and stretching her hands to the fire*]   Burrr! It's cold out here still! I thought you said the room was warm? [*She notices how he's dressed.*] All ready for the journey, eh? Soon we'll be skiing down the stairs, wha'? Praying to all the   180 saints you know to see me out, eh?

[*She puts the jersey on over her head before the mirror over the fireplace, and pats it down smoothly over her breast and shoulders.*]

ANGELA   We have to face the hard, cold facts, now haven't we, dear?

MULLIGAN   We've got to think now of what would become of me if you   185 were discovered here.

ANGELA [*mockingly*]   Really? Of course, when one thinks of it, that becomes the one important problem.

MULLIGAN [*not noticing the mockery*]   It is, actually. You see, Angela, the head of my department's a grand Knight of Columbanus, an uncom-   190 promising Catholic, strict in his thought of life, and if he heard of anything like this, I'd—I'd be out in the bleaker air, quick; the little gilt I have on life would be gone; I'd run to ruin! God help me!

ANGELA [*prompting him*]   And then there's Father Demsey?

MULLIGAN   Then there's Father Demsey whose right-hand man I am in the   195 Confraternity and at all Saint Vincent de Paul meetings, with his "We can safely leave that matter with Mr. Mulligan," or "John Jo will do this for us." You see, it's a matter of importance to more than me. So, come on—we betther get off at once.

ANGELA [*rising from the chair, and drinking the glass of wine*]   Angela's 200 bright eyes, her scarlet lip, fine foot, straight leg, and quivering thigh have lost their charm for Mr. Mulligan. He's all for go-ahead godliness now! [*She pours out another glass of wine and drinks it.*] And what is to become of me? You don't care, and I don't care either.

[*She moves about the room in a slow, semi-reckless rhythm as she* 20 *lilts—*MULLIGAN *following her trying to get her quiet again.*]

ANGELA [*lilting and moving about*]

I don't care what becomes of me,
I don't care what becomes of me.

MULLIGAN [*shuffling after her as she moves as well as he can—in a low,* 210 *anguished voice*]   Angela, please! Sit down, do!

ANGELA [*lilting*]

I don't care if I'm out till two,
I don't care for the man in blue.

MULLIGAN [*following her*]   Please, Miss Nightingale, be serious! The land- 215 lady'll hear you, and then we'll be done!

ANGELA [*lilting*]

I don't care what the people say,
Here, there, and everywhere;

MULLIGAN [*appealing to the ceiling*]   Saint Curberisco, help me!   220

ANGELA [*in a final burst*]

For I'm going to be married in the morning,
So tonight, boys, I don't care!

[*Facing towards* MULLIGAN]   Sometime or other, we have to face out of all we get into: face out of getting into bed with a woman no 225 less than face out into silence from the glamour of prayer; face out of summer into winter; face out of life into death!

MULLIGAN [*crossing himself*]   Your talk's near blasphemy, Angela! Now you're going where you shouldn't venture. You'll bring a curse down on me, if you're not careful! Please be more discreet.   230

ANGELA   They're facts.

MULLIGAN   We're not fit for facts now.

ANGELA [*facing him fiercely*]   You stand there mustering up moans for yourself, and never once realise that you've ruined me! Yes, ruined me!   235

MULLIGAN [*startled*]   Oh, God, d'ye hear her! Ruined you? Oh, come, now, don't thry to act the innocent.

ANGELA   It's you who's acting the innocent, but it won't work. I was only an innocent kid till I met you. You led me on and destroyed all confidence in the goodness of me own nature! You never, never ceased 240 from persuasion till you got me here. I wasn't even to take off my hat, if I was the least bit suspicious. We were just to sit quiet discussing Yeats's poems. You were to sit ice-bound in your chair.

MULLIGAN [*indignantly*]   I led you on! Angela Nightingale, you're inventing things. It was you insisted on coming, because you didn't like 245 restaurants. A sorry thing for me I ever listened to you!

ANGELA [*ignoring his remarks*]   It's me's the sorry soul for listening to you. You promised a quiet hour of poetry, but we were hardly here when you began to move. Yeats's poems soon flew out of your head and hand. You got as far as "I will arise and go now, and go to Innis- 250 free"; then before the echo of the line was hushed, you had me clapped down on your knee. [*She becomes tearful.*] That was the start of my undoing. What am I going to do!

MULLIGAN [*lifting his eyes to the ceiling*]   There's lies! [*Facing her*] Astounded I was, when without a word of warning, I found you fit- 255 ting into me lap! [*Coming closer to her—fervently*] The thruth is, if you want to know, that all the way to here, I was silently praying to a bevy of saints that you'd stay torpid in any and every emergency of look or motion!

ANGELA   You took care to leave your saints out on the doorstep; ay, and 260 shut the door in their faces, too. You gave your solemn word, before I'd take one step to this place, that you'd be as harmless as an image in a looking-glass. I trusted you. I had heard you were a good boy. I thought you were a gentleman.

MULLIGAN   What about your uplifting can-can round the table while I 265 was reading Yeats's poems?

ANGELA [*going her own way*]   You made me believe you'd keep the width of a world between us while we were together, so's to avoid accidents. You said anyone who knew you would tell me you had a profound respect for girls; that you were slow in love-making.   270

MULLIGAN [*with insistence*]   The can-can; what about the can-can around the table?

ANGELA [*with a great wail in her voice*]   And then you stunned me with your speed!

MULLIGAN [*with even greater insistence*]   I'm asking you what about the 275 can-can you danced around the table while I was thrying to read "I will arise and go now, and go to Innisfree"?

ANGELA [*acting the innocent*]   What can-can? What are you talking about? I don't know what you mean by can-can.

MULLIGAN   I mean the dance that uplifted your skirt out of the way of 280

your movements and juggled a vision of spiritual desolation into a
mirage of palpitating enjoyments.

ANGELA [*appealing to the world at large*]   Oh, d'ye hear the like o' that!
Meanness is most of you to try to put the cloak of your own dark way
round my poor shoulders! The dance I did could be done by an in-   285
nocent figure in a nursery rhyme. You were bent on this awful mischief from the first. I sensed it when I walked with you—something
evil hovering near. Oh, why didn't I follow me intuition! [*She begins
to be hysterical.*] And I thought you such a nice man; and now, after
fencing me in with shame, you're making out I gave you the stuff to   290
make the fence around me. Oh, the infamy of it! [*She moves rapidly
up and down the room, clasping and unclasping her hands.*] Oh, what
shall I do, where shall I go, what shall I say!

MULLIGAN [*getting very frightened*]   Angela, calm yourself. Speak lower,
or you'll wake Miss Mossie, and we'll be ruined. Sit down; do, please!   295

ANGELA [*fluttering about and staggering a little*]   I'm undone, undone
completely. I won't be able to look any honest woman in the face; I
won't be able to shake the hand of any honest man I meet; my future's
devastated! [*She presses a hand to her heart.*] I'm not feeling well;
not at all well; you'd better get Miss Mossie.   300

MULLIGAN [*horrified and very agitated*]   Angela!

ANGELA [*staggering towards the chair*]   Not well at all. I feel I'm going to
faint! No, no; yes, yes—I am going to faint!
[*She sinks down on the chair, stretches out, and closes her eyes.*]

MULLIGAN [*falling down on a knee before her—well frightened now*]   305
Angela, don't! Angela, dear, wake up! [*Lifting his eyes to the ceiling*]
Saint Correlliolanus, come on, and deliver us from utther desthruction!

ANGELA [*plaintively and faintly*]   Wather!

MULLIGAN [*panic-stricken*]   No, wine! [*He rises from his knee, pours out
a glass of wine, and brings it to her.*] Oh, Angela, why did you let   310
yourself get into such a state? Here, take it quietly in sips. [*As she
drinks it*] Sip, sip, sip. That should do you good. Hope no one heard
you. Miss Mossie sleeps with one ear cocked. [*He strokes her hand.*]
You'll soon be all right, and able to slip away in a few minutes.

ANGELA [*noticing the ring on the hand stroking hers*]   Pretty ring; garnet   315
set in gold; precious garnet didn't you say?

MULLIGAN [*none too sure of what he should say*]   Yep. Not much value
though.

ANGELA   Why's it on the little finger?

MULLIGAN   Knuckle's too big on the right one; won't go over it.   320

ANGELA [*fingering it*]   Let me see it in me hand. [*He hesitates, then takes
it off, and gives it to her with reluctance. Putting it on the engagement
finger*] Fits me to a nicety. How did you come by it?

MULLIGAN   An uncle left it in my care when he went on a job to Hong

Kong. He never came back, and as no one asked about it, I made it 325
my own.

ANGELA   Oh? Lucky one. [*She looks up into his face, smiling archly, dis-
displaying the finger with the ring on it*] Looks like we were an engaged couple, John Jo, dear, wha'?

MULLIGAN   An engaged couple? [*With an uneasy and constrained laugh*] 330
Yis! Funny thought, that; quite. Feeling betther?

ANGELA   Seem to; hope it won't come over me again.

MULLIGAN [*fervently*]   God forbid! What about taking off our shoes, and
making a start? [*He takes off his.*]

ANGELA [*taking off her shoes*]   I suppose we must go sometime.   335

MULLIGAN [*trying to speak carelessly*]   Let's have the ring back, dear.

ANGELA [*as if she'd forgotten it*]   The ring? Oh, yes; I near forgot. [*She
fiddles with it; then suddenly straightens herself to listen.*] Is that the
sound of someone at the door below?

MULLIGAN [*agitated again*]   Oh, God, it it's Halibut home from the dance 340
we'll have to wait till he settles down! I wish you'd gone when the
going was good!

ANGELA [*who has taken off her shoes—rising from the chair.*]   Come on,
we'll chance it!

MULLIGAN [*pushing her back*]   Chance it! We can't afford to chance it. 345
[*Going over to the door leading to rest of the house*] I'll reconnoitre
down, and make sure the way's clear, before we chance it.
[*He goes out of the room, is absent for a few moments, while* ANGELA
*swallows another glass of wine; then he returns hastily, a hand held up
warningly for silence.*]   350

MULLIGAN [*in a frightened whisper*]   Near ran into him on the stairs.
Thank God it was so dark. Just had time to turn back. We'll have to
wait now till he settles in. [*He listens at the door, shuts it suddenly,
and glides over to* ANGELA.] Quick! He's gone by his own place, and is
coming up here! [*He catches her by the arm, hurries her across the* 355
room, and shoves her into the bedroom.] Get in, and keep silent
for God's sake!
[*As he shoves her in, a knock is heard at the sitting-room door.* MULLI-
*gan shuts the bedroom door, slides over to the chair, sits down, takes
the book from the table, and pretends to be reading.*   360
   Another knock is heard at the door, then it opens, and MR. DANIEL
HALIBUT *is seen standing there. He is a man of twenty-five, a little
below medium height, inclining to be plump. His hair is reddish, and
a thick moustache flowing from his upper lip hides his mouth. Sometimes his hand tries to brush it aside, but the moment the hand is* 365
*removed, it falls back into its old place at once. A fawn-coloured
overcoat covers an informal evening-suit—dinner-jacket and black tie.
A black homburg hat is on his head. He comes in as one who is full*

of himself as if he had done himself well at the dance, and as one who 370
feels himself a man of the world above the cautious and timorous
MULLIGAN. *His hat and coat are damp.*]

HALIBUT [*coming into the room*]   Ha, there you are, me son, rotten night
out; sleet. Coming up, I could have sworn I seen you coming down
the stairs.

MULLIGAN [*in pretended surprise*]   Me coming down the stairs? At this 375
time of the morning? What would I be doing on the stairs at this
hour?

HALIBUT   Well, what are you doing up at this time of the morning?

MULLIGAN   I found it impossible to sleep, so got up to see if a bit of
Yeats's poetry would make me drowsy.   380

HALIBUT   Is it Yeats, is it? God, man, he wouldn't let you sleep; drive you
nuts! All people liking Yeats are all queer. He's all questions. What am
I? Why am I? What is it? How did it come? Where will it go? All
bubbles. Stuck up in the top of his ould tower, he sent the bubbles
sailing out through a little loophole to attract the world outside. And 385
all the little writers copied them, and blew bubbles of their own, till
you could see them glistening among the things of the althar, or
shining in the hair of the girl you were courting.

MULLIGAN [*with an obvious yawn*]   Well, Yeats has made me sleepy, anyway. [*He flings the book on the table, and goes to get out of the* 390
chair.] I'll be off to bed again.

HALIBUT [*shoving him back into the chair*]   Wait till I tell you. You should
ha' been at the dance. There never was a grander occasion; divel a
grander ever! The place was fair gushing with girls. And only a few
who'd make you shut your eyes if they were sitting on your knee. A 395
hilariously hopeful whirlwind of skirt and petticoat, John Jo, when a
waltz was on!

MULLIGAN [*getting up and edging* HALIBUT *towards the sitting-room door*]
Go to bed, now, like a good fellow. I'm tired. We'll talk about it to-
morrow. Goodnight.   400

HALIBUT [*edging* MULLIGAN *back towards the fireplace*]   Wait till I tell you.
You are a boyo. You'd never guess who was there? Your old flame
of a week—Jessie! She told me things! When will you wake up? When
he asked me out for the first time, says she, I expected a hilarious
night at a dance or a music-hall, says she; I near fainted, says she, 405
when, instead, he asked me to go with him to Benediction! Mulligan's
management of maidens! Oh, John Jo, when will you wake up?

MULLIGAN [*annoyed, pushing* HALIBUT *towards the door*]   If I elect to
keep from danger, that's my affair. Looka, Dan, I've got to get up
early to go to Mass on my way to the office, so be a good fellow, and 410
go. I'm not concerned with girls.

HALIBUT   Betther if you were. [*He pushes* MULLIGAN *back toward the
fireplace again.*] You'd sleep betther at night for one thing. [*He puts*

an arm around MULLIGAN, *and forces him into being a partner.*]
Roamin' in the gloamin', eh? Oh, boy! [*Lilting*] With a lassie by yeer 415
side. Oh, it's lovely to go roamin' in the' gloamin'!

MULLIGAN [*angrily—struggling from* HALIBUT'S *hold, and rather roughly
forcing him to the door*]   Aw, lay off it, damn it, Dan! I'm in no
mood for a Highland fling! Please go to your own room, and leave me
in peace—I'm done in! [*He shoves him out and closes the sitting-room* 420
door.]

HALIBUT [*as he's being shoved out*]   All right, if that's the way you feel.
It'd be a good thing to put your hand on a girl's knee, and chance it.
[MULLIGAN *listens at the door for a few moments. Then he gets down*
on his knees, and puts an ear to the floor. He rises, goes to the bedroom 425
door, opens it, and calls ANGELA *out.*]

MULLIGAN   Now, Angela; now's our time. No delay, please.

ANGELA [*going behind the curtains on the windows*]   What kind of a night
or morning is it? [*From behind the curtains*] Christ! It's snowing or
something! [*She comes from behind them, goes to the door, and takes* 430
one of MULLIGAN'S *coats hanging there.*] I must have a coat.
[ANGELA *puts the coat on.*]

MULLIGAN [*in a faint protest*]   Eh, Angela, that's me best one.

ANGELA [*taking an umbrella from the stand*]   And an umbrella, too.

MULLIGAN   That's me best umbrella.   435

ANGELA   Never mind, dear. I'll let you have it back when you hand me
into the taxi on the all-night rank. Let's hurry now, boy. [MULLIGAN
opens the door cautiously, listens a moment; takes a torch from a
pocket, and shines it forth, then leads the way from the room, shut-
ting the door gently behind him. Both of them are in their stockinged 440
feet. After a few moments have passed, the door suddenly flies open,
and ANGELA *hurries in, followed by* MULLIGAN *wearing a look of agony*
on his face. They carry their shoes under their arms. As she comes in]
You louser, you'd have let me go off without it! Didn't care a damn
once you were rid of me. And all I have for another fortnight is in that 445
handbag!

MULLIGAN [*appealingly*]   Speak lower, Angela, or you'll have the Mossie
one down on top of us! I just can't remember you having a handbag
when you first came in.

ANGELA [*angrily*]   You can't remember! Well, I had one, and a good one, 450
too, and I've got to get it—see! D'ye mean to hint I'm making it up?

MULLIGAN [*in agony*]   No, no; but for God's sake, speak easy; please,
Angela!

ANGELA [*leaving her shoes down, and pulling the cushions off the settee and*
throwing them on the floor]   Well, then, find it for me. Mind you, 455
had I been down the street when I missed it, I'd have banged the
door down to get in to get it!

MULLIGAN [*leaving his shoes down, and pulling the table about, pulling the*

chairs from the wall, and pulling the umbrella-stand away, to look 460
behind them]   This is terrible! I'll be ruined if I'm discovered. What
colour was it? Where had you it last? Where d'ye think you could have
put it?

ANGELA   I don't know, fool. It was a dark-green one I bought last week,
and gave five pounds for. I got confused and forgot about everything
when you started to pull me on to your knee. 465

MULLIGAN   But we can't stay to look for it. Miss Mossie'll soon be going
about with her candle in her hand.

ANGELA   I'm not going without it! I think I remember you snatching it
outa me hand when you started to pull me on to your lap.

MULLIGAN   Oh, give over about me pulling you on to me lap, and give us 470
a hand to look for it! *[He runs into the bedroom, and starts to search
there, flinging the bedclothes about. In bedroom]* I can't see it anywhere here, so I can't.

ANGELA *[tearfully]*   And I was to come here only for a quiet glass of wine
and a biscuit. That's what you said, and kept repeating; and I be- 475
lieved you, oh, I believed you!

MULLIGAN *[coming out of bedroom]*   No sign of it there.

ANGELA *[marching up and down the room, clasping and unclasping her
hands]*   Oh, isn't this a nice end to a quiet glass of wine and a biscuit! 480

MULLIGAN   Get a hold of yourself. What sort was it?

ANGELA   A pure morocco leather one, dark green, with initials on it fili-
greed in mother o' pearl.

MULLIGAN *[impatiently]*   Yis, yis; *[anxiously]* but how much was in it altogether? 485

ANGELA   Fifteen pounds odd.

MULLIGAN *[aghast]*   Good Lord!

ANGELA   And the lipstick you couldn't find musta been in it too; silver-
cased and all; and a lovely bracelet watch waiting to be mended. Oh,
what will I do! Oh, yes, and a silver brooch I wanted to get a pin for. 490
What will I do, what will I do?

MULLIGAN   You slip off, and when I come back, I'll search high and low
for it.

ANGELA *[with rising nervous tension]*   And how am I to fare till you find
it? You wouldn't turn a hair if I was willing to go in my shift! John 495
Jo Mulligan, you're a dasthard! It would be the price of you to let
Miss Mossie and the whole house know the sort you are!

MULLIGAN   For God's sake, Angela! What d'ye want me to do; only tell
me what you want me to do?

ANGELA *[moving about distracted]*   And to think I thought I was safe with 500
you! *[Her glance falls on the cupboard, and she makes a bee-line for
it.]* Could it have got in here?

MULLIGAN *[hastily]*   No, no; it couldn't have got in there.

ANGELA [*drawing out a leather wallet*]   What's this?

MULLIGAN [*going over to take wallet from her*]   Nothing there but a few 505
private letters, and a lot of bills.
[*But before he can reach her to get it away, she has whisked a bundle of notes from it.*]

ANGELA [*giggling—a little hysterical*]   John Jo's hidden treasure. [*She
counts them rapidly.*] Eighteen pounds ten. All fresh ones too. Nice 510
to handle.

MULLIGAN   They're not mine. I'm minding them for a friend. You can put
them back.

ANGELA [*mockingly*]   At once, dear. I'll mind them for you, dear. [*She
takes a cheque-book out of the wallet.*] A cheque-book, too. [*As he 515
comes closer*] Keep your distance, keep your distance, or I'll claw the
gob off you!

MULLIGAN   I was only going to give you a few of them to tide you over,
dear.

ANGELA [*fiercely*]   You were? How sweet of you! I'll have them all, you 520
primly-born yahoo. And more [*She raises her voice.*] And more!

MULLIGAN [*whisperingly*]   All right, all right, only keep calm; keep quiet.

ANGELA [*indicating the cheque-book*]   Make me out a cheque for five
pounds like a decent, honest man.

MULLIGAN [*taking a fountain pen from his pocket, and settling down to 525
write*]   All right; anything to pacify you.

ANGELA [*patronisingly patting his head*]   You're not the worst, John Jo.
You're really a pleasant chap when you get going. Make a cheque out
for ten, darling, to compensate for the goods in the handbag. Ten,
dear; that's all now. Well, we've had a right good time together. Pity 530
I can't stay longer. See you again soon, when you're feeling frisky, eh?
Naughty boy! [*She has taken the cheque from the dazed* MULLIGAN,
*put it in his wallet, and now straightens herself to go, taking her shoes
off the floor, and putting them under an arm. At the door*] I know
my way down, so don't you stir. I'll steal away like a maid of Araby. 535
I'll be seeing you. Be good.
[*Dazed and stunned,* MULLIGAN *sits still for a few seconds; then he
gets up from the chair to look around him.*]

MULLIGAN [*rising from the chair*]   Fully-fledged for hell, that one, and
you never noticed it! Oh, John Jo, John Jo! [*He suddenly stiffens.*] 540
She had no handbag! She never had a handbag! Oh, Christ, she's
codded me! [*He looks in the cupboard, then looks over the table.*]
She's taken away me wallet, too! Me umbrella!
[*He runs out of the room to follow her, so agitated that he leaves door
wide open behind him. There are a few moments of silence; then* 545
MISS MOSSIE *appears at the open door with a lighted candle in a can-
dlestick in her hand. She is a short, stout woman of thirty-five or so.
She is dressed in a brown skirt reaching to her ankles, and we get a*

glimpse of black stockings sinking into a pair of stout black shoes. Her
dark hair is gathered into a knob, and made to lie quiet on the nape   550
of her neck. She wears a yellow jumper, and a brown Jaeger topcoat
is flung over her shoulders. She wears spectacles. She looks into the
room for a moment, a look of perplexed anxiety on her face, then
turns aside to call to HALIBUT.]

MISS MOSSIE   Mr. Halibut, Mr. Halibut, come up, come up quick! [HALIBUT   555
appears at the door. He is now wearing a pair of blue pyjamas, cov-
ered by a dressing-gown of dark red, and his bare feet are slippered.]
Oh, Mr. Halibut, what can the matter be? Oh, dear, what can the
matter be?

HALIBUT [*agog with excitement*]   What's up, Miss Mossie?   560

MISS MOSSIE [*coming into the sitting-room, followed by* HALIBUT]   Looka
the state of the room; and Mr. Mulligan's just run out into the street
in his stockinged feet!

HALIBUT [*astonished*]   No? How d'ye know he went out into the street?

MISS MOSSIE   I seen him go. I heard something stirring when I was putting   565
on me jumper, so I looked out, and there was Mr. Mulligan scuttling
down the stairs. Walking in his sleep, he musta been. He had an air
on him as if he was enraptured within himself; a look as if he was
measuring life and death together to see which was tallest.

HALIBUT   Is that right? Coming back from the dance, I thought I saw   570
him on the stairs, too, but when I came up, he was sitting reading
Yeats's poems. Said he couldn't sleep. I warned him against the
poems.

MISS MOSSIE [*coming over to the bedroom door, and opening it*]   Oh,
looka the state of this room, too! Everything flung about.   575

HALIBUT [*awed*]   Looks like he had a wild fit, or something!

MISS MOSSIE   Something terrific! This isn't just disarray, Mr. Halibut—it's
an upheaval! You don't think it could be that something suddenly went
wrong in him?

HALIBUT [*startled by a thought*]   Wrong in him, Miss Mossie? What could   580
go wrong in him?

MISS MOSSIE   A quietly-disposed man like Mr. Mulligan doesn't do this
[*indicating disorder of rooms*] without something whizzing within
him.

HALIBUT [*frightened*]   You mean in his mind?   585

MISS MOSSIE [*firmly*]   We must act. We can't let him roam the streets or
do any harm here. I'll phone the police and a doctor, and I'll slip
out for the constable that usually stands at the street corner. [*They
move to the sitting-room door.*]   I'll go now. You stay on the lobby
here in the dark, and watch over him if he comes back.   590

HALIBUT [*dubiously*]   I'm not a strong man, Miss Mossie.

MISS MOSSIE   After all, Mr. Halibut, we don't want to be murdhered in our
beds.

HALIBUT [*crossing himself*]   God forbid, Miss Mossie!

MISS MOSSIE   And the odd thing is, he'd be doing it with the best inten-   595
tions. If he comes back, he may still be asleep, so don't shout at him
and wake him too suddenly. Just humour him, unless he gets violent.

HALIBUT [*picturing in his mind all that might happen*]   Ay, violent—that's
the danger!

MISS MOSSIE   Then you'll just have to close with him, and hold him till   600
the constable comes.

HALIBUT [*panic-stricken*]   Close with him? Hold him till the constable
comes? But, woman alive, I'm not gifted that way!

MISS MOSSIE   You'll do your best, I know; if he overcomes you, it won't
be your fault.   605

HALIBUT   Don't you think it would be only prudent to have a poker handy?

MISS MOSSIE   Too violent-looking. [*Indicating a corner of the lobby*]
There's the bit of curtain-pole I use to push the window up—you can
keep that handy; but don't let him guess why you have it. [*She takes
the key from the inside and puts it in the keyhole on the outside of*   610
the door.] There now, if the worst comes, you can fly out and lock him
safely within the room.

HALIBUT   It sounds easy, but it's really a desperate situation.

MISS MOSSIE   Don't let him see you're frightened. Keep him under command. That's what me sisther did with me when I used to walk in my   615
sleep a few years ago.

HALIBUT [*stricken with confused anxiety*]   What, you used to sleep-walk,
too?

MISS MOSSIE   That's why I dhread the habit coming back to me, for then
you never know whether you're always asleep and never awake, or   620
always awake and never asleep. I'll be off now. You'll be quite safe
if you only keep your wits about you.

[*She goes off with her candle, leaving a world of darkness to poor*
HALIBUT. *There is a silence for a few moments, then the watcher in*
the darkness, and any who are listening, hear a patter of feet on stairs   625
outside, and the voice of MULLIGAN *calling out loudly the name of*
MISS MOSSIE *several times. Then a great bang of a closing door; dead*
silence for a moment, till MULLIGAN *is heard calling again.*]

MULLIGAN [*outside*]   Dan, Dan, are you awake? Dan Halibut, are you
awake, man? [MULLIGAN *appears on the lobby just outside the sitting-*   630
room door. He is talking to himself, a haggard, lost, and anxious look
on his face, and he is a little out of breath. His coat and hat are
damped by the falling sleet outside; his feet wet. He pauses on the
lobby, and waves his electric torch about till its beam falls on the
silent and semi-crouching HALIBUT.] Oh, it's here you are? Thought   635
you were in bed fast asleep. Called you, but got no answer. What a
night! Twenty-eight pounds ten gone with the wind! [*He lifts a*
cushion from the floor to look under it.] It's not there! [*He flings it*

viciously away. To HALIBUT] What has you here in the dark and the cold? 640

HALIBUT   Just shutting the window to keep it from rattling.

MULLIGAN [*going into the sitting-room*]   We must do something. Miss Mossie's gone rushing hatless out into the darkness and the sleet. Hatless, mind you! Looked as if she was sleep-walking again. A one-time habit of hers, did you know? You'll have to go after her. 645

HALIBUT [*coming a little way into the room, but staying close to the door, holding the sprig of curtain-pole behind his back*]   I know, I know; but what were you doing out in the sleet and the darkness *yourself?* And in your stockinged feet, too, look at them!

MULLIGAN   Me? Couldn't sleep; felt stifled; went out for some fresh air. 650 Didn't think of shoes. Something whizzing in me mind. [*A little impatiently*] But you dress and go after Mossie. See what's wrong with her. Several times, before you came, she came into my room, fast asleep, at dead of the night, with a loving look on her face. We can't afford to let ourselves be murdhered in our sleep, Dan. [*He flops into* 655 *chair.*] Saint Fairdooshius, succour me this night.

HALIBUT [*bewildered with anxiety, eyes lifted to ceiling in a low appeal*] Oh, sweet Saint Slumbersnorius, come to me help now! [*To* MULLIGAN] All right; yes. I'll settle you in first. You go to bed, John Jo, quiet. Go to bed, go to bed, and go asleep, and go asleep! 660

MULLIGAN [*looking at* HALIBUT *curiously—a little impatiently*]   I've told you I can't sleep. Twenty-eight pounds ten, and my fine leather wallet gone forever!

HALIBUT [*in a commanding sing-song way*]   Never mind. Put them out of your thoughts, and go to bed, go to bed, and go to sleep, and go to 665 sleep—I command!

MULLIGAN [*half rising from his chair so that* HALIBUT *backs towards the door—staring at* HALIBUT *in wonderment*]   What's wrong with you, Halibut? [*He sinks back into the chair again, and* HALIBUT *returns into the room.*] Me best coat and best umbrella, too! Gone. 670 [*His glance happens to fall on his hand, and he springs out of the chair with a jump, sending* HALIBUT *backing swiftly from the room again.*]

MULLIGAN   Me ring! I never got it back!

HALIBUT [*straying cautiously back into the room again*]   Money, best coat, best umbrella, wallet, and ring! When did you lose all these 675 things, man?

MULLIGAN   A minute or so ago; no, no, an hour ago; two hours ago; more. [*He leans his arms dejectedly on the table, and buries his head on them.*] I di'n't lost them, Dan; I gave them away, flung them all away!

HALIBUT   In an excess of charity of having too many possessions, or what? 680 You know, I've warned you, John Jo; often warned you.

MULLIGAN [*raising his head from his arms—resentfully and suspiciously*] Warned me? How warned me?

HALIBUT   I warned you that running out to devotions morning and night, and too much valuable time spent on your knees, would upset you 685 one day or another. And, now, you'll have to admit that these things couldn't have happened to you if you had had a girl with you tonight.

MULLIGAN   [*with a wail of resentment*]   Oooh! Don't be a blasted fool! [*He notices that Halibut has something behind his back.*] What's that you have behind you?   690

HALIBUT   [*trying to be carelessly funny*]   Me tail. Didn't you know? I'm a wild animal. [*He wags the piece of curtain-pole.*] Now, the wild animal says you're to go to bed, go to bed, and go to sleep, and go to sleep. Obey the wild animal at once!

MULLIGAN   [*slowly rising from the chair, staring anxiously and suspiciously* 695 *at* HALIBUT]   What's amiss with you, Halibut? Are you sleep-walking, too? Leave down that curtain-pole. Don't be acting the goat, man. [*Coaxingly—as* HALIBUT *brings the piece of curtain-pole to his front*] Go on, Dan, oul' son, leave the thing down!

HALIBUT   As soon as you're safely settled in bed, John Jo. Then I'll pop out 700 after Mossie. To bed; to bed; and go to sleep, go to sleep—I command!

MULLIGAN   [*fear having come on him—suddenly seizes the wine-bottle by the neck, and holds it as a club, running to window, swinging back the curtains, and trying to open it*]   God Almighty, I'm alone with a 705 lunatic! [*Shouting—as he tries to open the window*] Help!

HALIBUT   I'll not let you destroy yourself—come away from that window, or I'll flatten you!

MULLIGAN   [*wheeling round, still holding bottle by the neck to use it as a club, and facing towards* HALIBUT]   Looka, Halibut, leave that club 710 down. [*Coaxingly*] Now, be sensible, Dan, like a good chap, and drop that club.

HALIBUT   Drop that bottle first, I say; drop that bottle first!

MULLIGAN   Drop that club, I tell you. [*Fiercely*] Drop that club!

HALIBUT   [*dancing up and down—panic-stricken*]   Put that bottle down! 715 Put it down, and go to bed, I tell you!

MULLIGAN   [*dodging about*]   Drop that club at once, Halibut!

HALIBUT   Put that bottle down immediately!

MULLIGAN   I command you!

HALIBUT   I command you!   720

[*They have been dodging about without coming near to each other;* HALIBUT *swinging the piece of curtain-pole to and fro in front of him for protection. In one of the blind swings, the pole slips from his hand, and sails out through the window, causing a great sound of falling glass. They both stare at the window—dumbfounded for a few* 725 *moments.*]

MULLIGAN   [*excitedly*]   Aha, I've got you now!

[*But* HALIBUT *has fled from the room, banged the door after him, and*

locked it from the outside. MULLIGAN *hurries to the door and presses*
his back to it. Then MISS MOSSIE'S *voice is heard outside.*   730

MISS MOSSIE [*outside*]   Oh, what's happened? I feared it would end in
violence! Mr. Halibut, Mr. Halibut, are you much hurted?

MULLIGAN [*shouting through the door to* MISS MOSSIE]   Miss Mossie; here,
Miss Mossie!

MISS MOSSIE [*from outside*]   Oh, Mr. Mulligan, what have you done to   735
poor, innocent Mr. Halibut? We've found him lying in a dead faint
out here on the lobby.

MULLIGAN [*indignantly—shouting outwards*]   Poor, innocent Mr. Halibut! What has he not tried to do to me! He rushed in here, lunacy
looking out of his eyes, and tried to shatther me with a club, with a   740
club; tried to murdher me! Now he's locked me in.

MISS MOSSIE [*soothingly*]   Now isn't that a shame! What a naughty man he
is! Never mind now. You go to your chair and sit down by the fire,
and I'll get the key to open your door. Everything will be all right,
Mr. Mulligan.   745

MULLIGAN [*indignantly*]   Everything isn't all right now! I'll live no longer
in the same house with Halibut!

MISS MOSSIE [*coaxingly*]   Do go and sit down by the fire, Mr. Mulligan,
there's a dear. I'll bring you a hot drink, and we'll talk about things;
do, now, like a good man. [*Mulligan goes to the fireplace, and sits*   750
down in the armchair. He lights a cigarette and puffs it indignantly.
After a few moments, the door opens, and MISS MOSSIE *lets into the*
room a big, topcoated and helmeted policeman, the doctor with his
case, wearing an anxious look on his face, and a nurse, enveloped with
a dark-blue cloak on the left side of which is a white circle surrounding   755
a large red cross. She carries the usual nursing-suitcase in her hand.
MISS MOSSIE *is in the midst of them, and* HALIBUT, *in the rear, with a*
ghastly pale face, rises on his tiptoes to gaze over their shoulders. All
but HALIBUT *form a semicircle round* MULLIGAN'S *back, who puffs away,*
unconscious of the entrance of the crowd. Bending sidewise from be-   760
hind the policeman to speak to the sitting MULLIGAN]   Now, Mr.
Mulligan, we'll see what all this little disturbance was about, and
what was the cause of it, and then we'll be all—er—O.K., eh? And
I've brought in a few kind friends to help me.

MULLIGAN [*rising from his chair in blank surprise, and almost echoing* MISS   765
MOSSIE]   A few friends to help you? [*He turns around to face* MISS
MOSSIE, *but is confronted by the big, helmeted policeman, the doctor,*
and the nurse. He slides back into the chair almost in a dead faint.
Falling back into the chair] Good God!

QUESTIONS

1. O'Casey's opening stage directions are longer than those of Synge in
    Riders to the Sea. Compare the two sets of stage directions. Does

O'Casey give the reader any information of a different sort from that of Synge?

2. What things in Mulligan's first speech arouse questions in the reader's mind?

3. What departures from usual social norms are we aware of up to the entrance of Angela?

4. How are the differing characters of Mulligan and of Angela brought out in their conversation? What are they arguing over?

5. What is there in the situation and dialogue that makes the reader not take their predicament too seriously? Which one do you laugh at more? Why?

6. From the references to the poetry of Yeats and Angela's quotation at lines 200–201 from Shakespeare's *Romeo and Juliet* (II, 1, lines 17–19)—"Angela's bright eyes, her scarlet lip . . ." what do you take to be the educational and social level of the characters?

7. What effects are created by the business of Mulligan's unlocking and locking the cupboard, Angela's singing, and his frequent appeals to saints? What is funny about their argument at lines 238–293?

8. O'Casey invents a succession of complications that delay Angela's departure, maintain suspense, and arouse laughter. Enumerate them, and the effect of each one.

9. A good dramatist has a reason for the details he uses. Why did O'Casey set his story in a sleety night and require coats and an umbrella among the properties?

10. When Mulligan realizes that he has been cheated, what is the reader's reaction, to sympathize or laugh at him? Why?

11. Why is it comic for Miss Mossie to say, "He had an air on him as if he was enraptured . . ."? What is the connection between the search for the handbag and the actions of Miss Mossie? What does she think has happened to Mulligan?

12. How do Halibut's reactions and comments create further humor?

13. After Mulligan returns to his flat, what mistaken ideas do each of the two men arrive at regarding the other's behavior?

14. Why is their "fight" a comic thing?

15. How does the element of surprise contribute to the comic effect as the play ends?

16. Mulligan represents himself as a pious and respectable person. Why do we regard him as a figure of fun and refuse to feel sorry for him?

17. What satirical element does this play have? Against what is satire directed?

18. To what extent and in what respects is the comedy of *Bedtime Story* based on (1) physical situations, (2) misunderstandings, and (3) character?

SECTION THREE

POEMS

Reading Poems

I

When we look at a poem on a page or listen to a poem recited, we see or hear words arranged in such an order that they have meaning. So our judgments of poems as works of art must be based on consideration of the words chosen, of the way in which the words are arranged, and of the total meanings that the word arrangements communicate.

But the words in prose are also arranged in meaningful order. If we heard Portia's reply to Shylock in *The Merchant of Venice*, "The quality of mercy is not strain'd, it droppeth as the gentle rain from heaven upon the place beneath," without knowing that Shakespeare wrote these words as poetry, we would not be able offhand to distinguish an essential difference between her statement and a statement in prose—for example, "The likelihood of rain now is not great; it seems as though the forage crops can safely be harvested this fall." Even if we restore the look of poetry to Shakespeare's lines, thus,

> The quality of mercy is not strain'd,
> It droppeth as the gentle rain from heaven
> Upon the place beneath,

we have merely made clearer the rhythmical pattern in which the words of the statement were arranged. The prose statement may also be given the look of poetry, thus:

> The likelihood of rain now is not great;
> It seems as though the forage crops can safely
> Be harvested this fall.

Actually the two statements have the same rhythm.

But analysis reveals differences between the statements.

1. They are about different subjects. The first is about that forgiving, pitying frame of mind, that attribute of character, called mercy. The second is about weather and crops.

2. The persons who made the statements are different: a lawyer pleading for a client; a weather forecaster, or reporter, giving information.

3. The intentions of the speakers are different. We may say that the first statement is informative, for it describes mercy; but those in the play who hear the speech, and those who read it, are not interested in the value of the statement as information. The intention of the speaker is persuasion: to persuade a vengeance-bent man to be merciful to one over whom he has power. The statement has value only if Shylock's feelings can be touched by it, or if the reader's own feelings are so touched that he contrasts the ideal virtue set forth by Portia with the vindictiveness of Shylock. This speech affects our feelings, our attitudes, our judgment upon a fellow man. But the statement from the weather and crop report is intended only to convey information; it has value only to those who can make use of it, the farmer and the hay buyer. Most readers will read it without emotion; some, because of their financial interests, may read it with relief, with joy, or with disappointment; but its value can be judged finally only by its truth. The weather and the harvest alone can prove the worth of the statement. Its value is also temporary: when the haying season is over, the statement will be valueless except to a historian.

4. The fourth difference between the two statements is highly important, namely, the manner in which their meanings are conveyed. Both statements are easily intelligible, but the techniques of communication are not the same. We can bring this point out by changing the words of the statements. For the second statement, let us substitute, "There is little probability of rain now; farmers, therefore, can cut hay this fall without fear of its getting wet." The intention of the writer is still clear; the efficacy of the statement is just as great as before. The reader is interested in the statement as fact or not-fact, and therefore the way in which the conclusion—no rain—is worded, matters not at all.

Let us consider now the way in which the other statement is communicated. Portia has told Shylock that he must be merciful. Shylock demands, "On what compulsion must I? tell me that." Portia might reply that no one can compel another person to have mercy. This is the bare "meaning" of her speech. But her purpose is persuasion, to influence Shylock toward a change of heart. So she expands the statement: "It droppeth as the gentle rain from heaven upon the place beneath." For this amplification she uses figurative language, she employs imagery; she creates a picture of rain falling. The linguistic symbol R-A-I-N cannot be seen or heard without arousing sense impressions: the look of rain, the feel of rain, the sound rain makes. To help communication, Portia uses her *imagination*: she combines two ideas, making one clarify the other. She asks herself what mercy is like, what she can compare it to, in order to make this merciless man understand it. Her imagination supplies the answer: Mercy cannot be compelled; rain, also, cannot be compelled—in this one respect mercy is like rain.

Portia uses the method we all customarily use when we want to make the unfamiliar, familiar—the method of comparison. This method is particularly valuable when the unfamiliar is an abstraction. "Mercy" is an abstraction, a quality without any physical substance, an idea existing only in the mind. Mercy itself cannot be seen or heard, tasted or touched. That is, it is not *concrete*. Rain, however, is not only familiar to everybody, but is also concrete; it can be seen and heard, touched, tasted, felt. Portia's statement concerning mercy is thus given additional meaning, given more value for its purpose, through the comparison of mercy to the familiar and concrete substance rain.

5. Finally, the amount conveyed and the messages themselves are different. The poetic statement conveys more in a richer way than does the prose statement, because of the compactness and concentration of the poetry. One might at first wonder why Shakespeare used so many words. Why not say, "Mercy cannot be compelled; it falls like rain," and be through? Such a comparison would not clearly communicate Portia's intention because it could include the rain that causes floods, and the rain lashed from thunderclouds by gales. Such rain is not like mercy. "It droppeth as the *gentle* rain. . . ." From all possible kinds of rain, one is selected, that which most exactly fits the intended meaning. But is not the rest of the passage— "from heaven upon the place beneath" (how else and upon what else could the rain drop?) obvious and thus superfluous? No, it is not; although if these words were changed to "from clouds upon the earth," they would be superfluous. Portia is illustrating the idea that mercy is not *strained* (that is, constrained). What place can compel rain to fall upon it? None. If people begged for rain, whom would they implore but heaven, a divine power? Heaven lets the gentle rain fall upon whatever place may be beneath, the will of inhabitants having no power to enforce rainfall. Thus it is suggested that mercy, like rain from heaven, comes from heaven and is therefore a divine quality; so that he who shows mercy is among the finest of men, having in him something of the divine. The words "clouds" and "earth" will not suggest this meaning and are, therefore, *in this statement*, without metaphorical value.

Portia's poetic statement, being imaginative, being basically metaphorical, uses the technique of comparison; it uses concrete imagery to illustrate an abstraction. The concrete illustration makes mercy more real to us; that is, it makes us *realize* a significant thing about mercy. The suggestions of the words chosen serve to clarify the thought, and, further, these words have an emotional appeal that other words close in denotative meaning do not possess. If we remove the image or change the wording, then we lessen the communication between writer and reader.

This is not true of the weather report, where only the facts are important and where emotion has no place. Whether the weather forecaster is vengeful or merciful, sorrowful or glad, his feelings cannot influence the weather. And of course he should not use his imagination in writing his report. He might write, "As little rain will fall this month as on the hot Sahara sands," but the comparison would not efficiently clarify the idea. Readers would prefer to know exactly how much rain he predicts.

We may say, then, that poetry uses language to communicate statements that will influence our feelings and attitudes. It is distinguished by imagination; it employs comparisons and concrete terms and words that have high power of suggestion.

Nevertheless, the contrast we have just observed is a contrast of extremes: a direct, flat, unemotional, unimaginative, utilitarian, and informative statement in prose, and a subtler, imaginative, figurative poetic statement full of feeling. But all prose is not devoid of feeling and imagination; prose ranges from the baldest statement of fact to impassioned outbursts of feeling.

At one extreme we find scientific statements; of all statements they are the least emotional. A scientist must be objective; professionally, he must "discount the human element"—that is, private hates and loves, loyalties and prejudices, must be kept out of the laboratory and out of his statement of results. Because words have powers of suggestion that blur their exact denotation, scientists develop specialized vocabularies that are emotionally neutral. For their most precise statements scientists abandon words and use only numerals and letters, which can have no emotional influence. Feelings must not be allowed to distort the truth.

The scientist, *as a scientist,* must "discount the human element." But in an educational conference an excited scientist once cried, waving his arms: "I say that a single *fact* has more influence in the world than mountains of poetry!" He was not in his laboratory; he was speaking, not as a scientist, but as a man solving a problem in communication. For the successful communication of his own feeling, he adopted the method of comparison, employing in fact the figure of speech know as hyperbole, that is, an exaggerated comparison. He used the technique of a poet. Yet he was speaking, of course, in prose.

Statements of physical scientists, which describe the behavior of phenomena outside of man, are the farthest distance from poetry. Not quite so far removed are the statements of social scientists, for their vocabulary is less specialized and their subject is man—the "human element." History and biography are still nearer to poetry. Historians and biographers are free to exploit most of the emotional resources of language; they are hampered only by the recorded facts of the period or life they deal with. Fiction, being entirely invented, does not have the shackle of recorded fact. Any novel will offer examples of imaginative, emotion-evoking communication.

Other prose forms, such as advertising, editorials, sermons, and other examples of oratory are obviously intended to influence our feelings, opinions, and attitudes. In them, language is frequently exploited with great skill.

Yet poetry is commonly more intense, more symbolic, more rhythmic and musical than prose. Language in poetry is used more vividly and is more concentrated; it tingles with a higher voltage of imagination. Almost everyone is capable of little spurts of poetic imagination; consider, for instance, the maid who was asked by her mistress why she was always laughing and happy and who replied, "Why, ma'am, I jest wears the world like a loose garment." With the half-dozen words of that symbolic comparison, she expressed her attitude very effectively. In poets this power of imagination is stronger, fuller, and more frequently available than with most of us.

Poets are acutely aware of the power of words, and in their best poems they use words with startling precision, with unusual freshness and originality, as does Emily Dickinson for example, in the following stanza:

> I'll tell you how the sun rose,—
> A ribbon at a time,
> The steeples swam in amethyst,
> The news like squirrels ran.

Poets are fine judges of word values too; they must know all the steps along the way from the most neutral or colorless term to that which is richest in associations. For example, the abstract term "capital punishment" is comparatively neutral; at the opposite extreme the statement "He suffered death on the Cross" rouses a powerful emotion. Because of its centuries of use among Christians, the word "cross" has immense symbolic value.

Most poetry has a more regular rhythm than prose, and the great majority of it is written in the regularly recurring units of rhythm called meters. The element of form is very important in poems; their intense effects depend on the arrangement of comparatively few details. Lines are grouped in stanzas of identical patterns of rhyme and line length. Especially significant is the fact that most poetry takes the form of metrical patterns called verse. *Verse* comes from the Latin word *versus*, "a turning." Unlike prose, lines of verse do not go clear to the right margin of the page; they turn back at a given point, usually predetermined by the poet according to his metrical design.

The following statement is written in prose: "Broken in pieces all asunder, Lord, hunt me not, a thing forgot, once a poor creature, now a wonder, a wonder tortured in the space betwixt this world and that of grace." Set up in a stanza, as George Herbert arranged these words in "Affliction," the turns of the lines (technically, each line is a *verse*) have a special effect:

> Broken in pieces all asunder,
> Lord, hunt me not,
> A thing forgot,

Once a poor creature, now a wonder,
A wonder tortured in the space
Betwixt this world and that of grace.

When the eye goes back to start a new line, the reader feels an effect quite different from that of prose, and the voice also responds to the turning. Thus we see that the stanza *form* makes us realize the pressure of feeling behind the statement through the tension created by constraining the statement, with its grammatical pattern, into the pattern of rhyme and meter required by the stanza.

Poets usually pay more attention to the sounds of the words they use than do prose writers. As G. L. Raymond has said in *Poetry as a Representative Art* (p. 9), "Certain words—and they are those which skilful writers always prefer to use, if they can—sound more like what they mean than others do." There are innumerable examples of poetic sound effects, from the obvious imitation of sound in Dryden's "Song for St. Cecilia's Day":

The double, double, double beat
Of the thundering drum

and the hearty alliteration of Browning in "How They Brought the Good News from Ghent to Aix":

The broad sun above laughed a pitiless laugh,
'Neath our feet broke the brittle bright stubble like chaff

to the affecting deep "cello music" of Shakespeare's Sonnet 30:

I sigh the lack of many a thing I sought,
And with old woes new wail my dear time's waste

and the slow sonority of Tennyson's "The Princess":

Ancient rosaries,
Laborious Orient ivory, sphere in sphere.

None of these word choices and sound effects is accidental. For poetry is the greatest of word arts, through which interpretations of experience are made distinctive and memorable.

Each element in a poem—all the devices of organization and form, the rhythm, the word values, the figures of speech, the music—combines with the other elements to produce a certain artistic effect. And the satisfactions that come from perceiving how the elements of poetry function are perennial. As Swinburne declared, "Art knows nothing of time; for her there is but one tense, and all ages in her sight are alike the present; there is nothing old in her sight, and nothing new." So long as people exist who understand a language, so long will the poetry of that language exist for their contemplation, pleasure, and enlightenment.

II

The poems that follow have been arranged in a baker's dozen of groups, some of which are based on subject matter, some on formal concerns, and some on theme. Within each group there is a general movement from simple to more complex, although no iron-clad consistency has been insisted upon here any more than in the categories themselves.

The poems of the first group are concerned with nature. "Winter" is a good example of how a poet shows the effects of winter on both animals and man. "Water Moment" is a vivid portrayal of the struggle for existence in nature. The last poem in the group, "Keep in the Heart the Journal Nature Keeps," is a more abstract and philosophical presentation of the round of nature's year.

The second group focuses upon the musical elements of poetry. Here are opportunities for many fine contrasts: for example, the colloquialism and percussive onomatopoeia of "Song for the Clatter Bones" with the very different meter and the sad sonority of "On the Beach at Fontana"; the delicate sound effects without onomatopoeia of "The Turtle" and the verbal imitation of a musical instrument in "Player Piano"; the use of poetic music to intensify emotion in "In Memoriam," and the combinations of descriptive and onomatopoetic diction with emphatic rhythm in "Inversnaid"; finally, the contrasting portrayals of railroad trains in the last two poems.

With an understanding of the matching of music and meaning in poetry now well established, we come to the third group, which contains folk ballads and poems in which such ballads are more or less imitated. The first three are old folk ballads, and the others are contemporary imitations of certain ballad techniques.

The fourth group also has a formal basis; it comprises several sonnets and some fourteen-line poems that we might call near-sonnets. (Sonnets appear in other sections of the collection as well.)

Each poem of the fifth group presents an account of an incident with more or less interpretive comment. Such topics as these might not be thought promising for treatment in poetry—an auto wreck, for example, a boy being whipped, or the replacing of stones in a wall by two farmers —but each poem here has its excellence and demonstrates that poetry is not something divorced from life but that, as Wordsworth wrote, "The objects of the Poet's thoughts are everywhere."

The poems of the sixth group are devoted to the presentation of characters and the interpretation of human character. The portrayal may be ironic, as in "Miniver Cheevy," sympathetic, as in "A Song in the Front Yard," or warmly understanding or appreciative, as in "Ruth" and "To My Mother." The technique of the dramatic monologue is illustrated by Browning's famous "My Last Duchess," and self-analysis is shown in the poems of Brontë and Thoreau. Animal comparisons are used in interesting ways for character analysis by Holbrook and Schwartz.

The seventh group contains brief and relatively more subtle poems, some of which obey the canons of imagism, and which show how much can be accomplished poetically by reference to physical things that can be made to produce an appeal to the imagination.

In the poems of the eighth group homage is paid to beautiful things. The relation of a later poem to an earlier one is demonstrated by placing together Waller's "Go, Lovely Rose" and Pound's "Envoi (1919)." Poe's tribute to a woman is succeeded by reports on aesthetic experiences by Keats and Millay. The section closes with the complex "Ode on a Grecian Urn," which represents the English ode tradition.

Since love poetry is strongly represented in Anglo-American literature, the ninth group comprises poems in this idealistic tradition, the earliest by Shakespeare and Donne and the most recent by Frost and MacLeish.

In the tenth group attitudes toward the death of men in war are represented. Shirley's poem is excellent for studying symbolic techniques; the dignified patriotism of Emerson's "Concord Hymn" is followed by the satire of Cummings; and the pieces by Housman and Smith show different methods and degrees of ironic pathos.

The elegiac mood is of course pronounced in the poems on the theme of death in the eleventh group. The irony and general application of Dickinson's "One Dignity Delays for All" is in contrast with the personal grief conveyed by the other poems, each with a different poetic technique.

In the twelfth group various aspects of the modern world are held up to view. The first three poems in different ways bring out contrasts of contemporary life and older civilizations, and the next three take up more specific situations: Booth's poem makes us think about special privilege; Jarrell's poem explains the life of twentieth-century soldiers; and Simpson's poem focuses on aspects of Nazi persecution. Hoffman's "The Arrival" illustrates allegory as applied to American history. Hecht's poem vividly contrasts an execution in modern Europe with one in the Renaissance. The next two pieces wittily present two types of modern people. The sardonic "Your Attention Please" makes readers feel what nuclear warfare might well be like.

The final section is a kind of extension of the preceding group into more abstract and philosophical territory. Here such themes as the following are given poetic treatment: in what spirit to face the problems of life, the rival claims of spontaneity and of discipline, the value of freedom, dynamism versus contemplation, the difficulties and obligations of reform, which values are most permanent, and finally, what may be hoped for amid the viciousness of modern life. The book is brought to a close with the substantial and relatively complex and philosophical "Prayer for My Daughter" by Yeats and "Waking Early Sunday Morning" by Robert Lowell.

Elements of Nature

Winter

RICHARD HUGHES

Snow wind-whipt to ice
  Under a hard sun:
Stream-runnels curdled hoar
  Crackle, cannot run.

Robin stark dead on twig,   5
  Song stiffened in it:
Fluffed feathers may not warm
  Bone-thin linnet:

Big-eyed rabbit, lost,   10
  Scrabbles the snow,
Searching for long-dead grass
  With frost-bit toe:

Mad-tired on the road
  Old Kelly goes;   15
Through crookt fingers snuffs the air
  Knife-cold in his nose.

Hunger-weak, snow-dazzled,
  Old Thomas Kelly
Thrusts his bit hands, for warmth,   20
  'Twixt waistcoat and belly.

ANALYSIS

Organization The author presents a winter scene in five stanzas.
Stanza 1 shows the severity of the cold, which has caused a hard freeze, so

From *Confessio Juvenis* by Richard Hughes. Reprinted with permission of Chatto and
Windus Ltd., London.

that the landscape is covered with ice. The next four stanzas make us see the effect of the winter on four creatures: a robin has been frozen to death; a very thin linnet is suffering from lack of warmth; a hungry rabbit is trying to scratch through ice to get at some grass to eat; and an old man is also hungry and suffering and is walking along the road. The man, Old Kelly, is presented last in the series of creatures. He appears in a position of climax in the poem, and two stanzas are devoted to him. Kelly is little better off than the other creatures, being hungry, weak, cold, and inadequately clothed. The implication is that even human beings must suffer in winter; winter spares no kind of being.

Musical Elements   At this point, a few words of general explanation are needed. The experienced reader of poetry is aware of stanza units and of other formal devices of organization such as meter and rhyme. The meters—that is, measures—of English poetry are expressed in feet. A foot in poetry is the smallest unit in which stressed and unstressed syllables are combined. To see just how a poet has handled the rhythm of his lines, readers often make a little record of the rhythmic flow of the words by *scanning* the lines. To scan means to divide the verses into feet and to mark the unstressed syllables (usually with -) and the stressed syllables (usually with /). The poetic feet most frequently used in English poetry are

1.   The iamb (- /), as in "agáin"

2.   The anapest (- - /), as in "wīth a smíle/ on hēr líps"

3.   The trochee (/ -), as in "píty"

4.   The dactyl (/ - -), as in "ámbūlance"

Two exceptional feet not used as basic meters but only as variations, or substitutions, within lines, are

5.   The spondee (/ /), as in "Slów, slów,/frésh fóunt"

6.   The pyrrhic (- -), as in the fourth foot of
     "Thē expéc-táncy/and róse/of thē/fáir státe"

Now let us return to the musical elements of "Winter." We are aware of each stanza as a four-line unit with rhymes coming at the ends of lines 2 and 4. Furthermore, the poet composed each stanza according to a repeated pattern of beats in each line: lines 1 and 3 have three feet; lines 2 and 4, two feet. The dominant meter is trochaic and dactylic, but the poet has introduced some feet that are iambic, anapestic, or spondaic. This is the scansion of stanza 1:

     Snów wínd/-whípt tō/íce
     Úndēr ā/hárd sún:

Stream-runnels/curdled/hoar

Crackle,/cannot run.

The first foot of line 1 is a trochee, a stressed syllable followed by an unstressed syllable. The first foot of lines 2 and 3 is a dactyl, a stressed syllable followed by two unstressed syllables. The second foot of line 2 is a spondee, two equally stressed syllables. And the second foot of line 4 is an anapest, two unstressed syllables followed by a stressed syllable. The third foot in lines 1 and 3 is incomplete, or catalectic; the unstressed syllable of the trochee has been omitted.

The poet has used enough stressed syllables (as in the second foot of line 2) to slow down the lines and make them rather stiff. They are anything but tripping; they cannot be read fast. This stiffness is suited to the ice-stiffened landscape and the icy cruel winter day. The poet has also used alliteration—the repeating of the same consonant sound at the begining of stressed syllables—a device that for ages English poets and readers have liked. The alliterative sounds also tend to slow down the movement of the lines. We note especially the *t* and *k* sounds in stanza 1—"whipt to," "curdle," "crackle," "cannot;" the *st, d, t,* and *g* sounds in stanza 2—"stark dead," "twig," "stiffened;" the *g, d, st,* and *t* sounds in stanza 3—"long-dead grass," "frost-bit toe;" and the *k, g, n, t,* and *b* sounds in the last two stanzas—"Kelly goes," "crookt fingers snuffs," "knife-cold," "nose," "hunger-weak," "Thomas Kelly," "thrusts," "bit hands," " 'twixt waistcoat," and "belly." Consonantal sounds predominate, and these prevailingly explosive sounds prevent the poem from being read in a smooth and flowing fashion.

Furthermore, the bringing together of consonants requires unusual effort to enunciate the words and thus stiffens some lines even more: "whipt to" (1),[1] "crackle, cannot" (4), "stark dead on twig" (5), "long-dead grass" (11), "frost-bit toe" (12), "mad-tired" (13), "crookt fingers snuffs" (15), " 'twixt waistcoat" (20). After reading the lines aloud, we can appreciate how deliberately the poet worked to achieve this harsh, difficult music that is in keeping with the scene and spirit of the poem.

Diction   "Winter" illustrates what has been said about how poets use figures of speech and language of unusual precision. The words of the poem have been carefully chosen to convey vivid pictures and exact meanings. Note that "wind-whipt" is basically a metaphor, that is, a figure of comparison in which one thing is said to be another because of identical qualities they have. Thus, the wind is a whip; both wind and whip inflict pain by a forceful movement called lashing. Hughes uses "wind-whipt" to reveal, metaphorically, the force of the wind. The sun is not warm and comforting but "hard." We need to know the meanings of "runnels" and "curdled hoar." Runnels are tiny channels or streamlets, and the ice of the

---

[1] Numbers in parentheses throughout Section Three refer to lines in the poem being discussed.

small streams looks cloudily white like curdled milk; when the sun shines on it the ice shows a crackling, but it is not melted and remains stiff. The dead robin is frozen stiff; "stark" is a vigorous word meaning strong, harsh, stiff, bleak. The poet imagines that even the song of the bird has been caught inside it and frozen up. The plight of the linnet is brought out by the compressed term "bone-thin," and we can visualize the rabbit clearly because of the adjective "big-eyed." It is not a usual word to describe a rabbit; it makes us appreciate the creature's thinness too. "Scrabbles," meaning scratches or scrapes, is a word that makes us see the actions of the rabbit by the marks it leaves on the icy snow.

"Mad-tired" is the emphatic term introducing Kelly. It can mean "out of his mind with fatigue" or "not right in the head and tired from wandering aimlessly." With fingers bent round his nose Kelly tries to warm them a bit with his breath. But "crookt" is a more precise, powerful adjective than "bent." His fingers have been made crooked with age and stiffened with cold; in fact, his hands are "bit hands." To call them "bit," without mention of the frost that bit them (like a fierce animal?) seems to make the pain in them greater. We sometimes speak of a wind like a knife. Here the poet has called the air "knife-cold," a term emphatic and satisfying to one who remembers how such winter air affects the breather. "Hunger-weak" and "snow-dazzled," along with "mad-tired," are the only words in the poem that interpret the inner condition of one of the creatures. These interpretive terms make Kelly's state seem even worse than that of the linnet and rabbit. But the poet ends with another pictorial element, that of Kelly thrusting his hands under his waistcoat (vest) for warmth; we realize when we complete our mental picture of the scene that he has no overcoat, the waistcoat clearly being his chief outer garment.

Theme   The poet lets his scene speak for itself. It tells us that winter is harsh and causes suffering to the creatures who have to be out in such cold. The poem makes the situation real and vivid for us by means of its several examples. The climactic example shows a man reduced to the condition of animals. As normal readers we understand the situation so clearly exhibited to us, and we probably feel regretful about the suffering and sorry for the sufferers. Many poets of the nineteenth century would have diluted such a poem by advising the reader to feel pity or even to do something to help the sufferers. But the twentieth-century poet does not wish to insult his reader's intelligence or imaginative powers by addressing him like a preacher or editorial writer.

We can admire this poem for its precision and functional beauty. All its parts work together to produce an effective scene, a rendition of winter that is convincing because of its organization, its well-chosen language, and its fitting word music.

Water Moment

EDMUND BLUNDEN

The silver eel slips through the waving weeds,
And in the tunnelled shining stone recedes;
The earnest eye surveys the crystal pond
And guards the cave; the sweet shoals pass beyond.
The watery jewels that these have for eyes,   5
The tiger streaks of him that hindmost plies,
The red-gold wings that smooth their daring paces,
The sunlight dancing about their airs and graces,
Burn that strange watcher's heart; then the sly brain
Speaks, all the dumb shoal shrieks, and by the stone   10
The silver death writhes with the chosen one.

QUESTIONS

1. This is in part a poem of observations and description, in part a poem of interpretation. What does the observer see as he looks into the pond?
2. Where can the poem be divided into its three parts of beginning, middle, and end?
3. What do the "shoals" of line 4 refer to?
4. Which terms are most effective in communicating the pictorial elements of the scene?
5. "Earnest eye" and "sweet shoals" are not descriptive terms like "waving weeds" and "shining stone." From what point of view do they interpret the experience of the poet? Of the eel?
6. What terms make the "sweet shoals" seem especially attractive? If the "strange watcher" were human and his heart *burned* for something, what feelings would he be experiencing? Love? Hatred? Anger? Envy? Desire? How do you relate lines 5–9 to "the chosen one" of line 11?
7. Analyze and explain the ironical effect created by the close of the poem.
8. What is the prevailing meter of the poem? prevailing rhyme scheme? What metrical variations do you find in the last four lines? To what parts do they give emphasis? How does "brain" (9) function in the rhyme scheme?
9. "Airs and graces" would ordinarily be applied to whom?

From *English Poems* by Edmund Blunden. Reprinted by permission of A. D. Peters & Company.

10. Since the shoal is "dumb," what is the sense of "shrieks"?
11. What does "silver death" mean? What are the connotations of "writhes"? Compare the last line with the first line in terms of rhythm and connotations.
12. Whether or not a human being can really understand an eel's feelings and reactions when it captures its prey, this poetic account of the event makes it interesting. A scientific book on eels (Leon Bertin, *Eels: A Biological Study*, London, 1956, pp. 18–19) says:

> Fishermen and naturalists of all times have recognized the existence of many kinds of eels by their colour and by the shape of the head. The big eels caught in the autumn generally have brilliant and contrasting colours, which the ordinary eels do not have. Their black backs contrast with their coppery flanks and especially with the brilliant white underparts. These are called Silver Eels, and are the sexually-mature individuals taken in the course of their migration towards the Sargasso Sea.

What are the main differences between the scientific account and the poetic one by Blunden?

Keep in the Heart the Journal Nature Keeps

CONRAD AIKEN

    Keep in the heart the journal nature keeps;
    Mark down the limp nasturtium leaf with frost;
    See that the hawthorn bough is ice-embossed,
    And that the snail, in season, has his grief;
    Design the winter on the window pane;   5
    Admit pale sun through cobwebs left from autumn;
    Remember summer when the flies are stilled;
    Remember spring, when the cold spider sleeps.

    Such diary, too, set down as this: the heart
    Beat twice or thrice this day for no good reason;   10
    For friends and sweethearts dead before their season;
    For wisdom come too late, and come to naught.
    Put down "the hand that shakes," "the eye that glazes";
    The "step that falters betwixt thence and hence";
    Observe that hips and haws burn brightest red   15
    When the North Pole and sun are most apart.

Note that the moon is here, as cold as ever,
With ages on her face, and ice and snow;
Such as the freezing mind alone can know,
When loves and hates are only twigs that shiver.   20
Add in a postscript that the rain is over,
The wind from southwest backing to the south,
Disasters all forgotten, hurts forgiven;
And that the North Star, altered, shines forever.

Then say: I was a part of nature's plan;   25
Knew her cold heart, for I was consciousness;
Came first to hate her, and at last to bless;
Believed in her; doubted; believed again.
My love the lichen had such roots as I,—
The snowflake was my father; I return,   30
After this interval of faith and question,
To nature's heart, in pain, as I began.

QUESTIONS

1. Some poems are dominated by a single metaphor. This poem is dominated by the metaphor of keeping a journal or diary. Note down all the references in the first three stanzas to entries in a diary. In what sense does nature keep a journal?
2. The poet tells himself (and the reader): "Keep *in the heart* the journal nature keeps." If one does so, what attitude will one have toward the phenomena of nature? Will he think nature is planned and regular or capricious and without plan?
3. What are the concrete examples of nature's behavior in lines 2–6 supposed to illustrate? In what other lines do you find similar illustrations?
4. Line 4 speaks of things happening "in season." Which seasons are mentioned in lines 5–8? Why are the seasons mentioned in a particular order?
5. Where do references to renewed life or renewed hope come in stanzas 1–3? With what elements of nature do these references contrast?
6. "Then say" of line 25 is like a conclusion reached after considering the evidence presented in stanzas 1–3. State this conclusion in your own words.
7. How is the poet (or reader) able to know the heart of nature (26)? What relation does he believe he has with nature? (Remember that the snowflake of line 30 is a form of water.) Explain the reference to pain in line 32.
8. Often a poet sets up a rhyme scheme in his first stanza and follows the same rhyme scheme in the other stanzas of a poem. Has Aiken done that here? The first and last lines of the first stanza rhyme. Does the

final word of line 4 play any part in the rhyme scheme? What other lines rhyme?

9. What examples of alliteration do you note in stanzas 1, 2, and 4? What examples of assonance (similarity of vowel sounds) are in stanza 3? What sort of vowel music does stanza 3 have?

10. The hawthorn (3) is also known as may; it is associated with spring flowers and maying. Is "hawthorn" a more effective word to use than "apple" or "maple" or "hemlock"? Explain. Is "bough" a better word than "twig" in line 3? What is the exact meaning of "embossed"?

11. How can hips and haws *burn* (15)? To what extent does Aiken use similes and metaphors in this poem?

12. In some poems the lines are mostly run-on lines; that is, the sense continues unchecked by any mark of punctuation, as from line 9 to line 10: "the heart/Beat twice or thrice." Other poems have lines that are mostly end-stopped; that is, a mark of punctuation requires a pause after the last word of the line, as does the semicolon at the end of line 1. Are the lines of this poem mostly run-on or mostly end-stopped? How does the answer to this question bear on the question of the movement of the poem? Is it fast or slow; gay or grave; formal or informal?

13. What kind of human being does the speaker in this poem seem to be?

Sound Effects

Song for the Clatter Bones

FREDERICK ROBERT HIGGINS

God rest that Jewy woman,
Queen Jezebel, the bitch
Who peeled the clothes from her shoulder-bones
Down to her spent teats
As she stretched out of the window   5
Among the geraniums, where
She chaffed and laughed like one half daft
Titivating her painted hair—

King Jehu he drove to her,
She tipped him a fancy beck;   10
But he from his knacky side-car spoke
"Who'll break that dewlapped neck?"
And so she was thrown from the window;
Like Lucifer she fell
Beneath the feet of the horses and they beat   15
The light out of Jezebel.

That corpse wasn't planted in clover;
Ah, nothing of her was found
Save those grey bones that Hare-foot Mike
Gave me for their lovely sound;   20
And as once her dancing body
Made star-lit princes sweat
So I'll just clack: though her ghost lacks a back
There's music in the old bones yet.

ANALYSIS

Theme Many painters have painted biblical scenes or scenes from classical stories, translating these scenes into life as the artist knew it, creat-

From *The Gap of Brightness*. Reprinted by permission of The Macmillan Company and Macmillan & Co., Ltd.

ing faces, costumes, and environment of the artist's own time and place. The various Annunciations, Madonnas, and Crucifixions by medieval and Renaissance German, Flemish, Italian, and Spanish painters illustrate the point. And many stories from the Bible have been retold in poetry: for example, Milton's *Samson Agonistes*, the story of Samson and Delilah in the form of a Greek tragedy; "King David" by Stephen Vincent Benét, the story of David and Bathsheba in ballad form; "The Daniel Jazz" by Vachel Lindsay, the story of Darius and Daniel in the form of a Negro folktale or sermon.

Similarly, Higgins has presented the climax of a biblical story, the death of Queen Jezebel, in terms of Irish life—as if Jezebel were an Irish woman, King Jehu an Irishman, and the speaker an Irish player of the bones (a percussion instrument of bone or hard wood, flat pieces held between the fingers and clacked together to beat out the time for music or dancing).

The story of Jezebel is related in I Kings 16, 17, 19, 21, and in II Kings 9. Read it, and you will see why her name is commonly thought of as a synonym for a bad woman. The idea that the speaker of the poem should be a bones player was probably suggested by II Kings 9:35. And the poem projects the idea that the spirit of Jezebel still lives in the bones.

Having Jezebel lean from an upper window among geraniums gives the setting of the incident an Irish realism. The "fancy beck" with which she greets King Jehu is an Irish colloquial term; and the chariot in which an Old Testament king would be expected to ride is turned into an Irish vehicle, a "knacky side-car" (look up "knacky" in the dictionary). "Beat/The light out of Jezebel" sounds like an Irish phrase too, though there is also another reason for using it. And "half daft/Titivating her painted hair" sounds a bit British, as well as line 17; "planted in clover" is another colloquial expression that fits with the rest.

Musical Elements   This poem is especially striking because of its sound effects. Of course the title suggests something of the kind of sounds we would expect to find in the poem. When the bones are between the player's fingers, they rattle, clatter, knock, and give a lively percussive accompaniment to music or dancing. But even having in mind the general idea of a percussive poem based on the sounds of the bones, we should hardly be prepared for such an extraordinary sound performance as the poet has created.

The poem has three eight-line stanzas; in each stanza lines 2 and 4 rhyme, as do lines 6 and 8. Lines 3 and 7 of each stanza have internal rhymes (line 3, stanza 1, has assonance, not rhyme, in "clothes" and "bones"). Thus the poem has a richness of corresponding sounds.

Besides the rhymes there are many examples of alliteration: *j* in "Jewy" and "Jezebel;" *b* in "Jezebel," "bitch," and "bones;" *t* in "titivating her painted;" *k* and *b* in "beck," "knacky," "spoke," "break," and "neck;" *l, f, b* in "like Lucifer," "fell," "feet," "beat," "light," "Jezebel;" *k* in "corpse" and "clover;" and *m* in "Mike" and "me."   With the alliteration the poet has interwoven assonance: most noticeable are the short *a* of "chaffed," "laughed," and "daft;" the long *a* of "titivating," "painted hair," and "grey," gave;" the long *o* of "so," thrown," "window," and of "corpse" and "clover;" the long *e* of "feet" and "beat;" and the short *a* of "clack," "lacks," and "back." Predominating are the cutting and explosive *k*'s and *b*'s. But in the second half of stanza 2 Jezebel's fall is expressed with smooth *l*'s and *o*'s. Then at the end the percussive clatter of "knacky," "break," and "neck" (lines 11–12) is made even more pronounced by "clack," "lacks," and "back."

There is only sparing use of onomatopoeia (words that are vocal imitations of sounds) in the poem: "laughed" (7) and "clack" (23); but these sounds are reinforced and echoed by many similar ones.

In a poem about clatter bones we might well expect a strong rhythm, and Higgins has used one here. It is mainly iambic with three beats in lines 1, 2, 4, 5, and 6, and four beats in lines 3 and 7 (the lines with internal rhyme). In some places the poet has produced a syncopated effect by displacing the regular metrical accent and bringing beats together, as in lines 3 and 4

Down to her spent teats
As she stretched out of the window,

and by introducing an extra short syllable, as in line 15

Beneath the feet of the horses and they beat

and line 24

There's music in the old bones yet.

But there is a notable change of rhythm and sound in lines 13–14. Line 13 has two smooth anapestic feet

she was thrown/from the window

and suddenly the lines become smooth with consonants that are continuants (not explosive sounds but sounds that can be continued as long as the breath holds out): *v, n, l, f*—and the deep long *o* vowel.

Organization and Diction   The short poem is concentrated on the end of Jezebel. The poet organized it chronologically: Stanza 1 tells of Jezebel's behavior as Jehu arrived; stanza 2 of her death; and stanza 3 of what happened to her bones.

The diction, as already indicated, is based on colloquial Irish terms. All the words applied to Jezebel in stanza 1 are disrespectful. Her unqueenly behavior is conveyed by "tipped him a fancy beck" in stanza 2, and her appearance, as the speaker imagined it, by "dewlapped neck." But the poet compares her fall to that of Lucifer, one of the rebellious angels thrown down from Heaven after war with God. (Milton described his fall in *Paradise Lost,* Book I, lines 740–746.) His fall is the symbol of a fall from greatness, a descent from high rank (and Jezebel was a king's daughter). *Lucifer* in Latin means "bearer of light;" his light faded to darkness. In this story the king's horses "beat/The *light* out of Jezebel." "Light" is equivalent to life. The reader who recognizes the allusion to Lucifer can better appreciate the irony of the situation in the poem.

Line 17 briefly and disrespectfully sums up what happened to Jezebel's body. But another aspect of her story is touched on in the reference to dancing in line 21; and this links up with the use of the bones made from parts of her skeleton. The last line brings to mind the expression "There's life in the old bones yet." "Bones" has a multiple meaning: it refers to the musical instrument, to the bones of the pleasure-loving queen, and perhaps to the bones of the player (his life or spirit). What kind of music is in the old bones yet? The last line suggests the lively, dancing music of a vigorous, naughty spirit that cannot be subdued. Thus Jezebel's bones would be appropriate as his chosen instrument.

On the Beach at Fontana

JAMES JOYCE

Wind whines and whines the shingle,
The crazy pierstakes groan;
A senile sea numbers each single
Slimesilvered stone.

From whining wind and colder   5
Grey sea I wrap him warm
And touch his trembling fineboned shoulder
And boyish arm.

Around us fear, descending
Darkness of fear above   10
And in my heart how deep unending
Ache of love!

Trieste 1914

QUESTIONS

1. Look up the meaning of the words "shingle," "crazy," and "senile" as used here.
2. This is another poem in which the musical elements are carefully planned. What onomatopoetic words (words imitating sounds) occur in lines 1–2? What sound predominates in lines 3–4? What sound in nature is this sound intended to represent?
3. The movement of the verse is one of the most important of the musical elements. The basic meter is iambic. But the first foot, "wind whines," is a spondee (two equal stresses), which gives strong emphasis and also slows up the line. Compare it with the second foot, "and whines." What other spondaic feet are there in the poem?
4. How does the meter of the last line differ from that of lines 4 and 8?
5. Which of the lines are run-on? Which words at the beginning of lines are given strong emphasis (increasing the emotional tension of the reader) by the running-on of the previous lines?
6. What is the atmosphere of the scene? Which words do the most to establish the atmosphere?
7. Why are the two characters of stanza 2 at the pier? Who may they be —a mother and son, two brothers, a father and son, a wife and her husband, a girl and her sweetheart? Whoever they may be, it is most important for the reader to be aware of their feelings. What fundamental human feelings are they experiencing?
8. How do you account for the "trembling shoulder"? What is the effect of "boyish arm"? Why should the characters feel fear? Indicate what pressures they are under.
9. Compare the music and atmosphere of this poem with those of "Song for the Clatter Bones."

The Turtle

OGDEN NASH

The turtle lives 'twixt plated decks
Which practically conceal its sex.
I think it clever of the turtle
In such a fix to be so fertile.

From *Verses from 1929 On* by Ogden Nash, by permission of Little, Brown and Co. Copyright 1940, by Ogden Nash.

QUESTIONS

1. "The Turtle" is an example of what is called light verse. In content, it amounts to no more than a witty remark. But in style it is elegant and accomplished; it represents a graceful and effective poetic result achieved mainly by alliteration and perfectly selected diction. Test this statement by substituting other words for some Nash used. Compare "lives between solid decks" and "lives 'twixt plated decks"; "very nearly hide its sex" and "practically conceal its sex." What differences are there in alliteration, distinction, and memorability?
2. Make other substitutions for " 'twixt," "practically," "conceal," "think," "clever," "fix," and compare effects with those of the original.
3. Contrast the sound patterns in this quatrain (four-verse stanza) with those of Milton's sonorous line "And let the bass of Heav'n's deep organ blow."
4. Consider the alliterative pattern of the quatrain—*t, l, ks, p, ch, s, k,* and *f*—and indicate how these sounds interact to produce a distinctive music that is perfect for Nash's purposes.

In Memoriam (VII)

ALFRED, LORD TENNYSON

> Dark house, by which once more I stand
>   Here in the long unlovely street,
>   Doors, where my heart was used to beat
> So quickly, waiting for a hand,
>
> A hand that can be clasp'd no more—   5
>   Behold me, for I cannot sleep,
>   And like a guilty thing I creep
> At earliest morning to the door.
>
> He is not here; but far away
>   The noise of life begins again,   10
>   And ghastly thro' the drizzling rain
> On the bald street breaks the blank day.

QUESTIONS

1. Alfred Tennyson's close friend Arthur Henry Hallam, who was engaged to marry Tennyson's sister, died suddenly in Vienna at the age of twenty-three. Tennyson was shocked and grieved and he wrote a long elegy called *In Memoriam A. H. H.* for his friend. In this section he

tells how he goes at dawn to Hallam's house. What aspects of the house are emphasized in stanza 1? Which words in stanza 1 receive emphasis because they are noniambic feet?

2. What is the subject of the verb "behold" (6)?

3. This poem is a good example of artistic combining of connotative diction, alliteration, and variations of meter. Connotations are suggested or implied meanings words have because of their associations; so "horse," "nag," and "steed" have different connotations. Consider the connotations of "dark," "unlovely," and "like a guilty thing I creep." Although the poem begins with "dark," it ends with "day." But what is a "blank day"? What are the connotations of the other words in lines 11–12?

4. Contrast the effect of alliteration in line 2 with that in line 12.

5. Contrast the meter of line 12 (note the vigorous accents) with that of lines 10–11.

6. Tennyson uses no words that directly express his feelings. What terms would you use to interpret his feelings?

Player Piano

JOHN UPDIKE

> My stick fingers click with a snicker
> And, chuckling, they knuckle the keys;
> Light-footed, my steel feelers flicker
> And pluck from the keys melodies.
>
> My paper can caper; abandon   5
> Is broadcast by dint of my din,
> And no man or band has a hand in
> The tones I turn on from within.
>
> At times I'm a jumble of rumbles,
> At others I'm light like the moon,   10
> But never my numb plunker fumbles,
> Misstrums me, or tries a new tune.

QUESTIONS

1. Who is the speaker in this poem?

2. In what meter is it written? What is its pattern of end rhymes—that is, rhymes at the ends of verses? What internal rhymes do you find?

3. Which are the chief alliterative sounds in each stanza? What alliterative links join stanza 1 to stanza 2 and stanza 2 to stanza 3?
4. What paper is referred to in line 5? What sort of music or dance is suggested by "caper" and "abandon"? Look up "snicker" and "dint" if you need to.
5. What aspect of the player piano is emphasized in each stanza?
6. Considering the total poem as a combination of meaning and music, what is the proportion of music to meaning in that combination? What satisfactions does the reader gain from the poem?
7. Compare this poem with "Song for the Clatter Bones."

Inversnaid

GERARD MANLEY HOPKINS

This darksome burn, horseback brown,
His rollrock highroad roaring down,
In coop and in comb the fleece of his foam
Flutes and low to the lake falls home.

A windpuff-bonnet of fáwn-fróth   5
Turns and twindles over the broth
Of a pool so pitchblack, féll-frówning,
It rounds and rounds Despair to drowning.

Degged with dew, dappled with dew
Are the groins of the braes that the brook treads through,   10
Wiry heathpacks, flitches of fern,
And the beadbonny ash that sits over the burn.

What would the world be, once bereft
Of wet and of wildness? Let them be left,
O let them be left, wildness and wet;   15
Long live the weeds and the wilderness yet.

QUESTIONS

1. It would be well to look up the following words: "burn," "coop," "comb(e)," "flute" (v.), "twindles," "pitch" (n.), "fell" (adj.), "degged," "groins," "braes," "heathpacks," "flitches," and "bereft."
2. The stream Hopkins writes about is in Scotland. Which of his words are Scottish? Which ones are considered dialect or obsolete?
3. The poem has an emphatic rhythm. How many beats are there in each line? Hopkins wrote poetry in which he counted only beats; any line

can have many or few unaccented syllables. Here the number of syllables per line varies from seven to eleven. What changes in meter do you observe that account for the special music of different lines?

4. What onomatopoetic word governs the music in line 2? What examples of assonance support the onomatopoeia? Is there onomatopoeia in lines 5–6?

5. Describe your picture of the stream as you visualize it.

6. What verbs describe the movement of the stream in stanzas 1–3? Which words in the poem seem particularly unusual and vivid? What impression is made by "darksome," "rollrock," "windpuff-bonnet," "broth," "degged," "groins," "treads through," and "beadbonny ash"?

7. Where has Hopkins used alliteration? Contrast the alliteration of stanza 1 with that of stanzas 2, 3, and 4.

8. In line 8 what unusual use has Hopkins made of "rounds"? What happens to Despair? Is this the poet's own temptation to despair?

9. How does the point of view change in stanza 3? How does stanza 4 differ from stanzas 1–3 in both language and purpose?

10. In stanza 4 "wet," "wildness," and "weeds" are significant words. What difference is there between "wildness" and "wilderness"? If we substitute "water" or "moisture" for "wet," and "plants" for "weeds," what different effect would be created in the poem?

11. What opinion expressed in stanza 4 does Hopkins want us to agree with? What does this opinion represent in terms of human life and values of living?

Crossing

PHILIP BOOTH

STOP LOOK LISTEN
as gate stripes swing down,
count the cars hauling distance
upgrade through town:
warning whistle, bellclang,   5
engine eating steam,
engineer waving,
a fast-freight dream:
B&M box car,
boxcar again,   10

From *Letter from a Distant Land* by Philip Booth. Copyright 1953 by Philip Booth. Originally appeared in *The New Yorker*. Reprinted by permission of The Viking Press, Inc.

Frisco gondola,
eight-nine-ten
Erie and Wabash,
Seaboard, U.P.,
Pennsy tankcar,   15
twenty-two, three,
Phoebe Snow, B&O,
thirty-four, five,
Santa Fe cattle
shipped alive,   20
red cars, yellow cars,
orange cars, black,
Youngstown steel
down to Mobile
on Rock Island track,   25
fifty-nine, sixty,
hoppers of coke,
Anaconda copper,
hotbox smoke,
eighty-eight,   30
red-ball freight,
Rio Grande,
Nickel Plate,
Hiawatha,
Lackawanna,   35
rolling fast
and loose,
ninety-seven,
coal car,
boxcar,   40
CABOOSE!

QUESTIONS

1. What is being described and from what point of view?
2. What meter has Booth used? Why is it suitable for this poem?
3. Explain the significance of the last word, "CABOOSE!"

The Express

STEPHEN SPENDER

> After the first powerful plain manifesto
> The black statement of pistons, without more fuss
> But gliding like a queen, she leaves the station.
> Without bowing and with restrained unconcern
> She passes the houses which humbly crowd outside,   5
> The gasworks and at last the heavy page
> Of death, printed by gravestones in the cemetery.
> Beyond the town there lies the open country
> Where, gathering speed, she acquires mystery,
> The luminous self-possession of ships on ocean.   10
> It is now she begins to sing—at first quite low
> Then loud, and at last with a jazzy madness—
> The song of her whistle screaming at curves,
> Of deafening tunnels, brakes, innumerable bolts.
> And always light, aerial, underneath   15
> Goes the elate meter of her wheels.
> Steaming through metal landscape on her lines
> She plunges new eras of wild happiness
> Where speed throws up strange shapes, broad curves
> And parallels clean like the steel of guns.   20
> At last, further than Edinburgh or Rome,
> Beyond the crest of the world, she reaches night
> Where only a low streamline brightness
> Of phosphorous on the tossing hills is white.
> Ah, like a comet through flames she moves entranced   25
> Wrapt in her music no bird song, no, nor bough
> Breaking with honey buds, shall ever equal.

QUESTIONS

1. What is being described and from what point of view?
2. Explain the functioning of onomatopoeia in the poem in lines 1–2 and
   11–16. Contrast the onomatopoetic effect of lines 13–14 with that of
   Tennyson's famous lines, "The moan of doves in immemorial elms/And
   murmur of innumerable bees."
3. In what meter is the poem written?

4. Explain the figurative language in lines 1–2. A simile is a figure of comparison in which a similarity between two things is asserted, using "like" or "as." How does the simile "like a queen" (3) make you think of the express? Explain the figurative language in lines 4–7.
5. Contrast this poem with "Crossing" in respect to meter, onomatopoeia, figures of speech, and theme. Why is "The Express" unmistakably British and "Crossing" unmistakably American?

Ballads and Near Ballads

Lord Randal

ANONYMOUS

"Where have you been, Lord Randal, my son?
Where have you been, my handsome young man?"
"I've been to my sweetheart's, mother; make my bed soon,
For I'm weary wi' hunting, and I fain wad lie down."

"What gat ye for your dinner, Lord Randal, my son?   5
What gat ye for your dinner, my handsome young man?"
"O eels and eel broth, mother; make my bed soon,
For I'm weary wi' hunting, and I fain wad lie down."

"Where did she get them, Lord Randal, my son?
Where did she get them, my handsome young man?"   10
"On hedges and ditches, mother; make my bed soon,
For I'm weary wi' hunting, and I fain wad lie down."

"I fear you are poisoned, Lord Randal, my son!
I fear you are poisoned, my handsome young man!"
"O yes, I am poisoned, mother; make my bed soon,   15
For I'm weary wi' hunting, and I fain wad lie down."

"What do you leave your father, Lord Randal, my son?
What do you leave your father, my handsome young man?"
"My lands and castles, mother; make my bed soon,
For I'm weary wi' hunting, and I fain wad lie down."   20

"What do you leave your mother, Lord Randal, my son?
What do you leave your mother, my handsome young man?"
"My gold and silver, mother; make my bed soon,
For I'm weary wi' hunting, and I fain wad lie down."

"What do you leave your sweetheart, Lord Randal, my son?   25
What do you leave your sweetheart, my handsome young
            man?"
"A rope to hang her, mother! Make my bed soon,
For I'm sick to my heart, and I fain wad lie down."

ANALYSIS

"Lord Randal" is a Scottish folk ballad, a compact poem, originally sung, that tells a story. It employs a few terms of the Northern English dialect: the shortened "wi'" for "with," and "wad" for "would," and "gat" for "got." "Fain" is an old term meaning "gladly." Like many ballads "Lord Randal" proceeds by questions and answers. We learn from lines 1 and 3 that Lord Randal's mother is asking the questions and that Lord Randal is replying. Like many ballads this ballad uses refrains. "Lord Randal, my son;" "my handsome young man;" "mother; make my bed soon,/For I'm weary wi' hunting, and I fain wad lie down" are repeated in stanza after stanza.

But each stanza supplies a little more information. This way of telling a story in ballads is called *incremental repetition*. The pattern of question and answer continues, but with each stanza the amount of information is slightly increased. Stanza 1 tells us that the young man has visited his sweetheart; stanza 2 that he ate "eels and eel broth;" stanza 3 that the "eels" were taken from hedges and ditches. Real eels do not live in such places. So in stanza 4 the mother immediately draws a conclusion from his statement (and his appearance): he has been poisoned, as he admits in his reply.

Stanza 5 lets us know (by another ballad formula) that his case is hopeless; he is going to die. The composer of the ballad cleverly works up to the final stanza. He uses the order of climax in the three last questions: father, mother, and—sweetheart. Lord Randal's last reply informs us that he holds his sweetheart guilty of treachery and of his murder. Thus the last stanza makes a strong dramatic impact.

The best folk ballads tell their stories with much compression. The story is reduced to its essentials, and it is told rapidly. We might say that the ballad maker rushes on to the last act of his drama. And ballads are told in the manner of drama, with frequent use of conversation and with practically no comment. Ballads are objective rather than subjective.

In "Lord Randal" we are not told what happened between the lover and his sweetheart. We know nothing of the motives that led her to poison him. The spotlight is thrown firmly on the meeting with his mother, after the poison from the snakes has had time to do its work. In this one brief scene, what can the poet do by way of characterization? The mother shows herself concerned, like any normal mother, over the condition of her son. Lord Randal does not at first admit his true condition. Presumably he wishes to spare his mother the knowledge that he is about to die, so he makes the excuse that he is "weary wi' hunting." We may think of him as a considerate son, brave and rather stoical. Is he then without feeling? No, for he feels that the guilty woman should be punished for her crime and because in the very last line the refrain is changed to "I'm sick to my heart," a phrase with a double meaning: (1) he is physically sick, but (2) he is also heartsick because his sweetheart has treacherously betrayed him. In a world where such a thing could happen, a loving and trusting man might gladly "lie down"—be glad to depart from a place so evil. So we know from that last little change of wording that Lord Randal is not an insensitive person. The surprise after the refrain has been used six times makes the effect of "sick to my heart" a powerfully emotional one.

Ballad makers were not educated people. Therefore we seldom find much distinction of diction in ballads. It was easier for minstrels to compose songs and for audiences to understand them when they were sung if the songs had ordinary language, with many oft-repeated phrases and formulas. Ballads do not always have perfect rhymes either. The genius of ballad makers is usually shown in the compactness of organization, rapidity of narrative, and the effective arrangement of the parts of their poems. "Lord Randal" is a fair example.

As for meter and music, ballads use rather simple meters and pay little attention to musical elements. They are at times irregular in meter, but irregularities are easily taken care of in the singing; and the fact that ballads are sung throws importance onto actual musical notes and away from word music. The majority of the lines in "Lord Randal" have a four-beat rhythm, although line 3 of each stanza has five feet, as do lines 17, 21, and 25. The feet are frequently anapestic (– – /), as in line 4 of each stanza, although in some places iambs and dactyls are used instead. When the ballad is sung, the tune carries the lines along with no metrical difficulty.

Hind Horn

ANONYMOUS

In Scotland there was a babie born,
And his name it was called young Hind Horn.

He sent a letter to our king
That he was in love with his daughter Jean.

He's gien to her a silver wand,   5
With seven living lavrocks sitting thereon.

She's gien to him a diamond ring,
With seven bright diamonds set therein.

"When the ring grows pale and wan,
You may know by it my love is gane."   10

One day as he looked his ring upon,
He saw the diamonds pale and wan.

He left the sea and came to land,
And the first that he met was an old beggar man.

"What news, what news?" said young Hind Horn;   15
"No news, no news," said the old beggar man.

"But there is a wedding in the king's ha,
That has halden these forty days and twa."

"Will ye lend me your begging coat?
And I'll lend you my scarlet cloak.   20

"Will you lend me your beggar's rung?
And I'll gie you my steed to ride upon.

"Will you lend me your wig a hair,
To cover mine, because it is fair?"

The auld beggar man was bound for the mill,   25
But young Hind Horn for the king's hall.

The auld beggar man was bound for to ride,
But young Hind Horn was bound for the bride.

When he came to the king's gate,
He sought a drink for Hind Horn's sake.   30

The bride came down with a glass of wine,
When he drank out the glass, and dropt in the ring.

"O got ye this by sea or land?
Or got ye it off a dead man's hand?"

"I got not it by sea, I got it by land,   35
And I got it, madam, out of your own hand."

"O I'll cast off my gowns of brown,
And beg wi you frae town to town.

"O I'll cast off my gowns of red,
And I'll beg wi you to win my bread."   40

"Ye needna cast off your gowns of brown,
For I'll make you lady o many a town.

"Ye needna cast off your gowns of red,
It's only a sham, the begging of my bread."

The bridegroom he had wedded the bride,   45
But young Hind Horn he took her to bed.

QUESTIONS

1. The Scottish dialect of this ballad has a few differences from standard English: "gien" (5) for "given"; "lavrocks" (6) for "larks"; "gane" (10) for "gone"; "a'" (17) for "all"; "ha" (18) for "hall"; "halden" (20) for "holden," that is, "been held"; "twa" (20) for "two"; "rung" (23) for "staff"; "wi" for "with"; "frae" (40) for "from"; "needna" (43) for "need not." What does the use of dialect add to the poem?
2. This poem may be divided into three main parts. What are they?
3. Did Princess Jean return Hind Horn's love? Show evidence.
4. If she did love him, why is she being married to another man?
5. Why are the wedding festivities extended to forty-two days or more?
6. Explain the significance of the magic ring in the story. In how many ways is it used?
7. What is the hero's purpose in asking for "a drink for Hind Horn's sake" (30)?
8. When Jean brings Hind Horn the wine, why does she not recognize him?
9. What is in her mind when she asks the question at line 34?
10. According to lines 37–40, what does she assume? What do these lines tell the reader about her affections?
11. What does the reader discover from lines 41–42?
12. To what extent is dialogue used in the poem? Compare this ballad for dramatic quality with "Lord Randal."
13. What is the prevailing meter of this ballad?
14. Point out places where the rhymes are imperfect.
15. Why did the poet think he had to include the final couplet? What is the effect of this couplet?

Helen of Kirconnell

ANONYMOUS

> I wish I were where Helen lies,
> Night and day on me she cries;
> O that I were where Helen lies,
>   On fair Kirconnell lea!
>
> Curst be the heart that thought the thought,   5
> And curst the hand that fired the shot,
> When in my arms burd Helen dropt,
>   And died to succour me!

O think na ye my heart was sair,
When my Love dropp'd and spak nae mair!   10
There did she swoon wi' meikle care,
   On fair Kirconnell lea.

As I went down the water side,
None but my foe to be my guide,
None but my foe to be my guide,   15
   On fair Kirconnell lea;

I lighted down my sword to draw,
I hacked him in pieces sma',
I hacked him in pieces sma',
   For her sake that died for me.   20

O Helen fair, beyond compare!
I'll mak a garland o' thy hair,
Shall bind my heart for evermair,
   Until the day I die!

O that I were where Helen lies!   25
Night and day on me she cries;
Out of my bed she bids me rise,
   Says, "Haste, and come to me!"

O Helen fair! O Helen chaste!
If I were with thee, I'd be blest,   30
Where thou lies low and taks thy rest,
   On fair Kirconnell lea.

I wish my grave were growing green,
A winding-sheet drawn owre my e'en,
And I in Helen's arms lying,   35
   On fair Kirconnell lea.

I wish I were where Helen lies!
Night and day on me she cries;
And I am weary of the skies,
   For her sake that died for me.   40

QUESTIONS

1. Note the following variations from standard English: "burd" (7) for "maid"; "sair" (9) for "sore"; "nae mair" (10) for "no more"; "meikle" (11) for "much"; "sma" (18) for "small"; "mak" (22) for "make"; "taks" (31) for "takes"; "e'en" (34) for "eyes" "owre" (34) for "over."
2. What are the feelings of the speaker at the opening of the poem? Who is the speaker?

3. What difference in terms of objectivity does the use of the first person here bring out in comparison with the two preceding ballads?
4. According to stanza 2, how did Helen lose her life?
5. What sequence of actions is indicated by stanzas 3–5?
6. What has the speaker accomplished in stanza 5?
7. What happens in stanzas 6–10?
8. Explain how stanzas 6–10 create an atmosphere in this ballad different from that of "Lord Randal" and "Hind Horn." Which of the three ballads is the most lyrical?
9. What is the rhyme pattern of the ballad? What part is played here by refrain?
10. In stanzas 6–10 which terms are most effective in showing the character of Helen and the feelings and state of mind of the speaker?

Carentan O Carentan

LOUIS SIMPSON

Trees in the old days used to stand
And shape a shady lane
Where lovers wandered hand in hand
Who came from Carentan.

This was the shining green canal   5
Where we came two by two
Walking at combat-interval.
Such trees we never knew.

The day was early June, the ground
Was soft and bright with dew.   10
Far away the guns did sound,
But here the sky was blue.

The sky was blue, but there a smoke
Hung still above the sea
Where the ships together spoke   15
To towns we could not see.

Could you have seen us through a glass
You would have said a walk
Of farmers out to turn the grass,
Each with his own hay-fork.   20

The watchers in their leopard suits
Waited till it was time,
And aimed between the belt and boot
And let the barrel climb.

I must lie down at once, there is   25
A hammer at my knee.
And call it death or cowardice,
Don't count again on me.

Everything's alright, Mother,
Everyone gets the same   30
At one time or another.
It's all in the game.

I never strolled, nor ever shall,
Down such a leafy lane.
I never drank in a canal,   35
Nor ever shall again.

There is a whistling in the leaves
And it is not the wind,
The twigs are falling from the knives
That cut men to the ground.   40

Tell me, Master-Sergeant,
The way to turn and shoot.
But the Sergeant's silent
That taught me how to do it.

O Captain, show us quickly   45
Our place upon the map.
But the Captain's sickly
And taking a long nap.

Lieutenant, what's my duty,
My place in the platoon?   50
He too's a sleeping beauty,
Charmed by that strange tune.

Carentan O Carentan
Before we met with you
We never yet had lost a man   55
Or known what death could do.

QUESTIONS

1. Carentan is a town in the French region of Normandy at the base of the Cotentin peninsula. What twentieth-century event is the poet likely to be writing about?

2. Compare this poem in terms of ballad characteristics with the three poems preceding it.

Ballad of the Bread Man

CHARLES CAUSLEY

Mary stood in the kitchen
Baking a loaf of bread.
An angel flew in through the window.
We've a job for you, he said.

God in his big gold heaven,   5
Sitting in his big blue chair,
Wanted a mother for his little son.
Suddenly saw you there.

Mary shook and trembled,
It isn't true what you say.   10
Don't say that, said the angel.
The baby's on its way.

Joseph was in the workshop
Planing a piece of wood.
The old man's past it, the neighbours said   15
That girl's been up to no good.

And who was that elegant feller,
They said, in the shiny gear?
The things they said about Gabriel
Were hardly fit to hear.   20

Mary never answered,
Mary never replied.
She kept the information,
Like the baby, safe inside.

It was the election winter.   25
They went to vote in town.
When Mary found her time had come
The hotels let her down.

The baby was born in an annex
Next to the local pub.   30
At midnight, a delegation
Turned up from the Farmer's Club.

They talked about an explosion
That cracked a hole in the sky,
Said they'd been sent to the Lamb & Flag   35
To see God come down from on high.

A few days later a bishop
And a five-star general were seen
With the head of an African country
In a bullet-proof limousine.   40

We've come, they said, with tokens
For the little boy to choose.
Told the tale about war and peace
In the television news.

After them came the soldiers   45
With rifle and bomb and gun,
Looking for enemies of the state.
The family had packed and gone.

When they got back to the village
The neighbours said, to a man,   50
That boy will never be one of us,
Though he does what he blessed well can.

He went round to all the people
A paper crown on his head.
Here is some bread from my father.   55
Take, eat, he said.

Nobody seemed very hungry.
Nobody seemed to care.
Nobody saw the god in himself
Quietly standing there.   60

He finished up in the papers.
He came to a very bad end.
He was charged with bringing the living to life.
No man was that prisoner's friend.

There's only one kind of punishment   65
To fit that kind of a crime.
They rigged a trial and shot him dead.
They were only just in time.

They lifted the young man by the leg,
They lifted him by the arm,   70
They locked him in a cathedral
In case he came to harm.

They stored him safe as water
Under seven rocks.
One Sunday morning he burst out   75
Like a jack-in-the-box.

Through the town he went walking.
He showed them the holes in his head.
Now do you want any loaves? he cried.
Not today, they said.   80

QUESTIONS

1. What does this poem have in common with Higgins' "Song for the Clatter Bones"?
2. Point to examples of diction that give the ballad its particular tone. Which stanzas seem to you to show the most wit?
3. Comment on the effect of the two similes in the next-to-the-last stanza.
4. Why is the protagonist of the poem called "the bread man"? What widely prevalent attitude is the final stanza meant to indicate?

A Frosty Night

ROBERT GRAVES

"Alice, dear, what ails you,
    Dazed and lost and shaken?
Has the chill night numbed you?
    Is it fright you have taken?"

"Mother, I am very well,   5
    I was never better.
Mother, do not hold me so,
    Let me write my letter."

"Sweet, my dear, what ails you?"
"No, but I am well.   10

The night was cold and frosty—
   There's no more to tell."

"Ay, the night was frosty,
   Coldly gaped the moon,
Yet the birds seemed twittering   15
   Through green boughs of June.

"Soft and thick the snow lay,
   Stars danced in the sky—
Not all the lambs of May-day
   Skip so bold and high.   20

"Your feet were dancing, Alice,
   Seemed to dance on air,
You looked a ghost or angel
   In the star-light there.

"Your eyes were frosted star-light;   25
   Your heart, fire and snow.
Who was it said, 'I love you'?"
   "Mother, let me go!"

QUESTIONS

1. Who is the first speaker? What causes the first speaker to ask the questions in stanzas 1 and 3? Is the first speaker curious, concerned, or alarmed?
2. What causes the second speaker to reply as she does in stanzas 2–3?
3. Why does the first speaker stop asking questions in stanzas 4–7? Why is the first speaker able to make the descriptive statements of stanzas 4–7?
4. What is the purpose of the references to May and June in stanzas 4 and 5? What is the meaning of line 26?
5. On what experience is the poem focused? Which line lets us know most precisely what has happened?
6. Which lines are in trochaic meter, which in iambic? Should lines 5 and 7 be read as three-foot lines or four-foot lines?
7. In what ways is this poem similar to "Lord Randal"?
8. If the author's name were not attached to this poem, how would a reader know that it is a literary ballad—a poem composed for reading, more or less in imitation of a folk ballad—and not a folk ballad?

Nostalgia

KARL SHAPIRO

My soul stands at the window of my room,
   And I ten thousand miles away;
My days are filled with Ocean's sound of doom,
   Salt and cloud and the bitter spray.
Let the wind blow, for many a man shall die.   5

My selfish youth, my books with gilded edge,
   Knowledge and all gaze down the street;
The potted plants upon the window ledge
   Gaze down with selfish lives and sweet.
Let the wind blow, for many a man shall die.   10

My night is now her day, my day her night,
   So I lie down, and so I rise;
The sun burns close, the star is losing height,
   The clock is hunted down the skies.
Let the wind blow, for many a man shall die.   15

Truly a pin can make the memory bleed,
   A world explode the inward mind
And turn the skulls and flowers never freed
   Into the air, no longer blind.
Let the wind blow, for many a man shall die.   20

Laughter and grief join hands. Always the heart
   Clumps in the breast with heavy stride;
The face grows lined and wrinkled like a chart,
   The eyes bloodshot with tears and tide.
Let the wind blow, for many a man shall die.   25

QUESTIONS

1. What contrast is set up in lines 1–2?
2. Where is the poet as he writes "ten thousand miles away"?
3. Note the contrasts in stanza 1 and stanza 2: "sound of doom" and "bitter spray" with "gilded edge" and "selfish lives and sweet." How does the familiar old life of his soul seem now to the poet?
4. What are the constituents of the soul as indicated by stanza 2?

5. What further element of nostalgia is introduced in stanza 3? (Be sure you know what "nostalgia" means.) What do lines 11 and 13 suggest about the geography of the poem?

6. Does "pin" have the same signficance as when we say, "I don't care a pin about it"? What has the metaphor of a bleeding memory to do with nostalgia?

7. What unfamiliar world (17) has made the "inward mind" explode? What has been the result of the explosion?

8. Why is simple, spontaneous laughter impossible to the poet? Note the references to heart, face, and eyes (lines 21–24). Explain the metaphor about the heart. The simile of line 23 compares the face to a chart. When one reads this chart, what does he find that was not there before? What elements of the poet's life are indicated by "tears and tide"?

9. Point out examples of alliteration in the poem.

10. What attitude is suggested by the refrain? In a situation where "many a man shall die" what should one single man do or expect?

11. To what extent does this poem resemble a ballad?

Sonnets and Near Sonnets

Sonnet 73

WILLIAM SHAKESPEARE

That time of year thou mayst in me behold
When yellow leaves, or none, or few, do hang
Upon those boughs which shake against the cold,
Bare ruin'd choirs where late the sweet birds sang.
In me thou see'st the twilight of such day   5
As after sunset fadeth in the west,
Which by and by black night doth take away,
Death's second self, that seals up all in rest.
In me thou see'st the glowing of such fire
That on the ashes of his youth doth lie   10
As the death-bed whereon it must expire,
Consum'd with that which it was noursh'd by.
    This thou perceiv'st, which makes thy love more strong,
    To love that well which thou must leave ere long.

ANALYSIS

Form   The experienced reader will quickly identify this poem as a sonnet; it has fourteen lines with a certain rhyme pattern—*ababcdcdefefgg*—which, with the punctuation, indicate that the poem is a Shakespearean, or English, sonnet. There are periods at the ends of lines 4, 8, and 12. Thus the three quatrains—lines 1–4, 5–8, and 9–12—are units, and lines 13–14 constitute a couplet which is the final unit. The logical relationship of these units provides the key to the understanding of the structure of the whole sonnet.

Quatrain 1 says that a person called "thou" may behold a time of year in the poet, a time of year which other details indicate is autumn, that is, the period of old age. Quatrain 2 begins "in me thou see'st the twilight," and quatrain 3 begins "In me thou see'st" a dying fire. All three quatrain units begin in the same way. They have a parallel grammatical structure, and all three express the same idea. The repetition of the basic idea is appropriately set forth by a repeatedly used grammatical pattern. The experienced reader is quick to catch these signals showing that the poet has used the principles of parallelism and repetition. Then the reader sees that the final couplet is a conclusion drawn from the preceding material.

Figurative Language   This sonnet, like many other poems, consists almost entirely of figures of speech—of metaphors and a simile. In quatrain 1 the main figure is the metaphor of autumn—a "time of year . . ./When yellow leaves, or [either] none, or few, do hang/Upon those boughs which shake against the cold." The poet uses symbols by which autumn is universally known, yellow leaves, denuded boughs, and cold weather. "Shake against the cold" renders in more specific and pictorial terms the condition of autumn. In line 4 another autumnal detail is added, also by means of a metaphor; the boughs are "bare ruin'd choirs where late the sweet birds sang." We know that in late autumn the summer birds have left. The birds were singers; so the trees in which they sang can be called choirs— now bare and also "ruin'd" by comparison with their full-leaved beauty of summer, when the "choir-singers" occupied them.

Quatrain 2 uses the metaphor of twilight, the last part of the day before night as autumn is the declining part of the year before winter. Twilight and sunset are symbols of old age. The blackness of night replaces the twilight. Night is a symbol of death. In fact, the poet in line 8 makes this metaphor specific by calling night "death's second self," that is, the twin of death. As night is the time of rest and sleep (for a few hours), so death brings an everlasting rest.

In quatrain 3 Shakespeare symbolizes old age by the metaphor of a fire—not a blazing fire but a glowing one of mere embers lying amid ashes. These are the ashes of youth—the used-up years of greater strength and vigor which were like logs giving much heat. In line 11 Shakespeare uses the simile of a deathbed for the ashes. As a human being dies on a bed, the fire will die in the ashes, which will gradually reduce ventilation and smother the flame. The wood from which the ashes came once fed the fire— just as the earlier years of life supported the man through maturity into old age. But now the too-many years, used up in living, will bring the life to an end.

The poet has beautifully—that is, appropriately, with all parts functioning to express the theme—stated the situation. And although the theme is repeated, Shakespeare has proceeded in a logical way toward a kind of climax. He has gone from the larger to the smaller. Autumn lasts for three months, and late autumn for some weeks; the life of the summer is only gradually leaving. A day is much shorter than a season, and twilight is only a brief part of the day. (The quicker passage of time is indicated by "by and by" in line 7, which in Shakespeare's day meant "immediately.") And a fire, unless fed continually, lasts only a little while, less than a day. In quatrain 2 night is spoken of as death's twin, and in quatrain 3 we are brought even to the poet's deathbed. Thus the time left to the writer is made to seem shorter and shorter, and the pathos of his approaching death all the more keen.

A reader is impressed by the fact that this sonnet is well planned; without being monotonous in its structure, it is very symmetrical. Each quatrain has a basic metaphor—autumn, twilight, and a dying fire—and each metaphor is developed by a secondary figure of speech—the metaphor of choirs develops boughs, the metaphor of death develops night, and the simile of the deathbed develops ashes. These figures of speech are not simply ornamental; *they are the poem itself*. If they were removed, there would be no poem.

As we can tell from other sonnets of Shakespeare, this sonnet is addressed to a young man friend. In effect, the final couplet tells him: "You understand *now* what my condition is; therefore, since I have so short a time left, your love (or friendship: *love* is the usual term for friendship in Shakespeare's work) will be all the stronger." This is the typical way in which Shakespeare's sonnets close—with a brief statement of a logical conclusion or a kind of moral based on the preceding twelve lines.

Musical Elements   Musical elements are not very pronounced in this poem, although as usual in Shakespeare's sonnets we find some alliteration: for example, *b* and *c* in lines 3–4, *s* in quatrain 2 (especially line 8), and *l* in lines 13–14. There is a kind of harmony, too, in the balance of "consum'd" and "nourish'd" (12) and even more in that of "love" and "leave" (14), because they have almost the same sound.

When I Have Fears That I May Cease To Be

JOHN KEATS

When I have fears that I may cease to be
   Before my pen has glean'd my teeming brain,
Before high-piled books, in charact'ry,
   Hold like rich garners the full-ripen'd grain;
When I behold, upon the night's starr'd face,   5
   Huge cloudy symbols of a high romance,
And think that I may never live to trace
   Their shadows, with the magic hand of chance;
And when I feel, fair creature of an hour!
   That I shall never look upon thee more,   10
Never have relish in the faery power
   Of unreflecting love!—then on the shore
Of the wide world I stand alone, and think
Till Love and Fame to nothingness do sink.

John Keats was born in 1795 and died of tuberculosis in 1821. He was deeply in love with a girl named Fanny Brawne whom he could not marry. on account of his illness. If his situation had been different, he would probably not have written this poem.

In lines 5–8 Keats speaks of "cloudy symbols" of romance in the heavens and of tracing the shadows of these symbols. He probably has in mind the Platonic concept of divine origin of poems. As imagined and then put into words by an earthly poet, the original divine idea has a less pure form, being only the "shadow" of the perfect original.

QUESTIONS

1. What is the rhyme scheme of the poem?
2. What marks of punctuation are at the end of lines 4, 8, 14? What are the main units of the poem? How do the units differ from those of Shakespeare's Sonnet 73? Is this poem a sonnet?
3. The poem begins with "When I have fears." What other clauses are grammatically parallel with this one? What clauses parallel "that I may cease to be"?
4. What is the main clause that finally completes the sentence after the three "when" clauses?
5. Besides his life, what is the poet fearing the loss of?
6. Explain the full metaphor implied by "glean'd" and "teeming." How is this metaphor developed further by the simile "like rich garners"? "Pen," "brain," and "books" are being compared to what?
7. In line 5 the starry night is made more specific by what metaphor? In line 7 "trace" implies that Keats, a poet, is thinking of himself in terms of what metaphor?
8. Why does Keats wait till lines 9–14 to introduce the topic of love? What previous topic is this parallel with?
9. Keats uses hyperbole (the figure of exaggeration) in line 9. In what sense is his hyperbole about the girl effective?
10. What effect does the repetition of "never" have?
11. How do you imagine the "shore of the wide world"? What is the other part of the metaphor? Is there anything on the other side of the shore? Why does the author say he is alone? What thoughts could make Love and Fame seem unimportant?
12. Does this poem make more or less use of figurative language than Shakespeare's Sonnet 73?
13. Point out examples of assonance and alliteration.
14. What is there about the pressures life put on Keats that makes this poem have a different effect from Shakespeare's Sonnet 73? With what terms would you describe the effect—irony, sadness, disgust, sympathy, pathos, pride?

Promise of Peace

ROBINSON JEFFERS

> The heads of strong old age are beautiful
> Beyond all grace of youth. They have strange quiet,
> Integrity, health, soundness, to the full
> They've dealt with life and been attempered by it.
> A young man must not sleep; his years are war   5
> Civil and foreign but the former's worse;
> But the old can breathe in safety now that they are
> Forgetting what youth meant, the being perverse,
> Running the fool's gauntlet and being cut
> By the whips of the five senses. As for me,   10
> If I should wish to live long it were but
> To trade those fevers for tranquility,
> Thinking though that's entire and sweet in the grave
> How shall the dead taste the deep treasure they have?

QUESTIONS

1. What qualities of old age does Jeffers contrast with what qualities of youth? In what setting do you imagine he sees the heads of old people? What does "attempered" mean?
2. How do you interpret the war metaphor (5–6)? Why is a young man's "civil war" worse than his "foreign war"?
3. How is "in safety" (7) related to the preceding lines, and what does it signify?
4. What image does Jeffers intend us to visualize through his "fool's gauntlet" metaphor (9–10)? Discuss the significance of "fool's" and "whips."
5. This poem raises the question of the value of life in old age. Should a person wish to have a long life? Is life worth living after one has become aged? What is Jeffers' answer? What might make a person prefer to be dead? What treasure do the dead have? What attitude do "entire" and "sweet" (13) convey?
6. What contrast of ideas does the last line bring out? This line is very striking, partly because of its meter but more because of the force and connotations of "taste" and "deep." Scan the line and show its accents. What is a deep treasure? Explain the various suggestions that "deep" conveys.

7. Which rhymes receive emphasis? Which ones are almost concealed by the movement of the verse? Which lines are run on? Which words receive the most emphasis at the beginnings of lines through variations of meter? What variations of meter do you find within the lines?
8. This is a fourteen-line poem. Is it a sonnet? Explain your answer in terms of the rhyme scheme and organization.
9. Compare this poem with Shakespeare's Sonnet 73.

you shall above all things be glad and young

E. E. CUMMINGS

you shall above all things be glad and young.
For if you're young,whatever life you wear

it will become you;and if you are glad
whatever's living will yourself become.
Girlboys may nothing more than boygirls need: 5
i can entirely her only love

whose any mystery makes every man's
flesh put space on;and his mind take off time

that you should ever think, may god forbid
and(in his mercy)your true lover spare: 10
for that way knowledge lies,the foetal grave
called progress,and negation's dead undoom.

I'd rather learn from one bird how to sing
than teach ten thousand stars how not to dance

QUESTIONS

1. This poem has fourteen lines. Is it a sonnet?
2. What unusual things about the way the poem is printed strike one's attention?
3. Is the poem addressed to a girl? Consider lines 6, 9–10, and 13. Who is the speaker supposed to be—father, lover, friend?
4. What is the meaning of "become" (3, 4)? Is it a double meaning?
5. What seems to be the significance of "living" (4)? How do you think the author would describe a person who is really "living"?

6. Does "nothing more than" (5) mean *only* or *most of all*? How is the "Girlboys . . . boygirls" related to line 4?

7. How does the word arrangement of line 6 force the reader to pay unusual attention (and give special stress in reading) to the words of that line?

8. What sort of appeal must the "her" of line 6 have in order to win the writer's love?

9. What, according to lines 9–14, should a glad and young person do? What is the lover to be spared from?

10. A familiar line in Shakespeare's *King Lear* (Act III, scene 4, line 21) would come into many readers' minds upon reading line 11. How does Shakespeare's line add extra meaning to line 11?

11. Look up "foetal" and "doom." What is "undoom" likely to mean? To use the metaphor of "foetal grave" for progress may seem puzzling. Is there anything about the shape, position, or condition of a foetus that helps one to comprehend the metaphor?

12. What is the significance of "one" and "ten thousand" (13–14) in terms of the values of life? What tendency in the modern world may the poet be criticizing?

13. Do birds sing and stars dance because of their knowledge?

14. If the poet learns how to sing (from one bird), does he have "knowledge" (11)? Is the bird a teacher? What does the poet value most about the bird?

15. What would make the stars stop dancing? Is line 14 a hyperbole? Would the teacher teach ten thousand stars at once, or one at a time?

16. What sort of music does this poem have? What lines have noticeable alliteration?

17. Is the poet's language colloquial or formal? Does his choice of words or his phrasing influence your answer the more?

18. Is there any irony or satire in the poem? What tone of voice does the poet use?

19. Contrast this poem with Jeffers' "Promise of Peace."

Lilith
(*For a Picture*)

DANTE GABRIEL ROSSETTI

    Of Adam's first wife, Lilith, it is told
      (The witch he loved before the gift of Eve.)
      That, ere the snake's, her sweet tongue could deceive,
    And her enchanted hair was the first gold.

And still she sits, young while the earth is old,   5
   And subtly of herself contemplative,
   Draws men to watch the bright net she can weave,
Till heart and body and life are in its hold.

The rose and poppy are her flowers; for where
   Is he not found, O Lilith, whom shed scent   10
And soft-shed kisses and soft sleep shall snare?
   Lo! as that youth's eyes burned at thine, so went
   Thy spell through him, and left his straight neck bent,
And round his heart one strangling golden hair.

QUESTIONS

1. "Lilith" is an Italian, or Petrarchan, sonnet. Compare its rhyme scheme with that of Shakespeare's Sonnet 73. How does it differ from Sonnet 73 in its thought pattern?
2. Who was Lilith? What was the legend that was developed about her in the Middle Ages?
3. What idea is expressed in lines 1–4? In lines 5–8?
4. Why should the rose and poppy be flowers of Lilith? What aspects of the witch-woman do they represent?
5. What were the results of her influence upon Adam—and other men? What makes the last line so memorable—is it the image or the connotations of the words?
6. What is the relation of lines 9–14 to lines 1–8?

Contemporary Portrait

ARCHIBALD MAC LEISH

This woman mask that wears her to the bone
they say for certain is her soul's disguise:
such holes are cut in colored cloth for eyes
where the live lid winks beneath the painted one.

The eyes are hers, the mouth is not her own.   5
The mouth smiles soft, remembers well, complies,
laughs, lifts a little, kisses—these are lies
when at the lid the tragic look is shown.

Whether her soul in fear has made this mask
for easier wandering beneath our moon   10
or time has tricked her so, they never ask:
they know the false face hides the honest one.

And yet it's certain, when she comes to die,
this is the face that death will know her by.

QUESTIONS

1. What metaphor governs the whole poem?
2. Is this an Italian sonnet or an English sonnet? How does it differ in rhyme scheme and structure from the sonnets by Shakespeare and Rossetti?
3. Explain the contrast between eyes and mouth in lines 5–8.
4. Is this a portrait of a particular woman, or is it meant to represent many modern women? Is a woman any more likely to be required or expected to "wear a mask" than a man is? What sort of "lies" does the "woman mask" communicate to the world?
5. In lines 10–11 two possible reasons are suggested to account for the wearing of a mask. Considering that traditionally the moon (most changeable of heavenly bodies) represents the influence of changes and vicissitudes on human life, explain why either one of these reasons is likely to be the real one.
6. Will death know the woman by her "false face" or by "the honest one"? What does the final couplet suggest about the reality of modern women's lives?

Incidents

Auto Wreck

KARL SHAPIRO

Its quick soft silver bell beating, beating,
And down the dark one ruby flare
Pulsing out red light like an artery,
The ambulance at top speed floating down
Past beacons and illuminated clocks   5
Wings in a heavy curve, dips down,
And brakes speed, entering the crowd.
The doors leap open, emptying light;
Stretchers are laid out, the mangled lifted
And stowed into the little hospital.   10
Then the bell, breaking the hush, tolls once,
And the ambulance with its terrible cargo
Rocking, slightly rocking, moves away,
As the doors, an afterthought, are closed.

We are deranged, walking among the cops   15
Who sweep glass and are large and composed.
One is still making notes under the light.
One with a bucket douches ponds of blood
Into the street and gutter.
One hangs lanterns on the wrecks that cling,   20
Empty husks of locusts, to iron poles.

Our throats were tight as tourniquets,
Our feet were bound with splints, but now
Like convalescents intimate and gauche,
We speak through sickly smiles and warn   25
With the stubborn saw of common sense,
The grim joke and the banal resolution.

The traffic moves around with care,
But we remain, touching a wound
That opens to our richest horror.   30

Already old, the question Who shall die?
Becomes unspoken Who is innocent?
For death in war is done by hands;
Suicide has cause and stillbirth, logic.
And cancer, simple as a flower, blooms.   35
But this invites the occult mind,
Cancels our physics with a sneer,
And spatters all we know of denouement
Across the expedient and wicked stones.

QUESTIONS

1. Be sure you know the meanings of "deranged," "douches," "gauche," "saw," "banal," "occult," "denouement," and "expedient."
2. Who is speaking in this poem?
3. At what point in the incident of the wreck is the story begun? Which different details of sound and sight make the incident vivid in lines 1–14?
4. How does the focus of interest shift in lines 15–21? What further shift occurs in lines 22–30? How are lines 31–38 different from the other three sections of the poem?
5. What principle of organization has Shapiro followed?
6. Note the terms that describe the bell in line 1. Is the term "beating" better than "tolling" (the poet uses "tolls" in line 11)?
7. Judging by the repetition of the word "down" in lines 2, 4, 5, from what point of view is the scene visualized? What effect do the terms "floating" (4) and "wings" (a verb in line 6) have on the reader's idea of the scene?
8. The term "pulsing" (3) first suggests what about the red light? Why is "ruby" a better word than "red"? What significance is added to "pulsing" by the simile "like an artery"?
9. What aspect of the scene is expressed by the metaphors of line 8?
10. What different aspect does the ambulance take on because of the connotations of "stowed" (10) and "cargo" (12)?
11. Explain the psychological differences involved in the contrast of "deranged," applied to the spectators in line 15, and "composed," applied to the policemen in line 16. Why should the one group be deranged, the other composed? What is happening in lines 17–21?
12. What do the terms "ponds of blood" and "empty husks of locusts" make the reader think about the accident and its results? Are these terms that policemen would be likely to use?

13. How do the figures of speech in lines 22–24 explain the behavior of the crowd?
14. What are some of the saws, jokes, and resolutions that you might have spoken if you had been among the spectators?
15. Whose wound (29) is touched? Is "opens to our richest horror" an ambiguous phrase?
16. In line 32 would it be better to say "Who is guilty"?
17. How does the thought of lines 36–38 contrast with that of lines 33–34? How does the "occult mind" contrast with "our physics"? How does the "sneer" metaphor operate?
18. Why should the stones be called "expedient" or "wicked"?
19. In what metrical pattern is the poem written? How much of it is in unrhymed iambic pentameter—that is, blank verse? Do you think the poet ought to have put a greater emphasis on the musical element of the poem?

The Whipping

ROBERT HAYDEN

> The old woman across the way
>   is whipping the boy again
> and shouting to the neighborhood
>   her goodness and his wrongs.
>
> Wildly he crashes through elephant ears,   5
>   pleads in dusty zinnias,
> while she in spite of crippling fat
>   pursues and corners him.
>
> She strikes and strikes the shrilly circling
>   boy till the stick breaks   10
> in her hand. His tears are rainy weather
>   to woundlike memories:
>
> My head gripped in bony vise
>   of knees, the writhing struggle
> to wrench free, the blows, the fear   15
>   worse than blows that hateful
>
> Words could bring, the face that I
>   no longer knew or loved . . .

Well, it is over now, it is over,
   and the boy sobs in his room,   20

And the woman leans muttering against
   a tree, exhausted, purged—
avenged in part for lifelong hidings
   she has had to bear.

QUESTIONS

1. What gives regularity to the four-line stanzas of the poem?
2. What details of stanzas 2 and 3 are more specific and picture-forming than the material of stanza 1?
3. Analyze the figures of speech in lines 11–12. How are old wounds supposed to feel in rainy weather? Who is remembering, and why? (Note the material following the colon that occupies lines 13–18.)
4. What was the worst thing about the remembered whipping?
5. To what experience does the "Well, it is over now" apply? And to what, the following "it is over"?
6. What is the woman purged of after whipping the boy? Explain the psychological reaction suggested by the last two lines.
7. Has the poet made his account of this incident serve as a symbol of a universal human situation? If you think so, explain how he did it.

A Girl at the Center of Her Life

JOYCE CAROL OATES

There may be some way back
she thinks, past familiar homes
that will look painful now
and the hammer of cries in her blood,
past the unchanged sky that is any sky—   5
"What time is it?" is her mind's question.

This field is any field beyond the town,
and twenty miles from her parents' house.
Twenty miles takes you anywhere,
In the country you must curve   10
and calculate to get
where you're going, accounting for great

Reprinted by permission of Louisiana State University Press.

blocks of farms selfish with land, and creeks,
and uncrossable boneyards of rock and junk.
This is any field, then, being so far.   15

Its silence and its indifferent rustling
of mice and birds of any field
make her want to cry in a delirium:
"Let me be off to soak in hot water,
bright hot water, or to brush my hair   20
in a girl's fury drawing the hairs out
onto the gold-backed brush—"
At the place of her heart is
a hot closed fist.
It is closed against the man who waits   25
for her at the car. . . .

How to release to the warm air
such a useless riot of hate?
Lacking love, her casual song
fell swiftly to hate, a dark vengeance   30
of no form, and unpracticed—
A dragonfly skims near, like metal.
Into her eyesight burns the face
of this man, half a boy,
who stands puzzled   35
on one shore, she on another.
Her brain pounds. . . . Who will not see
what she has become? Who will not know?
There is no confronting this blunder
of pains and lusts opened   40
like milkweed, scattered casually with wind,
soft and flimsy, adhesive to human touch
and delicate as a pillow's suffocation.
A hypnosis of milkweed!
A young girl, in terror not young,   45
is no colt now but a sore-jointed cow
whose pores stutter for help, help,
and whose sweaty skin has gathered
seeds upon it, and tiny dry bits of grass.

QUESTIONS

1. What experience has happened to the girl mentioned in the title? Is
   it an incident that is being reported or something else? From whose
   point of view has the poet chosen to make the report?
2. What is the double meaning of "some way back"? Past what three

things should there be a "way back"? Why might "familiar homes" look painful? What things are brought together in the metaphor of line 4?

3. What extra significance beyond the literal meaning does "What time is it?" have for the girl? Note that it is "her mind's question."
4. The poet says that the sky is unchanged; it is "any sky." Why does the poet emphasize this and the fact that the girl is in "any field" (7, 15, 17), where there is "indifferent rustling"?
5. Why is distance stressed in lines 7–15?
6. What are the feelings of the girl in lines 1–15? What other feelings does she have in lines 15–26?
7. What do we know about the man mentioned in lines 25 and 34? Why is he "on one shore, she on another" (36)?
8. What further thought is brought out in lines 37–38?
9. If you are familiar with the way in which milkweed seeds come out of the pod and are scattered by the wind, you can analyze and understand the "like milkweed" simile which dominates lines 39–45. Pay attention to "no confronting," "blunder," the adjectives modifying "milkweed," and "hypnosis."
10. Explain the connotations of "colt" and "cow" in the metaphor of line 46. In the metaphor of line 47 the pores behave like what? What moral and emotional implications are conveyed by the details of lines 48–49?
11. In terms of meter, stanza, and rhyme how does this poem differ from "Two Sons" and "The Whipping"?
12. What elements in it make it more, or less, emotionally powerful and vivid than those poems?

Two Sons

ANNE SEXTON

Where and to whom
you are married I can only guess
in my piecemeal fashion. I grow old on my bitterness.

On the unique occasion
of your two sudden wedding days   5
I open some cheap wine, a tin of lobster and mayonnaise.

I sit in an old lady's room
where families used to feast
where the wind blows in like soot from north-northeast.

From *Live or Die*, by Anne Sexton, published by the Oxford University Press.

Both of you monopolized   10
with no real forwarding address
except for two silly postcards you bothered to send home,

one of them written in grease
as you undid her dress
in Mexico, the other airmailed to Boston from Rome   15

just before the small ceremony
at the American Church.
Both of you made of my cooking, those suppers of starch

and beef, and with my library,
my medicine, my bath water,   20
both sinking into small brown pools like muddy otters!

You make a toast for tomorrow
and smash the cup,
letting your false women lap the dish I had to fatten up.

When you come back I'll buy   25
a wig of yellow hair;
I'll squat in a new red dress; I'll be playing solitaire

on the kitchen floor.
Yes . . . I'll gather myself in
like cut flowers and ask you how you are and where you've   30
          been.

QUESTIONS

1. What incident has created the bitterness mentioned by the speaker in line 3? Why should the speaker feel that she is growing old?
2. What makes stanza 2 seem sarcastic? What are the connotations of stanza 3?
3. Why does the speaker use the word "monopolized" regarding the two sons? What does "no real forwarding address" imply about the past and the future relations of the sons and the speaker? What attitude regarding the incident is conveyed by lines 12–17?—think particularly of "silly," "bothered," and "small ceremony."
4. What do the four "my" items (18–20) and "sinking into small brown pools" signify? What are the connotations of "brown" and "muddy"?
5. Is the term "false women" (24) just name calling, or are the sons' wives false in some sense?
6. What would a yellow wig and a red dress do for the speaker?
7. What is the tone of the last sentence? What feelings or what attitude does it suggest?
8. What is the formal basis of the ten three-line stanzas in terms of meter and rhyme?

9. What terms best describe the speaker's feelings: is she possessive, jealous, resentful, spiteful, abandoned, forlorn, unreasonable? Does she feel betrayed, sorry for herself, cheated, insulted? Are her feelings justified? Are they believable?
10. What will the speaker's future be like?
11. Is the poem a monologue addressed to a listener, a soliloquy, or a letter?

Reasons for Attendance

PHILIP LARKIN

> The trumpet's voice, loud and authoritative,
> Draws me a moment to the lighted glass
> To watch the dancers—all under twenty-five—
> Shifting intently, face to flushed face,
> Solemnly on the beat of happiness.   5
>
> —Or so I fancy, sensing the smoke and sweat,
> The wonderful feel of girls. Why be out here?
> But then, why be in there? Sex, yes, but what
> Is sex? Surely, to think the lion's share
> Of happiness is found by couples—sheer   10
>
> Inaccuracy, as far as I'm concerned.
> What calls me is that lifted, rough-tongued bell
> (Art, if you like) whose individual bell
> Insists I too am individual.
> It speaks; I hear; others may hear as well,   15
>
> But not for me, nor I for them; and so
> With happiness. Therefore I stay outside,
> Believing this; and they maul to and fro,
> Believing that; and both are satisfied,
> If no one has misjudged himself. Or lied.   20

QUESTIONS

1. Describe the situation of the speaker in stanza 1.
2. Why is he tempted to go "in there"? Why does he reject the temptation?

3. How old a man is he? Is he indifferent to women?
4. He justifies his decision to "stay outside" and remain an observer by stating that he obeys the call of a bell. What does the bell stand for? He stresses the importance of being individual. How is this brought out in lines 15–17?
5. What do "this" and "that" refer to in lines 18 and 19?
6. If the speaker misjudged himself, would he be staying outside for another reason than the one given? If a person inside misjudged himself, why would he find himself unhappy?
7. What ironic possibility is suggested by the last two words?
8. What is the rhyme pattern of the stanzas? Is the tone of the poem conversational or formal? emotional or unemotional? Do the rhymes fit in with the tone?

Mending Wall

ROBERT FROST

Something there is that doesn't love a wall,
That sends the frozen-ground-swell under it,
And spills the upper boulders in the sun,
And makes gaps even two can pass abreast.
The work of hunters is another thing: 5
I have come after them and made repair
Where they have left not one stone on a stone,
But they would have the rabbit out of hiding,
To please the yelping dogs. The gaps I mean,
No one has seen them made or heard them made,   10
But at spring mending-time we find them there.
I let my neighbor know beyond the hill;
And on a day we meet to walk the line
And set the wall between us once again.
We keep the wall between us as we go.   15
To each the boulders that have fallen to each.
And some are loaves and some so nearly balls
We have to use a spell to make them balance:
"Stay where you are until our backs are turned!"

We wear our fingers rough with handling them.   20
Oh, just another kind of outdoor game,
One on a side. It comes to little more:
There where it is we do not need the wall:
He is all pine and I am apple orchard.
My apple trees will never get across   25
And eat the cones under his pines, I tell him.
He only says, "Good fences make good neighbors."
Spring is the mischief in me, and I wonder
If I could put a notion in his head:
"*Why* do they make good neighbors? Isn't it   30
Where there are cows? But here there are no cows.
Before I built a wall I'd ask to know
What I was walling in or walling out,
And to whom I was like to give offence.
Something there is that doesn't love a wall,   35
That wants it down." I could say "Elves" to him,
But it's not elves exactly, and I'd rather
He said it for himself. I see him there
Bringing a stone grasped firmly by the top
In each hand, like an old-stone savage armed.   40
He moves in darkness as it seems to me,
Not on woods only and the shade of trees.
He will not go behind his father's saying,
And he likes having thought of it so well
He says again, "Good fences make good neighbors."   45

QUESTIONS

1. The poet focuses on what situation? And on what incident connected with the situation?
2. If you divided this poem into sections, where would you make your divisions?
3. What is the basis of the casual comment about the "game" in lines 21–22?
4. What does the speaker mean by "spring is the mischief in me" (28)?
5. Using such a colloquialism helps to give a certain air or atmosphere to the poem. How would you describe its air?
6. In what meter is the poem written? Read it carefully to see which words receive emphasis. Pay particular attention to lines 7, 9, 27, 30, 32, 34, 36, and 37. Is the meter adjusted so that you hear the rhythms of a real storyteller's voice?
7. What broader application of the idea in lines 32–34 does the poet expect us to make?
8. What judgment about the neighbor's ideas are we led to make by the

simile of line 40? What double meaning does the poet intend by "moves
in darkness" (41)?

9. Contrast the attitudes or "philosophies" of the two wall-menders.
10. What name would you give to the "something"—"not elves exactly"—
"that doesn't love a wall"?

Juggler

RICHARD WILBUR

A ball will bounce, but less and less. It's not
A light-hearted thing, resents its own resilience.
Falling is what it loves, and the earth falls
So in our hearts from brilliance,
Settles and is forgot.   5
It takes a sky-blue juggler with five red balls

To shake our gravity up. Whee, in the air
The balls roll round, wheel on his wheeling hands,
Learning the ways of lightness, alter to spheres
Grazing his finger ends,   10
Cling to their courses there,
Swinging a small heaven about his ears.

But a heaven is easier made of nothing at all
Than the earth regained, and still and sole within
The spin of worlds, with a gesture sure and noble   15
He reels that heaven in,
Landing it ball by ball,
And trades it all for a broom, a plate, a table.

Oh, on his toe the table is turning, the broom's
Balancing up on his nose, and the plate whirls   20
On the tip of the broom! Damn, what a show, we cry:
The boys stamp, and the girls
Shriek, and the drum booms
And all comes down, and he bows and says good-bye.

If the juggler is tired now, if the broom stands   25
In the dust again, if the table starts to drop
Through the daily dark again, and though the plate

Lies flat on the table top,
For him we batter our hands
Who has won for once over the world's weight.   30

QUESTIONS

1. In a general sense this poem is rather like Larkin's "Reasons for Attendance"; both use an incident as the basis for a statement about art. Notice the comparison in lines 3–5 with the behavior of a ball. What causes the ball to fall? In what sense is Wilbur using the word "earth" (3)? What double meaning does "falls" have in line 3? How do we come to feel this way about "the earth"?

2. After stanza 1, "gravity" (7) might be thought a fine example of wit. Explain why.

3. What incident is the poet describing in stanza 2? How does "Learning the ways of lightness" contrast with the statement of lines 1–2? If the balls "alter to spheres" that have "their courses," what does "small heaven" (12) imply about the pattern the balls take?

4. Why does the artist give up his heaven in order to regain earth? What connotations do "broom," "plate," and "table" have?

5. Why is the artist's performance in stanza 4 more difficult and more wonder-provoking than his performance in stanza 2?

6. Wilbur says the artist "has won for once over the world's weight." Why can he not have a continual or lasting triumph? How does the material in the first part of stanza 5 parallel that at the beginning of the poem?

7. What rhyme pattern does Wilbur use? Is it regular throughout the five stanzas? Where does he use approximate rhymes? How has he varied his line lengths?

8. This poem is much admired for its wedding of sound and sense. Point out especially in stanza 4 how alliteration, run-on lines, rhymes, onomatopoeia, and rhythm combine to produce a masterly effect. Notice too how the stanza ends.

9. State the theme of the poem.

10. Compare the point of view, tone, and diction of this poem with those of Larkin's "Reasons for Attendance."

Character and Character Analysis

Miniver Cheevy

EDWIN ARLINGTON ROBINSON

Miniver Cheevy, child of scorn,
  Grew lean while he assailed the seasons;
He wept that he was ever born,
  And he had reasons.

Miniver loved the days of old   5
  When swords were bright and steeds were prancing;
The vision of a warrior bold
  Would set him dancing.

Miniver sighed for what was not,
  And dreamed, and rested from his labors;   10
He dreamed of Thebes and Camelot,
  And Priam's neighbors.

Miniver mourned the ripe renown
  That made so many a name so fragrant;
He mourned Romance, now on the town,   15
  And Art, a vagrant.

Miniver loved the Medici,
  Albeit he had never seen one;
He would have sinned incessantly
  Could he have been one.   20

Miniver cursed the commonplace
  And eyed a khaki suit with loathing;
He missed the mediæval grace
  Of iron clothing.

Miniver scorned the gold he sought,   25
    But sore annoyed he was without it;
Miniver thought, and thought, and thought,
    And thought about it.

Miniver Cheevy, born too late,
    Scratched his head and kept on thinking;   30
Miniver coughed, and called it fate,
    And kept on drinking.

QUESTIONS

1. Look up the meaning of "miniver" in a dictionary. With what era and what type of life is it associated? Does "Cheevy" sound like an aristocratic name? After considering this whole character sketch, answer the question: Why did Robinson choose "Miniver Cheevy" as the name for the man being characterized?

2. Stanza 1 introduces Miniver's situation. What is it, in general terms? After speaking of "reasons" in line 4, what things does the poet list in successive stanzas?

3. Does stanza 2 or stanza 3 provide the more specific material? Look up Thebes, Camelot, Priam. With what famous literary works are they connected?

4. In Miniver's opinion what is the condition of Romance and Art in the twentieth century?

5. By contrast, what did the Medici do for art? Why is the comment about the Medici better in stanza 5 than earlier or later?

6. In which stanzas is there a contrast of the old-romantic and the new-unromantic, and in which stanzas do we see only the present time? What does your answer tell about the organization of the poem?

7. Note down all the verbs with Miniver ("he") as subject. What do you learn from them?

8. The diction of the poem is very important. Where would you normally expect to read such terms as "Wept that he was ever born," "days of old," "steeds," "warrior bold," "albeit," "sore annoyed"? Explain what connotations these terms have.

9. Some of the diction is incongruous with the terms listed above. What associations have such terms as "neighbors" (12), "on the town" (15), "vagrant" (16), "clothing" (24), "scratched his head and kept on thinking" (30)? Why does the incongruity of diction produce a mock-heroic effect?

10. Is this poem witty? amusing? satirical? What feelings are aroused by the word "incessantly" (19)? by the fourth occurrence of the word "thought" (28)? Which terms and stanzas seem to be the funniest?

11. Why is it necessary that the last word be placed in the final position? If

the author had not cleverly held it back but had introduced it earlier, what different effect would it have had?

12. How is the first line of each stanza different in meter from most of the other lines? What is the prevailing meter?

13. In terms of beats per line the stanza pattern is 4-4-4-2. Can you think of any justification for the short fourth line in each stanza?

14. What is the effect of the double rhyme in lines 2 and 4 of each stanza?

15. Which lines and stanzas are given force and held together by alliteration? Compare for alliteration lines 1–2 with 5–6; 11–12 with 13–15; 17, 19 with 21–24.

16. What sort of pressures has life put upon Miniver Cheevy? What has been his response?

17. State the theme of the poem in one sentence.

Ruth

EVE MERRIAM

Why did you go?
Not for a lurid elopement, the perilous ladder placed
Under the guilty window, lover's panting hand, and the heart-
        pounding haste.

But to throw   5
Home and your own bedroom away, deliberately to depart
With a shabby little old woman whose hat wasn't even smart.

Surely you know
Her people have no money, they live hard with working hands.
No piano in the parlor, flowers on the table, nothing grand.   10

And when they say *Hello*
It's with a funny accent, not one you're used to at all.
There are brownish cabbage smells in the dark front hall.

Yet you know
That here you are more than the taken-for-granted daughter 15
Or shrugging sister—*aw, let Ruthie boil the water* . . .

For they bestow
Attention like a jewel, hung on your tiniest phrase,
They worry over your health and cloak you in velvet ways.

From *Family Circle*, by Eve Merriam. Copyright © 1946 by Yale University Press. Reprinted by permission of Yale University Press.

In calico   20
They speak your name: it wears a satin sound.
Among these foreigners family is found.

Oh,
They offer their love humble as everyday stew
And accept your kindness like a ribboned gift—*how wonderful* 25
         of you!
And so you go.

QUESTIONS

1. This poem is based on the book of Ruth in the Old Testament; therefore, unless you know this book well, you must read it in order to understand the poem. Note that Naomi is from Bethlehem in Judah, whereas
   Ruth is from the land of Moab, east of the Dead Sea. What difference
   between the two women is indicated in stanza 4?
2. What possible motivation for Ruth's leaving Moab is rejected in stanza
   1? What things about Naomi and her family that might keep Ruth
   from going with her are pointed out?
3. With the knowledge that the story of Ruth took place in ancient Judah,
   how do you interpret lines 6, 9, and 12? How is the author treating
   the story?
4. What element in the biblical story suggested that Ruth would be "more
   than the taken-for-granted daughter" among Naomi's people?
5. The connotations of the words in stanzas 6–8 are important—especially
   "bestow," "jewel," "velvet," "satin," and "ribboned gift." Explain how
   the connotations influence our judgments of the characters.
6. Explain the metaphor "In calico/They speak" (19–20). With what does
   it contrast? What similar contrast is brought out in lines 23–24?
7. How does the stanza pattern of this poem resemble that of Anne Sexton's "Two Sons"? What do the first lines of all the stanzas have in common? How are they given variety? Compare line 27 with line 1.
8. Compare Eve Merriam's treatment of Ruth and Naomi with Robinson's
   treatment of Miniver Cheevy.

A Song in the Front Yard

GWENDOLYN BROOKS

I've stayed in the front yard all my life.
I want a peek at the back
Where it's rough and untended and hungry weed grows.
A girl gets sick of a rose.

I want to go in the back yard now   5
And maybe down the alley,
To where the charity children play.
I want a good time today.

They do some wonderful things.
They have some wonderful fun.   10
My mother sneers, but I say it's fine
How they don't have to go in at a quarter to nine.

My mother she tells me that Johnnie Mae
Will grow up to be a bad woman.
That George'll be taken to jail soon or late.   15
(On account of last winter he sold our back gate.)

But I say it's fine. Honest I do.
And I'd like to be a bad woman too,
And wear the brave stockings of night-black lace,
And strut down the streets with paint on my face.   20

QUESTIONS

1. What kind of family has the speaker in the poem? Which lines provide the answer to the question?
2. What does "rose" (4) stand for? What term in line 3 especially contrasts with it? What things are suggested by "front yard," "back yard," and "alley"?
3. How is the rhyme scheme of the last stanza different from that of the other stanzas? Notice the special rhythm of line 12. How many anapestic feet does it have? Should *they* have a strong accent? if so, why?
4. Why should the speaker go so far (17) as "But I say it's fine. Honest I do"? Does she do so because she is so young?

5. Note the alliteration and assonance of the last two lines. Why is the *st* alliteration of the last line particularly effective? What is the connotation of "*night*-black lace" in the mind of the speaker?
6. Why is it better to write this poem in the first person than in the third?

To My Mother

GEORGE BARKER

> Most near, most dear, most loved and most far,
> Under the window where I often found her
> Sitting as huge as Asia, seismic with laughter,
> Gin and chicken helpless in her Irish hand,
> Irresistible as Rabelais, but most tender for   5
> The lame dogs and hurt birds that surround her,—
> She is a procession no one can follow after
> But be like a little dog following a brass band.
> She will not glance up at the bomber, or condescend
> To drop her gin and scuttle to a cellar,   10
> But lean on the mahogany table like a mountain
> Whom only faith can move, and so I send
> O all my faith, and all my love to tell her
> That she will move from mourning into morning.

QUESTIONS

1. This poem has fourteen lines, divided 8-6 like a sonnet. Point out the pattern of rhyme and consonance that Barker has used. (Consonance is the converse of rhyme: consonants in words at ends of lines are the same but the vowels differ, as in "deer" and "door.") To what extent does Barker use iambic pentameter? Should the poem be regarded as a sonnet?
2. The characterization is aided greatly by figures of speech. Interpret the simile of line 3. What does "seismic" imply? Does it create a visual image? How does line 4 complete the image? Does "helpless" really modify "gin and chicken"?
3. Explain the metaphor and simile of lines 7–8. What elements of character, personality, or appearance do these lines convey?

4. Read a little about Rabelais (see the article in *The New Century Hand-book of English Literature,* eds. Clarence L. Barnhart and William D. Halsey, for example) to appreciate what is implied by the allusion in line 5.
5. According to lines 1–8, what kind of woman was George Barker's mother?
6. Lines 9–10 have to do with her behavior during the bombing of London in World War II. Why are "glance," "condescend," and "scuttle" particularly valuable words in this part of the characterization?
7. How does the simile of line 11 contrast with the action of line 10 and fit in with the figure in lines 2–4?
8. What does the son's "faith" in his mother consist in? What is the significance of the word "move" (12–14) and the probable meaning of "from mourning into morning"?
9. What are the son's feelings toward his mother, and why does he have them?

My Last Duchess

ROBERT BROWNING

That's my last Duchess painted on the wall,
Looking as if she were alive. I call
That piece a wonder, now: Fra Pandolf's hands
Worked busily a day and there she stands.
Will 't please you sit and look at her? I said   5
"Fra Pandolf" by design, for never read
Strangers like you that pictured countenance,
The depth and passion of its earnest glance,
But to myself they turned (since none puts by
The curtain I have drawn for you, but I)   10
And seemed as they would ask me, if they durst,
How such a glance came there; so, not the first
Are you to turn and ask thus. Sir, 'twas not
Her husband's presence only, called that spot
Of joy into the Duchess' cheek: perhaps   15
Fra Pandolf chanced to say "Her mantle laps
"Over my lady's wrist too much," or "Paint
"Must never hope to reproduce the faint
"Half-flush that dies along her throat": such stuff
Was courtesy, she thought, and cause enough   20
For calling up that spot of joy. She had

A heart—how shall I say?—too soon made glad,
Too easily impressed; she liked whate'er
She looked on, and her looks went everywhere.
Sir, 'twas all one! My favour at her breast,   25
The dropping of the daylight in the West,
The bough of cherries some officious fool
Broke in the orchard for her, the white mule
She rode with round the terrace—all and each
Would draw from her alike the approving speech,   30
Or blush, at least. She thanked men,—good!
          but thanked
Somehow—I know not how—as if she ranked
My gift of a nine-hundred-years-old name
With anybody's gift. Who'd stoop to blame   35
This sort of trifling? Even had you skill
In speech—(which I have not)—to make your will
Quite clear to such an one, and say, "Just this
"Or that in you disgusts me; here you miss,
"Or there exceed the mark"—and if she let   40
Herself be lessoned so, nor plainly set
Her wits to yours, forsooth, and made excuse,
—E'en then would be some stooping; and I choose
Never to stoop. Oh sir, she smiled, no doubt,
Whene'er I passed her; but who passed without   45
Much the same smile? This grew; I gave commands;
Then all smiles stopped together. There she stands
As if alive. Will 't please you rise? We'll meet
The company below, then. I repeat,
The Count your master's known munificence   50
Is ample warrant that no just pretence
Of mine for dowry will be disallowed;
Though his fair daughter's self, as I avowed
At starting, is my object. Nay, we'll go
Together down, sir. Notice Neptune, though,   55
Taming a sea-horse, thought a rarity,
Which Claus of Innsbruck cast in bronze for me!

QUESTIONS

1. Investigate the meaning of "favour," "officious," "munificence," and "avowed."
2. The speaker in this poem is a Duke of Ferrara who lived in the sixteenth century. The poem is a dramatic monologue. The dramatic monologue has been compared with an iceberg, only a small portion of which is visible, the bulk of it being concealed by water. By means

of the few indications given during the speech, we must construct and understand the character of the speaker, and his motives, which are not necessarily explained. After studying the whole poem, we can answer the questions "What kind of man is the speaker?" and "Why does he speak and act as he does?"

3. To whom is the Duke talking? At what point do we discover who the listener is and what the setting and the situation are? What were they discussing before the Duke mentioned the painting of the Duchess? What should we infer that the listener does at lines 9–13?

4. What sort of woman was the "last Duchess"? What details about her behavior indicate this? How do lines 8, 14–15, and 21 fit into your interpretation of the Duchess?

5. What reasons did her husband have to criticize her? In the account he gives, how do you evaluate "stuff" (19), "too soon" (22), and "some officious fool" (27)? What does he intend the four details of lines 25–29 to demonstrate?

6 Why was the Duke unable to make his "will/Quite clear" (36–37) to her and teach her the lesson she needed? What different feelings would he have felt if she had "let/Herself be lessoned" (39–40) or if she had "plainly set/Her wits" to his (40–41)? What makes him so that he chooses "never to stoop"? Do you feel any sympathy for the Duke faced by this difficult problem?

7. Browning was asked regarding lines 45–46 if the Duke had commanded that the Duchess be killed. He replied "meditatively, 'Yes, I meant that the commands were that she should be put to death.' And then, after a pause . . ., 'Or he might have had her shut up in a convent.'" Regarding the Duke's attitude toward "*my* last Duchess," consider what he says about the painting (2–4), "if they durst" (11), and lines 42–46. What is your decision about his character and his motives?

8. What impression does he desire to make upon his listener? What sort of person do you take the listener to be? What special attentions does the Duke pay him?—notice lines 5, 9–10, 47–48, and 53–54.

9. What can be inferred from lines 48–53 regarding the Duke's courtesy, subtlety, interest in money, concern about the "fair daughter's self," and his pride?

10. The Duke points out two masterly works of art. How does he feel about them? Does he have the same collector's pride (and no more?) in both of them?

11. Describe the verse form of the poem. Is it rhymed or unrhymed? Are the lines chiefly run-on or end-stopped? How do these qualities affect it?

I Am the Only Being

EMILY BRONTË

I am the only being whose doom
No tongue would ask, no eye would mourn;
I never caused a thought of gloom,
A smile of joy, since I was born.

In secret pleasure, secret tears,   5
This changeful life has slipped away,
As friendless after eighteen years,
As lone as on my natal day.

There have been times I cannot hide,
There have been times when this was drear,   10
When my sad soul forgot its pride
And longed for one to love me here.

But those were in the early glow
Of feelings since subdued by care;
And they have died so long ago,   15
I hardly now believe they were.

First melted off the hope of youth,
Then fancy's rainbow fast withdrew;
And then experience told me truth
In mortal bosoms never grew.   20

'Twas grief enough to think mankind
All hollow, servile, insincere;
But worse to trust to my own mind
And find the same corruption there.

QUESTIONS

1. According to the first two stanzas what kind of life has the poet had
   through her eighteenth year? What has pride (11) led her to do?
   What happened when her soul "forgot its pride"?
2. Why does she say in stanza 4 that she can hardly believe her earlier
   feelings existed?
3. What three steps in her development are mentioned in stanza 5? What
   phenomena of nature do the metaphors of lines 17–20 refer to?
4. What ironical observation does her self-analysis lead her to in stanza
   6? How is the thought of line 23 related to the earlier part of the poem?
5. What main trait is emphasized in this self-characterization?

Sic Vita

HENRY DAVID THOREAU

I am a parcel of vain strivings tied
   By a chance bond together,
Dangling this way and that, their links
   Were made so loose and wide,
     Methinks,   5
   For milder weather.

A bunch of violets without their roots,
   And sorrel intermixed,
Encircled by a wisp of straw
   Once coiled about their shoots,   10
     The law
   By which I'm fixed.

A nosegay which Time clutched from out
   Those fair Elysian fields,
With weeds and broken stems, in haste,   15
   Doth make the rabble rout
     That waste
   The day he yields.

And here I bloom for a short hour unseen,
   Drinking my juices up,   20
With no root in the land
   To keep my branches green,
     But stand
   In a bare cup.

Some tender buds were left upon my stem   25
   In mimicry of life,
But ah! the children will not know,
   Till time has withered them,
     The woe
   With which they're rife.   30

But now I see I was not plucked for naught,
   And after in life's vase
Of glass set while I might survive,
   But by a kind hand brought
     Alive   35
   To a strange place.

That stock thus thinned will soon redeem its hours,
And by another year,
Such as God knows, with freer air,
More fruits and fairer flowers   40
Will bear,
While I droop here.

QUESTIONS

1. If you need to, look up "vain," "methinks," "sorrel," "nosegay," "Elysian fields," "rout," "mimicry," "rife." What does the Latin title mean?
2. By means of what metaphor is the whole poem developed? What is the relation of stanzas 2 and 3 to stanza 1?
3. What criticism of the poet's own character is implied by the first three stanzas?
4. What does the metaphor of weather (6) imply about the condition of the poet's life? How does mention of "violets" and "sorrel" make more precise and perceptible the image of stanza 1? What is ironic about "the law" (11) governing his character? How does "clutched" (13) and the material of line 15 further reinforce the dominant image? Where is personified Time mentioned besides line 13?
5. Notice the complex and beautiful stanza Thoreau uses. What is the rhyme scheme? the meter? How are the lines varied in length? Does Thoreau use an identical pattern in every stanza?
6. What cause of dissatisfaction is brought out in stanzas 4–5? What contrasting feeling does stanza 6 express? Stanza 6 makes a transition to the consolation of stanza 7. What is that consolation? Through what agricultural metaphor is it developed? How is "another year,/Such as God knows, with freer air," related to stanza 1?
7. Compare the form, mood, and basic idea of this poem with those of "I Am the Only Being" by Emily Brontë.

Me and the Animals

DAVID HOLBROOK

I share my kneebones with the gnat,
My joints with ferrets, eyes with rat
Or blind bat, blinking owl, the goat
His golden cloven orb. I mate like a stoat,
Or like the heavy whale, that moves a sea   5
To make a mother's gross fecundity.

From *Imaginings* by David Holbrook, Putnam, 1961.

I share lung's action with the snake;
The fish is cold, but vertebrate like me; my steak
Is muscle from a butcher's arm, a butcher's heart
Is some sheep's breast that throbbed; I start
At noise with ears which in a dog   10
Can hear what I cannot; in water I'm a frog.

I differ most in lacking their content
To be, no more. They're at the mercy of the scent,
Of hot, cold, summer, winter, hunger, anger,
Or ritual establishing the herd, smelling out the stranger: 15
I walk upright, alone, ungoverned, free:
Yet their occasional lust, fear, unease, walk with me
Always. All ways.

QUESTIONS

1. What is the theme of this poem?
2. What do stanzas 1 and 2 contribute to it? What impression is made by mentioning so many different creatures in stanza 1? How do stoats resemble ferrets? What qualities are connoted here by such terms as "rat," "blind bat," "blinking owl," "heavy whale"?
3. What paradox is suggested by bringing together "butcher's arm," "butcher's heart," and "sheep's breast"?
4. What different aspects of the theme are developed in stanza 3?
5. What word effectively contrasts with "occasional" in line 18? What does this contrast suggest about the condition of mankind? How does the last line gain emphasis?
6. What rhyme pattern has the author used? What meter and what pattern of line lengths? How does stanza 3 differ in form from the other stanzas?

The Heavy Bear Who Goes with Me
"the withness of the body"—Whitehead

DELMORE SCHWARTZ

The heavy bear who goes with me,
A manifold honey to smear his face,
Clumsy and lumbering here and there,
The central ton of every place,

The hungry beating brutish one   5
In love with candy, anger, and sleep,
Crazy factotum, dishevelling all,
Climbs the building, kicks the football,
Boxes his brother in the hate-ridden city.

Breathing at my side, that heavy animal,   10
That heavy bear who sleeps with me,
Howls in his sleep for a world of sugar,
A sweetness intimate as the water's clasp,
Howls in his sleep because the tight-rope
Trembles and shows the darkness beneath.   15
—The strutting show-off is terrified,
Dressed in his dress-suit, bulging his pants,
Trembles to think that his quivering meat
Must finally wince to nothing at all.
That inescapable animal walks with me,   20
Has followed me since the black womb held,
Moves where I move, distorting my gesture,
A caricature, a swollen shadow,
A stupid clown of the spirit's motive,
Perplexes and affronts with his own darkness,   25
The secret life of belly and bone,
Opaque, too near, my private, yet unknown,
Stretches to embrace the very dear
With whom I would walk without him near,
Touches her grossly, although a word   30
Would bare my heart and make me clear,
Stumbles, flounders, and strives to be fed
Dragging me with him in his mouthing care,
Amid the hundred million of his kind,
The scrimmage of appetite everywhere.   35

QUESTION

1. Compare this poem with Holbrook's "Me and the Animals" in respect
   to theme, figures of speech, diction, and form.

Images

The Storm

WILLIAM CARLOS WILLIAMS

A perfect rainbow! a wide
arc low in the northern sky
spans the black lake

troubled by little waves
over which the sun   5
south of the city shines in

coldly from the bare hill
supine to the wind which
cannot awaken anything

but drives the smoke from   10
a few lean chimneys streaming
violently southward

ANALYSIS

During the decade 1909–1918, a group of English and American poets aiming to improve poetry adopted a program that they called imagism. They believed that the heart of good poetry should be the image, that a good poem should be a highly concentrated work of art with firm, clear outlines, and that it should rely on suggestion more than on statement. Imagism required poets to be objective. It is another expression of the "less is more" philosophy of art.

The imagists believed also that a poet ought to create new rhythms and not be content to repeat old ones. They were influenced by the example of Japanese and Chinese poets whom they admired. The typical imagist poem is a brief composition in free verse presenting accurately perceived sense impressions, particularly visual impressions. William Carlos Williams frequently wrote poems according to the imagist program. "The Storm" is one of them.

What distinctive things about a storm might be communicated by imagistic methods? This is the list of items that Williams mentions: rainbow, sky, lake, waves, sun, city, hill, wind, smoke, chimneys. The first item, rainbow, lets us know that the poet is observing a scene just after a storm. These items might not seem to amount to much; but the poet's words are chosen so as to give distinction to the scene and make the sharply vivid details memorable. Furthermore, Williams uses "a perfect rainbow!" as the dramatic focus of his composition, and he tells us its position very precisely—"low in the northern sky"—and its relation to other parts of the landscape. It arches over—but the poet's word is more precise, vivid, and economical: it "spans"—a black lake, which is not placid but "troubled by little waves." The sun is shining "coldly"— a surprising detail, but a strong wind is blowing. Williams, however, does not tell us that a wind is blowing; he makes us *see* a picture showing its effects.

The motive force of his poem is of course in nouns, adjectives, verbs, and adverbs. The quality of the modifiers is especially important. The adjectives in particular make it possible for us to see in imagination the specific elements in the picture. We are shown "a *wide* arc," "*black* lake *troubled*," "*little* waves," "*bare* hill/*supine* to the wind," "a few *lean* chimneys," and "smoke . . . *streaming* violently southward." The modifiers are precise, and lift the material from the ordinary to the extraordinary: the lake is black (not blue); the hill is bare as if lying defenseless; lean chimneys seem alive and tense and very tall (fat chimneys would at once furnish a relaxed and diminished effect).

The two adverbs also contribute something: "coldly" fits in with the mention of the bare hill and the wind to make us feel the unusual atmosphere of the occasion; and "violently" does the most to make us aware of the quality of the wind. The term "troubled" applied to the lake is a participle signifying "agitated" or "disturbed" but is more forceful than these other terms. "Shines" and "awaken" are adequate though not extraordinary verbs, but "drives" and "streaming" furnish much vigor in the final unit of the poem.

Author's comment is reduced to a minimum. The poem contains only one bit of comment, the statement that the wind "cannot awaken anything." This suggests the chill of a wind which is the opposite of a warm spring wind helping to awaken life in the world. One might be tempted to think that the adjective "perfect" is also a comment; it does not, however, mean "this is the perfection of all rainbows" but "this is a complete, perfectly whole rainbow."

"The Storm" is organized in four three-line units of irregular verse. In each unit two items are presented: (1) rainbow and lake; (2) waves and sun; (3) hill and wind; (4) smoke and chimneys. One gets the impression of following the poet's eye from the sky to the earth and from north to south.

In material so stripped down does the imagistic technique permit the poet to communicate anything but a few pictorial details? Is there anything more here than a landscape? A reader may sense that the poem does do something more than describe; that it also suggests an idea or two as well as the poet's response to the scene. First, Williams in effect vouches for this as a true report; this is what I have just seen at the end of a storm. Therefore, in addition, this is the way nature is, capable of combining a perfect rainbow, sunshine, and cold, violent wind. Second, nature can not only do unexpected things, but exhibit dangerous yet wonderfully dynamic strength. This last thought is suggested especially when we feel the force of the words combined together in the final unit, of which the dynamic verbs, as we have said, are chief: "drives" and "streaming." "Lean" and "violently" complete this suggestive pattern of words, with its strong visual imagery.

The position of the words in the final unit has been skillfully planned. The terms have a successive and cumulative impact that builds up very impressively.

Except for the exclamation point after "rainbow" Williams does not use a single mark of punctuation in the poem, not even a period at the end. The lack of any stop may suggest the unceasing dynamism of nature, the violent forces of which have just been dramatically unleashed during the storm. It may also suggest that here we have a piece of sheer, raw experience torn off alive, as it were, from the space-time continuum eternally flowing on.

Overlooking the Desert

TU FU, ADAPTED BY KENNETH REXROTH

Clear Autumn. I gaze out into
Endless spaces. The horizon
Wavers in bands of haze. Far off
The river flows into the sky.
The lone city is blurred with smoke. 5
The wind blows the last leaves away.
The hills grow dim as the sun sets.
A single crane flies late to roost.
The twilit trees are full of crows.

QUESTIONS

1. The dates of Tu Fu, one of the greatest Chinese poets, are A.D. ca. 713–770. From what sort of place, and toward what in general, do you imagine him looking out upon the scene he reports in the poem? In what direction is he looking—for example, from left to right, near to far, far to near? What season is it and what time of day?
2. What does the word "gaze" suggest that would not be signified by other verbs meaning "look"? How can a river flow into a sky? What are we supposed to see?
3. What items does Tu Fu include? List them. Which words make you able to perceive them distinctly? Are the most important words of the poem nouns, verbs, adverbs or adjectives?
4. Compare Tu Fu's treatment of the wind with Williams' treatment of it in "The Storm."
5. Compare the effect of the last three lines of this poem with that of the final unit of "The Storm." Why does Tu Fu put those lines in the sequence they are in?
6. Is there any comment in this poem? Are any thoughts or feelings implied by the images Tu Fu uses?

Balloons

SYLVIA PLATH

Since Christmas they have lived with us,	
Guileless and clear,	
Oval soul-animals,	
Taking up half the space,	
Moving and rubbing on the silk	5
Invisible air drifts,	
Giving a shriek and pop	
When attacked, then scooting to rest, barely trembling.	
Yellow cathead, blue fish—	
Such queer moons we live with	10
Instead of dead furniture!	
Straw mats, white walls	
And these travelling	
Globes of thin air, red, green,	
Delighting	15

The heart like wishes or free
Peacocks blessing
Old ground with a feather
Beaten in starry metals.
Your small   20

Brother is making
His balloon squeak like a cat.
Seeming to see
A funny pink world he might eat on the other side of it,
He bites,   25

Then sits
Back, fat jug
Contemplating a world clear as water,
A red
Shred in his little fist.   30

QUESTIONS

1. According to line 11 the family are now living with some other things (visitors?) besides "dead furniture." In what sense are the balloons not dead? What qualities are attributed to the balloons in lines 1–8?
2. In which words of lines 1–8 do you feel the most startling precision?
3. What terms are applied to the balloons in lines 1–19?
4. What function do the two similes of stanza 4 perform? Why insist that the birds are "free peacocks"? Is the simile about the peacock too elaborate? What image do you perceive in the metaphor of "starry metals"?
5. How does the scene change in lines 20–30?
6. Explain the contrast in the "worlds" of line 24 and of line 28.
7. Describe the different effect you receive from

    Then sits back . . .

    and

    Then sits
    Back . . .

8. Compare lines 26–27 with the effect of

    A fat jug
    He sits back

9. Comment on the effect of the rhyme in line 30 and the pause after it.
10. How is the poem organized?
11. How does "Balloons" compare with the poems by Williams and Tu Fu in regard to (1) the use of images, (2) comment, and (3) suggestions of thought and feeling?

Troubled Woman

LANGSTON HUGHES

        She stands
        In the quiet darkness,
        This troubled woman
        Bowed by
        Weariness and pain   5
        Like an
        Autumn flower
        In the frozen rain,
        Like a
        Wind-blown autumn flower   10
        That never lifts its head
        Again.

QUESTIONS

1. What image constitutes the heart of this poem? What figure of speech
    is it?
2. What is the meaning of "troubled"? Which of the following terms is
    the most abstract? the most concrete?—"quiet darkness," "weariness and
    pain," "autumn flower," "frozen rain," "wind-blown autumn flower."
3. What words of the poem communicate the most precise image?
4. What connotations do "flower" and "autumn flower" have? How is
    "frozen rain" connected with the "troubled woman" who is the subject
    of the poem?
5. Why does the poet repeat in lines 9–10 almost the same thing he said
    in lines 6–7? What does the term "wind-blown" do for the poem? What
    is contributed by the last two lines?
6. State the theme of the poem.
7. To what extent does Hughes use rhyme? Do the rhymes help the poem
    in any way? Do you find any matching of music and meaning?
8. What things does the poet actually see? In which parts of the poem
    does he use remembered experience in order to interpret this experience?
9. Discuss the ratio of subjectivity to objectivity in this poem. How does
    it compare with that of the three preceding poems?

Happiness

MALCOLM LOWRY

Blue mountains with snow and blue cold rough water,
A wild sky full of stars at rising
And Venus and the gibbous moon at sunrise,
Gulls following a motorboat against the wind,
Trees with branches rooted in air—   5
Sitting in the sun at noon with the furiously
Smoking shadow of the shack chimney—
Eagles drive downwind in one,
Terns blow backward,
A new kind of tobacco at eleven,   10
And my love returning on the four o'clock bus
—My God, why have you given this to us?

QUESTIONS

1. What is the setting of this poem?
2. The poet mentions several points of time during a day: before dawn, sunrise, eleven o'clock, noon, four o'clock. What happens at each of these times?
3. How is each happening differentiated? For example, what makes the twelve o'clock event different from that of eleven and of four?
4. When does the writer see the things recorded in lines 1, 4, and 5? Does it matter at what time he observes them?
5. What holds all the items of the poem together?
6. How is the title of this poem different from the titles of the four preceding poems? What does the difference indicate about the direction of the poet's interest?
7. Compare the activity of the wind with that in the poems by Williams and by Tu Fu.
8. What do the words "rough," "wild," "furiously," and "drive" contribute to the poem? As used here, what do they suggest about the author's personality?
9. What emotion is the author trying to communicate in the last line?
10. How would you state the theme of the poem?
11. Which images of this poem are as sharp and precise as those of "The Storm"? Which are less sharp or more inexact? In what respects is "Happiness" less representative of imagism than "The Storm"?

Coming

PHILIP LARKIN

On longer evenings,
Light, chill and yellow,
Bathes the serene
Foreheads of houses.
A thrush sings,   5
Laurel-surrounded
In the deep bare garden,
Its fresh-peeled voice
Astonishing the brickwork.
It will be spring soon,   10
It will be spring soon—
And I, whose childhood
Is a forgotten boredom,
Feel like a child
Who comes on a scene   15
Of adult reconciling,
And can understand nothing
But the unusual laughter,
And starts to be happy.

QUESTIONS

1. What is the subject of the verb "bathes"? Are "chill" and "yellow" nouns or adjectives? How do they function grammatically in the sentence?
2. Point out the chief details of the setting of the poem.
3. Why is the garden bare? Why is the light as it is?
4. What are the parts of the metaphor in lines 1–4?
5. Explain the imagery of "fresh-peeled voice" in line 8.
6. What effect does the poet gain by repeating line 10 in line 11?
7. Explain the responses of the poet toward approaching spring as they are communicated in the simile of lines 12–19.
8. Is there anything in the observed scene for "unusual laughter" to correspond to?

9. Is the title a good one? What does "Coming" signify?
10. Compare "Coming" with Lowry's "Happiness." Is "Coming" mainly subjective or objective?

The Noonday April Sun

GEORGE LOVE

> when through the winding cobbled streets of time
> new spring is borne upon the voices of young boys
> when all around the grass grows up like laughter
> and visions grow like grass beneath our feet
> then roads run out like wine   5
> and eyes like tongues drink up the streams of longing
>
> o then remembrance rages at the tyranny of days
> and men within their shabby inward rooms
> get up to press their faces to the windowpanes
> and then run down in rivers to the sea of dreams   10

QUESTIONS

1. This poem also deals with the arrival of spring, the start of another year. In the metaphor of "streets of time" what impression is communicated? How do you visualize the metaphor of line 2? How is someone usually borne through streets? What would make voices of young boys suitable bearers of spring?
2. How do the roads of line 5 contrast with the city streets of line 1? What does the simile of line 5 contribute to our impression of roads?
3. How is the simile of line 3 appropriate to grass growing? What idea about visions is communicated by the simile of line 4?
4. Explain the complex statement made through the figures (similes and metaphor) of lines 5–6.
5. Why does remembrance (rather than hope, for instance) rage at "the tyranny of days"?
6. Do you think the "shabby inward rooms" are the actual rooms men live in, or are the shabby rooms a metaphor for their state of mind? If they are the latter, what is their state of mind?
7. Why is spring a time when men would do the things mentioned in lines 9–10? Are these things a kind of resistance to the "tyranny of days"? Or is resistance too strong a term to use?

From *New Negro Poets: USA*, edited by Langston Hughes. Reprinted by permission of Indiana University Press.

8. What does pressing the face to the windowpane symbolize? What is conveyed by the metaphor of line 10?
9. Do lines 7–10 end with rhymes?
10. Is the title a suitable one? How does it differ from the titles of the two preceding poems?
11. How does this poem compare with them for amount and complexity of figurative language?

Spring

ELEANOR MUNRO

Its coming rankles the swamp   where the brook spills
such a reek of things splitting and smoking,
and the mud banks   shuddering into green, and
        gas over the cabbage burning.
The deer ruts, scraping her neck down the teeth of a branch. 5

Pods crack and fall   puff till they tear
gnats' grubs, toadstools, bundles of black eggs,
and the flowers   sweet alyssum, cicely, sweet gale,
        and trillium, spreading the wood's lips.
The elm bud breaks its back and lifts from the twig.   10

I drift.   Where's my fashion gone?
Sunk in some brown wet, with leaves stuck to my back, I hear
the mud's murmur   nymphs calling,
        lids opening, tongues and toes unfolding.
Oh, why does he wait? Here are my arms. Oh, look!   15

QUESTION

1. Make a comparison between this poem and the poems by Larkin, Love, and Williams in terms of (1) form, (2) use of images, figurative language, and comment, (3) evocative words (for example, "rankles," "reek," and "ruts" in the first stanza), (4) subjective and objective elements, and (5) theme.

As by Water

W. S. MERWIN

Oh
Together
Embracing departure
We hoisted our love like a sail

And like a sail and its reflection   5
However
We move and wherever
We shall be divided as by water
Forever forever
Though   10
Both sails shudder as they go
And both prows lengthen the same sorrow

Till the other elements
Extend between us also.

QUESTIONS

1. The only mark of punctuation in the poem is one period. If the poem were punctuated conventionally, should punctuation marks be inserted, to make the poet's meaning unmistakable, after "reflection," after "however," or after "wherever"?
2. What does "embracing" signify?
3. Explain the pertinence of the simile in line 4.
4. In the simile of line 5 what things are the sail and the reflection being compared to?
5. What part does imagery play in the communication of the poet's idea here?
6. What is the usual meaning of "divided by water"? What does "divided as by water" (8) mean? After mentioning the element of water in line 8, the poet refers to "the other elements" in line 13. What are they? In what situation would they "extend between us also"?
7. How does this poem differ in its technique from the three preceding poems?
8. What is the theme of the poem?

Experiences of Beauty

Go, Lovely Rose

EDMUND WALLER

> Go, lovely Rose—
> Tell her that wastes her time and me,
> That now she knows,
> When I resemble her to thee,
> How sweet and fair she seems to be.   5
>
> Tell her that's young,
> And shuns to have her graces spied,
> That hadst thou sprung
> In deserts where no men abide,
> Thou must have uncommended died.   10
>
> Small is the worth
> Of beauty from the light retired:
> Bid her come forth,
> Suffer herself to be desired,
> And not blush so to be admired.   15
>
> Then die—that she
> The common fate of all things rare
> May read in thee;
> How small a part of time they share
> That are so wondrous sweet and fair!   20

QUESTIONS

1. Consult a dictionary to discover the special way Waller uses the following words: "shuns," "sprung," "abide," "uncommended," and "suffer."
2. When a man who is courting a girl sends her roses, he may send a message with them. What are the parts of this message? What object lessons is the rose instructed to teach the girl?
3. Time is mentioned in stanzas 1 and 4. Considering the last two lines,

explain the meaning of "wastes her time" (2). What different meaning does "wastes" have in "wastes . . . me"?

4. Does the poet pay compliments to the girl? What adjectives are applied to her? From the hints in the poem what do you think his experience with her has been?
5. How is the poem organized? Does stanza 4 have to be placed last?
6. In one sentence state the thought (or argument) of the poem.
7. What is the pattern of stanza 1? Does Waller follow the same stanza pattern throughout?
8. What is the basic meter of the poem? What is the purpose of the variations from the meter in lines 1, 3, and 4 of stanza 3? What is the effect of the run-on lines in stanzas 2 and 3?

Envoi (1919)

EZRA POUND

Go, dumb-born book,
Tell her that sang me once that song of Lawes:
Hadst thou but song
As thou hast subjects known,
Then were there cause in thee that should condone   5
Even my faults that heavy upon me lie,
And build her glories their longevity.

Tell her that sheds
Such treasure in the air,
Recking naught else but that her graces give   10
Life to the moment,
I would bid them live
As roses might, in magic amber laid,
Red overwrought with orange and all made
One substance and one colour   15
Braving time.

Tell her that goes
With song upon her lips
But sings not out the song, nor knows
The maker of it, some other mouth,   20
May be as fair as hers,

Might, in new ages, gain her worshippers,
When our two dusts with Waller's shall be laid,
Siftings on siftings in oblivion,
Till change hath broken down 25
All things save Beauty alone.

QUESTIONS

1. Look up the meaning of "envoi" (envoy) as a poetic term. Also, find out who Henry Lawes was, and check the meaning of "condone," "longevity," "recking," "amber," "overwrought," "braving," and "oblivion."
2. What points of resemblance do you note between this poem and Waller's "Go, Lovely Rose"? How do we know that Pound was thinking of Waller's poem when he composed this one?
3. Has Pound used the same stanza pattern as Waller's? Has he followed the same stanza pattern throughout?
4. Noting alliteration, assonance, rhymes, verse movement, line lengths, pauses, and run-on lines, comment on the quality of verbal music in this poem. Is it richer or less rich than the music of "Go, Lovely Rose"?
5. What messages is the book instructed to deliver to the lady?
6. What is the poet modestly apologizing about in stanza 1? According to line 7, what is the main purpose of the poet's book?
7. In stanza 2 Pound mentions both roses and time. To what is he comparing the roses in his simile (13)? Be sure you understand what happens when the roses are laid in amber. Why is amber called "magic amber"? How is the fate of these roses different from that of Waller's rose?
8. How does Pound's concept of time and its ravages differ from Waller's?
9. Obviously this poem could not exist as it does without Pound's knowledge of "Go, Lovely Rose." But now, having dealt with questions 6–19, answer this question: In what way do Pound's subject and purpose differ from Waller's?

To Helen

EDGAR ALLAN POE

Helen, thy beauty is to me
    Like those Nicèan barks of yore,
That gently, o'er a perfumed sea,
    The weary, way-worn wanderer bore
    To his own native shore. 5

> On desperate seas long wont to roam,
>   Thy hyacinth hair, thy classic face,
> Thy Naiad airs have brought me home
>   To the glory that was Greece
> And the grandeur that was Rome.   10
>
> Lo! in yon brilliant window-niche
>   How statue-like I see thee stand,
>   The agate lamp within thy hand!
> Ah, Psyche, from the regions which
>   Are Holy Land!   15

QUESTIONS

1. Look up "Nicaea," "barks," "yore," "wont," "hyacinth," "hyacinthine," "classic," "Naiad," "niche," "agate," and "Psyche."

2. Readers must be sure that they do not "read into" poems things that the poet does not say or intend to express. For instance, this poem is not a description of a woman; it is only indirectly concerned with her appearance. Poe says: "thy beauty is *to me*/Like . . . barks." Is this to be an objective or a subjective poem?

3. A poet may say, "Helen, your beauty reminds me of ships." Very well, of what aspect of ships? Here it is certainly not their appearance. What association with ships does Poe make in lines 3–5? Who might the wanderer be? (Scholars have conjectured that Poe may be alluding to Ulysses or Bacchus or Catullus. See *The Poems of Edgar Allan Poe*, ed. Killis Campbell [New York: Russell & Russell, 1962] p. 201; and J. J. Jones, "Poe's 'Nicéan Barks,'" *American Literature*, II [1931], pp. 433–438.) Where did these three make voyages? What is their connection with the classic world?

4. What would be the feelings of a weary wanderer upon reaching his "native shore" after a gentle voyage? What was Poe thinking of as *his own* native shore? Should we call the home he mentions in line 8 a cultural, intellectual, or artistic home? Or is it a refuge? By what things were the "glory" and "grandeur" of lines 9–10 represented?

5. What are desperate seas? With what term in stanza 1 does this phrase contrast? In what sense could the pressures put on Poe make his world of early nineteenth-century America seem like desperate seas in contrast to the classical world?

6. Both stanzas 1 and 2 deal with a homecoming. What different aspect of Helen's beauty in relation to Poe's arrival is each stanza concerned with?

7. In stanza 3 Poe says he sees Helen "statue-like." In what sense does he "see" her?

8. If she is standing still as a statue and holding up a lamp, what function is her beauty performing for Poe the observer (and also still the traveler)?

9. Why should he call her Psyche? What are the associations of the word "Psyche"?

10. What are the connotations of "Holy Land"? In view of the whole poem, what are "the regions which/Are Holy Land," (1) supposing they can be shown on a map; (2) supposing they cannot be shown on a map?

11. What variations of rhyme scheme and line length has Poe introduced into the three stanzas? What is the basic meter? In which lines do you find anapestic feet?

12. Which lines are distinctive and memorable on account of their alliteration?

13. Describe the difference in verse movement and effect of lines 9–10 and lines 14–15.

On First Looking into Chapman's Homer

JOHN KEATS

Much have I travell'd in the realms of gold,
    And many goodly states and kingdoms seen;
    Round many western islands have I been
Which bards in fealty to Apollo hold.
Oft of one wide expanse had I been told   5
    That deep-brow'd Homer ruled as his demesne;
    Yet did I never breathe its pure serene
Till I heard Chapman speak out loud and bold:
Then felt I like some watcher of the skies
    When a new planet swims into his ken;   10
Or like stout Cortez when with eagle eyes
    He star'd at the Pacific—and all his men
Look'd at each other with a wild surmise—
    Silent, upon a peak in Darien.

QUESTIONS

1. The reader will quickly perceive by the indentation of the lines, the rhyme scheme, and the punctuation, that this poem is a sonnet. What type of sonnet is it?

2. The title will be enough to inform some readers what "realms of gold"

stands for. This phrase is the key to the interpretation of the octave (first eight lines) of the sonnet. Other readers will have to interpret the realms, states, kingdoms, and islands through the metaphor of line 4, "Which bards in fealty to Apollo hold." Look up "bards," "fealty," "Apollo," "demesne," "serene," "ken," and "Darien." This metaphor makes poets, according to the medieval feudal system, into vassals of the god Apollo, their lord and inspirer; and thus we understand that "realms of gold" refers to poetic literature. "Gold" is a significant word. What are its connotations?

3. Homer's epics, translated by the Elizabethan poet George Chapman, are, according to the territorial metaphor of lines 1–4, a "wide expanse" ruled by "deep-brow'd" Homer. What impression do these terms give us of the works and of their author?

4. What terms indicate something of the quality of Chapman's translation?

5. At the end of line 8 we find a colon, a signal to go ahead and learn more. At this point Keats proceeds from the octave to the sestet (last six lines) of his sonnet. The transitional term here is "Then felt I." The poet's problem was how to express his feelings when he first read Chapman's Homer. Keats expresses them in two similes. What are they?

6. Many people are watchers of the skies—professional or amateur astronomers. But not many can be the first to observe a new planet. Perhaps Keats was thinking of such a watcher as Galileo or Herschel, the leading astronomer of the eighteenth century. The poet imagines the watcher's experience even to the movement of the planet. What word should he use? Such terms as "appears," "comes," "moves," or "enters" are commonplace and rather general. Such terms as "leaps," "flies," "darts," or "rises" lack dignity or exactness. But "swims" is a term of greater power and precision that strikes the imagination, especially when joined with "ken." Just what does "ken" take in? And what does "swims" imply about the areas of the skies?

7. How would the ordinary person try to explain his feelings? He might say, "I felt astonished"—but the poet instinctively turns to examples. Keats's second example presents another discoverer. It really does not matter that the name should be Balboa rather than Cortez. What matters is the experience of discovery. Probably only certain kinds of discoveries could be suitable for Keats's purpose. What kinds? Specifically, what makes the experience of the discovery of the Pacific Ocean suitable for the poet's purpose here?

8. What terms bring Cortez vividly before the imagination of the reader?

9. What other terms make the experience of astonishment at a discovery precise and powerful in the imagination?

10. What has Keats done in his sestet to make his discovery of Homer seem extraordinary to the reader?

On Hearing a Symphony of Beethoven

EDNA ST. VINCENT MILLAY

> Sweet sounds, oh, beautiful music, do not cease!
> Reject me not into the world again.
> With you alone is excellence and peace,
> Mankind made plausible, his purpose plain.
> Enchanted in your air benign and shrewd,   5
> With limbs a-sprawl and empty faces pale,
> The spiteful and the stingy and the rude
> Sleep like the scullions in the fairy-tale.
> This moment is the best the world can give:
> The tranquil blossom on the tortured stem.   10
> Reject me not, sweet sounds; oh, let me live,
> Till Doom espy my towers and scatter them,
> A city spell-bound under the aging sun,
> Music my rampart, and my only one.

QUESTIONS

1. Look up the dictionary meaning of "plausible," "benign," "shrewd," "scullions," "spell-bound," and "rampart."
2. What type of sonnet is this? Give evidence in detail. Compare it with the preceding poem by Keats.
3. What particular value of Beethoven's music is suggested in lines 1–4?
4. How is the statement in lines 3–4 emphasized by alliteration? What alliterative patterns do you note in lines 9–12?
5. The concept of music as an enchantment is developed in lines 5–8. This quatrain suggests the fairy-tale theme of the enchanted princess (or palace put to sleep in an enchanted wood). What sorts of people are "transformed" by Beethoven's music? What result does the enchanting power of music have upon them?
6. What is the difference between the "world" and the musical experience? Yet the music is something that "the world can give." Explain the metaphor of "the tranquil blossom on the tortured stem." What is the stem and what makes it tortured? How can a symphony concert be called a "tranquil blossom"?

7. In line 11 the poet repeats "Reject me not." What is the literal meaning of "reject"? From what to what would the poet be rejected?
8. How is the metaphor of the "city spell-bound" in line 13 related to lines 5–8?
9. What might be another term for "Doom"? To what point in life does line 12 refer?
10. The city metaphor applies to the poet herself. How do we know this? Against what is music to be the poet's rampart?

Ode on a Grecian Urn

JOHN KEATS

Thou still unravish'd bride of quietness,
  Thou foster-child of silence and slow time,
Sylvan historian, who canst thus express
  A flowery tale more sweetly than our rhyme:
What leaf-fring'd legend haunts about thy shape   5
    Of deities or mortals, or of both,
      In Tempe or the dales of Arcady?
What men or gods are these? What maidens loth?
    What mad pursuit? What struggle to escape?
      What pipes and timbrels? What wild ecstasy?   10

Heard melodies are sweet, but those unheard
  Are sweeter; therefore, ye soft pipes, play on;
Not to the sensual ear, but, more endear'd,
  Pipe to the spirit ditties of no tone:
Fair youth, beneath the trees, thou canst not leave   15
    Thy song, nor ever can those trees be bare;
      Bold Lover, never, never canst thou kiss,
Though winning near the goal—yet, do not grieve;
    She cannot fade, though thou hast not thy bliss,
      For ever wilt thou love, and she be fair!   20

Ah, happy, happy boughs! that cannot shed
  Your leaves, nor ever bid the Spring adieu;
And, happy melodist, unwearièd,
  For ever piping songs for ever new;
More happy love! more happy, happy love!   25
    For ever warm and still to be enjoy'd,
      For ever panting, and for ever young;
All breathing human passion far above,

That leaves a heart high-sorrowful and cloy'd,
    A burning forehead, and a parching tongue.   30

Who are these coming to the sacrifice?
    To what green altar, O mysterious priest,
Lead'st thou that heifer lowing at the skies,
    And all her silken flanks with garlands drest?
What little town by river or sea shore,   35
    Or mountain-built with peaceful citadel,
      Is emptied of this folk, this pious morn?
And, little town, thy streets for evermore
    Will silent be; and not a soul to tell
      Why thou art desolate, can e'er return.   40

O Attic shape! Fair attitude! with brede
    Of marble men and maidens overwrought,
With forest branches and the trodden weed;
    Thou, silent form, dost tease us out of thought
As doth eternity: Cold Pastoral!   45
    When old age shall this generation waste,
      Thou shalt remain, in midst of other woe
Than ours, a friend to man, to whom thou say'st,
    Beauty is truth, truth beauty,—that is all
      Ye know on earth, and all ye need to know.   50

QUESTIONS

1. Consult a dictionary for the meaning of these words: "sylvan," "legend," "Tempe," "Arcady," "timbrels," "sensual," "ditties," "cloyed," "Attic," "brede," "pastoral."
2. Keats uses three terms to address the ancient Greek urn in stanza 1. What are they? What aspect of the existence of the urn do the first two bring out? What different attribute is brought out by the third?
3. Sculpture is a space-art, whereas poetry is a time-art. This distinction is the basis of what Keats says in lines 3–4. What materials of a "flowery tale" does the poet perceive on the urn?
4. How do these materials contrast with what is said about the urn in lines 1–2?
5. Elements of contradiction are an essential part of this poem. Why is an unheard melody (11) a paradox? What unheard melody is Keats aware of as he views the urn? How can unheard melodies be sweeter than heard melodies? Be sure to read line 14 with a pause after the word "spirit." What is the grammatical function of the word "ditties" in the sentence?
6. Why does the poet tell the lover not to grieve (18)? What do the

trees (16, 21–22), the lover (17), and the musician (23) have in common?

7. What are the conditions of the immortality guaranteed in line 20?

8. In what respect is the love portrayed on the urn superior to the "breathing human passion" (28) that Keats or any reader might feel?

9. What kind of occasion is described in stanza 4? Why does Keats call the priest "mysterious"? How does the spirit of the urn scene in stanza 4 contrast with that of stanza 1?

10. In stanza 3 the poet finds reason to congratulate the ancient lovers. What different feeling does he express about the townsfolk of stanza 4 (38–40)? Where does the empty town exist?

11. What terms used in stanza 5 make it a kind of parallel to stanza 1? Why do you think Keats felt that the urn led him beyond the limits of thought? Comment on the effectiveness of the simile in line 45. Why is eternity a very difficult concept to deal with?

12. Would it be fair to say that the urn is an analogy of eternity? How is its "eternal" life of pure being better than ordinary nature? What is implied about it by "Cold Pastoral!" (45)?

13. Keats says it is going to remain "a friend to man." Why? Its statement "Beauty is truth, truth beauty" has been a source of much discussion and disagreement. Perhaps it is reasonable to say: The beauty of the urn represents truth because it is eternal; and truth must be beautiful because it is the heart of the eternal reality. There have also been varied interpretations of the final statement. Does the urn also say this to man? Does the poet say it to man? Does the poet say it to the urn?

14. What paradox of art and life does the urn embody?

15. Does Keats use the same stanza form throughout the ode? What is his rhyme scheme?

16. Point out what different rhythmical effects Keats gets by varying the position of the caesura in his lines. Compare lines 3, 7, 9, 10, 12, 13, 14, 15, 20, 30, 38, 39, 40, 45, 49, 50.

17. To what extent does Keats use run-on lines? What effects do they have on the rhythm?

Love

Sonnet 116

WILLIAM SHAKESPEARE

Let me not to the marriage of true minds
Admit impediments. Love is not love
Which alters when it alteration finds,
Or bends with the remover to remove.
O, no! it is an ever-fixed mark   5
That looks on tempests and is never shaken;
It is the star to every wand'ring bark,
Whose worth's unknown, although his height be taken.
Love's not Time's fool, though rosy lips and cheeks
Within his bending sickle's compass come;   10
Love alters not with his brief hours and weeks,
But bears it out even to the edge of doom.
  If this be error and upon me proved,
  I never writ, nor no man ever loved.

QUESTIONS

1. The first statement of the sonnet echoes the marriage service from the Book of Common Prayer of the Church of England: "If any of you know cause or just impediment. . . ." But Shakespeare is writing about a marriage of true *minds*. What, then, woud "love" presumably mean?
2. The sonnet is developed by contrasts of negative and positive. Show what these contrasts are, and their relation to the three quatrains of the sonnet.
3. Even under what extreme conditions does true love refuse to change?
4. What sort of "mark" would Shakespeare have in mind in the navigation metaphor of quatrain 2?
5. Be sure you know the meaning of "bark" and of "height" in reference to a star. Explain the contrast between "worth" and "height." How does this apply to love?
6. Time is personified in line 9. How does Shakespeare intend us to visualize him?

7. How does the poet support the idea that "Love's not Time's fool"?
8. What happens to "rosy lips and cheeks"? Are they the lips and cheeks of the lover, or the loved person, or both?
9. What does the phrase "edge of doom" imply?
10. To what extent is the physical aspect of love considered here? Is the poem entirely idealistic?
11. Explain the paradox of the final couplet.
12. Which lines begin with a strong accent? Explain the effect of the spondaic stresses in line 9.
13. In which lines is alliteration most prominent: 1–2, 4, 10, or 11–12?

The Soul Selects Her Own Society

EMILY DICKINSON

> The soul selects her own society,
> Then shuts the door.
> To her divine majority
> Present no more.
>
> Unmoved she notes the chariots pausing   5
> At her low gate;
> Unmoved, an emperor be kneeling
> Upon her mat.
>
> I've known her from an ample nation
> Choose one,   10
> Then close the valves of her attention
> Like stone.

ANALYSIS

Theme and Organization   The theme of the poem is stated in the first line. The rest of the poem develops this theme by means of concrete exemplification. The soul is treated as a woman—"she." This woman—Miss Soul, we might say—invites people of her choice, and no others, to visit her; she is "not at home" to anyone else. She is a self-possessed, independent person who knows her own mind so well that it is useless for a stranger, or, in fact, anyone she does not care to see, to present a card of introduction and expect admittance.

From *The Complete Poems of Emily Dickinson*, edited by Thomas H. Johnson and published by Little, Brown and Company.

Stanza 2 dramatizes the situation very vividly. Though Miss Soul lives in a modest house with a low gate and an ordinary doormat, she is not awed by wealth, grandeur, or rank of unwanted callers. Even if people come in chariots (which are expensive vehicles), she pays no attention. Even the extraordinary example of an emperor kneeling at this ordinary woman's door to show his humility and devotion does not alter her sense of values.

The soul's society is highly "select." In fact, to drive this point home, the poet tells us in stanza 3 that the soul, though having generous opportunities to choose her intimates—"from an ample nation"—may select only one individual and then pay no attention whatever to all of the other possibilities. A single intimate—it would be better to say "affinity"—is sufficient for the soul. The soul has exercised her "divine majority" vote to choose the perfect friend. That person (or that other soul) must be divinely ordained as comrade and soul-mate.

Musical Elements   The poem begins with a four-line stanza in which four iambic feet per line alternate with two iambic feet, the second lines and fourth lines rhyming. Stanza 2 has the same pattern. But in stanza 3 the second and fourth lines are shortened to a single emphatic iambic foot. In the three stanzas the first and third lines have an extra light syllable at the end with a double rhyme—except line 3, stanza 1,

To her/divine/majority

which, if read as a four-beat line, lacks the light syllable.

Actually, the first and third lines of the three stanzas are not perfect rhymes; we must call "society" and "majority," "pausing" and "kneeling," and "nation" and "attention" light rhymes, since only the last (unaccented) syllables rhyme. The second and fourth lines of stanza 1 end in perfect rhymes, but the second and fourth lines of stanzas 2 and 3 do not: "gate" and "mat," and "one" and "stone" have corresponding consonant sounds at the end, but the vowel sounds do not correspond. By these departures from regularity in meter and rhyme Emily Dickinson has made the short poem with its simple basic pattern seem less ordinary and more challenging to the reader's attention and interest.

The poet has used some alliteration. Repeated *s*'s provide pronounced alliteration in line 1; *m* in "more" (4) alliterates with *m* in "unmoved" (5, 7) and "mat" (8), and these *m*'s are supported by unstressed *m*'s in "majority," "emperor," and "ample"; and *n* alliterates in "notes," "kneeling," "known," and "nation."

The most emphatic sounds are the strong rhymes of lines 2 and 4 ("door," "more") and the resounding, deep *o* of "stone" in line 12, which echoes the *o* of "close" in line 11. The change in line length—the reduction of lines 10 and 12 to monometer—together with the *o* sound, makes the close of the poem convey great firmness and finality.

Diction   The diction of this poem is quite simple, in keeping with the imagined setting of the soul's house; the simplicity of the dwelling is suggested by "shuts the door," "low gate," and "mat." In contrast to these terms, "divine majority" is more distinctive; its abstractness helps to convey the sure dignity of the soul even though she is living in a humble dwelling. "Notes" (5) is well chosen to indicate the kind of attention briefly conceded to unwanted visitors.

The contrast of "ample nation" with "choose one" is striking. The word "one" could not be changed except with loss of economy. What other adjective but "ample" might convey the breadth of choice available to the soul? Other possibilities such as "broad" and "extensive" tend to stress too much physical area and not the number of people; whereas "populous" has both a literalness and an unfortunate explosiveness of sound that make it less suitable.

But the words which carry the highest poetic voltage occur in the last two lines. First, the metaphor of "valves" suggests the utmost tightness of closing. Valves of machinery, valves of the heart, valves of marine creatures —all suggest the stubbornest refusal to open. Second, though these are the valves of attention, they are not stone valves. Yet the soul closes them "like stone," and the simile which ends the poem with the monometric line gives the poem, as we have said, great finality. Stone is hard, immovable, and impenetrable; it suggests sternness. Think, for example, of a "stony heart." But stone is also used to provide protection; behind the valves of attention closed like stone, the soul has secure privacy with her select kindred soul. Sound and connotations are used here to create a matching of music and meaning most effective for the close of the poem.

Point out the similarity of ideas in this poem and in Shakespeare's Sonnet 116.

Sonnet 55

WILLIAM SHAKESPEARE

> Not marble, nor the gilded monuments
> Of princes, shall outlive this powerful rhyme;
> But you shall shine more bright in these contents
> Than unswept stone besmear'd with sluttish time.
> When wasteful war shall statues overturn,   5
> And broils root out the work of masonry,
> Nor Mars his sword nor war's quick fire shall burn
> The living record of your memory.
> 'Gainst death and all-oblivious enmity

Shall you pace forth; your praise shall still find room   10
Even in the eyes of all posterity
That wear this world out to the ending doom.
   So, till the judgement that yourself arise,
   You live in this, and dwell in lovers' eyes.

QUESTIONS

1. Look up the meaning of "besmeared," "sluttish," "broils," "oblivious,"
    "doom."
2. From the ancient Greek poets through the Romans to the Renais-
    sance poets of France came the tradition of "poetic immortality"—
    that a loved person or patron would remain known in future ages
    through the deathless poems about that person. How do the first two
    lines of this poem fit in with that tradition?
3. What other commemorative devices are contrasted with poetry in
    lines 1–4? What are the connotations of "marble" and "gilded" monu-
    ments?
4. What word in line 4 contrasts with "bright" (3)? To what sort of person
    is time being compared in line 4? How do you know? For what pur-
    pose is the poet making the comparison?
5. What destructive acts are emphasized in quatrain 2? What does
    Shakespeare mean by "living record" (8)?
6. What is the "all-oblivious enmity" of line 9?
7. In which lines has Shakespeare repeated his assurance of "poetic im-
    mortality"? Considering lines 12–13, how long is this "immortality"
    to be?
8. Explain what phase of the subject is taken up in each quatrain and in
    the final couplet.
9. In what sense will the person Shakespeare writes about dwell in fu-
    ture lovers' (friends') eyes? As one whose fine qualities deserve re-
    membrance? As a kind of model of perfection?
10. Show how alliteration gives power and memorability to lines 1, 2,
    3–4, 5, 10–11, 12.
11. What difference in emphasis is there between "shall you step out" and
    "shall you pace forth" (10)? Explain the metrical effect of Shakes-
    peare's words.
12. Scan line 12. Where does the caesura come? Which foot is irregular?
    Which words receive the most emphasis?
13. Compare the organization and development of this sonnet with the
    organization and development of Sonnet 116.

A Valediction: Forbidding Mourning

JOHN DONNE

As virtuous men pass mildly away,
  And whisper to their souls to go,
Whilst some of their sad friends do say,
  The breath goes now, and some say, no:

So let us melt, and make no noise,   5
  No tear-floods, nor sigh-tempests move,
'Twere profanation of our joys
  To tell the laity our love.

Moving of th' earth brings harms and fears,
  Men reckon what it did and meant,   10
But trepidation of the spheres,
  Though greater far, is innocent.

Dull sublunary lovers' love
  (Whose soul is sense) cannot admit
Absence, because it doth remove   15
  Those things which elemented it.

But we by a love so much refin'd
  That ourselves know not what it is,
Inter-assured of the mind,
  Care less, eyes, lips, and hands to miss.   20

Our two souls therefore, which are one,
  Though I must go, endure not yet
A breach, but an expansion,
  Like gold to aery thinness beat.

If they be two, they are two so   25
  As stiff twin compasses are two,
Thy soul the fixt foot, makes no show
  To move, but doth, if th'other do.

And though it in the center sit,
  Yet when the other far doth roam,   30
It leans, and hearkens after it,
  And grows erect, as that comes home.

Such wilt thou be to me, who must
   Like th'other foot, obliquely run;
Thy firmness makes my circle just,   35
   And makes me end, where I begun.

QUESTIONS

1. Define "valediction," "profanation," "laity," "trepidation," "innocent," "sublunary," and "elemented" as used here.
2. Stanzas 1 and 2 go together. How does stanza 2 complete the death-bed simile of stanza 1?
3. In these stanzas there is a contrast of good taste (quietness) and bad taste or vulgarity (noise and violence). Describe the tone in which Donne writes.
4. How much noise does an ice cube make when it melts? What is the poetic connotation of "melt"?
5. The second part of the deathbed simile is developed first by metaphors of floods and tempests, and then by an implied metaphor of religion (the religion of love). Considering how the priesthood and the laity are contrasted in a religion, explain the significance of "profanation."
6. In the Ptolemaic cosmology the term "trepidation of the spheres" was used to account for irregularities in the revolutions of the planets. What is the purpose of the contrast between the "moving of th' earth" and the much more extensive quaking of the spheres?
7. Donne moves to another phase of his subject with stanza 4. What is his opinion of the love of "sublunary" lovers? Medieval and Renaissance literature contains many references to things governed by the moon or "under the moon," the most changeable of planets; such things are changeable.
8. If the very soul of the sublunary lovers is "sense," then they depend on the physical senses, sight and touch in particular. Thus they can't bear to be out of sight of each other; they even feel that they need to touch each other constantly in order to be sure of their love. What contrast with idealistic (or Platonic) love is brought out in stanza 5? What is the significance of "inter-assured"? Why is it that the idealistic lovers "care less" about losing the contact of eyes, lips, and hands?
9. John Donne was the chief member of the metaphysical school of poetry, and after the fashion of metaphysical poets he draws a logical conclusion (note the word "therefore," line 21) in stanza 6, based on the statements of stanzas 4 and 5 and on the assumption that the souls of the lovers are really one soul. What is this conclusion?
10. "Breach" and "expansion" take on more exact meaning from the simile of making gold leaf (24). Explain what Donne is suggesting about the souls of lovers while the man is away on his journey.

11. In stanza 7 Donne begins the final section of his poem by considering the possibility that the lovers really have two souls and not one soul. If so, their situation is still extraordinary; he compares it to "twin compasses" (the kind used to draw circles, not to point to the north). Which foot of the compass is pressed down in the center of the circle? What is the other compass foot doing? What is the relation of the woman foot and the man foot of the compass?

12. Explain how we visualize the images of "leans," "hearkens," and "grows erect." What are the connotations of these terms?

13. What is the effect of the last stanza of the poem, and particularly of the words "firmness," "just," "where I begun"?

14. What similarities does this love lyric have with Shakespeare's Sonnet 116?

"Not Marble nor the Gilded Monuments"

ARCHIBALD MAC LEISH

The praisers of women in their proud and beautiful poems,
Naming the grave mouth and the hair and the eyes,
Boasted those they loved should be forever remembered:
These were lies.

The words sound but the face in the Istrian sun is forgotten.   5
The poet speaks but to her dead ears no more.
The sleek throat is gone—and the breast that was troubled
                    to listen:
Shadow from door.

Therefore I will not praise your knees nor your fine walking
Telling you men shall remember your name as long   10
As lips move or breath is spent or the iron of English
Rings from a tongue.

I shall say you were young, and your arms straight, and your
                    mouth scarlet:
I shall say you will die and none will remember you:
Your arms change, and none remember the swish of your
                    garments,   15
Nor the click of your shoe.

Not with my hand's strength, not with difficult labor
Springing the obstinate words to the bones of your breast
And the stubborn line to your young stride and the breath to
           your breathing
And the beat to your haste   20
Shall I prevail on the hearts of unborn men to remember.

(What is a dead girl but a shadowy ghost
Or a dead man's voice but a distant and vain affirmation
Like dream words most)

Therefore I will not speak of the undying glory of women.   25
I will say you were young and straight and your skin fair
And you stood in the door and the sun was a shadow of leaves
           on your shoulders
And a leaf on your hair——

I will not speak of the famous beauty of dead women:
I will say the shape of a leaf lay once on your hair.   30
Till the world ends and the eyes are out and the mouths broken
Look! It is there!

QUESTIONS

1. Where did MacLeish get the title of this poem? According to the first stanza, what poetic tradition is he denying?
2. What foot pattern is the poet using in his stanzas? How many feet are in each line—is the pattern 5, 5, 5, 2 or 5, 5, 6, 2 or something else? (Consider lines 27, 21, 2–3, 6–7, 22, 31.)
3. Is there a prevailing meter? Is the rhythm monotonous? How much variation of meter does MacLeish employ? How many different metrical forms does every fourth line take?
4. The musical elements are important in giving the poem its particular flavor. In which lines is alliteration especially pleasing? Which lines are made slow and sonorous by means of assonance?
5. How do the run-on lines in stanzas 3 and 5 make them different from the other stanzas?
6. What details of the woman's appearance does the poet mention? Are adjectives important in communicating these details?—for example, "sleek" throat, "fine" walking, "young" stride, skin "fair." What is the difference in the effect of these terms and of "the swish of your garments" and "the click of your shoe"?
7. In his poem "Ars Poetica" MacLeish wrote:

A poem should be equal to,
Not true.

For all the history of grief
An empty doorway and a maple leaf.

Relate this "equal to" principle to the last two stanzas of this poem. Consider lines 3–4, 14, 25, 28, and then explain what MacLeish was trying to communicate to readers in future times.

My Love Is Like a Red Red Rose

ROBERT BURNS

My love is like a red red rose
    That's newly sprung in June:
My love is like the melodie
    That's sweetly play'd in tune.

So fair art thou, my bonnie lass,   5
    So deep in love am I:
And I will love thee still, my dear,
    Till a' the seas gang dry.

Till a' the seas gang dry, my dear,
    And the rocks melt wi' the sun: 10
And I will love thee still, my dear,
    While the sands o' life shall run.

And fare thee weel, my only love,
    And fare thee weel awhile!
And I will come again, my love,   15
    Tho' it were ten thousand mile.

QUESTIONS

1. Burns uses some words of Scottish dialect: "a'" for "all"; "gang" for "go"; "weel" for "well." Perhaps you should look up "sprung" and also "bonnie" and "lass," especially for their connotations.
2. How is the first simile to be interpreted? A girl does not literally look like a rose; in what sense can a girl be like a rose? What qualities of the girl is the poet trying to convey with this simile?
3. What does Burns gain by repeating the word "red"? How is "red red rose" different from "very red rose" or "big red rose"? What different impression would we receive from "pale red rose" or "wee red rose"?
4. The second simile may seem more unusual even than the first. In what

sense can a girl resemble a melody? What does line 4 add to the basic simile?

5. If "sweetly" were replaced by "neatly," "clearly," or "quickly," how would the effect be changed?
6. Explain how the transition is made from the girl to the lover in lines 5–6.
7. How does the content of stanzas 2–4 differ from that of stanza 1?
8. Why could we call lines 7–10 examples of hyperbole? When do you think a poet is justified in using the figure of hyperbole?
9. How should we visualize "the sands o' life"?
10. Contrast the purpose and ideas of this lyric with those of another love poem.

The Silken Tent

ROBERT FROST

She is as in a field a silken tent
At midday when a sunny summer breeze
Has dried the dew and all its ropes relent,
So that in guys it gently sways at ease,
And its supporting central cedar pole,   5
That is its pinnacle to heavenward
And signifies the sureness of the soul,
Seems to owe naught to any single cord,
But strictly held by none, is loosely bound
By countless silken ties of love and thought   10
To everything on earth the compass round,
And only by one's going slightly taut
In the capriciousness of summer air
Is of the slightest bondage made aware.

QUESTIONS

1. Look up "relent," "guys," "pinnacle," "strictly," and "capriciousness."
2. Is this fourteen-line poem a sonnet? The poem consists of only one sentence. Is it a single unit, or are there within the sentence any of the usual sonnet divisions such as 8, 6; 4, 4, 4, 2; 4, 4, 3, 3; and 8, 3, 3?

3. What is the principal clause of the sentence? At what point can we put a period and have a complete thought?

4. What is the basic figure of speech of the poem? By what specific details is this figure developed?

5. What does "sunny" (2) contribute to the poem? How can a breeze be sunny?

6. What are the connotations of certain important terms; for example, "silken" (1, 10), "pinnacle to heavenward," "capriciousness," and "bondage"?

7. Is "pole" (5) definitely a symbol? If so, a symbol of what? Comment on the importance of the three adjectives modifying "pole."

8. Explain the metaphor of "ties" (10).

9. Point out examples of alliteration with *d, s, p,* and *c.*

10. What has Frost succeeded in communicating about another human being?

11. For ideas, purpose, and organization compare this poem with another love poem.

Death in War

The Glories of Our Blood and State

JAMES SHIRLEY

The glories of our blood and state
 Are shadows, not substantial things;
There is no armour against Fate;
 Death lays his icy hand on kings:
  Sceptre and Crown   5
  Must tumble down,
And in the dust be equal made
With the poor crooked scythe and spade.

Some men with swords may reap the field,
 And plant fresh laurels where they kill: 10
But their strong nerves at last must yield;
 They tame but one another still:
  Early or late
  They stoop to fate,
And must give up their murmuring breath   15
When they, pale captives, creep to death.

The garlands wither on your brow;
 Then boast no more your mighty deeds!
Upon Death's purple altar now
 See where the victor-victim bleeds.   20
  Your heads must come
  To the cold tomb:
Only the actions of the just
Smell sweet and blossom in their dust.

QUESTIONS

1. Look up "glories," "blood," "state," "sceptre," "laurels," "nerves," "murmuring," and "garlands." Pay attention to earlier meanings and connotations of most of these terms.

407

2. In some books this poem is called "Death the Leveler." Certain lines suggest the medieval concept of the Dance of Death, for which Holbein and others made illustrations that show Death tapping all sorts of people, from highest to lowest, unexpectedly on the shoulder, as if saying, "Come and dance with me. Your time has come." In which stanza is this idea especially strong?

3. What two personifications do you observe in stanza 1?

4. The poet says, "Glories are shadows." In what sense should we understand "shadows"?

5. The poem makes use of symbols. What do "sceptre and crown" (5) and "scythe and spade" (8) symbolize? Look up "metonymy," and explain how these terms are examples of that figure. How are they related to the Dance of Death? Do not "poor" and "crooked" suggest more about the users of scythe and spade than about the implements themselves?

6. Why is "icy" (4) a good word to use? What are the connotations of "tumble" (6)? What is the difference between a tumble and a fall? Consider the end of the nursery rhyme of Jack and Jill and the effect of such a title as *The Decline and Tumble of the Roman Empire*.

7. In what meter and rhyme scheme is this poem written? Why is it suitable to have lines 5–6 of each stanza twice as short as the others?

8. Since in line 9 men are reaping the field with swords, what kind of field is the poet talking about? Explain how in this agricultural metaphor the men are planting "fresh laurels" in the reaped field. Be sure you understand the symbolism of laurels.

9. In stanza 3 "victor-victim" is the term applied to these men. Over whom are they victors? Whose victims do they become?

10. What is the double meaning of "murmuring" and the significance of the vivid words "pale" and "creep"?

11. What happens to make garlands wither (17)?

12. Point out sound effects of assonance, alliteration, and emphatic metrical variation in stanza 3.

13. How are lines 19–20 related to stanzas 1 and 2? What picture do these lines make the reader see?

14. What biblical association does the final word, "dust," have? How does it fit in with the agricultural metaphor? What metaphor has the poet used in the last two lines? How do these lines contrast with the rest of the poem?

15. What decisions regarding certain pressures of life do you think the poet was trying to make his readers agree to?

Concord Hymn
Sung at the completion of the Battle Monument, July 4, 1837

RALPH WALDO EMERSON

By the rude bridge that arched the flood,
    Their flag to April's breeze unfurled,
Here once the embattled farmers stood
    And fired the shot heard round the world.

The foe long since in silence slept;   5
    Alike the conqueror silent sleeps;
And Time the ruined bridge has swept
    Down the dark stream which seaward creeps.

On this green bank, by this soft stream,
    We set today a votive stone;   10
That memory may their deed redeem,
    When, like our sires, our sons are gone.

Spirit, that made those heroes dare
    To die, and leave their children free,
Bid Time and Nature gently spare   15
    The shaft we raise to them and thee.

ANALYSIS

This is an example of an occasional poem, that is, a poem written for a particular occasion, in this case the dedication of the Battle Monument at Concord, Massachusetts, on July 4, 1837. The monument commemorates the Battle of Concord, which occurred on April 19, 1775. Paul Revere had roused the minutemen to resist the British troops. Emerson imagined the scene on that day of 1775, the early "rude bridge," the April weather, and the "embattled farmers." The fight was the active beginning of the American Revolution. Since the War of Independence had such widespread effects, Emerson described the first shot as "the shot heard round the world." It would make Concord people proud to remember that shots fired by some farmers of their little village had achieved worldwide notice.

On such an occasion as the dedication of a monument an author often looks toward both past and future. Emerson's sense of past, present, and future determined the organization of the poem in four stanzas. Stanza 1 is about the battle; stanze 2 tells of the passage of time from 1775 to 1837; stanza 3 reminds the listeners of the act taking place on July 4, 1837 ("today"), and of the purpose of that act; finally, stanza 4 looks toward the future years both of the new monument and of the country whose beginning it commemorates.

Emerson speaks of three factors in the battle: the British soldiers, the American farmers, and the bridge where the minutemen drove the British back. All were gone by 1837. The monument is erected near the Concord River. In time the original bridge over the stream had had to be replaced. Emerson says, "And Time the ruined bridge has swept/Down the dark stream which seaward creeps." We customarily think of time as a stream. Emerson has personified time; but it seems as if for the moment the actual dark little river in Concord has metaphorically become the dark stream of time, which has "swept away" the bridge. "Dark" has connotations suggesting a thing of unknown or even sinister powers. Ordinarily the actual stream flows slowly toward the sea ("seaward creeps"). But the Time-stream metaphor suggests the continual movement of all things toward death or destruction; the sea is a symbol of eternity. (Many readers, reminded of the destructiveness of time, would think of some of Shakespeare's sonnets, like numbers 15, 55, 60, 64, 65, in which this is the main theme.) Thus stanza 2 develops the idea of the passage of time, during which the soldiers of both sides have died and the bridge has disappeared.

The summer stream is well described in stanza 3 as "soft"; both "green bank" and "soft stream" suggest a peaceful atmosphere—the peace of the place has long ago been restored after the violence of the famous battle of the past. But the present act of devotion is in memory of the past action of heroic ancestors, who are to be remembered through the "votive stone" on into the future. This thought is tenderly expressed in line 12 through the balance and alliteration of "sires" (past) and "sons" (future)— who will, like the foe and the conquerer and the bridge, also share in the common fate of death and destruction. Can anything survive it?

The possibility that something may survive is suggested in the final stanza. Here Emerson addresses (or apostrophizes) the spirit of independence and love of liberty, which induced the minutemen to fight and caused some of them to die. The heroes died and left their children fatherless and perhaps in poverty and difficulties. But whatever deprivations the children suffered, they were *free*. Thus the act of the father-heroes was not irresponsible but sacrificial. Their sacrifice ensured for their children freedom from foreign domination, a legacy of the greatest value.

Thinking of the mysterious future and the changes certain to occur, Emerson asks the spirit to "bid Time and Nature [the effects of storm, sun, rain, frost and flood] gently spare/The shaft we raise to them and thee." Following the tiny pause after "them," the final foot emphasizes "thee" (the spirit). The shaft of stone should survive a long time, and so should the memory of the ancestors. But more important than the heroic ancestors themselves is the spirit of independence that they represented and that every American should hope will survive throughout the future.

For this poem (which at the dedication was sung to the tune of "Old Hundred") Emerson chose a simple metrical and stanzaic pattern, which he used with dignity: the iambic tetrameter quatrain rhyming *abab*. In a few places he varied the meter as shown in the following examples:

Line 1—"By the/rude bridge"

Line 3—"Here once"

Line 8—"Down the/dark stream"

Line 9—"On this/green bank,/by this/soft stream"

Line 12—"When like/our sires"

Line 13—"Spirit"

Extra accents serve to slow up lines 8 and 9, which also have deep sounds, especially the assonating *ee* of "stream," "seaward," "creeps," "green," and "stream." Emerson also used much alliteration to strengthen his lines, the *f* in lines 2–5, the *s* in lines 5–10 and 12, *m* and *d* in line 11, *d* in lines 13–14, and *th* in line 16. Emerson matched music and meaning throughout.

Another element in the music of the poem is the verse movement, which is regular but with appropriate variation in placement of caesuras and in run-on lines. There are tiny pauses which the good reader observes even without punctuation in line 1 after the second foot, in line 3 after the first, in lines 4–5 after the second, in line 6 in the middle of the third (after "conqueror"), in line 8 after the second, and in line 12 after the third. And there are still other variations of the verse movement in lines 9, 12, 13, and 14 because of commas requiring more pronounced pauses. The run-on lines 7, 13, and 15 throw strong emphasis on the words that follow in the early part of the next lines. In this respect music and meaning go very well together in lines 7–8 with "swept/Down the dark stream." Similarly there is a dramatic emphasis as we pass from line 13 to line 14—"Spirit, that made those heroes dare/To die,"—where the *d*-alliteration and the comma after "die" combine with the *enjambement* to lift "die" into utmost deserved prominence.

All these are items that repeated readings may cause the reader to appreciate and to realize why this is an immortal poem of our literature.

next to of course god america i

E. E. CUMMINGS

"next to of course god america i
love you land of the pilgrims' and so forth oh
say can you see by the dawn's early my
country 'tis of centuries come and go
and are no more what of it we should worry   5
in every language even deafanddumb
thy sons acclaim your glorious name by gorry
by jingo by gee by gosh by gum
why talk of beauty what could be more beautiful than those heroic happy dead   10
who rushed like lions to the roaring slaughter
they did not stop to think they died instead
then shall the voice of liberty be mute?"

He spoke. And drank rapidly a glass of water

QUESTIONS

1. This poem has fourteen lines. Is it a sonnet?
2. Lines 1–13 are in quotation marks. Consider the whole poem, and then explain who speaks these lines and on what kind of occasion.
3. What impression do you receive from the first five words?
4. What is the implication of "and so forth" (2)? What is the purpose of running quotations together in lines 2–4?
5. Which lines contain the most colloquial diction? What contrasts of language do you note in the poem?—for example, the shifts from line 4 to line 5 and from line 7 to line 8.
6. Do these contrasts suggest two different speakers? If not, then what is the character of the one speaker? Which lines represent his own, genuine voice? What do the other lines represent?
7. What do the words "*thy* sons acclaim *your* glorious name" suggest about the speaker's level of culture? What is the effect of line 8? What impressions of the speaker do you get from lines 9–10?
8. What should be our opinion of those who "did not stop to think"? If they had stopped to think, what might have been the result?

9. What logical connection is there between line 13 and the preceding lines? What opinion does the poet wish us to have about the mental powers of the speaker?
10. Why is line 14 separated from the rest of the text? What impression does line 14 make on the reader?

Here Dead Lie We

A. E. HOUSMAN

Here dead lie we because we did not choose
To live and shame the land from which we sprung.
Life, to be sure, is nothing much to lose;
But young men think it is, and we were young.

QUESTIONS

1. This poem has distinction because of the way in which the words are arranged. Suppose we rearrange them: "We lie here dead because we did not choose to live and shame the land which we sprung from. To be sure, life is nothing much to lose, but we were young, and young men think it is." Comment on the differences in emphasis, rhythm, and tempo created by Housman's arrangement of the text. Which words in the poem are most important?
2. In what meter is the poem written? Scan the poem, and indicate the effects of variations of meter, of run-on lines, and of position of pauses.
3. With what feelings is the reader made to respond to the deaths of these soldiers?
4. This poem and the poems just preceding it by Shirley, Emerson, and Cummings deal with somewhat similar situations or topics. Discuss these four poems, explaining the different attitudes expressed in them.

What Is That Music High in the Air?

A. J. M. SMITH

A voice from the heroic dead,
Unfaltering and clear,
Rings from the overhead
And zips into the ear;

But what it was it said   5
Or what it meant to say,
This clarion of the sacred dead,
I cannot tell today;

And tomorrow will be late,
For the ear shall turn to clay   10
And the scrannel pipe will grate,
Shiver, and die away,

A sigh of the inconsequential dead,
A murmur in a drain,
Lapping a severed head,   15
Unlaurelled, unlamented, vain.

QUESTIONS

1. "Scrannel" means thinly harsh and grating. "Scrannel pipe" in line 11 should bring to mind Milton's scornful use of the term in his elegy "Lycidas": "their lean and flashy songs/Grate on their scrannel pipes of wretched straw." How do the terms "inconsequential," "murmur," "unlaurelled," and "vain" of stanza 4 contrast with the terms used in stanza 1?
2. What attitude of the world toward "the heroic dead" does this poem emphasize?
3. Contrast the ideas expressed in this poem with those of the poems by Emerson and Housman.

From *Collected Poems* by A. J. M. Smith. Reprinted by permission of Oxford University Press, Canadian Branch.

Death

One Dignity Delays for All

EMILY DICKINSON

One dignity delays for all,
One mitered afternoon,
None can avoid this purple,
None evade this crown.

Coach it insures and footmen,   5
Chamber, and state, and throng,
Bells also in the village
As we ride grand along.

What dignified attendants,
What service when we pause,   10
How loyally at parting
Their hundred hats they raise!

How pomp surpassing ermine
When simple You and I
Present our meek escutcheon   15
And claim the rank to die!

QUESTIONS

1. Ordinary people sometimes feel that there is a great difference between their lives and the lives of "great" people. Their feelings may take various forms, such as "I envy aristocrats all the attention they get" or "Wouldn't it be nice to be treated with the dignity that kings and queens receive?" or "Surely I'm entitled to more attention than people give me; why do they ignore me?" The poem announces that "one dignity delays for all," but it never explains precisely what the

From *The Complete Poems of Emily Dickinson*, edited by Thomas H. Johnson, published by Little, Brown and Company.

dignity is. So the reader's problem is to decide what this delayed dignity may be; that is, what special attention will everyone receive if he waits long enough?

2. Much of the effect of the poem comes from the connotations of the words. What connotations do "mitered," "purple," and "crown" have? Line 4′ says high rank is certain. But few people will actually receive a crown. Does "crown" mean something like the crown of life? Why is it fitting to place "crown" in the position of climax at the end of stanza 1?

3. Stanzas 1 and 4 are quite abstract. What more specific activities are represented in stanzas 2 and 3? What are the connotations of the nouns in lines 5–6?

4. Somewhere in his reading of the poem the reader discovers that many of the terms can have double meanings. What kind of coach is the poet referring to? What kind of footmen? Where *is* the chamber? Consider carefully the significance of "state." What are the bells ringing for? What do "we ride" in?

5. Line 8 assures us of grandeur. Do you think "ride grand" is sarcastic? Certainly there is irony in stanza 3. What are the double meanings of "service," "loyally," "parting"?

6. In lines 9, 10, 11, 13 we read "what" and "how." Does the emphasis they receive mean that the poet is deeply impressed? If so, by what? Why end stanzas 3 and 4 with exclamation points?

7. "Pomp," "ermine," and "escutcheon" are generally related to what sort of people and occasions? What is a "meek" escutcheon? "Simple You and I" finally claim a high rank—we become a person with a title, like a lord or king. Thus we are "entitled"—to what that we never had before? Just what is the artful effect of putting the final word where it is?

8. What is a "mitered afternoon"? Are there other metaphors in the poem?

9. Indicate where alliteration is used. What effect does the repetition of words have in the poem?

10. Does the poem have a regular rhyme pattern? What is its dominant meter? Where do you find emphatic variations of this meter?

11. The poet simply makes a statement, presents a scene, and asks no questions. But what deep and ironic question regarding human behavior does the poem dramatically bring to mind?

She Dwelt among the Untrodden Ways

WILLIAM WORDSWORTH

> She dwelt among the untrodden ways
>   Beside the springs of Dove,
> A maid whom there were none to praise
>   And very few to love:
>
> A violet by a mossy stone   5
>   Half hidden from the eye!
> —Fair as a star, when only one
>   Is shining in the sky.
>
> She lived unknown, and few could know
>   When Lucy ceased to be;   10
> But she is in her grave, and, oh,
>   The difference to me!

QUESTIONS

1. Note the organization of the poem. What situation is presented in stanza 1? How is stanza 2 related to stanza 1? Which stanza is the more concrete and imagistic? What point already made does stanza 3 touch on? What new ideas are introduced?
2. Explain the connotations of "violet" and "star" in the figures of speech of stanza 2. How do these relate to the last two lines of the poem?
3. Contrast the poem with the following prose account: "Miss Lucy Jones, aged 19, died September 30 after a short illness, at her home in Dove township. She is survived by her mother, Mrs. John Jones, and a brother, Sam Jones, both of Dove township. Her untimely death will be regretted by those of her acquaintance. Interment will be at Pigeon Hill churchyard, October 3, at 2 P.M."
4. Compare the feelings about death expressed in this poem and in "One Dignity Delays for All."
5. Is the expression of grief in this poem restrained or unrestrained? Is it effective? Why or why not?
6. What meter and rhyme scheme has Wordsworth used? This is a pattern of verse often used in ballads. What ballad in this book has the same pattern?

Elegy

EDNA ST. VINCENT MILLAY

Let them bury your big eyes
In the secret earth securely,
Your thin fingers, and your fair,
Soft, indefinite-coloured hair,—
All of these in some way, surely,   5
From the secret earth shall rise;
Not for these I sit and stare,
Broken and bereft completely:
Your young flesh that sat so neatly
On your little bones will sweetly   10
Blossom in the air.

But your voice, . . . never the rushing
Of a river underground,
Not the rising of the wind
In the trees before the rain,   15
Not the woodcock's watery call,
Not the note the white-throat utters,
Not the feet of children pushing
Yellow leaves along the gutters
In the blue and bitter fall,   20
Shall content my musing mind
For the beauty of that sound
That in no new way at all
Ever will be heard again.

Sweetly through the sappy stalk   25
Of the vigourous weed,
Holding all it held before,
Cherished by the faithful sun,
On and on eternally
Shall your altered fluid run,   30
Bud and bloom and go to seed:
But your singing days are done;
But the music of your talk

Never shall the chemistry
Of the secret earth restore.
All your lovely words are spoken.
Once the ivory box is broken,
Beats the golden bird no more.

35

QUESTIONS

1. An elegy is a serious, meditative poem—in modern times a poem on death, and frequently a poem inspired by the death of a particular person. This poem was written after the death in 1918 of the author's fellow student at Vassar, Dorothy Coleman. What idea is expressed in lines 1–11? Explain how lines 12–24 make a contrasting continuation to the statement of line 7.
2. How is this same contrast carried on in stanza 3? The poet says that certain elements of the dead girl will not be lost to the world. Explain why not. What element will be lost?
3. In what respect does the poet feel consoled after the death of her friend? In what respect inconsolable?
4. In what meter is the poem written? Sometimes it is easier to decide the question of meter by scanning other lines than the first line. After you have considered the meter of lines 5, 7, 16, and 19, you should be able to determine with more assurance how lines 1–4 and the rest should be read. A few lines are shorter than the others. Which ones?
5. What is the purpose of the numerous concrete details in lines 12–20?
6. Does the phrase "secret earth" have special connotations? Comment on the significance of "musing mind" (21) and "faithful sun" (28).
7. Which lines have the most alliteration? What part does alliteration play in the music of the poem? At what places do you find special emphases on words because of run-on lines? Is the rhyme pattern regular or irregular? Do you find it effective?
8. What do "ivory box" and "golden bird" (37–38) symbolize?

In Memoriam (XI)

ALFRED, LORD TENNYSON

Calm is the morn without a sound,
    Calm as to suit a calmer grief,
    And only thro' the faded leaf
The chestnut pattering to the ground:

Calm and deep peace on this high wold,   5
    And on these dews that drench the furze,
    And all the silvery gossamers
That twinkle into green and gold:

Calm and still light on yon great plain
    That sweeps with all its autumn bowers,   10
    And crowded farms and lessening towers
To mingle with the bounding main:

Calm and deep peace in this wide air,
    These leaves that redden to the fall,
    And in my heart, if calm at all,   15
If any calm, a calm despair:

Calm on the seas, and silver sleep,
    And waves that sway themselves in rest,
    And dead calm in that noble breast
Which heaves but with the heaving deep.   20

QUESTIONS

1. This is one of the many sections making up Tennyson's long elegy in-
    spired by the death of his friend Arthur Henry Hallam. Hallam died in
    Vienna, and his body was brought back to England by ship. At what
    point in the poem is the voyage alluded to?
2. What word is frequently repeated in the poem? Presumably it is the
    key word of the poem. To what circumstances is this word applied?
    What makes this word so significant?
3. What is the time of year? What references are there to the season?
4. To what items of visual imagery does Tennyson draw attention?
    Where is he standing as he sees them? Are they put together harmoni-
    ously?
5. What does the description of landscape and season lead up to?
6. Note the punctuation of the poem. How many sentences are there?
    What is the syntactical relation among the stanzas?
7. Which terms are especially precise and picturesque?
8. What terms would you apply to the music of this poem? Which words
    are emphatically important for their sounds? Where is alliteration evi-
    dent?

Funeral

WILLIAM JAY SMITH

Now he is gone where worms can feed
Upon him, a discarded rind,
God's image, and a thinking reed,
   In blindness blind

As any taxidermist's owl.   5
He who was tall and fleet and fair
Is now no more; the winds howl,
   The stones stare.

Your double who went dressed in black
And beat the lions to their cage   10
Lies in blood; the whips crack,
   The beasts rage.

Don your somber herringbone
And clap your top hat to your head.
The carriage waits; the axles groan;   15
   While prayers are said,

Rest your hot forehead on the plush;
And hear, beyond the measured, sad
Funeral drums, above the hush,
   The lions pad   20

Instantly through some sunless glade,
The body's blood-fed beasts in all
Their fury, while the lifted spade
   Lets earth fall.

QUESTIONS

1. What situation is indicated by the title and the first four words? The
   "he" is described by three epithets, one of which is "a thinking reed."
   This is the term used by Pascal in a famous statement: "Man is only a
   reed, the weakest thing in nature; but he is a thinking reed." What dif-

ferent aspects of man are indicated by the three terms used? Is there
any reason to speak of the corpse as a taxidermist's owl?

2. What happens as we move from line 6 to line 7? Can we think that
   winds are literally howling during the funeral? How can stones stare?
   What emotions are suggested by these terms?

3. Lions are mentioned in stanzas 3 and 5, and in stanza 6 they are called
   "the body's blood-fed beasts." What sort of furious "beasts" inhabit the
   body? What do the lions then symbolize?

4. In stanza 4 the poet is evidently speaking to a mourner, perhaps himself, and in stanza 3 we learn that the dead man was the mourner's
   double. What is the dead man given credit for doing? What is the
   mourner doing in stanzas 4–5?

5. When the funeral is over, what will the mourner have to do?

6. What is the rhyme pattern of each stanza? In each stanza how does line
   4 differ metrically from the other lines? How does the final line of
   stanzas 2, 3, and 6 differ from the final lines of the other stanzas? What
   image does the final line bring to the imagination, and what feelings
   does it create? How is the music of the final line matched to its meaning? Point out how the last three lines are made emphatic by alliteration.

Do Not Go Gentle into That Good Night

DYLAN THOMAS

Do not go gentle into that good night,
Old age should burn and rave at close of day;
Rage, rage against the dying of the light.

Though wise men at their end know dark is right,
Because their words have forked no lightning they   5
Do not go gentle into that good night.

Good men, the last wave by, crying how bright
Their frail deeds might have danced in a green bay,
Rage, rage against the dying of the light.

Wild men who caught and sang the sun in flight,   10
And learn, too late, they grieved it on its way,
Do not go gentle into that good night.

Grave men, near death, who see with blinding sight
Blind eyes could blaze like meteors and be gay,
Rage, rage against the dying of the light.   15

And you, my father, there on that sad height,
Curse, bless me now with your fierce tears, I pray.
Do not go gentle into that good night.
Rage, rage against the dying of the light.

QUESTIONS

1. This poem is a villanelle, a fixed form of verse with five three-line stanzas and a final four-line stanza, using only two rhymes. Lines 1 and 3 are used alternately as refrains: line 1 at the end of stanzas 2 and 4 and as the third line in stanza 6; and line 3 at the end of stanzas 2 and 5 and again as the final line. Show in what different grammatical ways the refrain lines 1 and 3 are worked into statements in the course of the poem.

2. Who is being addressed in this poem? What tone or mood does the poet create by using "burn," "rave" (2), "fierce" (17), and the repeated "rage, rage"?

3. In what particular sense are "close of day" and "dying of the light" being used? Therefore, what double meaning has "good night"?

4. What four different kinds of men are mentioned in the poem? What common experience are they all encountering? Do they all meet it in the same way?

5. With what four different metaphors does the poet interpret the responses of the four kinds of men?

6. Why should wise men "know dark is right" (4)? What is signified by "the last wave by" (7)? What kind of occupation is implied by "caught and sang the sun in flight" (10)? In what does the wild men's wildness consist? What kind of effect does Thomas accomplish by bringing together the contradictory terms "blinding sight" (13)? Should we connect them with brightness? with sight? with insight? What "sad height" has the poet's father reached? If you visualize the height, what visual image do you perceive?

7. What would the father's cursing represent (17)? How would his "fierce tears" constitute a blessing?

8. In what ways does this poem differ from the preceding poems concerned with death?

The Modern World:
Social Criticism

Cargoes

JOHN MASEFIELD

Quinquireme of Nineveh from distant Ophir,
Rowing home to haven in sunny Palestine,
With a cargo of ivory,
And apes and peacocks,
Sandalwood, cedarwood, and sweet white wine.　　　　5

Stately Spanish galleon coming from the Isthmus,
Dipping through the Tropics by the palm-green shores,
With a cargo of diamonds,
Emeralds, amethysts,
Topazes, and cinnamon, and gold moidores.　　　　10

Dirty British coaster with a salt-caked smoke stack,
Butting through the Channel in the mad March days,
With a cargo of Tyne coal,
Road-rail, pig-lead,
Firewood, iron-ware, and cheap tin trays.　　　　15

QUESTIONS

1. This poem is about cargoes delivered by three different ships: a quinquireme, a galleon, and a coaster. Look up the meanings of these words. In what historical period was each ship used?
2. Read the book of Jonah and I Kings 9–10 in the Bible. Look up Nineveh and Ophir. What connotations do these names have?
3. What do the cargoes mentioned in stanzas 1–2 have in common? What are "gold moidores"?

4. What contrasting connotations do the words of stanza 3 have? Point out some examples of the contrast.
5. Mark the metrical accents of the poem. Some of the lines can be read as six trochaic feet, but to think of the long lines as having four main beats makes them easier to read. Note the difference between lines 3–4 and lines 1–2 in each stanza. How is the last line of each stanza different in meter from line 1?
6. What parallel patterns of organization in terms of content, grammar, stanza patterns, and meters do you observe?
7. The poem shows a significant variation amid prevailing unity. Point out both variation and unity.
8. What comment concerning human history is suggested by the juxtaposition of stanza 3 with stanzas 1–2?

New York

AE (GEORGE WILLIAM RUSSELL)

> With these heaven-assailing spires
> All that was in clay or stone
> Fabled of rich Babylon
> By these children is outdone.
>
> Earth has spilt her fire in these   5
> To make them of her mightier kind;
> Has she that precious fire to give,
> The starry-pointing Magian mind,
>
> That soared from the Chaldean plains
> Through zones of mystic air, and found   10
> The Master of the Zodiac,
> The Will that makes the Wheel go round?

QUESTIONS

1. The meaning of this poem depends largely on allusions and on the rich associations accumulated around certain terms. The reader had better begin by getting information about Babylon, Babel, Magi, Magian, Chaldea, Chaldean, and Zodiac. What sort of associations do they have?

From *Vale and Other Poems.* Reprinted by permission of Diarmuid Russell, and A. M. Heath & Company Ltd.

2. Russell mentions New York's "heaven-assailing spires" in line 1. What heaven-assailing tower of the ancient world are we supposed to think of? Babylon had a great reputation for wealth and luxury (look up references to Babylon in the Bible); why does Russell say the stories of "rich Babylon" were in clay?

3. Russell was a man of Europe, a visitor to New York. Why would a person from the Old World think the people of New York were children (4)?

4. What tribute does Russell give to the New Yorkers in lines 5–6? What does the word "fire" signify in stanza 2?

5. What is the distinction between the fire of line 5 (the fire that "earth has spilt") and that of line 7 ("that precious fire")? What connotations does "soared" have (9)?

6. The poet's thought moves from tall buildings to the Chaldean seekers of knowledge, especially astronomy and astrology, to the creative forces behind the observed phenomena of the heavens. Why can the Zodiac be called a wheel? With what profound perceptions is Russell crediting the Chaldeans?

7. What then is the basis of the question that he asks about the people of New York in the second half of the poem? What modern equivalent of an ancient failure does the poem thus suggest?

Cities

JOHN PRESS

The gadgets, the machines, the luxuries
Confine us in a monstrous padded room,
The future, like a mausoleum, waits,
Preparing to receive us in its gloom.

We are cut off from converse with the dead,   5
Forget the words, cannot communicate,
And in our isolation are attacked
By new and strange perversities of hate.

Yet from our wounded cities there may spring
A union with the dead, the sense of time,   10
The knowledge that the pattern is made up
Of all men's folly, love, despair and crime.

From *Guy Fawkes Night*. Reprinted by permission of John Press, and A. M. Heath & Company Ltd.

The exiles and the hunted refugees
May learn that there is precedent for pain,
May trace their wanderings back to Abraham   15
And know the common brotherhood of Cain.

Linked with the dead by timeless suffering,
We can accept the world that they have made
And, like them, bearing grief and joy, may walk
In calm assurance to the welcoming shade.   20

QUESTIONS

1. If you need to, look up "monstrous," "mausoleum," "perversities," "precedent."
2. What view is given of the contemporary city in stanza 1? What is the purpose of a padded room? The author says that gadgets, machines, and luxuries "confine" us. If we were unconfined, where would we be? Explain the simile that conveys the idea of a gloomy future.
3. What accounts for our isolation, which is the topic of stanza 2?
4. If we can understand the pattern of history, what will give us "a union with the dead"?
5. If modern people know about the experiences of Abraham and Cain, what comfort will the knowledge give to some of them? Which ones? Why are Abraham and Cain effective examples? Could any other names be substituted for theirs?
6. Some modern people feel like outsiders in the world; A. E. Housman, for example, wrote: "I, a stranger and afraid,/In a world I never made." What reason does Press give in stanza 5 for accepting the world made by our forebears? What would give us a feeling of assurance as we look ahead? How does the close of the poem contrast with stanza 1?
7. What meter and rhyme scheme does the poem have? Where is the verse movement of the poem made interesting and agreeable by means of run-on lines and pauses?

Siasconset Song

PHILIP BOOTH

The girls
of golden summers whirl
through sunsprung
bright Julys

From *Letter from a Distant Land* by Philip Booth. Copyright 1951 by Philip Booth. Originally appeared in *The New Yorker*. Reprinted by permission of The Viking Press, Inc.

with born right   5
sky-bright
star-night
eyes;

everywhere
their tennis-twirl   10
of young gold
legs and arms,
they singsong
summer-long
I-belong   15
charms;

and through
the summer sailing swirl
they cut like
shining knives   20
in sun-told
never old
ever gold
lives.

QUESTIONS

1. Explain the complex pattern of rhymes and line lengths of this poem. Which rhyme appears in all three stanzas? Show how music matches meaning.
2. Which terms are repeated in the poem? What terms have favorable connotations or suggest attractive images?
3. Where do you find social criticism in the poem? Which terms suggest that under attractive appearances there is something to be criticized? Why is the title appropriate?

A Lullaby

RANDALL JARRELL

For wars his life and half a world away
The soldier sells his family and days.
He learns to fight for freedom and the State;
He sleeps with seven men within six feet.

He picks up matches and he cleans out plates;   5
Is lied to like a child, cursed like a beast.
They crop his head, his dog tags ring like sheep
As his stiff limbs shift wearily to sleep.

Recalled in dreams or letters, else forgot,
His life is smothered like a grave, with dirt;   10
And his dull torment mottles like a fly's
The lying amber of the histories.

QUESTIONS

1. What sacrifices does war require of the soldier? Whose freedom does he learn to fight for? How much freedom does he have? What details in the poem relate to the question of his freedom? What possible contradiction is there in fighting for freedom and the State with a capital S (3)? Does the poet intend an irony here?
2. What aspects of the soldier's life are indicated in stanza 2? What are the effects of the similes of line 6 and the connotations of "crop" and "like sheep" (shorthand for bells on sheep)?
3. In what sense is "his life" used (1, 10)? What approximation of the poetic import of "smothered," "like a grave," and "dirt" in line 10 can you express?
4. Amber is fossil resin exuded from cone-bearing trees ages ago; insects caught in that resin may still be seen preserved in amber. With these data in mind, explain "dull torment mottles" and "lying amber" of the metaphor in lines 11–12.
5. Which rhymes are perfect? imperfect? What is the rhyme pattern?
6. What do you feel is the purpose of this poem—social criticism? satire of the military establishment? giving a truthful picture of army life? revealing how dreadful a lot the soldier has? trying to create pity through irony?

A Story about Chicken Soup

LOUIS SIMPSON

In my grandmother's house there was always chicken soup
And talk of the old country—mud and boards,
Poverty,
The snow falling down the necks of lovers.

Now and then, out of her savings   5
She sent them a dowry. Imagine
The rice-powdered faces!
And the smell of the bride, like chicken soup.

But the Germans killed them.
I know it's in bad taste to say it,   10
But it's true. The Germans killed them all.

In the ruins of Berchtesgaden
A child with yellow hair
Ran out of a doorway.

A German girl-child—   15
Cuckoo, all skin and bones—
Not even enough to make chicken soup.
She sat by the stream and smiled.

Then as we splashed in the sun
She laughed at us.   20
We had killed her mechanical brothers,
So we forgave her.

The sun is shining.
The shadows of the lovers have disappeared.
They are all eyes; they have some demand on me—   25
They want me to be more serious than I want to be.

They want me to stick in their mudhole
Where no one is elegant.
They want me to wear old clothes,
They want me to be poor, to sleep in a room with many
        others—   30

Not to walk in the painted sunshine
To a summer house,
But to live in the tragic world forever.

QUESTIONS

1. What does chicken soup stand for? How does the land of chicken soup
    contrast with "the old country"? Which country do you presently find
    is the old country? Explain the significance of the concrete details about
    the old country in lines 2 and 4.

2. Be sure you know what "dowry" means. What situation is called up by
    lines 7–8? What do lines 9–11 tell us about the speaker's old-country
    relatives? Why were they killed? Why is it appropriate to speak of a
    "Grandmother's" house in line 1—not that of someone else?

3. Why, out of all the towns in Germany, does the author place section 2 of his poem in Berchtesgaden? Note the successive images of the child. Discuss them in terms of camera snapshots; and in terms of the thoughts of the men who see the child. Who are the men? Why is the child's hair yellow? Why use the word "cuckoo" (16)?

4. Why are the child's brothers called mechanical (21–22)? What relation is there between line 17 and lines 21–22?

5. How does section 3 of the poem differ from sections 1 and 2? Explain the significance of sunshine, the details of lines 27–30, "a summer house," and "the tragic world" in section 3.

6. What sort of meter and stanza form has the author chosen for this poem?

7. Would you describe this poem as a narrative poem, an allegory, a didactic poem, an illustrative incident suggesting a theme, or what?

8. What comments about human nature and about the twentieth-century world are suggested by this poem?

The Arrival

DANIEL HOFFMAN

> They burdened him, even though duty-free,
> His Father's bags. So did the oldtime guide-
> Book that weighed one down. It seemed nobody
> Used that dialect these days in this town
> That towers too high for any human need.   5
> Some things his Pa had said though did prove wise
> —Precepts recalled too late as he strolled down
> The wharf, his pockets and valise picked clean.
> Thus unencumbered, feet on solid ground,
> Remembered caravels that came to find   10
> A different land from what in fact they'd found.
> Agape at topless towers, he set his mind
> To reckon what he'd come to find or found.

QUESTIONS

1. The title of the poem and several terms in the first few lines—"duty-free," "bags," "guide-/Book," and "town"—indicate that a young traveler has arrived at a destination. How is the reader to interpret this situation?

By the time he has read through line 5 he may begin to wonder whether the situation is actual or symbolic or allegorical. Does the capitalized "His Father" stand for God? If so, then "the oldtime guide-/ Book" must be the Bible. But if "His Father" is the young man's actual human father, the guidebook must stand for the principles for living which have been passed on by the older generation. Then the poem would be about changes in values that a carefully reared youth discovers when he leaves home and sees that the world does not follow the principles taught by his parents. (Which statement in the poem leads us to say this?) In either case we have an allegory, with the guidebook taking on a significance that in its literal use it does not possess: that is, it means the Bible, God-given rules for living; or it means rules for right living taught by the older generation. If Father means God, then the allegorical pattern of ideas is more extensive than in the other case. But in line 10 the traveler calls to mind certain caravels—small sailing ships used by the Spanish in the fifteenth and sixteenth centuries. He is thinking of the ships of Columbus, and the reference in line 11 to "a different land from what in fact they'd found" suggests that the poem is meant to tell us something about the development of America. How should "burdened" (1), "weighed one down" (3), and "too high for any human need"(5) be interpreted? What would have happened to him if he had not been so burdened and weighed down? How would the town be different if human need had been the criterion for building?

2. Should we regard the reference to the "town/That towers too high for any human need" as similar to the reference to the tall buildings of New York in Russell's poem?

3. What situations in the city has the newly arrived traveler got himself into? Judging by lines 7–8, what sort of "wise" precepts had the father passed on to the son?

4. Consider the connotations of "feet on solid ground." What are the implications of line 9? How is the young man like the voyagers in the caravels?

5. "Topless towers" comes from Christopher Marlowe's *Doctor Faustus.* When Faustus sees Helen of Troy he cries: "Was this the face that launch'd a thousand ships,/And burnt the topless towers of Ilium?" Is there any connection between ancient Troy and the modern city?

6. Why is the young traveler so uncertain at the end? Why does he have to *reckon* "what he's come to find"? Has he found something different from that?

7. How would you state the theme expressed in this allegorical poem?

"*More Light! More Light!*"

ANTHONY HECHT

Composed in the Tower before his execution
These moving verses, and being brought at that time
Painfully to the stake, submitted, declaring thus:
"I implore my God to witness that I have made no crime."

Nor was he forsaken of courage, but the death was horrible,   5
The sack of gunpowder failing to ignite.
His legs were blistered sticks on which the black sap
Bubbled and burst as he howled for the Kindly Light.

And that was but one, and by no means one of the worst;
Permitted at least his pitiful dignity;   10
And such as were by made prayers in the name of Christ,
That shall judge all men, for his soul's tranquility.

We move now to outside a German wood.
Three men are there commanded to dig a hole
In which the two Jews are ordered to lie down   15
And be buried alive by the third, who is a Pole.

Not light from the shrine at Weimar beyond the hill
Nor light from heaven appeared. But he did refuse.
A Lüger settled back deeply in its glove.
He was ordered to change places with the Jews.   20

Much casual death had drained away their souls.
The thick dirt mounted toward the quivering chin.
When only the head was exposed the order came
To dig him out again and to get back in.

No light, no light in the blue Polish eye.   25
When he finished a riding boot packed down the earth.
The Lüger hovered lightly in its glove.
He was shot in the belly and in three hours bled to death.

No prayers or incense rose up in those hours
Which grew to be years, and every day came mute   30
Ghosts from the ovens, sifting through crisp air,
And settled upon his eyes in a black soot.

QUESTIONS

1. This bitterly critical poem depends for its effect on the contrast between two inhumanly cruel deeds several centuries apart and on allusions to the German writer Goethe. Judging by the language, the sentence construction, and the references to the Tower and the stake, what was the setting for the deed described in stanzas 1–3?

2. Note the alliteration in lines 7–8. How do the sounds of the alliterating words and the images they convey affect the reader? What irony comes out in "howled for the Kindly Light"? (Be sure to emphasize "by" in line 11.) What bit of consolation regarding the deed is stressed in stanza 3?

3. How does the style change in stanzas 4–8? What were the time and place of this second incident?

4. Goethe (1749–1832), the famous apostle of culture, lived much of his life at Weimar, a town of central Germany not far from Buchenwald (look up Buchenwald if you don't know about it). So Weimar is the seat of the Goethe shrine. Goethe's last words, "More light! More light!", were very appropriate, since he was dedicated to intelligence and enlightenment. Note the references to "no light" in lines 17, 18, and 25. Considering the whole poem, how do you interpret the title?

5. Why were the two Jews willing to bury the Pole? Why did the Pole obey orders when they were given a second time? Contrast the acts recorded in stanzas 4–8 with those of stanzas 1–3.

6. How should an informed reader, knowing of the German executions of Jews, interpret the reference to "ghosts from the ovens" (31)? What impression does line 32 make?

7. State the theme of the poem.

Bay-Breasted Barge Bird

WILLIAM JAY SMITH

The bay-breasted barge bird delights in depressions
And simply flourishes during slumps;
It winters on hummocks near used-car lots
    And summers near municipal dumps.

It nests on the coils of old bed springs,   5
And lines its nest with the labels from cans;

It feeds its young on rusty red things,
    And bits of pots and pans.

The bay-breasted barge bird joyfully passes
Where bulldozers doze and wreckers rumble,   10
Gazing bug-eyed, when traffic masses,
    At buildings that feather and crumble.

It wheels and dips to the glare and thunder
Of blasted rock and burning fuel
While the red-hot riveted sun goes under   15
    On every urban renewal.

It flaps long wings the color of soot,
It cranes a neck dotted with purple bumps;
And lets out a screech like a car in a crack-up
    As it slowly circles the dumps.   20

QUESTIONS

1. The poet has used interesting metrical variations in this poem. Consider the effect of the vigorous anapestic rhythm in line 1. Compare it with the effect of only two anapestic feet in line 3. Explain how line 5 differs metrically from line 3 and line 6 and how line 11 differs metrically from lines 7, 15, and 19. Are lines 9 and 1 identical in meter? Which syllables are accented in line 18?

2. In which lines is alliteration the most pronounced? Is alliteration more evident in stanza 1 or stanza 2, in stanza 3 or stanza 4?

3. How is the rhyme scheme of stanzas 1 and 5 different from that of stanzas 2, 3, and 4?

4. Does the strange creature described here seem attractive or unattractive? Why?

5. What aspects of life give the barge bird the greatest pleasure? How would you describe the spirit of the barge bird?

6. Is the poem humorous? Is it only a fantasy, or are there American people that the barge bird may represent? Is the poem a piece of satire?

The Managers

W. H. AUDEN

In the bad old days it was not so bad:
    The top of the ladder
Was an amusing place to sit; success
    Meant quite a lot—pleasure
And huge meals, more palaces filled with more   5
    Objects, books, girls, horses
Than one would ever get round to, and to be
    Carried uphill while seeing
Others walk. To rule was a pleasure when
    One wrote a death-sentence   10
On the back of the Ace of Spades and played on
    With a new deck. Honours
Are not so physical or jolly now,
    For the species of Powers
We are used to are not like that. Could one of them   15
    Be said to resemble
The Tragic Hero, the Platonic Saint,
    Or would any painter
Portray one rising triumphant from a lake
    On a dolphin, naked,   20
Protected by an umbrella of cherubs? Can
    They so much as manage
To behave like genuine Caesars when alone
    Or drinking with cronies,
To let their hair down and be frank about   25
    The world? It is doubtful.
The last word on how we may live or die
    Rests today with such quiet
Men, working too hard in rooms that are too big,
    Reducing to figures   30
What is the matter, what is to be done.
    A neat little luncheon
Of sandwiches is brought to each on a tray,
    Nourishment they are able

To take from one hand without looking up   35
    From papers a couple
Of secretaries are needed to file,
    From problems no smiling
Can dismiss. The typewriters never stop
    But whirr like grasshoppers   40
In the silent siesta heat as, frivolous
    Across their discussions,
From woods unaltered by wars and our vows
    There drift the scents of flowers
And the song of birds who will never vote   45
    Or bother to notice
Those distinguishing marks a lover sees
    By instinct and policemen
Can be trained to observe. Far into the night
    Their windows burn brightly   50
And, behind their backs bent over some report,
    On every quarter,
For ever like a god or a disease
    There on the earth the reason
In all its aspects why they are tired, the weak,   55
    The inattentive, seeking
Someone to blame. If, to recuperate
    They go a-playing, their greatness
Encounters the bow of the chef or the glance
    Of the ballet-dancer   60
Who cannot be ruined by any master's fall.
    To rule must be a calling,
It seems, like surgery or sculpture; the fun
    Neither love nor money
But taking necessary risks, the test   65
    Of one's skill, the question,
If difficult, their own reward. But then
    Perhaps one should mention
Also what must be a comfort as they guess
    In times like the present   70
When guesses can prove so fatally wrong,
    The fact of belonging
To the very select indeed, to those
    For whom, just supposing
They do, there will be places on the last   75
    Plane out of disaster.
No; no one is really sorry for their
    Heavy gait and careworn
Look, nor would they thank you if you said you were.

QUESTIONS

1. What is unusual about the rhymes that Auden has used in this poem? Does the poem have a regular pattern of accents?

2. Instead of "bad old days" what phrase would we be more likely to expect? What assumptions has Auden made about the course of history to cause him to call the old days bad?

3. What does he mean by "the top of the ladder"? Note that he calls it an "amusing" place. What made it amusing? What sort of amusement would arise from the last item in the list: "to be/Carried uphill while seeing/Others walk"? What elements of success are represented by lines 9–12?

4. Auden says success meant "quite a lot." How vivid and how worthy do the satisfactions of old-time success seem to you?

5. What sort of diction has the author used? Consider "quite a lot" (4); "get round to" (7); "jolly" (13); "to let their hair down" (25). Is the diction more formal in the second half of the poem?

6. What are the main topics of this poem? What is the first one? What topic is discussed in lines 13–26? What new one is introduced with line 27? What is being discussed in the last part, lines 62–79?

7. How would you describe the humor of the poem? Is it verbal? Does it come from anticlimax or from placing together incongruous or ridiculous images? How do you respond to the picture of a modern business or political figure naked on a dolphin, "protected by an umbrella of cherubs" (21)?

8. How does the life of modern men at the top of the ladder differ from that of their predecessors as Auden describes it in lines 29–39?

9. Why would the life of nature seem frivolous to them? How is it ironically different from theirs (41–49)?

10. Why do they have to work so hard? Why will they receive little satisfaction from their recuperative playing?

11. What rewards does the author decide the rulers of the modern world will gain from practicing their calling (62)?

12. What additional reward may be a comfort to them? But what sarcasm lies behind the phrase "the very select indeed" (73)? Assuming that "they do" (75) means "they do guess wrong," what will be the proof that these men belong to the "very select indeed"?

13. With what attitude has Auden approached his subject? Is the poem satirical? Is Auden critical of the managers? Is he at all sympathetic with them?

14. Do you find a matching of music and meaning in "The Managers"?

Your Attention Please

PETER PORTER

The Polar DEW has just warned that
A nuclear rocket strike of
At least one thousand megatons
Has been launched by the enemy
Directly at our major cities.   5
This announcement will take
Two and a quarter minutes to make,
You therefore have a further
Eight and a quarter minutes
To comply with the shelter   10
Requirements published in the Civil
Defense Code—section Atomic Attack.
A specially shortened Mass
Will be broadcast at the end
Of this announcement—   15
Protestant and Jewish services
will begin simultaneously—
Select your wavelength immediately
According to instructions
In the Defense Code. Do not   20
Take well-loved pets (including birds)
Into your shelter—they will consume
Fresh air. Leave the old and bed-
ridden, you can do nothing for them.
Remember to press the sealing   25
Switch when everyone is in
The shelter. Set the radiation
Aerial, turn on the geiger barometer.
Turn off your Television now.
Turn off your radio immediately   30
the Services end. At the same time
Secure explosion plugs in the ears
Of each member of your family. Take
Down your plasma flasks. Give your children
The pills marked one and two   35
in the C.D. green container, then put
Them to bed. Do not break

The inside airlock seals until
The radiation All Clear shows
(Watch for the cuckoo in your   40
perspex panel), or your District
Touring Doctor rings your bell.
If before this, your air becomes
Exhausted or if any of your family
Is critically injured, administer   45
The capsules marked "Valley Forge"
(Red pocket in No. 1 Survival Kit)
For painless death. (Catholics
Will have been instructed by their priests
What to do in this eventuality.)   50
This announcement is ending. Our President
Has already given orders for
Massive retaliation—it will be
Decisive. Some of us may die.
Remember, statistically   55
It is not likely to be you.
All flags are flying fully dressed
On Government buildings—the sun is shining.
Death is the least we have to fear.
We are all in the hands of God,   60
Whatever happens happens by His Will.
Now go quickly to your shelters.

QUESTIONS

1. What relation has the title to the poem? Does the author intend his title to carry a double meaning?
2. No one has yet had to carry out instructions given in a broadcast like this. What details has the author used in order to make the situation vivid and specific?
3. How many tons are there in a thousand megatons? What alterations of normal life are represented by the "specially shortened Mass?" What aspect of American life is reflected in lines 16–17? What is the effect of placing lines 20–24 immediately after the part about religious services?
4. The poem does not contain any figurative language. What purpose do you think the author had in excluding it? Is this work really any different from a piece of prose?
5. What is there about "Valley Forge" that makes it a suitable name for capsules in a survival kit? What use is, ironically, to be made of the capsules? Why is the parenthetical material of lines 48–50 necessary? What effect do lines 43–50 have on the reader?

6. Note the arrangement of lines 51–54. How do lines 53 and 54 receive emphasis? What is the effect of the word "decisive"? And of "Some of us may die" immediately afterward? Is this an understatement?

7. What are the last lines intended by the speaker to make the listeners feel? What do the readers of the poem feel about them? What is the special meaning of line 59? Will everyone feel sure that line 61 expresses the truth?

8. What is the theme of the poem? Why do you think the author wrote it? Did he have a didactic purpose?

The Human Situation: Values

Terence, This Is Stupid Stuff

A. E. HOUSMAN

"Terence, this is stupid stuff:
You eat your victuals fast enough;
There can't be much amiss, 'tis clear,
To see the rate you drink your beer.
But oh, good Lord, the verse you make,   5
It gives a chap the belly-ache.
The cow, the old cow, she is dead;
It sleeps well, the horned head:
We poor lads, 'tis our turn now
To hear such tunes as killed the cow.   10
Pretty friendship 'tis to rhyme
Your friends to death before their time
Moping melancholy mad:
Come, pipe a tune to dance to, lad."

Why, if 'tis dancing you would be,   15
There's brisker pipes than poetry.
Say, for what were hop-yards meant,
Or why was Burton built on Trent?
Oh many a peer of England brews
Livelier liquor than the Muse,   20
And malt does more than Milton can
To justify God's ways to man.
Ale, man, ale's the stuff to drink
For fellows whom it hurts to think:
Look into the pewter pot   25
To see the world as the world's not.

And faith, 'tis pleasant till 'tis past:
The mischief is that 'twill not last.
Oh I have been to Ludlow fair
And left my necktie God knows where,   30
And carried half-way home, or near,
Pints and quarts of Ludlow beer:
Then the world seemed none so bad,
And I myself a sterling lad;
And down in lovely muck I've lain,   35
Happy till I woke again.
Then I saw the morning sky:
Heigho, the tale was all a lie;
The world, it was the old world yet,
I was I, my things were wet,   40
And nothing now remained to do
But begin the game anew.

Therefore, since the world has still
Much good, but much less good than ill,
And while the sun and moon endure   45
Luck's a chance, but trouble's sure,
I'd face it as a wise man would,
And train for ill and not for good.
'Tis true, the stuff I bring for sale
Is not so brisk a brew as ale: 50
Out of a stem that scored the hand
I wrung it in a weary land.
But take it: if the smack is sour,
The better for the embittered hour;
It should do good to heart and head   55
When your soul is in my soul's stead;
And I will friend you, if I may,
In the dark and cloudy day.

There was a king reigned in the East:
There, when kings will sit to feast,   60
They get their fill before they think
With poisoned meat and poisoned drink.
He gathered all that springs to birth
From the many-venomed earth;
First a little, thence to more,   65
He sampled all her killing store;
And easy, smiling, seasoned sound,
Sate the king when healths went round.
They put arsenic in his meat
And stared aghast to watch him eat;   70

They poured strychnine in his cup
And shook to see him drink it up:
They shook, they stared as white's their shirt:
Them it was their poison hurt.
—I tell the tale that I heard told.　　　　　　　　75
Mithridates, he died old.

QUESTIONS

1. Look up the following words if you are unsure of their meaning: "hop-yards," "sterling," "scored," "smack," "store," "aghast."

2. In this poem Housman assumes the personality of an English country fellow who writes verses. What does his friend find to criticize about his poetry in lines 1–14? What sort of poetry would the friend like him to write?

3. In his reply, lines 15–20, what does the poet suggest would liven his friend up more than poetry could? Finding out what Burton-on-Trent is most famous for gives a part of the answer.

4. Lines 21–22 are an allusion to John Milton's statement of his purpose in writing *Paradise Lost* (Bk. I, line 26). They refer to the existence of evil in the world. How does malt produce its "justification" of God's ways?

5. What shortcoming, in turn, does the poet in lines 23–26 accuse his friend of having?

6. What point in the argument is the poet making with the incident he tells in lines 27–42?

7. The poet, we might say, discusses his responses to, or interprets, the "metaphysical pressures" of life. What two reasons does he give in lines 43–58 for having a bitter attitude?

8. Express lines 63–64 in your own words. Look up the story of Mithridates of Pontus. What is a "mithridate?" Which particular lines in the third section does the anecdote about Mithridates illustrate and support?

9. The poem is written in tetrameter (four-beat) couplets, a type of verse that may seem singsong and monotonous unless the poet provides considerable variation of meter and verse-movement. Housman varies the meter by using two sorts of 4-beat lines here, as in line 1 with seven syllables:

Terence,/this is/stupid/stuff,

and line 2 with eight syllables:

You eat/your vic/tuals fast/enough.

Which of these is an iambic line and which a trochaic line? Does Housman use more iambic lines or more trochaic lines?

10. Which lines have a varied verse movement because of pauses required by punctuation within the lines? How many such lines are there? In which lines is there a pause in the middle of a foot? Which of the seventy-six lines are run-on?

11. How much alliteration does Housman use here? Which five examples of alliteration seem to you the most emphatic?

12. Do you think the poem would be better if it were any more musical or any less musical?

13. What are some examples of colloquial British diction in the poem? Why must the last section seem less like the talk of a country fellow than the rest?

In Humbleness

DANIEL HOFFMAN

Neither malt nor Milton can
Explain to God the ways of Man:
Hobnailed troops have ever trod
Upon the flocks who know that God
Has a passion, plan, or mind,   5
Or that the Universe is kind.

Come flood, come war, come pestilence,
Come Man at last to Common Sense:
At last admit, in humbleness,
Whatever spire he dares erect   10
Of either faith or intellect
Can be but his sarcophagus;

Yet even in that iron tomb
Man stirs again, as in the womb:
Tunnels free, then, word by word,   15
Rebuilds, and is again interred.
Read this in the histories:
Newsweek, or Thucydides.

QUESTIONS

1. Consult a dictionary for the meaning of "passion," "sarcophagus," "interred."
2. Many writers, and especially poets, are great readers. They often have in mind the works of other writers, and sometimes they allude to these works in their own. They expect readers to recognize such allusions. Hoffman's allusion in line 1 shows that he had what poem in mind as he started to write this one? But how has he reversed the idea of the other poem?
3. What concept of God and the universe is suggested by stanza 1? What bad "ways of Man" are suggested? What are the denotation and the connotation of "hobnailed troops" and of "flocks" (lines 3–4)?
4. What connection is there between the items of stanza 2, line 1, and stanza 1?
5. What person might erect a spire of faith? of intellect? Does spire have only a metaphorical meaning here or a literal one also? (Note "word by word," line 15.)
6. Against the tendency of man to feel pride in spires of faith and intellect, why does Hoffman emphasize humbleness (9)?
7. Explain the metaphor "his sarcophagus" (12). Why call the sarcophagus an "iron" tomb? What does "as in the womb" add to the metaphor?
8. What history did Thucydides write? Why couple *Newsweek* with such a famous historian? What effect does the mention of *Newsweek* have? What theory of cultural history does stanza 3 support?
9. Could this poem be entitled "Renaissance"? Would you call the tone of the poem pessimistic, cynical, satirical, disgusted, reasonable, resigned, sad, ironical, hopeful, or something else?
10. Where does Hoffman depart from using rhymed couplets? How has he avoided monotony in his tetrameter verses?

"Long Live the Weeds"
Hopkins

THEODORE ROETHKE

> Long live the weeds that overwhelm
> My narrow vegetable realm!
> The bitter rock, the barren soil

That force the son of man to toil;   5
All things unholy, marred by curse,
The ugly of the universe.
The rough, the wicked, and the wild
That keep the spirit undefiled.
With these I match my little wit   10
And earn the right to stand or sit,
Hope, love, create, or drink and die:
These shape the creature that is I.

QUESTIONS

1. How is this work a poetic equivalent of Brahms's *Variations on a Theme by Haydn*?
2. The phrase providing the title is in the last line of a poem by Gerard Manley Hopkins. As Hopkins uses it, what idea about the world does it represent? Both Hopkins and Roethke see a value in weeds. How does the value Roethke perceives differ from that of Hopkins?
3. What other things besides weeds does Roethke praise? What good do they do for mankind?
4. What nonliteral meaning is suggested by "narrow vegetable realm," "barren soil," and "the wild" (2, 3, 7)?
5. Judging by lines 7–8, what would constitute defilement of the spirit for Roethke?
6. Compare the form and music of this poem with the one by Hopkins. How closely did Roethke imitate Hopkins?

Recollection of Childhood

RICHARD EBERHART

O the jungle is beautiful the jungle is wild
Here are the rodents and the butterflies,
The thorn tree prickles and the shady grottoes,
And I'll lie in the sun all day, and the shade.

And here is the orchard, bulging big fruit,   5
Adazzle in the eyes all red and golden,
There is the barn, and the many cows,
Hurray for the hay, I'll fall and tumble in the hay.

And below the happy pasture green and moist
I'll walk it to the shady grove by the river,   10
Swim the clear stream, the chalk cliff climb,
Bursting with desire still—cease action never,

But in the natural world of happy forms
Bird, beast, tree, fern, earth and rain and sun
Live melodious love, and touch above   15
All fingered air the very god of love.

QUESTIONS

1. According to this poem, how did things make the author feel when he was a child?
2. He says "the jungle is wild" (in recollection), but is it dangerous and frightening? What does "jungle" refer to?
3. Which words have the pleasantest connotations? Is there a difference between the satisfactions of stanza 1 and stanza 2? Of stanza 2 and stanza 3?
4. In line 15 Eberhart suggests that childhood was a time to "live melodious love." What made it possible for him to think he could do so? Explain the metaphor of "all fingered air." What is the significance of "the very god of love"?
5. Compare this poem for its form, rhythm, and melody with Roethke's "Long Live the Weeds" and Hopkins' "Inversnaid." How does it compare with them in its attitude toward wild, unrestrained things?

The Nobel Prize

BORIS PASTERNAK

I am like a beast tracked down.
Somewhere men live in freedom and light,
But the furious chase closes in,
And I cannot break out from my plight.

A dark forest, the edge of a pond,   5
And a log of fir-tree uprooted.
To the world my escape has been cut.
Then befall, what to me is allotted.

Reprinted by permission of G. P. Putnam's Sons from *The Poetry of Boris Pasternak*, translated by George Reavey. Copyright © 1959 by G. P. Putnam's Sons.

What so dreadful a deed have I dared?
Am I a murderer then or a bandit?   10
To oblige the wide world to shed tears
At the beauty of my native land.

So be it! On the brink of the grave,
I believe in a time very near
When the spirit of good that men crave   15
Will prove stronger than evil and fear.

January 1959

QUESTIONS

1. Boris Pasternak, a famous Russian writer, was awarded the Nobel
   Prize for literature in 1958, especially on account of his novel *Doctor
   Zhivago*. So this is an occasional poem. Find out what happened to
   Pasternak that made him write stanza 1. Explain the basic simile of
   stanza 1.
2. What is the difference in mood between stanza 2 and stanza 3?
3. Which is the most idealistic of the four stanzas?
4. Compare the connotations of the words in this poem and its spirit with
   those of the preceding piece by Eberhart.

On the Move
"*Man, You Gotta Go.*"

THOM GUNN

The blue jay scuffling in the bushes follows
Some hidden purpose, and the gust of birds
That spurts across the field, the wheeling swallows,
Have nested in the trees and undergrowth.
Seeking their instinct, or their poise, or both,   5
One moves with an uncertain violence
Under the dust thrown by a baffled sense
Or the dull thunder of approximate words.

On motorcycles, up the road, they come:
Small, black, as flies hanging in heat, the Boys,   10
Until the distance throws them forth, their hum
Bulges to thunder held by calf and thigh.

Reprinted by permission of Faber and Faber Ltd. from *The Sense of Movement* by
Thom Gunn.

In goggles, donned impersonality,
In gleaming jackets trophied with the dust,
They strap in doubt—by hiding it, robust—   15
And almost hear a meaning in their noise.

Exact conclusion of their hardiness
Has no shape yet, but from known whereabouts
They ride, direction where the tires press.
They scare a flight of birds across the field: 20
Much that is natural, to the will must yield.
Men manufacture both machine and soul,
And use what they imperfectly control
To dare a future from the taken routes.

It is a part solution, after all.   25
One is not necessarily discord
On earth; or damned because, half animal,
One lacks direct instinct, because one wakes
Afloat on movement that divides and breaks.
One joins the movement in a valueless world,   30
Choosing it, till, both hurler and the hurled,
One moves as well, always toward, toward.

A minute holds them, who have come to go:
The self-defined, astride the created will
They burst away; the towns they travel through   35
Are home for neither bird nor holiness,
For birds and saints complete their purposes.
At worst, one is in motion; and at best,
Reaching no absolute, in which to rest,
One is always nearer by not keeping still.   40

QUESTIONS

1. The "one" mentioned in line 6 is evidently the poet, an observer. What
    thoughts about the birds come to him as he watches their movements?
    With what precise and with what metaphorical terms has he described
    their movements? What contrast between the birds and himself does
    he bring out in lines 5–8? What part do the metaphors of dust and of
    thunder play in expressing this contrast?
2. Set down the complicated rhyme scheme of the stanzas.
3. Who are the "Boys" introduced in line 10? What specific terms in the
    description make these persons seem distinctive? Why is "bulges" (12)
    an effective word to use? How does their dress make them seem posi-
    tive and lacking doubt? Explain the sense of "trophied with the dust."
4. From the observations in stanza 3 the observer speculates about men in

general. What contrast between the riders and the birds does he make? How are the riders characteristic of mankind? What are some of the things imperfectly controlled by mankind with which men must venture to face the future? Put a strong emphasis on "from" in line 24. How do the riders go off from routes usually taken? How can the reader apply this idea to all mankind?

5. In stanza 4 the observer approves of the riders. Why? In what way is their action "a part solution" (25)? How are they something like the birds? What do they (and all human beings) lack that birds have? By what is the movement divided and broken: thought, self-consciousness, conscience, doubt? Do you think "joins the movement" has a double meaning? Reading line 32, we might ask "toward what"? Is there any specific answer to that question? How does line 32 express the theme of the poem?

6. How do birds "complete their purposes" (37)? What does holiness stand for at the opposite extreme from birds, so that saints can also complete their purposes? Even if these motorcycle riders cannot complete their purposes, what satisfactions do they have, "at worst" and "at best"? Look up "absolute." What would "rest" mean in relation to an absolute? What view of the place of the dynamic and of the static in life is expressed in this poem? Why do you think the poet included the epigraph following the title?

A Fire-Truck

RICHARD WILBUR

Right down the shocked street with a siren-blast
That sends all else skittering to the curb,
Redness, brass, ladders and hats hurl past,
    Blurring to sheer verb.

Shift at the corner into uproarious gear   5
And make it around the turn in a squall of traction,
The headlong bell maintaining sure and clear,
    Thought is degraded action!

Note   Line 8 echoes a notion entertained by Henry Adams in his "Letter to American Teachers of History" (1910).—R.W.

Beautiful, heavy, unweary, loud, obvious thing!
I stand here purged of nuance, my mind a blank.   10
All I was brooding upon has taken wing,
        And I have you to thank.

As you howl beyond hearing I carry you into my mind,
Ladders and brass and all, there to admire
Your phoenix-red simplicity, enshrined   15
        In that not extinguished fire.

QUESTIONS

1. Look up "skittering," "sheer," "uproarious," "squall," "traction," "de-
    graded," "purged," "nuance," "phoenix." With which verbs does the
    author emphasize the essence of the experience in stanzas 1–2? What
    nouns and adjectives contribute to the sense of violent action? Why
    is the street "shocked"? What does "verb" (4) imply?
2. Lines 1–8 are one sentence. What is the subject of "hurl," "shift," and
    "make"? What do lines 1–2 modify? The climax of the first sentence is
    in line 8; how is the idea expressed there related to the fire truck?
3. Notice the different number of syllables in some lines—for example,
    lines 3, 6, 7, 10, 13. How many beats are there in the first three lines of
    each stanza? How many in the fourth line? With what differences of
    rhythm has the author matched the music to the meaning?
4. How does the idea expressed in stanza 3 differ from that of stanzas 1–2?
    What happened to the poet's thoughts as he watched the fire truck?
    How does he feel about this matter? What is the tone of line 12? Why
    was he purged of nuance? For what reason would he value nuance?
5. The language of stanza 3 is less distinguished than that of the other
    stanzas. Point out examples of triteness. Why ought stanza 3 be more
    commonplace in diction?
6. What has happened to the fire truck in stanza 4? What idea does stanza
    4 give about the relative values of thought and action? How often can
    the image of the fire truck die and be reborn? What keeps the fire truck
    in existence? What is the signifcance of the allusion to the phoenix?
    What three meanings does "that not extinguished fire" have?
7. At the end of the poem how does the proposition of line 8 look?

Thrushes

TED HUGHES

Terrifying are the attent sleek thrushes on the lawn,
More coiled steel than living—a poised
Dark deadly eye, those delicate legs
Triggered to stirrings beyond sense—with a start, a bounce,
      a stab   5
Overtake the instant and drag out some writhing thing.
No indolent procrastinations and no yawning stares,
No sighs or head-scratchings. Nothing but bounce and stab
And a ravening second.

Is it their single-mind-sized skulls, or a trained   10
Body, or genius, or a nestful of brats
Gives their days this bullet and automatic
Purpose? Mozart's brain had it, and the shark's mouth
That hungers down the blood-smell even to a leak of its own
Side and devouring of itself: efficiency which   15
Strikes too streamlined for any doubt to pluck at it
Or obstruction deflect.

With a man it is otherwise. Heroisms on horseback,
Outstripping his desk-diary at a broad desk,
Carving at a tiny ivory ornament   20
For years: his act worships itself—while for him,
Though he bends to be blent in the prayer, how loud and
      above what
Furious spaces of fire do the distracting devils
Orgy and hosannah, under what wilderness   25
Of black silent water weep.

QUESTIONS

1. Look up "attent," "poised," "writhing," "indolent," "procrastinations,"
   "ravening," "obstruction," "deflect," "orgy," "hosannah."
2. What would cause a thrush to be attent on the lawn? What makes the

poet feel that the thrushes are terrifying? What words suggest that the
bird is a machine?

3. What kind of stirrings would be "beyond sense"? Interpret the metaphor
    "overtake the instant." What "writhing thing" does the thrush drag out?

4. In what respects does the bird differ from a human being in its actions?
    Which words contribute most to show the difference?

5. What four possible reasons does the poet suggest may make the thrush
    behave as it does? Explain the connotations of the phrase "bullet and
    automatic/Purpose." Which term is more concrete, "bullet" or "auto-
    matic"? How do the two adjectives work together?

6. What is the poet demonstrating by bringing together "Mozart's brain"
    and "the shark's mouth"? How does the last part of stanza 2 relate to
    the thrushes of stanza 1?

7. What contrast is brought out in stanza 3? What three kinds of action
    are exemplified in lines 17–20? What prevents a human being from
    being naturally a part of the universal harmony? Of what verbs is
    "devils" the subject?

8. Compare the ideas in this poem on action with those in the poems by
    Gunn and Wilbur.

The Tide Rises, the Tide Falls

HENRY WADSWORTH LONGFELLOW

The tide rises, the tide falls,
The twilight darkens, the curlew calls;
Along the sea-sands damp and brown
The traveller hastens toward the town,
    And the tide rises, the tide falls.   5

Darkness settles on roofs and walls,
But the sea, the sea in the darkness calls;
The little waves, with their soft, white hands,
Efface the footprints in the sands,
    And the tide rises, the tide falls.   10

The morning breaks; the steeds in their stalls
Stamp and neigh, as the hostler calls;
The day returns, but nevermore
Returns the traveller to the shore,
    And the tide rises, the tide falls.   15

QUESTIONS

1. Look up the meaning of "curlew," "efface," and "hostler."
2. Scan line 3 to identify the basic meter. Compare the meter of line 3 with that of lines 1, 2, 6, 7, 8, 11, and 12; how do the pauses affect the the variations of rhythm in lines 1, 2, 7, and 8?
3. What is the rhyme pattern? Which rhyme is used throughout the three stanzas?
4. What details create a picture in stanza 1? What element receives the main emphasis in stanza 2? How much time elapses during stanza 2?
5. Where does Longfellow use alliteration? Compare the effect of the *s* and *f* sounds in stanza 2 with that of the alliteration in stanza 3. Does the poet create onomatopoeia? What effect comes from the running-on of line 11? Comment on the matching of music and meaning.
6. What is the mood of this poem? Which words do the most to create the mood? How does the refrain affect the mood?
7. What literal account of a journey is given here? Readers will probably feel that the poem suggests more than this literal account. If the poem is symbolic, what does it symbolize? Who is the traveler? What might darkness, the sea, waves, tide, and shore symbolize?

The Horsemen

GENE BARO

Those lathered horses galloping past
with breathless riders come not this way back:
we look, scanning the east, searching the west;
only an old mule walks the muddy track.

Under grey skies promising rain again,   5
we hear the pounding hooves, or so it seems;
but there comes again only drumming rain
and we are sunk in wayside country dreams.

Sometimes, lying in love, or close to sleep,
the heart heaves suddenly and thunders on.   10
Those wild horsemen had not that furious leap;
a cry is at the lips, and then is gone.

QUESTIONS

1. Stanza 1 expresses a contrast. What is it? Which words in line 4 have strongest connotations? How do their connotations contrast with those of lines 1–2?
2. If stanza 2 represents the situation that "we" have, what is our world like? How does it differ from the world of the past? Why do the "breathless riders" not return?
3. What is the closest that "we" can come to the experience spoken of in lines 1–2?
4. Why does the cry (12) remain unuttered?
5. Would you call this poem symbolic or allegorical?

The New Sun

JOHN WAIN

The new sun rises in the year's elevation,
Over the low roof's perspective.

It reveals the roughness of winter skin
And the dinginess of winter clothes.

It draws, with a hard forefinger,   5
a line under the old ways.

Finis! the old ways have become obsolete,
The old skin, the old clothes.

The same sun, like a severe comet,
rises over old disappointments.   10

It makes us cry out in agony,
this peeling away of old sorrows.

When the sun foretells the death of an old sorrow,
the heart prophetically feels itself an orphan;

a little sniveling orphan, and the sun   15
its hard-hearted parish officer.

Dear gods, help us to bear the new sun!
Let our firm hearts pray to be orphaned!

From *Weep before God* by John Wain, by permission of Macmillan & Co. Ltd., London, The Macmillan Company of Canada Limited, and John Cushman Associates, Inc.

QUESTIONS

1. How can the sun be called new? "The new sun" that gives the poem its title—at what time of year does it make its appearance? What evidence can you give for your answer?
2. In lines 7–8 what things are equated with "old ways"?
3. What do you think are likely examples of "old disappointments" and "old sorrows" (10, 12)? What sort of experience would cause feelings of agony and orphan-like loneliness?
4. In the witty metaphor of lines 15–16, why is the sun called "hard-hearted"?
5. What kind of man would utter the prayer of lines 17–18? Or in what spirit does Wain utter that prayer? Why would he believe that we are better for being "orphaned"?
6. State the idea of the poem. What has Wain gained by expressing it through poetic symbolism?

The Horse Chestnut Tree

RICHARD EBERHART

Boys in sporadic but tenacious droves
Come with sticks, as certainly as Autumn,
To assault the great horse chestnut tree.

There is a law governs their lawlessness.
Desire is in them for a shining amulet   5
And the best are those that are highest up.

They will not pick them easily from the ground.
With shrill arms they fling to the higher branches,
To hurry the work of nature for their pleasure.

I have seen them trooping down the street   10
Their pockets stuffed with chestnuts shucked, unshucked.
It is only evening keeps them from their wish.

Sometimes I run out in a kind of rage
To chase the boys away: I catch an arm,
Maybe, and laugh to think of being the lawgiver.   15

I was once such a young sprout myself
And fingered in my pocket the prize and trophy.
But still I moralize upon the day

And see that we, outlaws on God's property,
Fling out imagination beyond the skies,   20
Wishing a tangible good from the unknown.

And likewise death will drive us from the scene
With the great flowering world unbroken yet,
Which we held in idea, a little handful.

QUESTIONS

1. Investigate the meaning of "sporadic," "tenacious," "droves," "amulet," and "tangible."
2. Who is the speaker? What does "tenacious" imply about the boys? What is lawless about their behavior? Can lawlessness be ruled by law? Explain the paradox in line 4.
3. Why do the boys not pick the horse chestnuts off the ground? What is the tone of line 7?
4. What is the unusual phrase "shrill arms" supposed to make us aware of?
5. What is the meaning of line 12?
6. Why does the speaker say "a kind of rage" (13)? Why can he not be really enraged?
7. When he moralizes "upon the day," he sees a parallel between it and mankind's situation in the universe. Make a detailed list of the parallels between the boys and mankind, according to the explicit explanation in the last two stanzas.
8. Do you find any rhymes in the poem? What form has the author given his composition?
9. What sort of voice is speaking here? Consider the colloquialism of stanzas 5–6.

A Prayer for My Daughter

WILLIAM BUTLER YEATS

Once more the storm is howling, and half hid
Under this cradle-hood and coverlid
My child sleeps on. There is no obstacle
But Gregory's wood and one bare hill
Whereby the haystack- and roof-levelling wind,   5
Bred on the Atlantic, can be stayed;
And for an hour I have walked and prayed
Because of the great gloom that is in my mind.

I have walked and prayed for this young child an hour
And heard the sea-wind scream upon the tower,   10
And under the arches of the bridge, and scream
In the elms above the flooded stream;
Imagining in excited reverie
That the future years had come,
Dancing to a frenzied drum,   15
Out of the murderous innocence of the sea.

May she be granted beauty and yet not
Beauty to make a stranger's eye distraught,
Or hers before a looking-glass, for such,
Being made beautiful overmuch,   20
Consider beauty a sufficient end,
Lose natural kindness and maybe
The heart-revealing intimacy
That chooses right, and never find a friend.

Helen being chosen found life flat and dull   25
And later had much trouble from a fool,
While that great Queen, that rose out of the spray,
Being fatherless could have her way
Yet chose a bandy-legged smith for man.
It's certain that fine women eat   30
A crazy salad with their meat
Whereby the Horn of Plenty is undone.

In courtesy I'd have her chiefly learned;
Hearts are not had as a gift but hearts are earned
By those that are not entirely beautiful;   35
Yet many, that have played the fool
For beauty's very self, has charm made wise,
And many a poor man that has roved,
Loved and thought himself beloved,
From a glad kindness cannot take his eyes.   40

May she become a flourishing hidden tree
That all her thoughts may like the linnet be,
And have no business but dispensing round
Their magnanimities of sound,
Nor but in merriment begin a chase,   45
Nor but in merriment a quarrel.
O may she live like some green laurel
Rooted in one dear perpetual place.

My mind, because the minds that I have loved,
The sort of beauty that I have approved,   50
Prosper but little, has dried up of late,
Yet knows that to be choked with hate
May well be of all evil chances chief.
If there's no hatred in a mind
Assault and battery of the wind   55
Can never tear the linnet from the leaf.

An intellectual hatred is the worst,
So let her think opinions are accursed.
Have I not seen the loveliest woman born
Out of the mouth of Plenty's horn,   60
Because of her opinionated mind
Barter that horn and every good
By quiet natures understood
For an old bellows full of angry wind?

Considering that, all hatred driven hence,   65
The soul recovers radical innocence
And learns at last that it is self-delighting,
Self-appeasing, self-affrighting,
And that its own sweet will is Heaven's will;
She can, though every face should scowl   70
And every windy quarter howl
Or every bellows burst, be happy still.

And may her bridegroom bring her to a house
Where all's accustomed, ceremonious;

For arrogance and hatred are the wares   75
Peddled in the thoroughfares.
How but in custom and in ceremony
Are innocence and beauty born?
Ceremony's a name for the rich horn,
And custom for the spreading laurel tree.   80

QUESTIONS

1. This is an occasional poem. The occasion that prompted it was the birth of Yeats's daughter on February 24, 1919. Why would such an event inspire the poet to compose a poem concerned with human values in the years ahead? What is his feeling about "the future years"? (Consider lines 7–8 and 13–16.)

2. What is the poetic significance of the storm and wind mentioned in lines 1–6 and 9–12? How are the storm and wind related to the baby?

3. Probably the legend of Venus coming from the sea makes the connection between stanza 2 and stanza 3. What distinction does Yeats make between one who is "granted beauty" and one who is "made beautiful overmuch"? The idea of choosing right in line 24 leads to two examples of women who were involved in wrong choices. What two phases of the life of Helen of Troy are indicated in lines 25 and 26? The "great Queen" of line 27 is Venus. How do lines 28–29 fit into her legend?

4. What does Yeats think is the value of courtesy (33)? Explain the metaphor of the "hidden tree" and the simile of the linnet (41–42). Point out the effectiveness in sound and sense of "magnanimities of sound" (44) and of the words in lines 47–48.

5. What do you judge would be the quality of the minds and the beauty mentioned in lines 49–50? To what contrasting idea does Yeats turn in stanza 7?

6. Stanza 8 carries this idea to its climax. "The loveliest woman born" (59) was the beautiful but fanatical Maude Gonne, Irish Nationalist leader. Is the example of such a woman an effective one? Point out the irony involved in the passage from "Plenty's horn" in line 60 to the "old bellows" of line 64.

7. Look up the basic meaning of "radical" (66). What are the conditions of the happiness spoken of as potential in line 72?

8. How does the final stanza bring together the important concepts dealt with earlier in the poem? What does the poet see as the superiority of a life based in ceremony and custom?

9. What rhyme scheme does Yeats use here? In each stanza which three lines are shorter than the others? Which stanzas do you think are finest —that is, in which do the pressure of feeling and Yeats's poetic skill drive the words most tellingly through the turns of the verse?

10. Where does Yeats use alliteration emphatically?

Waking Early Sunday Morning

ROBERT LOWELL

O to break loose, like the chinook
salmon jumping and falling back,
nosing up to the impossible
stone and bone-crushing waterfall—
raw-jawed, weak-fleshed there, stopped by ten   5
steps of the roaring ladder, and then
to clear the top on the last try,
alive enough to spawn and die.

Stop, back off. The salmon breaks
water, and now my body wakes   10
to feel the unpolluted joy
and criminal leisure of a boy—
no rainbow smashing a dry fly
in the white run is free as I,
here squatting like a dragon on   15
time's hoard before the day's begun!

Vermin run for their unstopped holes;
in some dark nook a fieldmouse rolls
a marble, for hours on end, then stops;
the termite in the woodwork sleeps—   20
listen, the creatures of the night
obsessive, casual, sure of foot,
go on grinding, while the sun's
daily remorseful blackout dawns.

Fierce, fireless mind, running downhill.   25
Look up and see the harbor fill:
business as usual in eclipse
goes down to the sea in ships—
wake of refuse, dacron rope,
bound for Bermuda or Good Hope,   30
all bright before the morning watch
the wine-dark hulls of yawl and ketch.

I watch a glass of water wet
with a fine fuzz of icy sweat,
silvery colors touched with sky,   35
serene in their neutrality—
yet if I shift, or change my mood,
I see some object made of wood,
background behind it of brown grain,
to darken it, but not to stain.   40

O that the spirit could remain
tinged but untarnished by its strain!
Better dressed and stacking birch,
or lost with the Faithful at Church—
anywhere, but somewhere else!   45
And now the new electric bells,
clearly chiming, "Faith of our fathers,"
and now the congregation gathers.

O Bible chopped and crucified
in hymns we hear but do not read,   50
none of the milder subtleties
of grace or art will sweeten these
stiff quatrains shovelled out four-square—
they sing of peace, and preach despair;
yet they gave darkness some control,   55
and left a loophole for the soul.

No, put old clothes on, and explore
the corners of the woodshed for
its dregs and dreck: tools with no handle,
ten candle-ends not worth a candle,   60
old lumber banished from the Temple,
damned by Paul's precept and example,
cast from the kingdom, banned in Israel,
the wordless sign, the tinkling cymbal.

When will we see Him face to face?   65
Each day, He shines through darker glass.
In this small town where everything
is known, I see His vanishing
emblems, His white spire and flag-
pole sticking out above the fog,   70
like old white china doorknobs, sad,
slight, useless things to calm the mad.

Hammering military splendor,
top-heavy Goliath in full armor—

little redemption in the mass   75
liquidations of their brass,
elephant and phalanx moving
with the times and still improving,
when that kingdom hit the crash:
a million foreskins stacked like trash . . .   80

Sing softer! But what if a new
diminuendo brings no true
tenderness, only restlessness,
excess, the hunger for success,
sanity of self-deception   85
fixed and kicked by reckless caution,
while we listen to the bells—
anywhere, but somewhere else!

O to break loose. All life's grandeur
is something with a girl in summer . . .   90
elated as the President
girdled by his establishment
this Sunday morning, free to chaff
his own thoughts with his bear-cuffed staff,
swimming nude, unbuttoned, sick   95
of his ghost-written rhetoric!

No weekends for the gods now. Wars
flicker, earth licks its open sores,
fresh breakage, fresh promotions, chance
assassinations, no advance.   100
Only man thinning out his kind
sounds through the Sabbath noon, the blind
swipe of the pruner and his knife
busy about the tree of life . . .

Pity the planet, all joy gone   105
from this sweet volcanic cone;
peace to our children when they fall
in small war on the heels of small
war—until the end of time
to police the earth, a ghost   110
orbiting forever lost
in our monotonous sublime.

QUESTIONS

1. Check the meaning of "obsessive" (22), "yawl," "ketch" (32), "dregs,"
    "dreck" (German dröck) (59), "lumber" (61), "precept" (62), "pha-
    lanx" (79), "diminuendo" (82), "rhetoric" (96).

2. What would you expect in the first part of a poem entitled "Waking Early Sunday Morning"? How does the salmon simile suggest the experience of the poet in lines 1–10? What does he mean by "unpolluted joy" (11)? What might pollute it? What sort of person would feel that a boy enjoyed "criminal leisure"?

3. Explain the dragon and hoard simile (15–16).

4. What setting for the poem is implied in stanza 4? What activities are other people engaging in, and what is the poet doing, as implied by stanzas 4–8?

5. Judging by stanzas 6–9, what are the poet's feelings about the present state of Christianity? How does the verse movement of line 53 match the meaning of the statement about the hymns? But what does Lowell give the hymns credit for?

6. To appreciate the reference to St. Paul in stanzas 8–9, you ought to reread I Corinthians 13. What is the meaning of line 66?

7. Note that Lowell uses some repetition, as with lines 1 and 89, 45 and 88. What feelings of modern man do these lines bring out?

8. What are the poet's conclusions—or should we say fears?—about the future of the world? Try to give examples for various aspects of our time mentioned in stanza 14.

9. Compare the theme and verse technique of this poem with those of Yeats's "Prayer for My Daughter."

Index

AE (George William Russell), 425
"After the Theater," 77
Aiken, Conrad, 95, 310
"Arrival, The," 431
"As by Water," 384
Auden, W. H., 436
"Auto Wreck," 348

"Ballad of the Bread Man," 333
"Balloons," 377
Barker, George, 365
Baro, Gene, 455
"Bay-Breasted Barge Bird," 434
"Bedtime Story," 275
Bennett, Jr., Lerone, 35
Bierce, Ambrose, 24
Blunden, Edmund, 309
Böll, Heinrich, 130
Booth, Philip, 321, 427
Bowen, Elizabeth, 72
Bradbury, Ray, 111
Brodeur, Paul, 158
Brontë, Emily, 369
Brooks, Gwendolyn, 364
Browning, Robert, 366
Burns, Robert, 404

"Careless Talk," 72
"Carentan O Carentan," 331
"Cargoes," 424
Causley, Charles, 333
"Chaser, The," 4
Chekhov, Anton, 77
"Cities," 426
Collier, John, 4
"Coming," 381
"Concord Hymn," 409

"Contemporary Portrait," 346
"Convert, The," 35
"Cost of Living, The," 48
"Crossing," 321

Dahl, Roald, 139
Dickinson, Emily, 396, 415
"Do Not Go Gentle into That Good Night," 422
Donne, John, 400

Eberhart, Richard, 447, 457
"Elegy," 418
Emerson, Ralph Waldo, 409
"Envoi (1919)," 386
"Everything That Rises Must Converge," 170
"Express, The," 323

"Farewell! Farewell! Farewell!" 95
"Fire-Truck, A," 451
"First Views of the Enemy," 191
Frost, Robert, 356, 405
"Frosty Night, A," 335
"Funeral," 421

"Girl at the Center of Her Life, A," 351
"Glories of Our Blood and State, The," 407
"Go, Lovely Rose," 385
Graves, Robert, 335
Gunn, Thom, 449

"Happiness," 380
Hayden, Robert, 350
"Heavy Bear Who Goes with Me, The," 372

Hecht, Anthony, 433
"Helen of Kirconnell," 329
"Here Dead Lie We," 413
Higgins, Frederick Robert, 313
"Hind Horn," 327
Hoffman, Daniel, 431, 445
Holbrook, David, 371
Hopkins, Gerard Manley, 320
"Horse Chestnut Tree, The," 457
"Horsemen, The," 455
Housman, A. E., 413, 442
Hughes, Langston, 379
Hughes, Richard, 305
Hughes, Ted, 453

"I Am the Only Being," 369
"In Humbleness," 445
"In Memoriam VII," 318
"In Memoriam XI," 419
"Inversnaid," 320

Jarrell, Randall, 428
Jeffers, Robinson, 343
"Jockey, The," 64
Joyce, James, 316
"Juggler," 358
"Just Lather, That's All," 30

Keats, John, 341, 389, 392
"Keep in the Heart the Journal Nature
    Keeps," 310
Krause, Ervin D., 183

Larkin, Philip, 355, 381
"Lilith," 345
London, Jack, 13
"Long Live the Weeds," 446
Longfellow, Henry Wadsworth, 454
Lowell, Robert, 462
"Lullaby, A," 428

McCullers, Carson, 64
MacLeish, Archibald, 346, 402
Malamud, Bernard, 48
"Managers, The," 436
Marquerie, Alfredo, 56
Masefield, John, 424
"Me and the Animals," 371
"Mending Wall," 356

Merriam, Eve, 362
Merwin, W. S., 384
Millay, Edna St. Vincent, 391, 418
Miller, Arthur, 222
"Miniver Cheevy," 360
"More Light! More Light!" 433
Munro, Eleanor, 383
"My Lady Love, My Dove," 139
"My Last Duchess," 366
"My Love Is Like a Red Red Rose," 404

Nash, Ogden, 317
"New Sun, The," 456
"New York," 425
"next to of course god america i," 412
"Nobel Prize, The," 448
"Noonday April Sun, The," 382
"Nostalgia," 337
"Not Marble nor the Gilded Monu-
    ments," 402

Oates, Joyce Carol, 191, 351
O'Casey, Sean, 275
O'Connor, Flannery, 170
O'Connor, Frank, 81
"Ode on a Grecian Urn," 392
"On First Looking into Chapman's
    Homer," 389
"On Hearing a Symphony of Beetho-
    ven," 391
"On the Beach at Fontana," 316
"On the Move," 449
"One Dignity Delays for All," 415
"Overlooking the Desert," 376

Pasternak, Boris, 448
Plath, Sylvia, 377
"Player Piano," 319
Poe, Edgar Allan, 387
Porter, Peter, 439
Pound, Ezra, 386
"Prayer for My Daughter, A," 459
Press, John, 426
"Promise of Peace," 343

"Reasons for Attendance," 355
"Recollection of Childhood," 447
"Riders to the Sea," 211
Robinson, Edwin Arlington, 360

Roethke, Theodore, 446
Rossetti, Dante Gabriel, 345
Russell, George William (AE), 425
"Ruth," 362

Schwartz, Delmore, 372
"Self-Service Elevator," 56
Sexton, Anne, 353
Shakespeare, William, 339, 395, 398
Shapiro, Karl, 337, 348
"She Dwelt among the Untrodden Ways," 417
Shirley, James, 407
"Should Wizard Hit Mommy?" 152
"Siasconset Song," 427
"Sic Vita," 370
"Silken Tent, The," 405
Simpson, Louis, 331, 429
Smith, A. J. M., 414
Smith, William Jay, 421, 434
"Snake, The," 183
"Song for the Clatter Bones," 313
"Song in the Front Yard, A," 364
"Sonnet 55," 398
"Sonnet 73," 339
"Sonnet 116," 395
"Soul Selects Her Own Society, The," 396
"Spoiler, The," 158
"Spring," 384
"Storm, The," 374
"Story about Chicken Soup, A," 429
"Story of a Conscience, The," 24
Synge, John Millington, 211

Téllez, Hernando, 30
Tennyson, Alfred, Lord, 318, 419
"Terence, This Is Stupid Stuff," 442

Thomas, Dylan, 422
Thoreau, Henry David, 370
"Thrower-Away, The," 130
"Thrushes," 453
"Tide Rises, the Tide Falls, The," 454
"To Helen," 387
"To My Mother," 365
"Troubled Woman," 379
Tu Fu, 376
"Turtle, The," 317
"Two Sons," 353

"Ugly Duckling, The," 81
Updike, John, 152, 319

"Valediction: Forbidding Mourning, A," 400
"View from the Bridge, A," 222

Wain, John, 456
"Waking Early Sunday Morning," 462
"Waller, Edmund," 385
"Water Moment," 309
"What Is That Music High in the Air?" 414
"When I Have Fears That I May Cease To Be," 341
"Whipping, The," 350
Wilbur, Richard, 358, 451
Williams, William Carlos, 374
"Winter," 305
"Wonderful Ice Cream Suit, The," 111
"Wordsworth, William," 417

Yeats, William Butler, 459
"you shall above all things be glad and young," 344
"Your Attention Please," 439